P9-CRL-045

# IBM WebSphere

## Deployment and Advanced Configuration

# IBM Press Series—Information Management

## On Demand Computing Books

***On Demand Computing***
Fellenstein

***Grid Computing***
Joseph and Fellenstein

***Autonomic Computing***
Murch

***Business Intelligence for the Enterprise***
Biere

## DB2 Books

***The Official Introduction to DB2 for z/OS***
Sloan

***High Availability Guide to DB2***
Eaton and Cialini

***DB2 Universal Database v8.1 Certification Exam 700 Study Guide***
Sanders

***DB2 Universal Database v8.1 Certification Exams 701 and 706 Study Guide***
Sanders

***DB2 for Solaris: The Official Guide***
Bauch and Wilding

***DB2 Universal Database v8 for Linux, UNIX, and Windows Database Administration Certification Guide, Fifth Edition***
Baklarz and Wong

***Advanced DBA Certification Guide and Reference for DB2 Universal Database v8 for Linux, UNIX, and Windows***
Snow and Phan

***DB2 Universal Database v8 Application Development Certification Guide, Second Edition***
Martineau, Sanyal, Gashyna, and Kyprianou

***DB2 Version 8: The Official Guide***
Zikopoulos, Baklarz, deRoos, and Melnyk

***Teach Yourself DB2 Universal Database in 21 Days***
Visser and Wong

***DB2 UDB for OS/390 v7.1 Application Certification Guide***
Lawson

***DB2 SQL Procedural Language for Linux, UNIX, and Windows***
Yip, Bradstock, Curtis, Gao, Janmohamed, Liu, and McArthur

***DB2 Universal Database v8 Handbook for Windows, UNIX, and Linux***
Gunning

***Integrated Solutions with DB2***
Cutlip and Medicke

***DB2 Universal Database for OS/390 Version 7.1 Certification Guide***
Lawson and Yevich

## More Books from IBM Press

***Developing Quality Technical Information: A Handbook for Writers and Editors***
Hargis, Carey, Hernandez, Hughes, Longo, Rouiller, and Wilde

***Enterprise Messaging Using JMS and IBM WebSphere***
Yusuf

***Enterprise Java Programming with IBM WebSphere, Second Edition***
Brown, Craig, Hester, Stinehour, Pitt, Weitzel, Amsden, Jakab, and Berg

# IBM WebSphere

## Deployment and Advanced Configuration

WebSphere

Roland Barcia, Bill Hines, Tom Alcott, and Keys Botzum

An Imprint of PEARSON EDUCATION
Upper Saddle River, NJ • New York • San Francisco
Toronto • London • Munich • Paris • Madrid
Capetown • Sydney • Tokyo • Singapore • Mexico City
www.phptr.com

Library of Congress Cataloging-in-Publication Data
A CIP catalog record for this book can be obtained from the Library of Congress
LOC Number: 2004106052

Acquisitions Editor: John Neidhart
Marketing Manager: Robin O'Brien
Managing Editor: Gina Kanouse
Senior Project Editor: Sarah Kearns
Copy Editor: Ben Lawson
Indexer: Angie Bess
Proofreader: Sheri Cain
Composition: Jake McFarland
Cover Design Director: Sandra Schroeder
Cover Design: Alan Clements
Manufacturing Manager: Dan Uhrig



Prentice Hall PTR offers excellent discounts on this book when ordered in quantity for bulk purchases or special sales. For more information, please contact: U.S. Corporate and Government Sales: 1-800-382-3419, corpsales@pearsontechgroup.com. For sales outside the U.S., please contact: International Sales, 1-317-581-3793, international@pearsontechgroup.com.



ISBN: 0-13-146862-6
Text printed on recycled paper
5 6 7 8 9 10 08 07
Fifth Printing February 2007

Pearson Education Ltd.
Pearson Education Australia Pty., Limited
Pearson Education South Asia Pte. Ltd.
Pearson Education Asia Ltd.
Pearson Education Canada, Ltd.
Pearson Educacion de Mexico, S.A. de C.V.
Pearson Education—Japan
Pearson Malaysia S.D.N. B.H.D.

*For Our Fathers*

*Allan Alcott*
*Rolando Barcia*
*John R. Botzum 1927-2003*
*William J. Hines 1934-2003*

## About the Authors

**Roland Barcia** is a Consulting I/T Specialist with IBM's Software Services for WebSphere, and he specializes in helping enterprise clients implement WebSphere, J2EE, and Web services solutions.

*First and foremost, I would like to thank God, who without his mighty hand, nothing would be possible. Next, I would like to thank my loving wife, Blanca, who's exhibited great patience, support, and love while I worked on this book. I would like to thank my children: Savannah, Alyssa, Joseph, and Amadeus, who constantly remind me daily of what is important. I would like to thank my parents, Maria and Rolando Barcia, who have always been there for me. I would like to thank my brilliant co-authors for writing this book with me. I would like to thank my mentor, Kyle Brown, who has provided me with many opportunities to succeed and for creating the opportunity for this book. I would like to thank my manager, Albert Scardino, for always supporting my career moves. I would also like to thank the following people for various different reasons: Nery Leon, Michael Kenna, Peter Bahrs, Robert Thimsen, Gang Chen, Matthew Oberlin, Geoffrey Hambrick, Robert Conlon, Alain Ratsimbazafy, George Klarmann, David Salkeld, Sree Ratnasinghe, my ISSW teammates, and anyone else I may have forgotten.*

**Bill Hines** is a Certified Consulting I/T Specialist with IBM's Software Services for WebSphere. His expertise includes installation, configuration, tuning, dynacache, security, troubleshooting, and design/architecture of enterprise J2EE WebSphere applications.

*I'd like to thank my mom, wife Patty, daughters Jenn and Brittany, son Derek, sisters Patty and Donna, and the rest of my extended family for their love, support, patience, and encouragement; my friends for being there; my co-workers for sharing their knowledge; IBM and my manager Lou for his support and for hiring me into the best job I've ever had; and my co-authors for including me in their prestigious presence.*

*"Nothing in the world can take the place of persistence"—Calvin Coolidge*

**Tom Alcott** is an IBM Consulting I/T Specialist and a member of IBM's World Wide WebSphere technical sales support team, assisting customers in both the United States and abroad.

*The dictionary defines "patience" as "the act of being patient," for which several definitions are offered, two of which are especially appropriate when writing a book. The first definition is "bearing pains or trials calmly or without complaint"; the second is "manifesting forbearance under provocation or strain." Thanks to my mother for her lessons in patience when I was growing up. Thanks to my wife Barbara for her support and patience as evenings working on the book turned to late nights and early mornings, and a number of weekends also fell prey to this effort. Thanks also to my fellow authors for their patience and perseverance, both of which were tested during this endeavor, especially the latter for Bill and Keys with the loss of their fathers. At times I'm sure we all wondered why we were doing this; I know I did, but I'm glad we saw this through.*

**Keys Botzum** is a Senior Consulting I/T Specialist with IBM Software Services for WebSphere. He has over 10 years' experience in large-scale distributed system design and now specializes in security.

*I'd like to thank my mother for teaching to speak and write "The King's English." Thanks to her, I can be understood. I'd like to thank many of my great teachers in high school and college that made me write and write well. My contribution to this book could never have been written without your help long ago. I remember you, Mr. Bonstingle, Karen O'kane, and more. And I'd like to thank my co-authors for making this all possible.*

---

The three of us would especially like to thank Keys for participating despite his eternally high demand and tremendous workload. This book is many times better than it would have been without his insistence on quality throughout.

**—Roland Barcia, Bill Hines, and Tom Alcott**

# Technical Reviewers and Contributors

## Technical Reviewers

Chris Ruegger
Pete Van Sickel
Matt Oberlin
Mike Capern
Kyle Brown
Gary Albeli
Julie Strong

## Contributors

Pete Van Sickel
Matt Oberlin
Mike Capern
Kyle Brown
Chris Ruegger
Wayne Beaton
Gang Chen
Kareem Yusuf
Sam Pearson
Mitch Johnson
Lori Adington
Kevin Sutter
Keith Blake
Katherine Reichard
Brian Martin
Bert Laonipon
Alexandre Polozoff
Gale Botwick
Melissa Modjeski
Stacy Joines
Ruth Willenborg
Trey Williamson
Subbarao Meduri
Madhu Chetuparmbil
Gabe Montero
Leigh Williamson
Barry Seale
Bobby Woolf
Ken Ueno
Yuki Sohda
Stephen Brand

# Table of Contents

# Foreword

Just as there are two sides to every coin, there are two sides to each WebSphere project. And just as you can't have one side of a coin without another, you can't leave off one half of your WebSphere project and expect the other to succeed. I'm speaking, of course, about the two major roles involved in J2EE projects—not only application developers (or J2EE programmers) but also the role that's most often overlooked—the application deployer.

The bookshelves of any large bookstore will be well laden with books on how to develop code for J2EE application servers. In fact, most bookstores will have several that I've contributed to. It's easy for a developer to find a good, reliable source of information on how to do his job. However, that's not quite the case with a WebSphere deployer.

Why is this true? Well, I believe that one reason is that even though J2EE has always defined the different roles like deployer and system administrator, the emphasis has always been on the development role because it is the one that the authors and readers of the J2EE specs identify with the most.

This book is one of the first efforts to address this inconsistency. You see, the issue is that deployment is difficult—in many ways, planning and executing a successful application deployment is as difficult as developing the application itself. There are a myriad of issues to consider—is your topology sufficient to meet your application performance needs? Are both your network and applications secured from external intrusion and unauthorized internal access? Do you have a plan for managing upgrades to your application and to the software (application servers, databases, third-party libraries) on which your application depends? If you don't have the right answer for any of these questions, your application will not meet your user's needs, no matter how well it's written.

Unfortunately, WebSphere system administrators and deployers often get the short end of the stick when educational resources are assigned. While it's often easy in many development shops to obtain authorization for a class on J2EE development, it's often harder to find a good class on administration and harder to justify the expense. Thus, there exists an urgent need for guides like the book you now hold.

This book is a wonderful resource; not only does it contain detailed instructions on how to carry out the real work of building and deploying applications, but more importantly, it also provides a wealth of information on best practices for application deployment.

I have immense respect for the authors of this book—they are the true experts in their field. When someone needs an answer on application security, topology design, or deployment, no group is more qualified to provide it than the authors assembled for this book. They've done a great job of capturing that knowledge here, and I'm sure you'll benefit from it. So sit back, grab a cup of coffee, and start reading—you'll find that the process of building and deploying your WebSphere applications will be better as a result.

**Kyle Brown**
Senior Technical Staff Member
IBM Software Services for WebSphere
Author of *Enterprise Java Programming with IBM WebSphere,* Second Edition

# PART I

# Introduction to WebSphere and Deployment

CHAPTER 1

# Introduction

It takes rigorous planning, design, and architecture to build a house. Houses are built from components where each component depends on other components in order for the house to work. For example, a good roof can only rest successfully upon a strong frame. A strong frame needs to lie upon a solid foundation. Even the foundation requires that the ground be adequately prepared. If, at any point, short cuts are taken or mistakes are made, the house will not be as sturdy, and, depending upon the severity of the weaknesses, the house may crumble.

If we apply this analogy to the development of Java 2 Enterprise Edition (J2EE) applications, applications are the visible parts of the house—the roof, walls, windows, etc. Applications provide the functionality we desire, as do walls or windows. The unseen parts of the house (the framing, the foundation, the earth itself) and the processes used to build the house are the infrastructure. Without proper infrastructure, applications, as with houses, will fail. The purpose of this book is to talk about the unseen and overlooked parts of large-scale J2EE application deployment.

This book is part of a series of three books that targets users of WebSphere Application Server (WAS):

- *Enterprise Java Programming with IBM WebSphere,* Second Edition [Brown 2004]
- *IBM WebSphere System Administration* [Williamson 2004]
- This book

The first book focuses on the complex design and architectural issues surrounding building complex J2EE applications and is focused on developers. The second book describes in detail the WAS administrative tools for managing and deploying applications and is focused on administrators. The third, this book, covers the uneasy ground that is often overlooked.

This book will focus on the critical but often neglected portion of assembling, deploying, and administering the applications that run under the WAS environment. This book is focused on those individuals that span the gap between development and administration. Here, we focus on the complex processes that take an application from development to production. We provide expert advice on how to build and deploy applications as well as on how to configure WAS. This advice is based on our years of experience building, deploying, and managing large and complex WAS applications.

## Who Should Read This Book

As we've already said, this book is focused on the uneasy gap between development and administration. If you are the person who stays late at work trying to get the application builds installed or the person whom everyone expects to magically figure out how to configure WAS to make the application run smoothly, this book is for you. We've been there.

By necessity, since this book focuses so much on administration, we will assume you are familiar with WAS administration. If you are not, read and understand [Williamson 2004] or the equivalent first. While this book is not intended for developers, by necessity, you must be familiar with J2EE packaging and the basics of WAS development.

## Why Concentrate So Much on Deployment?

It is reasonable to ask, "Why is so much of this book focused on application deployment?" It may seem that one can simply create the application using a tool like WebSphere Studio and then just drop it into production. In some rare cases, this approach works; but it does not work for enterprise-scale applications. Applications that serve hundreds, thousands, and even millions of users must be treated with rigorous processes to avoid catastrophe.

Enterprise application development must meet specialized requirements, different even from small-scale application development. Here, we will list some of the key aspects of enterprise application development as justification for the rigorous processes that we will be advocating throughout this book:

- Enterprise-class systems provide mission-critical functionality and must therefore be carefully deployed. We cannot risk deploying an application into production (or developing our applications in production) if it might cause an outage.
- Applications must be rigorously tested prior to production deployment. Applications must be developed in a separate development environment, rigorously tested in well-defined test environments, and then deployed into production. Good rigorous testing includes not only testing the functionality of the application, but also testing the application for non-functional requirements such as performance, scalability, security, etc.
- Applications depend on other applications. Applications often need to communicate with each other over various communication mediums. This leads to complex system integration challenges that must be carefully planned for and tested.

- Applications and the infrastructure on which it runs is network-accessible. This means that applications are vulnerable to attacks from all over the world. In fact, Internet-accessible applications are often under constant attack. This means applications must be designed with security in mind right from the start.
- J2EE applications are component-based. Component-based applications are split up into smaller subunits, and the units need to be assembled to create the total application.
- Applications now heavily rely on the services of the underlying infrastructure, which is non-trivial and complex in its own right.

Based on the reality just discussed, we need rigorous procedures for building, deploying, and testing enterprise-class applications. This requires a new way of thinking about application deployment. While we would like to cover all aspects of rigorous enterprise application deployment, that is impractical. Instead, this book focuses on these three key areas:

- Application assembly and build
- Application and infrastructure configuration and administration
- Application and configuration verification

These three major points are critical to successful application deployment. At the same time, "speed of development" and time-to-market are crucial success factors for many enterprises. Thus, we need to ensure that our rigorous procedures can be executed frequently, reliably, and quickly. As such, automation is a key objective. Manual procedures may take too long to execute and are subject to human error. Throughout this book, you will see examples of automation. We will provide you with scripts for automated build, deployment, and administration. You can use these as the basis for automated rigorous procedures in your organization.

## How This Book Is Organized

This book is organized to provide the reader information in a practical and concrete way. Most of the chapters will start by introducing concepts and features and why they are important. They will then discuss the practices needed to implement and use the concepts or features successfully. Finally, where applicable, many chapters will conclude with the use of an example that includes automation to illustrate the concepts.

Our main objective is to help you effectively use the powerful WAS platform to run your J2EE applications by providing information in a practical and concrete way. In keeping with that objective, this book is divided into five parts as follows:

- **Part I, "Introduction to WebSphere and Deployment"**—Chapters 1 through 5 will introduce the reader to key aspects of WebSphere, including the basics of J2EE applications and WAS architecture. We will also provide a quick-start chapter to help readers set up their environments so they can follow the examples in this book. And, most importantly, the section will introduce the basic build and deployment automation procedures that will be referenced throughout this book.

- **Part II, "J2EE Deployment and Administration"**—Chapters 6 through 14 will discuss the key J2EE technologies supported by WAS: Servlets, JDBC, Java 2 Connectors, Enterprise Java Beans, Container Managed Persistence Entity Beans, transactions, Java Messaging Service, Message Driven Beans, and other J2EE resources such as JavaMail and Client Containers. The chapters will provide guidance and tips on deployment and administration related to those technologies. In keeping with the key themes of this book, automation examples will be used frequently. We will also develop and enhance chapter-by-chapter a sample that demonstrates many of the J2EE technologies that the reader will be able to deploy.
- **Part III, "Managing WebSphere Application Server Infrastructure"**—Chapters 15 through 19 will discuss several advanced aspects of WAS administration and the management of the WAS infrastructure to support application development, testing, and production deployments. Topics include advanced considerations for build and deploy, ideal development and test environments, Java management extensions, security, and caching.
- **Part IV, "WebSphere Application Server Network Deployment"**—Chapters 20 through 23 are focused on topics related to multi-node WAS environments built using WAS Network Deployment (WAS ND). We'll discuss WAS ND, clustering, distributed session management, and using edge components for high availability and scalability.
- **Part V, "Problem Determination and Server Tools"**—The final two chapters will discuss numerous tools and procedures for problem determination and performance management.

In addition to the core chapters, there will be four appendices. Appendix A will provide a reference listing the WAS-supported ANT tasks. Appendix B will provide a summary deployment checklist to help readers determine if they have done what is necessary to deploy WAS applications. The deployment checklist will provide a general place to get a summary of the techniques used in this book. Appendix C will describe the setup needed to run the samples in this book. This includes the installation of the application server and the setup of dependencies such as the DB2 database. Appendix D will contain an overview of how to configure and use the Web Services Gateway that is new in WAS V5.

The rest of this chapter introduces you to the WebSphere platform, WebSphere Application Server, and some of the WebSphere tools.

## Introduction to WebSphere

Although many of the ideas in this book can be applied in many contexts, this book will focus on WebSphere Application Server (WAS). We are going to highlight just a few key points of relevance to readers of this book. To learn more about the WebSphere platform, refer to [Brown 2004] or IBM's web site at http://www.ibm.com/websphere.

Very briefly, the WebSphere name is a branding of a group of closely related products. These products include development tools (e.g., WebSphere Studio), runtime platforms (e.g., WebSphere Application Server), and higher end integration products (e.g., WebSphere Portal). WebSphere Application Server was one of the first products in the WebSphere family. As a result, the name WebSphere is often associated exclusively with the Application Server. Unfortunately, this is not accurate. In this book, we use WAS or Application Server to mean one of the editions of WebSphere Application Server. We will generally not distinguish between the WAS editions unless it is crucial to the discussion. Nonetheless, it is sometimes helpful to understand the different editions.

WAS is made up of several editions to meet different needs:

- **WebSphere Application Server, Express Edition**—WebSphere Application Server, Express supports a J2EE web container but not an EJB container.
- **WebSphere Application Server**—The cornerstone of the WebSphere product family. WAS 5.X is a J2EE 1.3-compliant application server that provides complete support for all aspects of the J2EE programming model. WAS (the base edition, sometimes called the core server) is targeted for small, departmental applications that can be deployed on a single server machine.
- **WebSphere Application Server, Network Deployment Edition**—WAS ND provides the ability to deploy applications that support failover and load balancing across multiple server machines.
- **WebSphere Application Server, Enterprise Edition (now called WebSphere Business Integration Server Foundation)**[1]—This provides programming model extensions that go above and beyond the J2EE specification. Some of the capabilities address common problems faced by enterprise-scale application developers that have not yet been incorporated into the J2EE specification, such as support for asynchronous beans and dynamic query capabilities to the EJB Entity Beans. Other changes are truly unique to IBM's vision of enterprise development (for example, Process Choreographer).
- **WebSphere Application Server for zOS**—This product is a version of WAS specifically targeted at the zOS (OS/390) platform. It is fully compliant with the J2EE 1.3 specification, and code written for WAS will deploy and run without change on this platform. Likewise, it shares the same web-based administrative console feature as WAS. However, some of the advanced capabilities of the zOS platform allow the product to take advantage of that platform's unique scalability in ways that differ from the scalability mechanisms used in WAS ND.

Our book will focus on WAS and WAS ND because they provide the cornerstone of the WebSphere family of products. We will describe how to use WebSphere Application Server to provide the foundation needed for applications. Our goal is not to provide a comprehensive

1 As we write this chapter, WebSphere Business Integration Server Foundation V5.1 has been released.

manual with exhaustive WAS administration details. [Williamson 2004] will provide the WAS administrative reference that we recommend everyone have on their desk. Our goal is to provide guidance on how to best use the powerful tools available to you.

WebSphere Studio is an IBM product specifically targeted at developers who are developing applications for WAS. Like WAS itself, it comes in many editions. WebSphere Studio is thoroughly covered in [Brown 2004]. In this book, we will not focus on WebSphere Studio. If visual assembly is needed, we will be using the WebSphere Application Server Toolkit (ASTK) to assemble applications for deployment. Conveniently, the ASTK and WebSphere Studio share components. As a result, the examples used in this book that use the ASTK should work equally well with WebSphere Studio.

## Conclusion

In this chapter, we laid the foundation for the remainder of this book. We introduced you to the important topic of application deployment and provided an overview of the WebSphere Platform. In Chapter 2, we will introduce the J2EE application platform and discuss the characteristics of the applications that are meant to run inside WebSphere Application Server. We will also talk about J2EE application packaging.

CHAPTER 2

# J2EE Applications

In the last chapter, we introduced the purpose of this book and its intended audience. We also introduced WebSphere Application Server (WAS) and the different editions of WAS. In this chapter, we introduce the type of applications that run inside the WAS platform; specifically, we will talk about the J2EE platform as well as how applications are packaged for J2EE.

## Understanding J2EE and J2EE Applications

This section is not meant to provide a comprehensive introduction to each of the programmatic APIs in the J2EE platform. Instead, we will talk about the core components of the Java 2 Enterprise Edition (J2EE) platform as they relate to certain aspects of the WAS containers meant to run in a J2EE Application Server. J2EE is a specification that defines a set of technologies. The vision is such that any J2EE-compliant application can be deployed and run in any J2EE application server. As a practical matter, many applications are not completely portable. Nonetheless, a J2EE application is in a better position than other non-J2EE applications to be moved from one J2EE platform implementation to another.

The J2EE specification sits on top of the Java 2 Standard Edition (J2SE), which provides the underlying version of the JRE. WAS 5.x implements the J2EE 1.3 specification along with some features from J2EE 1.4. Table 2-1, taken from the J2EE 1.3 specification, and Table 2-2 illustrate the J2EE 1.3 and J2EE 1.4 components that are present in the current implementation of WAS 5.x.

> **NOTE**
>
> As you read this chart, keep in mind that the inclusion of an API in this chart does not mean that every method of the API is required by the specification. In many cases, such as with JAAS or JTA, only subsets of the full API are required. Readers are encouraged to read section 6 of the J2EE 1.3 specification to learn the precise details of the API support required.

**Table 2-1** J2EE 1.3 Components in WAS 5.x

| Optional Package | App Client | Applet | Web | EJB |
|---|---|---|---|---|
| JDBC 2.0 Extension | Y | N | Y | Y |
| EJB 2.0 | Y* | N | Y* | Y |
| Servlets 2.3 | N | N | Y | N |
| JSP 1.2 | N | N | Y | N |
| JMS 1.0 | Y | N | Y | Y |
| JTA 1.0 | N | N | Y | Y |
| JavaMail 1.2 | N | N | Y | Y |
| JAF 1.0 | N | N | Y | Y |
| JAXP 1.1 | Y | N | Y | Y |
| Connector 1.0 | N | N | Y | Y |
| JAAS 1.0 | Y | N | Y | Y |

* Client APIs only.

**Table 2-2** J2EE 1.4 Components in WAS 5.x

| J2EE 1.4 Technology |
|---|
| JAX-RPC (Java API for XML-based RPC) |
| SAAJ (SOAP with Attachments API for Java) |
| JMX (Java Management Extensions) |

While this list contains a large set of APIs, most applications make use of only the core components: Servlets, JSP, EJB, JDBC, and JNDI. JMS usage is also growing in popularity. [Brown 2004] provides programmatic instructions on how to develop J2EE applications.

The J2EE specification also defines some aspects of the J2EE Application Server. A J2EE Application Server runs or contains a set of J2EE containers in which an application is deployed. There are two server-based containers: the Web container and the EJB container. J2EE also defines two client containers, one for running applets and one for standalone clients. The specification defines the protocols used for components within the J2EE containers when communicating. For example, a web component such as a Servlet can call a Stateless Session Bean EJB using IIOP when the Web container and EJB containers are in separate JVMs or via multiple mechanisms when the containers are co-located. Figure 2-1 gives a high-level view of the containers that make up a J2EE server. Although all the possible communication protocols are listed in the figure, it is advisable to learn which protocols to use in which circumstance. For example, if a web component is in the same JVM as the EJB component, using a local call is preferred for performance reasons.

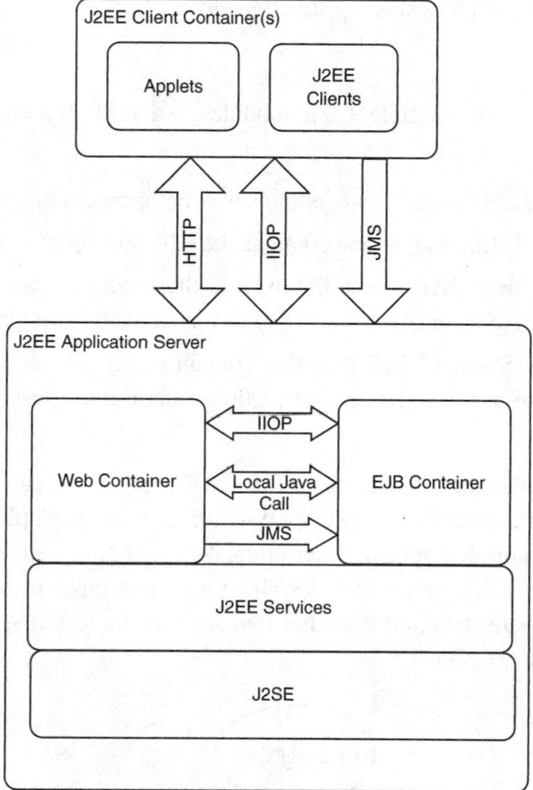


**Figure 2-1** J2EE containers.

The J2EE specification mandates how applications should be packaged for deployment. J2EE application components are combined into an Enterprise ARchive file (EAR). The EAR file may contain one or more J2EE modules as well as plain Java JAR files. This allows the J2EE application to be packaged into a single unit, simplifying the deployment effort since there is only one package to deploy. The J2EE server handles deploying the modules to the correct containers. One notable exception is client container deployment, which is not handled on the server. Chapter 14, "Client Applications," will cover the WebSphere Client Container in detail.

The J2EE 1.3 specification only defines the application packaging, not how the package is deployed into the server. In the future, the J2EE 1.4 specification will provide a common API for application deployment to which all J2EE servers must adhere.

## J2EE Packaging

In this section, we will look at the EAR file. As previously stated, an EAR file is a module that is made up of J2EE modules, utility JAR files, and a set of deployment descriptors that describe the modules. Deployment descriptors are XML files stored in the package that contains a description of the package and its components. For an EAR file, the J2EE specification mandates the existence of a deployment descriptor called *application.xml*.

### EAR File

An EAR file is made up of multiple J2EE modules. An EAR file can contain four distinct archives:[1]

- **WAR file**—A J2EE module that contains web components of an application.
- **EJB-JAR**—A J2EE module that contains the EJB portion of an application.
- **Application Client JAR**—A J2EE module that contains client components that run outside the J2EE Server Container. They run inside a lightweight J2EE client container.
- **Utility JARs**—Standard JAR files that contain utility classes used by the other J2EE modules. These utility JARs are not modules themselves, just code used by the J2EE modules.

Figure 2-2 illustrates the makeup of a J2EE EAR file. As you can see, it is a module and must contain at least one other J2EE module (WAR, EJB-JAR, or Application Client JAR). An EAR file must also contain deployment descriptors. As a matter of fact, each J2EE module contains its own deployment descriptor. In WAS, there are three types of descriptors. One type is mandated by the J2EE specification; the other two are specific to WAS. We will describe these descriptors in the coming sections.

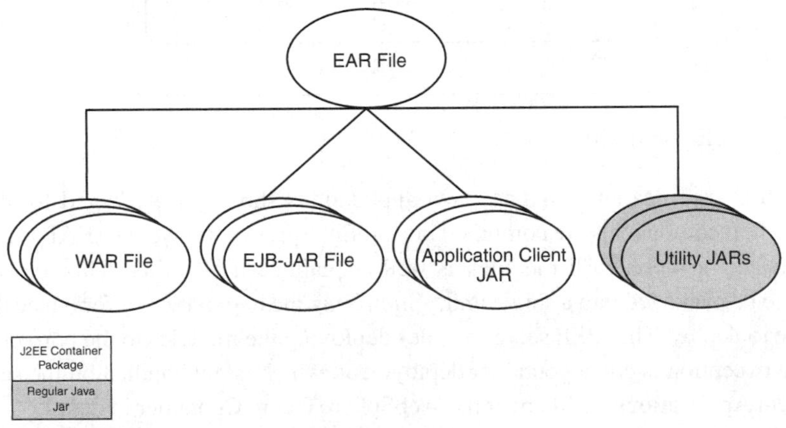


**Figure 2-2** EAR file makeup.

1 J2EE also defines the notion of a RAR file for the Java Connector Architecture (J2C). Chapter 8 will cover J2C.

## Deployment Descriptors

Deployment descriptors are a key part of J2EE deployments. These descriptors describe the contents of various J2EE modules and are used by the container when deploying an application. Standard J2EE deployment descriptors are those mandated by the J2EE specification:

- EAR file -> application.xml
- EJB-JAR file -> ejb-jar.xml
- WAR file -> web.xml
- Application Client -> application-client.xml

The application.xml file is covered in this chapter.

WAS includes two additional types of deployment descriptors that are unique. The IBM binding file (ibm-application-bnd.xmi) is used to map elements and references into the runtime environment, while the IBM extension file (ibm-application-ext.xmi) details the settings for IBM specific features, which are outside the J2EE specification.

The IBM binding file, as the name implies, binds something abstract about the compliant J2EE descriptor to a concrete runtime component. Elements in a J2EE application such as EJBs, resources such as JDBC Data Source, or security roles must be bound to a naming service or underlying concrete resource. Standard J2EE deployment descriptors define elements or references to other elements. The IBM binding file maps these elements or references to elements to the actual concrete name under which they are configured. Here are some examples:

- The ejb-jar.xml file defines an EJB named Stock. The binding file for the EJB module, called ibm-ejb-jar-bnd.xmi, says that the Stock EJB is defined in the JNDI naming service as ejb/Stock. A client uses the name ejb/Stock to find the EJB.
- The application.xml file in the EAR file defines a security role called TradeUser. The binding file for the EAR, called ibm-application-bnd.xmi, maps the TradeUser role to the trade group defined in the security registry.

The binding file can be created at development time using WebSphere tools such as WebSphere Studio. It can also be updated, replaced, or generated at deployment time. This allows great flexibility in binding abstract elements to different names at deployment time. Here are the specific binding files for each J2EE module:

- EAR file -> ibm-application-bnd.xmi[2]
- WAR file -> ibm-web-bnd.xmi
- EJB-JAR file -> ibm-ejb-jar-bnd.xmi
- Application Client JAR -> ibm-application-client-bnd.xmi

The other type of WAS-specific deployment descriptor is the IBM extension file. These files contain extensions that WAS provides that go beyond what the J2EE specification mandates.

2 The XMI file is a special type of XML file that stands for extensible markup inspection language.

Depending on the module, this file will have different elements that address different needs. For example, the web extension might specify a pre-compile option for JSPs. Here is the extension file for each module:[3]

- EAR file -> ibm-application-ext.xmi
- WAR file -> ibm-web-ext.xmi
- EJB-JAR file -> ibm-ejb-jar-ext.xmi

Figure 2-3 illustrates an EAR file and modules along with their descriptors. Notice the structure of the EAR and the contained modules. For an EAR file, all the modules must be put under the root of the EAR archive. Each archive (EAR and modules) must have a META-INF folder that contains the deployment descriptors (the WAR file puts its descriptors in a directory called WEB-INF).

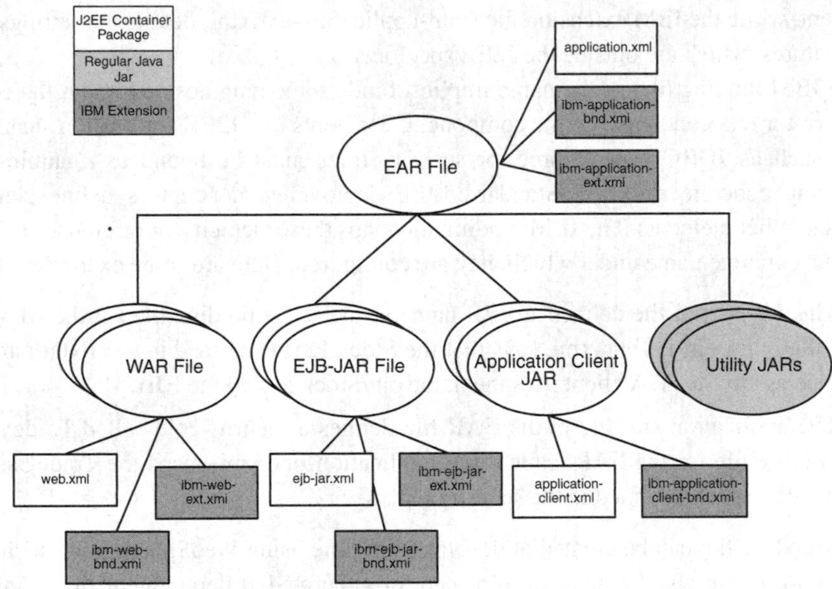


**Figure 2-3** Application archives and associated descriptors.

Java archives (JAR, ejb-jar, client-jar, etc.) contain another file called a MANIFEST.MF that is stored in the META-INF directory along with the other descriptors. For a standard JAR file, the MANIFEST describes Java elements of a JAR file. For J2EE modules, a MANIFEST plays a critical role; it is the J2EE-compliant way to specify *classpath* information for a J2EE module. Each utility JAR, Web module, and EJB module can specify in their MANIFEST the other JARs in the same EAR that are visible to them. This concept is illustrated in Figure 2-4. In the figure, the WAR file lists which other archives within the EAR are in the classpath. The EJB module does the same. Any other JAR not listed in the MANIFEST of the WAR or the EJB-JAR

3 Depending on the edition of WebSphere Application Server, there may be more or fewer extension files.

is not visible to its classpath. Any reference to a class stored in a JAR within the EAR that is not listed in the MANIFEST will cause a ClassNotFoundException at runtime. Be aware that a MANIFEST can only list JAR files that are stored in the EAR file. Furthermore, even though a WAR file is an archive, it cannot be listed on any MANIFEST since any Java artifacts within a WAR are only visible to the same WAR. There are other ways to specify classpath information in WAS that are beyond the J2EE specification. WAS classloading will be explained in more detail in Chapter 5, "WebSphere Application Server Architecture."

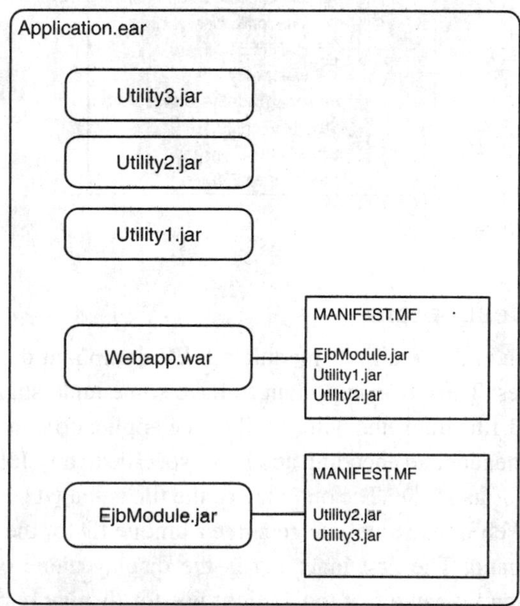


**Figure 2-4** Using the MANIFEST in J2EE modules.

One last file we will cover here is the was.policy file, which is used to specify what Java 2 security permissions the application needs. WebSphere Application Server supports the Java 2 Security model. The Java 2 Security model offers policy-driven, fine-grained access control to system resources from a Java Virtual Machine (JVM) perspective. Java 2 can protect resources such as the file system, system properties, socket connections, threads, and class loading. Application code must be explicitly granted the required permission in order to access protected resources. Security permission grants are specified in one of several policy files. In WAS, when deploying J2EE applications requiring Java 2 permissions, placing a was.policy file inside the EAR file in the META-INF directory is perhaps the simplest way to grant permissions to a particular application. This is what we will use in this book. The was.policy file follows standard Java 2 Security syntax, although WAS does provide some predefined variables you can use to point to your own application components within the EAR. To learn more about Java 2 security, refer to [Oaks 2002] and the Info Center.

Figure 2-5 illustrates the structure of the EAR file. As you can see, all the modules are stored in the root of the EAR, and all the descriptors are stored under the META-INF directory. The EAR file also contains a MANIFEST, but the MANIFEST has no relevance in determining the classpath of the modules.

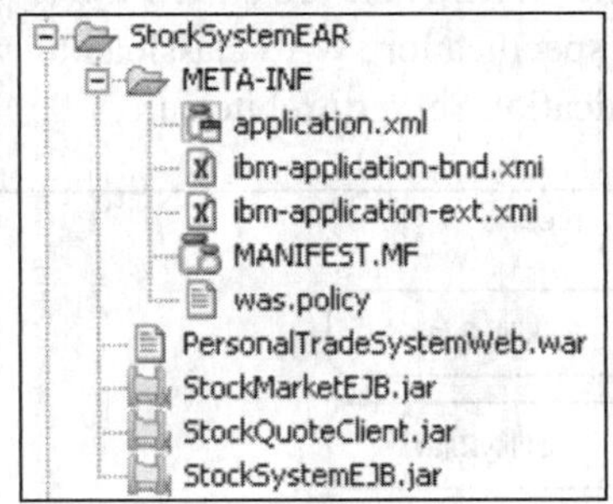


**Figure 2-5** EAR structure.

## EAR Deployment Descriptors

As stated, the application.xml is the EAR module's J2EE-compliant descriptor. All deployment descriptors are XML files. Thus, it is important to have some understanding of the structure of XML.[4] Code Snippet 2-1 illustrates the outer shell of the application.xml file. The first line contains the standard XML header and encoding and is not specific to any J2EE descriptors. The next line defines the location of its DTD.[5] The outer tag of the file is `<application>`, which can have an ID attribute as well. WebSphere tools can generate a unique ID for the descriptor so it does not have to be defined by hand. The first inner tag is the display name of the EAR file. This is intended to be a user-friendly name that tools might use for display purposes. After the display name, there are two major sections of an application.xml file—the module section and the security role section.

**Code Snippet 2-1** application.xml shell

```
<?xml version="1.0" encoding="UTF-8"?>
<!DOCTYPE application PUBLIC "-//Sun Microsystems, Inc.//DTD J2EE
➥Application 1.3//EN" "http://java.sun.com/dtd/application_1_3.dtd">
<application id="Application_ID">
  <display-name>StockSystemEAR</display-name>
  ...
</application>
```

4 A deployer does not need deep knowledge of XML, just the basic rules for the structure of an XML file.

5 DTD (Document Type Definition) is a standard file that describes the rules for a specific XML file. DTD files are being replaced by XML schemas as a standard for XML description.

The module section defines each J2EE module in the EAR. It is not required that any utility JAR files be defined, but all the J2EE-specific modules must be defined. Code Snippet 2-2 shows a few module definitions. The module tag also has a generated ID attribute. The first one is a web module, indicated by the nested tag `<web>`. Within the `<web>` tag, one must have a `<web-uri>` tag. Between the `<web-uri>` tags is the name of the WAR file within the EAR. Next is the web application context root, which is specific to WAR files. The context root is defined in the EAR deployment descriptor and defines how URL clients would access the application. In our example, the context root is "pts," so a URL would be formatted as `http://<network_name>/pts`.[6] The next module is an EJB JAR. Inside the `<module>` tag is the nested tag`<ejb>`. In between the `<ejb>` tag is the name of the EJB JAR. The last tag is for a J2EE application client, which uses the `<java>` tag to define the J2EE client JAR.

**Code Snippet 2-2** Module definitions in application.xml

```
<module id="WebModule_1060570931279">
  <web>
    <web-uri>PersonalTradeSystemWeb.war</web-uri>
    <context-root>pts</context-root>
  </web>
</module>
<module id="EjbModule_1062189285961">
  <ejb>StockSystemEJB.jar</ejb>
</module>
<module id="JavaClientModule_1063039430223">
  <java>StockQuoteClient.jar</java>
</module>
```

The next section of the application.xml file is the security roles section. J2EE security is based on the concept of roles. Roles are the abstract representation of the groups of users of an application. At deployment time, an administrator associates real users or groups with the role. The roles at the EAR-level are also defined in the corresponding modules. They are aggregated at the EAR-level and mapped to the users and groups in one convenient place. Code Snippet 2-3 illustrates how roles are defined in the application.xml file. Each security role has a surrounding tag called`<security-role>`. Within the tag are a description tag and the `<role-name>` tag. The name of the role is defined in between the `<role-name>` tag.

**Code Snippet 2-3** Security role definition in application.xml

```
<security-role id="SecurityRole_1041353400900">
    <description></description>
```

6 Web server proxies such as those used for Single Sign-on solutions might prefix the context root.

```
      <role-name>TRADEUSER</role-name>
    </security-role>
    <security-role id="SecurityRole_1062189469575">
      <description></description>
      <role-name>MQUser</role-name>
    </security-role>
    <security-role id="SecurityRole_1062189706216">
      <description></description>
      <role-name>NEWUSER</role-name>
</security-role>
```

The next file we discuss is the EAR-level binding file. Now, as stated earlier, binding files bind abstract notions to concrete implementations, so you might wonder, "What is concrete about an EAR module?" The answer is, "Not much." So why do we need a binding file? It is required because security roles are abstract and thus need to be bound to actual users and groups. In Chapter 3, "WAS Quick Start," you will have an opportunity to configure a security registry for WAS and see how roles are mapped to security groups. Code Snippet 2-4 shows a sample EAR binding file. Unlike the application.xml file, the binding file makes use of an XML schema for its definition. Within the root tags `<applicationbnd:ApplicationBinding>` is the authorization table. The authorization table is a map of roles to concrete users and/or groups. The binding file makes use of the generated ID attribute on the application.xml file. We will not go over the tags in detail; WebSphere Tools provide deployment descriptor editors that hide the complexity of deployment descriptors.

**Code Snippet 2-4** EAR-level binding file

```
<?xml version="1.0" encoding="UTF-8"?>
<applicationbnd:ApplicationBinding xmi:version="2.0" xmlns:xmi=
➥"http://www.omg.org/XMI" xmlns:applicationbnd="applicationbnd.xmi"
➥xmi:id="ApplicationBinding_1041353400900">
  <authorizationTable xmi:id="AuthorizationTable_1041353400900">
    <authorizations xmi:id="RoleAssignment_1041353400900">
      <role href="META-INF/application.xml#SecurityRole_
      ➥1041353400900"/>
      <groups xmi:id="Group_1062189248237" name="TRADE"/>
    </authorizations>
    <authorizations xmi:id="RoleAssignment_1062189469575">
      <users xmi:id="User_1062189469575" name="Admin"/>
      <role href="META-INF/application.xml#SecurityRole_
      ➥1062189469575"/>
```

```
    </authorizations>
    <authorizations xmi:id="RoleAssignment_1062189706216">
      <specialSubjects xmi:type="applicationbnd:Everyone" xmi:id=
      ➥"Everyone_1062189706216" name="Everyone"/>
      <role href="META-INF/application.xml#SecurityRole_
      ➥1062189706216"/>
    </authorizations>
  </authorizationTable>
  <application href="META-INF/application.xml#Application_ID"/>
</applicationbnd:ApplicationBinding>
```

The last descriptor in the EAR file is the EAR extension file. For the EAR file, there are only a few extension options:

- You can define the *reload interval* of an application. This flag tells the application server how often the application server should check to see if the application should be reloaded. It will cause the application to be stopped and restarted.
- The other flag indicates whether this EAR file supports shared sessions. The J2EE specification defines that there is one HTTP session per WAR file.[7] If an EAR file has multiple WAR files, they each have their own HTTP session. WAS allows all the WAR files within one EAR to share a single HTTP session. This feature is beyond the J2EE specification and thus affects the portability of the application if used.

Code Snippet 2-5 illustrates an EAR-level extension file. The extensions in the EAR file are defined as attributes on the root tag. You can see the `<applicationext:ApplicationExtension>` tag has a `reloadInterval` attribute and a `sharedSessionContext` attribute. Again, the deployment descriptor editors in ASTK (WebSphere Application Server Toolkit) or WebSphere Studio expose these features.[8]

**Code Snippet 2-5** EAR-level IBM extensions file

```
<?xml version="1.0" encoding="UTF-8"?>
<applicationext:ApplicationExtension xmi:version="2.0" xmlns:xmi=
➥"http://www.omg.org/XMI" xmlns:applicationext="applicationext.xmi"
➥xmi:id="ApplicationExtension_1" reloadInterval="20"
➥sharedSessionContext="false">
  <application href="META-INF/application.xml#Application_ID"/>
</applicationext:ApplicationExtension>
```

7 HTTP session will be covered in Chapter 6 and Chapter 23.

8 Unfortunately, not every feature is exposed and thus some require a hand edit, but ASTK and WebSphere Studio can be used to specify most features.

## WAS Policy File

While technically not an EAR deployment descriptor, since the was.policy file that is included with the EAR is used by WAS to control the access rights of code in the EAR, we will take a moment to describe a few WAS-specific points.

As we said earlier, the was.policy file follows the same format as a standard Java 2 policy file, but WAS adds some extra variables. Code Snippet 2-6 shows a portion of the was.policy file that we are using with the stock trade example. The basic format of a Java 2 policy file is a series of grants for code bases (JAR files or modules). Within each grant stanza is a series of permission statements that identifies the specific permissions to be granted. The Java 2 policy mechanism is based on positive grants—by default, code has no rights and must be granted permissions. In Code Snippet 2-6, we are giving the code the ability to write to a system property `cactus.contextURL` and read/write permissions to files under `${user.home}/junit.properties`.

As you examine the example, you'll notice two interesting variables that are expanded by WAS to have special meanings:

- **`${/}`**—This is the path separator for this operating system. WAS will automatically use a forward or reverse slash depending on the operating system.
- **`${application}`**—This means that the grant here applies to all code within the EAR. One can also use the `${ejbComponent}` or `${webComponent}` variables to refer to all EJBs or all WARs within the EAR. You can also list specific modules by just using their name (e.g., "StockEJB.jar").

Refer to the Info Center for more details on the variables you can use.

**Code Snippet 2-6** EAR-level was.policy file

```
grant codeBase "file:${application}" {
  permission java.util.PropertyPermission "cactus.contextURL", "write";
  ...
  permission java.io.FilePermission "${user.home}${/}junit.properties",
  ➥"read,write"
  ...
};
```

**SECURITY NOTE**

In the examples in this book, we grant significant Java 2 permissions because we want to enable the Cactus test framework that we use for our verification testing. Keep in mind that when you deploy these EARs to a production system, those excessive permissions should not be granted.

## Conclusion

In this chapter, relevant portions of the J2EE specifications were discussed. We also focused on the notion of J2EE containers and how J2EE packaging targets the containers. In the next chapter, an introduction to the application used throughout this book is provided. You will do some initial configuration of WAS and then deploy the sample application to WAS.

CHAPTER 3

# WAS Quick Start

It is now time to get our hands dirty. The goal of this chapter is to introduce you to the application used throughout the book and to deploy (or install) that application in its simplest form. Although this is not a development book, you will need some understanding of the application being deployed, and we will provide the appropriate background that deployers need from developers. You will configure WAS security in preparation for the deployment and then deploy and verify the application.

## Overview of Applications Used Throughout This Book

The application is called the Personal Trade System. This is a stock trading application with several use cases. Figure 3-1 illustrates the complete use case diagram.

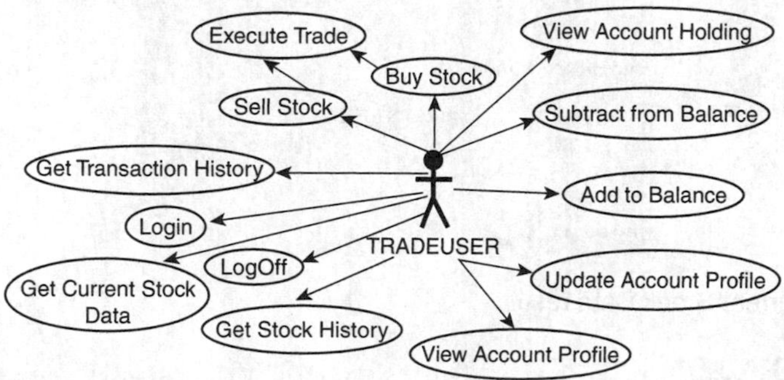


**Figure 3-1** Personal Trade System use case diagram.

- **Login**—This use case represents a login page to the system.
- **LogOff**—This use case implements an explicit logout function that invalidates all credentials and session data.
- **Get Current Stock Data**—This is a submission form where the user enters the symbol, and the system returns stock data. Figures 3-2 and 3-3 show the screens.

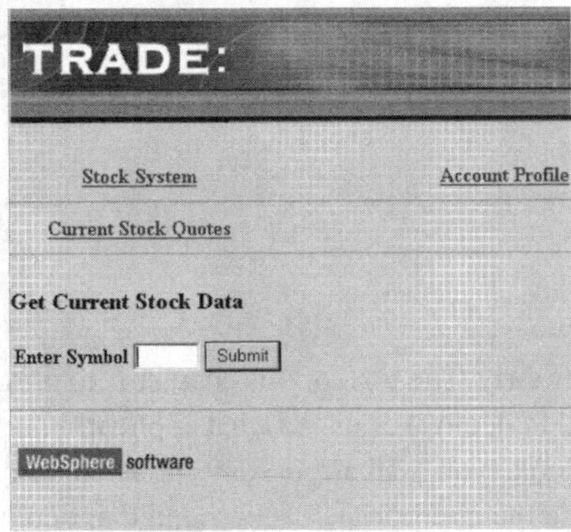


**Figure 3-2** Get Current Stock Data use case.

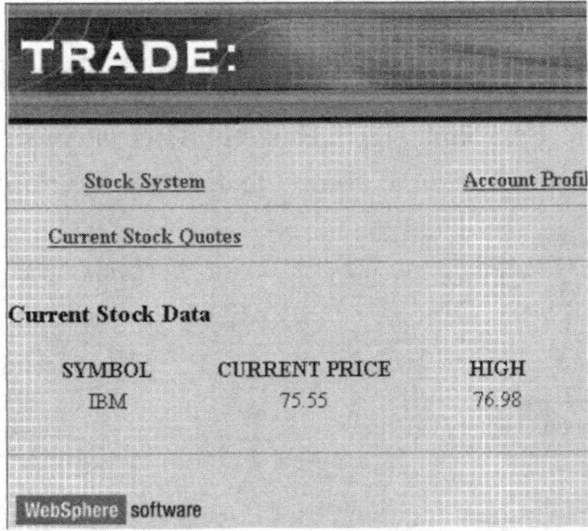


**Figure 3-3** Current Stock Data result.

- **Get Stock History**—This is similar to the prior use case. It returns stock price history.
- **View Account Profile**—This returns the personal information about the user, such as home and work addresses.
- **Update Account Profile**—This allows users to update certain aspects of the profile.

- **Add to Balance**—This allows a user to update his user account to add more funds. When a user buys or sells stock, the application will use the funds in the account.
- **Subtract from Balance**—This allows the user to withdraw funds from the account.
- **View Account Holding**—This allows the user to view the stocks he owns.
- **Sell Stock**—This allows a user to sell a particular stock that he holds.
- **Buy Stock**—This allows a user to buy a particular stock.
- **Execute Trade**—This is an extension of the Sell or Buy Stock use case. Trades are submitted asynchronously to a third party trader.
- **View Transaction History**—This is a log of all the executed trades.

The application itself follows a layered architecture. It uses the Struts Web application framework for the controller and presentation logic and Enterprise JavaBeans (EJBs) for the business logic and data access portions. Figure 3-4 illustrates the basic layering of the application.

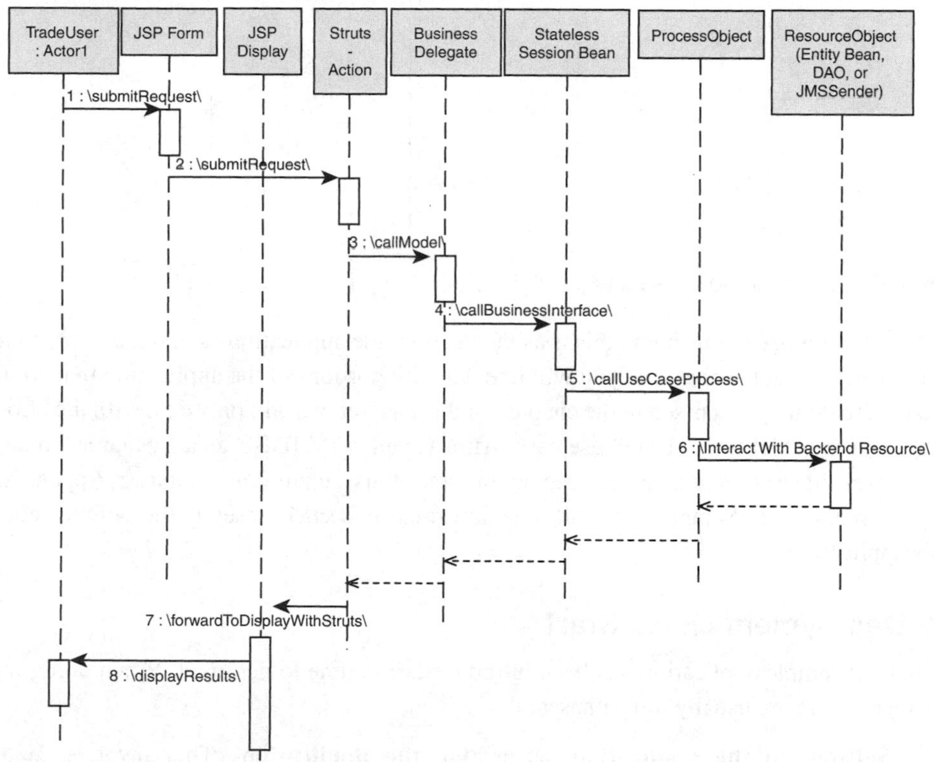


**Figure 3-4** Application layering.

Chapter 12, "JMS and Message Driven Beans," covers JMS and Message Driven Bean deployment for the "Execute Trade" use case. Figure 3-5 illustrates the basic layering for receiving asynchronous trade requests.

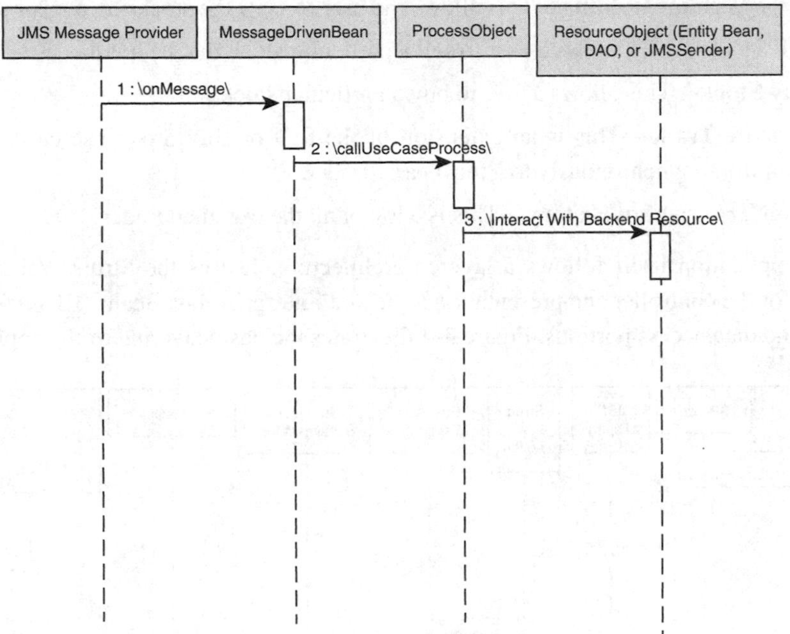


**Figure 3-5** Asynchronous use case.

For the purpose of this book, this is as much about the application as you are likely to need to know. Throughout the chapters, you will interact with portions of the application that are relevant to the technology discussed in the chapter. In this chapter, we will only deal with the "Login" use case and the "Get Stock Data" use case. After Chapter 7, "JDBC as a Resource," many of the exercises have some database interaction and thus require a database. Appendix C, "Setup Instructions for Samples," provides the information needed to set up the sample database for this application.

## WAS Deployment Quick Start

Now that the sample application has been introduced, it is time to deploy it. When doing initial deployment, there are usually three phases:

- **Setting up the application server for the application**—This involves creating resources the application needs, such as JDBC or JMS. It also involves other setup options, including security. In this chapter, we will deploy a version of the application that requires no external resources. However, the application does require security. We will configure a custom security registry for WAS.

- **Deploying the application**—The application server reads an EAR file and places the components where they will be used at runtime.
- **Verifying the deployment**—There should be a well-documented way to test the application to verify that deployment is successful. For example, if the application uses various J2EE resources, some test cases should exercise each of the resources used. In this chapter, the application is configured for security; thus, the test cases will include security verification. The verification will be a manual process of exercising the application through a browser. It will verify that security for the application works and that the application can receive web requests successfully.

## Configuring a File Sample Security Registry

Our first step will be to configure security. This is not accidental. Security should never be an afterthought; it should be part of the development process from the very beginning. In that spirit, all examples in this book are to be used with WAS security enabled. In this chapter, we will configure WAS to use a sample file registry; then, we will enable both WAS Security and Java 2 Security. This section will outline the steps of this setup and introduce the related security topics as needed. However, because this chapter is meant to be a WAS quick start, the descriptions will be brief. Throughout the rest of this book, many of the chapters will cover one aspect of security or another relevant to that chapter. Chapter 18, "Security," will be focused on security.

This exercise was tested on WAS Base version 5.1 on the Microsoft Windows 2000 platform. Depending on the version of WAS used, certain screenshots may not match exactly. It is worth mentioning again that any setup needed to run all the examples in this book is written in Appendix C:

1. Start the WebSphere Application Server (WAS). This can be done by going to a command prompt or shell, going to the bin directory of your WAS installation, and executing **startServer.bat server1**.[1]
2. Next, go the WebSphere Administrative Console. Typically, this is at http://localhost:9090/admin.[2]
3. If WAS security is not yet enabled, the administrative console does not prompt an administrator for a password. In this case, the user ID can be any made-up name so that WAS can audit any changes made to the configuration.
4. The admin console should show the homepage. On the left, you will notice the tree menu. This is the main instrument of navigation through the administrative console.

   The first step is to expand the Security portion of the tree. There will be more subentries. Expand the User Registries subentry. There are three types of registries:

1 Refer to Appendix C for installation and post installation instructions. Also, the troubleshooting section will have instructions on certain log files to look at for problem determination.

2 Different platforms may have different default ports. These are assuming the usual default ports.

- **Local OS**—Leverages the operating system for a security registry. For example, on the Microsoft Windows platform, it would use the users defined on the Windows machine. This is ideal for some development scenarios; however, a simple file registry may be more appropriate if you don't have the ability to easily modify your Windows user registry. Actually, this is the technique we use in this book.
- **LDAP Registry**—Makes use of an LDAP server for user information. LDAP is a very common solution for security registries. WAS supports many LDAP directories. LDAP is an ideal solution for production scenarios.
- **Custom Registries**—WAS provides a simple interface that you can extend to map to an underlying custom registry implementation. For example, a set of JDBC tables may contain a table for users and groups. You can write a Custom Registry to utilize these tables as a security registry. WAS ships with a sample File Registry that is simple to configure. We will use it here.

**NOTE**

User registries are configured on WebSphere so that applications can make use of J2EE security. Most of the time, applications are unaware of the underlying registries because application artifacts are secured using roles. The roles are mapped to users or groups at deployment time. Therefore, understand that the user registry choice is a contract between the application server and the security registry and therefore does not affect the portability of the application at all. In fact, it enforces a more portable solution to security without compromise. It is very common for developers to test using a file registry and deploy to a test server that is configured for an LDAP Registry. This independence from specific configuration issues is an important property of J2EE security.

Select **Custom**, as illustrated in Figure 3-6.

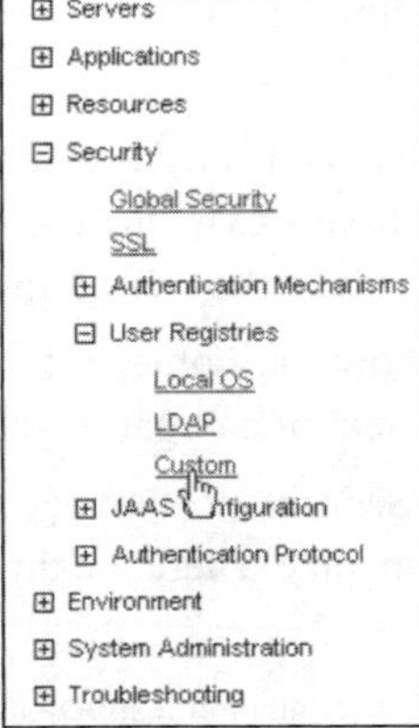


**Figure 3-6** Select Custom under User Registries.

5. This will bring the administrator to the Custom User Registry page. Here, you must provide the user name and password for WAS to use to authenticate to the underlying Registry. For the example registry in this book, use "adminUser" for the Server User ID and use "password1a" for the Server User password. You must also enter the Custom Registry Classname. We will use the File Sample provided with WAS. Enter **com.ibm.websphere.security.FileRegistrySample**. Press the **Apply** button, as shown in Figure 3-7. Next, click the **Custom Properties** Link.

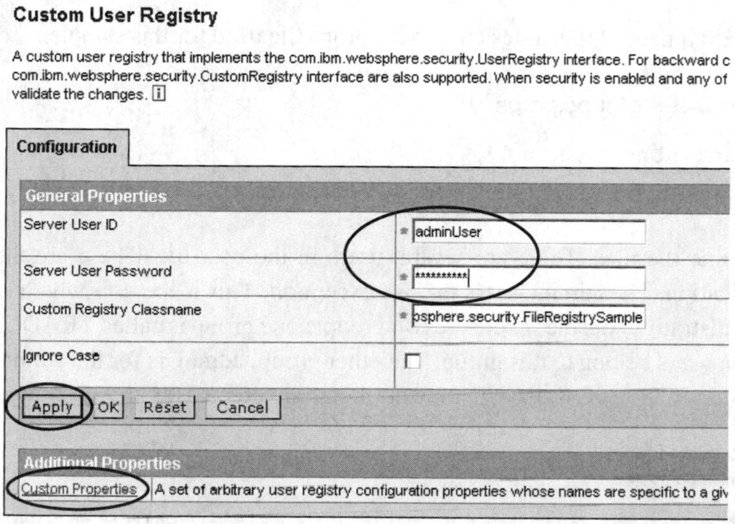

**Figure 3-7** Custom User Registry.

Under the Custom Properties, you must create two properties: **groupsFile** and **usersFile**. The value of the files is set to the actual location of the files that store the data for the user registry. If you extracted the zip file provided with this book to the C drive, the location of the files is **C:/WASDeployBook/UserRegistry/users.props and C:/WASDeployBook/UserRegistry/groups.props**. The format of the user file is as follows:

```
<user name>:<password>:<unique user identifier>:<identifiers
➥of groups user belongs to commas separated>:<Display Name>
```

Code Snippet 3-1 illustrates the users.props file included in the sample.

**Code Snippet 3-1** users.props

```
adminUser:password1a:123:987:AdminUser
bbird:password1a:234:876:BigBird
ckid:password1a:345:876:CiscoKid
lranger:password1a:456:876:LoneRanger
```

```
jbond:password1a:567:876:JamesBond
mshark:password1a:678:876:MikeShark
userid:password1a:789:876:UserIdentification
```

The format of the group file is as follows:

```
<group-name>:<group identifier>:<users that belong to the
➥group comma separated>:<display name>
```

Code Snippet 3-2 illustrates the groups.props file used for this sample.

**Code Snippet 3-2** groups.props

```
admin:987:adminUser:Admin
TRADE:876:bbird,ckid,lranger,jbond,mshark,userid:Trade_Users
```

Examine the files. There are several users in the user file. These are the users of the application. The adminUser is the one exception. This is the user who has access to the administrative console. There are two groups: one group is called TRADE. All the application users belong to this group. The other group, admin, is for the admin console user, adminUser. Press OK once; the file attributes are created, as shown in Figure 3-8.

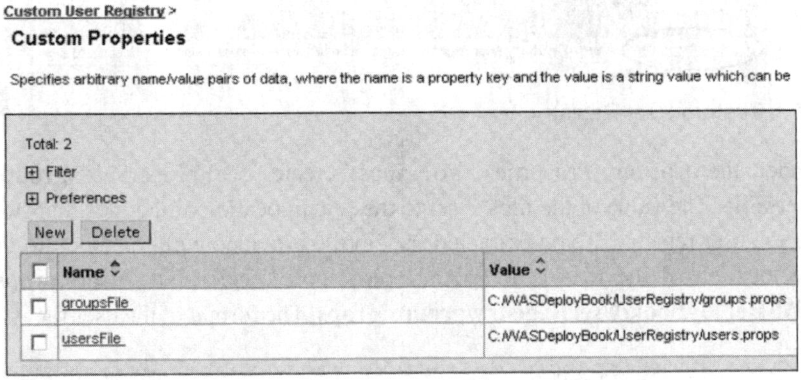

Custom User Registry >
**Custom Properties**

Specifies arbitrary name/value pairs of data, where the name is a property key and the value is a string value which can be

Total: 2
⊞ Filter
⊞ Preferences
New Delete

| | Name | Value |
|---|---|---|
| ☐ | groupsFile | C:\WASDeployBook\UserRegistry\groups.props |
| ☐ | usersFile | C:\WASDeployBook\UserRegistry\users.props |

**Figure 3-8** Custom Registry.

> **NOTE**
> It is important to remember that this file registry is not a production-quality solution. It is useful as an example of implementing a Custom Registry for demonstration of deployment, or for the Unit Test Environment inside WebSphere Studio. Remember, you should be using an LDAP Registry or other secure registry in production.

6. Once you press OK, you must save the changes. A save link should appear on the top of the page. If not, you can click the save link on the main menu. This will bring the admin console to the save page. Press the Save button. The configuration must be saved to make changes permanent. Changes made in the administrative console will not take effect until you explicitly save it.

**NOTE**

In general, when starting new projects, administrators tend to use the administrative console to set up initial test environments. However, repetitive human tasks are error-prone. WAS provides a scripting solution called wsadmin that calls the same JMX administrative objects that the WAS admin console uses. Furthermore, you can use ANT to script and automate certain tasks. JMX, wsadmin, and ANT will be explained and used in this book. As this book moves further along, the examples rely more on scripting.

7. Next, we need to configure an LTPA password. WAS supports two authentication mechanisms:

   - **SWAM (Simple WebSphere Authentication Mechanism)**—This mechanism is intended for development environments. SWAM does not support forwarding of credentials and requires no configuration.
   - **LTPA (Lightweight Third-Party Authentication)**—This mechanism is intended for distributed platforms. It supports forwarding of credentials. LTPA works with other mechanisms such as Single Sign-on and supports distributed environments through the use of cryptography.

   LTPA should be used for most environments. Chapter 18 will cover this in more detail. Under the **Security** tree menu item, expand **Authentication Mechanisms** and click the **LTPA** link, as shown in Figure 3-9.

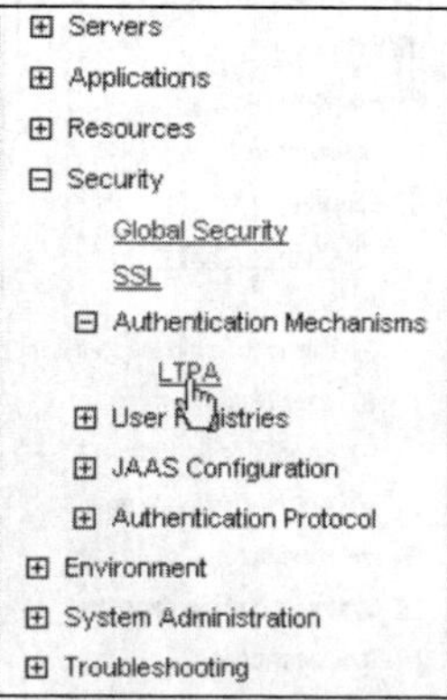


**Figure 3-9** Select LTPA.

8. On the LTPA page, enter a password, such as "password1a." Make sure to confirm the password and press **OK** when finished (see Figure 3-10). The keys will be generated automatically when security is first enabled. The LTPA key is essentially an index into the table used to re-create the credentials in case the request flows to a different application server as part of a request. This will be explained further in Chapter 18, "Security."

LTPA

Lightweight Third Party Authentication configuration settings. When security is enabled an changes. The LTPA keys are automatically generated the first time security is enabled. Aft the password and press OK or Apply to generate the keys (no need to press the Generat saved.

Configuration

Generate Keys | Import Keys | Export Keys

General Properties

| | |
|---|---|
| Password | * ********** |
| Confirm Password | * ********** |
| Timeout | * 120 |
| Key File Name | |

Apply | OK | Reset | Cancel

**Figure 3-10** LTPA key generation.

9. Next, we will enable security in WAS. In WAS, there is one active registry, in this case, the Custom File Registry. Back in the tree menu, expand **Security** and press the **Global Security** link, as shown in Figure 3-11. This will render the Global Security page.

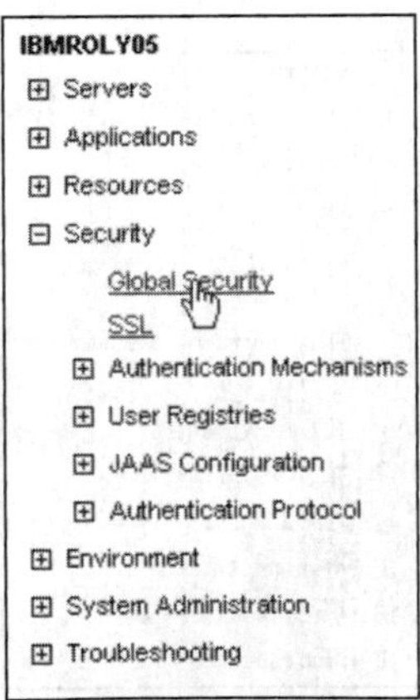


**Figure 3-11** Global Security link.

10. The first check box is Enabled, which enables security in WAS. Once enabled, WAS will enable applications to use J2EE security, using the Active Registry to acquire user and group information. There is much more to security that will be covered throughout this book. The second check box is for enabling Java 2 Security. The Java 2 Security model offers policy-driven, fine-grained access control to system resources from a Java Virtual Machine (JVM) perspective. Java 2 can protect resources such as the file system, system properties, socket connections, threads, and class-loading. Application Code must be explicitly granted the required permission in order to access protected resources. Chapter 18 will cover WAS and Java 2 Security. Check both boxes. On the Active Authentication Mechanism option, select **LTPA**. On the Active User Registry option, select **Custom**. This makes the configured Custom Registry the active registry, as shown in Figure 3-12. Press **OK**.

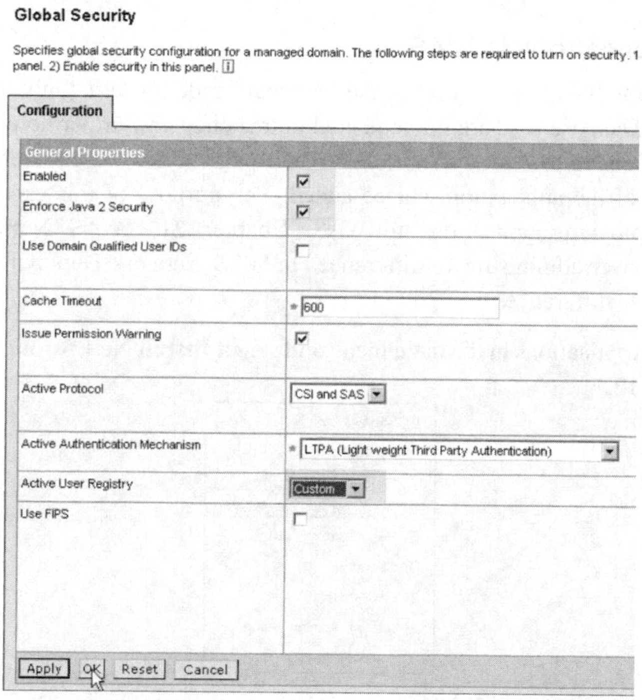

**Figure 3-12** Global Security page.

11. Save the configuration again. Log out of the admin console by pressing the logout link and close the browser.

12. Now that we have enabled security, we need to restart the server. Back in the command prompt, enter the command **stopServer.bat server1**. Once the server has stopped, restart the server by entering the command **startServer.bat server1**.[3]

3 Please refer to the troubleshooting chapter and Appendix C for examining logs in case of errors.

13. Once the server is started, bring up a new browser and go to the admin console URL. This time, the admin login page prompts for a user and a password. Now you must enter the user that is part of the registry and the one we specified when we configured the custom registry. Enter **adminUser** and **password1a**.

14. Remain logged in.

This completes the security configuration. For the rest of the book, WAS will be enabled for security and thus will support deployment for J2EE secure applications. You can also swap out the file registry for an LDAP registry. Chapter. 19 will cover some advanced LDAP configurations. Refer to [Mitra 2004] for a simple illustration on setting up an LDAP Registry for WebSphere in a development environment. Remember that the same users and groups that are bound to the application roles would have to be defined in the LDAP server unless you change the bindings at deployment time.

## Deploying Applications to WAS

In this section, we will deploy a subset of the Personal Trade System. Only the Login use case and Access Stock Data use case are implemented in this chapter. Furthermore, the Access Stock Data page is hard-coded to return a static JSP result page. Once we go over JDBC resources, dynamic portions of the application will be added. The purpose of this exercise is to become familiar with deploying applications to WAS. Chapter 21, "WAS Network Deployment Clustering," will cover administrative differences in WAS Network Deployment and will show some admin console differences.

1. Expand Applications in the main menu and select **Install New Application**, as shown in Figure 3-13.

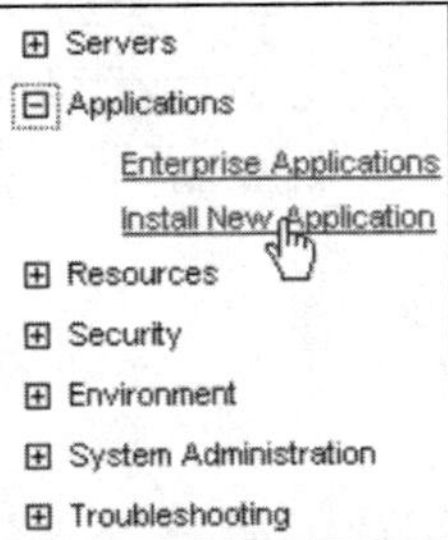


**Figure 3-13** Install New Application.

2. In the Preparing for the application installation page, select the **Browse** Button. The EAR file is located in C:\WASDeployBook\Chapter03\StockSystemEAR.ear; press **Next**. See Figure 3-14.

3. The next page allows the deployer to create the IBM binding deployment descriptor or to override the one packaged within the application. Also, you can select the default virtual host for all web applications within the EAR. We will keep the default values, as shown in Figure 3-15, and select **Next**.

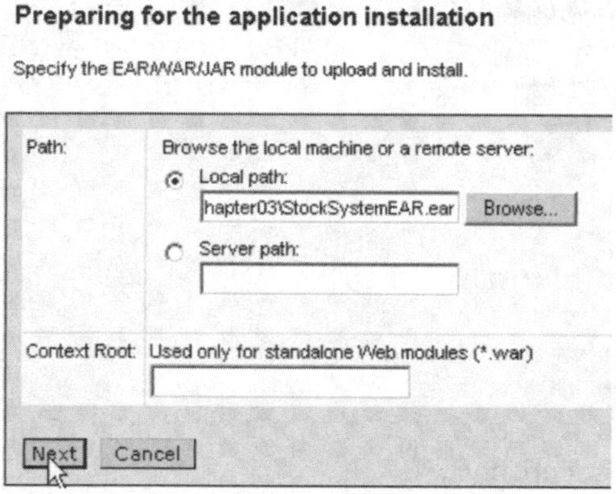

**Figure 3-14** Select the EAR file.

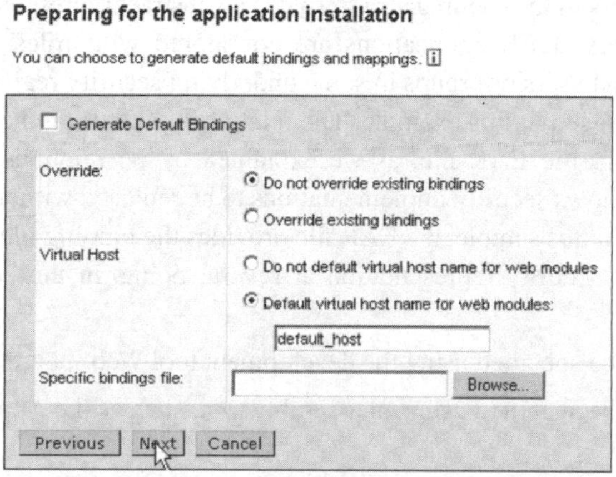

**Figure 3-15** Default binding and virtual host.

4. Depending on the submodules within the EAR, the number of steps will vary. Since the EAR file only contains a WAR file, the number of steps is small. In Chapter 9, "Enterprise JavaBeans," the application will add an EJB JAR file, and therefore there will be more steps. This first step has many options, but none of them are relevant here, so just click **Next**.
5. Step 2 allows you to map a specific web application within the EAR to a virtual host. EAR files may have more than one WAR file. Each WAR file can map to the same virtual host, or each can map to a different one. We will go over Virtual Hosts in Chapter 6, "J2EE Web Applications and the Web Container." Press **Next**.
6. Step 3 allows you to map the application to a particular application server. In WAS Base, there is only one server. This has more relevance in a network deployment where there are many servers. Press **Next**.

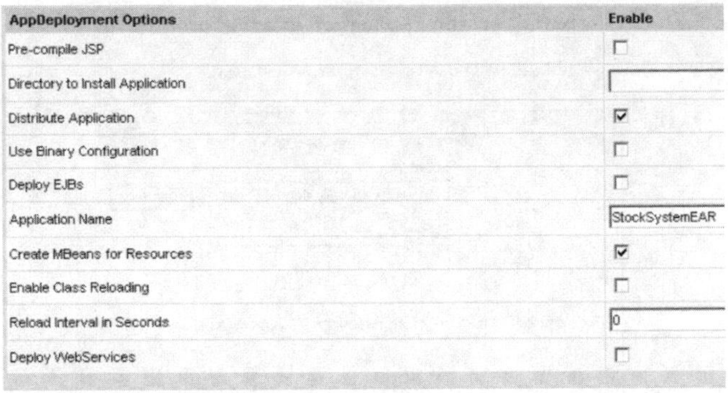

| AppDeployment Options | Enable |
|---|---|
| Pre-compile JSP | ☐ |
| Directory to Install Application | |
| Distribute Application | ☑ |
| Use Binary Configuration | ☐ |
| Deploy EJBs | ☐ |
| Application Name | StockSystemEAR |
| Create MBeans for Resources | ☑ |
| Enable Class Reloading | ☐ |
| Reload Interval in Seconds | 0 |
| Deploy WebServices | ☐ |

**Figure 3-16** Deployment options.

7. Step 4 allows the deployer to map a defined security role on the EAR to be mapped to groups or users in the user registry. A role is an abstract representation of some user or a group of users. J2EE applications are configured with roles. Those roles are then mapped to real users or groups in some underlying security registry, such as the sample File Registry used in this example. The relationship between them is maintained in the binding file of the EAR file, as we explained in the previous chapter. The level of abstraction allows security implementations to be replaced without having to change the application. In this sample, the EAR file provides the binding file. Roles can be mapped to the actual security representation at several points in the application deployment process:

   - They can be specified using the development tool WebSphere Studio.
   - They can be specified using an assembly tool, such as the Application Server Toolkit (ASTK).
   - They can be mapped at deployment time.

   Furthermore, a binding created at development or assembly time can be modified at deployment time, as shown here. As this book deals with more resources, advantages and disadvantages of the various approaches will be discussed. Right now, the role TRADEUSER, which is defined on the application deployment descriptor, is mapped to the group TRADE, which is defined in the Custom File Registry files. Leave the default values specified and press **Next**.

8. The last step is the Summary screen. Review the deployment settings and press **Finish**, as shown in Figure 3-17.

9. The deployment step should take a few seconds since there is only a small web application. Once done, there will be a link to save the deployment to the master configuration. Press the link; then on the Save page, press the **Save** button.

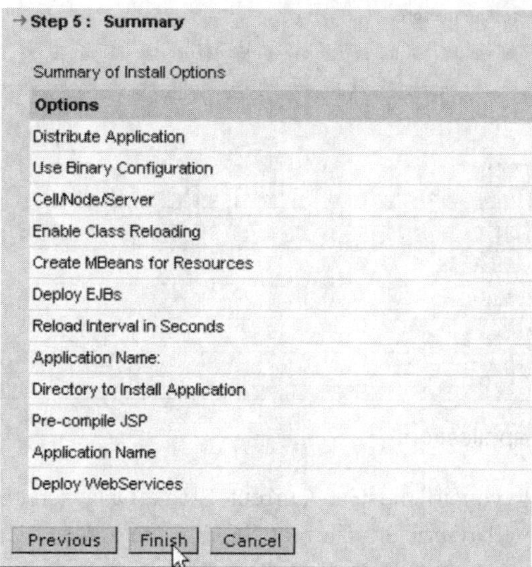


**Figure 3-17** Deployment summary.

The application has been successfully deployed. This has been a very simple deployment. As we talk about external resources such as JDBC and Enterprise Java Beans, there will be more settings to consider. Next, we verify the deployment.

## Verify Deployment

Verifying a deployment is an important task. For a simple application, having the deployer exercise some key functions in the application may be enough. For more complex applications, there should be scripted tests. Deployment verification should test that each resource works and ensure that security is working. Sometimes, running automated component tests with frameworks such as JUnit and Cactus is enough. For this chapter, exercising the login screen and stock data screen is sufficient:

1. From the tree menu, expand **Applications** and select **Enterprise Applications**.
2. The Status column next to StockSystemEAR should have a red X. This indicates the application is not started. Press the check box next to the StockSystemEAR and press the **Start** button, as shown in Figure 3-18. Once started, the status should show a green arrow.
3. Open a second browser[4] and go the following URL: http://localhost:9080/pts. This will bring you to the login screen. Log in with the user **bbird**. For the password, enter **password1a**. The Login screen is shown in Figure 3-19.

4 It's important that this really be a second browser. If this browser shares session cookies with the browser that you used to authenticate to the WAS admin console, re-authentication won't be necessary, and you won't see the login page.

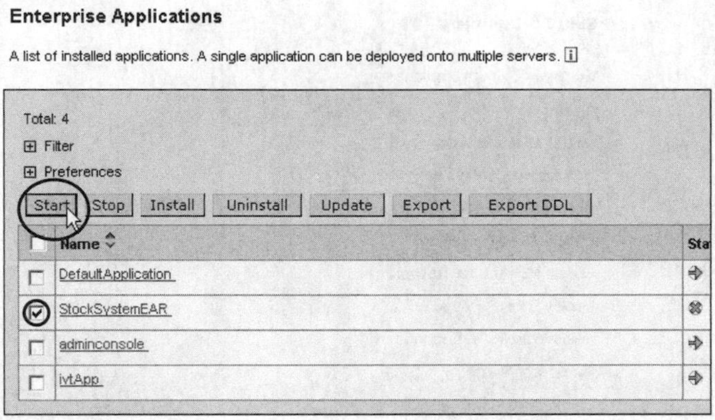

**Figure 3-18** Start an application.

4. This will bring you to the Get Current Stock Data screen. Enter **IBM** and press **Submit**. This will return the Current Stock Data screen. The returned data is hard-coded. We have not configured any external resources. You could enter any input, and the result will be the same.
5. When done, press the **Logout** link.

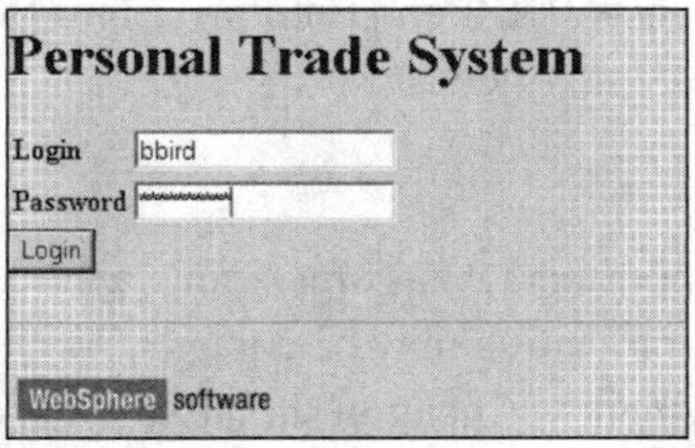

**Figure 3-19** Login screen.

6. Go back to the Enterprise Application screen in the admin console. Select the Stock-SystemEAR and press the Stop button. This will stop the application.
7. Again on the Enterprise Application Screen, select the StockSystemEAR and press Uninstall. This will uninstall the application. We will be installing newer versions as this book progresses, so we need to clean the environment.
8. Press the **Save** line and then the **Save** button on the save page. The configuration must be saved because the application is no longer deployed.
9. Log out of the admin console.
10. Back in the command prompt, stop the server by typing **stopserver server1 –user adminUser –password password1a**.

The application deployment has been successfully verified.

## Conclusion

In this chapter, we introduced you to the application used throughout this book. Next, you learned how to configure WAS for secure deployment. Then, the application was deployed and verified. The deployment in this chapter was quick and easy; however, most application modules are more complex. In the next chapter, we will discuss J2EE build models and introduce scripting techniques that will help manage deployment in an enterprise environment. The concepts in the next chapter will set up the way deployment is handled in the chapters that follow.

CHAPTER 4

# Build and Deploy Procedures

In the last chapter, we provided you with a quick start to WebSphere Application Server (WAS) by configuring and deploying the Personal Trade System. The deployment was simple and straightforward, using the WAS administrative console to do most of the work. With small applications, this approach is often sufficient. However, for most J2EE applications, deployment requires much more planning and process. In fact, the entire application lifecycle requires rigorous processes. In this chapter, we will focus on three closely related areas: builds, deployment, and server configuration. We will start by discussing some key reasons why rigor is important and then define some terminology that we'll be using for the rest of the chapter. Then we'll identify three common approaches to build and deploy. Following that, we will focus on automation. Automation of the build and deploy steps can reduce the amount of effort required to produce and then deploy an application. Automation can also reduce the likelihood of human error—not an insignificant concern in large and complex projects. In addition to automating the assembly and building of applications, we will offer advice on how to automate server configuration.

## Procedures Matter

The enterprise development model is more complex than traditional small application development—code must be written, compiled, assembled, and then deployed (presumably with some testing included). That is, after the code is compiled, the application must be assembled from a set of modules into a single application EAR. In addition, deployment includes the implicit concept of "binding," which is taking a built application and binding its contents to the target runtime environment. These two concepts are very powerful and give applications a great deal of flexibility, but they do require additional discipline. Build and deploy in these situations are core functions that must be carefully managed like anything else. Setting up high-quality procedures correctly can set the tone for the rest of the project.

In our experience, failing to develop solid procedures often will cause projects to experience serious problems and occasionally will result in project failure. In this book, we are assuming a rigorous approach to development, roughly like this:

- Developers write code following high-quality software engineering principles. This includes a configuration management system for their source code and other artifacts.
- Developers execute unit tests against their code before checking it into the repository.
- Code is **built** into a complete system following a well-defined procedure.
- Code is **deployed** to a runtime environment (an actual WAS instance) following some well-defined procedure.
- Deployments are verified using a well-defined set of component test cases. Component tests are essentially a subset of development unit tests and are focused on cross-component function and environment sanity.
- The target application server environment is **configured** using well-defined procedures.
- Multiple runtime environments are available for different purposes (development integration, system test, performance, etc.) as defined in Chapter 16, "Ideal Development and Testing Environments."

If you are not following procedures like these, your projects will suffer problems, quite possibly serious problems. Unfortunately, due to space constraints, we can't discuss every aspect of this basic approach. Instead, we are concerned here with the build, deployment, and server configuration steps. Notice that the preceding list makes no mention of automation. This is not an accident. Rigorous procedures can be developed without automation and will work fine for projects of a certain size. But for various reasons already discussed, automation can greatly benefit the basic approaches. Many parts of this book focus on using automation.

In this chapter, we will focus on moving an application out of the desktop development environment and into development integration. Because the deployment life cycle starts from the development environment, creating a rigorous process for moving a build out of development can set the tone for a successful deployment. Rigorous process in development can be a model for rigorous deployment in other environments, such as system tests or performance testing. We will focus on these other environments in Chapter 16.

## Development and Build Terminology

Before continuing with the remainder of this chapter, we need to define some common terms that we are going to be using. Some of this terminology may be familiar. In order to be consistent with terms, we define several here:

1. **Runtime or runtime environment**—A place where code can be executed. Basically, this is a system or set of systems that includes WAS and other needed components where application code is deployed for various purposes.

2. **IDE**—An Integrated Development Environment used by an application developer to write, compile, and unit test code. WebSphere Studio is an example of an IDE.
3. **Unit Test Environment (UTE)**—A runtime where developers run their unit tests. This runtime is often integrated with the IDE to offer developers quick testing and debugging. The WAS unit test environment inside WebSphere Studio is an example of a UTE. If developers do not have access to an IDE with a UTE, it is not uncommon for them to have a WAS install on their desktop for unit testing.
4. **Verification runtime**—A runtime needed to verify a successful build. This runtime is usually an application server and usually is located on the same machine where an official build is done. Depending on where the build is done, this runtime can be a UTE inside of an IDE, like WebSphere Studio, or a standalone WAS install on a dedicated build server.
5. **Code repository**—A place where developers store versions of code and code history to share with others. Examples of code repositories are Rational Clearcase and the Concurrent Versioning System (CVS). We will use CVS throughout this book because it is readily available. Appendix C, "Setup Instructions for Samples," has information about where you can obtain CVS.
6. **Golden Workspace**—A special term we use to represent a desktop snapshot of a deployable version of the code. This is essentially a version of the system loaded into a single IDE instance. This instance represents a final version before an official build.
7. **Build server**—A centralized server needed to run automated builds. A centralized build can be used to coordinate projects. Specialized build scheduling and publishing tools, such as Cruise Control or AntHill,[1] can be installed on a build server to add an extra level of automation.
8. **Binary repository**—A place to store packaged builds that are ready for deployment. Builds must be stored and versioned just like code.

## Build and Deployment Models

Now that we have outlined some key concepts, we are going to define three build and deployment models at increasing levels of sophistication. The three models are Assemble Connection Model, Assemble Export Model, and Assemble Server Model. We'll return to the discussion of server configuration later.

### Assemble Connection Model

The simplest possible method of build and deploy is the Assemble Connection Model. Figure 4-1 illustrates this model.

1 Cruise Control can be obtained from http://cruisecontrol.sourceforge.net/. AntHill can be obtained from http://www.urbancode.com/.

In this model, build, assembly, and verification steps are all performed from a desktop using either an IDE or an assembly tool. For example, WebSphere Studio contains tools for deploying both server configurations and applications directly from a WebSphere Studio workspace into a runtime environment.

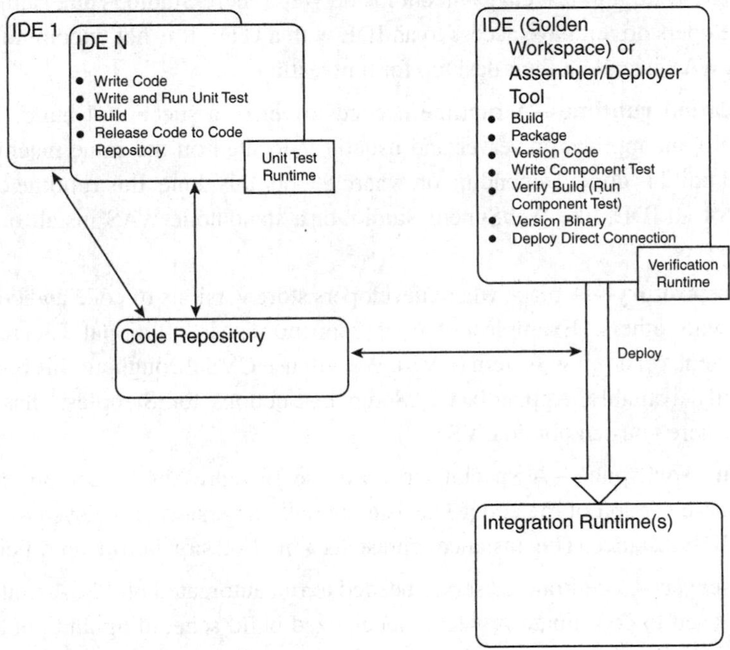


**Figure 4-1** Assemble Connection Model.

When using this model, it is essential to use a Golden Workspace as part of the official build and deploy process. That is, instead of deploying directly from an uncontrolled developer's desktop, use a dedicated desktop (or at least a dedicated workspace) for creating and exporting to the application server.

This model is simple for small development environments and it is easy to implement. However, it has major drawbacks:

- The development team makes use of *deployment shortcuts* available to developers. For example, WebSphere Studio has a remote server deployment feature that enables an application to be deployed directly from the development workbench.[2] No EAR is ever produced, and thus the deployment details are hidden from developers. Despite its

2 Another example of a "deployment shortcut" is deploying an application in an exploded format. Developers usually feel they need this to do quick deployment while making and debugging frequent changes. An IDE with an integrated UTE should make exploded deployments unnecessary.

simplicity, this deployment process is less portable because J2EE defines no way of deploying applications that are not in an EAR or one of the submodules.

- Because no EAR file is produced, there is no versioning of any EAR file. If an environment needs to rollback to a prior version, the build must be reproduced from the source. This can lead to unanticipated errors reproducing the correct build if the source repository tool is not sophisticated or if assemblers do not make use of code repositories correctly.
- It takes great discipline for developers to make this work. It is very difficult to consistently reproduce a build. Deploying directly from the IDE or application source places too many dependencies on idiosyncrasies.
- The process used in development and testing does not usually reflect the process used in production. This means the deployment process for production will mostly likely suffer from a lack of proper testing.
- This process does not scale well. As the artifacts and number of developers grow, the assembler and deployer become a bottleneck. Many artifacts and developers are feeding input to a human that is executing a manual process.

We strongly oppose this approach. We include it here only as a point of contrast to the next two approaches, which are more reasonable.

## Assemble Export Model

The key problem with the previous model is that the deployment step that is used during development does not in any way reflect what is typically done in production. That's unfortunate because this delays the finding of inevitable problems. In the Assemble Export Model, we recognize this weakness and move to a more robust model. Here, the development tools are used to produce the deployable package (either from a Golden Workspace or from deployment scripts). The deployable package is then delivered to the runtime environment and deployed using a well-defined procedure. Figure 4-2 illustrates this model.

This results in a process that is rigorous but potentially time-consuming, depending on the complexity of the application and deployment environment. It is also subject to human error. For systems of reasonable size, this approach will work. With large environments, however, this is often insufficient.

Nonetheless, this is a clear and defined way of producing an EAR file every time. The application is deployed to a runtime similar to how it will be done in production. Therefore, certain errors can be found in this model that could not be found in the previous model.[3] This approach has some nice advantages. Unfortunately, this model still suffers from some drawbacks:

3 For example, classpath errors seem to crop up later in deployment because the packaging of the application is often ignored when deploying using shortcuts. Producing an EAR file each time helps you think about package design earlier in the development lifecycle.

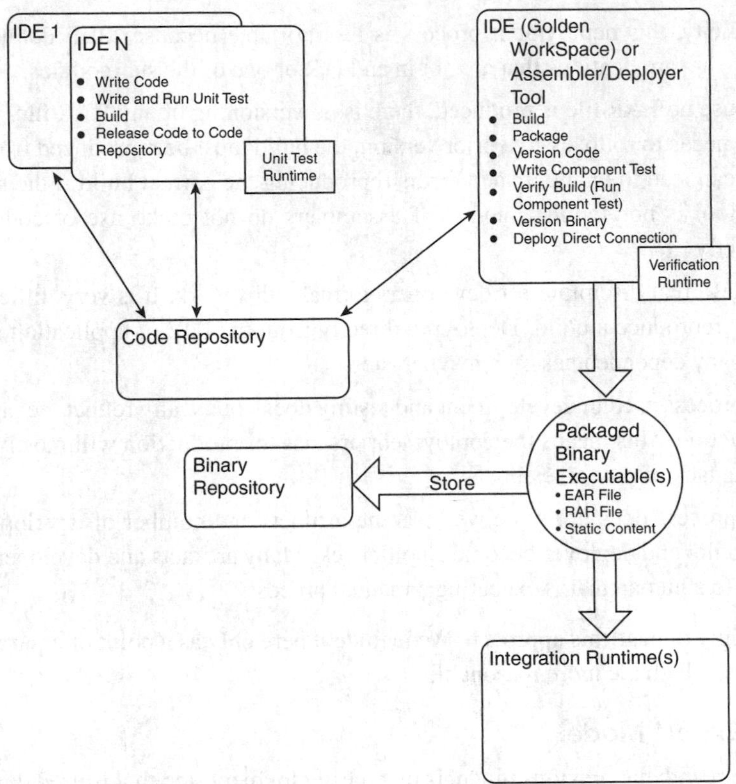


**Figure 4-2** Assemble Export Model.

- There is still a scalability issue because someone is needed to create the EAR file from within the IDE (admittedly, this is only a few mouse clicks) and then execute the deployment using the WAS admin tools. In addition, the application assembler has to verify that changes made by various developers work together. As the number of developers increases, this task can become more difficult for one individual.
- The build process is dependent on the development team. In some organizations, this is an issue in itself.

This model has been used successfully in numerous organizations. Furthermore, if the project grows to a larger size, it can be upgraded to the next model.

## Assemble Server Model

The Assemble Server Model expands on the previous model by externalizing the build process. That is, instead of performing builds from within an IDE or from a developer's workstation, builds are done in a separate environment. Obviously, externalizing builds from the IDE requires automation of the build step.

The need for this model is dependent on some key factors:

- **The size and complexity of the project**—Large development efforts often require an externalized build environment to coordinate many pieces.
- **Build and deploy frequency**—Projects with demanding schedules often require frequent building and testing in order to meet demanding schedules. There needs to be a way to manage and automate many of the tasks to allow this to happen. By moving builds to dedicated machines, additional opportunities for automation are created.
- **Multiple development teams**—Large development efforts often involve multiple development teams, sometimes under different management. In order to manage the different teams, it is best to have a designated environment for builds and one team responsible for it.

Figure 4-3 illustrates the Assemble Server Model.

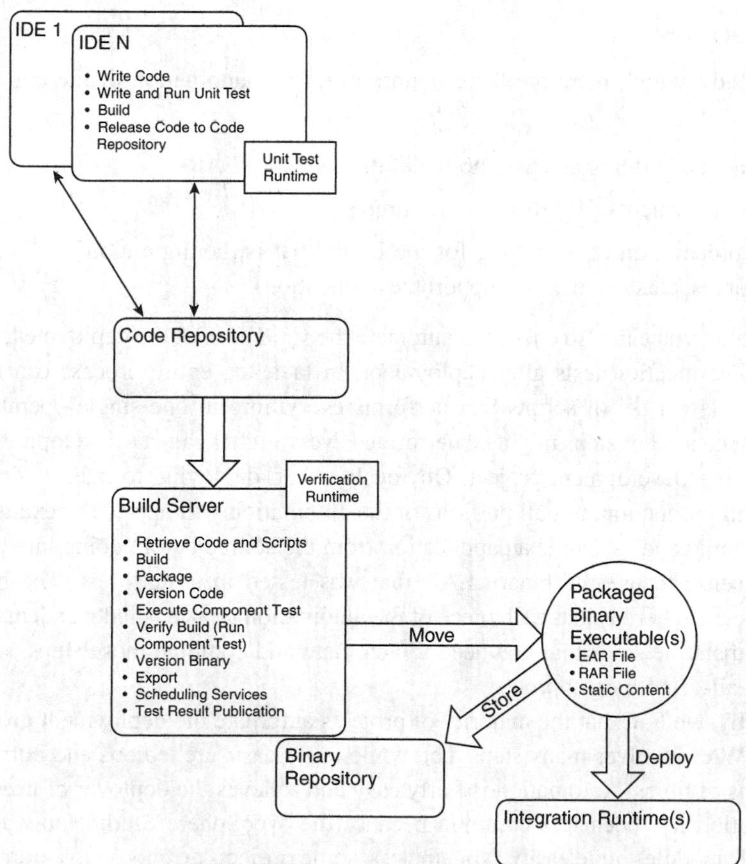


**Figure 4-3** Assemble Server Model.

This model solves many of the drawbacks in the other models. However, there are downsides:

- The initial planning and creation of scripts takes significant amounts of time. The scripts need to be tested and verified as much as the application itself.
- The build environment needs to be built and tested. Building environments sometimes takes extra effort that people don't always want to invest. In addition, you must consider that resources may not be available. Having an extra build machine may not be feasible.

Nonetheless, if this approach is combined with automation, there are long-term benefits to using this model, and it will end up saving time for large or complex projects. A server-side automated build is highly scalable because it does not generally depend on the number of artifacts or developers. Of course, substantial effort will need to be invested in the creation of automation scripts. In the next section, we'll talk more about automation.

## Automation

As we've already stated, there are three opportunities for automation of the build and deploy process:

- The actual building and assembling of the code into EARs
- The deployment of EARs onto a runtime
- The preparation of a runtime for the EAR (that is, configuration of the server (J2EE resources, clusters, etc.) to support the application)

In addition, you can also choose to automate the validation of the deployment by automatically running verification tests after deployment. In fact, the entire process can be combined together into a larger set of scripts that performs everything in one single operation. You can imagine that such a set of steps might be performed every night against a development integration environment on a development project. Obviously, when deploying to later environments like system test and production, not all portions of the automation will apply. For example, it makes little sense to build and assemble an application from the source before going into production. It makes more sense to use the binary EAR that was tested in system test. The beauty of the approach advocated here is that each piece of the automation puzzle is independent of the others. You can automate the steps that you need to automate and combine those steps as appropriate. This is not an all-or-nothing approach.

Generally, we find that the majority of projects automate the deployment process because deploying to WAS involves many steps that, while fairly easy, are tedious and boring when performed dozens of times. Automation is fairly easy and relieves the deployer of needless tedium. Build automation has been less common because the WebSphere Studio tools already create complete EAR modules quite easily. Nonetheless, some projects do choose to automate builds for good reasons:

- First, the corporate culture might be uncomfortable with developers creating builds and might prefer that a central-build organization build software. We described this when defining the Assemble Server Model.
- Second, the build process itself might be complicated by the combination of a number of modules from multiple sources (possibly multiple project teams).

While less common, there are situations where the build is automated but not the deployment step. It might be that the build process is very complex (perhaps a large application with many pieces), but the deploy step is fairly simple.

Automation can also be applied to server configuration. Some organizations may have many environments that require constant creation and re-creation of configurations.

We'll now discuss these different automation steps in turn.

## Build Automation

Scripting is the major vehicle for automating build tasks. There are a few scripting languages for building applications, but ANT has become the dominant language for building Java applications; therefore, ANT will be the scripting language driving the automation in this book. ANT is an XML-based scripting language that can be used to build Java and J2EE applications. If you are not familiar with ANT, we give an overview in Appendix A, "ANT with WebSphere Application Server."

There are many strategies to structuring ANT scripts. We will use an approach that is similar to the popular Model View Controller (MVC) paradigm. We are going to create scripts with a clear separation of concern. Some scripts work against specific artifacts and can be thought of as "model" scripts. Other scripts control the overall process and thus are "controllers":[4]

- Model scripts produce artifacts or perform a specific task. A model task, for example, will build a WAR file or check out source code from a repository.
- Controller scripts execute other scripts in a particular sequence to perform an overall flow. Controller scripts can interact with model scripts or other controller scripts. Models should be independent of controllers. The same model build should work with different controllers.

If we apply this approach to building a J2EE application, model scripts represent scripts that build specific modules, such as a JAR file, a WAR file, or an EAR file. Controller scripts execute each of the model scripts in sequence. This is illustrated in Figure 4-4.

Building model scripts requires knowledge of the domain. For example, writing a model script for building a WAR file requires that the script writer has knowledge of the structure of J2EE web applications. Throughout this book, as we illustrate various portions of WAS, we will show various model scripts.

4 The careful reader will note that we have no view scripts. We did say similar!

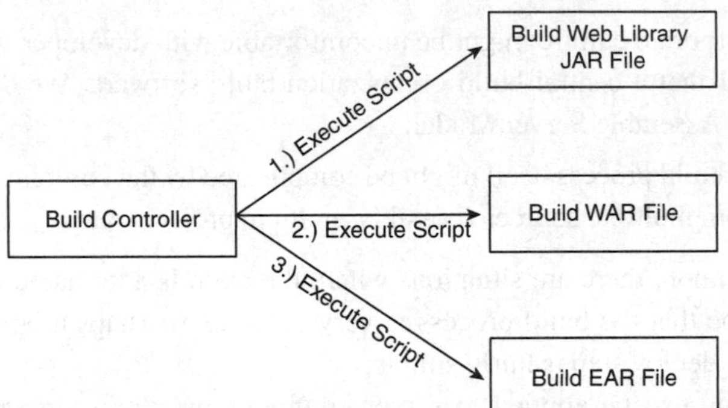


**Figure 4-4** Build controller.

Build controller scripts define the flow of the build process. Code Snippet 4-1 illustrates a sample controller script. Using the `<ant>` tag, a controller script can execute other ANT scripts. In this script, the controller calls each model script in sequence.

**Code Snippet 4-1** Controller snippet

```
<?xml version="1.0" encoding="UTF-8"?>

<project name="buildprojects" default="buildall">
  <!--  SETUP PROPERTIES FOR CONTROLLER SCRIPT -->
  <property name="srcroot" value="C:/SourceRoot" />
  <property name="buildhome" value="C:/build" />

  <target name="init">
    <delete dir="${buildhome}" />
    <mkdir dir="${buildhome}"/>
  </target>

  <!--BUILD ALL PROJECTS THAT MAKE UP THE TOTAL EAR -->
  <target name="buildprojects">

        <!--CALL BUILD FOR STANDALONE JAVA PROJECT THAT IS PART OF THE
        ➥WAR -->
    <ant dir="${srcroot}/PTSVerificationTest" inheritall="true" >
  <!--  OVERRIDE MODEL SCRIPT PROPERTIES WITH CONTROLLER PROPERTIES -->
      <property name="wasroot" value="${wasroot}" />
      <property name="srcroot" value="${srcroot}"/>
      <property name="buildhome" value="${buildhome}"/>
```

```
   </ant>
  <!--CALL BUILD MODEL FOR WAR : PREVIOUS BUILD SCRIPT -->
   <ant dir="${srcroot}/PersonalTradeSystemWeb/WebContent"
   ➥inheritall="true" >
     <property name="wasroot" value="${wasroot}" />
     <property name="srcroot" value="${srcroot}"/>
     <property name="buildhome" value="${buildhome}"/>
   </ant>
  <!--  CALL BUILD MODEL FOR EAR FILE -->
   <ant dir="${srcroot}/StockSystemEAR" inheritall="true" >
     <property name="wasroot" value="${wasroot}" />
     <property name="srcroot" value="${srcroot}"/>
     <property name="buildhome" value="${buildhome}"/>

   </ant>
  </target>

  <target name="clean" >

  </target>

  <target name="buildall" depends="init,buildprojects,clean" />
</project>
```

> **NOTE**
> It is our recommendation to design and build controller scripts before building model scripts. This enables you to think about the design of the build process first. We will elaborate on this in the following sections.

As you read the remainder of this book, you will see many examples of controller and model build scripts.

## Deployment Automation

Deployment of applications can be automated as well. There are two approaches: ANT and wsadmin. WAS comes with a set of ANT tasks to handle many deployment tasks (for example, installing and uninstalling an EAR file or stopping and starting applications). Appendix A has a list of the supported WebSphere ANT tasks and examples of their usage. Throughout the examples in this book, we will use the WAS ANT tasks to deploy the application. As you will see, the WAS ANT tasks are actually a wrapper to WAS's wsadmin configuration language. There is nothing to stop you from using wsadmin to do deployment rather than ANT. This is really dependent on how deployment happens; for example, when combining build and deployment automation as part of a development build process, using ANT is convenient because the build and the deployment happen in the same language. On the other hand, your administrators may prefer to use just wsadmin.[5] We will use both ANT and wsadmin extensively throughout this book.

Code Snippet 4-2 illustrates a portion of the ANT deployment script used in the samples throughout this book. It illustrates how you can install an EAR file using ANT. Throughout the examples in this book, we will utilize the `<wsInstallApp>` task. You can examine the installation scripts under the various sample directories for each chapter.

**Code Snippet 4-2 Installing an application with ANT**

```
<target name="install" description="Installs the application">
  <wsInstallApp ear="${earfile}"
          options="-server ${servername}"
          wasHome="${wasroot}"
          user="${username}"
          password="${password}"
          conntype="${conntypenname}"
          port="${portnumber}"
             host="${hostname}"
             />
</target>
```

## Combining Build and Deployment Automation

We have illustrated how you can automate the build and deployment process using scripting. We have also illustrated how you can use MVC to design the flow of scripts. We now illustrate how we can combine these concepts to create an automated build and deployment process. Figure 4-5 gives an overview of part of the build and deploy process used throughout this book.

We will follow the gray portions of the figure. There is one master controller that controls the total process by calling either model scripts or other controllers. The steps in the process are as follows:

1. The master controller first calls a model script that extracts source from a code repository into a temporary directory. Part of the source that is extracted from the code repository is actually the model scripts that build the J2EE modules. The source should be versioned as well.

5 With the rising popularity of ANT, you may also find that your administrators want to use ANT.

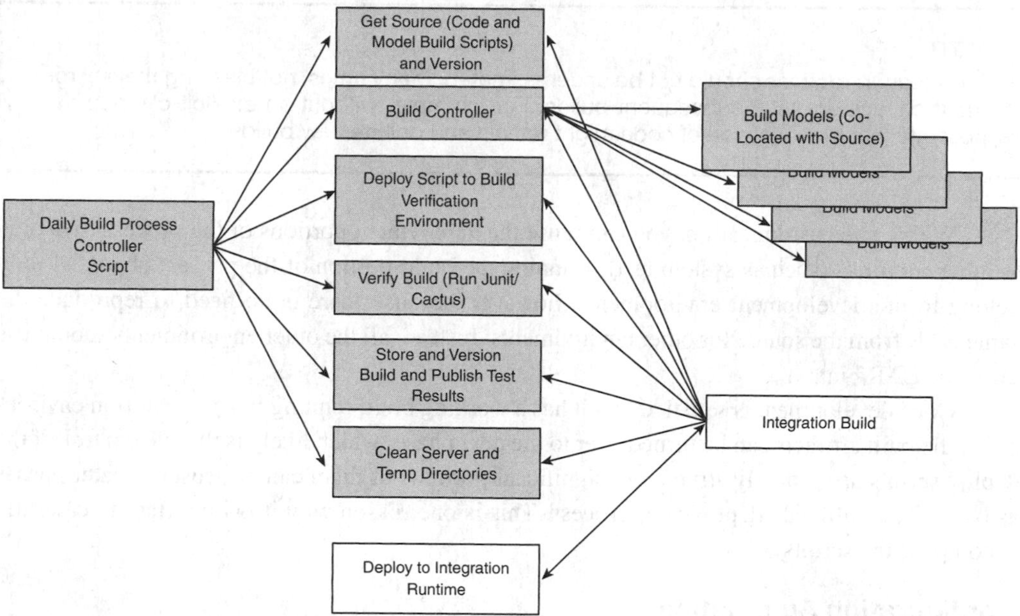


**Figure 4-5** Build process.

2. Next, the master controller runs the build controller. The build controller will look for the model build scripts in the source directory of each project extracted from the previous step.
3. After the build controller builds the StockSystem EAR file, the master scripts will call the model deploy scripts that install the application into a runtime environment.
4. Next, the master build script calls build verification model scripts. These are implemented using special ANT tasks that execute JUnit tests. The test results will be stored in a special directory created by the build.

> **NOTE**
> For every build, test results should be published somewhere associated with the build. In our book, we just overwrite the prior test results for simplicity.

5. Once finished, the master controller executes the versioning and publishing model tasks. This should include storing the EAR file in a binary repository and publishing the test results in some well-known location.
6. Finally, the master controller will execute the model script that cleans all of the intermediate directories. This step involves undeploying the application from the runtime environment and cleaning the build and source directories.

> **NOTE**
> The cleanup routines should not be underestimated. Many times, not cleaning the environment causes errors in subsequent builds. For example, without an explicit cleanup, it is possible that older version of code might remain and pollute new builds.

With some customization, you can reuse the deployment portions of the process to deploy to other runtimes (such as system test). Running the build portion of the process should strictly belong to the development environments, however, because there is no need to reproduce the same EAR from the source for other environments. Instead, all the other environments should use the same EAR binary.

Once development is satisfied that it has a working build running in an integration environment, the built artifacts can be turned over to the next phase, which likely is the system test. If the deploy scripts are properly structured, significant portions of them can be reused in later phases as part of the "official" deployment process. This is one reason why it is important to carefully decompose the scripts.

## Configuration Automation

We've discussed build and deploy automation. Now it is time to turn our attention to the last area of interest for this chapter: server configuration. Often, application-development projects start development without giving serious thought to server configuration. The development integration environment should be a testing ground for configuration procedures—either script or manual. Thinking about configuration procedures early in the process can help administrators set up the various testing and production environments later. As the development project begins, architects should begin to think about the flow of configuration. For example, consider an application that needs to access a relational database. Figure 4-6 illustrates an example configuration flow.

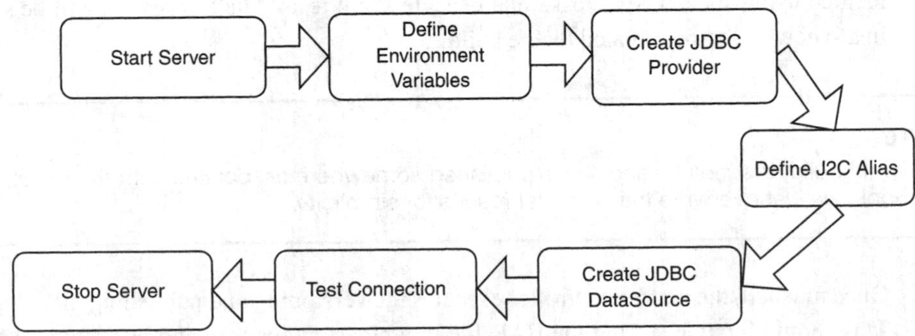


**Figure 4-6** Server configuration flow.

You'll notice that we are starting our script-development effort with a high-level design. Not surprisingly, this is not that different from how you design applications. When developing these scripts, keep in mind that it is crucial to keep these scripts up-to-date. An often-made mistake is that scripts are used initially, but then individual manual changes are made to the server configuration without modification to the original scripts. This results in the scripts becoming useless because they are no longer able to produce the required system configuration. Instead, the changes to configurations should be made as follows:

1. Incorporate the scripting change into the server configuration design.
2. Add changes to the scripts/flow.
3. Use the scripts to apply the changes to the server configuration.

During development, it may be acceptable to update the server configuration manually if application functionality and testing is a priority. But once that is done, go back and incorporate the changes into the scripts and test the scripts as a whole. This rigorous process will ensure quicker deployment as configurations get rolled out into new environments.[6]

To enforce configuration flow, configuration scripts can also follow the MVC paradigm. Here, model scripts are implemented using the *wsadmin* language while we will still rely on ANT as a controller for the configuration. Of course, you can use wsadmin as the controller as well. WAS contains a generic `<wsadmin>` ANT task to execute wsadmin scripts. Code Snippet 4-3 shows how you can use the task.

**Code Snippet 4-3 Executing wsadmin from ANT**

```
<!-- Generic ANT Caller , -->
<target name="genericWsadminCaller" description="Generic wsadmin task">
  <wsadmin
     wasHome="${wasroot}"
     user="${username}"
     password="${password}"
     conntype="${conntypenname}"
     port="${portnumber}"
     script="${scriptname}" />
</target>

 <!-- Call Create CreateWSVariables.jacl -->
 <target name="callCreateDBWSVariables">
   <antcall target="genericWsadminCaller">
     <param name="scriptname" value="CreateDBWSVariables.jacl"/>
   </antcall>
 </target>
```

6 It may also be necessary to create and test scripts that will undo any configurations because there may be a need to wipe out configurations to test the scripts.

In Code Snippet 4-3, we create a generic wsadmin task. From other tasks, we can pass wsadmin scripts using the `<antcall>` task. Using ANT as a controller, we can implement the flow as illustrated in Figure 4-7. This flow is very similar to that of our build and deployment process, except the ANT controller calls wsadmin scripts.

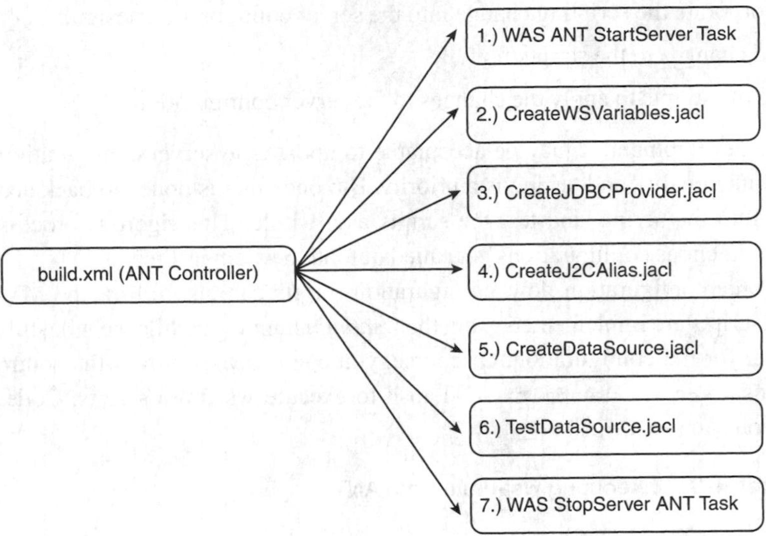


**Figure 4-7** Script design.

This type of script design is essential to building environments. Being able to reproduce environments from scripts is much more robust than using utilities that copy environments. WAS 4 had a tool called XMLConfig that allowed you to extract a configuration from one server and import it into another. This type of configuration-to-configuration promotion is error-prone, usually requires modification of scripts, and results in a process that is poorly controlled. For example, certain configurations may be OS-dependent or may have different directory structures. This means that the "copies" aren't perfect and that hand modification is needed. Instead, hand-built scripts can be designed to externalize properties into separate files to account for environment dependencies. With respect to control, the problem is that by copying an environment, you are making no decisions. You are merely making one environment look like another without any explicit control over configuration. During development and testing, it is not uncommon for people to make quick manual changes and then forget to back them out. When people copy environments, these random changes have an unfortunate tendency to end up in production without any clear reason. Instead, we strongly advocate using explicitly developed scripts.

## Adding Configuration Automation to Build and Deploy Automation

Because we chose to use ANT as our controller for configuration, you can easily add server configuration to the daily build process in development. Figure 4-8 illustrates adding the configuration controller to the overall build and deployment process.

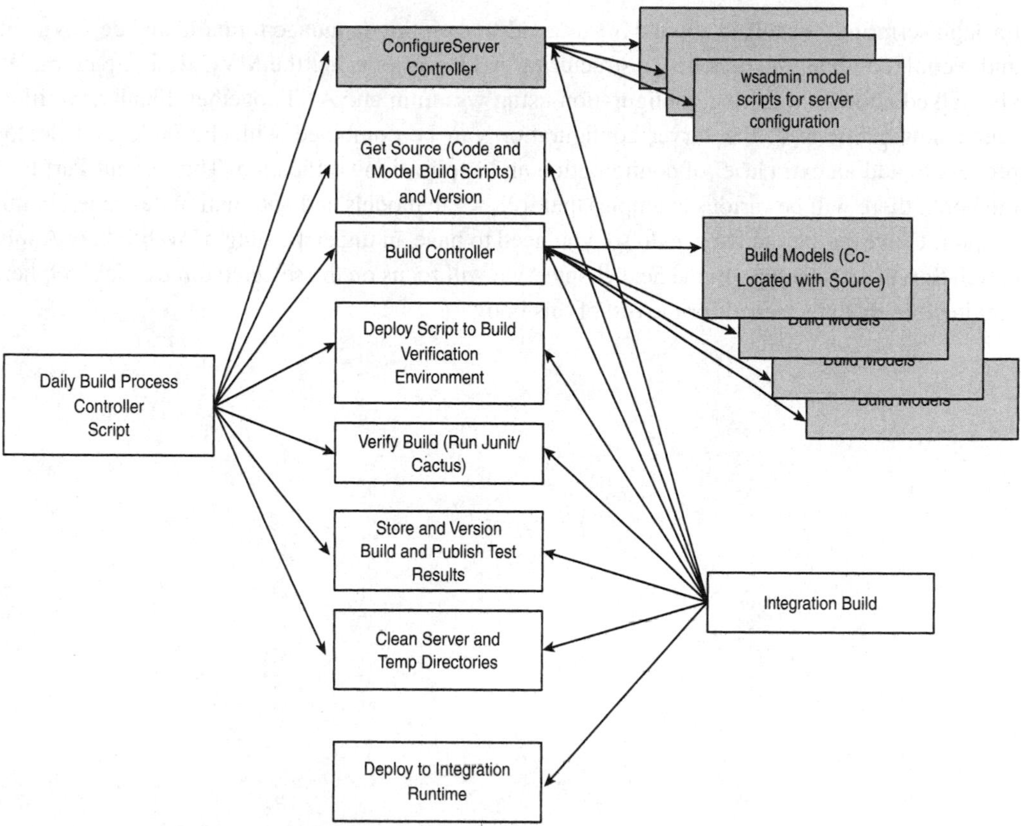


**Figure 4-8** Build, deployment, and configuration automation.

There are several advantages to this approach:

- Because the server gets configured each time during the build process, the configuration scripts are constantly being tested along with the application. The same verification tests verify both the application and the configuration.
- The same configuration scripts that are used by the development team are used by the administrators, ensuring more consistency and communication between the various teams an organization may have.

## Conclusion

In this chapter, we focused heavily on the importance of automation. All the automation samples in this book will use the combined build, deployment, and configuration processes shown in this chapter. We described three build and deployment models and offered advice on what type of projects would benefit from each model. We then focused heavily on implementing automation through scripting. We talked about ANT as an ideal scripting language for build and deployment, and we talked about the benefits of structuring ANT scripts using the MVC design pattern. We also talked about automating configuration using wsadmin and ANT together. Finally, we illustrated how portions of the server configuration can be combined with the build and deploy process to add an extra level of configuration and application verification. Throughout Part II of the book, there will be various examples that follow the models and automation described in this chapter. However, before we can do so, you need to have an understanding of WebSphere Application Server architecture. In the next chapter, we will focus on the selected topics of WebSphere architecture that are needed for the rest of this book.

CHAPTER 5

# WebSphere Application Server Architecture

WebSphere Application Server (WAS) V5 is a J2EE 1.3 (Java 2 Enterprise Edition) compliant runtime. This chapter covers the runtime architecture of WebSphere Application Server V5 (also referred to as WAS base), which is a single JVM (process) runtime. The discussion will include an introduction to the WAS runtime architecture, application and administrative clients, and the WAS implementation of various J2EE services such as JNDI (Java Naming and Directory Interface), Java classloaders, and other essential services. (We will discuss the WebSphere Application Server Network Deployment V5 in a later chapter.)

## Runtime Architecture

Architecturally, WAS V5 is considerably different from prior versions of WebSphere Application Server, though readers familiar with earlier versions of WAS will notice that WebSphere Application Server V5 bears a passing resemblance to the WAS V4.0 AE Single Server (AEs) edition. The key difference in WAS V5 from earlier versions is that the application server is designed to be a standalone process not dependent on other processes for administration or configuration information. This design provides improved fault tolerance and runtime performance. Figure 5-1 depicts the WAS V5 application server architecture as well as its interactions with the most common client types.

Each application server is a Java Virtual Machine (JVM) capable of running applications. The application server typically interacts with an external HTTP server to return a personalized response to a web client's request, though clients can also be "standalone" Java clients that communicate with EJBs running in WAS. As discussed earlier, application code is packaged in a J2EE Enterprise Application Archive (EAR) composed of EJBs and accompanying classes or in Web Application Archive (WAR) files composed of Servlets, JSPs, and ancillary classes. As required by J2EE, WAS provides containers for hosting J2EE application artifacts. These artifacts are typically Servlets and JSPs running in a web container and EJBs running inside an EJB container.

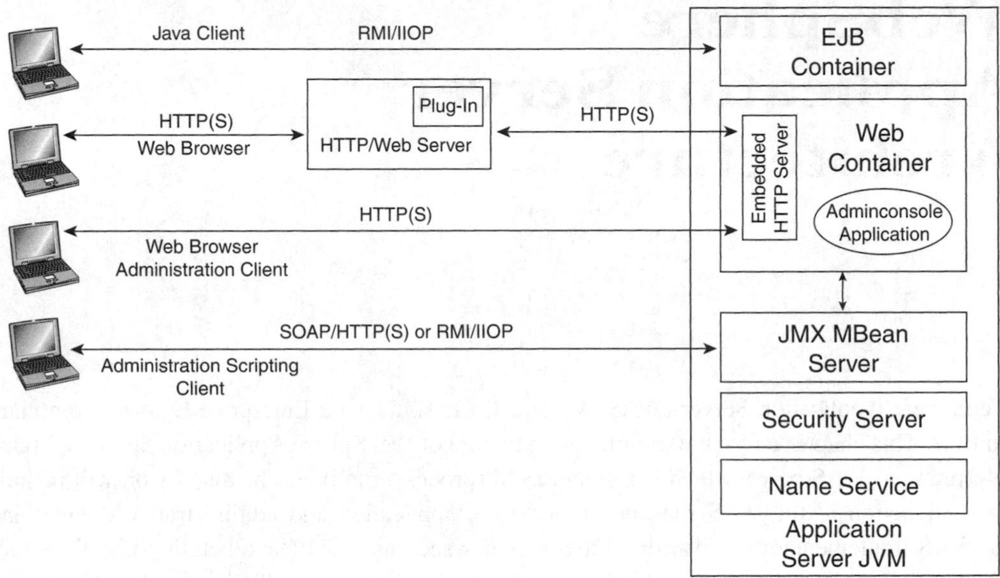


**Figure 5-1** WebSphere Application Server runtime and clients.

In WAS V5, administration is accomplished via a Java Management Extensions (JMX) MBean (Management Bean) server running as part of the application server process. The JMX server exposes a series of MBeans that provide for both runtime process and configuration management. The runtime and installed application configuration repository is stored in a set of XML and XMI documents on the local file system. In turn, the configuration management MBeans read and update these documents in response to commands from the WAS administrative clients. Each server also contains a security server that provides for authentication and authorization of both application and administrative client requests. (Both JMX and security will be discussed in more detail later in this book.) Though not depicted in Figure 5-1, each application server also contains a transaction manager that implements the JTA (Java Transaction API) specification and supports the JTS/OTS (Java Transaction Service/Object Transaction Service) transaction protocol over IIOP. Finally, there is a name server that provides a CORBA CosNaming implementation in support of the J2EE Java Naming and Directory Interface (JNDI) API. We'll return to the name service implementation later in this chapter.

## Application Clients

The most common client type is a web-browser client that interacts with Servlets or JSPs running in the web container. You'll notice that in Figure 5-1, an external HTTP server is used to support a web-browser client. Web requests that are served by WAS are typically forwarded from a standalone HTTP (or web) server, such as Apache or IIS, to the WAS web container by a WAS module known as the HTTP server plug-in that runs as part of the HTTP server process. This module is responsible for examining the URLs that the HTTP server receives and then forwarding requests for WAS applications to the WAS web container in WAS. In WAS base, this allows the HTTP server and WAS to be running on separate machines, allowing for construction of a DMZ (Demilitarized Zone) where the HTTP server resides between two firewalls, allowing WAS to run outside the DMZ.[1] In WAS-ND, the HTTP server plug-in also provides for workload management and client request failover. While it is possible to bypass the HTTP server and the WAS HTTP server plug-in and to send requests directly to the web container embedded HTTP server on port 9080,[2] this configuration is not recommended for the majority of deployments since essential elements (such as security and workload management) are not provided when the HTTP server plug-in is not employed.[3] (Note that workload management is only part of WAS-ND.)

Less frequently used is a Java application client that interacts with Enterprise JavaBeans running in the WAS EJB container. The necessity to distribute the client application to each of the client desktops and the use of an IIOP transport, which is usually not "firewall friendly," typically limits this client type to applications that are internal to an enterprise.

Although not depicted, Web services are another supported client type.

## Administration Clients

Runtime administration in V5 is accomplished via two alternative mechanisms: a web browser-based administration client or the wsadmin command-line scripting client, both of which interact with the JMX server running inside WAS. The browser-based client provides a GUI interface that is implemented as a web application running inside the web container alongside custom developed applications. It is depicted in Figure 5-2.

In order to provide separation between the administration application and custom applications, the web console is configured to use a different virtual host[4] than the one used for application requests. The browser is invoked using the URL http://hostname:9090/admin (port 9043 is the default for HTTPS). When logging in to the admin console application, a workspace is created for

1 WAS security including deployment scenarios with firewalls will be covered in Chapter 18, "Security."

2 Port 9080 is the default HTTP transport for the web container; the value for this can be modified as required, and is automatically incremented in WAS-ND as additional servers are created on a node.

3 Third-party products such as a Reverse Proxy Security Server can be used to provide authentication if desired.

4 Virtual hosts refer to the capability of most HTTP servers to support multiple logical hosts sharing one IP address on a server. Since the Servlet 2.3 specification (Section 3.6) prohibits sharing of Servlet context across virtual hosts, this provides a means of segregating applications since each virtual host has its own Servlet context or set of Servlet contexts. WAS provides for the definition of virtual hosts in order to facilitate the mapping of applications running in WAS to the corresponding HTTP server virtual hosts.

the user ID supplied, and all configuration changes are made in the workspace until the changes are saved to the configuration repository.[5] The creation of a workspace for each user ID, which occurs with both the browser console and wsadmin, allows multiple users to make changes. This function is useful in a WAS-ND cell with multiple servers and applications. If changes are made by multiple users to the same configuration artifact—say, the configuration for a given application server—the admin console application provides a warning of a save conflict, as depicted in Figure 5-3, while wsadmin throws a com.ibm.websphere.management.exception.ConfigServiceException.[6] In a large environment, manual procedures often need to be employed to ensure the separation of work by multiple administrators so that the changes made by one administrator do not conflict with the changes made by another.

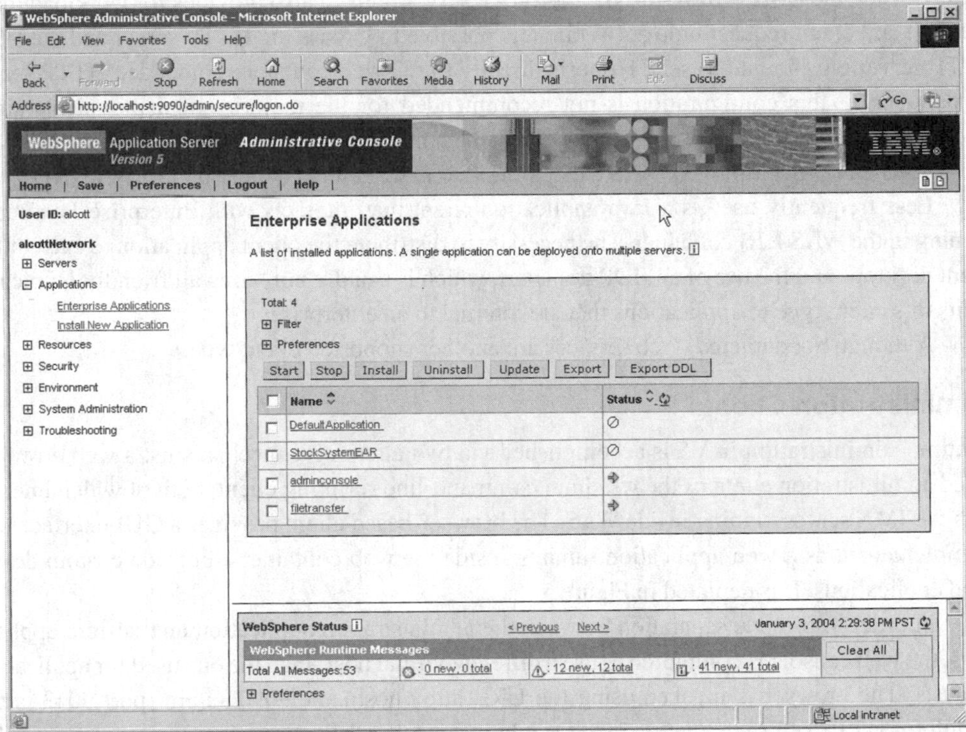


**Figure 5-2** Enterprise Application view in WAS browser administration client.

5 When running without security enabled, any user ID can be used for login. When security is enabled, a valid user ID and password must be used.

6 The option in the admin console to allow administrators to overwrite changes in the master repository has been the source of repository problems at several customer sites. As a result, the use of the overwrite option is not recommended. If an operational or administrative requirement makes use of this option unavoidable, you should be sure you have the latest WAS maintenance applied to take advantage of changes intended to remedy possible problems.

The wsadmin utility provides a Bean Scripting Framework (BSF) based mechanism for command-line administration. In the initial release of WAS V5, wsadmin operates using the Jacl language. (Jacl is Java implementation of TCL.) In WAS V5.1, Jpython was added as an option, and in time, additional BSF languages will likely be added. An example wsadmin session, which depicts listing the installed (or deployed) applications, is shown in Figure 5-4.

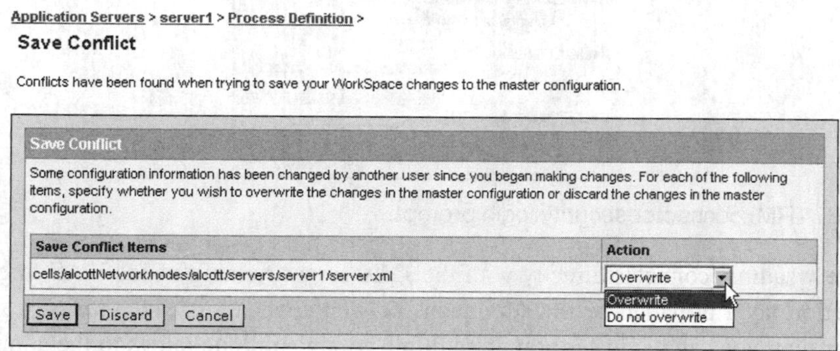


**Figure 5-3** Save Conflict dialog in WAS browser administration client.

Wsadmin can be invoked in multiple ways. The two most common are by opening an OS command shell and starting a wsadmin shell by typing "wsadmin" (.sh or .bat) or by invoking a script with a "-f <filename>" command. Wsadmin can also be extended by creating a properties file with a series of common scripts or commands for a given environment.

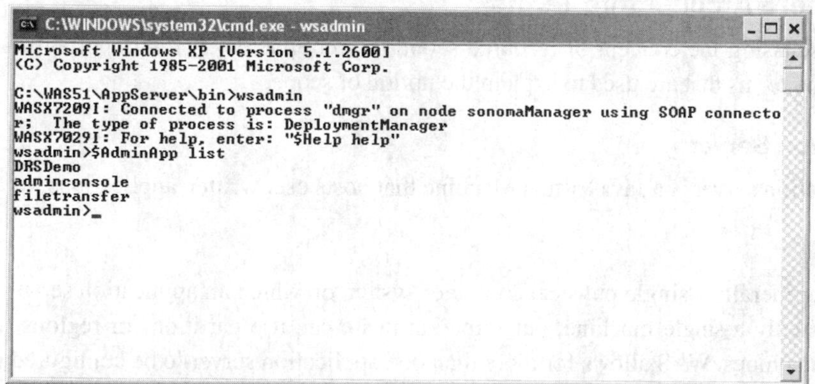


**Figure 5-4** wsadmin shell listing installed applications.

Both the browser adminconsole and wsadmin administration clients connect to WAS via an HTTP(S) transport. In addition, wsadmin offers the option to connect via RMI/IIOP. We prefer to use the RMI connector for wsadmin because when it's running secured, the RMI connector provides a login dialog prompt (see Figure 5-5) that is not available when running via SOAP over HTTPS. This dialog allows for the user ID and password to be provided at login. This differs from the SOAP connector, which requires that the login parameters either be provided as a clear text command-line argument or stored in a properties file. However, the RMI connector can also employ command-line arguments or a property file to provide the login properties.

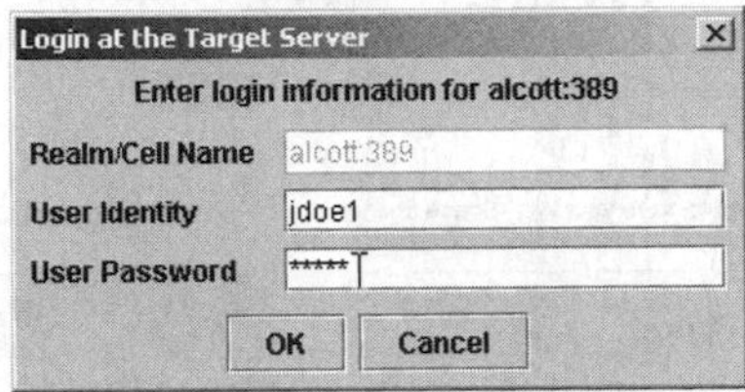


**Figure 5-5** RMI connector security login prompt.

Since wsadmin connects directly with the JMX server running inside WAS, it eliminates the abstraction layer provided by the adminconsole web application. Since scripts can be executed faster than you can navigate through multiple administration dialogs in the adminconsole application, scripted administration will likely be quicker than administering via the browser client. As we consider scripting to be an essential part of having a defined and repeatable process for administration and deployment of development and production environments, you will notice that this book makes extensive use of the command-line utilities in WebSphere Application Server V5.

## WebSphere Architecture Terms

Before discussing the concept of resource scope in WebSphere V5, it's important to explicitly define some terms that are used to explain the notion of scope.

### Application Server

An application server is a Java Virtual Machine that hosts user written applications.

### Node

A node is generally a single physical computer system on which an application server resides. A node is usually a single machine, but some hardware can use partitions or regions that mimic multiple machines. WAS allows for more than one application server to be configured on a given node, but in WAS base, each of these servers is "standalone" and is managed independently, while in WAS-ND, multiple servers can be configured and managed centrally. In WAS, a node name is normally the same as the host name for the computer.

## Cell

A cell is an administrative configuration concept. In WAS base, a cell is composed of one node and a single application server, which differs from WAS-ND, where a cell consists of one or more nodes, each with one of more application servers.

## WAS Resource Scope

Later in this book, we will discuss the WAS-ND in detail. It is worth mentioning that resources such as JDBC, JMS Providers, and resource adapters, as well as WebSphere variables such as a JDBC driver path, can be defined at different levels of visibility, or scopes. Although WAS base is only a single server, the resources are still scoped in its configuration. This allows WAS base servers with defined resources to be added to a WAS-ND installation without losing any of those defined resources. There are three scope levels:

- **Cell**—Variables defined at the cell level can be shared across node boundaries.
- **Node**—Variables and resources defined at the node level can be shared by all the servers on that node.
- **Server**—Resources defined at the server level are visible only to the server on which it was defined.

A server-scoped JDBC Provider definition for "server1" is illustrated in Figure 5-6. In this figure, the resource would be scoped to a node if there were no explicit server specified and would be cell-scoped if there were neither a server or node specified.

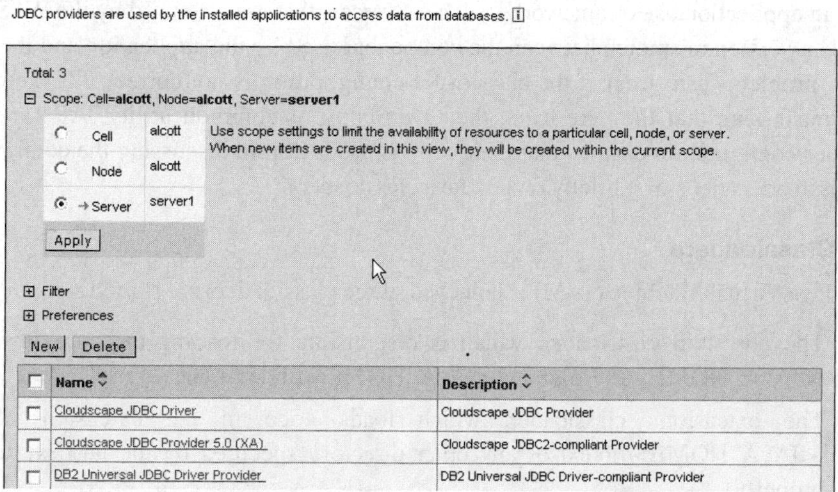


**Figure 5-6** Server-scoped JDBC Providers dialog in browser admin client.

Resource definitions are actually replicated to each server, so in essence, to say a resource is defined at a node scope is to say "every server on that node has a copy of the configuration." This figure depicts specifying the scope in WAS base.[7] We'll return to this subject briefly in Chapter 20, "WAS Network Deployment Architecture," since the "visibility of resources" is only truly meaningful with WAS-ND. Two WAS base servers cannot share resources through scoping. When using WAS base, every resource is visible to the one and only server, regardless of the scope. However, using the different scope definitions in WAS base has advantages:

- Existing servers can be upgraded to a WAS-ND cell and still have their resources configured correctly. This applies to resources scoped at both the node and server level. Cell-level definitions will be lost when a base server is federated into a WAS-ND cell. This is because, in WAS base, a node and a cell are synonymous, while in WAS-ND, these differ.
- Certain configuration scripts can be written generically and can be applied to both WAS base and WAS-ND. This allows the configuration scripts to be designed and developed early in the development process with WAS base and allows the scripts to be used in WAS-ND environments later.

## Classloaders in WebSphere

It's essential that anyone in the J2EE application component provider role (developer), the J2EE application assembler role (developer or architect), or the J2EE application deployer and administrator role (system administrator) understand classloaders. Classloader behavior affects how code executes and how property files are loaded. An incorrect classloader configuration may prevent the application or server from executing properly. A common source of classloader problems is when an application uses frameworks, such as Xerces, that are also used by the WAS runtime. If there is a version mismatch between the component used by the application and the one used by WAS, problems can occur if the classloader configuration is not correct. J2EE components need to make sure that they are using their own copy of common utility JARs and that the classloader configuration ensures that their copy is used. Before discussing the configuration of WAS classloaders, let's first briefly review Java classloaders.

### Java 2 Classloaders

When a Java Virtual Machine (JVM) is launched, three classloaders are started:

- The bootstrap classloader, which is responsible for loading the core Java libraries (<JAVA_HOME>/lib/rt.jar and <JAVA_HOME>/lib/i18n.jar)
- The extensions classloader, which loads code in the extensions directories (<JAVA_HOME>/lib/ext or any other directory specified by the java.ext.dirs system property)

7 After selecting the desired scope, be sure to select "Apply." Otherwise, the display will not reflect the selected scope; instead, it will reflect the prior scope and associated resources.

- The system classloader, which is responsible for loading the code that is found on java.class.path, which ultimately maps to the system CLASSPATH variable

The default for classloaders is to arrange them in a parent/child hierarchy. When a classloading request is presented to a classloader, it first asks its parent classloader to fulfill the request. This is known as request delegation. The parent, in turn, asks (or delegates to) its parent for the class until the request reaches the top of the hierarchy. If the classloader at the top of the hierarchy cannot fulfill the request, then the child classloader that called it is responsible for loading the class. If the child is also unable to load the class, the request continues back down the hierarchy until a classloader fulfills the request or until a ClassNotFoundException is produced by the classloader when the request reaches the bottom of the hierarchy. Perhaps the most important point to remember is that once a class is loaded by a classloader, any new classes that the class tries to load will reuse the same classloader or go up the hierarchy to find a class. A classloader can only find classes up in the hierarchy, not down.

To make this a bit more concrete, let's look at the hierarchy of the three JVM classloaders, depicted in Figure 5-7, and consider the following example. Assume there's a method called the "foo method" running in the system classloader. "Foo" (or "foo" if you prefer) can locate and use a class in all three classloaders. Contrast this with the "bar" method that is running in the extensions classloader; "bar" can only use and locate classes that are present in the extensions classloader and the bootstrap classloader. Finally consider the "foobar" class running in the bootstrap classloader; the only classes that "foobar" can use are those that are present in the bootstrap classloader.

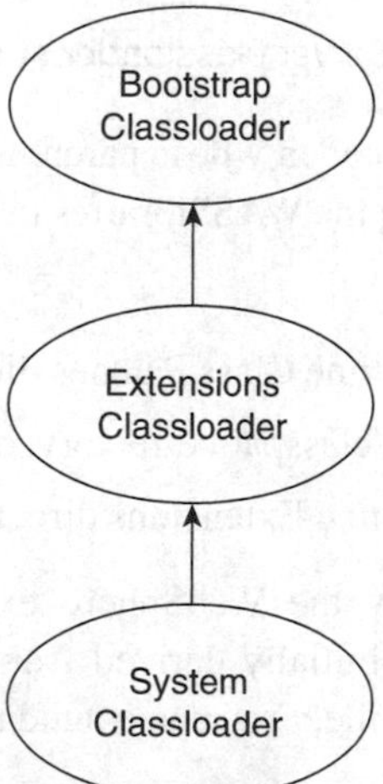


**Figure 5-7** Java 2 classloader structure.

## WAS Classloaders

WebSphere Application Server adds several classloaders to those provided by the Java Virtual Machine and provides options for changing the default delegation mode. The WAS classloader structure is illustrated in Figure 5-8.[8]

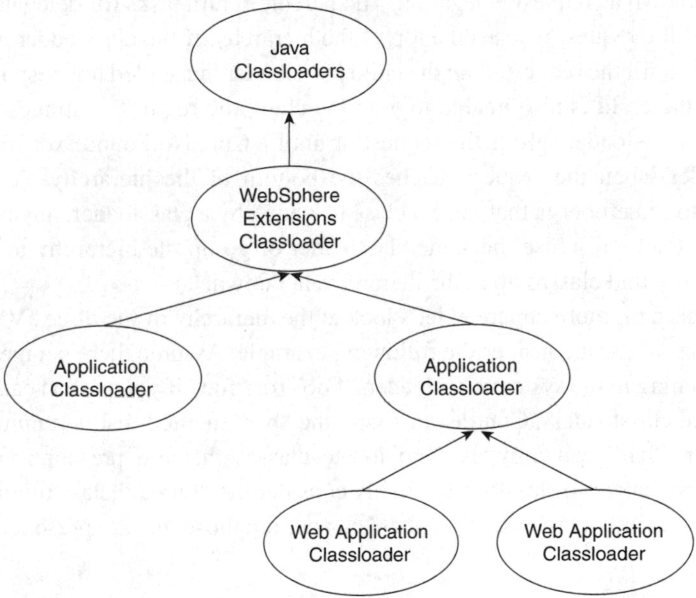


**Figure 5-8** WebSphere Application Server classloader structure.

The WebSphere extensions classloader, whose parent is the Java system classloader, shown in Figure 5-7, is responsible for loading the WAS libraries in the following directories:

- <JAVA_HOME>\lib
- <WAS_HOME>\classes (Runtime Class Patches directory, or RCP)
- <WAS_HOME>\lib (Runtime classpath directory, or RP)
- <WAS_HOME>\lib\ext (Runtime Extensions directory, or RE)

The WAS runtime is loaded by the WebSphere extensions classloader based on the ws.ext.dirs system property, which is initially derived from the WS_EXT_DIRS environment variable set in the setupCmdLine script file.[9] You can extend the list of directories and files loaded

8 For the sake of simplicity, the three Java classloaders just discussed are not all depicted; instead, these are depicted as "Java Classloaders" in Figure 5-8. If depicted, the Java classloaders would be in the same order as shown in Figure 5-7 with the system classloader as the parent to the WebSphere extensions classloader.

9 setupCmdLine is located in the <wasroot>/bin directory and is used to specify many of the OS shell environment variables, such as the path and classpath, when a WAS java process is started. If you look at the various command-line scripts in the <wasroot>/bin directory, you'll see that more than 50 scripts invoke setupCmdLine to create the correct execution environment.

by the WebSphere extensions classloaders by setting a ws.ext.dirs custom property to the Java Virtual Machine settings of an application server. However, this is not recommended because classes loaded from here can interfere with the WAS runtime and cause problems.

Next is the application classloader, where EJB modules, dependency JARs, resource adapter files, and shared libraries associated with an application are grouped together. Depending on the application classloader policy, the application classloader can be shared by multiple applications (EARs) or can be unique for each application. When configuring the application server classloader, a selection of MULTIPLE for this classloader means that each EAR file has its own classloader, which is the default. Specifying SINGLE means that all EARs installed in the application server share the same classloader. The dialog for specifying this is depicted in Figure 5-9.

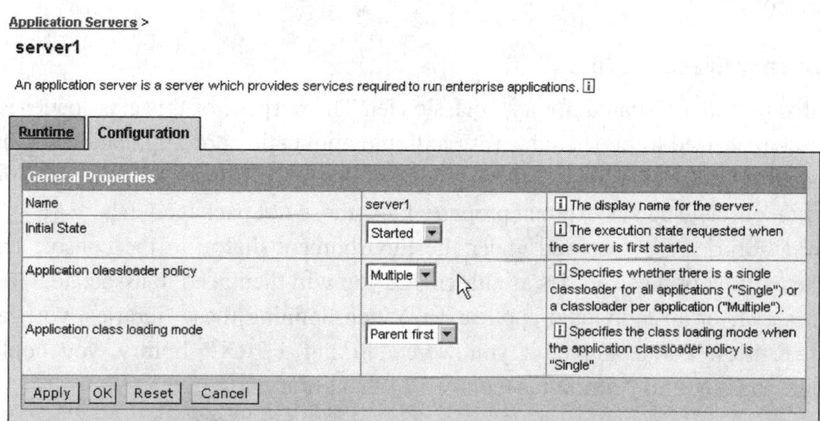
Application Servers >
server1
An application server is a server which provides services required to run enterprise applications.
Runtime
Configuration
General Properties
Name
server1
The display name for the server.
Initial State
Started
The execution state requested when the server is first started.
Application classloader policy
Multiple
Specifies whether there is a single classloader for all applications ("Single") or a classloader per application ("Multiple").
Application class loading mode
Parent first
Specifies the class loading mode when the application classloader policy is "Single"
Apply
OK
Reset
Cancel

**Figure 5-9** Application server classloader Configuration dialog.

With the enterprise application, there is the classloader for web modules. The default is for each web module to receive its own classloader (a WAR classloader) to load the contents of the WEB-INF/classes and WEB-INF/lib directory. By default, the application classloader is the parent of the WAR classloader. The default behavior can be modified by changing the application's WAR classloader policy (the default being MODULE). If the WAR classloader policy is set to APPLICATION, the web module contents are loaded by the application classloader (in addition to the EJBs, RARs, dependency JARs, and shared libraries).

As noted previously, the default is for a classloader to delegate a request for a class to its parent classloader, which is known as PARENT_FIRST delegation. WAS provides an option to specify PARENT_LAST delegation, which can be specified for the application classloader, the WAR classloader, and the shared library classloader. When PARENT_LAST is specified, the classloader first attempts to load classes from its local classpath before delegating the class loading to its parent. This option allows an application classloader to override and provide its own version of a class that exists in the parent classloader. A common example of this is an application that uses a version of Xerces that differs from the one used by the application server runtime. By specifying PARENT_LAST in this case, the version of Xerces packaged with the application is loaded first and used by the application without affecting the version used by WAS.

Another classloader option provided by WAS is to enable class reloading for web modules. This feature is especially useful in a development environment where a new version of a web application artifact (e.g., Servlet or JSP) can be loaded by the classloader without stopping and restarting the web application. If the application consists of EJBs in addition to Servlets and JSPs, it's best to stop and restart the entire enterprise application when making changes. If you don't, when the web components are reloaded and the EJB components are not, errors can result if the EJB components should have been updated as well. By restarting the application, you ensure that all dependencies between application components are reloaded, and you save yourself time spent debugging errors.

## Shared Library Classloaders

WAS V5 also provides a shared library[10] classloader. The purpose of this classloader is to define code libraries that need to be shared across multiple applications or application servers; hence, the term "shared library classloader." Typical uses of this are for Java and native libraries as well as for other resources, such as external property files (those not packaged in an EAR).

Shared libraries are specified under the Environment dialog in the console (see Figure 5-10). You can think of these entries as aliases that you will then need to associate with either an application server or an individual application. When defining these libraries, you can specify multiple JAR files. For example, if you were defining a JAXP library, you could specify jaxp-api.jar, sax.jar, and dom.jar as members of this library.

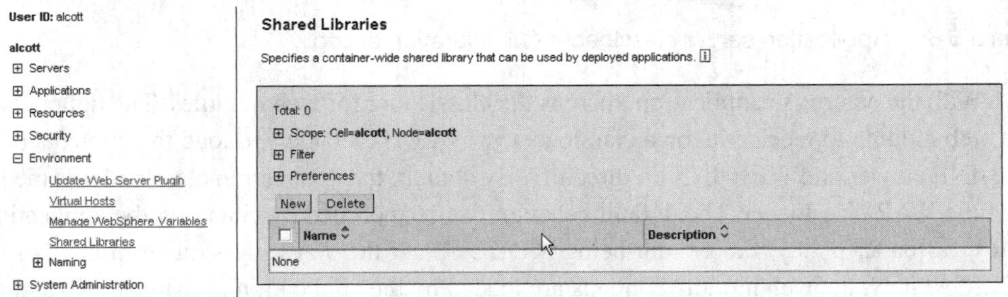


**Figure 5-10** Shared Libraries dialog in WAS admin browser.

It's important to understand the implications of how you choose to associate a library with an application server or an application. If the library is associated with the application server, then the library is loaded by another classloader that's independent of the application classloader, which enters the classloader hierarchy between the WebSphere classloader and the application

10 Don't confuse the term "shared library classloader" with an operating system shared library such as a DLL file on Windows or a shared object file on Unix.

classloader. As a result, the hierarchy looks like that depicted in Figure 5-11. You can add as many classloaders as you want to a server, and their placement in the classloader hierarchy will vary depending on how you configure them. Let's consider a couple of examples:

1. If you were to add four classloaders to a server and associate four libraries, one to each classloader, when you looked at the classloader hierarchy, you would see only one classloader, which would appear identical to the one in Figure 5-11, but there would be one significant difference—the classpath would be ordered as if there had been four separate classloaders.
2. If you were to specify two classloaders, again assigning them to a server, and were to mix their delegation modes, one with "parent first" and one with "parent last,"[11] multiple classloaders would be created.
3. In contrast to the first two examples, if you were to create a shared library and associate it with an application, then it would be loaded by the application classloader, essentially providing the equivalent of the application classloader shown previously in Figure 5-8.

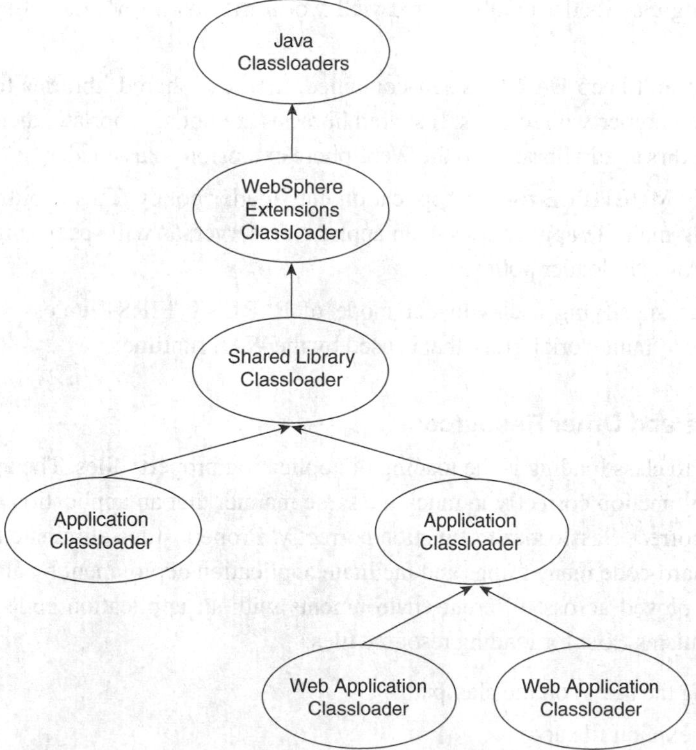


**Figure 5-11** WAS classloader structure with shared library classloader.

11 This precludes an equivalent classpath being accomplished with a single classloader.

In order to associate a shared library with a server classloader once the shared library is created, navigate to Application Servers > server > Classloader > Classloader_ID > Library Ref and enter the alias you specified when defining the shared library. To associate a library with an application, navigate to Enterprise Applications > application name > Libraries and then enter the alias.

One item to be aware of is that the native library feature will break if it contains any indirect references to other native libraries. If a native library loads other native libraries, you will have to include a proper native library path in the runtime environment of the application server. Also, when specifying libraries at the server level, you need to know if other applications in the server need different versions of the classes in the shared library, as this can lead to conflicts. Additionally, if the shared library is associated with the application, the shared library settings for the application must be reset after a code update.

In terms of packaging and classloader configuration, the following points summarize our recommendations:

- You should try to keep EAR files self-contained, as this is the easiest approach for avoiding classloader conflicts (and well worth the cost of additional space on the file system).
- If you can't keep EAR files self-contained, then use shared libraries for external JAR files and property directories. If shared libraries are not appropriate, then consider using ws.ext.dirs to add libraries to the WebSphere extensions classloader.
- Specify MULTIPLE for the application classloader policy. This avoids conflicts when running multiple applications in an application server, as will specifying MODULE for the WAR classloader policy.
- Plan on specifying a classloader mode of PARENT_FIRST unless your application utilizes a framework library that is used by the WAS runtime.

## Property Files and Other Resources

Closely related to class loading is the loading of application property files. The application relies on these files to function correctly in much the same manner that an application relies on classes loaded by the correct classloader to function correctly. Property files eliminate the need for the application to hard-code many things and facilitate application deployment by allowing an application to be deployed across different environments without application code changes. Three primary mechanisms exist for loading resource files:

- Placing the file(s) on the classpath
- Using explicit file access
- Using URL (Uniform Resource Locator) resources

Placing a file on the classpath typically involves the use of ResourceBundle() or getResourceAsStream() methods, either of which allow you to package resources as classes, allowing a developer to take advantage of Java's classloading mechanism to find resources. An example of the former would be:

```
ResourceBundle applicationResources =
  ResourceBundle.getResourceBundle(appPackage.
        someLocale, appClassLoader);
```

It should be clear from the preceding discussion on classloaders that if you choose to load resources from a classpath, you must make sure you understand which classloader is being used. If you don't, a common problem is that the property loading utility class may be using a different classloader than the caller (application artifact). The result is either a java.lang.NullPointer-Exception or, even worse, the application loads and uses an incorrect property file.

Explicit file access typically involves the use of the java.io API. The downside of this method is that reading external properties directly from a file is a violation of the EJB 2.0 specification (Section 24.1.12). While the Servlet specification presently contains no such restriction, that's not to say that this won't change in the future. In addition, it's best to try and employ a single method in applications that can be used by all application artifacts. This leaves URL resources.

URLs can be used to look up property files, which are defined as references to URL connection factories and are mapped to installation-specific URL resources. At first, the thought of using an external property file that is located via a URL would seem contrary to the normal practice of packaging all J2EE application artifacts inside an EAR file. However, in practice, though, it's very difficult, if not impossible, to edit property files in an EAR after deployment. It turns out to be far easier to configure a URL resource to point to an external property file through the WAS adminconsole (Resources > URL Providers) and maintain the property file. Furthermore, like other resources in WAS, the scope of the URL resource can be configured for the server, node, or cell. Even better, a URL reference does not require special application access permissions since the file is read by WAS runtime rather than application code, so application specific security considerations are not required. Last, since the URL resource can be looked up via JNDI, it's accessible by all J2EE application artifacts such as Servlets, JSPs, and EJBs.

## JNDI in WAS

As noted previously when discussing the V5 application server architecture, each application server has its own name server. The improvement in reliability that a distributed namespace provides comes at a cost in V5—the namespace is topology-dependent. In WAS base, this has little or no impact since application components, such as EJBs, are bound to the server root context of the server they are installed in, and WAS is a single server runtime, so there is only one server root context. This is depicted in Figure 5-12.

When specifying JNDI names corresponding to ejb-refs and resource-refs in WAS base, this can be simply "myEJB," since the EJB client is bootstrapped to the same server that the EJB is located in. In the single-server case, this is equivalent to a JNDI reference of cell/nodes/myNode/servers/myServer/myEjb, as shown in Figure 5-12. On the other hand, the picture becomes more complex when we discuss JNDI in Chapter 20. In the WAS-ND case, deploying an application to a cell requires that either the reference specify the EJB location (e.g., "cell/clusters/myCluster/myEjb") or that a namespace binding be created. While the impact of the additional contexts—or partitions, to be more precise—is more apparent in WAS-ND, in brief, the partitions function as follows:

- **System namespace partition**—This contains the structure of elements based on cell topology. In WAS base, the cell, node, and server are synonymous so there's no difference to be concerned with at this point. One thing to keep in mind, though, is that as its name implies, this namespace is controlled by the system; as a result, all contexts in the system namespace are read-only. You cannot add, update, or remove any bindings.
- **Server root partition**—As noted previously, this is where EJB homes and other resources for server applications are bound. These bindings are transient, and the server creates the required bindings at application startup, Since there is only one server in WAS base, there is only one server root context; in WAS-ND, however, there will be a server root context for each server in the cell.
- **Cell persistent partition**—As implied by its name, entries in this partition are part of the cell configuration and exist even when an application server is not running, and exist until explicitly removed, which has more meaning in a WAS-ND cell where there are multiple server objects. Bindings in this partition are static, such as part of an application setup or configuration, and are not created at runtime.
- **Node persistent partition**—These bindings function much like those in the cell persistent partition, but only have a node "scope" (recall the earlier discussion on resource scope), as opposed to cell scope.

The following example should help make this more concrete and that was obtained by dumping the namespace for the application associated with Chapter 9, "Enterprise JavaBeans," of this book:

```
(top)/nodes/alcott/servers/server1/ejb/StockFacadeHome
➥"com.deploybook.quote.ejb._StockFacadeHome_Stub"
```

In this case, StockFacadeHome is the JNDI reference assigned in the application for the Stock EJB.

If you've already installed the application associated with this book, you may want to dump the namespace so that you can examine this for yourself. There are two mechanisms for dumping the namespace. One is via the dumpNameSpace command-line script; the other is via the wsadmin command-line utility, which is what we'll demonstrate here.

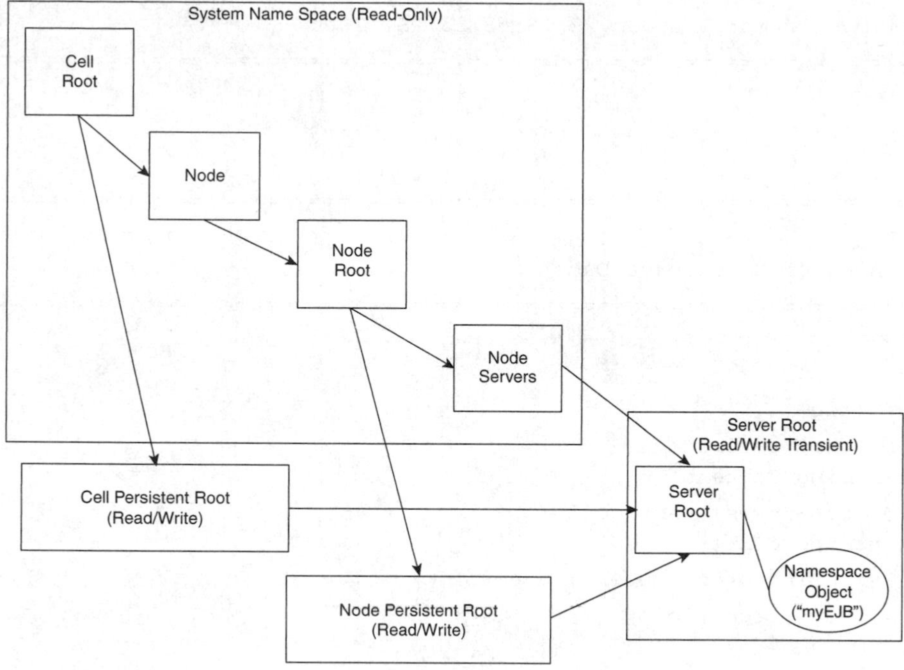


**Figure 5-12** WAS namespace.

First, you get a reference to the MBean associated with the name server:[12]

```
wsadmin>set serverMbean [$AdminControl queryNames
➥{*:*,type=NameServer}]
```

Then you invoke a name server dump:

```
wsadmin>$AdminControl invoke $serverMbean dumpServerNameSpace {{ }}
```

The result is shown in Code Snippet 5-1 (note especially the highlighted entry).

**Code Snippet 5-1** Example name space dump

```
" "
=========================================================================
➥=======
"Name Space Dump"
"   Starting context: (top)=alcott"
```

12 In WAS-ND, you would need to specify a specific server process since there are multiple name servers, one in each application server, Node Agent, and the Deployment Manager. In WAS-ND, the command would be wsadmin>set mbean [$AdminControl queryNames {*:*,type=NameServer,process=server1}].

```
"   Time of dump: Thu Jan 22 18:58:53 PST 2004"
==========================================================================
➥=======
" "
" "
==========================================================================
➥=======
"Beginning of Name Space Dump"
==========================================================================
➥=======
" "
"    1 (top)                                                      "
"    2 (top)/persistent
javax.naming.Context"
"    3 (top)/persistent/cell
javax.naming.Context"
"    3    Linked to context: alcott"
"    4 (top)/legacyRoot                                    javax.naming.
➥Context"
"    4    Linked to context: alcott/persistent"
"    5 (top)/domain                                        javax.naming.
➥Context"
"    5    Linked to context: alcott"
"    6 (top)/cells                                         javax.naming.
➥Context"
"    7 (top)/clusters                                      javax.naming.
➥Context"
"    8 (top)/cellname                                      java.lang.
➥String"
"    9 (top)/cell                                          javax.naming.
➥Context"
"    9    Linked to context: alcott"
"   10 (top)/nodes                                         javax.naming.
➥Context"
"   11 (top)/nodes/alcott                                  javax.naming.
➥Context"
"   12 (top)/nodes/alcott/cell                             javax.naming.
➥Context"
"   12    Linked to context: alcott"
"   13 (top)/nodes/alcott/servers                          javax.naming.
➥Context"
```

```
"   14 (top)/nodes/alcott/servers/server1                    javax.naming.
➥Context"
"   15 (top)/nodes/alcott/servers/server1/thisNode           javax.naming.
➥Context"
"   15     Linked to context: alcott/nodes/alcott"
"   16 (top)/nodes/alcott/servers/server1/cell               javax.naming.
➥Context"
"   16     Linked to context: alcott"
"   17 (top)/nodes/alcott/servers/server1/ejb                javax.naming.
➥Context"
"   18 (top)/nodes/alcott/servers/server1/ejb/StockFacadeHome"
"   18 com.deploybook.quote.ejb._StockFacadeHome_Stub"
"   19 (top)/nodes/alcott/servers/server1/eis                javax.naming.
➥Context"
"   20 (top)/nodes/alcott/servers/server1/eis/jdbc           javax.naming.
➥Context"
"   21 (top)/nodes/alcott/servers/server1/eis/jdbc/wstrade_CMP"
"   21                                                       WSTradeDS_CF"
"   22 (top)/nodes/alcott/servers/server1/eis/DefaultDatasource_CMP"
"   22                                                       Default_CF"
"   23 (top)/nodes/alcott/servers/server1/jta                javax.naming.
➥Context"
"   24 (top)/nodes/alcott/servers/server1/jta/usertransaction"
"   24                                                       java.lang.
➥Object"
"   25 (top)/nodes/alcott/servers/server1/DefaultDatasource"
"   25                                                       Default
➥Datasource"
"   26 (top)/nodes/alcott/servers/server1/jdbc               javax.naming.
➥Context"
"   27 (top)/nodes/alcott/servers/server1/jdbc/wstrade   WSTradeDS"
"   28 (top)/nodes/alcott/servers/server1/TransactionFactory"
"   28                                                       com.ibm.ejs.
➥jts.jts.Co
ntrolSet$LocalFactory"
"   29 (top)/nodes/alcott/servers/server1/services           javax.naming.
➥Context"
"   30 (top)/nodes/alcott/servers/server1/services/cache  javax.naming.
➥Context"
"   31 (top)/nodes/alcott/servers/server1/services/cache/
➥distributedmap"
```

```
"   31
com.ibm.websphere.cach
e.DistributedMap"
"   32 (top)/nodes/alcott/servers/server1/servername      java.lang.
➥String"
"   33 (top)/nodes/alcott/node                            javax.naming.
➥Context"
"   33     Linked to context: alcott/nodes/alcott"
"   34 (top)/nodes/alcott/persistent                      javax.naming.
➥Context"
"   35 (top)/nodes/alcott/nodename                        java.lang.
➥String"
"   36 (top)/nodes/alcott/domain                          javax.naming.
➥Context"
"   36     Linked to context: alcott"
" "
=======================================================================
➥=======
"End of Name Space Dump"
```

You may notice that only one of the two EJBs in the application is listed in the previous dump, that being the StockFacade EJB, while the StockEntity EJB is missing. That's because the Stock entity EJB in the application only has a local interface defined for it. Since local interfaces are not bound in the external namespace, they must be looked up in the java:comp/env namespace, which does not show up in a dumpNameSpace of the external namespace. A dump of the namespace, which contains an ejb-ref to the local interface, is required. In order to do one, we simply replace dumpServerNameSpace with dumpLocalNameSpace and invoke the name server MBean again in the following manner with wsadmin (see Code Snippet 5-2).

**Code Snippet 5-2** Example local name space dump

```
wsadmin>$AdminControl invoke $serverMbean dumpLocalNameSpace {{ }}

=======================================================================
➥=======
"Name Space Dump"
"   Starting context: (top)=local:"
"   Time of dump: Thu Jan 22 18:57:10 PST 2004"
=======================================================================
➥=======
" "
```

```
" "
==========================================================================
➥=======
"Beginning of Name Space Dump"
==========================================================================
➥=======
" "
"    1 (top)                                                          "
"    2 (top)/ejb                                          javax.naming.
➥Context"
"    3 (top)/ejb/ejb                                      javax.naming.
➥Context"
"    4 (top)/ejb/ejb/StockEntity com.deploybook.
➥quote.ejb.EJSLocalCMPStockHome_75076f8d"
"    5 (top)/ejb/ejb/StockFacadeHome com.
➥deploybook.quote.e jb.EJSLocalStatelessStockFacadeHome_fe9b3cc2"
" "
==========================================================================
➥=======
"End of Name Space Dump"
```

You'll also note that a local interface is defined for the QuoteFacade EJB in this dump in addition to the remote interface visible in the first dump and the local interface for the QuoteEntity EJB.

Many of the differences in the WAS V5 namespace manifest themselves only when running multiple application servers either in a cluster or in a cell. As a result, we'll defer further discussion of this until Chapter 20.

## Logging and Tracing in WAS

WAS employs the IBM RAS Toolkit for Java (JRAS) to provide features to enhance the Reliability, Availability, & Serviceability (RAS) of Java programs. JRAS provides the framework for the message logging and tracing that WAS provides for diagnostic purposes and includes loggers, handlers, events, and formatters. As a result, in order to debug a problem, you'll need to enable trace in WAS and work with the output from JRAS. Not only is JRAS employed by WAS, but it is also is available for use as a logging framework with user applications. One advantage afforded by JRAS over open-source frameworks such as Log4J and jLog is that it is included in the product support that comes with WebSphere Application Server.

For an application deployer or administrator, the most important tasks are correctly understanding the types of diagnostic trace available, how to enable them, and where to look for the trace output for them. The JRAS implementation in WAS offers two mechanisms for enabling trace, one that is persistent and one that is dynamic. We'll refer to these as "Configuration Trace" and "Runtime Trace," respectively.[13]

### Configuration Trace

The first WebSphere trace service is the Configuration Trace service. This trace is enabled by changing the server configuration files and, as a result, is stored persistently when the server is not running. This trace allows an administrator to trace the server from server process start. Unfortunately, the specification of a Configuration Trace does not take effect immediately on a running server; instead, a server shutdown and restart is required.

### Runtime Trace

The second trace service is the Runtime Trace service. Unlike Configuration Trace, Runtime Trace is not persisted to the server configuration files, so a trace specification does not survive a server shutdown. Runtime Trace does have the advantage of taking effect immediately, not requiring a server shutdown.

### Enabling Trace

Trace can be enabled either through the adminconsole (Servers > Application Servers > "server-name" > Logging and Tracing > Diagnostic Trace, then selecting the appropriate tab) or via the wsadmin command-line tool.

Enabling Runtime Trace with wsadmin requires two AdminControl commands that are used to change settings for active objects in WAS.

First, you obtain the completeObjectName for the trace service in the server and assign it to a variable:

```
wsadmin>set ts [$AdminControl completeObjectName type=
➥.TraceService,process=server1,*]
```

Second, you specify the trace specification:

```
wsadmin>$AdminControl setAttribute $ts traceSpecification
➥com.ibm.*=all=enabled
```

Once the command returns, you can view the trace in the "tracefile" located in the server log directory (for example, C:\WebSphere\ApplicationServer\logs\server1\logs\tracefile).

The mechanism for setting the Configuration Trace differs from Runtime Trace in that it requires use of AdminConfig instead of AdminControl because we're making a change to the server configuration, which will survive a server stop and restart.

13 Both Configuration Trace and Runtime Trace use JRAS. The only difference is that with Configuration Trace, the settings are persisted so they remain in effect after a server shutdown and restart, while Runtime Trace applies only to the currently running process.

First, you specify the server to be configured:

```
wsadmin>set server [$AdminConfig getid /Cell:alcott/Node:alcott/
➥Server:server1/]
```

Second, the trace service for the server is specified:

```
wsadmin>set tc [$AdminConfig list TraceService $server ]
```

Third, the trace specification is specified for the server trace service:

```
wsadmin>$AdminConfig modify $tc {{startupTraceSpecification
➥com.ibm.*=all=enabled}}
```

Last, the configuration is saved:

```
wsadmin>$AdminConfig save
```

As noted previously with Runtime Trace, by default, the trace is directed to the "tracefile" in the server log director (for example, C:\WebSphere\ApplicationServer\logs\server1\logs\tracefile).

Chapter 24, "Problem Determination," will delve into more detail on the use of WAS trace, including specifying trace settings, the format of WAS trace messages, and interpreting trace output. As a result, we'll defer further discussion of trace until then since the intent of this chapter is simply to discuss the WAS architecture and to introduce this material.

## Conclusion

This chapter introduced the various components that make up the WebSphere runtime architecture as well as the configuration of some of those components. We also used the wsadmin facility for configuring trace as well as for dumping the namespace.

# PART II

# J2EE Deployment and Administration

CHAPTER 6

# J2EE Web Applications and the Web Container

In Part I, "Introduction to WebSphere and Deployment," we laid the groundwork for this book. We introduced you to the WebSphere Application Server platform and introduced architecture for build and deployment procedures. We begin Part II, "J2EE Deployment and Administration," by focusing on J2EE web applications. This includes understanding the technologies that make up web applications. In addition, we will illustrate the structure of web modules. Then we illustrate the characteristics of the WebSphere Application Server (WAS) web container. Finally, we will use an exercise to illustrate automating the assembly and deployment of the Personal Trade System example application.

## J2EE Web Application Technologies

As stated in Chapter 2, "J2EE Applications," most J2EE applications make use of the core technologies: Servlets, JSP, JDBC, JNDI, and EJB. This chapter will focus on the web technologies, namely Servlets and JSPs. This is not a programming book, so only the role these technologies play in J2EE applications will be described.

### Servlets

Servlets are one of the earliest and most central technologies of the J2EE specification. Servlets are Java classes that process requests and construct responses dynamically. Responses are usually constructed HTML web pages that are returned to a browser; however, Servlets can generate other response types, such as other Java classes or XML documents. A developer is required to override one or more methods, and the web container will call one of these methods when the Servlet is invoked. The most commonly used type of Servlet is an HTTP Servlet. HTTP Servlets receive HTTP requests. The type of HTTP request determines the type of method called; for example, an HTTP POST request will make the web container call a doPost() method on the Servlet. The code in the Servlet does some work, constructs a response object, and returns it to the web container. The web container then translates the response object back into an HTTP Response Stream.

Servlet classes can be packaged in a WAR file or in a JAR file visible to the WAR's classloader. They are defined on the web.xml deployment descriptor. Using the web URI, the web container determines the target Servlet. Servlets can also forward requests to other Servlets; this allows different Servlets to handle different phases of the same request. J2EE web developers typically use a combination of Servlets and JSPs. JSPs are special forms of Servlets that are focused on rendering web pages instead of code execution.

## Java Server Pages

During the early days of Servlet programming, the HTTP response was constructed by writing HTML text into the Servlet's output stream. It was very common to see code such as in Code Snippet 6-1. Java developers needed to understand HTML. Furthermore, any changes in the HTML web design required the developers to change Java code and redeploy.

**Code Snippet 6-1 Servlet coding before JavaServer pages**

```
out.println("<HTML><HEAD></HEAD><BODY>");
out.println(dynamicData);
out.println("</BODY></HTML>");
```

Java Server Pages (JSP) addresses this limitation. With JSP, web developers develop web pages and insert dynamic pieces of Java where needed. JSP pages are then dynamically converted into a Servlet class by the container. Usually, the JSP compilation process is done the first time a JSP is invoked via a web request. The web container will then cache the generated Servlet class and use it on subsequent requests. This avoids the performance overhead of having to generate a Java class and then compile it on every web request.

It didn't take long to realize that JSP suffered from a similar problem as the Servlet—JSP pages had too much Java in them. JSPs then evolved to support custom tags. Custom tags allowed developers to hide Java code behind HTML-like tags. These custom tags make it easier for non-programmers to insert dynamic content (such as data read from a database) into JSP pages. Custom tags are packaged together in a tag library, and just like other J2EE constructs, tag libraries have descriptors. Tag libraries are defined in the web.xml file. We will talk about the web.xml file later in this chapter.

## Filters and Life-Cycle Listeners

J2EE 1.3 introduced a few new concepts to web applications. Filters are Java classes that are developed to handle pre- and post-processing of HTTP requests. Filters can be configured to intercept requests for a group of Servlets or JSPs. These filters execute before and after the underlying Servlets, making it possible for them to alter the input or output of the Servlet. This is very handy for generic functionality that is shared across Servlets or for altering the behavior of an existing Servlet without changing it.

Life-cycle listeners are another technology introduced in the Servlet 2.3 specification. They allow developers to develop code inside callback methods that can respond to certain web-related life-cycle events such as the creation of an HTTP session.

Both of these features are configured in the web.xml file, which we will cover later this chapter.

## J2EE Web Application Characteristics

J2EE web applications usually use a combination of Servlets and JSP. J2EE web applications have evolved to use the Model View Controller (MVC) design pattern. MVC is a way to structure code to separate the concerns of an application. In J2EE applications, the model usually represents the business logic and data. This layer is usually implemented using technology such as EJB, JDBC, and JavaBeans. The controller layer is usually implemented using Servlets. A Servlet will usually extract HTTP input and translate it to some specific input for the model. The controller will then invoke model objects. Once done, the Servlet will forward the request to a JSP. The JSP will extract dynamic data from the model for display and return the HTTP response back to a browser. Figure 6-1 illustrates this interaction.

Good web applications will follow some form of the classic MVC paradigm. It has become so common that popular frameworks have been created to implement generic controller and view functions using the MVC pattern. The most popular MVC framework for web development available today is Struts.

The Struts Framework uses a single Servlet controller to dispatch requests to Action classes. The controller uses a Struts configuration file to know what Action classes to invoke. The Struts controller also creates a Form Object based on the HTTP request. A Form Object is a plain JavaBean with data. The Form Object is passed into the Action as input. This hides the complexity of lower-level HTTP objects as developers interact with plain Java Objects rather than dealing with extracting parameters from an HTTP Stream. Developers code their controller logic in an Action that then returns some indication of success or failure. The Struts Framework uses this indication to know to which JSP to forward control.

Application development is beyond the scope of this book, but there are several Struts resources available, such as [Cavaness 2002]. Struts provides web applications with many other features such as special formatting tag libraries, validation, exception handling, internationalization, configuration division, and many other features. Other J2EE MVC frameworks exist. In addition, the J2EE specification has finalized a specification called JavaServer Faces. JavaServer Faces (JSF) is an evolution of Struts that makes JSP tag libraries feel more like thick GUI controls to the application developer. Development tools can implement drag and drop technology and deploy it to application servers such as WAS. More information on JSF can be found in [Barcia 2004: JSF Series] or [Mann 2004].

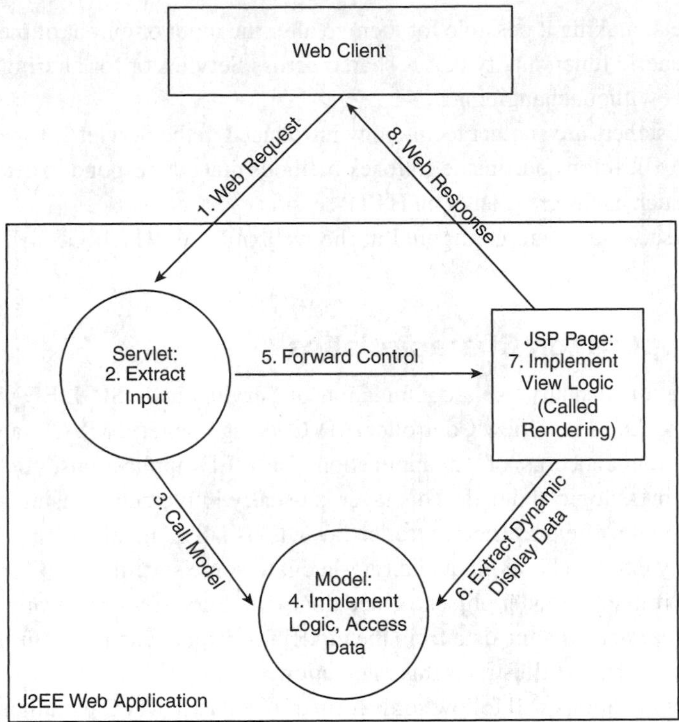


**Figure 6-1** Web applications using MVC.

The Personal Trade System is a Struts 1.1 application. Therefore, there will be one Struts controller Action Servlet. The Struts Framework uses a URL pattern to determine which Action class to go to. When describing the web.xml file later in this chapter, we will describe the Servlet mappings that give the web container the ability to find the correct Servlet. [Brown 2004] describes the programmatic details of Servlet and JSP development. It is important to understand that a web request or series of conversational requests involves the sharing and moving of data from component to component. Understanding this will help you understand the requirements a web container has to fulfill.

## HTTP Session

HTTP is a stateless protocol. This means the client makes a connection, sends a request, and receives a response, and the association with the client is finished. However, many web applications are conversational. Therefore, web applications need a way to keep track of specific clients during conversational interactions. J2EE supports a server-side object called HTTP session. The application server keeps an association between the user and his HttpSession object. The web application server will make the same HTTP session accessible to the Servlet method or JSP page serving the request. This makes it possible for application code to store state information in the HTTP session that is sure to be accessible on future requests. Chapter 22, "Session Management," will cover HTTP sessions in detail.

## WAS Web Container

The WAS web container processes web requests for Servlets, JSPs, and web resources hosted by WAS, such as HTML pages. When handling a web request for a Servlet, the web container creates a request object and a response object and then invokes the Servlet's method. Requests are received through an embedded HTTP server. Requests can be received directly from web clients or through an external HTTP server. An external HTTP server is configured with the WebSphere web server plug-in, which forwards requests to the application server. The web container uses the Session Manager to maintain session objects. Figure 6-2 illustrates the web container components within WAS.

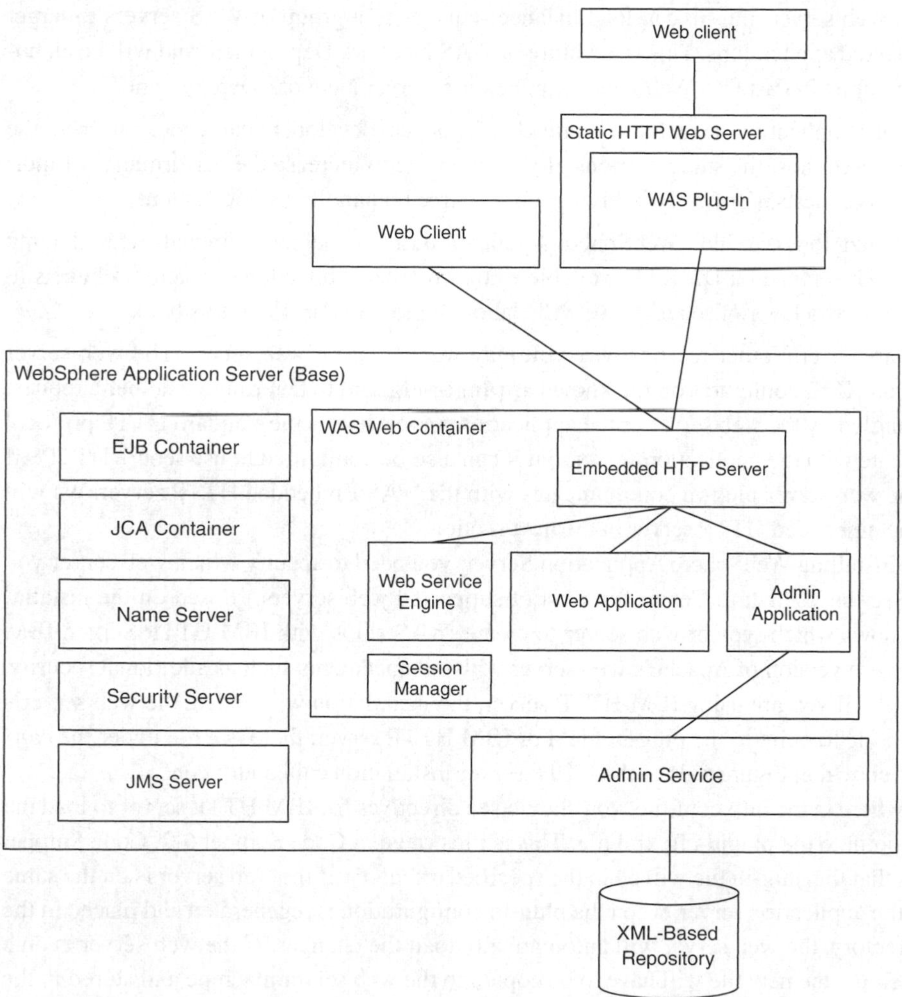


**Figure 6-2** WAS web container components.

## Web Container Components

As stated, the web container has several components. In this section, we describe the key components.

### Web Server Plug-In

As we showed in Figure 6-2, the web server plug-in is a component of WebSphere Application Server that is installed in an external web server such as IBM HTTP Server or Apache's web server. Fronting WebSphere Application Server with a web server is a preferred way of accessing the application server. There are several reasons:

- The web server plug-in can load balance requests to a group of WAS servers to target clustered applications. This is a feature of WAS Network Deployment and will be elaborated upon in Part IV, "WebSphere Application Server Network Deployment."
- If your application has a lot of static HTML pages, developers can choose to have the web server host the static portions of your web site to increase the performance of individual requests. [Brown 2002] is a good resource on handling static content.
- Organizations can hide WebSphere Application Server behind a firewall while having the web server in a DMZ be available to the Internet. This allows system architects to add an extra layer of security. We will elaborate more in Part IV of this book.

There are several other reasons why you may want to use a web server. The web server plug-in uses an XML configuration file known as **plugin-cfg.xml** to determine whether a request should be handled by the web server or the application server. It uses the standard HTTP protocol to communicate with the application server, but it can also be configured to use secure HTTPS if required. The web server plug-in communicates with the WAS Embedded HTTP server. We will talk about the embedded HTTP server in the next section.

When installing WebSphere Application Server, you need to specify which web server you are using. (See the WAS Info Center for a list of supported web servers.) Based on the installation, WAS knows which type of web server to create. WAS ships with IBM HTTP Server. IBM HTTP server is a version of Apache's web server with enhancements such as additional security. So for example, if you are using IBM HTTP server, the installation will update the web server's configuration file to point to the plug-in file. For IBM HTTP server, there is a file under the ***conf*** directory (as shown in Figure 6-3) of the HTTP server installation called http.conf.

Somewhere in the http.conf file, you should see directives for IBM HTTP server to load the plug-in and point to the plugin-cfg.xml file. This is illustrated in Code Snippet 6-2. Code Snippet 6-2 assumes that the plug-in file will be in the specified directory. If the web server is on the same machine as the application server, when the plug-in configuration is regenerated and placed in the expected directory, the web server will automatically load the changes. If the web server is on a separate machine, the new file will have to be copied to the web server machine and stored in the directory specified in the configuration file.

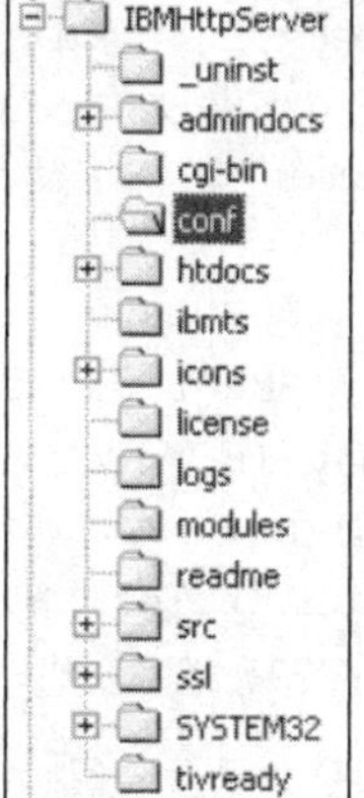


**Figure 6-3** IBM HTTP server.

**Code Snippet 6-2** http.conf file pointing to WebSphere Application Server web server plug-in

```
LoadModule ibm_app_server_http_module "C:\WebSphere5_1Base\AppServer/
➥bin/mod_ibm_app_server_http.dll"
WebSpherePluginConfig "C:\WebSphere5_1Base\AppServer/config/cells/
➥plugin-cfg.xml"
```

The plugin-cfg.xml file itself contains information about the WAS configuration. After certain changes in the WAS configuration, the web server plug-in needs to be updated so that it can handle requests properly. These changes include:

- Installing an application
- Creating or changing a virtual host
- Creating a new server
- Modifying HTTP transport settings
- Creating or altering a cluster

For example, Code Snippet 6-3 illustrates a piece of the plug-in that identifies a cluster of WAS servers. It identifies each host in the cluster, the port numbers (one with SSL), the various load-balancing settings, and various other settings. Some of these settings will be explained more thoroughly later in this book.

**Code Snippet 6-3** Web server plug-in snippet

```
<ServerCluster CloneSeparatorChange="false" LoadBalance="Round Robin"
➥Name="server1_IBMROLY05_Cluster" PostSizeLimit="-1"
```

```
RemoveSpecialHeaders="true" RetryInterval="60">
      <Server ConnectTimeout="0" ExtendedHandshake="false"
      ➥MaxConnections="-1" Name="IBMROLY05_server1"
      ➥WaitForContinue="false">
         <Transport Hostname="IBMROLY05" Port="9080" Protocol="http"/>
         <Transport Hostname="IBMROLY05" Port="9443" Protocol="https">
            <Property Name="keyring" Value="C:\WebSphere5_1Base\
            ➥AppServer\etc\plugin-key.kdb"/>
            <Property Name="stashfile" Value="C:\WebSphere5_1Base\
            ➥AppServer\etc\plugin-key.sth"/>
         </Transport>
      </Server>
      <PrimaryServers>
         <Server Name="IBMROLY05_server1"/>
      </PrimaryServers>
   </ServerCluster>
```

The web server plug-in configuration file can be generated manually through the WAS administrative console. Under the environment section, go into the WAS plug-in page. Figure 6-4 illustrates the manual plug-in regeneration page. The plug-in configuration can also be regenerated using wsadmin.

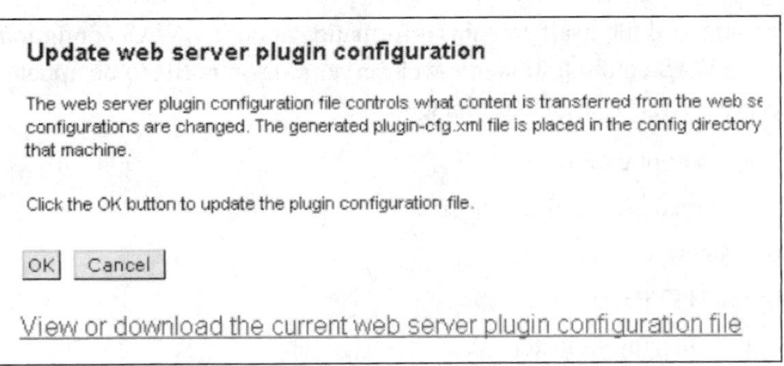


**Figure 6-4** Web server plug-in.

The plug-in file can also be generated using a command-line tool called GenPluginCfg (.bat for windows or .sh for Unix). This utility is located in the bin directory of the WebSphere Application Server. The WebSphere Server plug-in can also be generated using the wsadmin scripting language. An example is shown in Code Snippet 6-4.

**Code Snippet 6-4** Generating the web server plug-in using wsadmin

```
#---------------------------------------------------------------------------
➥-------
# Take care of environment settings
#---------------------------------------------------------------------------
➥-------

set scriptPath      [getShellEnvVariable "WSADMIN_SCRIPTS_HOME"]
set pluginCfgName   [getShellEnvVariable "PLUGIN_CFG_NAME"]
set pluginCfgDir    [getShellEnvVariable "SOURCE_PLUGIN_CFG_DIR"]

#---------------------------------------------------------------------------
➥-------
# Regenerate plugin
#---------------------------------------------------------------------------
➥-------

puts "\n ====== Regenerate plugin  ======"

regeneratePluginConfig $pluginCfgName $pluginCfgDir
```

You can consider adding web server plug-in generation to the build and deployment process, but it may not be worth doing so in a development or a development integration environment. Because these environments are usually only concerned with making sure the application works properly, adding this to a build and deployment process may not add much value but will add extra complication. However, if certain functionality in your application can only be tested under conditions that require a web server, you can add the wsadmin script that generates the plug-in as a model script after the installation of the application. Such conditions may be:

- Testing the links between dynamic portions of your web site and the static portions deployed on the web server
- Testing proper behavior of an application in a cluster of servers

In the automation example you will execute in this chapter, we will not assume the presence of a web server. However, if you are interested, you can add the wsadmin script right after the deployment of the application.

> **NOTE**
> If you do not test with the web server plug-in in your development or integration test environments, we recommend testing the application using the web server plug-in in every other test environment after development.

### Embedded HTTP Server

As stated, the plug-in communicates with WAS using HTTP. These requests are serviced by the embedded HTTP server within WAS. The embedded HTTP server is written in Java. It supports the functions of a web server. Accessing the embedded HTTP server is quite common during development; however, using an external HTTP server in production is recommended. Little configuration is needed for the embedded HTTP server other than port number changes or thread pools. Information on where to update these settings can be found in the WAS Info Center.

## Web Application Descriptors and Packaging

As stated in Chapter 2, web artifacts are packaged with several deployment descriptors into a web module called a WAR file. The WAR file is then packaged into an EAR. This section describes the structure of the web deployment descriptors and the structure of a WAR file.

### Web Deployment Descriptors

The main deployment descriptor in a web module is the ***web.xml*** file. The web.xml file contains many settings. Code Snippet 6-5 shows the shell of web.xml. Much like the application.xml file in the EAR file, it contains the standard headers. The `<web-app>` tags are the parent tags of the web.xml file.

**Code Snippet 6-5** web.xml shell

```
?xml version="1.0" encoding="UTF-8"?>
<!DOCTYPE web-app PUBLIC "-//Sun Microsystems, Inc.//DTD Web
➥Application 2.3//EN" "http://java.sun.com/dtd/web-app_2_3.dtd">
<web-app id="WebApp">
  <display-name>PersonalTradeSystemWeb</display-name>
  ...
</web-app>
```

The first embedded tag is the display name of the web application. After that, there are several sections. The next entry in the web.xml file is the context parameters, if they exist. Context parameters are available via the ServletContext object. Servlets can then access these parameters using the getInitParameter method on the ServletContext. Code Snippet 6-6 illustrates the context parameter entry in the deployment descriptor.

**Code Snippet 6-6** Context parameters

```
<!--INITIALIZATION PARAMETERS FOR WEB APPLICATION AS WHOLE -->
<context-param>
```

```
    <param-name>contextParam</param-name>
    <param-value>test</param-value>
  </context-param>
```

The next section defines any filters if available. Code Snippet 6-7 illustrates a filter definition. The definition includes the filter name, the display name, and the filter class that implements it. After all the filter definitions, the filter mapping section is defined. Whenever a Servlet or URL is requested, any filter mapped to it will execute before the requested Servlet or URL.

**Code Snippet 6-7** web.xml filter definition and mapping

```
<!--  FILTER DEFINITION -->
<filter>
  <filter-name>CheckUserFilter</filter-name>
  <display-name>CheckUserFilter</display-name>
  <filter-class>com.deploybook.trade.filters.CheckUserFilter</
  ➥filter-class>
</filter>

<!--  SERVLET OR URI THAT THIS FILTER IS MAPPED TO -->
<filter-mapping>
  <filter-name>CheckUserFilter</filter-name>
  <url-pattern>/stock/AccessStockQuote.do</url-pattern>
</filter-mapping>
<filter-mapping>
  <filter-name>CheckUserFilter</filter-name>
  <url-pattern>/stock/ViewStockQuote.do</url-pattern>
</filter-mapping>
```

After that, the next section defines any available life-cycle listeners. Listeners respond to any event on the web application. The listener specification requires only the class definition. Code Snippet 6-8 illustrates a listener definition.

**Code Snippet 6-8** Life-cycle listener

```
<listener>
  <listener-class>com.deploybook.trade.SessionListener</listener-class>
</listener>
```

The next section is the Servlet section. Much like the filter, first you must define all the Servlets in the web application. Then you must define the Servlet mapping. The Servlet mapping specifies which Servlets correspond to which URIs. Code Snippet 6-9 illustrates a Servlet definition and its corresponding Servlet mapping. A Servlet definition can take several initialization parameters specific to the application. The `<load-on-startup>` tag tells the container to have the Servlet load when the application is started in a specific order. If not specified, the Servlet will load at first invocation.

**Code Snippet 6-9 Servlet definition and Servlet mapping**

```
<!--Servlet Definition -->
<servlet>
  <servlet-name>action</servlet-name>
  <servlet-class>org.apache.struts.action.ActionServlet</servlet-class>
  <init-param>
    <param-name>config</param-name>
    <param-value>WEB-INF/struts-config.xml</param-value>
  </init-param>
  <init-param>
    <param-name>debug</param-name>
    <param-value>2</param-value>
  </init-param>
  <init-param>
    <param-name>detail</param-name>
    <param-value>2</param-value>
  </init-param>
  <init-param>
    <param-name>validate</param-name>
    <param-value>true</param-value>
  </init-param>
  <init-param>
    <param-name>config/stock</param-name>
    <param-value>WEB-INF/struts-stock.xml</param-value>
  </init-param>
  <load-on-startup>2</load-on-startup>
</servlet>
```

```
<!--Servlet Mapping - how it is accessed in a browser or web client-->
<servlet-mapping>
  <servlet-name>action</servlet-name>
  <url-pattern>*.do</url-pattern>
</servlet-mapping>
```

Servlet mappings can use wildcard characters to have different URI patterns map to the same Servlet. Struts applications will usually have a small amount of Servlets that are specialized and that make use of URI patterns. Some applications may use many Servlets with concrete URIs. These are all development decisions.

The next section defines some general features, and Code Snippet 6-10 illustrates some of the general entries. The first tags define any MIME mappings. Next is the welcome-file list. If any application enters a URL of the web application without specifying a specific resource, it will look for a resource on the list within the WAR file. After that, you can map HTTP error codes or Java exceptions to certain error pages.

**Code Snippet 6-10** General section

```
<!--  ANY MIME DEFINITION -->
<mime-mapping>
    <extension>*.doc</extension>
    <mime-type>word</mime-type>
  </mime-mapping>
  <!--  DEFAULT WEB RESOURCES FOR URL WITHOUT SPECIFIED URI -->
<welcome-file-list>
    <welcome-file>index.html</welcome-file>
    <welcome-file>index.htm</welcome-file>
    <welcome-file>index.jsp</welcome-file>
    <welcome-file>default.html</welcome-file>
    <welcome-file>default.htm</welcome-file>
    <welcome-file>default.jsp</welcome-file>
  </welcome-file-list>

  <!--  ERROR PAGE TO BE DISPLAYED IF WEB CONTAINER ENCOUNTERS THE
  ➥EXCEPTION -->
  <error-page>
    <exception-
type>org.apache.commons.validator.ValidatorException</exception-type>
    <location>/errors/error.jsp</location>
  </error-page>
```

```
<!--ERROR PAGE TO BE DISPLAYED IF SPECIFIC HTTP ERROR IS ENCOUNTERED-->
<error-page>
  <error-code>500</error-code>
  <location>/errors/error.jsp</location>
</error-page>
```

The next section defines references. Web applications can have references to tag libraries, resources, or EJBs. Tag library references point directly to a TLD file within the WAR file. A TLD file is an XML file that describes the tags within a tag library. Resources and EJB references are bound via the binding file. Resources are accessed through JNDI using a web application-specific local namespace. We explained this in Chapter 5, "WebSphere Application Server Architecture." The local namespace contains environment entries as well as references. The local namespace is created by WAS when an application is deployed. Code Snippet 6-11 illustrates references.

**Code Snippet 6-11** References

```
<!--  TAG LIBRARY DEFINITION  JSP PAGES WITHIN WAR CAN MAKE USE OF TAG
➥LIBRAIRES DEFINED -->
<taglib>
  <taglib-uri>http://jakarta.apache.org/taglibs/utility</taglib-uri>
  <taglib-location>/WEB-INF/lib/utility.jar</taglib-location>
</taglib>
<taglib>
  <taglib-uri>http://jakarta.apache.org/taglibs/mailer-1.1</taglib-uri>
  <taglib-location>/WEB-INF/lib/taglibs-mailer.jar</taglib-location>
</taglib>

<!--  A RESOURCE REFERENCE TO A JDBC RESOURCE.  SEE CHAPTER 7  -->
<resource-ref id="ResourceRef_1070208818046">
<res-ref-name>jdbc/DataSource</res-ref-name>
  <res-type>java.lang.Object</res-type>
  <res-auth>CONTAINER</res-auth>
  <res-sharing-scope>Shareable</res-sharing-scope>
</resource-ref>
```

The next section is the security section. It is illustrated in Code Snippet 6-12. First, security constraints are defined. A security constraint maps a resource to a role. Users that are mapped to the role or that belong to a group mapped to the role are allowed to access the resource. The security constraint also defines a user data constraint. This defines whether the request will go over SSL. The next section defines the login scheme. Web applications support several authentication methods:

- **Basic**—The user name and password are encoded by the browser and included in the HTTP request. The web server sends a request to the client, containing the realm name in which the user will be authenticated.
- **Client Certificate**—A PKI-based authentication is performed between the browser and the web server using client certificates. The web server then extracts the credentials from the certificate and forwards them to WAS along with the request.
- **Form**—This method allows the developer to control the look of the authentication request page. Application developers create their own custom pages that are displayed by WAS when a user ID and password is needed for authentication. The form is expected to perform an HTTP POST to j_security_check with the user's ID and password.
- **Digest**—This method is not supported by WAS.

The Personal Trade System uses FORM-based authentication. After the login section, all the roles are defined. These roles must exist in the web.xml file if any security constraints are to be defined. Also, the same roles must then be defined in the application. As stated in Chapter 2, the roles are mapped at an EAR level.

**Code Snippet 6-12** Security section

```
<security-constraint>
  <!--  WEB RESOURCES THAT ARE TO BE PROTECTED -->
<web-resource-collection>
<web-resource-name>StockConstraints</web-resource-name>
<description></description>
<url-pattern>/stock/AccessStockQuote.do</url-pattern>
<url-pattern>/stock/ViewStockQuote.do</url-pattern>
<url-pattern>/ServletRedirector</url-pattern>
</web-resource-collection>

<!--  ROLE THAT IS ALLOWED TO ACCESS WEB RESOURCES COLLECTION ABOVE -->
<auth-constraint>
   <description></description>
   <role-name>TRADEUSER</role-name>
</auth-constraint>
```

```
<!-- WEATHER THIS CONTRAINST WILL USE SSL -->
<user-data-constraint>
    <transport-guarantee>CONFIDENTIAL</transport-guarantee>
</user-data-constraint>
</security-constraint>

<!--  DEFINE THE TYPE OF AUTHENTICATION USED BY THE WEB APPLICATION -->
<login-config>
<auth-method>FORM</auth-method>
<form-login-config>
    <form-login-page>/login/login.jsp</form-login-page>
    <form-error-page>/login/loginFailure.jsp</form-error-page>
</form-login-config>
</login-config>

<!--  DEFINITION OF ROLE FOR WEB APPLICATION -->
<security-role>
  <description></description>
  <role-name>TRADEUSER</role-name>
</security-role>
```

In the last section, you can define environment variables. These environment variables can be accessed in the application using a JNDI call and are defined in the web application's local namespace. The environment setting is illustrated in Code Snippet 6-13.

**Code Snippet 6-13** Environment entries

```
<!--  SIMPLE STRING VARIABLE AVAILABLE TO JAVA CODE IN APPLICATION -->
<env-entry>
    <env-entry-name>var</env-entry-name>
    <env-entry-value>test</env-entry-value>
    <env-entry-type>java.lang.String</env-entry-type>
  </env-entry>
```

A web module contains a binding file as well. The binding file exists to bind EJB and resource references to the actual names that are defined on the server. In the next chapter, we will describe JDBC resources and thus introduce the binding for JDBC. The web extension file defines several settings for the web application that are beyond the specification. WebSphere tools generally generate these files and provide editors that expose the features; showing the structure of these files here might be too confusing.

## Packaging Web Application in WAR Files

The WAR file needs to be structured in a specific way, much like the EAR file. Figure 6-5 illustrates the structure of a web module. The web artifacts, such as JSP pages, HTML pages, and images, can be placed in the root. The META-INF directory contains only the MANIFEST.MF file, which is used to determine the classpath for a J2EE module. (We described this in Chapter 2.) Any web resource outside the WEB-INF can be directly accessed by web clients if file serving is enabled. Anything under the WEB-INF directory cannot be directly accessed. The WEB-INF directory contains all the necessary descriptors.

> **NOTE**
> Place only content intended to be served to web clients in the root of the WAR. All private information, including property files, XML configuration files, etc., should be placed within WEB-INF or within a containing EAR.

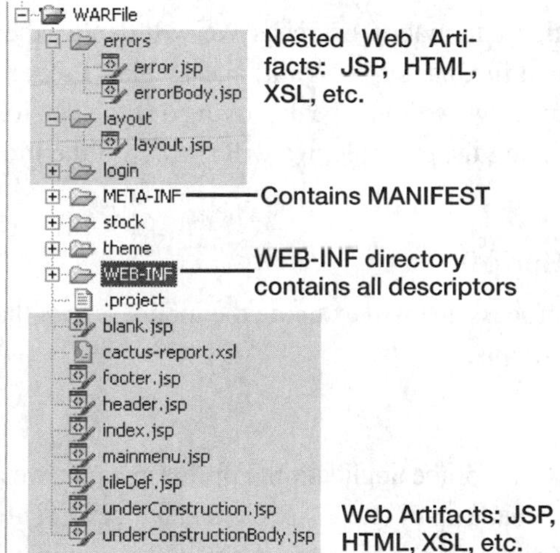


**Figure 6-5** WAR file structure.

The WEB-INF directory is also a good place to store configuration files, such as struts-config for the Struts Framework. Figure 6-6 illustrates the WEB-INF structure. The WEB-INF directory also contains two folders. The "classes" directory contains any Java classes that are part of the WAR file, such as Servlets. The lib folder contains jar files that are automatically in the classpath of any of the classes or JSP pages in the WAR file.

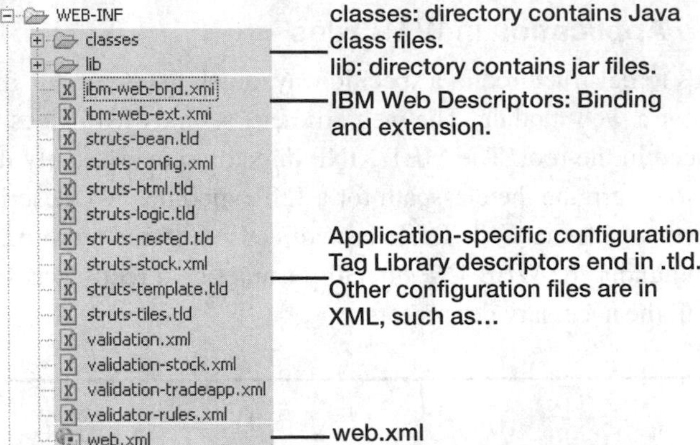


**Figure 6-6** WEB-INF structure.

## Automation

We are now ready for our first automation exercise. We will deploy the Personal Trade System using the process we outlined in Chapter 4, "Build and Deploy Procedures." Because we have only covered the web container, we will only be deploying a static version of the application with no data access. Before executing the example, we will show you the model scripts used to build the EAR file.

### Examining the Build Scripts

Before executing the build process, we will examine the model scripts that make up the build and deployment portions of the scripts.

#### Build Scripts

The goal is to build the EAR file for the application. For this chapter, we are only focused on web applications. Our EAR file is made up of one WAR file that has several utility JARs. Most of them are third-party JARs (libraries developed by someone else; for example, a utility tag library JAR that is part of Struts). There is one library JAR called PTSVerificationTests. This utility JAR includes the components tests that are executed by the verification tests. Figure 6-7 illustrates the EAR file.

The model scripts for building modules follow similar steps:

1. Create temporary folders.
2. Compile code.
3. Create module.
4. Place module in a specified directory.

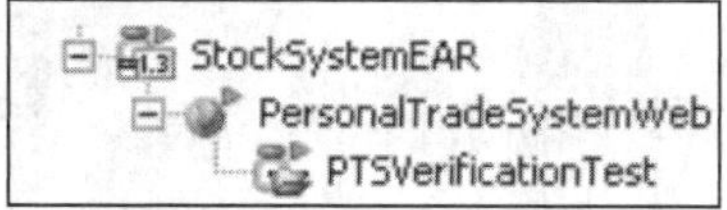


**Figure 6-7** EAR file.

Code Snippet 6-14 illustrates the build file for the WAR file. As you can see, it follows the basic steps just listed. There are a few ways you can create J2EE modules with ANT. See [Hatcher 2003] for the various options.

**Code Snippet 6-14** Model build script for WAR

```
...
<!--COMPILE TARGET FOR CLASSES PLACES in classes DIRECTORY WITHIN WAR-->
<target name="compile">
  <!--SOURCE LOCATION AND TARGET FOR CLASSES -->
  <javac srcdir="${srcdir}" includes="**/*.java"  destdir=
  ➥"${classesdir}" >
    <!--BUILD TIME CLASSPATH -->
    <classpath>
      <!-- WAS libraries for build time classpath -->
      <fileset dir="${wasroot}/lib"  casesensitive="no">
        <include name="*.jar" />
      </fileset>
      <!--THIRD PARTY JAR FILES FROM LIB DIRECTOY -->
      <fileset dir="${webcontent}/WEB-INF/lib"  casesensitive="no">
        <include name="*.jar" />
      </fileset>
      <!--WAR lib Projects developed by the same development team as a
      ➥separate jar -->
      <fileset dir="${war.lib.projects}"  casesensitive="no">
        <include name="*.jar" />
        <include name="*.zip" />
      </fileset>
      <!--EAR LEVEL JAR FILES -->
      <fileset dir="${ear.lib.dependencies}"  casesensitive="no">
        <include name="*.jar" />
        <include name="*.zip" />
      </fileset>
    </classpath>
```

```
  </javac>
</target>

<!--MOVE ANY JAVA PROJECTS DEVELOPED BY THE SAME DEVELOPMENT TEAM INTO
➥lib DIRECTORY -->
<target name="movewebproject">
  <copy  todir="${webcontent}/WEB-INF/lib">
  <fileset dir="${war.lib.projects}">
    <include name="*.jar"/>
  </fileset>
  </copy>
</target>

<!--BUILD WAR FILE FROM WEB CONTENT -->
<target name="buildweb">
  <zip zipfile="${output}/${warjarname}">
    <fileset dir="${webcontent}" />
    </zip>
</target>
...
```

The build controller that we illustrated in Chapter 4 will call all the build models in sequence.

## Deploy Script

WAS has several ANT tasks that aid in the deployment process. We utilize those ANT tasks in our deployment process. Code Snippet 6-15 illustrates the portion of the deployment script that installs the application.

**Code Snippet 6-15 Installing an EAR file with ANT**

```
<target name="install" description="Installs the application">
  <wsInstallApp ear="${buildhome}/${eardir}/${earname}"
        options="-server ${servername}"
        wasHome="${wasroot}"
        user="${username}"
        password="${password}"
```

```
            conntype="${conntypenname}"
            port="${portnumber}"
               host="${hostname}"
               />
</target>
```

The `<wsInstallApp>` tag installs an EAR file in the specified WebSphere Application Server. We also utilize other tasks, such as stopping and starting the server or the application. We also include the tasks for uninstalling the application. Appendix A, "ANT with WebSphere Application Server," will review the rest of the tasks.

The controller script will start the server, install the application, and start the application. This will enable you to install the application into the runtime and execute the verification tests.

## Running the Build Process

It is time to run the build. First, some preparations need to take place. The CVS repository with the source needs to be set up. Next, the server needs to be prepared. Then the properties in the scripts need to be updated to match the reader's environment. Finally, the process will be run, and the test result will be examined:

1. As stated, the sample uses CVS. Appendix C, "Setup Instructions for Samples," covers the installation of CVS. In this chapter, we will add a CVS repository. The version of CVS used in these samples is CVSNT 2.0.12 on Microsoft Windows 2000.[1] Bring up the CVSNT console and go to the Repositories tab. Select Add and enter **c:\cvs_chapter06**. (If you choose another directory, the build script needs to be modified.) The Repositories screen is illustrated in Figure 6-8.

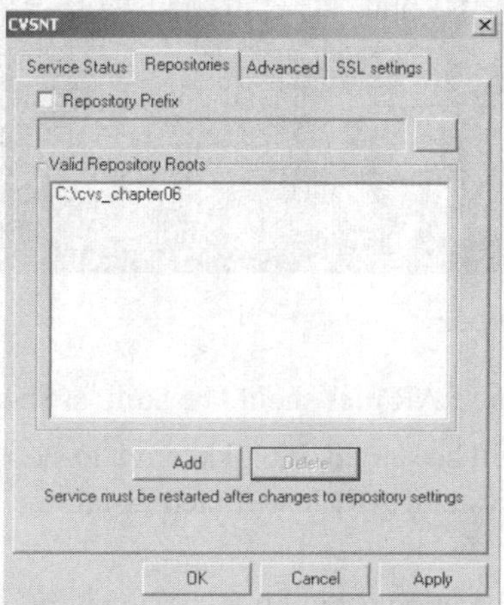


**Figure 6-8** CVS repository.

1 CVS on Windows is not recommended. People who use CVS usually run the CVS server on Unix- or Linux-based systems.

2. Next, click the **Service Status** tab and stop the CVS service. You can also stop the locking service because it is not used.
3. Next, go to the C:\WASDeployBook\Chapter06 directory and extract the **cvs_chapter06.zip** into the newly created directory. We are placing J2EE projects created in WebSphere Studio into CVS. In a real development environment, the Studio workbench will be connected to the repository.
4. Back in the CVS console, start the CVS service. Once started, you can close the console.
5. Before running the script, go to the ANTController directory under C:\WASDeployBook\Chapter06 and edit the build.properties file. Update the wasroot variable to the installation of WAS. Do the same for the RunBuildProcess.bat file.

   WAS ships with a BAT file within the bin directory of the WAS install called ws_ant.bat. This BAT file sets up the necessary classpath to execute standard ANT- and WAS-specific ANT tasks for deployment. However, to add third-party JARs, it is easier to use the ws_ant as a model and create your own BAT file. In this sample, the ws_ant bat file was used as a model and updated to add the JUnit and Cactus testing support to the ANT classpath. This is the purpose for the existence of the RunBuildProcess.bat file.
6. Open a command prompt, go to the C:\WASDeployBook\Chapter06\ANTController, and call RunBuildProcess.bat. This BAT file will execute the process controller with the appropriate classpath needed by the ANT engine.
7. Examine the console:
   - The source should be extracted from CVS, as shown in Figure 6-9.

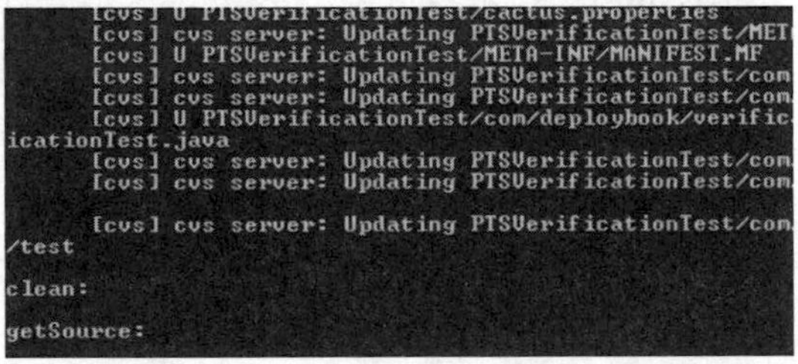

```
      [cvs] U PTSVerificationTest/cactus.properties
      [cvs] cvs server: Updating PTSVerificationTest/MET
      [cvs] U PTSVerificationTest/META-INF/MANIFEST.MF
      [cvs] cvs server: Updating PTSVerificationTest/com
      [cvs] cvs server: Updating PTSVerificationTest/com
      [cvs] U PTSVerificationTest/com/deploybook/verific
icationTest.java
      [cvs] cvs server: Updating PTSVerificationTest/com
      [cvs] cvs server: Updating PTSVerificationTest/com

      [cvs] cvs server: Updating PTSVerificationTest/com
/test

clean:

getSource:
```

**Figure 6-9** Extract CVS source.

   - The submodules and EAR files should be built, as shown in Figure 6-10.
   - The WAS server will be started. It will attempt to stop and uninstall any previous version of the StockSystemEAR. It will then install the application and start it. This is illustrated in Figure 6-11.
   - Next, the junit verification should run and be published to C:\testreport. Figure 6-12 shows a portion of the output for the verification test.
   - Next, the EAR will be placed in C:\earout, and the source and build directories will be cleaned, as shown in Figure 6-13.

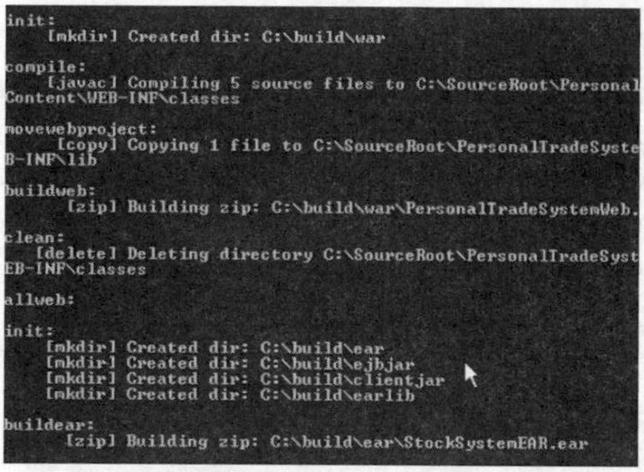

```
init:
     [mkdir] Created dir: C:\build\war

compile:
    [javac] Compiling 5 source files to C:\SourceRoot\Personal
Content\WEB-INF\classes

movewebproject:
     [copy] Copying 1 file to C:\SourceRoot\PersonalTradeSyste
B-INF\lib

buildweb:
      [zip] Building zip: C:\build\war\PersonalTradeSystemWeb.

clean:
   [delete] Deleting directory C:\SourceRoot\PersonalTradeSyst
EB-INF\classes

allweb:

init:
    [mkdir] Created dir: C:\build\ear
    [mkdir] Created dir: C:\build\ejbjar
    [mkdir] Created dir: C:\build\clientjar
    [mkdir] Created dir: C:\build\earlib

buildear:
      [zip] Building zip: C:\build\ear\StockSystemEAR.ear
```

**Figure 6-10** Build the EAR file.

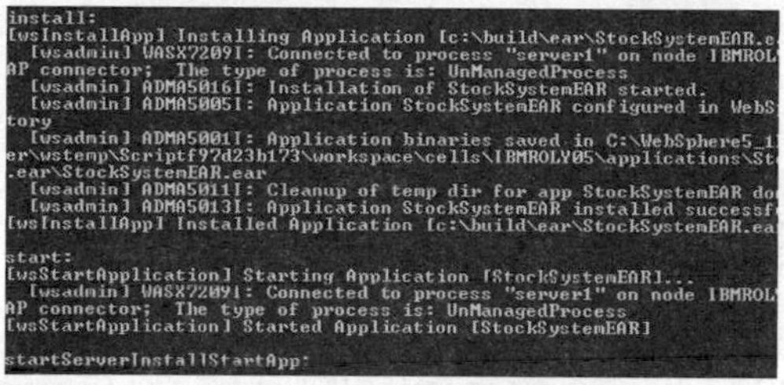

```
install:
[wsInstallApp] Installing Application [c:\build\ear\StockSystemEAR.e
  [wsadmin] WASX7209I: Connected to process "server1" on node IBMROL
AP connector;  The type of process is: UnManagedProcess
  [wsadmin] ADMA5016I: Installation of StockSystemEAR started.
  [wsadmin] ADMA5005I: Application StockSystemEAR configured in WebS
tory
  [wsadmin] ADMA5001I: Application binaries saved in C:\WebSphere5_1
er\wstemp\Scriptf97d23b173\workspace\cells\IBMROLY05\applications\St
.ear\StockSystemEAR.ear
  [wsadmin] ADMA5011I: Cleanup of temp dir for app StockSystemEAR do
  [wsadmin] ADMA5013I: Application StockSystemEAR installed successf
[wsInstallApp] Installed Application [c:\build\ear\StockSystemEAR.ea

start:
[wsStartApplication] Starting Application [StockSystemEAR]...
  [wsadmin] WASX7209I: Connected to process "server1" on node IBMROL
AP connector;  The type of process is: UnManagedProcess
[wsStartApplication] Started Application [StockSystemEAR]

startServerInstallStartApp:
```

**Figure 6-11** The server is started and the application is deployed.

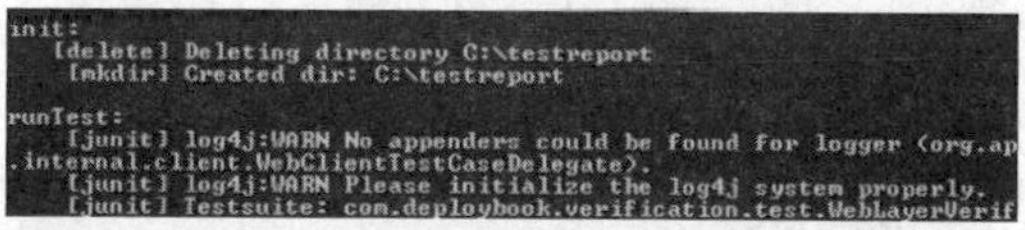

```
init:
   [delete] Deleting directory C:\testreport
    [mkdir] Created dir: C:\testreport

runTest:
    [junit] log4j:WARN No appenders could be found for logger (org.ap
.internal.client.WebClientTestCaseDelegate).
    [junit] log4j:WARN Please initialize the log4j system properly.
    [junit] Testsuite: com.deploybook.verification.test.WebLayerVerif
```

**Figure 6-12** The application verification test is run.

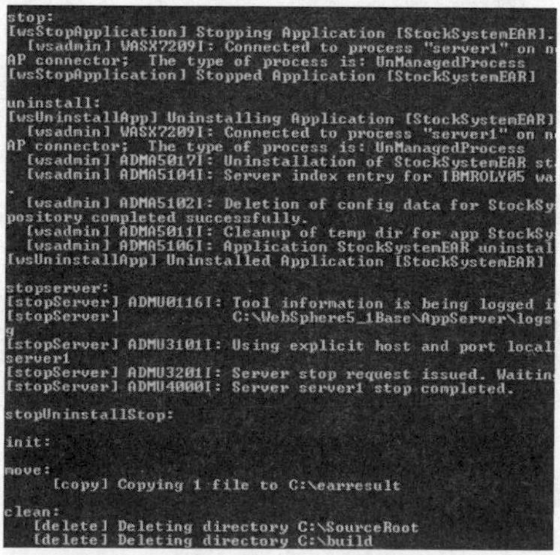

```
stop:
[wsStopApplication] Stopping Application [StockSystemEAR].
  [wsadmin] WASX7209I: Connected to process "server1" on n
AP connector;  The type of process is: UnManagedProcess
[wsStopApplication] Stopped Application [StockSystemEAR]

uninstall:
[wsUninstallApp] Uninstalling Application [StockSystemEAR]
  [wsadmin] WASX7209I: Connected to process "server1" on n
AP connector;  The type of process is: UnManagedProcess
  [wsadmin] ADMA5017I: Uninstallation of StockSystemEAR st
  [wsadmin] ADMA5104I: Server index entry for IBMROLY05 wa
.
  [wsadmin] ADMA5102I: Deletion of config data for StockSy
pository completed successfully.
  [wsadmin] ADMA5011I: Cleanup of temp dir for app StockSy
  [wsadmin] ADMA5106I: Application StockSystemEAR uninstal
[wsUninstallApp] Uninstalled Application [StockSystemEAR]

stopserver:
[stopServer] ADMU0116I: Tool information is being logged i
[stopServer]             C:\WebSphere5_1Base\AppServer\logs
g
[stopServer] ADMU3101I: Using explicit host and port local
server1
[stopServer] ADMU3201I: Server stop request issued. Waitin
[stopServer] ADMU4000I: Server server1 stop completed.

stopUninstallStop:

init:

move:
     [copy] Copying 1 file to C:\earresult

clean:
   [delete] Deleting directory C:\SourceRoot
   [delete] Deleting directory C:\build
```

**Figure 6-13** Publishing the EAR and cleaning up the environment.

8. If any errors are encountered, run with the -verbose option.
9. Go to c:\testreport and open **index.html**. It should display a general page with the test results, as shown in Figure 6-14. Click the only package **com.deploybook.verification.test** link. Next, click on the **WebLayerVerificationTest** class. The last screen will show the three test cases verified, as in Figure 6-15. Besides testing the functional requests, authentication is also verified.

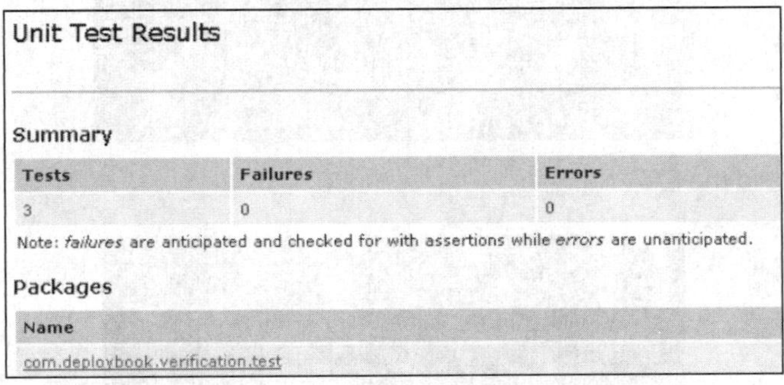
Unit Test Results

Summary

| Tests | Failures | Errors |
| --- | --- | --- |
| 3 | 0 | 0 |

Note: *failures* are anticipated and checked for with assertions while *errors* are unanticipated.

Packages

| Name |
| --- |
| com.deploybook.verification.test |

**Figure 6-14** The test summary.

The scripts will clean up the server environment and the build directories. The final EAR is located in C:\earout. You can deploy the EAR as in Chapter 3, "WAS Quick Start," to verify. Rerunning the script will override the EAR and test report. In a well-structured, repeatable environment, builds and test results names should be uniquely generated and stored in a build repository as well.

Unit Test Results

Class com.deploybook.verification.test.WebLayerVerificationTest

| Name |
| --- |
| WebLayerVerificationTest |

Tests

| Name | Status | Type |
| --- | --- | --- |
| testAuthentication | Success | |
| testAccessStock | Success | |
| testViewStock | Success | |

**Figure 6-15** A specific test case.

## Conclusion

In this chapter, J2EE web technologies and web applications were introduced. Then the WebSphere web container was examined. The web deployment descriptors and the anatomy of WAR files were illustrated. Finally, the reader automated the assembly and deployment of web applications into a WAS build verification environment. Thus far, our applications have been pure web applications with no external resources. In the next chapter, we will examine the use of JDBC in order to create more useful web applications.

CHAPTER 7

# JDBC as a Resource

In the last chapter, you learned about the web container and web application artifacts. But a developer cannot live by Servlets and JSPs alone. In most cases, those useful tools for writing web applications need some way to connect to the various types of backend data that give them purpose. JDBC is the most common way to accomplish that in J2EE applications since it is an interface to relational databases, which are the most common type of backend data store. In this chapter, we will do a quick review of JDBC and explore WebSphere Application Server (WAS) resources related to JDBC. We will also show some examples of how to administer and deploy JDBC resources using the wsadmin scripting facility. Finally, we will assemble and deploy a new version of the Personal Trade System that makes use of JDBC to access data.

## JDBC and J2EE Services

JDBC is one of the services that are available to J2EE applications. Other examples of services available to J2EE applications are Java Message Service (JMS) and JavaMail. With regard to the title of this chapter, you may think of the physical implementations of these abstract services (such as a JDBC data source that has been configured to point to a physical database) as resources for your application to use. The facilities to create and manage resources for the various J2EE services are grouped under the top-level Resources link in the WAS administrative console.

JDBC is the oldest, best known, and most used J2EE service. Its basic purpose is to facilitate the access and manipulation of tabular data sources (in most cases, relational databases) through Java application code. There are two main parts of JDBC—the API that J2EE application programmers use to access and change data, and the service provider interface API that companies use to develop JDBC drivers for the data sources that they provide to their customers. Notice that we carefully avoided saying "database." As of JDBC 2.0, the data source can be other types of tabular data, such as a spreadsheet or text file, in addition to the traditional relational database. However, we will focus here on relational databases.

## Resource References

When a J2EE application is developed, it may contain what might be thought of as "loose wires" to various resources. These must be connected when the application is installed in your particular environment. These "wires" are connected via JNDI. JNDI is an interface to naming services—in this case, the WAS Naming Service (covered earlier in this book). When a JDBC data source is created with the WAS administrative facilities, it is given a JNDI name. This name is considered to be the real JNDI name. Although programmers can access artifacts from JNDI directly, this is not flexible and in fact will not work in certain situations. In the previous chapter, we saw how a developer can define a resource reference on the web.xml file, as shown in Code Snippet 7-1.

**Code Snippet 7-1** JDBC resource reference

```
<resource-ref id="ResourceRef_1063514449762">
    <res-ref-name>jdbc/wstradeRef</res-ref-name>
    <res-type>javax.sql.DataSource</res-type>
    <res-auth>CONTAINER</res-auth>
    <res-sharing-scope>Shareable</res-sharing-scope>
  </resource-ref>
```

Rather than looking up the resource in code using the real name (jdbc/wstrade), applications should use the reference name (java:comp/env/jdbc/wstradeRef). Then the resource reference, defined in the web application's local namespace and accessible through the java:comp/env prefix, is mapped to the real data source in the binding file of the web application, as shown in Code Snippet 7-2.

**Code Snippet 7-2** Binding

```
<resRefBindings xmi:id="ResourceRefBinding_1063514449762" jndiName=
➥"jdbc/wstrade">
    <bindingResourceRef href="WEB-
INF/web.xml#ResourceRef_1063514449762"/>
  </resRefBindings>
```

The resource reference "id" attribute matches the binding file "id" attribute, which is the long number generated by WebSphere tools. A developer or deployer should never have to touch the binding file directly. The binding can be generated at development/assembly time using WebSphere Studio or the ASTK, as shown in Figure 7-1.

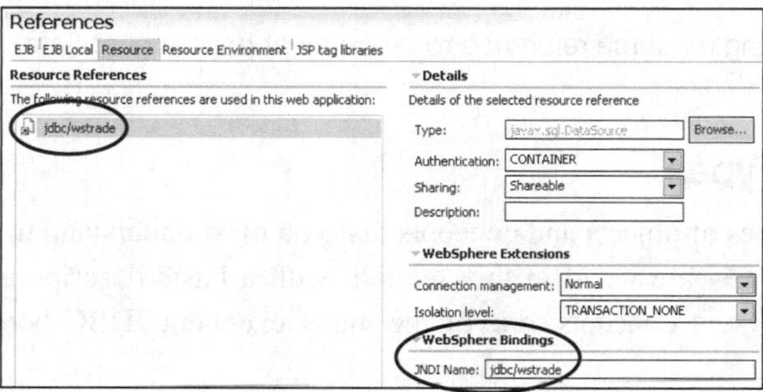


**Figure 7-1** Resource reference using developer/assembly tools.

However, as stated in the previous chapter, this binding information can also be specified during deployment. That is, the resource reference and data source can be matched during application installation, thereby connecting the "loose wire." Data sources such as database tables can even be physically created as part of the deployment process when the application is installed. This is another example of the portability of J2EE applications. A developer can build the application on his or her desktop with these "wires" connected to scaled-down versions of these resources, and when the application is deployed in production, the wires are connected to the "real" enterprise-level resources, all without changing any code. These resources, be they databases accessed with JDBC or email servers accessed with JavaMail, are accessed by the same J2EE APIs, regardless of their brand or size. In theory, if a company decides to switch the brand of database it uses, the code should not have to change. A new JDBC Provider (discussed in the next section) specific to the new brand of database and provided by the database vendor is plugged into the environment and connected to the application resource reference and life goes on. However, we must admit that since SQL isn't entirely portable, for very complex applications, perfect portability is not possible. That is of course why encapsulation and layering of applications is so important. Figure 7-2 illustrates that resource references can be mapped to data sources during installation rather than during assembly. The screen is one of the steps in the deployment wizard through the admin console of WAS. The resource reference to resource mapping can also be part of a scripted install.

**NOTE**

J2EE applications should always look up resources through resource references to benefit from the flexibility described. If an application looks up the resource directly, then the application is tied to a specific name on the server. Every server in the infrastructure then has to define the same exact names to match those in the application.

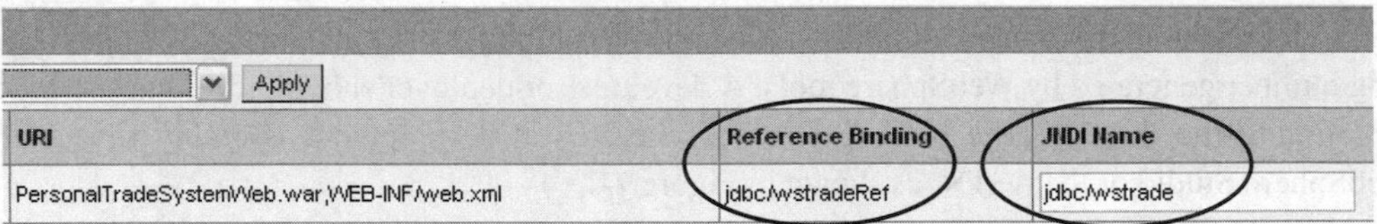


**Figure 7-2** Mapping resource reference to resource at deployment time.

## JDBC Object Types

There are several types of objects and concepts that you must understand in order to be comfortable with JDBC. A few are listed in this section, with a basic description of each. For more expanded definitions and concepts, one of the many excellent JDBC books on the market is recommended.

### JDBC Provider/Driver

JDBC Providers encapsulate what are traditionally known as "drivers." These are typically written by the vendor who provides the brand of backend data source that you are using. For example, if you are using IBM's DB2 database, you would typically install a JAR or ZIP file provided by IBM that contains its JDBC Provider for DB2. When that is done, you can use this new JDBC provider to create JDBC data sources for the specific DB2 databases that you would want to access from your applications.

Drivers are certified by Sun Microsystems and listed on the J2EE compatibility web site when they pass certification. They are also classified into "types," from Type 1 to Type 4. Today, most database vendors support one of two types in production use: Type 2 drivers, which include native code, and Type 4 or "thin" drivers that are written entirely in Java. There is no inherent advantage or disadvantage in either driver other than the theoretically easier installation with pure Java (no native database client installs are required). However, individual database vendors often implement the native drivers with more features than the thin drivers. Consult your database vendor's documentation for details.

> **NOTE ON DRIVER TYPES**
> Type 1 drivers are implemented by using a bridge to some other data access API, such as ODBC. Using a bridge can degrade performance and thus is not very practical. Type 3 drivers implement a protocol-neutral solution to JDBC drivers to allow one pure Java client JDBC driver to be used for multiple databases; however, this requires driver providers to create a server component of the JDBC driver to translate the neutral protocol on the database side.

### JDBC Drivers and Transactions

A transaction is a logical unit of work with one or more operations. For a transaction to be successful, all of the operations must succeed. We'll cover transactions in more detail in Chapter 11, "Transactions with WebSphere Application Server," but right now, you need to understand that there are two types of transactions that a JDBC driver can support: XA and non-XA transactions. Non-XA transactions are one-phase commit transactions involving only a single resource (e.g., a single connection to a single database). XA transactions support two-phase commits across multiple databases or even different types of resources (for example, JMS messages or Enterprise Information Systems). Generally, different data-source drivers provide XA functionality and non-XA functionality. Just be aware of this as you install applications. You'll need to know which type of transaction the application requires in order to determine the correct driver.

### IBM DB2 JDBC Drivers

You may be familiar with the JDBC drivers from IBM (DB2) and Oracle. These files have traditionally been named db2java.zip and classes12.zip, respectively. Making sure they are correctly in place has been a part of many J2EE application installs (and the lack of these has been the cause of many an administrator's headache!). To better understand the concepts covered thus far in this chapter, let's look at IBM's specific implementation:

- **DB2 JDBC driver**—db2java.zip may now be considered IBM's legacy driver, and it supports the DB2 CLI (call-level interface), which is an API to communicate directly with DB2. With its newest version of DB2 Universal Database (v8.1), IBM still provides this driver, but its use is deprecated. db2java.zip contains drivers for Types 2 and 4 and implements JDBC 2.1, but only the Type 2 driver supports XA.
- **DB2 Universal JDBC driver**—The newer DB2 Universal JDBC driver implements JDBC 2.1 and some portions of JDBC 3.0. This driver is found in the file db2jcc.jar. It is provided with DB2 Universal Database v8.1 or can be downloaded from IBM's web site. This implementation provides Type 2 and Type 4 drivers. Obviously, the Type 2 driver requires a native DB2 client install. This driver does not use CLI as the legacy db2java.zip does. It uses a technology called Distributed Relational Database Architecture (DRDA), which is also known as the Java Common Client (JCC) database driver. The Common Client (CCI) portion of the API is an interface that is part of J2EE Connector Architecture (J2C) to ensure that applications have a consistent API for interfacing with an Enterprise Information System (EIS). J2C and CCI are described in more detail in Chapter 8, "J2EE Connector Architecture."

**FIXES/CHANGES**

Use of the db2jcc driver requires a license JAR file named db2jcc_license_xxx.jar (the value of "xxx" is dependent on the platform). This license JAR was not present with the driver until PTF 2 of DB2 UDB v8.1.

As of PTF 2, only the Type 2 driver supports XA; however, this will change in a future fixpack.

Figure 7-3 shows the configuration panel for the IBM DB2 Universal Driver Provider just discussed. Consider the scope where you want to create the provider. Generally, this should be at the highest scope you have defined so that the provider can be used for all nodes/servers. For example, if you have configured a WAS cell, then you might want to create the driver there so that other nodes in the cell can use it. If the provider is application-specific and not to be used for multiple applications, you could give it a name such as TradeAppJDBCProvider and set the scope to only the nodes or application server(s) that the application runs on, as opposed to the entire cell. Note that the paths are rooted off the variable DB2UNIVERSAL_JDBC_DRIVER_PATH. Ensure that this WebSphere variable has been defined for the scope at which you chose to add this driver and not any lower scope,[1] as those will override the parent variable's value. The license JAR files are also visible here in the classpath.

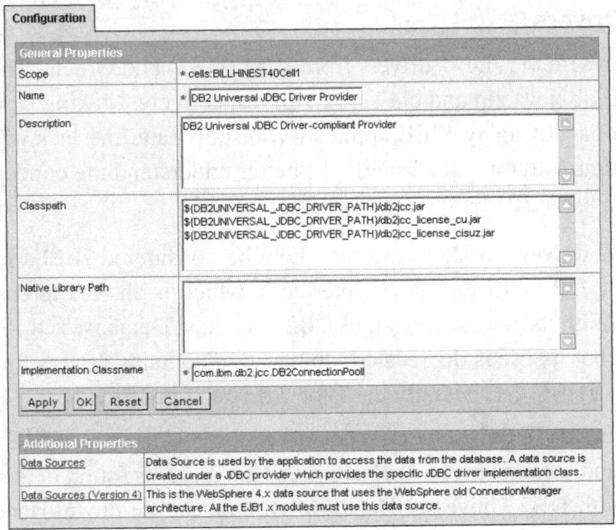


**Figure 7-3** JDBC Provider configuration.

> **NOTE**
> If you want to use SQLJ with this provider, you will have to add an entry to the classpath shown in Figure 7-3 for ${DB2UNIVERSAL_JDBC_DRIVER_PATH}/sqlj.zip.

Also notice the implementation class name for this JDBC Provider—DB2ConnectionPoolDataSource. This name is provided by WAS automatically for known JDBC Providers. If you are using a more obscure driver, you may have to provide the class name yourself. Consult the vendor's documentation for these details.

1 WAS install often defines these variables at the node scope with an empty value. You have to delete the definition to expose a definition at the cell scope. An empty definition overrides a definition with a value at a higher scope.

## JDBC Data Source

A data source is a resource that is the interface to a physical source of data, as its name implies. In most cases, this would be a database. If your environment has ten databases of the same type (for example, DB2) that are used by your applications, then it is likely you would create at least ten data sources in your application server environment, all under one DB2 JDBC Provider. Of course, you might create more than ten data sources if your individual applications will connect with slightly different properties (numbers of connections, security aliases, etc.). You might also define a few of those data sources under a separate JDBC Provider that provides more functionality such as XA transaction support. Each of these data sources would have properties such as the data source name, the JNDI lookup name, and connection pool settings. When the data source is registered in the environment, applications can use it to connect to, view, and manipulate the data it contains.

In WAS5, data sources are implemented using the J2EE Connector Architecture (J2C). We'll discuss that in more detail a bit later. In version 4, WAS had an internal component called a Connection Manager (CM) that managed connections for the application servers. Therefore, WAS5 provides the option to create both version 4 (CM) and version 5 (J2C) data sources. In general, J2EE 1.2-based applications or components of your application (such as Servlet 2.2 or EJB 1.1) must use the WAS4 CM-based data sources, while J2EE 1.3-based applications or components (such as Servlet 2.3 or EJB 2.0) must use the newer WAS5 J2C-based data sources.

Figure 7-4 shows the main configuration page for a JDBC data source. Let's take a look at a few items of interest for deployment:

- **Statement Cache Size**—The Statement Cache Size shown in this figure is a setting for the size the cache of prepared SQL statements[2] available for a JDBC connection. We need to emphasize that this cache exists *per connection*, not per data source. Therefore, when changing this setting, factor in the size of your connection pool. Tuning this setting is a good opportunity to improve performance for applications that use prepared SQL statements. See the Tuning section of the InfoCenter for helpful advice for tuning this setting. Caching the statement improves database access performance by saving the database from repeating the work it performs (e.g., compilation and access plans) when it sees a new statement. This parameter should be evaluated closely during performance/load testing. If these tests show a large number of prepared statement cache discards when using the Tivoli Performance Viewer (TPV), consider making the value here larger. We will discuss TPV in more detail in Chapter 25, "Performance Tuning Tools."
- **Component- or Container-managed Authentication Alias**—The aliases that are referred to in these fields are defined in the WAS administrative console under Security/ JAAS Configuration/J2C Authentication Data.

2. Only JDBC applications that use prepared statements can benefit from the prepared statement cache. Most JDBC applications should use prepared statements in their applications. See [Brown 2004] to learn how developers can use prepared statements.

Configuration

Test Connection

| General Properties | |
|---|---|
| Scope | * cells:BILLHINEST40Cell1 |
| Name | * WSTradeDS |
| JNDI Name | jdbc/wstrade |
| Container managed persistence | Use this Data Source in container managed persistence (CMP) |
| Description | DB2 Universal Driver Datasource |
| Category | |
| Statement Cache Size | 10 statements |
| Datasource Helper Classname | com.ibm.websphere.rsadapter.DB2U |
| Component-managed Authentication Alias | |
| Container-managed Authentication Alias | |
| Mapping-Configuration Alias | DefaultPrincipalMapping |

Apply OK Reset Cancel

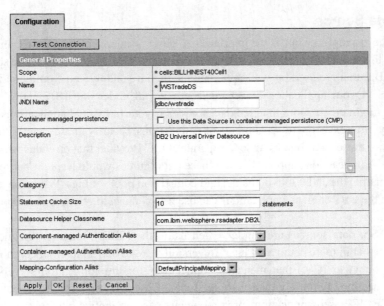

**Figure 7-4** JDBC data source, general properties.

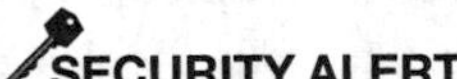

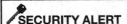

**SECURITY ALERT**

We recommend using container aliases rather than component aliases because container aliases are generally more secure. We'll discuss that in more detail later in Chapter 18, "Security."

From the general data source configuration page shown in Figure 7-4, there are links to edit custom properties specific to the database type. These contain properties such as the database name and, for the IBM JDBC provider that we are using, whether to use the data source as Type 2 or Type 4. Normally, there are separate JAR or ZIP files provided by data source vendors for Type 2 and Type 4 drivers; however, IBM has decided to package both in the same db2jcc.jar file with this particular driver.

There is also a link for connection pool settings from the main data source page. This leads to our next topic—connections and connection pooling.

## JDBC Connection

A connection is just what it sounds like—a conduit from your application to the backend JDBC data source to facilitate the sending of commands and the returning of results. Connections incur quite a bit of overhead, so they should be used sparingly. Applications should close connections as quickly as possible and should take advantage of the built-in connection pooling facilities discussed next.

## JDBC Connection Pool

Because connections are expensive to obtain and use, and because there are a limited number of connections that servers can realistically support, connection pools were created to better manage them. A connection pool is a JDBC resource that manages a set of open connections that are available to applications, thereby saving the overhead of continually opening and closing them. When applications are finished with a connection and issue a close() on it, the connection actually remains open and is returned to the pool instead of being destroyed. Older applications that still get their own connections directly by using the legacy DriverManager object or those that have home-grown connection pooling should be rewritten to take advantage of the JDBC standard connection-pooling facilities.

Applications should use connections for as short a period as possible and should always close them as soon as possible after use. If you notice during testing or monitoring that connections are not being turned over quickly, or that the pool is growing large, check with your developers; it is likely that they aren't returning every connection or are holding connections too long. See Chapter 24, "Problem Determination," for information on troubleshooting this type of problem.

Figure 7-5 shows the connection pool settings for a data source. These will not be discussed individually here as they are covered in [Williamson 2004]. However, take note that the pool size can be configured for minimum and maximum connections. This is a major tuning knob for applications that rely heavily on databases. It is important to tune these parameters carefully and not just "ratchet them up," as higher numbers will often result in worse performance. Final connection pool settings used in production should be a result of rigorous performance testing and tuning.

Configuration

| General Properties | |
|---|---|
| Scope | cells:BILLHINEST40Cell1 |
| Connection Timeout | 1800 seconds |
| Max Connections | 10 connections |
| Min Connections | 1 connections |
| Reap Time | 180 seconds |
| Unused Timeout | 1800 seconds |
| Aged Timeout | 0 seconds |
| Purge Policy | EntirePool |

Apply OK Reset Cancel

**Figure 7-5** Data source connection pool configuration.

## SQLJ

If your application programmers want to use SQLJ, you will have to choose a JDBC provider that has this feature and then likely enable it when creating the data source. SQLJ was defined in the 1999 SQL specification as an alternative to the standard JDBC API. It allows static SQL statements to be directly embedded into Java methods, allows Java methods to be used as SQL stored procedures, and extends some Java data types to those more familiar with database data types. When used in Java to issue SQL statements, this results in code that is more concise and database-like (but less Java-like) and that additionally often runs faster. However, SQLJ requires an extra translation to occur. This can be deemed as a benefit because when using SQLJ, SQL syntax and data types are checked for correctness at compile time, whereas in standard JDBC, the SQL is simply a static string that is not checked until runtime. As noted, SQLJ is useful only for static SQL. For dynamic SQL, JDBC is still the only alternative. In versions 5.01 and above, WAS provides support for SQLJ in application code, including both BMP and CMP types of EJBs.

## JDBC Isolation Levels

Isolation levels define the types of locks that are held on databases during a transaction. Applications have different requirements for data integrity and thus need a way to pass this information to the underlying database.

The JDBC API has a way to provide this functionality programmatically, but as you might expect in J2EE, a declarative approach is preferred. Unfortunately, the J2EE specification does not specify a declarative solution. WAS provides ways to declaratively specify isolation information. The simplest method that we'll describe in this chapter is to set the default isolation level on the resource reference to a data source. In later chapters, we'll discuss the WAS access intent architecture. In any case, since a declarative approach is used, the source code remains portable.

Transactional isolation is defined in terms of ***isolation conditions*** that describe what happens when two or more transactions operate on the same data. There are three conditions:

- **Dirty reads**—Occur when one transaction reads uncommitted changes made by a second transaction.
- **Nonrepeatable**—When the data retrieved in a subsequent read within the same transaction can return different results.
- **Phantom reads**—Occur when new records added to a database are detectable by transactions that started prior to the INSERT.

Transaction isolation levels are defined in terms of the isolation conditions we described. The lock technique used by any data store is vendor-specific. There are four isolation levels:

- **Read uncommitted**—This means a transaction can read uncommitted data. Dirty reads, nonrepeatable reads, and phantom reads are allowed.
- **Read committed**—This means a transaction cannot read uncommitted data of another transaction. Dirty reads are prevented, but nonrepeatable reads and phantom reads can occur.

- **Repeatable read**—This means the same as read committed but prevents nonrepeatable reads. Phantom reads can still occur.
- **Serializable**—These transactions have exclusive read and update access to the data, and all three conditions are prevented.

When thinking about isolation levels, it is useful to understand ***database locking***. This is how databases actually implement isolation. There are four types of locks:

- **Read locks**—These prevent other transactions from changing data read during a transaction until the transaction ends. This prevents nonrepeatable reads. Other transactions can read the data but cannot write to it. Read locks can happen at a record level, a block of records, or a whole table. That decision is entirely database-dependent.
- **Write locks**—These prevent other transactions from changing data until the current transaction is complete but allow dirty reads by other transactions and by the transaction itself.
- **Exclusive write locks**—These prevent other transactions from reading or changing the data until the current transaction is complete. They also prevent dirty reads by other transactions. Other transactions cannot read the data while exclusively locked.
- **Snapshots**—Some databases get around locking by providing a frozen view of the data that is taken when the transaction begins. This is sometimes referred as a snapshot of the data. Snapshots prevent all three conditions described previously but can be problematic because the data cached in the snapshot may not reflect the data actually stored in the physical table.

In WAS applications, you can indicate isolation levels declaratively or programmatically (e.g., by using resource APIs such as JDBC). The isolation-level information is passed to the resource, which then uses an appropriate locking technique to accomplish the desired affect. Strict isolation levels prevent more isolation conditions, but more performance overhead is added to the application. Application architects need to understand the business and data requirements in order to choose the correct isolation levels. Sometimes, applications can allow certain isolation conditions in order to gain performance. Usually, this is when data consistency is not that important to a particular application or when the usage patterns of the application are such that data consistency is maintained.

## Resource References and Isolation Levels

WAS uses resource references to declaratively attach information to a data source. In WAS, the isolation level of the data source is attached to the resource reference as well. Figure 7-6 illustrates the reference section of the deployment descriptor editor. Under the WebSphere Extensions section, you can select one of the four desired isolation levels.

**Figure 7-6** Resource reference and isolation.

> **NOTE**
> Attaching isolation levels to resource references is strongly recommended over programming them inside the application.

## J2EE Connector Architecture

JDBC was invented to provide a vendor-independent, portable, and standard way to access tabular data from Java. However, many applications also need to make other types of connections to a variety of Enterprise Information Systems (EIS) such as Enterprise Resource Planning (ERP) products (e.g., PeopleSoft, Siebel, SAP R/3) and transaction monitors such as IBM CICS. Because there was no standard way to do this (as there was for JDBC), these vendors were creating their own incompatible APIs. Because of this need, the J2EE Connector Architecture (J2C) was added to the J2EE specification. Using J2C, EIS resource adapters can provide the same benefits as the JDBC providers, and application developers using the J2C Common Client Interface (CCI) benefit from only having to learn one API to connect to these EIS systems and being able to write portable code to connect to EIS. Chapter 8 will discuss J2C in greater detail.

## Resource Adapter

A resource adapter is a J2C driver that connects at the Java system level to a backend EIS, much as a JDBC Provider provides a way to connect to a backend data source. Realizing this, IBM has implemented the WAS5 JDBC data sources on top of the J2C infrastructure. Thus, it leverages the common functions of J2C. This also means that when configuring JDBC resources, you may be confronted with J2C terminology. The next chapter will discuss J2C and resource adapters in greater detail.

# Automation

In the last chapter, we automated the building and deployment of the Personal Trade System. Now that we have covered JDBC, we have updated the example to use JDBC to access a DB2 database. In order to run the example, you must set up the database using the installation examples in Appendix C, "Setup Instructions for Samples." Because we need to access JDBC, we will add JDBC configuration to our build and deployment process. (The process was outlined in Chapter 4, "Build and Deploy Procedures.") Before running the example, we will examine the wsadmin JDBC scripts.

## Examining JDBC wsadmin Scripts

Some administrators prefer a graphical user interface, and others prefer the command line. Both approaches work well; however, many times you may not have a choice. In many shops, administrative consoles (even thin clients running in browsers) are prohibited by security policy and infrastructural constraints. Scripted administration is beneficial because of the ability to repeat certain tasks with less chance of errors caused by things like typos. Once scripts are tested, they can be run repeatedly with less concern for error, and they can be set to kick off at predetermined times or intervals. So as an example, let's explore how to configure our JDBC Provider and associated components from the command line using wsadmin scripting. wsadmin is a tool provided with WAS that allows for scripting administrative operations.

Our approach to configuring WAS for an application's JDBC provider and data source is:

1. Start the server. Although some wsadmin commands can be run without the server running, configuration commands are better run while the server is up.
2. Define a WAS variable for the actual location of the JDBC driver on the server. By doing this at the cell scope, the variable can be overridden at a lower scope (for example, an individual node) in case there is a different path to the JDBC provider on that particular machine. This can happen for many reasons; for example, not all machines in a WAS cell may run the same operating system—there could be a combination of Unix and Windows servers.

   While variable scopes give us the ability to set a general rule and override it as needed, this can also be the source of errors. For example, if NoClassDefFoundError appears on application server startup for JDBC driver classes, the WAS variable for the driver path may not be properly defined, not defined at all, or perhaps even unexpectedly defined at a lower scope. This commonly happens because WAS configures default variable names for popular databases; however, the path values for the variable are left blank.

3. Define the JDBC Provider. This will usually also be at a high scope, such as the cell, since organizations tend to use the same backend storage for all of their applications on each node.
4. Next, define the J2C authentication alias. This provides an identity under which to open connections with the database, as discussed earlier in this chapter.
5. Define the JDBC data source itself. This could be defined at a lower scope than the cell if only one node or application will use this data source due to special configurations required, such as when only one application has a need for XA transactions or to get to a specific database, such as the marketing database.
6. Test the connection.
7. Stop the server.

These seven steps will all be accomplished with separate wsadmin scripts for clarity in describing each step. However, there is no reason all seven could not be combined into one script or run in sequence from the command line. wsadmin is a very powerful facility, and you are encouraged to learn more from the WAS Info Center and [IBM WAS 5 Handbook].

### Adding a WAS Variable

The script shown in Code Snippet 7-3 adds the WAS variable DB2_UNIVERSAL_JDBC_DRIVER_PATH at the cell scope. Notice that the variable name, the path to the driver, and the variable description are all hard-coded into the script as variable definitions at the very top. This script could be changed so that these values could be passed in at runtime when executing the script with the ANT controller. Taking this approach would make the script much more extensible—it could be used to create any WAS variable, not just the one for this particular JDBC driver path.

**Code Snippet 7-3 Adding a WAS variable with wsadmin**

```
#-------------------------------------------------------------
# Create a WAS Variable for the driver path
#-------------------------------------------------------------


# Set variables for variable map
set variableName "DB2UNIVERSAL_JDBC_DRIVER_PATH2"
set jdbcDriverPath "C:/Program Files/IBM/SQLLIB/java"
```

```
set variableDesc "Path to the IBM JDBC driver file(s)"

# Set the cell name
puts "\nGetting the name of the cell we are on"
set cellName [$AdminControl getCell]
puts "\nAdd WAS variable $variableName on cell:$cellName"

# Get the variable Map
puts "\nGetting the variable map ID"
set vm [$AdminConfig getid /Cell:$cellName/VariableMap:/]

# Set the variable Map
set symname [list symbolicName "$variableName"]
set value   [list value "$jdbcDriverPath"]
set desc    [list description "$variableDesc"]
set temp    [list $symname $value $desc]
set attr_vals  [list entries [list $temp]]
set attrs   [list $attr_vals]

# Modify the variable map with new variable
puts "\nUpdating the variable map."
$AdminConfig modify $vm $attrs

# Save the Configuration
puts "\nSaving configuration"
$AdminConfig save

# Finish message
puts "\nDone!"
```

### Adding a JDBC Provider

The script shown in Code Snippet 7-4 adds a JDBC Provider at the cell scope. Notice that the driver and license JARs are concatenated into the classpath, the WAS variable we just created is being put to good use, and an existing driver of this type is removed if it already exists. **Be aware, however: If you are using WAS-ND, this script will remove all occurrences of this name in the cell level!**

**Code Snippet 7-4** Adding a JDBC Provider with wsadmin

```
#--------------------------------------------------------------
# Create a JDBC Provider
#--------------------------------------------------------------

# Set variables for JDBC provider
set jdbcProviderName "DB2UniversalJDBCDriverProvider"
set jdbcProviderDesc "DB2 Universal JDBC Provider"
set jdbcProviderClass " com.ibm.db2.jcc.DB2ConnectionPoolDataSource"
set driverClassPath
"\$(DB2UNIVERSAL_JDBC_DRIVER_PATH)/db2jcc.jar;\$(DB2UNIVERSAL_JDBC_
➥DRIVER_PATH)/db2jcc_license_cu.jar;\$(DB2UNIVERSAL_JDBC_DRIVER_PATH)/
➥db2jcc_license_cisuz.jar"

# Get the cell we are on
puts "\nGetting the name and ID of the cell we are on"
set cellName [$AdminControl getCell]
set cellID [$AdminConfig getid /Cell:$cellName/]
puts "\nInstall JDBC Provider on cell:$cellName Cell ID:$cellID"


#Remove any existing provider with the same name
puts "\nLooking for and removing any existing JDBC providers by this
➥name"
set providers [$AdminConfig getid /Cell:$cellName/JDBCProvider:
➥$jdbcProviderName/ ]
foreach provID $providers {
  puts "\nRemoving old entry $provID"
  $AdminConfig remove $provID
  $AdminConfig save
}

#Create provider on the target cell.
puts "\nCreating provider $jdbcProviderName on $cellName"
set attrib {}
lappend attrib [list classpath "$driverClassPath"]
lappend attrib [list implementationClassName "$jdbcProviderClass"]
```

```
lappend attrib [list name "$jdbcProviderName"]
lappend attrib [list description "$jdbcProviderDesc"]

$AdminConfig create JDBCProvider $cellID $attrib

# Save the Configuration
puts "\nSaving configuration"
$AdminConfig save

puts "\nDone!"
```

### Adding a J2C Authentication Alias

The script shown in Code Snippet 7-5 will create the J2C authentication alias that will be used to configure a data source for the Personal Trade System application in the next step.

**Code Snippet 7-5** Adding a J2C authentication alias with wsadmin

```
#---------------------------------------------------------
# Create a J2C Authentication Alias
#---------------------------------------------------------

# Set variables for authentication alias
set defaultUser1 "db2admin"
set defaultPassword1 "db2admin"
set aliasName "tradeDBAlias"
set aliasDescription "J2C alias for the Trade application"

# Get cell that we are on
puts "\nGetting the name and ID of the cell we are on"
set cellName [$AdminControl getCell]
set cellID [$AdminConfig getid /Cell:$cellName/]
puts "\nInstall JDBC Provider on cell:$cellName Cell ID:$cellID"

# remove any existing alias with the same name
puts "\nSearch for and remove the alias if it exists"
set secID [$AdminConfig getid /Cell:$cellName/Security:/]
set aliases [$AdminConfig list JAASAuthData $secID]
```

```
foreach al $aliases {
  set thisAlias [lindex [lindex [$AdminConfig show $al {alias}] 0] 1]
  if {($thisAlias == "$aliasName")} {
   puts "\nRemoving old JAAS Auth Alias:$thisAlias"
   $AdminConfig remove $al
   $AdminConfig save
  }
}

# Create the alias
puts "\nCreate the J2C Authentication Alias"
set alias_attr    [list alias $aliasName]
set desc_attr     [list description $aliasDescription]
set userid_attr   [list userId $defaultUser1]
set password_attr [list password $defaultPassword1]
set attrs         [list $alias_attr $desc_attr $userid_attr
➥$password_attr]

$AdminConfig create JAASAuthData $secID $attrs

# Save the Configuration
puts"\nSaving configuration"
$AdminConfig save

puts "\nDone!"
```

## Adding a JDBC Data Source

The script shown in Code Snippet 7-6 will create the JDBC data source, which will utilize the JDBC Provider and J2C authentication alias that were created in the prior steps.

**Code Snippet 7-6** Adding a JDBC data source

```
#-----------------------------------------------------------
# Create a JDBC Data Source
#-----------------------------------------------------------

# Set variables for JDBC data source
```

```
#JDBC provider
set jdbcProviderName "DB2UniversalJDBCDriverProvider"

# JAAS auth alias Users and passwords..
set aliasName "tradeDBAlias"

#DataSource and Connection Factory
set dsName "WSTradeDS"
set cmpDSName "WSTradeDS_CF"
set dsDescription "DB2 Data Source for the Trade application"
set databaseName1 "WSTRADE"
set jndiName "jdbc/wstrade"
set statementCacheSize "10"
set driverType "2"
set datasourceHelperClassname
"com.ibm.websphere.rsadapter.DB2UniversalDataStoreHelper"

puts "\nGetting the name and ID of the cell we are on"
set cellName [$AdminControl getCell]
set cellID [$AdminConfig getid /Cell:$cellName/]

puts "\nGetting the ID of the JDBC Provider"
set jdbcProviderID [$AdminConfig getid
/Cell:$cellName/JDBCProvider:$jdbcProviderName/ ]
set found 0
set foundCMP 0

#Look for existing Data Source and remove it
set list [$AdminConfig list DataSource]
foreach fnm $list  {if {[string compare $dsName [$AdminConfig
➥showAttribute $fnm name]] == 0} {$AdminConfig remove $fnm}}

puts "\nCreating the datasource $dsName"
set attrs2 [subst {{name "$dsName"} {description "$dsDescription"}}]
set ds1 [$AdminConfig create DataSource $jdbcProviderID $attrs2]

#Set the properties for the data source...
set propSet1 [$AdminConfig create J2EEResourcePropertySet $ds1 {}]
```

```
set attrs3 [subst {{name databaseName} {type java.lang.String} {value
➥"$databaseName1"}}]
puts "\nj2eeresourceproperty"
$AdminConfig create J2EEResourceProperty $propSet1 $attrs3

set attrs4 [subst {{jndiName $jndiName} {statementCacheSize
➥$statementCacheSize} {datasourceHelperClassname
➥$datasourceHelperClassname} {authMechanismPreference
➥"BASIC_PASSWORD"}}]
$AdminConfig modify $ds1 $attrs4

#Create the connection pool object...
$AdminConfig create ConnectionPool $ds1 {{connectionTimeout 1000}
➥{maxConnections 30} {minConnections 1} {agedTimeout 1000} {reapTime
➥2000} {unusedTimeout 3000} }

#Create Container Managed Alias
set authDataAliasList [list authDataAlias $aliasName ]
set mappingConfigAliasList [list mappingConfigAlias
➥DefaultPrincipalMapping ]
set mappingList [list $authDataAliasList $mappingConfigAliasList]

$AdminConfig create MappingModule $ds1 $mappingList

puts "\nSaving configuration"
$AdminConfig save

puts "\nDone Creating Data Source\n"
```

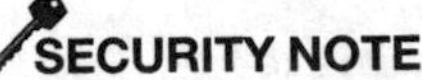

**SECURITY NOTE**

Here, we have used container aliases rather than component aliases because container aliases are generally more secure. We'll discuss that in more detail later in Chapter 18, "Security."

### Testing the Connection

The final script is a simple script that will actually test the data source by making a connection using the data source we created. Code Snippet 7-7 illustrates the test script.

**Code Snippet 7-7** Test connection

```
#Provider Name
set jdbcProviderName "DB2UniversalJDBCDriverProvider"

#DS Name
set dsName "WSTradeDS"

# Get the ID of the datasource
set myds [$AdminConfig getid/JDBCProvider:$jdbcProviderName/
➥DataSource:$dsName/]

#Test the connection
$AdminControl testConnection $myds

puts "\nConnection Tested\n"
```

After running the build and deployment process, you can check the admin console to verify that the configurations have been made. We have created WAS variables, a J2C authentication alias, and the JDBC resources. All these are accessible from the main tree menu, as shown in Figure 7-7.

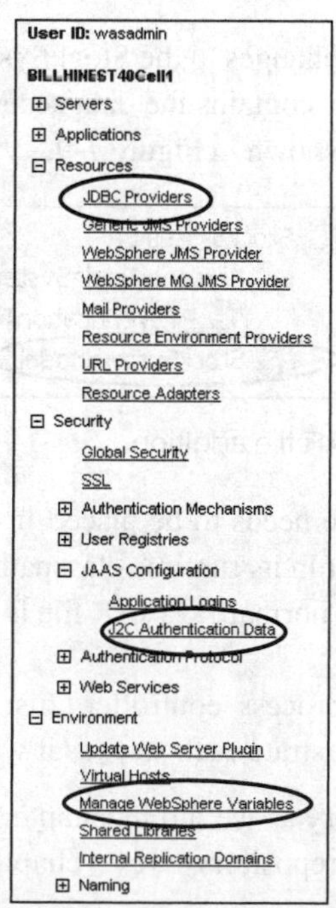


**Figure 7-7** Accessing configurations through the WAS admin console.

If you do not see the resource defined after running the build process, it is probably because you are not on the correct scope. On the JDBC Provider page, you can switch the scope you are looking at by selecting the desired scope and pressing Apply, as shown in Figure 7-8.

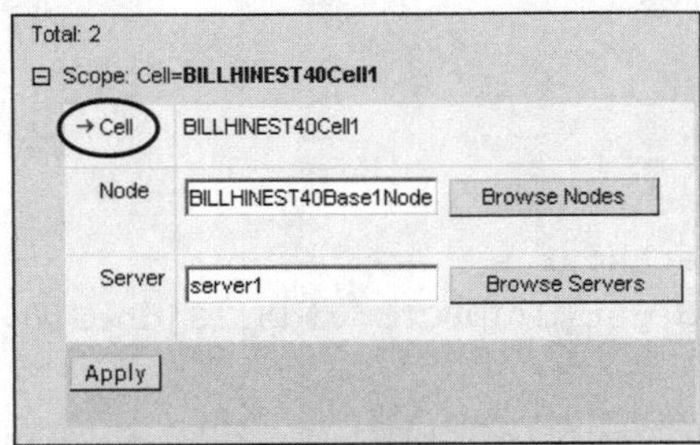


**Figure 7-8** Switch scopes.

## Running the Build and Deployment Process

In the last chapter, a static version of the Personal Trade System was deployed. In this chapter, the application has been updated to use the JDBC data source we created. Besides updating the code, the web.xml file now contains the resource reference definition we showed earlier in Figure 7-1. The binding file has also been generated at development time to match the JDBC resource we created in the server.

There are also some structural changes to the StockSystemEAR. There is a new utility JAR file called StockSystemModel, which contains the data access code. The StockSystemModel.jar has been placed at the EAR level, as shown in Figure 7-9.

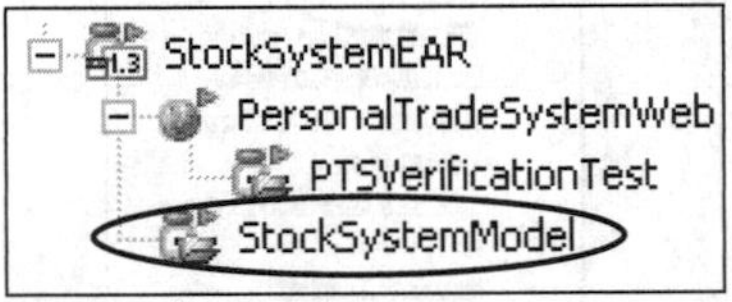


**Figure 7-9** StockSystemModel JAR file addition.

The StockSystemModel.jar file needs to be placed in the MANIFEST of the WAR file in order for the web application to see it in its runtime classpath. No entries are needed in the application.xml file of the EAR because a normal Java JAR file is not a J2EE module, as we explained in Chapter 2, "J2EE Applications."

We will now run the build process controller. Just like last chapter, we will run the BuildProcess.bat file. We will not illustrate each step, as it will be similar to the last chapter:

1. Create a new CVS repository as we did in Chapter 6, "J2EE Web Applications and the Web Container." Call this repository c:/cvs_chapter07. Also run the DB scripts as in Chapter 6.

2. Extract C:\WASDeployBook\Chapter07\cvs_chapter07.zip into the newly created c:/cvs_chapter07 repository. (If you desire to examine the EAR, you can import it into WebSphere Studio, as shown in Appendix C. The resulting EAR will be stored in the c:\earresult directory.)
3. Now, from a command prompt, go to C:\WASDeployBook\Chapter05\ANTController. Execute **RunBuildProcess buildDeployAndVerifyNoStop**, as shown in Figure 7-10. We are explicitly passing in the target name because the default behavior is to undeploy the application and stop the server after running the verification tests.

```
C:\WINNT\system32\cmd.exe

C:\WASDeployBook\Chapter05\ANTController>RunBuildProcess buildDeployAndVerifyNoS
top
```

**Figure 7-10** Run the build process without the undeployment and stop piece.

4. It will start the server, as shown in Figure 7-11.

```
startserver:
[startServer] ADMU0116I: Tool information is being logged in file
[startServer]            C:\WebSphere5_1Base\AppServer\logs\server1\startServer.
log
[startServer] ADMU3100I: Reading configuration for server: server1
[startServer] ADMU3200I: Server launched. Waiting for initialization status.
[startServer] ADMU3000I: Server server1 open for e-business; process id is 3408
```

**Figure 7-11** Start the server.

5. Create the configuration variables, as shown in Figure 7-12.

```
callCreateWSVariables:

genericWsadminCaller:
  [wsadmin] WASX7209I: Connected to process "server1" on no
AP connector;  The type of process is: UnManagedProcess

  [wsadmin] Getting the name of the cell we are on

  [wsadmin] Add WAS variable DB2UNIVERSAL_JDBC_DRIVER_PATH2

  [wsadmin] Getting the variable map ID

  [wsadmin] Updating the variable map.

  [wsadmin] Saving configuration

  [wsadmin] Done creating variable!
```

**Figure 7-12** Create WebSphere variables.

6. Next, the script will create the DB2 JDBC Provider, as shown in Figure 7-13.

```
callCreateJDBCProvider:

genericWsadminCaller:
  [wsadmin] WASX7209I: Connected to process "server1" on node
AP connector;  The type of process is: UnManagedProcess

  [wsadmin] Getting the name and ID of the cell we are on

  [wsadmin] Install JDBC Provider on cell:IBMROLY05 Cell ID:I
OLY05:cell.xml#Cell_1)

  [wsadmin] Looking for and removing any existing JDBC provid

  [wsadmin] Removing old entry DB2UniversalJDBCDriverProvider
sources.xml#JDBCProvider_1071990486200)

  [wsadmin] Creating provider DB2UniversalJDBCDriverProvider

  [wsadmin] Saving configuration

  [wsadmin] Done Creating JDBC Provider!
```

**Figure 7-13** Create the JDBC Provider.

7. Next, the script creates an authentication alias that the data source will use to authenticate to the data store. This will be explained later. This is illustrated in Figure 7-14.

```
callCreateJ2CAlias:

genericWsadminCaller:
  [wsadmin] WASX7209I: Connected to process "server1" on
AP connector;  The type of process is: UnManagedProcess

  [wsadmin] Getting the name and ID of the cell we are on

  [wsadmin] Install JDBC Provider on cell:IBMROLY05 Cell
OLY05:cell.xml#Cell_1)

  [wsadmin] Search for and remove the alias if it exists

  [wsadmin] Removing old JAAS Auth Alias:tradeDBAlias

  [wsadmin] Create the J2C Authentication Alias

  [wsadmin] Saving configuration

  [wsadmin] Done creating J2C Alias!
```

**Figure 7-14** Create a J2C alias.

8. Next, the data source is created, as illustrated in Figure 7-15.

```
callCreateDataSource:

genericWsadminCaller:
  [wsadmin] WASX7209I: Connected to process "server1" on node IBM
AP connector;  The type of process is: UnManagedProcess

  [wsadmin] Getting the name and ID of the cell we are on

  [wsadmin] Install JDBC Data Source WSTradeDS on cell:IBMROLY05

  [wsadmin] Getting the ID of the JDBC Provider

  [wsadmin] Installing DataSource

  [wsadmin] Creating the datasource WSTradeDS

  [wsadmin] j2eeresourceproperty

  [wsadmin] Saving configuration

  [wsadmin] Done Creating Data Source
```

**Figure 7-15** Create the JDBC data source.

9. The data source is then verified by testing the connection, as shown in Figure 7-16.

```
callTestDataSource:

genericWsadminCaller:
  [wsadmin] WASX7209I: Connected to process "server1" o
AP connector;  The type of process is: UnManagedProcess

  [wsadmin] Connection Tested
```

**Figure 7-16** Test the connection.

10. Finally, the server should be stopped, as shown in Figure 7-17.

```
stopserver:
[stopServer] ADMU0116I: Tool information is being logged in file
[stopServer]            C:\WebSphere5_1Base\AppServer\logs\server1
g
[stopServer] ADMU3101I: Using explicit host and port localhost:888
server1
[stopServer] ADMU3201I: Server stop request issued. Waiting for st
[stopServer] ADMU4000I: Server server1 stop completed.

fullConfigure:
```

**Figure 7-17** Stop the server.

11. The rest of the build process should be similar to Chapter 6. The build process should follow the procedure described in Chapter 4, minus the uninstallation and stopping of the server. Wait till the build completes, as shown in Figure 7-18.

```
outputEar:

init:

move:
      [copy] Copying 1 file to C:\earresult

clean:

clean:
   [delete] Deleting directory C:\SourceRoot
   [delete] Deleting directory C:\build

buildDeployAndVerifyNoStop:

BUILD SUCCESSFUL
Total time: 1 minute 49 seconds
```

**Figure 7-18** The build result.

12. Once the build is done, you can go into c:\testreport and open index.html to explore the verification test results. There should be a new ModelLayerVerificationTest entry. Follow the links and determine if the verification tests are successful.
13. Once you have examined the verification result, let's run the application. Open the browser and go to http://localhost:9080/pts.
14. Log in to the application as **bbird**. The password is **password1a**.

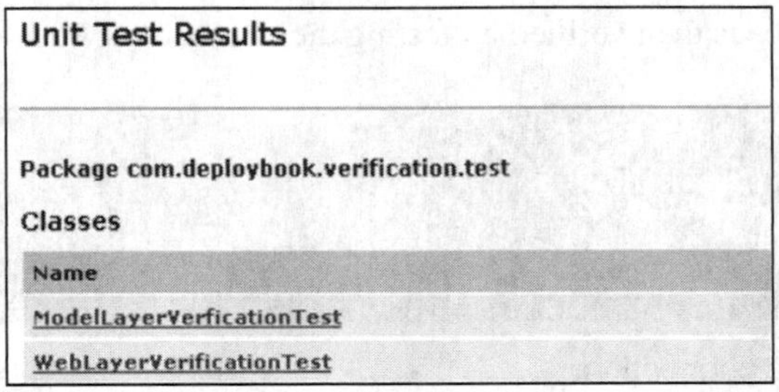

Unit Test Results

Package com.deploybook.verification.test

Classes

| Name |
| --- |
| ModelLayerVerficationTest |
| WebLayerVerificationTest |

**Figure 7-19** The verification test result.

**15.** Enter **IBM**, as shown in Figure 7-20, and press Submit.

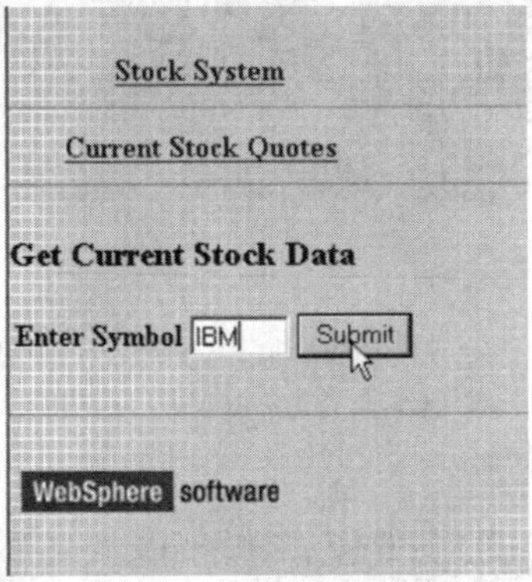

**Figure 7-20** Enter **IBM**.

**16.** The result should access the database and return data, as shown in Figure 7-21.

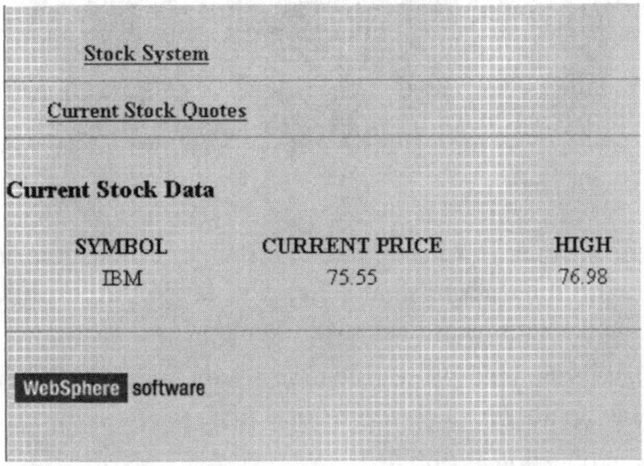

**Figure 7-21** Get result.

17. To ensure that dynamic data is being returned, enter **MSFT** as input.

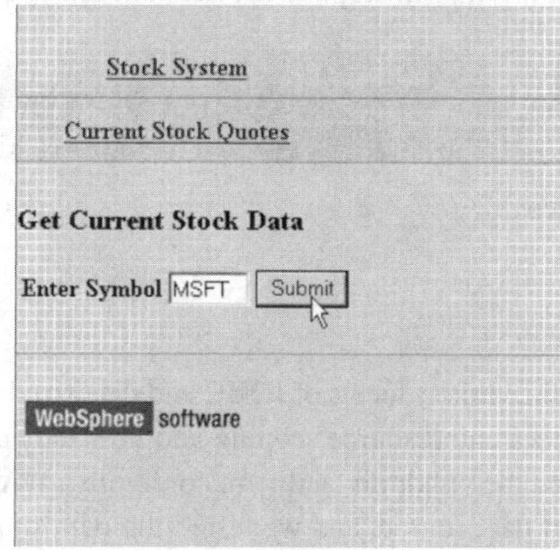


**Figure 7-22** Try different input.

18. Different data should be returned, as in Figure 7-23.

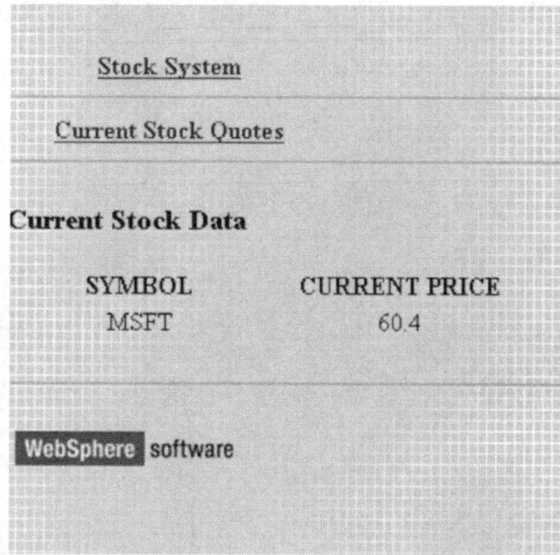


**Figure 7-23** Different results are returned.

**19.** Once done, go back to the command line and run **RunBuildProcess UndeployStop**, as shown in Figure 7-24. This will stop the application, undeploy it, and stop the server.

```
C:\WINNT\system32\cmd.exe
C:\WASDeployBook\Chapter05\ANTController>RunBuildProcess UndeployStop
```

**Figure 7-24** Stop the server.

## Conclusion

In this chapter, we explored the various facets of JDBC and discussed some practical applications for its use. Resource references and resource scoping and how they apply to deploying applications were discussed. We used the wsadmin facility to configure a WAS variable, JDBC Provider, J2C authentication alias, and data source, and we tested the data source. Finally, we assembled and deployed a dynamic version of the Personal Trade System using build and deployment process.

In addition, in this chapter, we discussed the J2EE Java Connector Architecture (J2C) and how WAS resources, such as JDBC, make use of J2C. In the next chapter, we will explore the J2C in detail.

# CHAPTER 8

# J2EE Connector Architecture

Since early J2EE incarnations, applications have taken advantage of JDBC for vendor-independent, portable, standard access to relational databases from Java. However, many applications also need to make other types of connections to a variety of other types of Enterprise Information Systems (EIS). These include Enterprise Resource Planning (ERP) products such as PeopleSoft, Siebel, and SAP R/3, transaction monitors such as IBM CICS and IMS, enterprise and object-oriented databases, and even applications written in other languages and running on other platforms. In early J2EE, there was no standard mechanism for this connectivity (as there was for databases with JDBC), so vendors created their own incompatible APIs. Because of the need for a common framework for enterprise system access, the J2EE Connector Architecture (J2C) was added to the J2EE specification. This chapter explores J2C and provides some wsadmin scripts for creating J2C resources.

**NOTE—THE NAME GAME**

JCA is commonly used as the acronym for J2EE Connector Architecture. However, we chose to use J2C in our text for several reasons:

1. JCA is defined on the Sun web site as belonging to Java Cryptography Architecture.
2. For consistency, acronyms beginning with a single "J" should indicate that it stands for "Java," while those beginning with "J2" should indicate "J2EE."
3. This is the convention used by the WebSphere Application Server product.

## J2C Architecture

The J2C architecture is much like that of JDBC. It is built around several layered components. See Figure 8-1, which we will discuss now in general and then later in detail (including system contracts and Common Client Interface) in the balance of this chapter.

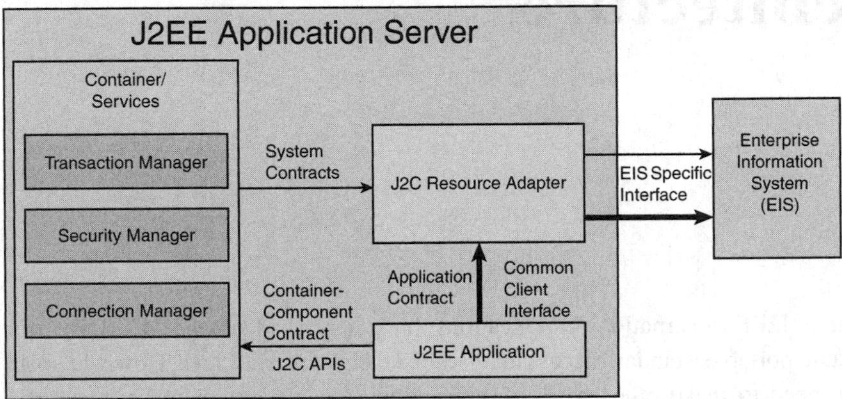


**Figure 8-1** J2C component interaction.

Essentially, a vendor provides a resource adapter that handles the low-level details of interacting with the enterprise information system. This is the "EIS-specific interface" shown in Figure 8-1. The adapter uses J2C-defined APIs for interacting with the J2EE container when necessary, and more importantly, the J2EE container uses J2C-defined APIs for controlling the adapter when necessary. These APIs are standardized and known as the Service Provider Interface (SPI), and they implement the system contracts shown in Figure 8-1. In addition to managing the connection, the APIs are used to handle errors and exceptions that may occur. In theory, any properly written adapter should be able to plug into any J2EE-compliant container. Of course, given the reality of variations in implementation and support for optional features, you should check with the adapter vendor to ensure that the adapter is supported and tested with the WebSphere Application Server (WAS) container.

In any case, the APIs discussed so far are system-level APIs that are contracts between the container vendor and the adapter vendor. J2EE application code does not have to work with these APIs. The J2C specification has defined the Common Client Interface (CCI) for that purpose. This is a fairly abstract framework that provides generic access to arbitrary enterprise systems. As you might expect, adapter vendors often need to provide additional enterprise system-specific helper classes to ease the integration with the enterprise system. For example, many adapter and tool vendors provide helper classes to translate from the enterprise system's data format to some simpler Java object-oriented format. You can think of a J2EE connector as being composed of two parts—a connector part for connecting to the backend EIS, and an adapter part for tasks like converting data formats, such as EBCDIC-to-ASCII or JavaBean data into CICS COMMAREA format. Going back to Figure 8-1 and the application interface to J2C, Java client applications can communicate directly to the resource adapter using CCI, as shown by the bold arrows. This is referred to as the "non-managed environment." The other arrows show the more common application interface through the J2EE application server ("managed environment"). Most applications don't use CCI directly, but rather depend on tools such as WebSphere Studio Application Developer Integration Edition (WSAD-IE) to generate easier-to-use beans that encapsulate this interface. Keep in mind that while Figure 8-1 shows the more traditional model of the application running inside the application server, it could also be a J2EE client application running remotely from the application server.[1]

We aren't going to go into details of the J2C programming model, but it is very similar in concept to the JDBC programming model. Applications look up resources, obtain connections from connection factories to the enterprise resources, perform operations against those connections, and then release the connections when done. Where possible, the container provides authentication and transactional information to the adapter. Thus, for adapters and resources that support it, the container can provide end-to-end identity propagation and transactional integrity. Unfortunately, this function is heavily dependent on the adapter and the underlying resource, so you'll need to check with the adapter vendor to determine what functionality your adapter supports.

Now that we've covered things at a high level, we are going to describe the details of J2C—resource adapters, connection factories, and more.

## J2C Resource Adapters

EIS vendors write J2C *resource adapters,* just as database vendors write JDBC providers. A resource adapter is a driver that connects at the system level to a backend EIS, much as a JDBC provider provides a way to connect to a backend data source. In fact, JDBC can use J2C and resource adapters—we will see that WAS5 JDBC data sources are run under the J2C infrastructure to leverage the common functions of J2C.

In keeping with the J2EE packaging model, resource adapters are packaged as modules, in this case as RAR files, with an extension of .rar. You would typically have a RAR file for each type of EIS that you are connecting to—for example, one for CICS and another for SAP. A RAR file is essentially a JAR file with some specific content—basically, code and an XML deployment descriptor with the filename ra.xml. The RAR file may also contain utility classes, native binary files, and documentation. While RAR files can be deployed to the container as part of an application deployment, it is best to install them to the container as a separate administrative operation. RAR files contain the resource adapter code written by the adapter vendor to comply with the J2C specification. As with any J2EE module, the deployment descriptor describes various details about the module. We'll discuss that in more detail later in this chapter.

When RAR files are deployed to the J2EE application server, they must be bound, as with any J2EE module. Various properties required by the J2C specification and the resource adapter vendor need to be set when deploying a RAR file to your application server.

1 J2EE and other types of client applications are covered in Chapter 14, "Client Applications."

### Connection Factories

Like JDBC data sources, J2C resources provide connection factories, and they provide them for the same reasons: to provide a common configuration point and to provide a pool of connections to improve performance. Just as with JDBC data sources, application code obtains connections from the connection pool (via a connection factory) and then releases the connection when done. The container manages the size of the connection pool and other details about obtaining connections. In the same way that there is one JDBC driver for each type of database you are using, you typically install one resource adapter for each type of EIS you are using. The adapter supports multiple configurations for connecting to its backend EIS. To facilitate multiple configurations, you create connection factories, which have settings for connections and connection pools to the EIS. Connection factories are given JNDI names and are matched to resource references in the application deployment descriptor at deploy time (just like any other J2EE resource).

## J2C System Contracts

The J2C 1.0 specification, as part of J2EE 1.3, requires adherence to system contracts for various types of resources/services. The contracts are transparently enforced by the application server and backend EIS by collaboration through the resource adapter code. The J2C 1.0 specification calls for the following system contracts:

- **Connection Management**—Pooling of connections for better performance and scalability, management of the connection factories.
- **Security**—Secure access to the EIS through J2C connections. The J2C specification provides ways of passing identity information from the J2EE container to the adapter and then on to the EIS. Given the myriad of security systems, the specification is quite flexible and requires little specific function out of the box. In fact, much of the security support is optional and is dependent on the function of the adapter and the EIS. WAS provides trivial many-to-one identity mapping using J2C authentication aliases. A single user ID/password combination can be used to authenticate to the underlying resource. However, there are more flexible approaches. These include custom J2C identity mappers (implemented as JAAS login modules) that make it possible for you to develop custom code that performs arbitrary mappings from the WAS identity of the user to some identity in the underlying EIS. For this to work, both the adapter and the EIS must support this more complex mapping model. To work efficiently, it must be possible to obtain new connections with different user identities very efficiently.[2]
- **Transactional Management**—This contract allows an application server to manage transactions over several resources. The resource adapter and backend EIS can participate in transactions controlled by the WAS transaction manager. Resource adapters can designate that they cannot participate in transactions or that they can participate in local (managed by the resource manager only, with no external transaction manager;

2 Some of these features are platform-dependent. For example, the CICS and IMS adapters for the z/OS operating system are unaware of this particular feature.

hence, "one-phase commit") or global (external transaction manager used to manage two-phase commit involving the resource adapter and other parties to the transaction) transactions.

Looking to the future, J2C 1.5, which will be part of the J2EE 1.4 specification as implemented in WAS v6, designates other system contracts:

- **Transaction inflows**—A resource adapter can propagate a transaction to an application server, along with transaction completion and crash-recovery details.
- **Message inflows**—The resource adapter can deliver messages from the EIS to endpoints in the application server. This contract allows message providers, such as JMS and JAXM (Java API for XML Messaging), to be plugged into an application server as resource adapters.
- **Life-cycle management**—This contract allows the application server to include the resource adapter in life-cycle events, such as bootstrapping the resource adapter on application startup and notifying the resource adapter of application server shutdown.
- **Work management**—This contract allows a resource adapter to carry out various tasks directly related to interfacing with the EIS by submitting work units to the application server. The application server then facilitates the work by creating threads and allocating other necessary resources so that the resource adapter does not have to be concerned with system-level tasks, such as creating, managing, and pooling threads. The resource adapter has input to the application server as far as the security and transactional context in which the work is performed.

### J2C Common Client Interface

The J2C Common Client Interface (CCI) is a programming API for applications that use J2C to interface with a backend EIS through the resource adapter. This is more interesting to application developers than deployers/administrators, so we will not go into detail on the CCI in this book.

## WAS J2C Implementation

Now that we've discussed some J2C generalities, let's move to specific J2C resources under WAS. We will use two examples of J2C implementation under WAS. First, we discuss the built-in Relational Resource Adapter (RRA) and how it is a "special" case, and then we install a more traditional resource adapter and discuss its settings and configuration in detail.

### WebSphere Relational Resource Adapter

WAS ships with a built-in J2C resource known as the WebSphere Relational Resource Adapter (RRA). This adapter is used by WAS to provide JDBC access to databases. Essentially, it connects JDBC drivers into the J2C framework that is part of WAS. By doing this, the JDBC and J2C resources can leverage the same common infrastructure. Since WAS includes the J2C RRA, it is a readily available example. However, because the JDBC infrastructure is managed in a separate area of WAS administratively, there are differences between this adapter and a more traditional resource adapter, as we will see.

As with other types of WAS resources, the configuration for the WebSphere RRA and other J2C components can be found in the resources.xml file, and this is modified using the WAS admin console's Resources section.

Figure 8-2 shows the resource adapters listing at Resources > Resource Adapters in the admin console. The WebSphere RRA can be seen here. Clicking on the link for the built-in resource adapter displays its configuration. As shown in Figure 8-3, this includes the path to the physical RAR file, links for accessing the connection factories and custom properties, and for viewing the adapter's deployment descriptor. Notice that there is a field to include a native path to any operating system–specific native files on which this resource adapter depends. Typically, these native files are shared libraries, which take the form of .dll files on a Windows machine or .so files on a Unix machine.

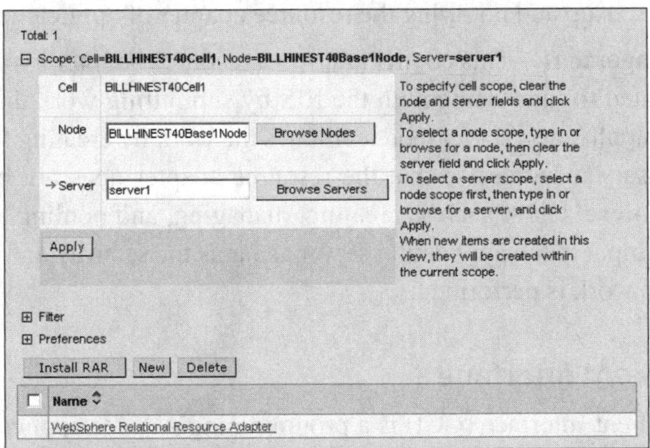


**Figure 8-2** WebSphere Relational Resource Adapter.

Configuration

| General Properties | |
|---|---|
| Scope | cells:BILLHINEST40Cell1:nodes:BILLHINEST40Base1Node:servers:server1 |
| Name | WebSphere Relational Resource Adapter |
| Description | Built-in Relational Resource Adapter for Container Managed Persistence |
| Archive Path | ${WAS_LIBS_DIR}/rsadapter.rar |
| Classpath | |
| Native Path | |

Back

| Additional Properties | |
|---|---|
| CMP Connection Factories | CMP Connection Factories are used by CMP beans to access any backend store. |
| Custom Properties | Properties that may be required for Resource Providers and Resource Factories. For example, most database vendors require additional custom properties for data sources that will access the database. |
| View Deployment Descriptor | View the Deployment Descriptor |

**Figure 8-3** WebSphere Relational Resource Adapter config.

## Relational Resource Adapter Connection Factories

As a J2C resource adapter, the WebSphere Relational Resource Adapter also provides connection factories. In this case, it provides them specifically for CMP Entity Beans, which can be accessed from the CMP Connection Factories link shown in Figure 8-3. It's important to note that, normally, connection factories are created directly on the resource adapter. But because the Relation Resource Adapter is special, its factories are created implicitly when creating the JDBC data source. In Chapter 7, "JDBC as a Resource," you might remember a check box labeled "Use this DataSource in container-managed persistence" on the page where a data source can be created. Selecting this check box creates a connection factory in the WebSphere Relational Resource Adapter. Clicking on the CMP Connection Factories link (shown in Figure 8-3) yields a page similar to Figure 8-4 if you have the WAS samples installed. Here, you can see connection factories that were created for various data sources that are included with the WAS samples, such as the Pet Store and Plants by WebSphere. You will configure a data source for CMP in the next chapter.

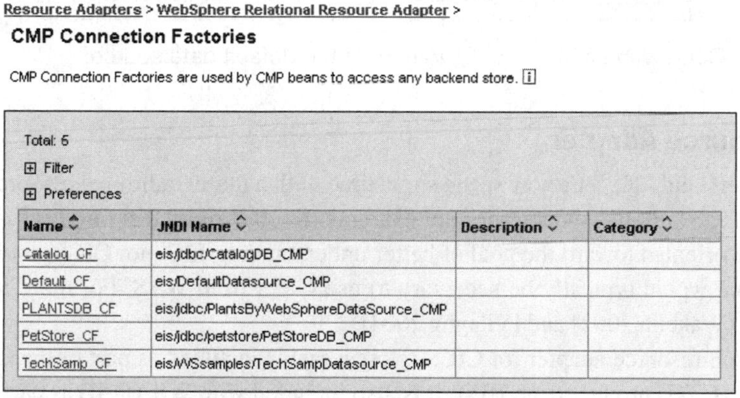

Resource Adapters > WebSphere Relational Resource Adapter >

**CMP Connection Factories**

CMP Connection Factories are used by CMP beans to access any backend store.

Total: 6

⊞ Filter

⊞ Preferences

| Name | JNDI Name | Description | Category |
|---|---|---|---|
| Catalog_CF | eis/jdbc/CatalogDB_CMP | | |
| Default_CF | eis/DefaultDatasource_CMP | | |
| PLANTSDB_CF | eis/jdbc/PlantsByWebSphereDataSource_CMP | | |
| PetStore_CF | eis/jdbc/petstore/PetStoreDB_CMP | | |
| TechSamp_CF | eis/WSsamples/TechSampDatasource_CMP | | |

**Figure 8-4** WAS samples and default connection factories.

Figure 8-4 shows the JNDI name for each connection factory in the list. Notice the convention of eis/<conn_factory_name>_CMP. Clicking on the **Default_CF** connection factory for the default JDBC data source shows additional detail, as shown in Figure 8-5. As we said, this RRA adapter is a special case—with normal adapters, you would also see a link to establish connection pool settings with connection factories. Since Default_CF is a connection factory for a JDBC data source, the connection pool settings are on the data source itself.

Figure 8-5 shows that a preferred means of authentication and a J2C authentication alias can be assigned. In choosing between component- and container-managed aliases, the same security issues apply as discussed in Chapter 7.

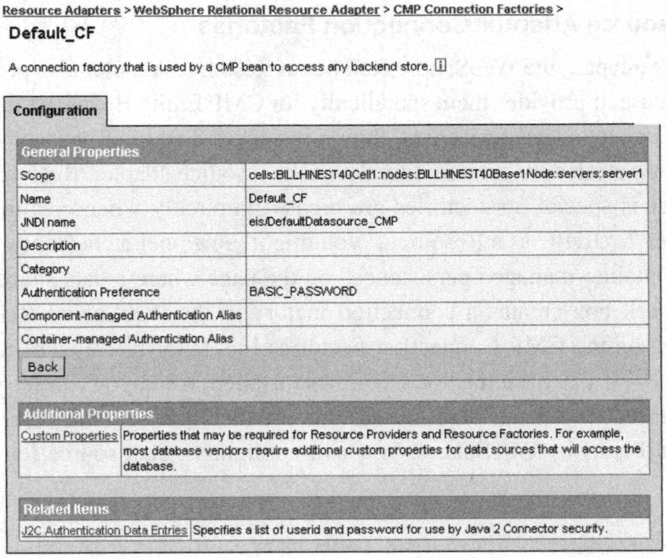

Resource Adapters > WebSphere Relational Resource Adapter > CMP Connection Factories >
**Default_CF**

A connection factory that is used by a CMP bean to access any backend store.

Configuration

General Properties

| | |
|---|---|
| Scope | cells:BILLHINEST40Cell1:nodes:BILLHINEST40Base1Node:servers:server1 |
| Name | Default_CF |
| JNDI name | eis/DefaultDatasource_CMP |
| Description | |
| Category | |
| Authentication Preference | BASIC_PASSWORD |
| Component-managed Authentication Alias | |
| Container-managed Authentication Alias | |

Back

Additional Properties

| | |
|---|---|
| Custom Properties | Properties that may be required for Resource Providers and Resource Factories. For example, most database vendors require additional custom properties for data sources that will access the database. |

Related Items

| | |
|---|---|
| J2C Authentication Data Entries | Specifies a list of userid and password for use by Java 2 Connector security. |

**Figure 8-5** Connection factory configuration for the default data source.

## CICS Resource Adapter

To better understand J2C, let's now spend some time with a more traditional resource adapter. We will use the CICS[3] resource adapter for our example. Keep in mind that our discussion and exercises here are oriented toward the goal of better understanding J2C, not CICS, so we will not do everything that would typically be necessary to use CICS from WAS. For more information in that area, see [Wakelin 2002] and [Vilaghy 2004].

The J2EE resource adapter for CICS (cicsesi.rar) is included as part of the CICS Transaction Gateway (CTG) product from IBM. It is also included with WSAD-IE as part of that developer tooling.[4] We will install it using wsadmin, review the configuration in the admin console, and then take a peek inside the ra.xml descriptor file.

### Installing the CICS Resource Adapter

As stated elsewhere in this book, when installing J2EE artifacts in a cell, it is good practice to install them at the cell scope for a single point of administration across all nodes. Unfortunately, this is not possible with RAR files. WAS cells can contain a heterogeneous mixture of servers, such as a combination of Windows and Unix machines. Resource adapters often contain binary

3 CICS (Customer Information Control System) is a family of application servers and connectors that provides industrial-strength, online transaction management and connectivity for applications.

4 Always check to ensure that the version level of adapters included with tooling is the latest and is appropriate for all platforms. For example, the CTG adapter included with WSAD-IE does not provide the same functionality as the one for z/OS 5.01 and should not be used with that operating system.

shared libraries, and there is no distribution mechanism at the cell level for this. The adapters use the native path to locate these executables, which could be different on some nodes or platforms. Because of these problems, J2C resource adapters have to be installed to the nodes directly, and this is enforced by both wsadmin and the admin console. **When using resource adapters in a cell environment, you should install to the nodes and then configure them at the cell scope.** Because of this issue, if you were to attempt to install an adapter using the console, you would find the steps a bit different from what you have seen in installing applications or JDBC resources. Referring to Figure 8-2, if you are installing a resource adapter, the panel used for scoping to the cell, node, or server is not used—when you press the **Install RAR** button, you are led to a page as shown in Figure 8-6, and you must select a node to install to. You can specify the location of the RAR file you wish to install (from either your local browser machine or the server) and specify which node the file is to be installed to.

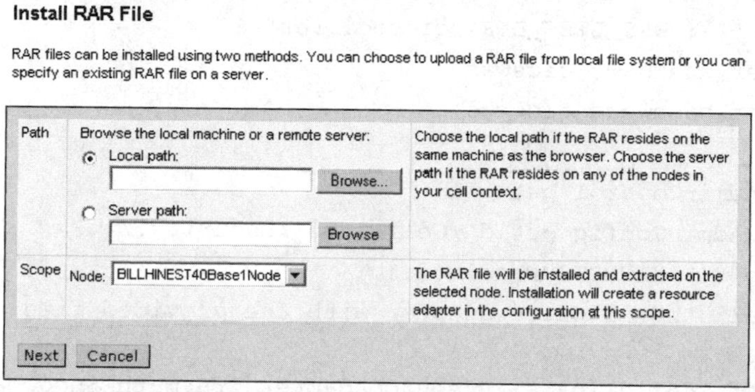

**Install RAR File**

RAR files can be installed using two methods. You can choose to upload a RAR file from local file system or you can specify an existing RAR file on a server.

| | | |
|---|---|---|
| Path | Browse the local machine or a remote server:<br>Local path: [ ] Browse...<br>Server path: [ ] Browse | Choose the local path if the RAR resides on the same machine as the browser. Choose the server path if the RAR resides on any of the nodes in your cell context. |
| Scope | Node: BILLHINEST40Base1Node | The RAR file will be installed and extracted on the selected node. Installation will create a resource adapter in the configuration at this scope. |

Next Cancel

**Figure 8-6** Admin Console pane for installing a RAR file.

Once the resource adapter has been physically installed using this page (or wsadmin), it can be defined at the cell level so that configuration data is managed centrally, as it is with applications and other resources. We will now proceed to install the adapter using wsadmin and then review how to configure it at the cell scope. Code Snippet 8-1 shows the wsadmin script to install the CICS resource adapter to a node.[5] The adapter could also be installed as part of an application install, but this practice is discouraged in favor of installing resource adapters separately to the container. This script also creates a J2C container alias and uses it for this adapter. Finally, a connection factory is created. If you were in a cell, you might just install the adapter and later create the connection factory after defining the adapter at the cell scope so that you only have to do it once and so that all nodes can use the connection factory configuration.

5 Notice that, for simplicity, the node name is coded into the script. In a production environment, this would probably be a variable that is passed into the script, so that the script is useful for installing the adapter to other nodes. Alternatively, the script could build a list of nodes and install the adapter to each one in a loop.

**Code Snippet 8-1 wsadmin script to install a resource adapter**

```
#---------------------------------------------------------------------------
➥-----
# Create a J2C resource adapter, authentication alias and connection
➥factory
#---------------------------------------------------------------------------
➥-----

set CONTAINER_ALIAS my-containerAuth-Alias
set cfName CICS_CF
set cicsCFjndiName  eis/cicsConnectionFactory
set DEFAULT_PRINCIPAL_MAPPING  DefaultPrincipalMapping
set rarpath ""\$(WAS_LIBS_DIR)/cicseci.rar""
set container_username cicswas
set container_password cicspwd

set cell [$AdminControl getCell]
set secid [$AdminConfig getid /Cell:$cell/Security:/]
set nodeName BILLHINEST40Base1Node
puts ""Install the resource adapter with the provided file: $rarpath to
➥$nodeName""
set ra [$AdminConfig installResourceAdapter $rarpath $nodeName {-
➥rar.desc ""IBM CICS Resource Adapter""}]
puts ""Creating a JAASAuthData object for container-managed
➥authentication""
set alias_attr    [list alias $CONTAINER_ALIAS]
set desc_attr     [list description ""J2C Container-managed
➥authentication alias""]
set userid_attr   [list userId $container_username]
set password_attr [list password $container_password]
set attrs [list $alias_attr $desc_attr $userid_attr $password_attr]
set contauthdata [$AdminConfig create JAASAuthData $secid $attrs]
puts ""Creating connection factory $cfName""
set name_attr     [list name $cfName]
set jndi_attr     [list jndiName $cicsCFjndiName]
set authmech_attr [list authMechanismPreference BASIC_PASSWORD]
set map_auth_attr [list authDataAlias $CONTAINER_ALIAS]
set map_configalias_attr [list mappingConfigAlias
➥$DEFAULT_PRINCIPAL_MAPPING]
```

```
set map_attrs     [list $map_auth_attr $map_configalias_attr]
set mapping_attr  [list mapping $map_attrs]
set attrs [list $name_attr $jndi_attr $authmech_attr $mapping_attr]
set cf [$AdminConfig create J2CConnectionFactory $ra $attrs]
puts ""\nSaving configuration""
$AdminConfig save

puts ""\nDone!\n""
```

After running the script shown in Code Snippet 8-1, we can return to the admin console and look up all adapters for the node we installed to. Figure 8-7 shows that we are viewing adapters at the node scope, and the newly installed ECIResourceAdapter is now visible. This name came from the ra.xml deployment descriptor. We could have overridden it in our script by providing a new name with rar.name, just as we overrode the description from the deployment descriptor with rar.desc. Notice that while this adapter has a check box to use for deleting it, the built-in Relational Resource Adapter does not because it is a critical part of the WAS infrastructure and should never be deleted.

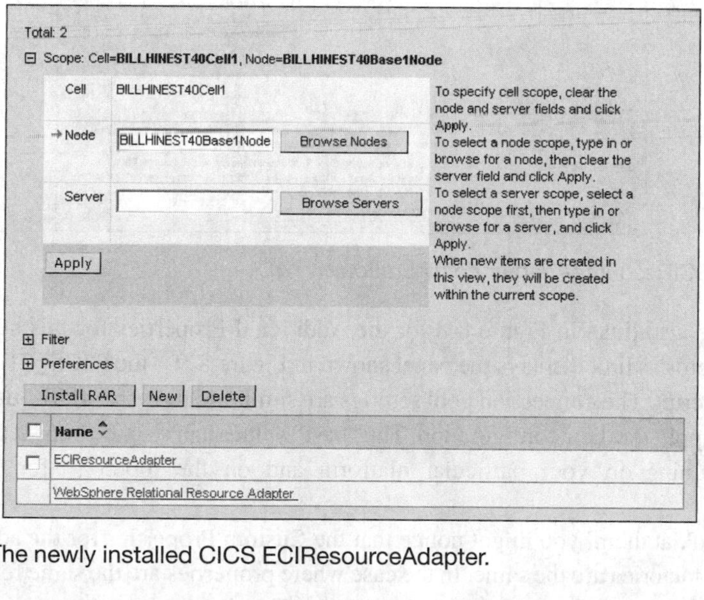

**Figure 8-7** The newly installed CICS ECIResourceAdapter.

Clicking on the adapter presents the Configuration page, as shown in Figure 8-8. There are no native shared libraries installed with this adapter, so a native path was not necessary. However, if we were accessing CICS with a "local:" URL to the same server, we would then need to specify a native path to its shared libraries. The installed path is InstalledConnectors rooted off a WAS variable named CONNECTOR_INSTALL_ROOT. In some cases, you may need to add other

JAR files to the Classpath field shown in this figure. For example, the CICS resource adapter does not include the JAR file needed to support applications using WSDL. For that, an additional JAR file would need to be added to this Classpath field.

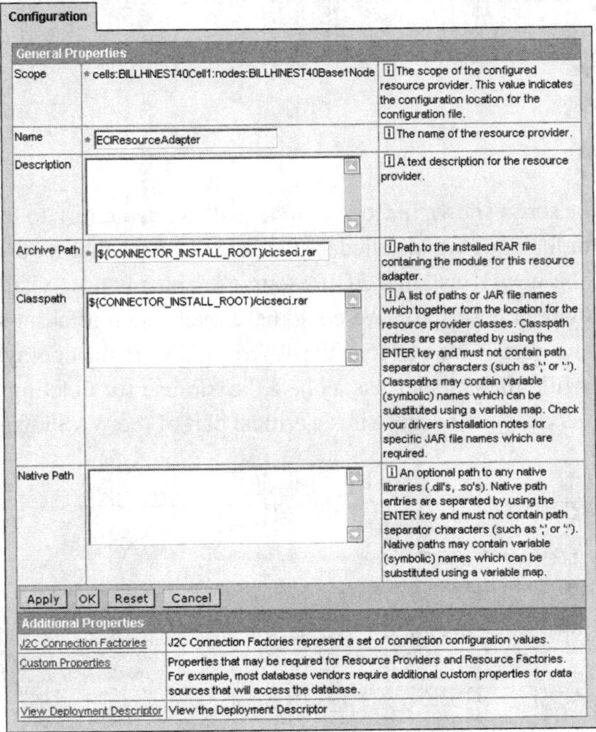
Configuration
General Properties
Scope
* cells:BILLHINEST40Cell1:nodes:BILLHINEST40Base1Node
The scope of the configured resource provider. This value indicates the configuration location for the configuration file.
Name
* ECIResourceAdapter
The name of the resource provider.
Description
A text description for the resource provider.
Archive Path
* ${CONNECTOR_INSTALL_ROOT}/cicseci.rar
Path to the installed RAR file containing the module for this resource adapter.
Classpath
${CONNECTOR_INSTALL_ROOT}/cicseci.rar
A list of paths or JAR file names which together form the location for the resource provider classes. Classpath entries are separated by using the ENTER key and must not contain path separator characters (such as ';' or ':'). Classpaths may contain variable (symbolic) names which can be substituted using a variable map. Check your drivers installation notes for specific JAR file names which are required.
Native Path
An optional path to any native libraries (.dll's, .so's). Native path entries are separated by using the ENTER key and must not contain path separator characters (such as ';' or ':'). Native paths may contain variable (symbolic) names which can be substituted using a variable map.
Apply
OK
Reset
Cancel
Additional Properties
J2C Connection Factories
J2C Connection Factories represent a set of connection configuration values.
Custom Properties
Properties that may be required for Resource Providers and Resource Factories. For example, most database vendors require additional custom properties for data sources that will access the database.
View Deployment Descriptor
View the Deployment Descriptor

**Figure 8-8** ECIResourceAdapter configuration.

There are also links in Figure 8-8 for the Additional Properties for this adapter. The J2C Connection Factories link displays the panel shown in Figure 8-9—the CICS_CF factory that we created in our script. The connection pool settings are similar to those for JDBC data sources, and similar issues apply for their configuration. The "best" values can only be known through diligent performance tuning on your particular platform and on the topology for your particular applications.

If you look at them, you might notice that the Custom Properties for the adapter itself and the connection factories are the same. In the case where properties are the same for all connection factories, you should configure them on the adapter. For those properties that are specific to a connection factory, you should configure them at that scope. These properties will be specific to the adapter you are installing, so you should always follow the adapter vendor's recommendation and documentation when setting the properties. They typically contain the settings necessary to connect to the backend EIS, such as server name, URL string, port number, security information, and trace level settings for troubleshooting problems.

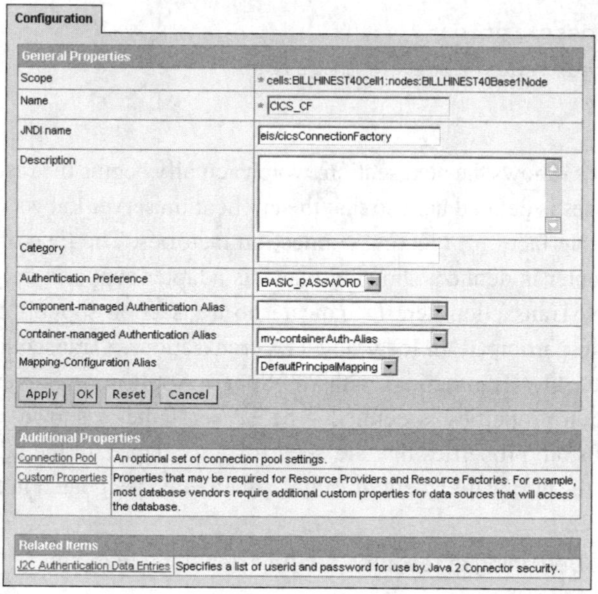

Configuration

General Properties

| | |
|---|---|
| Scope | * cells:BILLHINEST40Cell1:nodes:BILLHINEST40Base1Node |
| Name | * CICS_CF |
| JNDI name | eis/cicsConnectionFactory |
| Description | |
| Category | |
| Authentication Preference | BASIC_PASSWORD |
| Component-managed Authentication Alias | |
| Container-managed Authentication Alias | my-containerAuth-Alias |
| Mapping-Configuration Alias | DefaultPrincipalMapping |

Apply OK Reset Cancel

Additional Properties

| | |
|---|---|
| Connection Pool | An optional set of connection pool settings. |
| Custom Properties | Properties that may be required for Resource Providers and Resource Factories. For example, most database vendors require additional custom properties for data sources that will access the database. |

Related Items

| | |
|---|---|
| J2C Authentication Data Entries | Specifies a list of userid and password for use by Java 2 Connector security. |

**Figure 8-9** CICS_CF Connection Factory configuration.

## Resource Adapter Deployment Descriptor—ra.xml

After installing the resource adapter, the contents can be viewed under the InstalledConnectors directory of your install root. Under InstalledConnectors/cicsesi.rar/META-INF, we find the ra.xml deployment descriptor. Let's look at a few of the more interesting sections of that file. Code Snippet 8-2 shows the opening stanza. Here, you can see the default adapter name ECIResourceAdapter, which we saw in the admin console after installing. There is also a description (which we overrode in our script), as well as other important information, such as the vendor name, EIS type, and version of the adapter. spec-version indicates that this adapter is compliant with version 1.0 of J2C.

**Code Snippet 8-2** Opening stanza of ra.xml for the CICS adapter

```
<connector>
<display-name>ECIResourceAdapter</display-name>
<description>CICS J2EE ECI Resource Adapter</description>
<vendor-name>IBM</vendor-name>
<spec-version>1.0</spec-version>
<eis-type>CICS</eis-type>
<version>5.0.1</version>
<license>
```

```
<description></description>
<license-required>true</license-required>
</license>
```

Code Snippet 8-3 shows the next section, which actually begins the resource adapter definition. A series of classes is defined here so that the application server knows which classes implement the necessary interfaces for creating connection factories. The type of transaction support provided by this adapter is defined, showing that this adapter supports only local transactions. It could designate NoTransaction here to indicate no transaction support or XATransaction to indicate the ability to participate in local and JTA transactions. (Transactions are discussed in more detail in Chapter 11, "Transactions with WebSphere Application Server.") Next in ra.xml, a series of configuration properties is defined—the ServerName is shown here as an example. These map to the custom properties that are seen for this adapter in the admin console, and in some cases (such as the port value), default values are already designated in the XML file.

**Code Snippet 8-3** Beginning of resource adapter definition in ra.xml

```
<resourceadapter>
<managedconnectionfactory-class>com.ibm.connector2.cics.
➥ECIManagedConnectionFactory</managedconnectionfactory-class>
<connectionfactory-interface>javax.resource.cci.ConnectionFactory
➥</connectionfactory-interface>
<connectionfactory-impl-class>com.ibm.connector2.cics.
➥ECIConnectionFactory</connectionfactory-impl-class>
<connection-interface>javax.resource.cci.Connection</connection-
➥interface>
<connection-impl-class>com.ibm.connector2.cics.
➥ECIConnection</connection-impl-class>
<transaction-support>LocalTransaction</transaction-support>
<config-property>
<description>ServerName</description>
<config-property-name>ServerName</config-property-name>
<config-property-type>java.lang.String</config-property-type>
<config-property-value></config-property-value>
</config-property>
```

The next section of the deployment descriptor specifies security information. Code Snippet 8-4 shows the start of this section. The authentication-method stanza tells the container what authentication mechanisms the adapter recognizes—BasicPassword is supported by WAS, although there are other possibilities, such as Kerberos. The credential-interface identifies how authentication information is transmitted from the container to the adapter. The reauthentication-support attribute indicates to the container whether the adapter can change the identity on an existing connection. Most of these attributes are of little interest to an average user of an adapter, but as a deployer, you should carefully read the documentation for the adapter you have selected. Next, there is an XML stanza that essentially lists Java 2 permissions required by the adapter. The container will grant the adapter these permissions when executing the Java code in the adapter.

**Code Snippet 8-4** Security properties in the ra.xml

```
<authentication-mechanism>
<description></description>
<authentication-mechanism-type>BasicPassword</authentication-mechanism-
➥type>
<credential-interface>javax.resource.spi.security.PasswordCredential
➥</credential-interface>
</authentication-mechanism>
<reauthentication-support>true</reauthentication-support>
<security-permission>
<security-permission-spec>
grant {
permission java.net.SocketPermission ""*"", ""resolve"";
      };
</security-permission-spec>
</security-permission>
```

## Configuring the CICS Resource Adapter at the Cell Scope

Now that we have successfully installed the resource adapter using wsadmin and explored it using the admin console, let's configure it at the cell scope so that the changes we make can be made once and pushed down to all nodes in the cell. Return to the Resource Adapters page in the console and set the scope to Cell. As shown in Figure 8-10, the only adapter shown should be the built-in RRA.

At this point, we have installed the CICS adapter and want to configure it so that it is known at the cell scope. To accomplish this, we do not want to press **Install RAR** here, but rather the **New** button. This brings us to a page, as shown in Figure 8-11, where we have already entered the resource adapter name and selected the appropriate archive path from the list of our previously installed adapters on the nodes.

Total: 1

⊟ Scope: Cell=**BILLHINEST40Cell1**

→Cell BILLHINEST40Cell1

Node [Browse Nodes]

Server [Browse Servers]

[Apply]

To specify cell scope, clear the node and server fields and click Apply.
To select a node scope, type in or browse for a node, then clear the server field and click Apply.
To select a server scope, select a node scope first, then type in or browse for a server, and click Apply.
When new items are created in this view, they will be created within the current scope.

⊞ Filter

⊞ Preferences

[Install RAR] [New] [Delete]

| ☐ | **Name** |
|---|---|
| | WebSphere Relational Resource Adapter |

**Figure 8-10** Resource adapters at the cell scope.

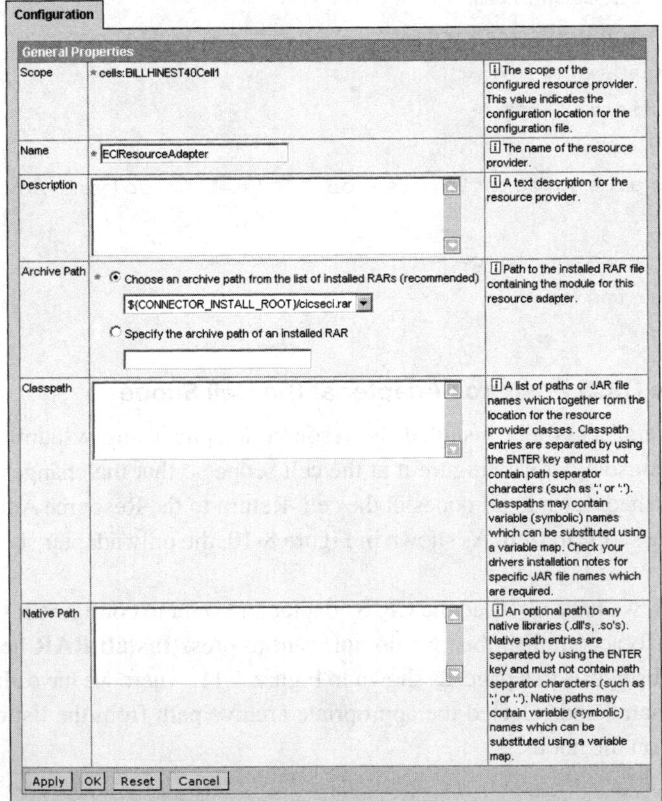
Configuration
General Properties
Scope
* cells:BILLHINEST40Cell1
The scope of the configured resource provider. This value indicates the configuration location for the configuration file.
Name
* ECIResourceAdapter
The name of the resource provider.
Description
A text description for the resource provider.
Archive Path
Choose an archive path from the list of installed RARs (recommended)
${CONNECTOR_INSTALL_ROOT}/cicseci.rar
Specify the archive path of an installed RAR
Path to the installed RAR file containing the module for this resource adapter.
Classpath
A list of paths or JAR file names which together form the location for the resource provider classes. Classpath entries are separated by using the ENTER key and must not contain path separator characters (such as ';' or ':'). Classpaths may contain variable (symbolic) names which can be substituted using a variable map. Check your drivers installation notes for specific JAR file names which are required.
Native Path
An optional path to any native libraries (.dll's, .so's). Native path entries are separated by using the ENTER key and must not contain path separator characters (such as ';' or ':'). Native paths may contain variable (symbolic) names which can be substituted using a variable map.
Apply
OK
Reset
Cancel

**Figure 8-11** Configuring the resource adapter at the cell scope.

Press **OK** here to define the resource adapter at the cell scope. After saving, the definition should then be visible on all nodes. Code Snippet 8-1 had a section of wsadmin code that creates a connection factory on the resource adapter after it adds it to the node. As an alternative, we could have extracted the section of wsadmin code before running it and instead run it against the cell at this point, and the connection factory would be pushed down and configured on all nodes in the cell.

## Conclusion

In this chapter, we learned about an important J2EE resource foundation—the J2EE Connector Architecture. You can use this part of the J2EE specification in your applications, whether they are accessing ubiquitous relational databases or more obscure types of Enterprise Information Systems. The coming improvements and responsibilities in J2C with version 1.5 demonstrate its significance to the J2EE 1.4 architecture, as implemented by WAS v6. Performance and stability benefits should greatly outweigh any effort required in rewriting legacy code that may connect to these systems using proprietary or home-grown APIs. That is consistent with a founding principle of J2EE—focus on the business logic and allow the infrastructure to do the rest. In the next chapter, we will begin our discussion of Enterprise JavaBeans.

CHAPTER 9

# Enterprise JavaBeans

Enterprise JavaBeans is a core technology in the J2EE platform. Enterprise JavaBeans are server-side components that run inside a managed environment, in our case, the EJB container inside WebSphere Application Server (WAS). The EJB container provides services to applications so that developers do not have worry about creating low-level system code. These services include:

- **Resource pooling**—Connections to resources, such as JDBC, are pooled to allow for better use of those resources. Any resource defined on a J2EE server is easily accessible to EJB applications.
- **Transaction management**—Transactional coding is not easy and requires advanced knowledge of low-level code. EJB applications have their transactions managed implicitly by the EJB container, allowing developers to concentrate on business logic rather than writing transactional code.
- **Concurrency**—EJB containers handle most multithreading and concurrency issues for you. This includes client access to Enterprise Beans, as well as managing access to shared resources from the Enterprise Beans themselves.
- **Security**—EJB methods are secured implicitly so that developers do not have to worry about writing security code.
- **Persistence**—Applications that wish to use Entity Beans can have persistence managed by the container rather than allowing the developer to write data access code.
- **Object distribution**—EJBs can be deployed on different servers on a network and can be accessed by clients remotely.

In this chapter, we are going to discuss the different types of Enterprise JavaBeans (EJBs), their structure, how to assemble them, and how to deploy them to WAS. This chapter provides an introduction to the deployment process for EJBs under the WAS container. In later chapters, we delve into specific EJB types, such as Entity Beans and Message Driven Beans, as well as container services, such as transactions. In this chapter, we focus on deploying EJBs and become familiar with the various tools used in doing so.

We will not cover EJB programming in much detail. We refer you to [Brown 2004] for an in-depth discussion of the architectural role EJBs should play in an application. However, configuration and deployment of the EJBs are also important and are covered in greater detail in the coming chapters.

## Introduction to Enterprise JavaBeans

In this section, we provide a basic introduction to Enterprise JavaBeans and their deployment descriptors. A deployment descriptor defines the beans and classes that make up an EJB and includes additional attributes such as how an EJB behaves in a transaction, how it is secured, and the relationships between beans.

### Enterprise JavaBean Types

In the EJB 2.0 specification, there are three major types of Enterprise Java Beans: Session Beans, Entity Beans, and Message Driven Beans. Each one serves a very different purpose, and they can be used together or independently. We will proceed with a brief introduction of each.

#### Session Beans

Session Beans are EJBs that are meant to control the *flow* of an application, and they are usually entry points to the business logic layer. Clients expect Session Beans to perform some task, such as "retrieve the current stock price for symbol IBM." They do not represent data but usually interact with *other* objects that represent data, such as Entity Beans. They can also directly interact with databases via JDBC or with enterprise systems using other APIs, such as J2EE connectors.

There are two types of Session Beans: Stateless Session Beans and Stateful Session Beans. Stateless Session Beans maintain no conversational state between client calls. This means that a client cannot rely on getting the same instance of the bean on subsequent calls. In fact, the beans are typically pooled and shared among clients. On the other hand, Stateful Session Beans maintain the conversational state between the client and the bean, so client requests will be directed to a specific bean instance on all calls.

> **NOTE**
> Stateful Session Beans are typically used in combination with Java client applications, such as Swing applications. Web applications usually interact with Stateless Session Beans because web applications maintain a state via HTTP session, which generally scales more effectively in large systems. For example, application servers usually have better solutions for replicating a conversational state across multiple servers for the HTTP session. Scalability problems can arise in large-volume web sites because of Stateful Session Beans.

## Entity Beans

Entity Beans are EJBs that represent data. They usually map to a data store such as a relational database and retrieve, update, insert, or delete data from that database. Entity Beans may have simple "get" and "set" methods for updating their persistent state and may also have simple logic methods that update or present the data in a more specialized way. For example, rather than calling getCounter(), performing some math, and then calling setCounter(), you may choose to implement an increment method on the bean.

EJB containers use the term *persistence* to define how the EJB container stores and loads data between the underlying data store and the bean instance. There are two types of persistence: Container Managed Persistence and Bean Managed Persistence. Container Managed Persistence (CMP) delegates responsibility to the EJB container for how the data is accessed, updated, and cached. Bean Managed Persistence (BMP) means that the developer is responsible for coding this type of data access into his or her Entity Beans.

## Message Driven Beans

Message Driven Beans act as asynchronous listeners. Rather than clients interacting synchronously as with Session and Entity Beans by invoking methods, Message Driven Beans (MDB) rely on the arrival of an asynchronous message to begin processing business logic. In other words, a Message Driven Bean is bound to some destination that contains messages left by the client. The client does not wait for a response. As an analogy, a mailman leaves a message in a mailbox and does not wait for a person to retrieve it. The person can come an hour later and read his or her mail. In the EJB 2.0 specification, Message Driven Beans receive a JMS[1] message and process that message. Therefore, clients use the Java Message Service (JMS) API to send messages to a queue or topic.[2] Clients send messages to destinations rather than to specific MDBs. Message driven beans are tied to that destination and wait for a messaging broker to trigger an event signaling that a message has arrived. The EJB container then reads that message and passes it to the Message Driven Bean.

1 In version 2.1 of the EJB specification, Message Driven Beans have been expanded to support other messages besides JMS, such as JavaMail.

2 Clients can use any API supported by a JMS Provider; for example, WebSphere MQ supports other programming languages besides Java.

Message Driven Beans are configured to a JMS connection factory and destination at deployment time. This binding information tells the container which destination a Message Driven Bean listens to. Chapter 12, "JMS and Message Driven Beans," will focus on this topic.

Figure 9-1 summarizes the types and subtypes of EJBs.

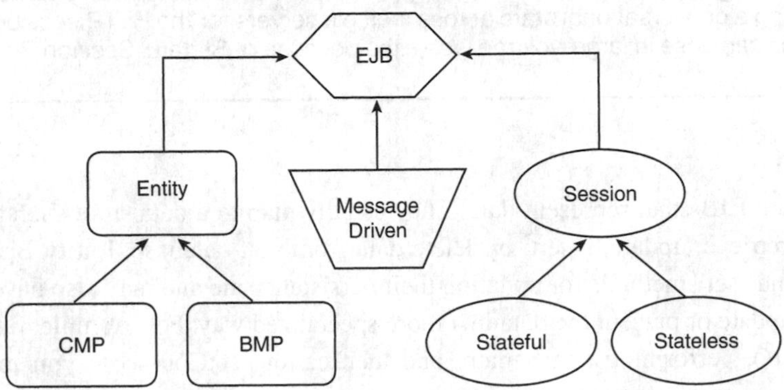


**Figure 9-1** EJB types.

## Enterprise JavaBean Elements

Like all J2EE components, EJBs are packaged together as a module or JAR file. This section details the elements that make up an EJB module.

### EJB Java Code

An Enterprise JavaBean is made up of several related classes that are visible to the deployer:

- **Home interface(s)**—The home interface is a factory interface used to create or/and find instances of the Enterprise Bean from other areas of application code, such as a Servlet. As of version 2.0 of the EJB specification, you are allowed to create two home interfaces—local and remote. The local home interface is only accessible to EJB clients from within the same Java Virtual Machine (JVM), while a remote interface is accessible from within the same JVM or another JVM via a remote call. The EJB developer provides the interface by extending a base EJBHome or/and EJBLocalHome interface from their bean but does not provide the object that implements the home interface. The container implements the defined home interfaces with generated code. Knowing your Enterprise Bean type is important because the behavior of the home interface depends on the bean type. For Session Beans, a create() method usually creates a new bean instance or selects one from a pool. Clients then use that bean instance to issue method calls on the bean to execute logic.

For an Entity Bean, home interfaces behave differently. Entity Beans represent data and usually map to some underlying data store, so the results of executing methods on the home interface are quite different from those of a Session Bean. The home of an Entity Bean has create(), find(), and move() methods. When a client issues a create(), the call usually corresponds to the creation of data in the underlying data store. For example, if an Entity Bean is mapped to a relational database, a create call usually maps to a SQL INSERT. Entity Bean home interfaces' find() methods allow clients to find an instance of an Entity Bean and usually invoke a SQL SELECT.[3] Find() methods return either a reference to a bean interface or a collection interface if the result was more than one row in the database. Local home interfaces return local interface references, and remote home interfaces return remote references. Remove() methods delete the persisted state of the Entity Bean and usually correspond to a SQL DELETE.

Message Driven Beans do not have home interfaces since they are not called directly from clients.

An Enterprise Bean client uses the home interface to locate or create an instance of its bean. Enterprise Bean clients obtain an instance of the home interface by looking up the object using JNDI (Java Naming and Directory Interface).

- **Remote/local interface(s)**—The remote/local interface provides the signatures of the business method that are accessible to the client. Clients never interact directly with the business implementation; they interact with references to this interface. This decouples the client from the code that implements the business logic. As long as they keep the interface contract, the implementation can change without the client needing to change. Message Driven Beans have no remote/local interface for the same reason they do not have a home interface.
- **Bean class**—The bean class is where the application methods are implemented. The bean class does not directly implement the local or remote interfaces. This is because the bean class is not directly accessed from the client. The container is responsible for delegating method calls the client makes through the bean interfaces to the bean class through generated code.

  The bean class will extend javax.ejb.SessionBean, javax.ejb.EntityBean, or javax.ejb.MessageDrivenBean and implement a variety of methods defined on these interfaces. Depending on the bean type, some methods must be overridden from the inherited classes. Also, the bean class needs to have methods that match the business method signatures on the remote/local interface. They can also have other methods that are not exposed to the client, such as private helper methods (used by other methods on the bean class).

3 Because CMP Beans use an abstract schema, finder methods map to defined EJB QL. EJB QL queries are defined in the deployment descriptor. The EJB container uses the EJB QL to generate queries—in most cases, SQL—against the underlying data store.

Figure 9-2 illustrates the relationship between EJB clients, the remote interfaces, and the implementation. Notice the clients never interact with the bean class. Local and remote clients can call the remote interface.

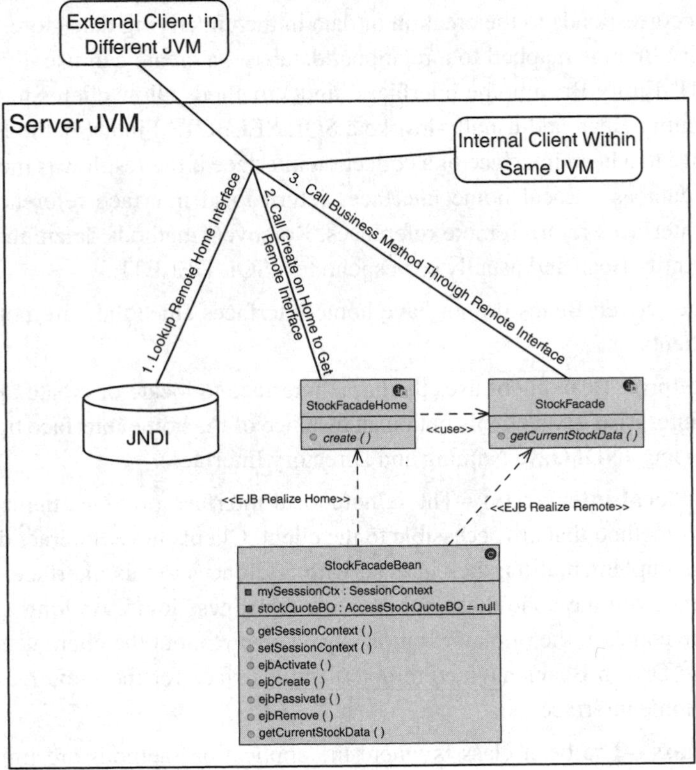


**Figure 9-2** EJB clients interacting with remote interface.

Internal clients can also use the local interface, as shown in Figure 9-3. Local interfaces are not accessible to clients outside the JVM.[4]

Message Driven Beans only have a bean class that must implement an onMessage() method to process incoming messages.

- **Key class**—EJB packages may also contain key classes that are associated with Entity Beans. Key classes uniquely identify an Entity Bean and usually correspond to primary keys in a database.

4 Even though the Name Server is pictured, an application is allowed to store objects anywhere it wants as long as it adheres to the JNDI specification.

- **Generated deployment code**—As long as developers code to the EJB contract and provide the necessary deployment descriptors, EJB deployment tools can be used to generate the deployment code needed to be packaged along with the EJB module. Within the EJB module, this generated code provides the necessary code to allow the EJB to interact with the container to benefit from the container services and EJB clients to access the Enterprise Beans within the module. In addition, the generated code allows the container to interact with external resources on behalf of the EJB.

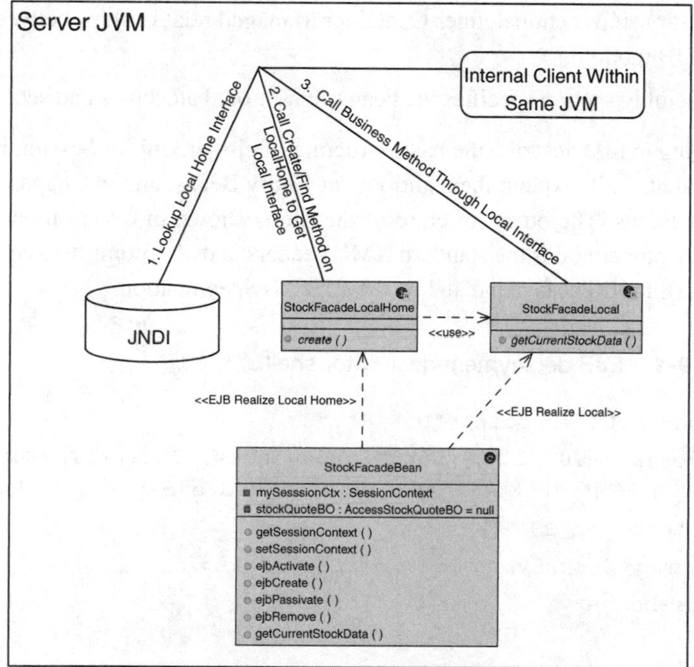


**Figure 9-3** Local EJB client interacting with client interface.

An EJB module might also contain ordinary Java classes that the Enterprise Beans need.

## Standard EJB Deployment Descriptor

Enterprise JavaBeans usually implement the business logic layer (or model layer) of an application, and they interact with enterprise data. These interactions involve the coordination of transactions, securing business logic, and integrating with other systems. Enterprise Beans leverage the EJB container to provide the application with these services. An EJB developer provides the necessary data in deployment descriptors for the container to run your application correctly. This deployment descriptor is ejb-jar.xml.

Every EJB module contains a standard deployment descriptor called ejb-jar.xml. Much like a web deployment descriptor, an EJB deployment descriptor is an XML file used to describe all the EJBs inside an EJB module as well as how they are assembled. The standard EJB deployment descriptor is divided into three parts:

- The Enterprise Bean section defines the type of each bean, the standard classes of each bean (home interface, business interface, key class, and bean class), and the security identity of the bean. Entity EJBs also require persistent field and EJB-QL information.
- The relationship section defines Container Managed relationships between Entity Beans in the EJB module.
- The assembly section specifies the bean transactional attributes and security roles.

We are going to first describe the basic structure of ejb-jar.xml for Session Beans. After we have completed that, we'll explain the additions for Entity Beans, and in Chapter 12, we'll cover Message Driven Beans. The outer structure of the file is shown in Code Snippet 9-1. The EJB deployment descriptor contains the standard XML headers and also points to a compliant EJB 2.0 deployment descriptor DTD as mandated by the EJB 2.0 Specification.

**Code Snippet 9-1** EJB deployment descriptor shell

```
<?xml version="1.0" encoding="UTF-8"?>
<!DOCTYPE ejb-jar PUBLIC "-//Sun Microsystems, Inc.//DTD Enterprise
➥JavaBeans 2.0//EN" "http://java.sun.com/dtd/ejb-jar_2_0.dtd">
<ejb-jar id="ejb-jar_ID">
  <display-name> StockSystemEJB</display-name>
  <enterprise-beans>
    ...

  </enterprise-beans>

  <assembly-descriptor>

    ...

  </assembly-descriptor>
</ejb-jar>
```

Within the <enterprise-beans> tags, each EJB type has a separate set of tags. Session Beans are surrounded by the <session> tag. Code Snippet 9-2 shows the definition of a StockFacade Session Bean.

**Code Snippet 9-2 EJB deployment descriptor Session Bean definition**

```
<!--  SESSION BEAN DEFINITION -->
<session id="StockFacade">
<!--  EJB NAME AND CLASSES THAT MAKE UP THE EJB -->
<ejb-name>StockFacade</ejb-name>
<home>com.deploybook.stock.ejb.StockFacadeHome</home>
<remote>com.deploybook.stock.ejb.StockFacade</remote>
<local-home>com.deploybook.stock.ejb.StockFacadeLocalHome</local-home>
<local>com.deploybook.stock.ejb.StockFacadeLocal</local>
<ejb-class>com.deploybook.stock.ejb.StockFacadeBean</ejb-class>

<!--  TYPE OF SESSION BEAN-->
<session-type>Stateless</session-type>
<!--  WHO HANDLES THE TRANSACTION?  CONTAINER OR YOUR OWN CODE -->
<transaction-type>Container</transaction-type>

<!--  EJB LOCAL REFERENCE TO ANOTHER BEAN  -->
<ejb-local-ref id="EJBLocalRef_1057121846690">
  <description></description>
  <ejb-ref-name>ejb/Stock</ejb-ref-name>
  <ejb-ref-type>Entity</ejb-ref-type>
  <local-home>com.deploybook.stock.ejb.StockLocalHome</local-home>
  <local>com.deploybook.stock.ejb.StockLocal</local>
  <ejb-link>Stock</ejb-link>
</ejb-local-ref>

<!--  IDENTITY UNDER WHICH THE BEAN RUNS -->
<security-identity>
  <description></description>
  <user-caller-identity />
</security-identity>
</session>
```

As stated, the Bean Section describes the beans:

- The first part defines the name, type, and classes that make up the bean.
- The `<transaction-type>` tag determines whether you want the container to manage transactions for this bean. This is accomplished by specifying a value of *Container*. A value of *Bean* specifies that the developer will code transaction logic directly in the bean class.
- Next, you can specify references to resources or other EJBs. Each EJB component is independent of others and has its own local namespace. This is different from a web application, which has one local namespace for the whole web application.
- The security identity is also defined in the bean section. The `<security-identity>` tag defines what security identity the EJB is.[5] There are several options for security identity:
  - An EJB can run under the identity of the client that calls it. This is done by specifying `<user-caller-identity>`.
  - An EJB can run as a specific role. Roles are defined in the assembly section. Once defined, an EJB can assume the role as its identity.

    The EJB 2.0 specification mandates that the `<security-identity>` property of an EJB be defined on the whole EJB[6] and not on each method.

For CMP Entity Beans, the Enterprise Bean section defines more properties. Code Snippet 9-3 shows an example of an Entity Bean definition.

**Code Snippet 9-3** EJB deployment descriptor Entity Bean definition

```
...
<entity id="ContainerManagedEntity_1057120180353">
    ...
  <!--ADDITIONS TO DEPLOYMENT DESCRIPTOR FOR CMP ENTITY BEAN -->

  <!--  WHO HANDLES PERSISTENCE?  -->
<persistence-type>Container</persistence-type>
<!--  CLASS THAT IMPLEMENTS PRIMARY KEY -->
  <prim-key-class>com.deploybook.stock.ejb.StockKey</prim-key-class>
  <!--  IS CMP ALLOWED TO HAVE LOOPBACK BEHAVIOR -->
  <reentrant>False</reentrant>
  <!--  CMP VERSION THAT THE CONTAINER SHOULD FOLLOW FOR THE BEAN  -->
```

5 The security identity *does not* secure your EJB from clients; instead, it is done in the assembly section.

6 WAS allows the security identity to be defined on an EJB method-level.

```
  <cmp-version>2.x</cmp-version>
  <!--   NAME OF ABSTRACT SCHEMA FOR CMP, SEE CHAPTER 8 -->
  <abstract-schema-name>Stock</abstract-schema-name>

  <!--   CMP PERSISTENT FIELDS   -->
  <cmp-field id="CMPAttribute_1057120180444">
    <field-name>symbol</field-name>
  </cmp-field>
  <cmp-field id="CMPAttribute_1057120180454">
    <field-name>currentprice</field-name>
  </cmp-field>
  <cmp-field id="CMPAttribute_1057120180464">
    <field-name>currentdayvolume</field-name>
  </cmp-field>
  <cmp-field id="CMPAttribute_1057120180474">
    <field-name>openprice</field-name>
  </cmp-field>
  <cmp-field id="CMPAttribute_1057120180484">
    <field-name>dayhighprice</field-name>
  </cmp-field>
  <cmp-field id="CMPAttribute_1057120180494">
    <field-name>daylowprice</field-name>
  </cmp-field>
  ...
</entity>
```

In addition to describing the bean classes, CMP Entity Beans have fields relative to persistence:

- The `<persistence-type>` tag specifies the persistence type for the bean. A value of *Container* specifies that the container is handling persistence. A value of *Bean* specifies that the persistence is handled by code in the Entity Bean. In other words, the developer codes the data access code.
- The `<prim-key-class>` defines the key class that will be used to uniquely identify a specific Entity Bean.
- The `<reentrant>` tag specifies whether you want to allow your bean to have loopback behavior. For example, *EJB A* calls a method on *EJB B*, and then *EJB B* calls a method back on *EJB A* within the same thread of execution. This behavior is dangerous and

could cause dead locks. Session Beans by default are not reentrant. Entity Beans can be configured to be reentrant by specifying a value of *true*. However, this is strongly discouraged.

- The `<cmp-version>` tag specifies what version of the CMP specification the bean is implemented in. The EJB 2.0 specification mandates that containers must be backward-compatible. WAS supports both the 1.1 and 2.0 version of the CMP specification.
- The `<abstract-schema-name>` tag defines the schema name for a CMP Entity Bean. Every Entity Bean has a unique schema name. We will talk about abstract schemas in the next chapter.
- Finally, you must define each persistent field in your CMP. The `<cmp-field>` tag must correspond to some persistent field in the bean. We will elaborate on CMP in the next chapter.

For applications that use Container Managed relationships, the relationship section would come after the bean section. The relationship section will be examined in the next chapter.

The assembly section defines attributes for bean behavior. The two main areas that the assembly section defines are transactions and security access. Code Snippet 9-4 illustrates an assembly section.

**Code Snippet 9-4** EJB deployment descriptor assembly section

```
<assembly-descriptor>
<!--  SECURITY ROLE VISIBLE TO EJB APPLICATION -->
  <security-role>
    <description></description>
    <role-name>TRADEUSER</role-name>
  </security-role>
<!--  MAPPING EJB METHODS TO SECURITY ROLE FOR SECURITY  -->
  <method-permission>
    <role-name>TRADEUSER</role-name>
    <method>
      <ejb-name>Stock</ejb-name>
      <method-name>*</method-name>
    </method>
    <method>
      <ejb-name>StockFacade</ejb-name>
      <method-name>*</method-name>
    </method>
    <method>
```

```
            <ejb-name>StockFacade</ejb-name>
            <method-intf>Home</method-intf>
            <method-name>*</method-name>
        </method>
    </method-permission>
    <!-- FOR CONTAINER MANAGED TRANSACTION, CHOOSING HOW AN EJB METHOD
    ➥SHOULD BEHAVE TRANSACTIONALLY -->
    <container-transaction>
        <method>
            <ejb-name>StockFacade</ejb-name>
            <method-name>*</method-name>
        </method>
        <trans-attribute>Required</trans-attribute>
    </container-transaction>

</assembly-descriptor>
```

- The `<security-role>` tag defines security roles. Just like web artifacts, Enterprise Bean methods are secured using roles. All the roles must be defined before they can be used to secure any EJB.
- The `<method-permission>` section maps roles defined in the previous section to specific EJB methods. This is how an EJB is secured. As part of the deployment process, roles are mapped to actual groups or users. EJB methods are matched with roles, much as security constraints map web artifacts to roles. For example, you might only want to allow users with the *manager* role to call a method on an EJB that returns employee salaries. You can use the wildcard character * to signify all the methods on the EJB interfaces.[7]
- The `<container-transaction>` section defines how EJB methods behave transactionally if the application uses Container Managed Transactions (CMT). By defining a transactional attribute on an EJB method, you can define how the code in that method behaves transactionally. Any transactional resources that are used within the EJB method will be part of the transaction. The way that Container Managed EJB methods behave in transactions is mandated by the EJB specification. There are six transaction attributes you can attach to a method:

7 There is also the notion of marking EJB methods as unchecked. This signifies that those methods can be accessed by any client and overrides any other role that the method is mapped with. The assembly section can also include an excludes list. The *excludes list* is basically the opposite of the unchecked methods. These methods are not callable by any client. Usually, this is used as a temporary marker for methods that have been deployed but have not been secured.

- **Required**—If the caller has an active transaction, the code in the EJB method becomes part of it. If not, the container will start a new one before calling your method and end it either by committing or rolling it back after the method.
- **RequiresNew**—When the EJB method is called, the container will start a new transaction before calling your method and end it either by committing or rolling back after the method returns. If the caller has another existing transaction, the caller's transaction will be paused until the method returns.
- **Mandatory**—The caller must have started a transaction already; if not, the container will throw an exception to the caller and won't allow execution of the method.
- **Never**—The caller must not have a transaction active. If the caller does, the container throws an exception and doesn't allow execution.
- **Supports**—If the caller has a transaction, the called EJB method will become part of the caller's transaction. If not, the container will not start a transaction but will still execute the method. Thus, if there is no transaction, any call to a resource within the EJB's context will execute in autocommit mode.[8]
- **NotSupported**—If the caller has a transaction, it will suspend that transaction until the EJB method returns and will execute the EJB method in autocommit mode. Otherwise, the method will just execute in autocommit mode.

The transaction behavior is dependent upon the client calling the EJB methods through the remote or local interface. In addition to the usual clients, such as Servlets or Java client applications, an EJB client can be another EJB or even the same EJB. An EJB acting as a client must go through a defined interface, remote or local, of the bean it is calling for the container to be aware of the call and apply any transactional semantics. If an EJB bean class, however, calls one of its own methods through a simple Java method call, it does not go through the container, and thus no transactional decision is made. In order to give you a better understanding of CMT, we will give you some examples in Chapter 11, "Transactions with WebSphere Application Server."

## WAS EJB Deployment Descriptor

As stated in Chapter 2, "J2EE Applications," an EJB module has IBM-specific deployment descriptors. The binding file is responsible for binding information about the bean either in code or in the EJB deployment descriptor to defined entities within the WAS runtime. There are three specific tasks the binding file accomplishes in an EJB module:

- Define the JNDI name for the EJB on WAS.
- Map any reference defined on a bean to the actual JNDI name under which it is registered on the server.
- Define a data source for CMP Entity Beans to use for data access.

8 Autocommit mode means any single update to a resource is committed as soon as it is completed; multiple related operations are not grouped and committed together.

The binding file name inside an EJB module is **ibm-ejb-jar-bnd.xmi.** WebSphere tools can generate the binding file, and it can be maintained using editors. Code Snippet 9-5 illustrates a portion of an EJB binding file. The binding in the example defines the JNDI name for the StockFacade Session Bean and maps the reference to the Stock Entity Bean to the actual JNDI name under which the Entity Bean is mapped.

**Code Snippet 9-5** IBM binding definition for Session Bean

```
...
<!--  BINDING FOR STOCKFACADE SESSION BEAN - DEFINES BEAN UNDER
➥ejb/StockFacade -->
<ejbBindings xmi:id="EnterpriseBeanBinding_1040603043703" jndiName=
➥"ejb/StockFacade">
    <enterpriseBean xmi:type="ejb:Session" href="META-INF/ejb-jar.
➥xml#StockFacade"/>
<!--  MAPS THE REFERENCE TO THE STOCK ENTITY BEAN -->
    <ejbRefBindings xmi:id="EjbRefBinding_1057121846690" jndiName=
➥"ejb/Stock">
      <bindingEjbRef xmi:type="common:EJBLocalRef" href="META-INF/
      ➥ejb-jar.xml#EJBLocalRef_1057121846690"/>
    </ejbRefBindings>
  </ejbBindings>
```

The file is difficult to read and contains generated unique numbers appended to certain attributes. As an alternative, Figure 9-4 illustrates the deployment descriptor editor available in WebSphere Studio or the ASTK. Any binding information is clearly marked as WebSphere Binding and contains simple text fields for entering the information.

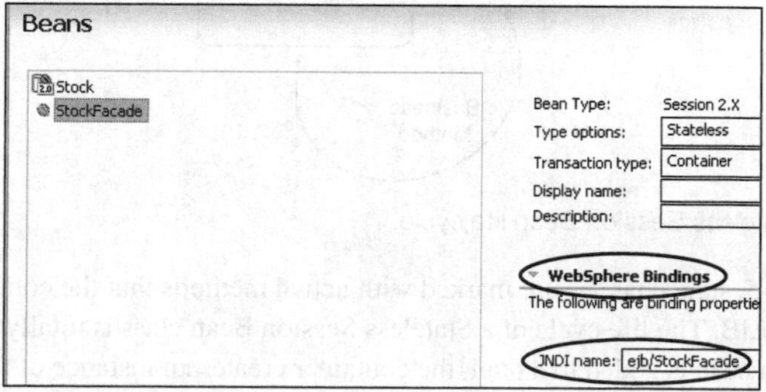


**Figure 9-4** EJB binding.

An EJB module also has an extension file called **ibm-ejb-jar-ext.xml** that contains definitions for features in WAS that extend the standard EJB specification. The file looks similar to the binding file, and many extensions are editable through the EJB deployment descriptor editor. Different EJB extensions will be illustrated throughout this book.

Not all extensions in the WAS EJB module are located in the ibm-ejb-jar-ext.xmi file. For example, the EJB specification does not specify how to map an Entity Bean to some underlying data element, such as a database table. That is defined in a file called **map.mapxmi**. This will be discussed in the next chapter.

## EJB Life Cycle

The EJB specification mandates the life cycle of EJB components within the container, specifically the bean class. Different Session Bean types have different life cycles. Since Stateless Session Beans do not maintain any state for a client, there are two states in the Session Bean life cycle: "does not exist" and "method-ready pool." Figure 9-5 illustrates the expected life cycle of a Stateless Session Bean.

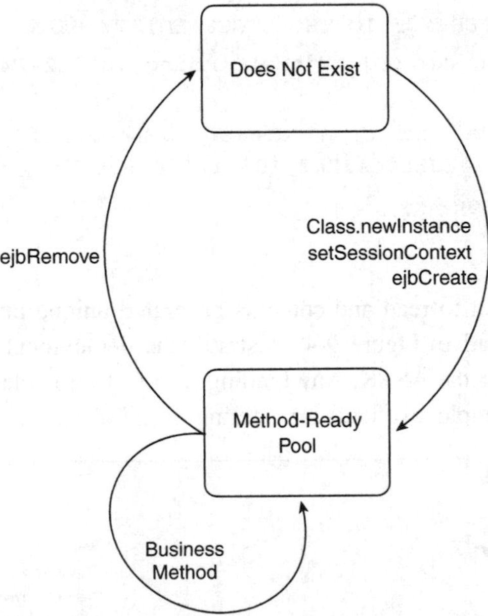


**Figure 9-5** Stateless Session Bean life cycle.

In Figure 9-5, state changes are marked with actual methods that the container calls on the bean class of the EJB. The life cycle of a Stateless Session Bean class is totally controlled by the container. When a bean is added to a pool, the container creates an instance of the bean class and calls setSessionContext() and ejbCreate() only once per bean instance. When the bean instance is not needed because the pool size may be reduced, the container will call ejbRemove(). Although clients call create() on the home interface to get a Session Bean instance, you cannot assume that a client calling a Stateless Session Bean's home create() corresponds to a call to ejbCreate() on the Bean class. In fact, with Stateless Session Beans, the container will rarely call ejbCreate(). Bean instances are either serving client requests, waiting to serve requests, or they do not exist.

Stateful Session Beans have a different life cycle because each bean instance is expected to maintain state for a client until the client is finished with the bean or some timeout occurs. The life cycle of a Stateful Session Bean is expected to start with client issuing a create() on the home interface of the Stateful Session Bean. A client can hold on to a reference and expect the state to be active until it calls remove() or the bean times out.

The container is free to passivate the bean instance in response to demands in workload. This means that the container copies the state of the bean to some secondary storage and frees the in-memory instance for another client to use or to save resources during inactivity. The mechanism for saving the state is up to the J2EE vendor; WAS will serialize any state to the local file system.[9] When the client issues another method call, the bean is reactivated, and the state is restored.

Stateful Session Beans are not very scalable because the server must maintain this state for each client, using valuable server resources. In addition, Stateful Session Beans cannot be workload managed because each client must return to the same server (the server that owns the client state). Figure 9-6 illustrates the life cycle of a Stateful Session Bean.[10]

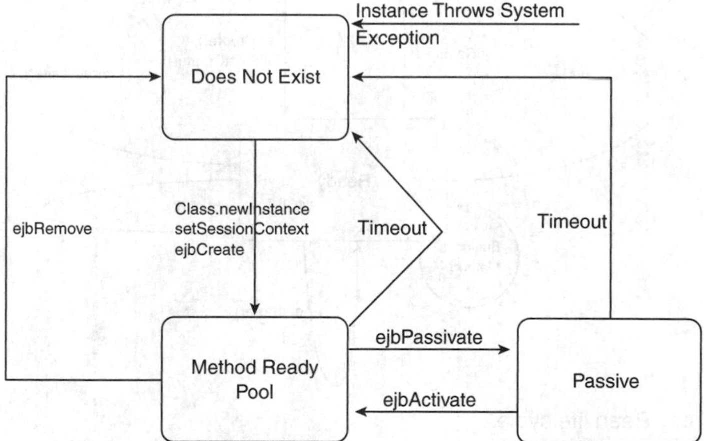


**Figure 9-6** Stateful Session Bean life cycle.

9 Developers must make Stateful Session Bean data serializable in order for the state to be serialized. This is a frequent cause of application failure.

10 WAS does not cluster the bean class of a Stateful Session Bean. In order to have some scalability or failover, developers should rely on HTTP session for client state. WAS has multiple techniques for replicating HTTP session state across a cluster. This will be explained in Part IV of this book.

Entity Bean instances are mapped to some underlying persistent store and therefore have a special life cycle as well. Entity Beans have a pooled state and a ready state. In a pooled state, a bean instance is not associated with any underlying persistent data. Bean instances in this state receive home method and finder method calls. Entity Bean instances move into ready state when they are associated with some underlying persistent data. Entity Beans can be passivated and activated like Stateful Session Beans to allow the container to manage resources. However, unlike Stateful Session Beans, Entity Beans are typically backed by an enterprise quality persistent store (such as a relational database). The Entity Bean life cycle is shown in Figure 9-7.

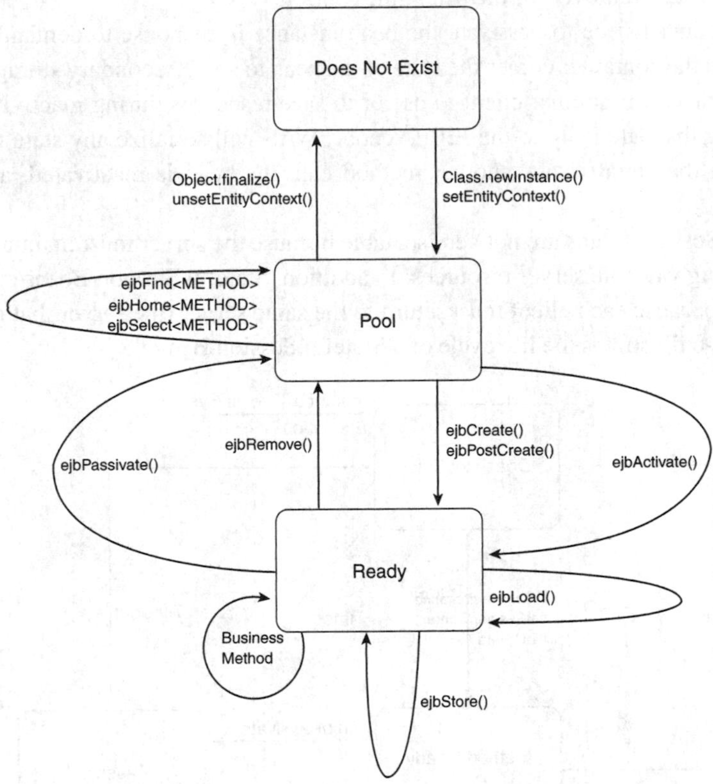


**Figure 9-7** Entity Bean life cycle.

Message Driven Beans have a life cycle that is similar to Stateless Session Beans. We will cover that in Chapter 12.

## Enterprise JavaBean Deployment with WAS

In this section, we will illustrate a manual deployment of an application with Enterprise Beans. We will demonstrate an automated deployment in the next chapter. By walking through the steps manually, you should gain a better understanding of the underlying concepts, which will help when it comes to automating deployment. There are a few more steps in deploying EJB applications, and by seeing them illustrated, you will understand some key concepts. WebSphere Application Server provides full support for deployment of 2.0 Enterprise JavaBeans. In this section, the reader will be shown how to examine an EJB module using the Application Server Toolkit (ASTK). The reader will then deploy an application with an EJB JAR file to WAS. Because we deployed a web application in the web application chapter, only the differences relevant to EJBs will be highlighted.

## Enterprise JavaBean Module

Bring up the ASTK and open an empty workspace to C:\WASDeployBook\Chapter09\workspace. Import the StockSystem.ear file in the C:\WASDeploy\Chapter09 directory. Under the J2EE Perspective, there are several ways to look at an EJB module. The J2EE Hierarchy view gives us a view of all the beans in the package divided by type, as well as some information about the deployment descriptor. Figure 9-8 shows the StockSystemEJB JAR in J2EE Hierarchy view. From the J2EE Hierarchy view, you can see one Session Bean called StockFacade and one Entity Bean called Stock. The J2EE Hierarchy view reads the EJB deployment descriptor to form its display.

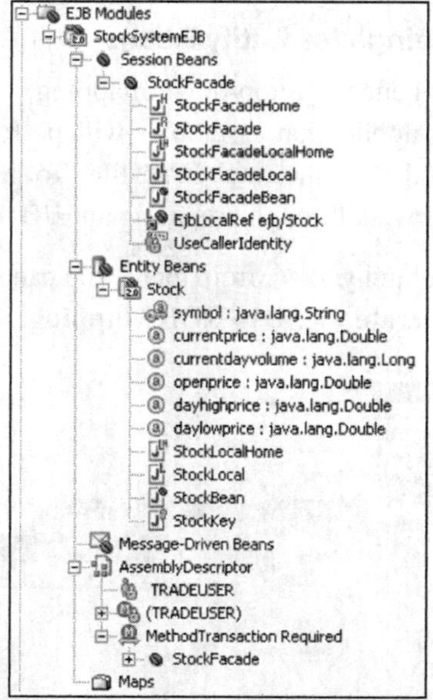


**Figure 9-8** J2EE Hierarchy view.

To get a better understanding of how the EJB module is structured, switch to the Project Navigator view, as shown in Figure 9-9. The figure highlights the EJB classes and deployment descriptors. However, understand that each package really represents a hierarchy. For example, com.deploybook.stock.ejb is really the folder structure com/deploybook/stock/ejb.

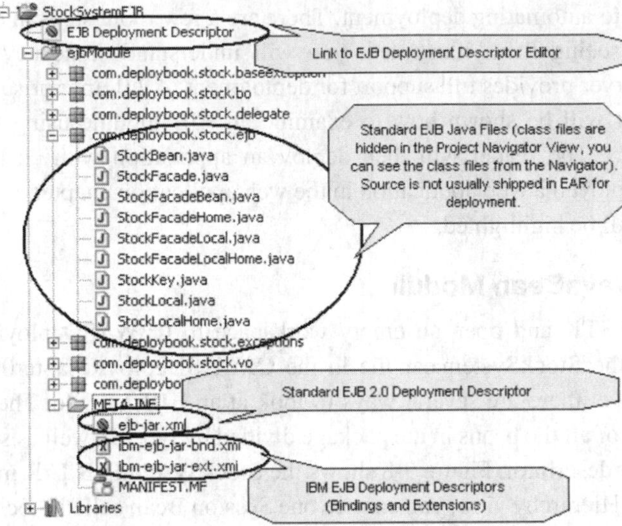


**Figure 9-9** Project Navigator view.

## Generating Database Mappings for Entity Beans

Now we will use the ASTK to generate a top-down mapping[11] to a database for Entity Beans. Generally, a lead developer or application assembler will perform this task. The actual WAS administrator is more concerned with the final EAR file. To get a better appreciation for the assembly steps, this section will walk through preparing an EJB module for deployment:

1. Switch to the J2EE Hierarchy view; from there, you can right-click the StockSystemEJB module and select **Generate > EJB to RDB Mapping...** as shown in Figure 9-10.

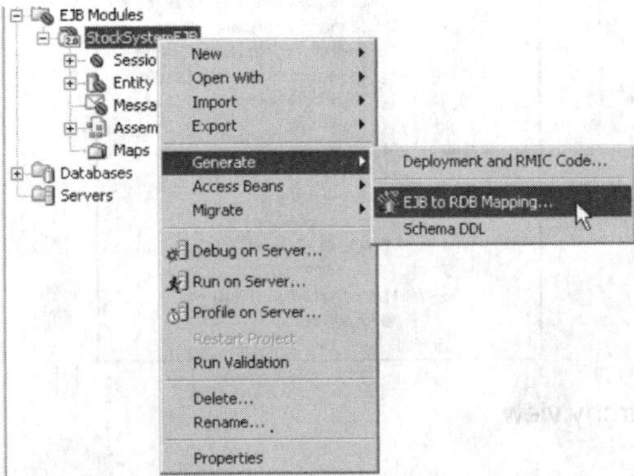

**Figure 9-10** EJB to RDB Mapping.

11 Keep in mind that the focus of this chapter is deployment of EJBs. The use of top-down mapping is shown to be able to create a quick database schema for the example. In the next chapter, we will deploy an existing set of Entity Beans with a more robust mapping.

2. On the first screen, you can create a new backend folder or use an existing one. Press **Next**.
3. The next screen allows us to select our mapping strategy. There is a choice of top-down or meet-in-the-middle. If there were no Entity Beans in the project, bottom-up would be highlighted. Select **top-down** to generate the database schema for the Stock Entity Bean. Press **Next**.
4. On the next screen, we will enter the database information. For Target Database, enter **DB2 Universal Database V8.1**. For Database name, enter **WSTRADE**. For schema name, enter **CHAPTER09**, as shown in Figure 9-11.

> **NOTE**
> Throughout this book, a different schema name is given for each chapter. This allows you to have different virtual databases. Leaving the schema name blank is a valid option as well. This enables you to use any schema at deployment time without regenerating the mappings based on a schema change.

5. Ensure Generate DDL is selected. Press **Finish**.

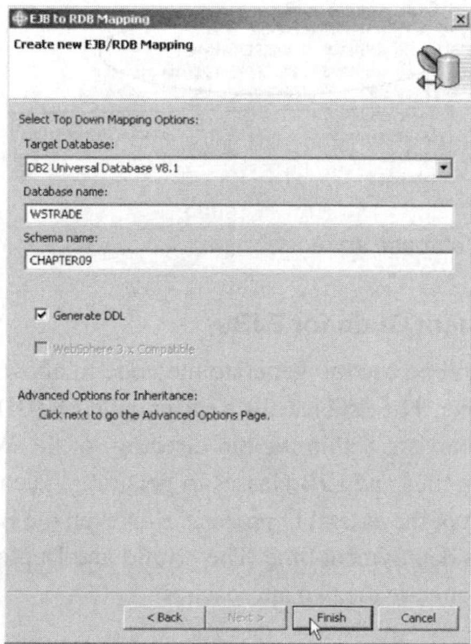


**Figure 9-11** Top-down generation.

6. Pressing **Finish** will create the needed files. It will also open the mapping editor and update the J2EE Hierarchy view with mapping information. Close the mapping editor.

Switch back to the Project Navigator view. An examination of the EJB module will show a new backend folder. Within the folder, there are several generated files:

- Map.mapxmi contains the configuration for the mapping between the Stock Entity Beans and the newly generated schema.
- The table.ddl contains the SQL necessary to create the tables in the database.
- The other three files maintain the database schema. You can use the Data Perspective to update the schema information. These files are more useful for meet-in-the-middle or bottom-up mapping.

Figure 9-12 shows the generated files.

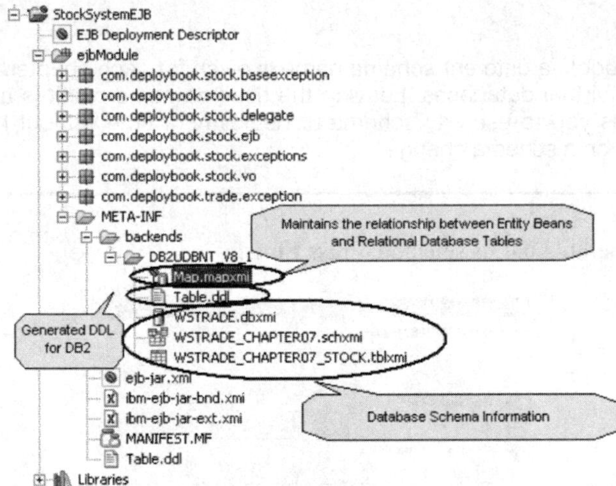


**Figure 9-12** Generated database artifacts.

## Generating the Deployment Code for EJBs

In this section, the ASTK will be used to generate the code to allow the EJB application to run within the WAS EJB container. The ASTK calls a script called **EJBDeploy.bat**[12] to generate the deploy code. This script file exists within the bin directory of the WAS install. EJBDeploy.bat will use all the configuration files and EJB classes to generate the code. In this sample, EJBDeploy.bat can be called as part of the assembly process. However, the EJB deployment code generation can also be deferred to deployment time. The "Build and Deployment Analysis" section at the end of the chapter will compare the two approaches:

1. Go to the J2EE Hierarchy view, right-click the StockSystemEJB module, and select **Generate > Deployment and RMIC Code**, as shown in Figure 9-13.
2. This will bring up the RMIC Deployment Wizard; ensure that both StockFacade and Stock are selected and press **Finish**.

12 On Unix platforms, the EJBDeploy utility will not have the BAT extension.

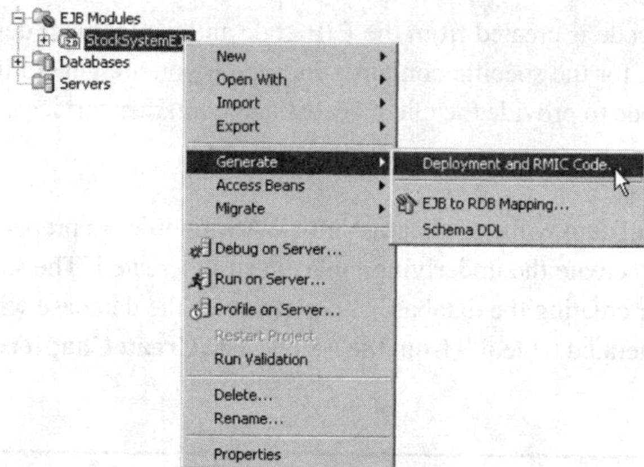


**Figure 9-13** Generate Deployment and RMIC Code.

The Generation Wizard will generate all the necessary code. Switch back to the Project Navigator view and expand the StockSystemEJB project, as shown in Figure 9-14, to see the newly generated code.

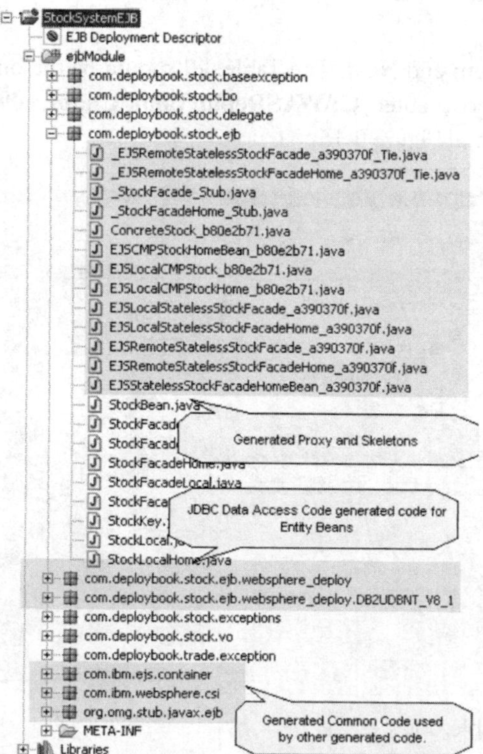


**Figure 9-14** The generated code.

The generated code is created from the EJB code and deployment descriptors provided by the developer to work for the specific container for which you are generating it. The code interacts with container code to provide the client access and container services.

## Deploying to WAS

In this section, you will deploy the application into WAS. In order to prepare for the deployment, the database scripts to create the underlying tables must be created. The samples with this book provide the scripts for creating the database and populating the database with test data. You only need to export the generated table.ddl from the ASTK. The **CreateChapter09Tables.bat** file will call table.ddl.

> **NOTE**
> If you are using top-down mapping, this would be a good opportunity to also apply security on the created tables. DBAs usually have separate scripts to apply permissions.

1. Export the file from ASTK by right-clicking the table.ddl file in the DB2 Backend folder.[13]
2. Select **File System** and **Next**. The Table.ddl should be the only file checked. In the To directory text box, enter **C:\WASDeployBook\Chapter09\CreateDBScript**. Click **Finish**, as shown in Figure 9-15.

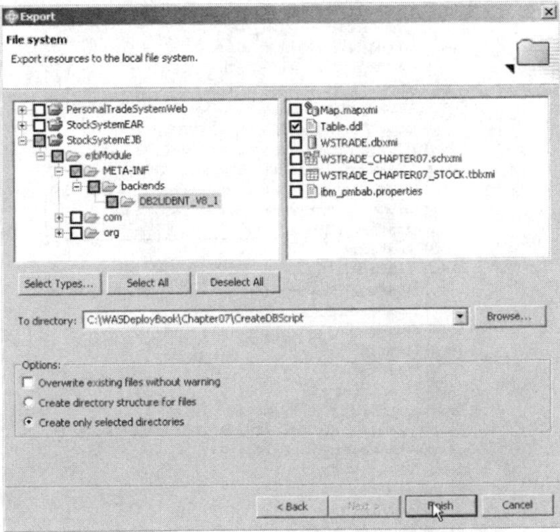


**Figure 9-15** Export table.ddl.

13 There is also a copy of it in the META-INF folder; the META-INF folder contains the Table.ddl for the active backend. ASTK can have multiple backend mappings, but only one mapped at runtime.

3. Open the file C:\WASDeployBook\Chapter09\CreateDBScript\CreateChapter09Tables.bat and modify the user and password for your database.
4. Open your DB2 command prompt and go to the C:\WASDeploy\Chapter09\CreateChapter09Tables.bat directory. Type **CreateChapter09Tables**.
5. From the main menu of the ASTK, select **File > Export**. Select EAR file from the list and press **Next**. Select **StockSystemEAR** from the list and export to **C:\WASDeployBook\Chapter09\StockSystemEARDeployable.ear**.
6. Start the server from a command prompt; make sure the directory is the <WAS-INSTALL>\bin directory. Enter **startserver server1**.
7. Once the server is started, open a browser and go to the admin console URL: http://localhost:9090/admin. Log into the admin console with the admin user ID and password.
8. Alter the data source created in Chapter 7, "JDBC as a Resource," to support Container Managed Persistence. Expand Resources and click **JDBC Providers**. On the JDBC Providers Page, select the DB2 Universal **JDBC Driver Provider** driver. On the Provider page, scroll down to the Additional Properties section and select **DataSources**.
9. Click on the **WSTradeDS** link. To enable the CMP support, check the box next to Container managed persistence, as shown in Figure 9-16. Press **OK**. Save the configuration by clicking the Save link and then the Save button.

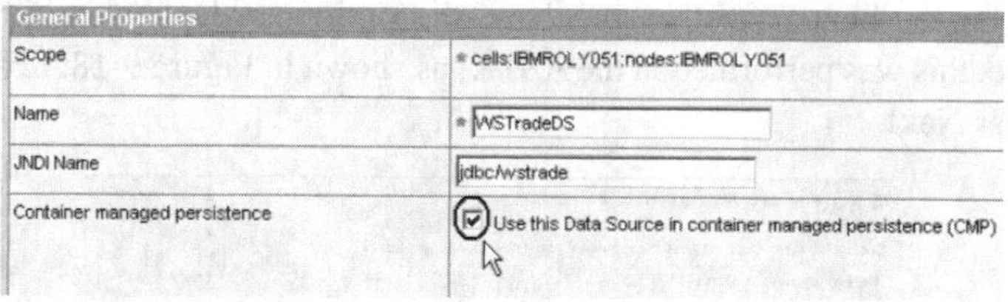

**Figure 9-16** Enable CMP for Data Source.

10. Back on the menu tree, expand Applications and select the **Install Application** link. Click **Browse**, go to the **C:\WASDeployBook\Chapter09** directory, select the **StockSystemEARDeployable.ear** file, and select **Next**.
11. The second page controls binding generation. You can choose to generate the **ibm-ejb-jar-bnd.xmi** file and control how to generate it, as shown in Figure 9-17. For this example, use the one generated by ASTK. In many situations it will be appropriate to specify different information. For example, as an application moves from environment to environment (for example, QA > UAT > Performance Test > Production), you may have to point to differently named resources on each environment. Leave the defaults and go to the next page. Press **Next**.

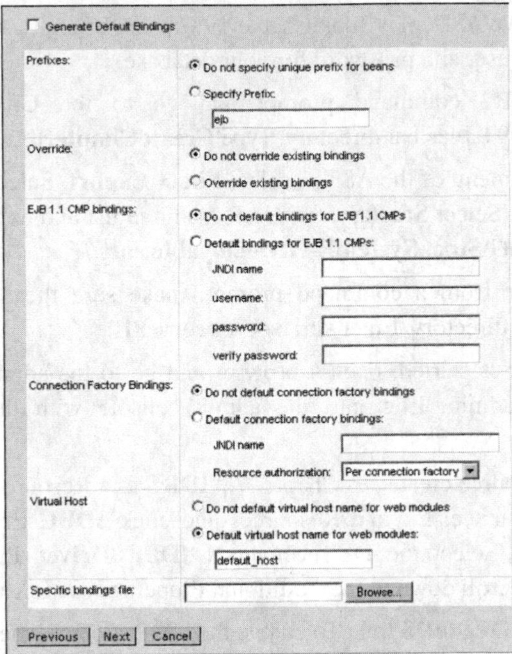


**Figure 9-17** Generate binding at deployment time.

12. Notice on the next page that you have the option to deploy the EJB code. In this example, this was performed in the ASTK, as shown in Figure 9-18. Leave it unchecked and press **Next**.

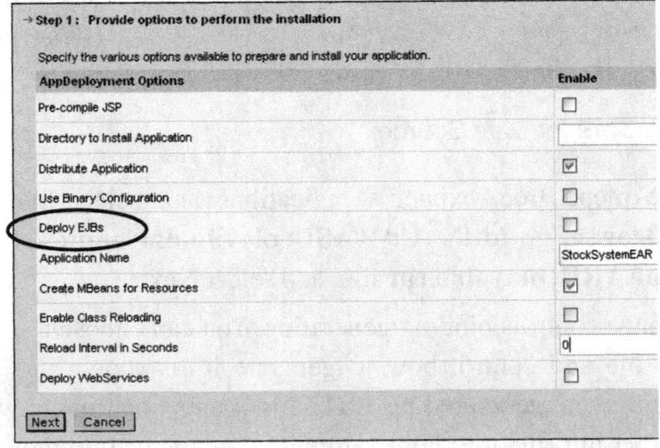


**Figure 9-18** Deploy EJBs.

13. On the next page, you can select the default backend ID for all the Entity Beans in the module, as shown in Figure 9-19. An EJB module can have multiple backends inside the EJB JAR, but only one at runtime will be active. Leave the value and select **Next**.

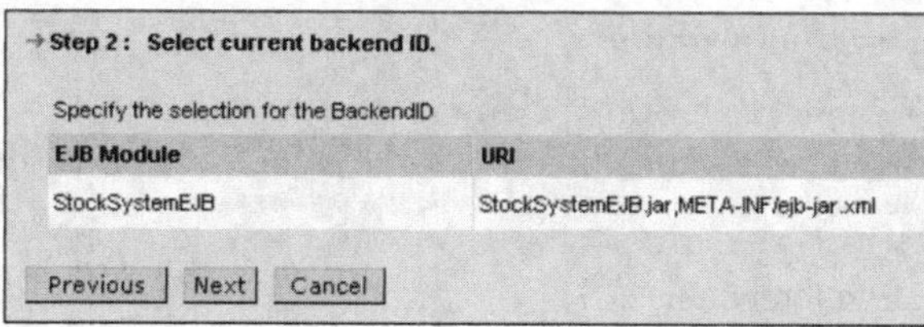


**Figure 9-19** Select CMP backend.

14. Next, you can define the actual names for the EJBs in JNDI. The binding in the EJB JAR had them defined already, so the names are populated by the entries in the binding, as shown in Figure 9-20. It is common for developers to enter these using WebSphere Studio. This can be performed in the ASTK or during the deployment process. Leave the defaults and press **Next**.

**Figure 9-20** JNDI definition for EJB.

15. Next, you can bind a default data source for all the Entity Beans inside the module, as shown in Figure 9-21. The name should be jdbc/wstrade, and the authentication type should be Container. Leave the defaults and press **Next**.

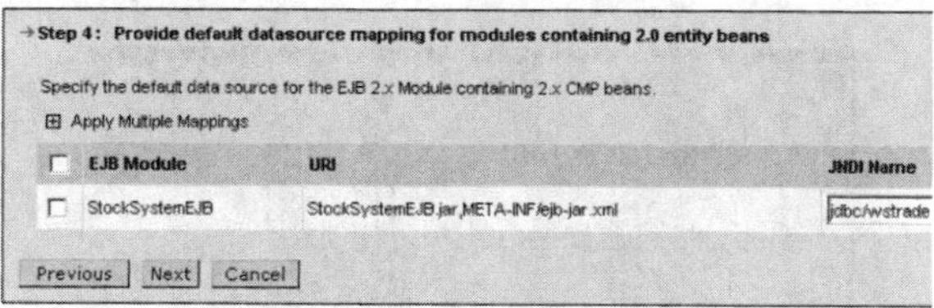


**Figure 9-21** Bind default JDBC data source for CMP.

16. On the next screen, you can map each specific Entity Bean to a data source, again ensuring that the JNDI name is jdbc/wstrade and that the authentication type is Container. Press **Next**.

17. Next, you can map the EJB references to the actual names under which they are defined (see Figure 9-22). The Stock Entity Bean is looked up under the context of the StockFacade Session Bean. Because the real name that the Entity Bean is registered under can change, the Session Bean looks up the Entity Bean using a local reference binding. If the Entity Bean name changes, you must change the resource mapping. This information was already provided in the binding as well, so leave the default and press **Next**.

→ **Step 6 : Map EJB references to beans**

Each EJB reference defined in your application must be mapped to an Enterprise bean.

| Module | EJB | URI | Reference I |
|---|---|---|---|
| StockSystemEJB | StockFacade | StockSystemEJB.jar,META-INF/ejb-jar.xml | ejb/Stock |

**Figure 9-22** Map EJB references.

18. Press **Next** on the Virtual Host Screen.
19. Press **Next** on the Server Selection Screen.
20. Ensure that the TRADEUSER role maps to the TRADE group. Our EJB module uses the same role to protect the EJB methods as the web application did. All EJB methods should be protected using roles.
21. On the Summary Page, review the options and Press **Finish**. Once completed, save the deployment to the Master Configuration.
22. The application has been deployed. You now need to start the application and then test it.
23. From the Tree Menu, expand Application and click **Enterprise Applications**.
24. On the main frame, press the Check button next to StockSystemEAR and press the Start button. The status should change from a red X to a green Go arrow.
25. Open a browser and go to the application URL as you did in Chapter 3. Log in and enter **IBM** as the symbol. The data should return. To ensure that the application is returning dynamic data, enter MSFT as a symbol and submit again. The resulting data should change, as in Figure 9-23. Log out and close the application browser when finished.

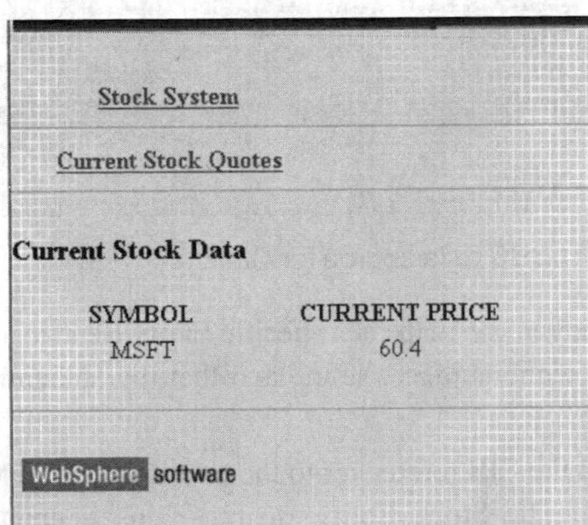


**Figure 9-23** Dynamic data.

26. Go back to the Enterprise Application page, check the StockSystemEAR application, and press **Stop**. Once the status of the application is stopped, check the application again and press **Uninstall**.

27. Save the changes to the configuration.
28. Log out of the console.
29. Close the ASTK.
30. Stop the server by issuing stopserver server1 –user adminUser -password password1a from the CMD line.

## Build and Deployment Analysis

As in Chapter 3, "WAS Quick Start," the application was deployed using the administrative console mainly to outline the extra steps when an application contains Enterprise JavaBeans. Going forward, the samples will rely on scripts. Nonetheless, this exercise provided some important lessons. In general, applications that have Enterprise JavaBeans follow certain steps. How you perform these steps may differ, but the tasks still need to be completed:

1. Code development, compile, build, and package are performed by the developer and assembler.
2. If an application uses CMP, the Entity Beans needs to be **mapped to the underlying data store**. This is performed by the developer or assembler. There are several mapping strategies:
   - The top-down approach was used in this chapter. Top-down approaches are usually used for application packages that can run on multiple databases, such as a generic rules engine or when the application does not make use of existing databases. Once generated, a DBA should use the file as the basis for proper production quality database creation scripts. The table.ddl is not enough; it is only a starting point. The DBA will likely update the file with DBA optimizations, such as creating indexes. Changes made to the Entity Bean schemas means that the database scripts need to be regenerated and optimizations need to be reapplied.
   - The meet-in-the-middle approach is a more common occurrence. This is where the developer creates Entity Beans and then maps them to an existing database. In this case, someone else is maintaining the database schema. Changes in the database schema then have to be incorporated into the process. Generally, a change in database schema requires an import of the schema and a remapping phase. This can be cumbersome. This is usually handled by the developer or assembler.
   - The bottom-up approach is another strategy where Entity Beans are generated from the database schema. This approach is useful for fast prototypes, but it is usually not a valid approach. The decision is usually a development issue; however, the assembler and deployer must know the process.
3. Generation of EJB deployment code can be performed by the developer, assembler, or deployer. You can generate the deployment code at build time or deployment time:

- Build-time generation is performed in the ASTK/WebSphere Studio or can be accomplished using scripts. Developers actually do this generation often if they use an IDE such as WebSphere Studio. Developers need to unit test code. The actual generation that is part of an official build should not be undertaken by developers; it should be performed by the assembler. When doing builds from a tool, it is essential that the code is generated from the Golden Workspace and not shared between developers. To enforce this, the source control plug-ins for WebSphere Studio or the ASTK can be configured to ignore certain files during the checking in and out process. This avoids development-time generated code from entering the official build.
- Deployment-time generation is an extra step for deployers. This means you must make sure the application is properly tested after it has been generated using the new runtime. This can be performed by using build verification tests. This is usually required when developers do not have a tool such as WebSphere Studio that does this for them. However, developers can make use of the WebSphere ANT tasks to do it at build time and not at deployment time so that the details are hidden.

4. The **build** is completed by the assembler. There are generally two approaches to building—using a tool as shown in this chapter or using the automated scripts.
5. Assuring resources are defined. Development should **document** all the resources needed by the application. Then the deployer should make sure they are defined and verified.
6. **Binding** can be performed by the developer, assembler, or deployer. EJB applications tend to have much more binding information. Because they usually implement the model layer, they almost always interact with external resources. Furthermore, an Enterprise Bean can have references to other Enterprise Beans. Knowing when to bind is important:
   - Doing bindings at build time means that you know the build will stay the same throughout environments. However, this means that each environment has to be configured with the same JNDI names for resources throughout all environments in the infrastructure.
   - Generating bindings at deployment time means you have flexibility in maintaining different JNDI names in each environment. However, the deployment process must be documented in more detail because the EAR is incomplete as it moves through the environment and requires a binding step at deployment time to work. This can be simplified through automation.

   Many times, development provides default bindings, but administrators use special scripts to update them at deployment time.

> **NOTE**
> Generating deployment code in production environments is a high risk because there is a higher probability of failure due to the extra activity. It is highly recommended that deployment code be generated as part of the build process and deployed with the generated code already packaged.

## Conclusion

In this chapter, EJB technology was introduced. We went over some programming model basics and learned about the various deployment descriptors. We examined the structure of an EJB JAR using the ASTK, and we deployed the EJB application using the administrative console. In the next chapter, we will focus on Container Managed Persistence (CMP) and some advanced EJB settings. Furthermore, we will deploy a much bigger EJB application by incorporating many of the other use cases of the Personal Trade System. Rather than using the administrative console, we will use our automated build process to accomplish the same tasks.

CHAPTER 10

# CMP and Advanced EJB Settings

In the last chapter, we provided an introduction to Enterprise JavaBeans and learned how to deploy EJB applications in WebSphere Application Server (WAS). In this chapter, we are going to focus on Container Managed Persistence (CMP) Entity Beans. First, we will discuss some basic CMP concepts. Then we will discuss the WebSphere Persistence Manager. We will then address some advanced EJB settings that can enhance performance, usually for CMP Beans, but sometimes for Session Beans as well. Finally, a new version of the Personal Trade System will be deployed. This version of the application will include most of the use cases described in Chapter 2, "J2EE Applications." We will deploy the application using our automated build and deployment process.

## Understanding CMP 2.0

Persistence is a term used to define how applications read and write data from a data store such as a database. JDBC coding is an example of persistence. A developer uses JDBC to create, update, read, and delete data from a relational database. CMP is an abstraction layer for managing persistence in J2EE applications. Developers code to an object-oriented programming model and then map these objects to an underlying persistence store, such as a relational database, using mapping tools. The mapping is then used to generate code that the container uses to persist the data (for example, SQL statements to save the bean properties to a database). CMP is not the only choice for persistence inside J2EE applications, but using CMP enables applications to leverage the persistence services provided by the J2EE application server. The WAS CMP engine includes a number of powerful features related to caching as well as the usual CMP features required by the J2EE specification, such as relationships.

In this section, we will introduce some CMP concepts. The concepts illustrated in this chapter address the CMP specification version 2.0.[1]

## Abstract Schema

With the introduction of EJB 2.0, the CMP model changed dramatically. The biggest change is the introduction of the abstract schema. Because CMP is an abstraction, it is only natural that an abstract data model is needed. Abstract schemas provide a view of data that is independent of the underlying data store. This abstraction allows CMP code to be independent of any data store technology or vendor. The abstract schema is made up of abstract accessors on bean classes and a set of XML elements within the deployment descriptor that define the persistent fields of the bean class and relationships between different beans within the EJB module. This level of abstraction gives the container provider more freedom in persistence implementation. Let's look at a portion of the EJB deployment descriptor. Code Snippet 10-1 illustrates the abstract schema portion of the Stock Entity Bean. Every Entity Bean defines one abstract schema.

**Code Snippet 10-1 Abstract schema for Stock Entity Beans**

```
<entity id="ContainerManagedEntity_1057120180353">
. . .
 <abstract-schema-name>Stock</abstract-schema-name>
 <cmp-field id="CMPAttribute_1057120180444">
   <field-name>symbol</field-name>
 </cmp-field>
 <cmp-field id="CMPAttribute_1057120180454">
   <field-name>currentprice</field-name>
 </cmp-field>
 <cmp-field id="CMPAttribute_1057120180464">
   <field-name>currentdayvolume</field-name>
 </cmp-field>
 <cmp-field id="CMPAttribute_1057120180474">
   <field-name>openprice</field-name>
 </cmp-field>
 <cmp-field id="CMPAttribute_1057120180484">
   <field-name>dayhighprice</field-name>
 </cmp-field>
 <cmp-field id="CMPAttribute_1057120180494">
```

1 The CMP specification usually changes a great deal from version to version. Expect EJB 2.1 to have minor changes, but expect EJB 3.0 to change the persistent model quite a bit.

```
    <field-name>daylowprice</field-name>
  </cmp-field>
  <security-identity>
    <description></description>
    <use-caller-identity />
  </security-identity>
</entity>
```

The abstract schema name on the Entity Bean tag is analogous to a table in a database. This terminology sometimes confuses database administrators who view a schema as a collection of database tables. The data type of the CMP field is defined on the bean class. Thus, for every CMP field on your definition, you must have a corresponding abstract getter and setter method on your bean class, as shown in Code Snippet 10-2. Notice the getSymbol() and setSymbol() definitions. These correspond to the symbol field name in the descriptor.

**Code Snippet 10-2** Abstract getters and setters

```
/**
 * Get accessor for persistent attribute: symbol
 */
public abstract java.lang.String getSymbol();
/**
 * Set accessor for persistent attribute: symbol
 */
public abstract void setSymbol(java.lang.String newSymbol);
```

## Container Managed Relationships

Many data stores have the notion of relationships among different data constructs. For example, in our application, we have a data element called Stock. The Stock element has its own fields such as price and symbol. A Stock element also has stock history. For each day of trading, there is a stock history element. So, one Stock Data element has many StockHistory elements, as illustrated in Figure 10-1. Therefore, this relationship needs to be represented in the data model. Relationships can have cardinality; for example, in our application, the Stock Data construct has a one-to-many relationship with the StockHistory construct. This means that *one* Stock Data object can have *many* related StockHistory objects, as Figure 10-1 shows. Relationships can also be one-to-one or many-to-many.

To implement and maintain relationships, Entity Beans use the notion of a Container Managed Relationship field (CMR field). A CMR field represents a reference either to some other

Entity Bean or a collection of Entity Beans within the same EJB module. The bean class has abstract methods to obtain references to another related bean. In the deployment descriptor, you must create a relationship and define the relation role for each bean, which in turn defines the CMR field for the bean. You must also define whether you can navigate from one side of the relationship to the other. (For a developer, this specifies whether you can obtain a reference to another related Entity Bean through the abstract programming model if you have a reference to one of the Entity Beans.) You can also define the cardinality of the relationship. As stated, Entity Beans can have a one-to-one relationship, one-to-many relationship, or a many-to-many relationship. Code Snippet 10-3 illustrates a one-to-many relationship in the bean section of the deployment descriptor.

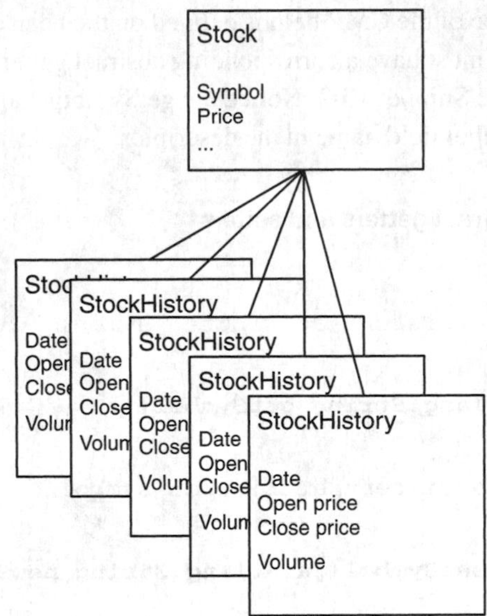


**Figure 10-1** Stock-to-stock history relationship.

**Code Snippet 10-3** One-to-many relationship in a EJB deployment descriptor

```
<!-- Relationship between 2 Beans -->
<ejb-relation>
<description></description>
  <!-- RELATIONSHIP NAME -->
  <ejb-relation-name>Stockhistory_To_Stock</ejb-relation-name>
  <!-- STOCK SIDE OF THE RELATIONSHIP -->
  <ejb-relationship-role id="EJBRelationshipRole_1057120180634">
    <ejb-relationship-role-name>stock</ejb-relationship-role-name>
```

```
        <!-- ONE STOCK HAS MANY STOCK HISTORY -->
        <multiplicity>Many</multiplicity>
        <!-- NAME OF OTHER ENTITY BEAN, IN THIS CASE STOCKHISTORY, THAT
        ➥IS RELATED TO STOCK-->
        <relationship-role-source>
          <ejb-name>Stockhistory</ejb-name>
        </relationship-role-source>
                 <!-- HOW STOCKHISTORY REFERS TO STOCK -->
        <cmr-field>
          <cmr-field-name>stock</cmr-field-name>
        </cmr-field>
    </ejb-relationship-role>

    <!--  STOCKHISTORY SIDE OF THE RELATIONSHIP -->
    <ejb-relationship-role id="EJBRelationshipRole_1057120180644">
      <ejb-relationship-role-name>stockhistory</ejb-relationship-
      ➥role-name>
      <!--  EACH STOCK HISTORY CORRESSPONDS TO ONE STOCK -->
        <multiplicity>One</multiplicity>
    <!--  NAME OF OTHER ENTITY BEAN, IN THIS CASE STOCK, THAT IS RELATED
    ➥TO STOCKHISTORY -->
      <relationship-role-source>
        <ejb-name>Stock</ejb-name>
      </relationship-role-source>
      <!--  HOW STOCK REFERS TO STOCKHISTORY -->
      <cmr-field>
        <cmr-field-name>stockhistory</cmr-field-name>
  <!--  BECAUSE A STOCK CAN HAVE MANY STOCK HISTORY, A STOCK ENTITY BEAN
  ➥CONTAINS MANY STOCKHISTORY BEANS STORED IN A COLLECTION -->
        <cmr-field-type>java.util.Collection</cmr-field-type>
      </cmr-field>
    </ejb-relationship-role>
  </ejb-relation>
```

Every relationship has two sides represented by roles. Each side of the relationship needs to know information about the other side. Figure 10-2 illustrates the relationship between the Stock and Stockhistory Entity Beans in UML format. The figure is a graphical representation of the XML deployment descriptor definition of the relationship.

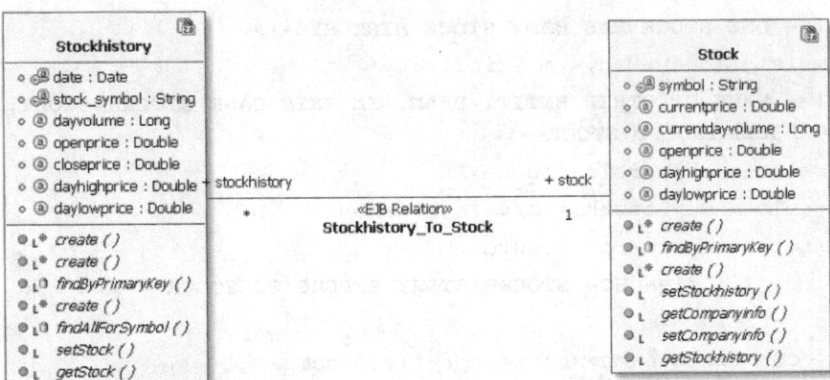


**Figure10-2** EJB relationship in UML.

## EJB Query Language (EJB-QL)

As stated in the last chapter, Entity Beans have finder methods on the home interface that allow clients to find existing Entity Beans. In CMP Entity Beans, a finder is matched to an EJB-QL statement. EJB-QL is an SQL-like language that queries against the abstract schema. EJB containers such as WAS use the EJB-QL definitions to generate queries to the underlying data store. For example, if our CMP implementation is mapped to a relationship database, an EJB-QL query such as **select object(o) from Stockhistory o where o.stock.symbol =?1** will translate to something like **SELECT * FROM STOCKHISTORY,STOCK WHERE STOCK.SYMBOL = ?** in SQL. An EJB-QL statement can navigate across relationships as well (this is similar to how you can create an SQL statement using a JOIN). An EJB-QL statement is defined in the bean section of each bean. Code Snippet 10-4 illustrates an EJB-QL definition.

**Code Snippet 10-4** EJB-QL in the EJB deployment descriptor

```
<query>
<description></description>
  <query-method>
    <method-name>findAllForSymbol</method-name>
    <method-params>
      <method-param>java.lang.String</method-param>
    </method-params>
</query-method>
  <ejb-ql>select object(o) from Stockhistory o where o.stock.symbol =?1
</ejb-ql>
</query>
```

Queries are defined at the end of the bean definition. You must have a query definition for each finder on the home interface or each select method on the bean class (except for the findByPrimaryKey() method). An EJB book such as [Monson-Haefel 2002] is a good source for information on writing good EJB-QL. Finally, be aware that EJB-QL is defined statically during development. There is no dynamic query facility[2] in the base version of WAS 5.x. This static nature limits the types of things you can do using EJB-QL; i.e., your queries must be known at compile time, not runtime.

## WebSphere Persistence Architecture

The WebSphere persistence manager exists for the purpose of supporting the CMP model. The persistence manager interacts with the runtime-generated concrete CMP bean instances to implement the abstract schema and persist the data to the actual data store. The WebSphere Persistence Manager provides a layer of abstraction between the underlying resource such as a JDBC driver and the concrete bean implementation. The concrete bean is the actual persistent class that is generated when running the EJB Deploy Generation tool. As we learned in Chapter 7, "JDBC as a Resource," resources such as JDBC make use of the J2EE Connector Architecture (J2C). The Persistence Manager is implemented as a J2C Adapter. Thus, the generated Concrete Bean uses the J2C Client Connector Interface (CCI) to communicate to the Persistence Manager. Having the Persistence Manager as layer of indirection between the resource adapter and the Entity Bean implementation gives the container freedom to plug in different adapters, such as an SQLJ Adapter. Having the concrete bean use the CCI API also makes it possible for the container to use non-relational backends. Figure 10-3 illustrates a high-level view of where the persistence manager comes into play.

In Chapter 7, we stated that resources such as a JDBC data source are bound to a specific JNDI name inside WebSphere Application Server. The Persistence Manager then operates above the different relational resource adapters. The Persistence Manager is also bound with its own JNDI name. When the developer binds the CMP to a data store, the CMP is bound to the JNDI name of the persistence manager. Binding CMP Entity Beans to the Persistence Manager allows a layer of abstraction. This abstraction allows you to change the underlying resource adapter without the CMP knowing about it. The Persistence Manager is only an abstraction of relational resource adapters. If your CMP implementation uses another type of data store, it needs some other type of J2C-based persistence manager.

From a configuration point of view, it is not necessary to explicitly point to the J2C Adapter, although doing so would not be incorrect. One can configure the CMP data source directly to the JNDI name of the underlying resource. We did this last chapter by configuring the CMP Bean directly to the DataSource JNDI name. At deployment time, the container will find the corresponding J2C wrapper. This reduces the complexity of deploying CMP Beans.

2 WebSphere Application Server Enterprise Edition version 5.0 (Renamed WBI Server Foundations in version 5.1) has a dynamic query feature that allows a developer to pass EJB-QL at runtime in Java code. This feature also extends the EJB-QL language to support more flexible queries.

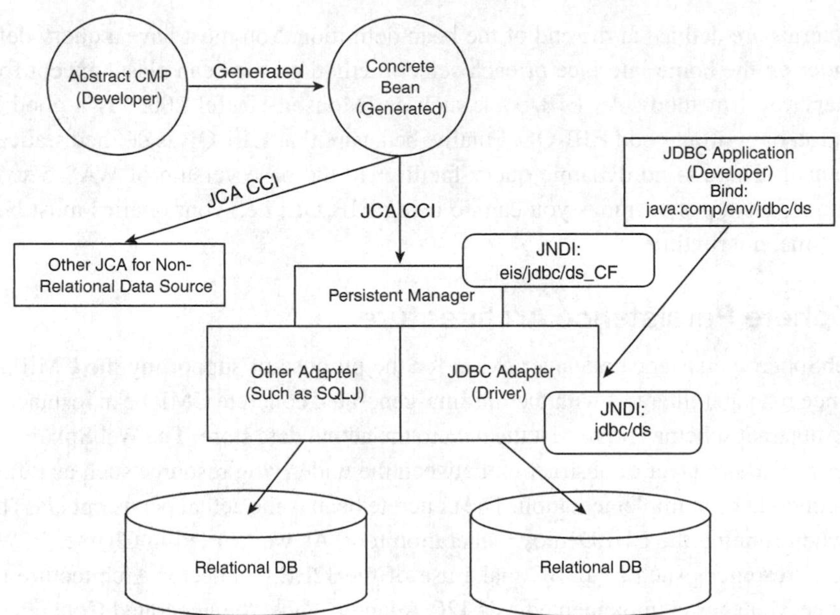


**Figure 10-3** WAS persistence manager overview.

## Bean and Data Caching

The EJB container provides caching capabilities to your Enterprise Beans. Database applications often need caching facilities in order to reduce the number of round trips between the database and the application server. This provides better performance for applications in some scenarios. Because CMP (and EJBs in general) provides abstraction at many levels, understanding where caching can happen can be a challenge. Figure 10-4 illustrates some of these concepts.

On the top layer, there is a set of CMP objects that have the data in the format the programmer uses. For example, the Stock Entity Bean is an object with loaded data members inside the memory of the application. Underneath the CMP layer is the data access layer, usually JDBC. JDBC provides objects in the form of tabular ResultSets; for example, in the figure, we have a JDBC ResultSet retrieved from the underlying STOCK table. Data accessed from the database is moved into the ResultSet Object. Then data is moved from the ResultSet object into the CMP objects. WebSphere maintains a cache at both the JDBC ResultSet level and at the CMP Bean level. As you might imagine, there are tunable cache controls that affect each of these layers. Through careful study of these controls and appropriate application, significant performance gains can be achieved. The next several sections discuss each of the controls in turn.

### Configuring the Bean Cache

All Enterprise Beans (Session Beans, Entity Beans, and Message Driven Beans) in the 2.0 version have a bean class. All beans inside of a container share a bean cache for active bean instance pools for each type of stateless, message-driven, and entity EJB. Figure 10-5 illustrates an example of two clients accessing two different beans. The bean cache maintains all the active instances of EJBs deployed in a particular container.

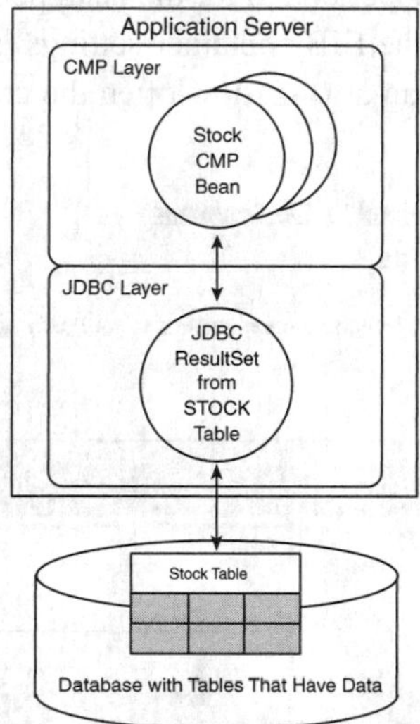


**Figure 10-4** CMP bean and data cache.

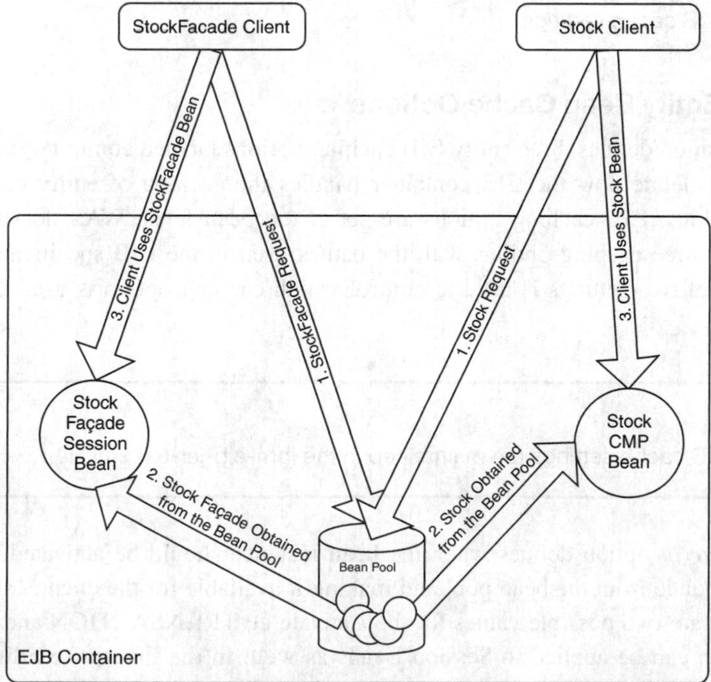


**Figure 10-5** Clients using the bean pool.

In the last chapter, we illustrated that EJB components are made up of several interfaces. The interfaces provide a view for the client, while the bean class contains the majority of your implementation. In order to manage the client load in a multithreaded environment, the EJB container pools all bean classes. The upper bound for the bean pool can be set in the admin console. The setting is accessible through the EJB container settings of a particular server, as shown in Figure 10-6. On this screen, you can also set how often the container removes unused beans by setting the Cleanup interval.

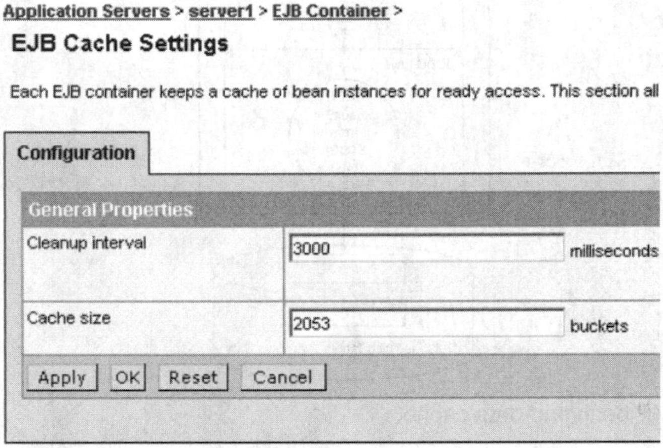

**Figure 10-6** EJB cache settings.

## Configuring Entity Bean Cache Options

The EJB specification defines three entity EJB caching options labeled commit option A, B, and C. These options define how the EJB container handles the caching of entity bean instances between transactions. EJB caching options are set at the bean level. WAS doesn't explicitly expose the same three caching options with the names used in the EJB specification. Instead, the combination of two settings is used to control which caching option is used: *Load at* and *Activate at*.

> **NOTE**
> All of these EJB cache settings are maintained in the ibm-ejb-jar-ext.xmi file.

The *Activate at* option defines when the bean instance should be activated. This means taking a bean instance from the bean pool and making it available for the client. In version 5 of WAS Base, there are two possible values for the Activate at: TRANSACTION and ONCE. The Activate at option can be applied to Session Beans as well. In the Enterprise Edition of WAS version 5, there is a third option called Activity Sessions. Activity Sessions add a new level of caching not addressed by the EJB specification, sometimes called Option C+. Activity Sessions will be explained next chapter.

The *Load at* option defines when the data should be loaded from the data store into the bean instance. This option only applies to Entity Beans. There are two possible options: TRANSACTION and ACTIVATION. Using these options, you can effectively configure the system to meet the requirements of options A, B, or C. We'll return to that in a moment.

Figure 10-7 illustrates activating and loading concepts. Activating applies to both Session Beans and Entity Beans, while loading only applies to Entity Beans. The setting controls *when* the activation and loading occur and control when data and bean instances are cached.

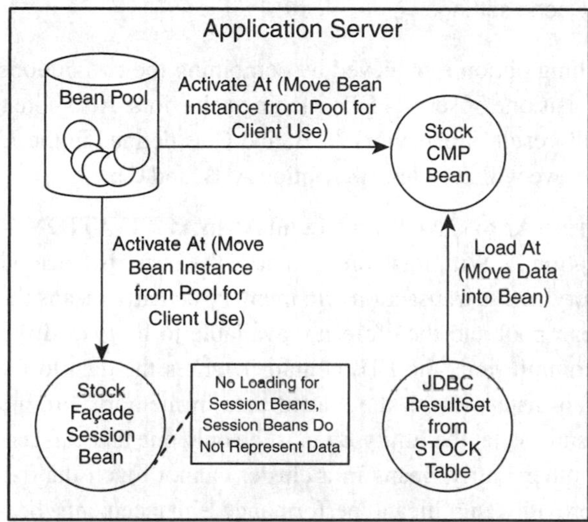


**Figure 10-7** Activating bean instances and load data.

Code Snippet 10-5 shows a piece of the ibm-ejb-jar-ext.xmi file. This file shows how you define the caching option on an EJB. You must embed a `<beanCache>` tag within the `<enterpriseBean>` tag and define these options.

**Code Snippet 10-5** Setting the beanCache option in extended deployment descriptor

```
<ejbExtensions xmi:type="ejbext:ContainerManagedEntityExtension"
➥xmi:id="ContainerManagedEntityExtension_1057120180655" name="Stock">
   <enterpriseBean xmi:type="ejb:ContainerManagedEntity" href="META-
   ➥INF/ejb-jar.xml#ContainerManagedEntity_1057120180353"/>
   <beanCache xmi:id="BeanCache_1064686904857" activateAt=
   ➥"TRANSACTION" loadAt="TRANSACTION"/>
 </ejbExtensions>
```

The EJB deployment descriptor editor within the ASTK (and WebSphere Studio) can be used to set these options. Under the bean tab, you select your bean and scroll down to the IBM Extensions section. There, you will see the Bean Cache section, as shown in Figure 10-8.

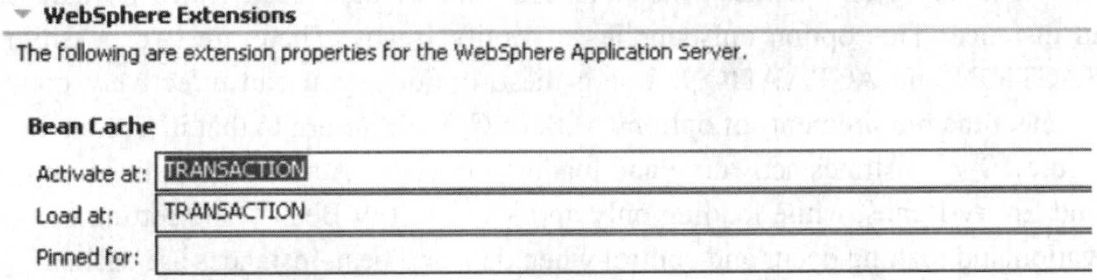

WebSphere Extensions
The following are extension properties for the WebSphere Application Server.
Bean Cache
Activate at: TRANSACTION
Load at: TRANSACTION
Pinned for:

**Figure 10-8** Bean Cache settings.

The desired caching option is achieved by combining the two options. Let's examine how combining values gives us one of several EJB caching behaviors. Also note that three of the combinations listed actually result in behaviors A, B, and C as defined in the J2EE specification (In describing each setting, we will also describe option A, B, and C):

- **Setting Activate At to ONCE and Load At to ACTIVATION**—This is equivalent to EJB cache option A. With this configuration, the bean instance with the loaded data is kept in memory across transactions (in memory actually means the bean instance is not inside the bean pool and therefore not available to be loaded with different data). At transaction commit time, the EJB container writes the data to the persistent store but keeps the bean instance with the loaded data in memory. From an application standpoint, this assumes that the Entity Bean is the only one that can access the data. External programs or other Entity Beans in a cluster cannot touch the data, or else the data is dirty. This provides significant performance enhancements because the application usually retrieves the data from the cache and not the data store. The cache is maintained at both the CMP level and the JDBC ResultSet level. This is illustrated in Figure 10-9.

  As you might expect, there are tradeoffs. First, the bean pool is used to maintain this bean cache. Second, memory resources are being used to hold the ResultSet Data in memory. Most significantly, this model assumes that no other party, even another application server, is accessing the same data. In practice, this is very hard to guarantee. In spite of its limitations, this setting is ideal for read-only data.

- **Setting Activate At to ONCE and Load At to TRANSACTION**—This setting is equivalent to EJB commit option B. Unlike the previous option, this setting allows for shared access to the underlying data store. At the start of every transaction, data is loaded from the database. Only the bean instances are cached, not the data within it. This setting does not give you great caching benefits from a data access standpoint but avoids the overhead of accessing the total bean pool. However, if the number of users to a particular server is high, users may have to wait long if there is no bean instance available in the pool. This option is illustrated in Figure 10-10.

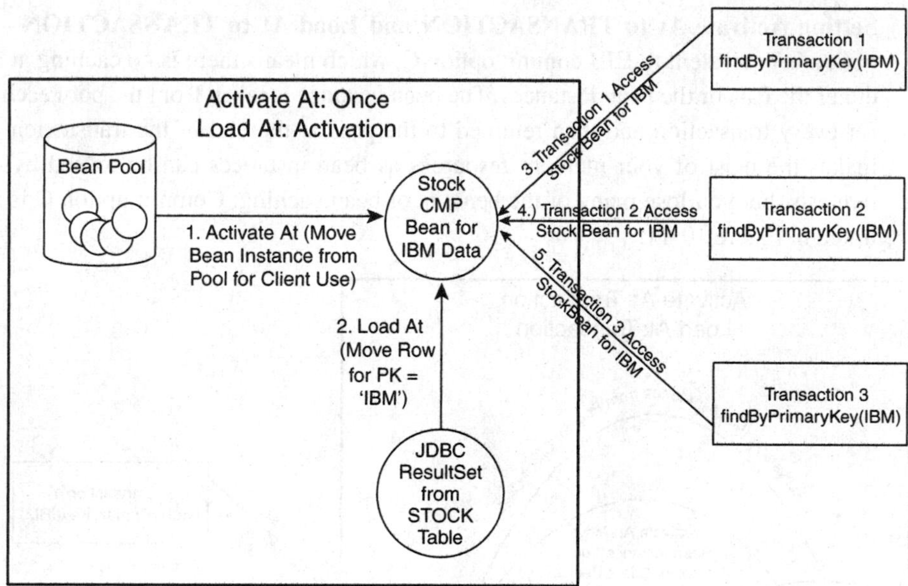


**Figure 10-9** Commit option A.

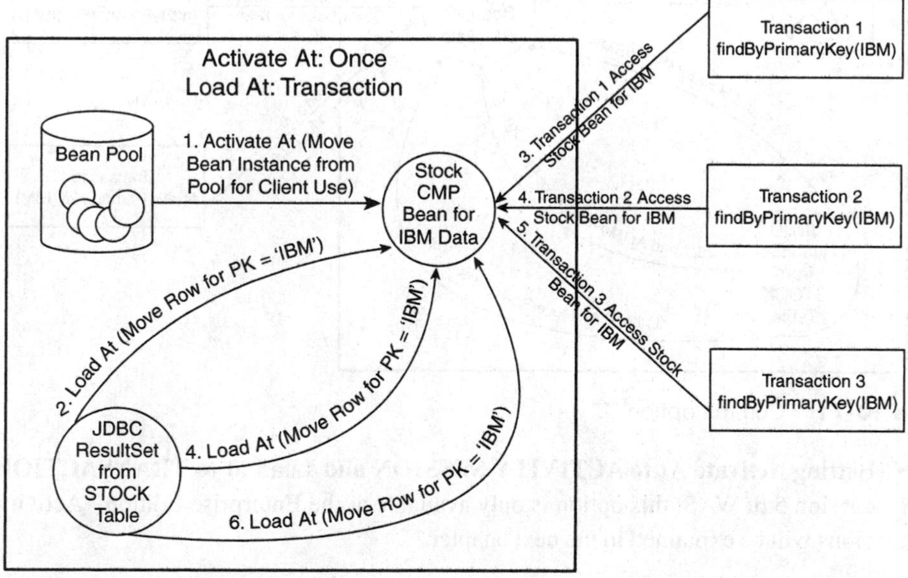


**Figure 10-10** Commit option B.

- **Setting Activate At to TRANSACTION and Load At to TRANSACTION**—This option is equivalent to EJB commit option C, which means there is no caching at all of either the data or the bean instances. The bean instance is taken from the pool each time for every transaction and then returned to the pool at the end of the transaction. This makes the most of your memory resources as bean instances can be reused by other requests, but you lose many of the benefits of bean caching. Commit option C is illustrated in Figure 10-11.

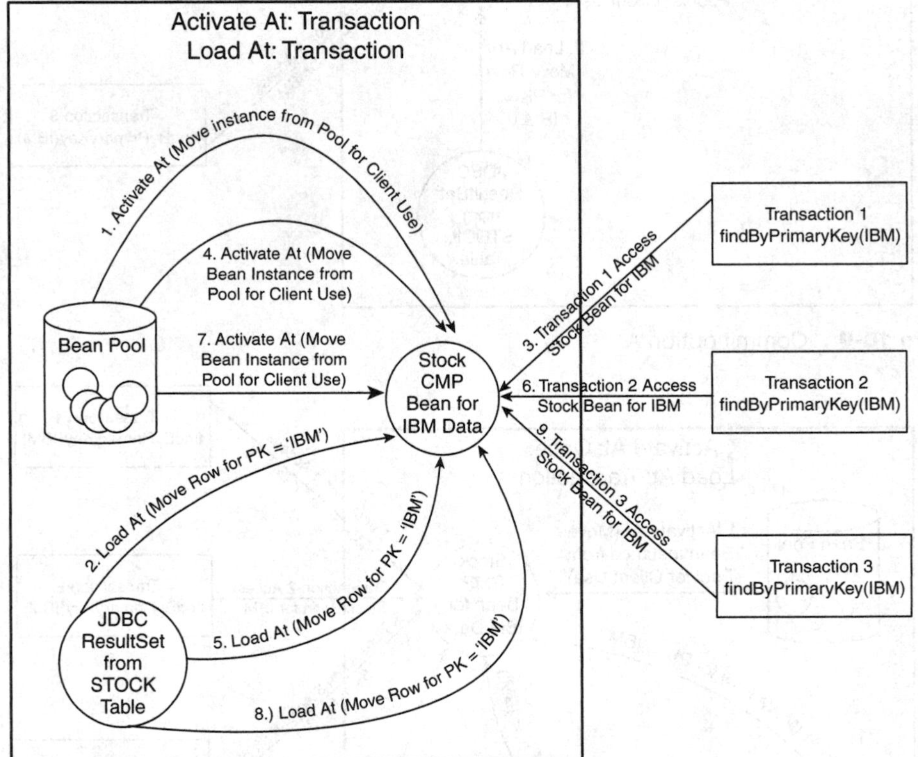


**Figure 10-11** Commit option C.

- **Setting Activate At to ACTIVITY SESSION and Load at to TRANSACTION**—In version 5 of WAS, this option is only available at the Enterprise Edition.[3] Activity Sessions will be explained in the next chapter.

The other possible combinations are not supported. Figure 10-12 summarizes the concepts.

As stated, the bean cache options can be configured using the deployment descriptor editor. The bean cache options also allow you to specify an expiration for bean instances that are cached, as shown in Figure 10-13.

3 Renamed to WBI Server Foundations in version 5.1.

| Load At \ Activate At | Once | Transaction | Activity Session |
|---|---|---|---|
| Activation | A | Unsupported | Unsupported |
| Transaction | B | C | C+ |

**Figure 10-12** EJB caching options.

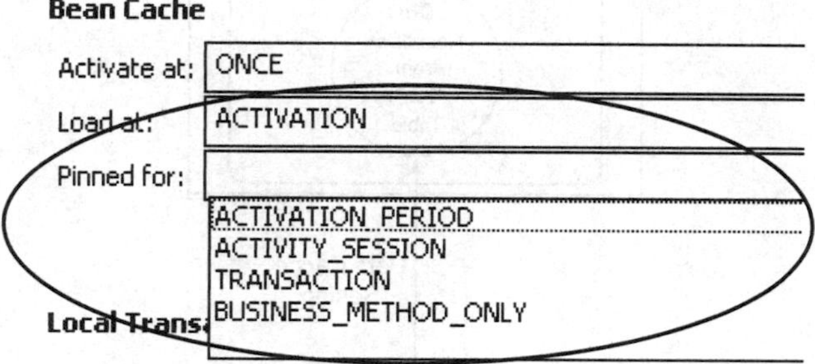


**Figure 10-13** Bean cache life cycle.

The option that controls the bean cache expiration is called Pinned for. In other words, it defines the expiration of the Activate at and Load at option. There are four possible settings:

- **ACTIVATION_PERIOD**—The period where the bean remains activated. The lifespan of this setting is controlled by the cleanup interval of the total bean cache illustrated back in Figure 10-5.
- **ACTIVITY_SESSION**—This option keeps the bean instance around for the Activity Session. Again, in version 5.X, this option is only available in the Enterprise Edition.
- **TRANSACTION**—Keeps the bean instance around only for the transaction scope. So for example, if you apply this option for commit option A, your bean instance will expire when the application issues a commit. This example is not too practical because it defeats the purpose of configuring a bean cache.
- **BUSINESS_METHOD_ONLY**—This setting keeps the bean cache around during the invocation of a business method. For example, not all business methods have transactions, so there has to be a way to specify how the bean should behave in these occurrences.

## Configuring EJB Data Cache

The EJB specification only addresses how bean instances are pooled but not necessarily how the underlying data is cached in the application server. In our example, as illustrated in Figure 10-14, the specification does not address how specifically data is cached in the JDBC ResultSet.

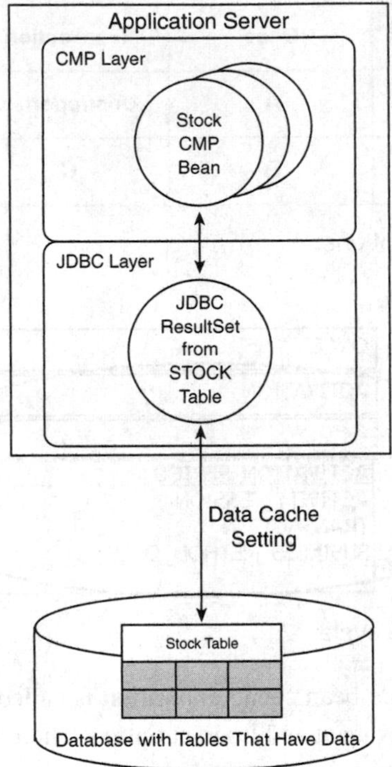


**Figure 10-14** Data cache settings.

WAS also allows you to configure caching for the underlying data. When data caching is configured, data is cached the first time the data is accessed. When making use of data caching, having a way to refresh caches can help in situations where data gets updated occasionally on the backend (for example, if some other user or system alters it). Figure 10-15 illustrates the data cache options. It is also accessible under the Bean tab under the IBM Extensions section.

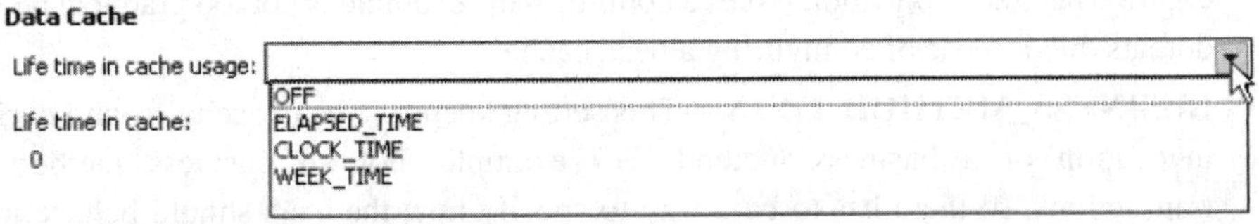

**Data Cache**

Life time in cache usage:
OFF
ELAPSED_TIME
CLOCK_TIME
WEEK_TIME

Life time in cache:
0

**Figure 10-15** Data cache.

There are two settings, as shown in Figure 10-15. The Life time in cache usage setting determines the expiration scheme used. This setting controls when the cache expires. Once a cache expires, the data will be reloaded when accessed again. There are four possible options:

- **CLOCK_TIME**—This value represents a particular time of day, in seconds. Using CLOCK_TIME enables you to specify that all instances of this bean type are to have their cached data invalidated at 12 AM. This setting is useful for data that may only be updated at a specific time (for example, a batch routine that runs each night at midnight). We will give an example of CLOCK_TIME in this section.
- **WEEK_TIME**—The same as CLOCK_TIME, except that cache is expired on a specified weekly basis. When WEEK_TIME is used, the value of Life time in cache can represent more than 24 hours but not more than 7 days.
- **ELAPSED_TIME**—The value of Life time in cache is added to the time at which the transaction in which the bean instance was retrieved is completed. The resulting value becomes the time at which the cached data expires. For example, if I set the value of ELAPSED_TIME to one hour, and the Entity Bean is accessed at 3:00 PM, the data will expire at 4:00 PM.
- **OFF**—The value of Life time in cache is ignored. Beans of this type are cached only in a transaction-scoped cache. The cached data for this instance expires after the transaction in which it was retrieved is completed.

The usage value helps determines what allowable values can be used for the Life time in cache value. For example, if you are using CLOCK_TIME, you need to be able to designate a time with values such as AM/PM. The EJB deployment descriptor editor is dynamic and accommodates the input control for the option. For example, Figure 10-16 illustrates how to enter the settings when the CLOCK_TIME is used.

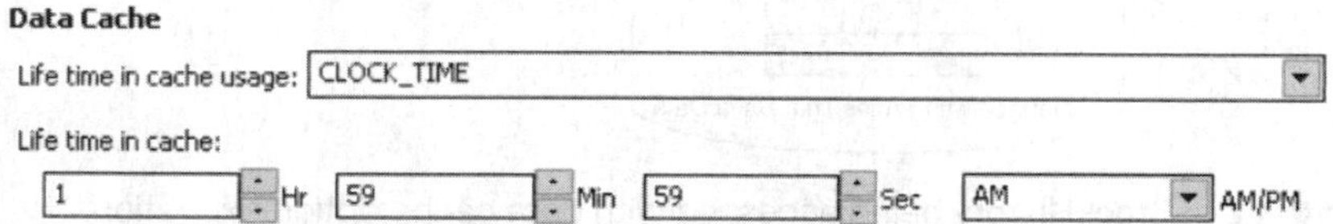


**Figure 10-16** Data cache with CLOCK_TIME.

The figure illustrates the setting of the StockHistory Entity Bean that we will deploy in this chapter. The StockHistory Entity Bean is updated every night by a batch job that starts at midnight. The batch job adds a new entry to the StockHistory Table, adding the daily activity. This is the only time that the StockHistory gets updated. Because of this, the StockHistory Entity Bean is invalidated at 1:59:59 AM. The next time the StockHistory is accessed, it will be loaded and cached until the next night. Figure 10-17 illustrates how the Stock History Entity Beans behaves in the data cache situation we just configured.

In order to accomplish data caching correctly, you must understand how your application accesses data.

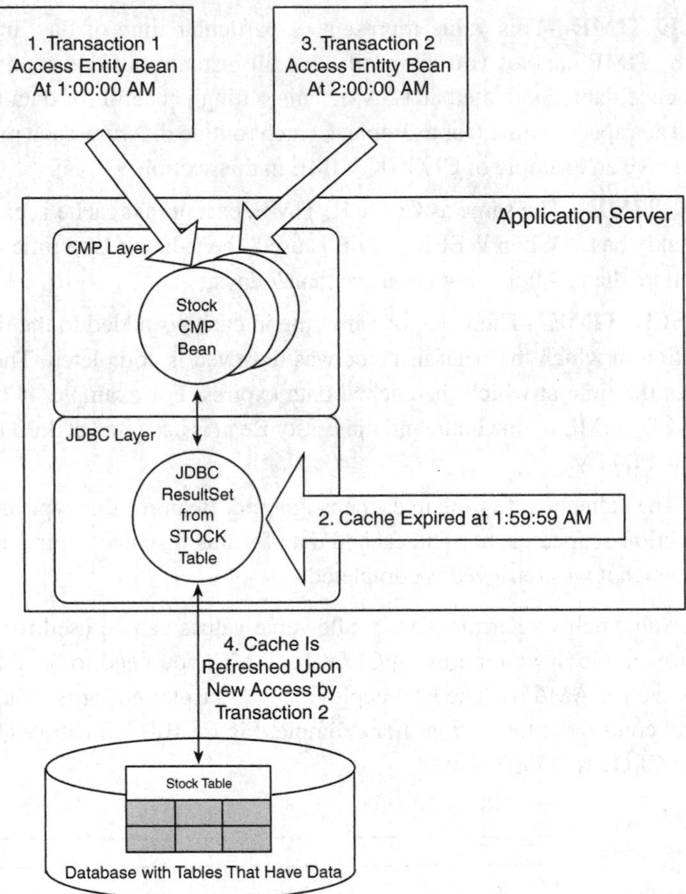


**Figure 10-17** StockHistory being accessed with data cache option expiration.

> **NOTE**
> The data cache options make sense when using commit option B and commit option C. Since commit option A caches the data in the bean instances, it will not reload data from the underlying JDBC objects and therefore make the data cache useless.

## Distributed Cache Synchronization

As of version 5.0.2 of WAS, the data cache can be programmatically invalidated. Explicit control can greatly increase cache usage. For example, if you programmatically invalidate the cache when a batch job completes, you will never have "stale" data as you would if the batch job finished at 12:30 AM and the cache is statically configured to invalidate at 2:00 AM. The cache can be invalidated and in fact can be invalidated in a distributed way. This explicit control can be applied, for example, to WAS in a clustered environment where the cache may be distributed to several servers. In order to make this mechanism work, WAS uses a broadcast mechanism. For example, Figure 10-18 gives an example of how the Stock Facade Session Bean updates the stock data and then invalidates the cache by programmatically calling the invalidation API. There are four steps here:

1. The client updates data that is tied to a cache. The other servers that are caching the data need to be notified.
2. The Stock Facade Session Bean calls the Invalidation API.
3. WAS receives the request and notifies all the data caches that are caching the data.
4. The cache is invalidated, and the Entity Bean refreshes the data cache upon the next access.

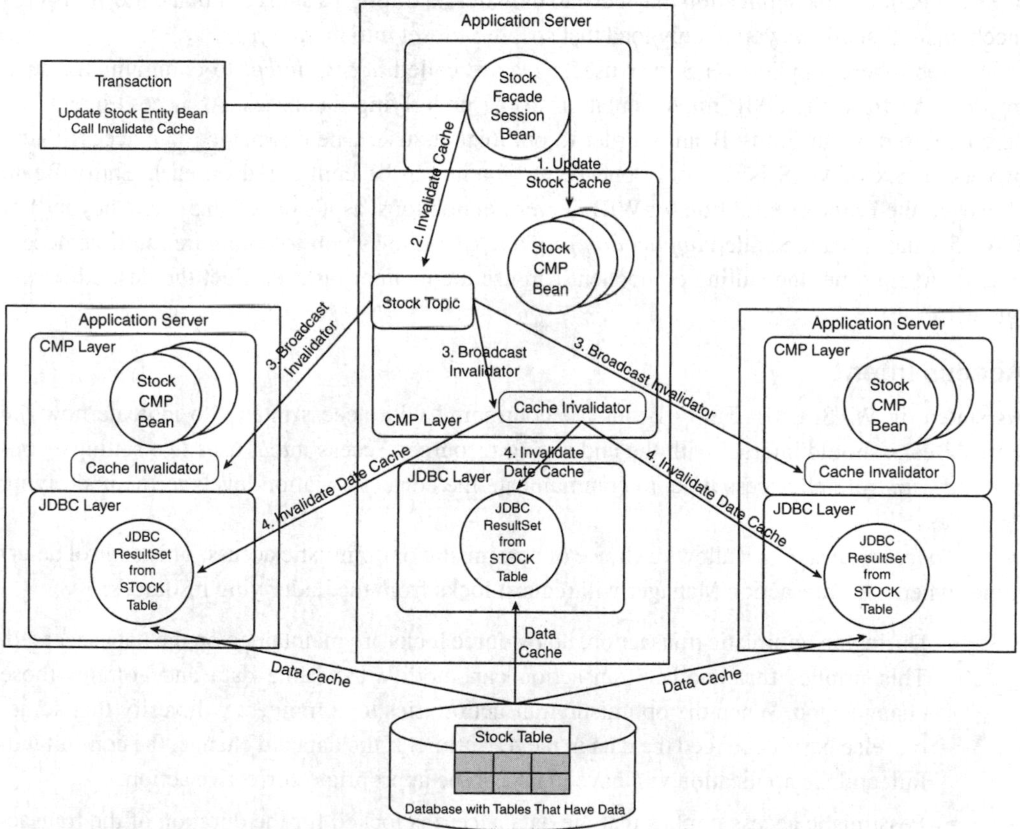


**Figure 10-18** Distributed cache.

The API is fairly simple but requires basic knowledge of the Java Messaging Service (JMS). WAS uses the JMS Publish and Subscribe model to implement the notification. JMS will be covered in Chapter 12, "JMS and Message Driven Beans." The WebSphere Information Center has the details of the invalidation API.[4]

## Dealing with Isolation Levels in CMP

In Chapter 7, we learned how JDBC uses resource references to communicate the desired isolation level to the underlying database. This allows the database to acquire the correct type of lock for the specific transaction. However, with CMP, the database layer is abstracted, and therefore we need a way to communicate desired isolation levels to the underlying data store. In addition, there are other settings that need finer-grain control. For example, earlier, we illustrated that we can have a collection of CMPs. An application may need to iterate through the collection. With large collections, the application may need to only iterate through a subset of that data. We need a mechanism that allows you to only load that specific subset into memory.

WebSphere Application Server uses a feature called *access intent* to communicate such information from the CMP implementation to the underlying databases. An access intent can be configured on an Entity Bean in order to optimize its use. One downside to an access intent in version 5.x of WAS is that only one access intent can be configured on each Entity Bean. However, the Enterprise Edition (or WBI Server Foundations, as it's called in 5.1 and beyond) of WAS 5.x has a feature called *application profiling* that allows you to configure multiple access intents. At runtime, the calling component can use a container task to select the desired access intent.

### Access Intent

As stated, in WAS, CMP Entity Beans are configured with access intents to indicate how the Entity Beans should interact with the underlying resource. Access intent uses two settings, concurrency control and access type, to communicate the correct isolation levels to the underlying database.

*Concurrency control* allows a choice of pessimistic or optimistic access. This control determines when the Transaction Manager will request locks from the underlying resources:

- During an optimistic transaction, no resource locks are maintained on the data accessed. This implies that another transaction can modify the same data and commit those changes, too. When the optimistic transaction tries to commit, it will verify that someone else hasn't changed the data in the meantime. If the data did change, the commit will fail, and the application will have to take some appropriate corrective action.
- Pessimistic access implies that the data access is locked for the duration of the transaction. At a minimum, no one else will be able to modify that EJB instance. The benefit of this option is that it provides maximum data integrity. The trade-off is paid in terms of concurrency since locking is required.

4 See the article, "Explicit Invalidation in the Persistence Manager Cache" (http://publib.boulder.ibm.com/infocenter/wasinfo/topic/com.ibm.websphere.nd.doc/info/ae/ae/rejb_lifetime.html).

Typically, optimistic approaches improve concurrency (meaning multiple transactions can be operating on the same data at the same time more frequently), and therefore throughput is increased, but the application needs to be structured in a way that it handles the problems that may occur if there is an update conflict. Pessimistic access is often easier to use but results in lower concurrency because locks are held for a longer duration.

*Access type* refers to whether an application intends to read or update an Entity Bean. Typically, read access results in less contention. In order to achieve the correct isolation level, the access type setting is combined with the concurrency setting to achieve the desired result. Read and update can be combined with optimistic and pessimistic approaches.

If you use pessimistic read, there is no way to escalate the intent later to perform an update. For example, if a transaction specifies read intent, and then it calls a method that actually updates, the container will throw UpdateCannotProceedWithIntegrityException. The container will prevent you from trying to load the same EJB in the same transaction using incompatible access intents.

If you start by loading an EJB with a pessimistic read intent and then subsequently try to load the same EJB with an update intent, you'll get the InconsistentAccessIntentException. Pessimistic update is the most stringent form of intent—the most demanding in terms of isolation. Three combinations are available for pessimistic update:

- **WeakestLockAtLoad**—This variation implies that, although the update intent is specified, a read lock is acquired first. Then, if the transaction really updates, a lock escalation will be pursued. This option allows for better concurrency than if an update lock was attempted at the beginning, but it may result in deadlocks. This is the default access intent for Entity EJBs in WebSphere.
- **Exclusive**—This implies that an update lock on instances is acquired immediately. Phantom and non-repeatable reads are also not admitted. This is the most restrictive option and has to be used with care when applied to large result sets, such as in finder methods.
- **No collision**—This option behaves like an exclusive lock but allows EJB instances to be cached in memory. Therefore, the isolation level requirements are not so stringent. However, this option can be used safely only if the database tables where the EJB are persisted aren't shared with any other program or even WAS servers, or else data inconsistency may occur.

As we stated, isolation information is not the only configurable attribute you can define on an access intent. An access intent also contains attributes to help deal with the loading of collections of Entity Beans. When dealing with collections, remember that we need to deal with both data loading into the underlying result sets as well as data being loaded from the result sets into the bean instance. Access intents affect both these settings. There are three settings:

- **Read-Ahead Hint**—This applies to Entity Beans with Container Managed Relationships. At the time a getByPrimaryKey is performed, the container uses the read-ahead hint to control optional prefetching of the data for the specified related objects.

For example, while getting a Stock Bean by primary key, the container could get not only the stock information but also the information for all the related stock history. This option is beneficial if the caller that is looking up the stock is then going to be using the related StockHistory Beans. This is illustrated in Figure 10-19.

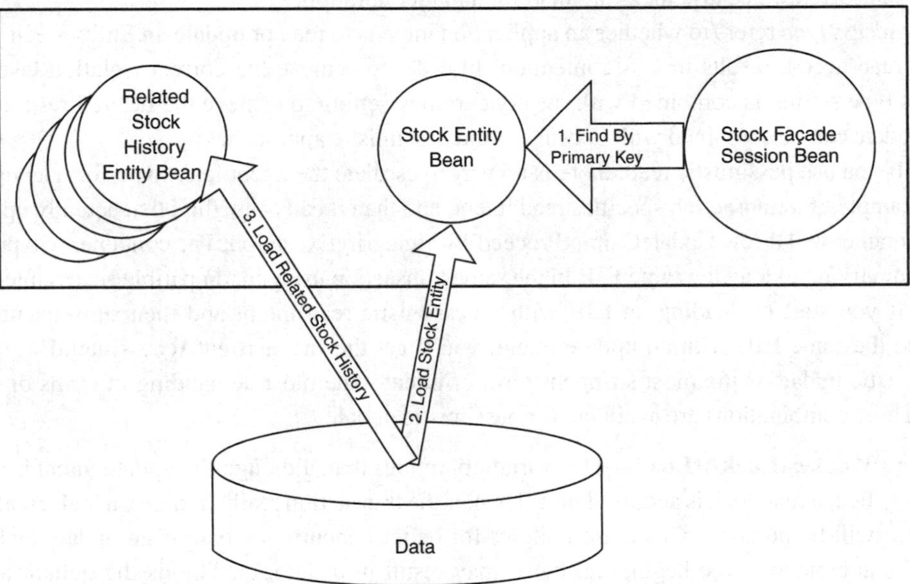


**Figure 10-19** Container loading related beans with read-ahead hint.

> **NOTE**
> The CMP specification has certain restrictions when using collections that are tied by a relationship. For example, a collection accessed through a CMR-based collection reference is only valid in the same transaction in which it was fetched. This is the default behavior; however, certain settings in WAS may allow you to break portability. These can increase performance but affect the portability of the application.

- **Collection Scope**—This controls the life cycle for collections that are not preloaded (which means there is no read-ahead hint configured). When you call a finder method optimistically (as defined in the previous section), you get a lazy collection back from the container (a collection without the data loaded). The collection can be loaded in memory "in chunks" so that as you iterate through it, the elements that you are looking for are already in memory. However, as stated in the previous note, such a lazy collection will normally expire at the transaction boundary. You can extend this scope by specifying "activity session" for the collection scope and have the collection survive multiple transactions, as long as they all take place within the same activity session (as stated, this will affect the portability of your CMP implementation). Activity Sessions will be described in the next chapter. The *Collection Increment* is used to control the number of instances to be pre-fetched.

- **Resource Manager Pre-Fetch Increment**—This suggests how many RDB rows should be preloaded in a single operation. As stated, the data from a database is first loaded into a result set. The pre-fetch increment represents how data is loaded into the result set. Setting this translates to setting fetch size in the JDBC API. This parameter may be completely ignored by a number of database implementations that have their own optimization mechanisms for pre-fetching data. In some cases, this number may differ from the collection increment discussed before (which controls the number of instances to be pre-fetched in the WebSphere cache). For instance, you may have a data mapping where a single instance is scattered across multiple tables.

Figure 10-20 illustrates both the Collection Scope and Resource Manager Pre-Fetch.

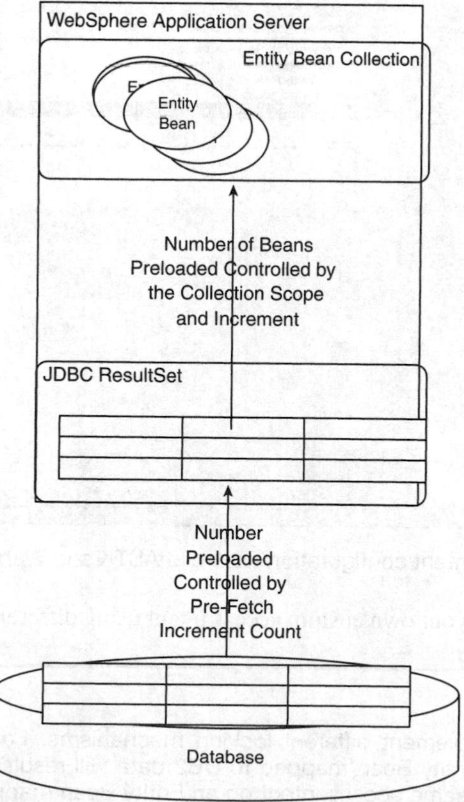


**Figure 10-20** Pre-Fetch versus Collection Increment Count.

When configuring an access intent on an Entity Bean, you can select one of the predefined access types, as shown in Figure 10-21. These predefined types match the access type and concurrency control options we described before:

- wsOptimisticRead
- wsOptimisticUpdate
- wsPessimisticRead
- wsPessimisticUpdate
- wsPessimisticUpdate-WeakestLockAtLoad
- wsPessimisticUpdate-Exclusive
- wsPessimisticUpdate-NoCollision

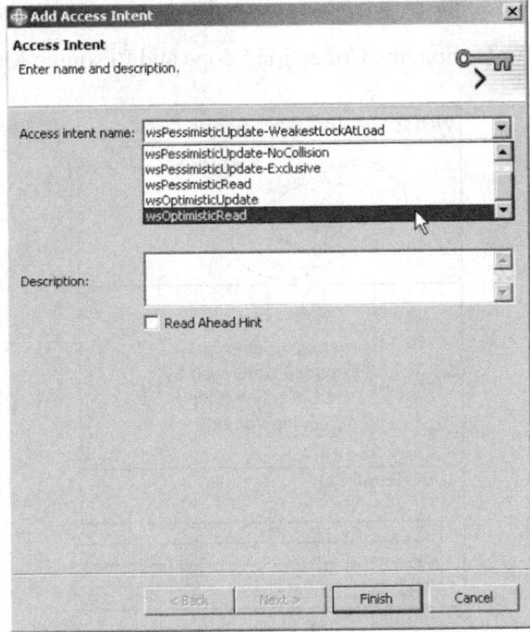


**Figure 10-21** Access Intent configuration wizard in ASTK and WebSphere Studio.

You can also create your own custom access intent using different combinations of settings.

> **NOTE**
> Database vendors implement different locking mechanisms. For example, a particular access intent on an Entity Bean mapped to DB2 data will result in DB2 having different locks than that of the same access intent on an Entity Bean mapped to Oracle data. The WAS Info Center contains information on isolation levels and access intent inside WAS and their mappings in various databases.

## Application Profiling

In some scenarios, there is the need for J2EE applications to be able to specify different access intents on the same Entity Beans depending on the business task that is using them. For example, an application may have an Entity Bean representing a bank account. When the end user is just checking his balance, the access intent is to read the data. However, when making a withdrawal or deposit, the application access intent is to update the data.

Unfortunately, access intent is statically associated with the methods of the Entity Beans. Once the intent is defined on a method, any client calling that method will use the same intent. So to accomplish dynamic access behavior, the developer would have to create two Entity Beans, one called AccountRead and one called AccountUpdate. Both Entity Beans would be mapped to the same table. Having to create multiple Entity Beans for the same data is wasteful for a programmer. With *application profiling*, the intent can be associated with a "task." This feature makes it possible to fine-tune the data access behavior of applications based on the specific needs of each use case. This function is called application profiling because it allows you to associate a certain data access profile with individual application tasks. Figure 10-22 illustrates the concept. The calling Session Bean is marked with a task. Based on the task, the correct access intent is used by the Entity Bean.

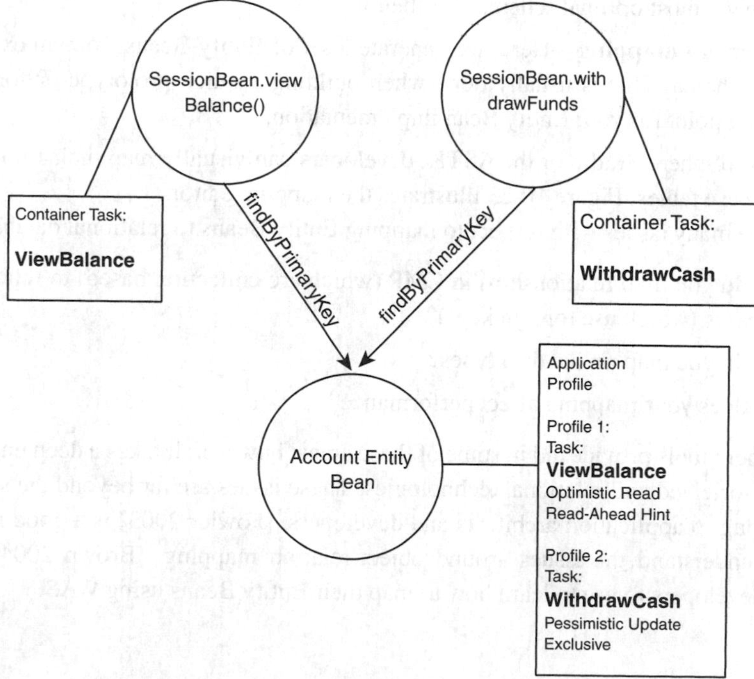


**Figure 10-22** Application profile.

The application profiling feature is available in the Enterprise Edition of WebSphere Application Server version 5.x.[5] Using this approach greatly simplifies the programming model and provides a powerful way to control Entity Bean behavior.

## Schema Mapping

Entity Beans need to be mapped to the underlying data representation. WAS application developers who deploy Entity Beans usually make use of the tools provided within WebSphere Studio or the ASTK to map Entity Beans to the underlying data store. WAS provides three different ways to map a set of Entity Beans to an underlying data store:

- **Top-down mapping**—This mapping generates an actual database schema out of an existing set of Entity Beans. With this methodology, no database exists yet, and the Entity Bean model will be used to create your database. Top-down mapping can be generated at application deployment time as well.
- **Meet-in-the-middle mapping**—Here, we map an existing set of Entity Beans to an existing data base. This is the most common mapping technique since most applications are built around an existing database and because both developers and DBAs want to create the most optimal schemas for their use.
- **Bottom-up mapping**—Here, we generate a set of Entity Beans from an existing database schema. This is usually done when building a quick prototype or for creating a starting point for your Entity Bean implementation.

Using WebSphere Studio or the ASTK, developers can visually map their Entity Beans to relational database tables. Figure 10-23 illustrates the mapping editor.

There are many issues with respect to mapping Entity Beans to relational databases:

- How do you map relationships in CMP (which are collection based) to relationships in databases (which use foreign keys)?
- How do you map unlike data types?
- How does your mapping affect performance?

WebSphere tools provide aid in some of these areas; however, it takes a deep understanding of both object-oriented and relational technologies. These issues are far beyond the scope of this book and belong to application architects and developers. [Fowler 2003] is a good resource for architects to understand the issues around object-relation mapping. [Brown 2004] is a good resource for developers to use to learn how to map their Entity Beans using WAS.

5 In version 5.1, WAS Enterprise is called WBI Server Foundations.

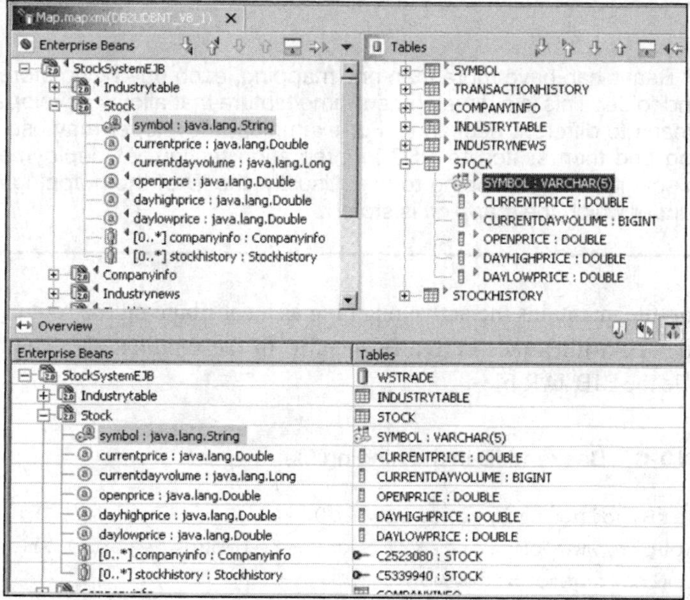


**Figure 10-23** CMP Mapping Editor.

It is not uncommon, however, for an assembler or deployer to import an EAR file into the ASTK and open the mapping file to examine the mappings. The mapping file is called map.mapxmi. It is located under the backend folder within the META-INF directory, as shown in Figure 10-24.

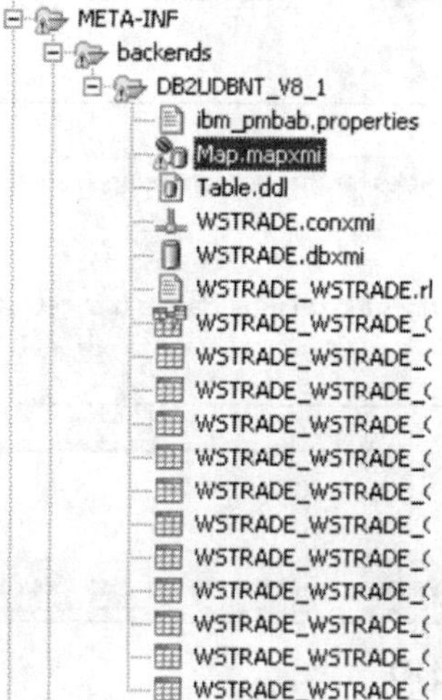


**Figure 10-24** Map file location.

> **NOTE**
>
> A set of CMP Beans can have more than one mapping, each one being stored in an individual backend folder. This is a development-time feature that allows developers to switch their Entity Beans to different backends. For example, a developer may use Cloudscape for unit testing and then switch to DB2 in integration testing. At deployment time, the deployer can specify which mapping to use. Usually, the ID of the mapping matches the folder name under which the mapping is stored.

The binding file maintains the active mapping as an attribute on the root tag of the binding file. Code Snippet 10-6 illustrates currentBackendId in the binding file. The ID matches the folder name inside the EJB JAR file.

**Code Snippet 10-6** Backend ID in the binding file

```
<ejbbnd:EJBJarBinding xmi:version="2.0"
xmlns:xmi="http://www.omg.org/XMI" xmlns:ejbbnd="ejbbnd.xmi" xmlns:ejb=
➥"ejb.xmi" xmlns:common="common.xmi"
xmi:id="EJBJarBinding_1040603043703" currentBackendId="DB2UDBNT_V8_1">

...

</ejbbnd:EJBJarBinding>
```

This entry can be set on the overview page of the deployment descriptor editor, as shown in Figure 10-25.

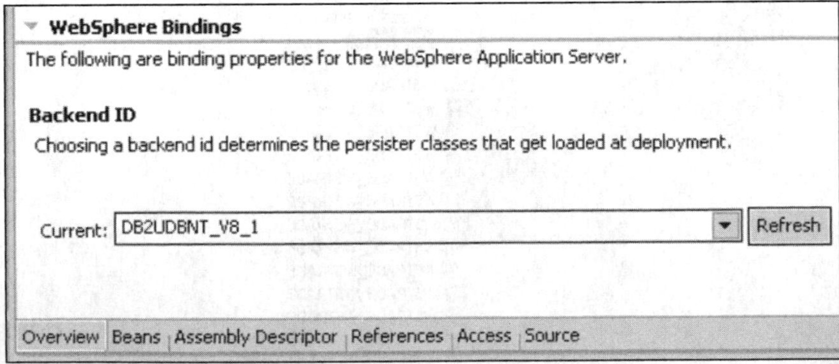


**Figure 10-25** Current backend ID.

## So Why Does the Deployer Care?

CMP is an abstraction of data access code such as JDBC. The JDBC code for CMPs is generated by WebSphere Application Server (WAS) tools. The code is generated based on the mapping between the data access layer and the beans themselves. The mapping is maintained in a file and used as metadata to properly generate code. The abstraction layer presents a challenge for diagnosing errors. This means that there will be two levels of errors, one for the CMP abstract layer and one for the generated data access layer. Many times, developers need both errors to fix problems with mappings or CMP code. Figure 10-26 illustrates how the layering in CMP affects the different roles involved and how they may translate to runtime errors.

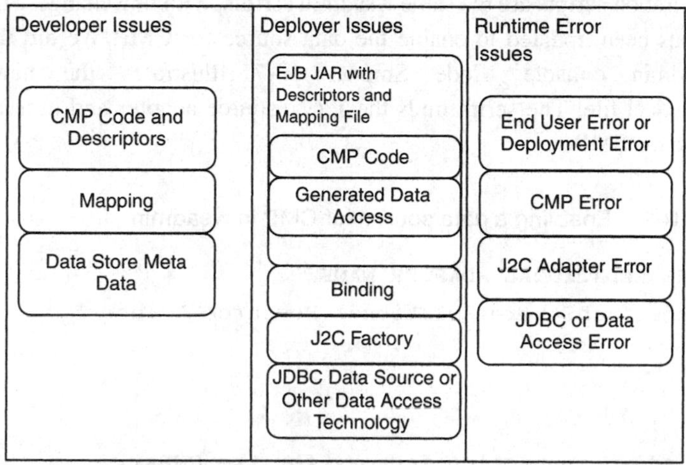


**Figure 10-26** Affect of CMP to various roles.

The concepts in the figure summarize what we have explained in this chapter. Often, applications have a mix of non-CMP data access code and CMP code, making diagnosing errors more of a challenge. In general, a deployer and administrator will have to interact directly with developers to understand how to solve errors.

WAS trace helps diagnose many errors, as we learned in Chapter 5, "WebSphere Application Server Architecture." To deal with CMP errors, you can use the following trace strings:

- **RRA=all=enabled:PMGR=all=enabled**—This shows the underlying SQL for the CMP executed at runtime.
- **com.ibm.ws.ejbpersistence.*=all=enabled**—This shows persistence manager trace messages.
- **com.ibm.ws.rsadapter.*=all=enabled**—This shows WAS interacting with various resource adapters.
- **com.ibm.ws.db2.*=all=enabled**—This shows WAS interacting with DB2.[6]

The WAS Info Center also has different trace string options.

6 Similar trace strings can be enabled for specific databases.

## Automation

Now that we have discussed CMP and some advanced EJB settings, we will deploy a new version of the Personal Trade System Application. This time, the application will be more complete and will contain most of the use cases introduced in the beginning of the book, except for the actual Trade execution, which will be added later in this book. CMP is used to implement the data access layer. Some of the settings talked about in this chapter are used in this version of the application. As an exercise for yourself, you may want to import the resulting EAR file into an ASTK or WebSphere Studio workspace and view the options we used for access intent and caching. We will use our build process to deploy the application.

The configuration scripts are the same wsadmin scripts, with one change—the Data Source Creation script has been updated to enable the data source for CMP. We did this last chapter through the admin console. Code Snippet 10-7 illustrates the new portion of CreateDataSource.jacl file. The script finds the J2C resource adapter and uses it to enable the JDBC data source for CMP.

**Code Snippet 10-7** Enabling a data source for CMP in wsadmin

```
#SET WEBSPHERE RELATIONAL ADAPTER NAME
set adapterName "WebSphere Relational Resource Adapter"

...

#Now we will add a connection factory for the CMPs..
puts "Creating the CMP Connector Factory for WSTradeDS"
puts "Finding the Resource Adapter"
set rsadapter [$AdminConfig list J2CResourceAdapter $cellID]
set attrs12 [subst {{name $cmpDSName} {authMechanismPreference
➥BASIC_PASSWORD} {cmpDatasource $ds1}}]
set cf1 [$AdminConfig create CMPConnectorFactory $rsadapter $attrs12]

#Set the properties for the data source.
set authDataAliasList [list authDataAlias $aliasName ]
set mappingConfigAliasList [list mappingConfigAlias
DefaultPrincipalMapping ]
set mappingList [list $authDataAliasList $mappingConfigAliasList]

$AdminConfig create MappingModule $cf1 $mappingList
```

We also have a build script for the EJB project. Besides compiling and packaging the EJB, the EJB build script also uses the WAS EJB Deploy ANT task to generate the EJB deploy code. Code Snippet 10-8 illustrates how we use the WAS EJB deploy ANT task.

**Code Snippet 10-8** ejbDeploy ANT task

```
<target name="generateejbdeploy" depends="buildejb">
  <wsejbdeploy inputJar="${ejbjardir}/${predeployjar}"
          wasHome="${wasroot}"
          outputJar="${ejbjardir}/${ejbjarname}"
          failonerror="false"
          trace="false" />
</target>
```

The EJB ANT task takes an EJB JAR without deployment code and creates a new EJB JAR with the generated code.

> **NOTE**
> You can generate the code either as a separate step, as shown previously, or at deployment time as an attribute into the Install ANT task. However, this means that the deploy code needs to be generated for every environment in which the same EAR is deployed.

You are ready to begin:

1. Like the previous chapters, create a new repository in CVS and call it C:/cvs_chapter10.
2. Extract C:\WASDeployBook\Chapter10\cvs_chapter10.zip into the new repository.
3. Next, run the C:\WASDeployBook\Chapter10\CreateDBScript.bat script in a DB2 command window to create the tables needed for this exercise.
4. Next, let's run the build process we described previously. From the command prompt, go to the C:\WASDeployBook\Chapter10\ANTBuildScripts directory and enter **RunBuildProcess buildDeployVerifyNoStop**.
5. Examine the command prompt as before. Notice that first the server is configured. As stated, the data source creation also includes enabling it for CMP, as shown in Figure 10-27.

```
[wsadmin] Installing DataSource

[wsadmin] Creating the datasource WSTradeDS

[wsadmin] j2eeresourceproperty
[wsadmin] Creating the CMP Connector Factory for WSTradeDS
[wsadmin] Finding the Resource Adapter

[wsadmin] Saving configuration

[wsadmin] Done Creating Data Source
```

**Figure 10-27** Enabling data source for CMP.

As stated, another difference is that the EJB build process includes generating the EJB deployment code. Figure 10-28 shows a portion of the EJB deploy screen.

```
generateejbdeploy:
[wsejbdeploy] Working Directory does not exist. Creating.

[wsejbdeploy]

[wsejbdeploy] Starting workbench.

[wsejbdeploy]

[wsejbdeploy]   20031007_1915-WB212-AD-V511D-W5
[wsejbdeploy]

[wsejbdeploy] Creating the project.

[wsejbdeploy]

[wsejbdeploy]   Creating EJB Project...
[wsejbdeploy]

[wsejbdeploy]   Creating EJB Project... Opening: /StockSystemEJBPreDeploy
[wsejbdeploy]
```

**Figure 10-28** Generate EJB deployment code.

Once the build is complete, you can examine the verification test by going to c:\testreport and opening index.html. There should be two test suites—one for the model layer and the other for the web layer. Figure 10-29 illustrates the test suites.

**Unit Test Results**

**Package com.deploybook.verification.test**

**Classes**

| Name |
|---|
| ModelLayerVerficationTest |
| WebLayerVerificationTest |

**Figure 10-29** Verification test.

Examine the test results of the various use cases.

6. Once you have examined the test results, open a new browser, go to http://localhost:9080/pts, and log in as user **bbird** and password **password1a**. The menu has

more choices, as shown in Figure 10-30. Examine the application by going through the various menus and exercising the application. Everything except an actual trade execution is implemented.

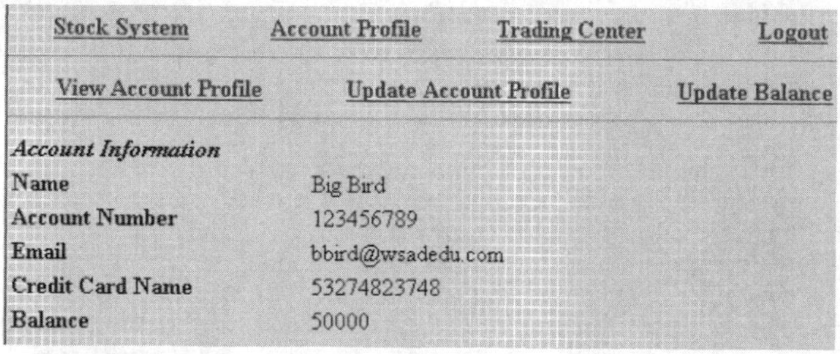

Stock System Account Profile Trading Center Logout

View Account Profile Update Account Profile Update Balance

| *Account Information* | |
|---|---|
| Name | Big Bird |
| Account Number | 123456789 |
| Email | bbird@wsadedu.com |
| Credit Card Name | 53274823748 |
| Balance | 50000 |

**Figure 10-30** Account Profile page.

7. Undeploy and stop the application by running the same BAT file and passing in the UndeployStop target as shown: **RunBuildProcess UndeployStop**.

## Conclusion

In this chapter, we provided a more thorough explanation of CMP Entity Beans. We illustrated the WAS Persistence Manager and the services that it provides. We also illustrated the various caching options for EJBs. Specifically, we showed that WAS caches both at the bean level and the underlying ResultSet level. In addition to caching, we illustrated how WAS uses access intents and application profiling to allow Entity Bean implementation to optimize database access. Finally, as in previous chapters, we provided an automated example of deployment.

Careful design and rigorous testing should be applied when using many of the options described in this chapter. Incorrect tuning of these settings can lead to horrible performance and even data inconsistency. Many of the settings described in this chapter require strong knowledge of transaction management for correct tuning. For that reason, we will shift our focus to WAS transactional support in the next chapter.

CHAPTER 11

# Transactions with WebSphere Application Server

WebSphere Application Server (WAS) targets applications that interact with data from enterprise data sources. Enterprise applications are not simple applications. They often perform significant non-trivial actions that require multiple steps. For example, a typical bank money transfer application needs to move money from one account to another. This actually involves deducting money from one account in some resource and depositing funds into another account, possibly in a different resource. Consider what would happen if the application fails right after the deduction step. Because the money was never deposited into the target account, if some specific compensating action isn't taken, money will actually disappear, and the system will be inconsistent. This problem is addressed through the use of transactions. This chapter focuses on the transactional support in WAS, which includes the mandated J2EE function as well as significant enhancements. In this chapter, we will introduce some transactional concepts and provide an overview of how J2EE applications use transactions. We also describe some advanced features of the WAS transaction manager as well as how to handle transactional failure scenarios. Finally, we introduce some troubleshooting techniques.

## Introduction to Transactions

A transaction is a logical unit of work with one or more operations. The operations succeed or fail as a single unit. Thus, if we return to our example from a moment ago, if the application fails prior to completing the money transfer, all intermediate steps are undone. It's as if they never occurred. What makes transactions so powerful is that the "undo" step is done automatically by the transactional system. A programmer is not required to code undo operations.[1] The programmer simply starts a transaction (implicitly or explicitly) and then performs a series of

1 Undo actions are sometimes referred to as compensating transactions.

transactional operations against resources. If anything goes wrong, the transactional system will ensure that the steps are rolled back.

Those who are interested in learning more about transactions from the developer's perspective should refer to [Brown 2004].

## ACID Properties

We just informally defined transactions, but a more formal definition is important. A system is considered to be transactional if it meets the following properties, often referred to as ACID:

- **Atomic**—A transaction must execute completely or not at all.
- **Consistent**—The application logic or data store settings do not allow for inconsistent data.
- **Isolated**—A transaction must be allowed to execute without interference from other processes or transactions.
- **Durable**—All the data changed during the course of a transaction must be written to some type of "permanent" data store before the transaction is successfully completed. This means that if the system fails after committing a transaction, it is expected that the data changes made will be recovered after the restart—that is, they are persistent.

Transactions can be applied to different type of data stores as well as messaging systems. In J2EE, we refer to these as resources. Resources involved in a transaction are controlled by a Resource Manager (RM). It is up to the RM to enforce and guarantee that the ACID properties are maintained for transactions using that resource. Typically, relational database management systems (RDBMS), such as IBM DB2 and messaging-based systems, including Java Message Service (JMS) providers such as IBM WebSphere MQ, can fulfill the roles of *Resource Managers*.

## Transactional Scope

In order for operations to be grouped together, they must be under the same transactional scope. There are various ways to scope transactions, but in general, they accomplish the same thing. There is usually some *begin* operation that starts the transaction. Then there is either a *commit* operation or a *rollback* operation that ends the transaction. All of the resource operations between the beginning and end operations are part of the same transaction. If any of the operations fail, the transaction is rolled back. J2EE developers can also explicitly call a rollback operation to force an undo of any of the previous operations under the same transaction. The piece of code that controls the scope of the transaction, whether it is generated, hard-coded in the application, or coded in the database, is said to *demarcate* the transaction. Data that is updated in a transaction is called *uncommitted* until the commit operation occurs. Transactional scope can be extended using concepts such as nested transactions, compensating transactions, or extended transactions. These concepts are beyond the scope of this book. [Smolenski] is a good resource for those who are interested.

## Distributed Transactions

J2EE provides for distributed transactions. That is, in addition to the simple case of a single resource accessed from a single application server, J2EE application servers support multiple resources being accessed from multiple application servers participating in the same transaction. Essentially, a transaction with a single resource is referred to as a *local transaction*, while a transaction that spans multiple resources or application servers is referred to as a *distributed* (or global) *transaction*. Distributed transactions must adhere to the same ACID properties as non-distributed transactions, but there is an inherent complexity revolving around the synchronization of the participants (or resources). Since the coordination of several Resource Managers is necessary in this case, J2EE application servers such as WAS provide a *Transaction Manager (TM)*. The TM is responsible for coordinating with all of the RMs involved in a single transaction.

The *two-phase commit protocol (2PC)* has been widely adopted as the protocol of choice for coordinating distributed transactions. It is based on the Open System Interconnection (OSI/DTP) standard. This protocol guarantees that the work is either successfully completed by all participants (Resource Managers and other Transaction Managers) or not performed at all. The goal is to ensure that each participant in a global transaction takes the same action (everybody commits or everybody rolls back). The TM initiates the two-phase commit after all of the work of the transaction is complete and needs to be committed. The flow is as follows:

1. **First phase**—All participants are asked by the TM to *prepare* to commit. If a given RM can guarantee to commit its work, it replies affirmatively, agreeing to accept the outcome decided by the TM. Once this is done, the RM can no longer unilaterally abort the transaction. The RM is said to be in the ready-to-commit or *prepared state*. If a Resource Manager cannot guarantee that it will be able to commit, it responds negatively to the prepare request and rolls back its work (unilateral rollback).
2. **Second phase**—A Transaction Manager tells all Resource Managers to *commit* if all are in the ready-to-commit (prepared) state. Otherwise, the TM tells all RMs to roll back. All RMs commit or roll back as directed and return status to the TM. If an RM returns a failure at this stage, it is violating the 2PC protocol, and this is considered heuristic damage. Such failures should never occur, but unfortunately, we do occasionally see these problems. In that case, the outcome is not transactional, and manual intervention is required.

In order for a TM to communicate with RMs as part of a 2PC protocol, a standard interface is desired. The standard interface used is the *XA interface*. This interface defines the XA APIs used by the Transaction Manager when talking to transactional Resource Managers, as well as TX APIs for applications that are controlling the transaction. Keep in mind that in J2EE applications, standard Java APIs are defined that wrap the function of XA and TX; thus, neither is directly used, but it is helpful to understand the basic model of interaction. As you look at Figure 11-1, also notice that applications use the Resource Manager API such as JDBC to interact with the resource.

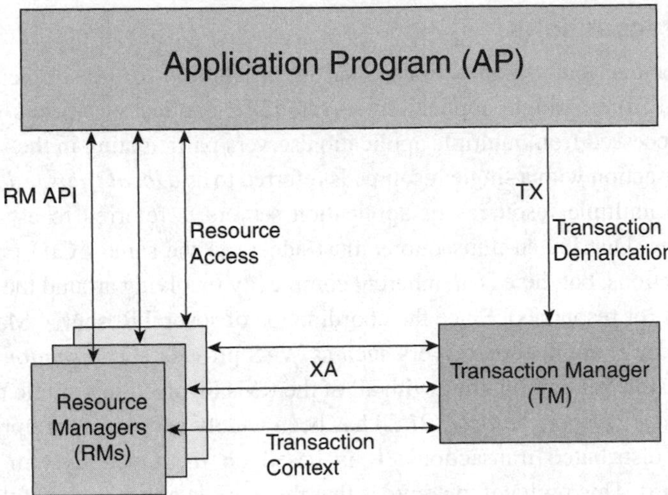


**Figure 11-1** XA contract.

If Resource Managers and Transaction Managers follow the contract, applications that use multiple resources can expect there to be a single global transaction. Figure 11-2 illustrates a more complete picture of WebSphere Application Server playing the role of TM coordinating an XA transaction between a JDBC Provider and a JMS Provider. The diagram is complex as it shows far more detail regarding how WAS internal components interact with the Resource Managers. From an administrator's standpoint, it is important to understand the phases of the transactional process. The figure illustrates a complete, successful 2PC commit. During steps 1–11, the application is executing its business logic. The Transaction Manager also does some initial setup. However, the 2PC has not started yet. It is not until step 12 where the 2PC starts. Let's go over the steps in Figure 11-2:

1. The application issues a begin, either explicitly through the Java Transaction API (JTA) or implicitly by the EJB container.
2. The Transaction Manager *enlists* the JDBC resource. This is usually triggered by the application asking for a JDBC connection.
3. The application issues a JDBC operation, such as an INSERT.
4. The application closes the JDBC connection.
5. The Transaction Manager *delists* the resource when the application is done with it.
6. The application asks for a JMS session. The Transaction Manager enlists the JMS resource.
7. The application issues a JMS operation; in this example, the application publishes a message.

8. The application closes the JMS session, marking that it is done with the resource.
9. The Transaction Manager delists the JMS resource.
10. The application issues a commit, either implicitly through the EJB container or explicitly through the JTA API.
11. The WAS Transaction Manager writes transaction and XA resource information to the transaction log. This is only done once for a resource. Subsequent XA transactions with the same resource will not have this step.

    At this point, the Transaction Manager starts the 2PC process.
12. The Transaction Manager asks the JDBC resource to prepare to commit. The underlying resource will write its transaction record to its log. Then the resource returns a vote of "yes."
13. Next, the Transaction Manager asks for the JMS resource to "prepare" to commit. The resource returns a vote of "yes."
14. At this point, the Transaction Manager writes the information to its transaction log. This is the first time that the WebSphere Application Server writes the information needed to recover a transaction in the prepare phase. The end of this operation marks the end of the prepare phase. At this point, the logs have enough information to handle most recovery scenarios because all of the resources have prepared to commit and thus have written records to their logs.
15. The Transaction Manager now asks the JDBC resource to commit the work. This means making the logged information permanent.
16. The Transaction Manager asks the JMS resource to commit its work.
17. The Transaction Manager records the success of the commit. This marks the end of the 2PC process.
18. The commit method returns to the application. The application code at this point can assume the work has been persisted and committed.

We've described here the normal situation where everything works as it should. As you might imagine, things can sometimes go wrong. Later in this chapter, we will cover recovery scenarios for when things go wrong.

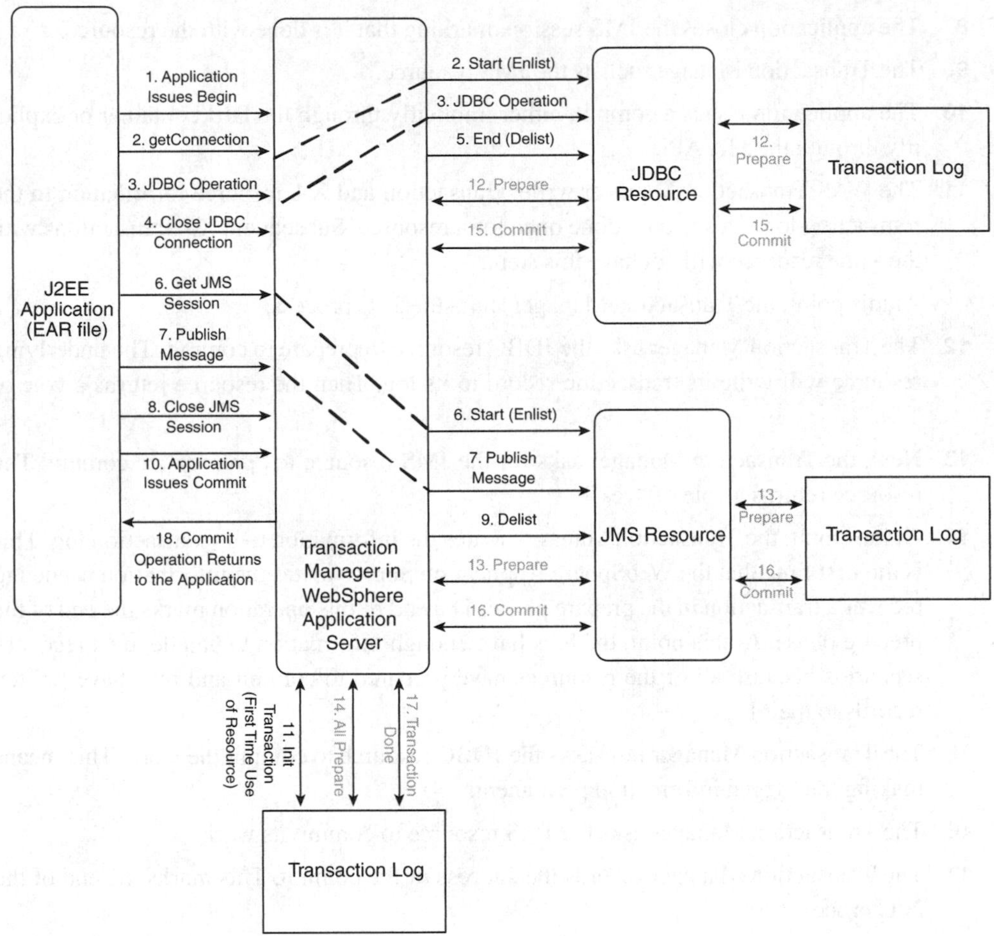


**Figure 11-2** 2PC.

## J2EE Applications and Transactions

We've discussed some of the basics of transactions, and now we'll turn our attention to how J2EE supports transactions. The J2EE specification defines several standards that application servers and J2EE applications need to follow. Although many of the details are more relevant to developers, an understanding of the J2EE model is important.

### J2EE Transaction Model

There are two important APIs in the J2EE transaction model: the Java Transaction Service (JTS) and the Java Transaction API (JTA). JTS is the Java implementation of OMG Object Transaction Model (OTS). OTS is a low-level API that allowed CORBA developers to work with transaction managers and resource managers directly. JTS is used internally by the application server to flow transactions over the IIOP protocol (the protocol defined by the CORBA specification) to other EJB applications in an interoperable way.

Because JTS development is difficult, the JTA API was introduced. The JTA API contains some low-level APIs as well as a high-level API. The low-level APIs are used by the J2EE container behind the scenes. The high-level API is meant for use by applications. This API is known as the UserTransaction object. UserTransaction includes some simple demarcation methods, such as begin, commit, and rollback. The UserTransaction object is accessible programmatically via JNDI and also on the EJB context.

## Using Transactions

J2EE applications can manage their transactions declaratively or programmatically. For programmatic management, applications that need container support must use the UserTransaction object. Web applications use JNDI to access this object, while EJB applications can access the UserTransaction object through the EJB context object. Alternatively, applications also can rely on the API provided by the native resource, such as JDBC, to manage transactions, but this is not recommended because it is outside container control. This is particularly important since only the container can manage two-phase commit transactions. Furthermore, writing code to the resource transactional APIs forever limits that code from participating in Container Managed Transactions and may severely hinder reuse. If two components need to be used together in one transaction, this is impossible without changing the code if the components use native resource transactions.

Code Snippet 11-1 illustrates an example of how web or J2EE client applications programmatically demarcate transactions.

**Code Snippet 11-1** Sample web application code

```
//LOOKUP UserTransaction OBJECT in the JNDI
UserTransaction bmtTran = ( UserTransaction ) initialContext.lookup
➥("java:comp/env/UserTransaction");
   try {
...

     //  Begin the transaction processing
     bmtTran.begin();
     // execute business logic within the transaction context

     ...
     // Successfully End the transaction process
     bmtTran.commit();
   } catch ( Exception ex )
   {
```

```
        // Rollback the transaction in event of an exception
        bmtTran.rollback();
        ...
    }
```

## Enterprise JavaBeans

Enterprise JavaBeans can manage transactions implicitly or explicitly. In Chapter 9, "Enterprise JavaBeans," we introduced Container Managed Transactions (CMT). This is how the EJB technology implicitly manages transactions. Code Snippet 11-2 highlights a portion of the EJB deployment descriptor illustrated in Chapter 9. Under the bean definition, a developer specifies 'Container' to indicate that transactions are going to be managed by the container. A developer can also choose Bean, which means that the developer is explicitly coding transaction control inside the EJB business methods using the JTA or the Resource Manager's API. CMP Entity Beans, however, always use CMT.

**Code Snippet 11-2** Choosing to use Container Managed Transactions

```
<!--  SESSION BEAN DEFINITION -->
<session id="StockFacade">
    <!--  EJB NAME AND CLASSES THAT MAKE UP THE EJB -->
        <ejb-name>StockFacade</ejb-name>
...

<!-- WHO HANDLES THE TRANSACTION?  CONTAINER OR YOUR OWN CODE -->
        <transaction-type>Container</transaction-type>
...
</session>
```

Under Container Managed Transactions, the developer then selects one of the six transactional attributes we defined in Chapter 9. These attributes are relevant only for an EJB that uses Container Managed Transactions. Code Snippet 11-3 illustrates a bean that is specifying the transaction REQUIRED attribute.

**Code Snippet 11-3** Specifying the transactional attribute to a bean method

```
<!--  FOR CONTAINER MANAGED TRANSACTION, CHOOSING HOW AN EJB METHOD
➥SHOULD BEHAVE TRANSACTIONALLY -->
    <container-transaction>
      <method>
        <ejb-name>StockFacade</ejb-name>
```

```
        <method-name>*</method-name>
      </method>
      <trans-attribute>Required</trans-attribute>
    </container-transaction>
```

Even though the transaction is container managed, J2EE provides a means for application code to indicate that a transaction should be rolled back. Application code can force a rollback by calling the setRollbackOnly() method on the EJB context object. Code Snippet 11-4 illustrates this. Be aware that this is different than explicitly calling a rollback on the UserTransaction Object. The setRollbackOnly() method is only a marker passed back to the container. The container will perform the actual rollback of the transaction.

**Code Snippet 11-4 Rolling back explicitly under CMT**

```
try
    {
      updateAccountBO.updateAccountProfile(accountVO);
    }
    catch(FinderException e)
    {
    //TELL THE CONTAINER TO ROLLBACK UNDER CMT
    mySessionCtx.setRollbackOnly();
      throw new AccountException(e.getLocalizedMessage());
    }
  }
```

Enterprise Beans that utilize Bean Managed Transactions (BMT) can manage transactions using the UserTransaction object. However, unlike web applications, they must access the object not through JNDI but through the EJB Context object. This is shown in Code Snippet 11-5. The returned UserTransaction object is used the same way as it is in web applications. BMT can also use the resource manager's API if there is only one resource, but this is discouraged.

**Code Snippet 11-5 How BMT EJB applications access the UserTransaction Object**

```
mySessionCtx.getUserTransaction();
```

## Transaction Propagation

Components that wish to participate in the same transaction within a J2EE application need to be part of the same *transaction context*. When a new transaction is started, whether explicitly through code or implicitly by the container, the Transaction Manager creates a transaction context and associates it with the running thread. If during that transaction, another J2EE component is called that needs to be part of that transaction, it will have access to the same transaction context. To better understand some of these concepts, let's look at some scenarios. The semantics of the EJB transactional attributes were described in Chapter 9.

### Stateless Session Bean Set to REQUIRED Calls Entity Bean in Same Application Server Set to REQUIRED

In this scenario, one EJB calls another EJB in the same application server. The Stateless Session Bean has a transaction set to REQUIRED and it calls an Entity Bean that is also set to REQUIRED. Because the Entity Bean is set to REQUIRED and the calling Session Bean has a transaction, the entity needs to be part of the same transaction. The thread of execution will continue to hold the same transaction context while the Entity Bean is executing. Figure 11-3 illustrates this scenario.

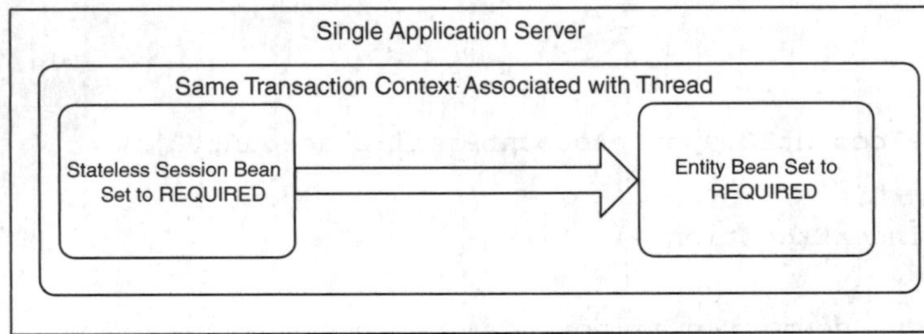


**Figure 11-3** Session Bean set to REQUIRED calls Entity Bean in same application server set to REQUIRED.

### Web Component with Transaction Calls EJB Component in Same Application Server Set to REQUIRED

Similar to the last scenario, a local web component explicitly starts a container transaction and calls a local EJB set to REQUIRED. The transactional context created in the web layer stays on the thread of execution and is passed to the EJB context. This scenario is illustrated in Figure 11-4.

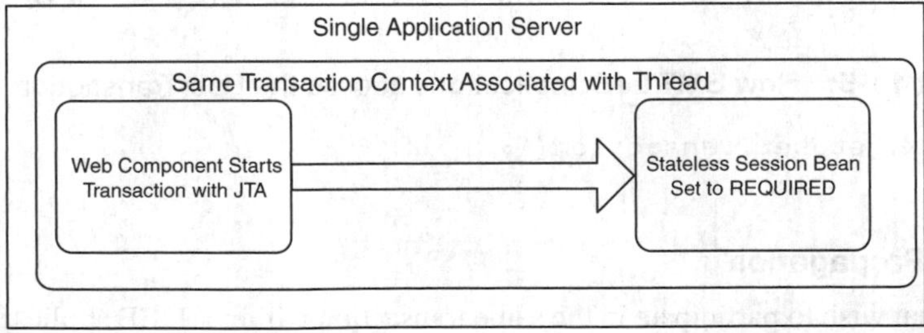


**Figure 11-4** Web component calls EJB in same application server.

### Web Component with Transaction on Server A Calls Remote EJB on Another Application Server B Set to REQUIRED

This scenario is the same as the previous one, except the EJB is remote and located on a different server. In addition, Server A starts the transaction, and Server B participates in it. This is the scenario where the Transaction Manager will utilize JTS to pass the transactional context over to a remote component. The transactional context is serialized over the IIOP protocol and transferred to another application server. The application server will associate that same transactional context to the thread of execution. If there is a failure in Application Server B or an explicit rollback, Application Server A will be informed and will clean up the transaction.

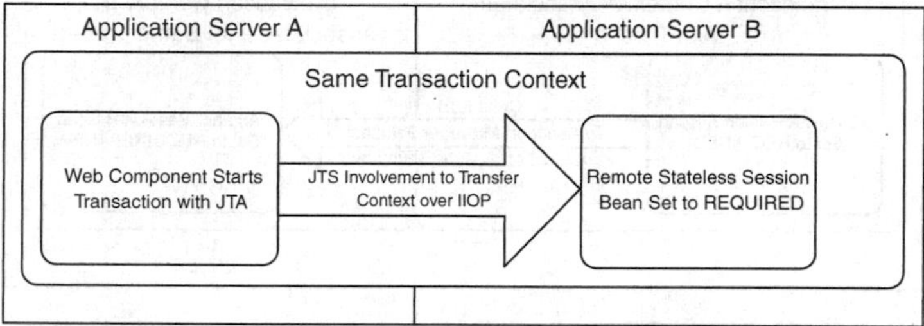


**Figure 11-5** Web component with a transaction calls a remote EJB set to REQUIRED.

### Web Component with No Transaction Calls Remote EJB Set to REQUIRED

In this case, the web component has no transaction. Application Server B will see there is no transactional context and create a new transaction. The Transaction Manager in Application Server A is not involved. As stated in Chapter 9, REQUIRED states that if the caller has no transaction, the container will start a new one; otherwise, the EJB will participate in the transaction of the caller.

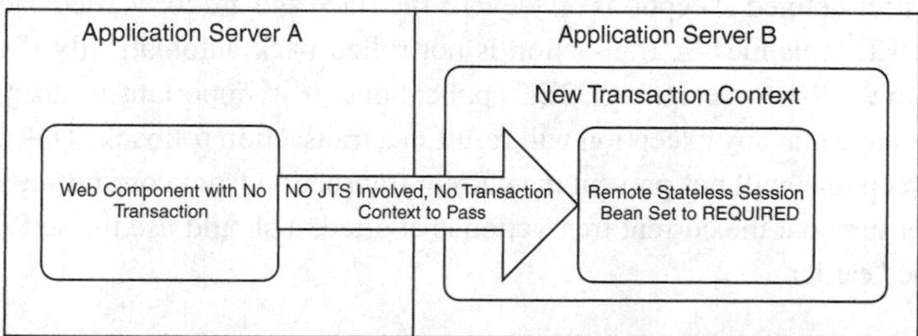


**Figure 11-6** Web component with no transaction calls a Remote EJB set to REQUIRED.

### One EJB Set to REQUIRED Calls Another EJB in Same Application Server Set to REQUIRES_NEW

Under this scenario, an EJB set to REQUIRED calls another EJB set to REQUIRES_NEW. Because REQUIRES_NEW states that no matter what the transactional state of the caller, a new transaction will be started, and the Transaction Manager will pause the first transaction and associate the thread of execution with a new transaction. Once that transaction is finished, the thread of execution will be associated back with the original transaction.

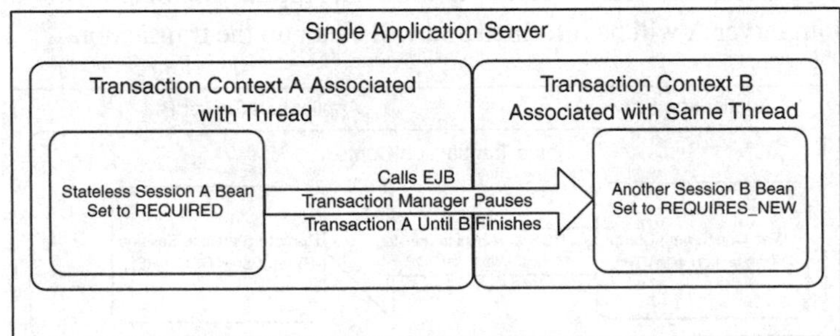


**Figure 11-7** EJB set to REQUIRED calls EJB in same application server set to REQUIRES_NEW.

There are several other combinations, but the scenarios illustrated should be helpful.

### Exceptions and Container Managed Transactions

J2EE applications, like any Java application, can raise exceptions. In the J2EE sense, there are two types of exceptions: application exceptions and non-application exceptions. If a non-application exception (sometimes referred to as a system exception) is thrown by an EJB, the EJB container will automatically roll back the current transaction. Application exceptions, on the other hand, are user-defined exceptions on the EJB interface and are forwarded back to the caller per the usual J2EE semantics. A transaction is not rolled back automatically if an application exception is thrown. When designing J2EE applications, it is important to keep this in mind. Many people assume that any exception will result in a transaction rollback. This is not the case. In fact, most exceptions will not prevent the current transaction from committing. If an application wishes to ensure that the current transaction is aborted, it should use the setRollBackOnly() method described earlier.

## WebSphere Application Server Transaction Manager

We've spent some time describing the various Java APIs for transaction management and how WebSphere Application Server implements transactions. Figure 11-8 may be useful in understanding how these pieces fit together.

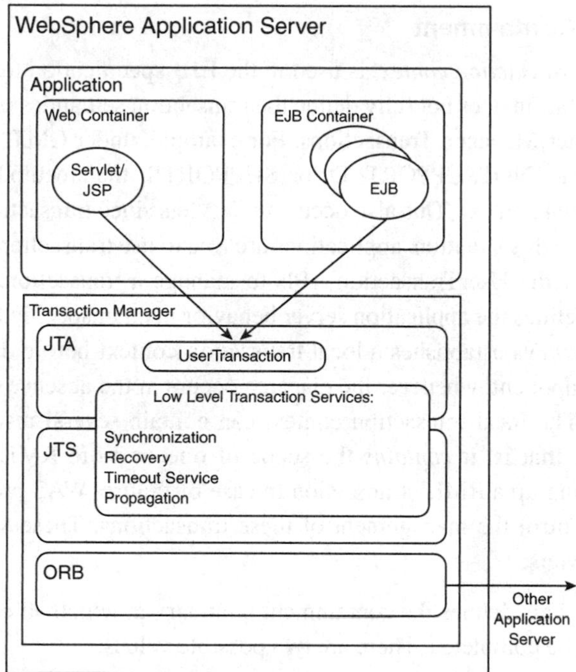


**Figure 11-8** WebSphere Application Server Transaction Manager.

## WebSphere Transactional Enhancements

So far, we have focused on the basic functions of a Transaction Manager and how WAS supports those functions. As you might expect, WAS provides a number of extensions to the basic J2EE-mandated transactional function that are useful in several scenarios. We are going to describe three of them in this section:

- **Local Transaction Containment**—The J2EE specification defines the concept of an unspecified transaction. This occurs when an EJB method is executing, quite literally, without a specified transaction. WAS addresses this ambiguity by defining an IBM-specific feature known as Local Transaction Containment.
- **Last Participant**[2]—WAS provides a way for a single non-XA resource to participate in a two-phase commit with other XA aware resources.
- **Activity Sessions**[2]—WAS provides some extensions that extend the transactional model to support situations that aren't truly transactional.

2 These features are only available in WAS Enterprise Edition V5.0.x or WBI Server Foundation version 5.1.

## Local Transaction Containment

The term *unspecified transaction context* is used in the EJB specification to refer to the cases in which the EJB specification does not fully define the transaction semantics of an Enterprise Bean method under Container Managed Transactions. For example, under CMT, if an EJB method is demarcated as NEVER, NOTSUPPORTED, or SUPPORTS, that method may run under an unspecified transactional context. This also occurs in Servlets since transactional attributes aren't specified on Servlets. In this situation, applications are free to use transactional capabilities of the underlying resource or the UserTransaction APIs to manage a transaction. A local transaction containment (LTC)[3] defines the application server behavior in an unspecified transaction context.

The container always establishes a local transaction context before dispatching a method on an EJB or web component, whenever the dispatch occurs in the absence of an existing global transaction context.[4] The local transaction context can contain several resource manager local transactions (RMLT); that is, it *contains* the scope of one or more RMLTs and provides the opportunity for cleaning up a RMLT transaction in case of failure. WAS provides the following specific settings to control the management of these transactions. These settings are available both on EJBs and Servlets:

- **Boundary**—This defines the containment boundary at which all contained local transactions must be completed. There are two possible values:
  - **BeanMethod (default)**—The local transactions must be resolved within the same bean method (or service method for Servlets) in which they were started. In version 5.x, this is the only available option for base server.
  - **ActivitySession**—The local transactions must be resolved within the scope of any ActivitySession in which they were started. In version 5.x of WebSphere Application Server, Activity Sessions are only available in the Enterprise Edition (or WBI Server Foundation).
- **Resolver**—Specifies the component responsible for initiating and ending the local transactions. It must be one of the following:
  - **Application**—It is up to the application code to resolve the transactions.
  - **ContainerAtBoundary**—The transaction is resolved by the container as defined by the boundary setting.
- **Unresolved**—Defines the action that the container will take if the local transaction is unresolved at the end of the local transaction context. This applies when the resolver is Application. The unresolved-action element is either commit or rollback. WAS will automatically take this action if the transaction is not complete when the context ends (typically when the method ends).

3 LTC is a WAS extension and not part of the J2EE specification.

4 Among other things, this means that a local transaction cannot be shared across bean methods; e.g., if bean A calls bean B, any local transaction will not be propagated to bean B.

The last setting is perhaps the most interesting. This indicates what WAS will do if an application starts its own transactions and then neglects to complete them (rollback or commit). This is very handy because it prevents a number of subtle bugs related to developers forgetting to commit transactions (we've seen these mysterious hanging transactions all too often).

The local transaction containment settings are part of the extended deployment descriptor (ibm-web-ext.xmi or ibm-ejb-jar-ext.xmi). It can be set for EJBs using the deployment descriptor editor within Studio or the ASTK, as shown in Figure 11-9. You can access this menu from the Beans tab after selecting the bean of interest.

**NOTE**

While WAS provides support for using native resource manager APIs and then managing that access using local transaction containment, to build portable EJB applications, the EJB Bean must be written to avoid using the native resource APIs to demarcate transactions. EJBs should rely on Container Managed Transactions in order to best utilize the capabilities of the J2EE container. For transactional web applications that do not choose to use the EJB technology, local transaction containment may be a viable option. However, even then, we recommend considering adding a simple Stateless Session Bean layer to manage transactions.

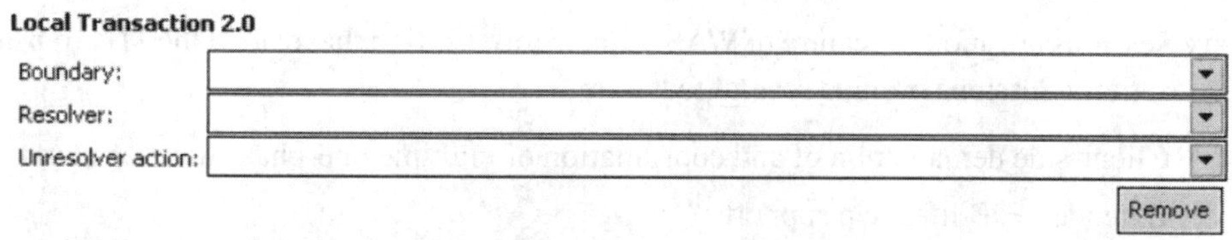

**Local Transaction 2.0**

Boundary:

Resolver:

Unresolver action:

Remove

**Figure 11-9** LTC settings.

## Last Participant Support

Ordinarily, all participants in a two-phase commit process must be two-phase commit-capable. With the Last Participant Support (LPS), you can use a single one-phase commit (1PC)-capable resource with any number of two-phase commit (2PC)-capable resources in the same global transaction. The global transaction commit processing still takes place in two phases. At phase 1, all the two-phase commit resources are prepared using the two-phase commit protocol. During phase 2, the one-phase commit resource is called to commit first if all the two-phase resources successfully prepared. This way, if the 1PC resource fails, WAS can simply rollback the other resources. On the other hand, if the 1PC commit resource succeeds, WAS can commit the remaining resources. Figure 11-10 illustrates the concept.

Unfortunately, LPS is not a complete substitute for using a resource that fully supports 2PC. It should only be used when you want to commit a one-phase-capable resource (which has no 2PC support) with other 2PC resources and you want to get as close as 2PC as possible. LPS introduces a hazard of a mixed commit result because 1PC resources can't completely participate in the 2PC protocol. For example, if the WAS does not get a response from the 1PC resource,[5] it has no way of knowing the status. Thus, WAS can't know whether the 1PC resource committed or not and thus does not know how to proceed. In this case, manual intervention will be required to resolve the state of the data in the 1PC resource.

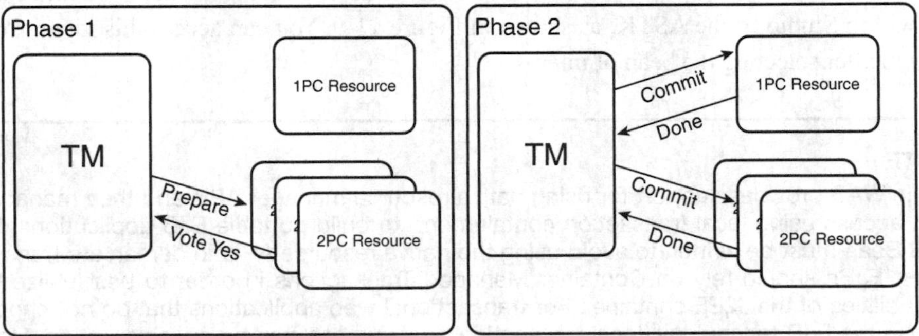


**Figure 11-10** Last Participant Support.

### Activity Sessions

Activity Sessions are another feature of WAS 5 Enterprise Edition that extend the JTA transaction model.[6] Activity Sessions provide several features:

- Client-side demarcation of and coordination of multiple one-phase units of work
- Extended EJB lifecycle support
- Extensions to local transaction support
- A long-running transaction semantic
- Association with HttpSession to scope contexts to the lifecycle of HTTP clients
- Provides for distributed context distribution using the OMG Activity service

Activity Sessions provide an alternative unit of work to the 2PC model, but they are not a replacement because Activity Sessions suffer a higher chance of mixed outcomes. However, they do provide a level of coordination if one has to deal with multiple non-XA resources in some reasonably coordinated way. Activity Sessions can even be used to group multiple 2PC transactions to provide some level of long-running transaction semantics.

Activity Sessions are a large topic, and the details are beyond the scope of this book. We refer interested readers to [Kovari 2003].

5 A network failure could occur when the response was being transmitted.

6 Activity Sessions are not part of the current J2EE specification; however, Activity Sessions are being worked on for future versions of J2EE as JSR 95: J2EE TM Activity Service for Extended Transactions.

## Distributed Transaction Failure Recovery

We've spent quite a bit of time describing how transactions are supposed to behave: Each RM and TM nicely commits or rolls back as required. However, as you might imagine, in the real world, things don't always work that way. Sometimes, there can be more serious failure involving the loss of a participant. That is, an RM or TM might simply fail. By fail, we don't mean that the RM or TM decides to rollback; we mean that it may have crashed and disappeared (at least briefly). In this situation, the TM has to handle some more complex error scenarios through what we call the recovery process. We describe those here. Failures can occur at any time or any place. When dealing with XA transactions, there are three types of failures to consider:

- Failures before the 2PC started
- Failures during the prepare phase
- Failures during the commit phase

The first case is the simplest. As stated earlier, any failure before the 2PC process begins is a presumed rollback. This includes simple failures such as applications rolling back the transaction or a communication failure in the middle of a JDBC operation and more complex failures such as the TM itself failing (e.g., the application server crashes). In any case, if a failure occurs at this early stage, the TM and RMs will simply rollback the transaction. This is particularly easy since no persistent transactional state has yet been written by the TM.[7]

Any failure during the prepare phase of the 2PC transaction also always implies a rollback. Failure during the prepare phase can happen only because the Resource Manager fails or the Transaction Manager fails:

- If any RM fails during the prepare call, or if the TM itself fails before writing the commit record to the log (signifying the end of the prepare phase), then the outcome has to be 'rollback.' In the case where the TM is still up, the TM will call a rollback on any RM that may already have voted yes during the prepare phase.
- In the case where the TM itself fails, the outcome is still to rollback, but it's now up to the TM recovery mechanism to ensure that a rollback is called on all resources. In the case of WAS, when the server restarts, the recovery process will involve rolling back any transactions that failed during the prepare phase.

A failure during the commit phase of the 2PC transaction is much more difficult to handle. The transaction must commit since this is required by the specification. However, this gets complicated:

- In the case that the TM itself fails, when the TM recovers, it will contact all the RMs and issue the commit command.

7 This is known as "the presumed abort optimization."

- In the case of a RM failure, the overall transaction still needs to commit. Thus, the TM will retry periodically while the client is waiting. Eventually, the TM can timeout and report an error of an incomplete outcome. Some manual intervention may be needed at this stage, such as some operator going into the specific resource and committing the transaction. When a decision is made independently of the TM, this is referred to as a *heuristic decision*.

The recovery mechanisms involved are very detailed and beyond the scope of this book. There are many scenarios that can happen during the 2PC process. Those scenarios multiply when the number of resources involved is large. For applications that require strong transaction support, reading and understanding a good resource on XA is critical. The [Spille 2004] article series provides a detailed explanation of the steps involved in transaction recovery.

## Advanced Recovery Considerations

In WAS, since WAS acts as the Transaction Manager, there is a routine recovery check process during the server initialization. The process involves checking the transaction log files for any outstanding unresolved transactions. If it finds any outstanding transactions, the TM will contact the participating Resource Managers and send the appropriate commit/rollback decision. If the Resource Manager is unavailable, WAS will schedule recovery retries on an asynchronous thread. Until this completes, those transactions remain *in-doubt*. It should be noted that after the TM completes its first attempt to contact the RMs about outstanding transactions, new transactions can be accepted. However, it is quite possible that they will end up deadlocking.

If transactions are not resolved with the underlying Resource Managers, the Resource Managers will be waiting for the WAS transactional decision regarding the in-doubt transactions. *In this situation, serious problems can result since the RM is holding locks and resources that could be blocking other applications.* You must make provisions to resolve those transactions. If the transactions are held because an RM is down, you should endeavor to restart it. If this is not possible, transactions will have to be manually forced.

If the transactions are held because the application server is unable to restart (perhaps because of a machine failure), you can either manually resolve the transactions or restart the application servers on a backup machine.

Unfortunately, restarting an application server on a backup machine is not as simple as it may seem. In addition to the obvious requirements—same fix levels, transactional logs, directory structure, and J2EE configurations—if WAS-ND is being used, the backup machine must use the same hostname and IP address since the transactional logs contain embedded host and IP address information (in support of distributed multi-machine transactions).

The WAS transaction logs are located under the *tranlog* directory in the WAS install. The *tranlog* directory will have a subdirectory for each server. Figure 11-11 illustrates the transaction log directory makeup.

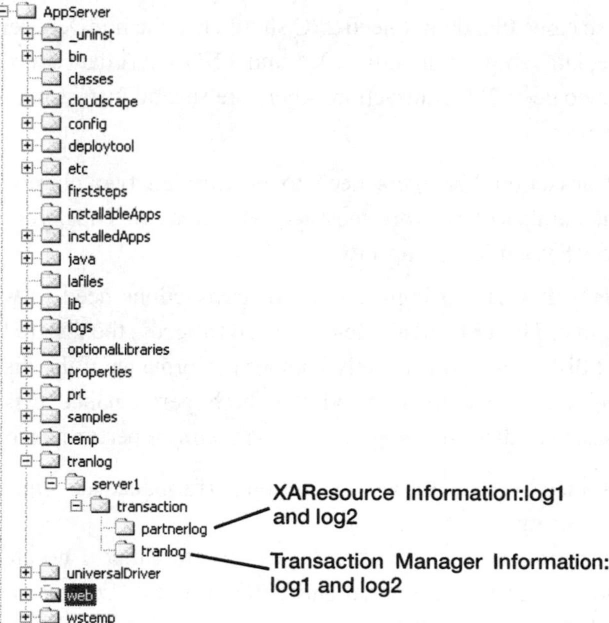


**Figure 11-11** Transaction log.[8]

Highly available systems that use 2PC should make a habit of having a spare server and shared fault tolerant disk arrays for these situations. Because the transaction logs are critical components, applications with critical transactional requirements should use highly available disk systems such as RAID. If the transactional logs are lost (or cannot be moved), an administrator manually has to go to each resource manager and force the transactions to an appropriate state (commit or rollback). Not only is this tedious and difficult, but it also requires application knowledge. If the administrator forces a transaction to the wrong state on the Resource Manager, the system can end up in an inconsistent state.

## Transaction Performance

Transactions add overhead to applications; thus, you should carefully consider the performance implications of transactions and use them appropriately. This is **not** a recommendation to avoid transactions! We are simply encouraging you to understand how to use transactions in a way to give the best performance possible for your application. The first, and perhaps most obvious, point is that distributed transactions (often called XA transactions) require more overhead than local transactions. Thus, if your application can be written to properly use only a single resource, this will result in the best performance.[9]

8 This directory structure is new in WAS V5.1. In 5.0, the resource information was stored in the same directory as the tranlog in files called XAResource1 and XAResource2.

9 The application code will still use the J2EE transaction mechanisms, just one resource.

Application use cases that do not need 2PC should use the non-XA version of the resource drivers. For example, DB2 ships with both an XA and a NON-XA data source.

Assuming you do need 2PC transactions, there are several infrastructure factors that affect transaction performance:

- Because Transaction Managers need to go through two phases during the commit process, the number of network messages is increased. Thus, you should validate that your network has sufficient capacity.
- Environments that have a high number of transactions need to worry about the disk access required. The TM and all the RMs need to access the disk to log information. The high rate of disk writes can severely hamper performance if the disks are poorly tuned. Where appropriate, we recommend that high performance disk arrays and RAID techniques such as disk stripping be used to maximize performance.

Two more optimizations to improve transaction performance are supported by WAS: read-only and connection sharing.

The read-only optimization takes advantage of the fact that if no changes are made to a resource, there is no need to go through an entire 2PC process. During the prepare phase, if a Resource Manager detects that all of the accesses to this resource in the transaction were read-only, it informs the Transaction Manager of this. As a result, during the second phase of 2PC, this RM will be skipped, and there is no need to write to the transaction log.

Connection sharing is another optimization for transactions. Obviously, each separate resource requires its own connection. But there is also the issue of multiple connections to the same resource. During a transaction, WAS will attempt to share a single connection to the same resource if possible. When a single connection is used to a resource, there is less overhead, and fewer single connections must be created. Furthermore, the commit phase will go much faster. In fact, it can degenerate into a single-phase commit if only one resource is accessed. Thus, applications need to be designed to share connections.

You can avoid the overhead of creating additional connections to a single resource inside the scope of a transaction if the following conditions are met:

1. The JNDI name used to reference the underlying connection factory must be the same for all participant components in the transaction.
2. Resource authentication must be the same.
3. If the underlying resource is a relational DB, then the isolation level, catalog, typemap, and read-only attributes must be identical.
4. Last and most importantly, the resource must be marked as "Shareable."

In brief, the application components in the scope of a transaction must all specify the same connection properties for a particular resource. Assuming all these conditions are met, the runtime will then attempt to share a connection. This basically means that within the same transaction or LTC, multiple calls to getConnection() on the same connection factory will return the same logical connection. One side effect of this is that the transaction (or LTC) owns the connection for the length of its scope and does not return the connection to the pool until the transaction scope is finished. In low-resource situations, this may cause transactions to wait and affect performance. In these situations, unsharable connections should be used. It's important to note that even if all these conditions are met, the runtime may choose not to share the connection based on workload and runtime object availability.

By avoiding creating a new connection or getting a reference to an existing connection, scalability and performance can be improved since fewer "server shared resources" (connection objects) are required to satisfy application requests.

Connection sharing can be applied both to JDBC and JMS resources. Setting a sharable scope to a connection is done on the resource reference, as illustrated in Code Snippet 11-6.

**Code Snippet 11-6** Setting a connection as shareable on a resource reference

```
<resource-ref id="ResourceRef_1063514449762">
    <res-ref-name>jdbc/wstradeRef</res-ref-name>
    <res-type>javax.sql.DataSource</res-type>
    <res-auth>CONTAINER</res-auth>
  <!-- SETTING A CONNECTION AS SHAREABLE -->
    <res-sharing-scope>Shareable</res-sharing-scope>
</resource-ref>
```

Deployment of your applications and EJBs can also impact transaction performance. If one application calls EJBs that are running in another application server, a distributed transaction will be created. This will occur even if you're only using a single resource manager for the EJBs in both application servers. Thus, for best performance, all the EJBs required in a transaction should be packaged in one EAR and deployed into a single application server (or server clone in a WAS-ND server cluster).[10]

## Transaction Troubleshooting

Troubleshooting transactions can be quite difficult. Knowing the available tools for troubleshooting problems in advance of problems is advisable. WebSphere Application Server ships with the Tivoli Performance Viewer, which has a section for viewing transaction statistics. You should also become familiar with the management tools of the underlying resources. For example, if you are using a database, become familiar with the tools from the database vendor for monitoring active connections. It may be necessary as well to enable trace for the underlying client resource drivers, such as the DB2 packages. We illustrated this in Chapter 10, "CMP and Advanced EJB Settings."

10 There are other issues related to application maintenance that make packaging all application components into a single EAR a good idea. Refer to Chapter 15, "Advanced Considerations for Build," for a discussion of this.

Finally, if all else fails, you can rely on the WAS trace facility to provide detailed information on the state of a transaction. The following trace strings will provide you with useful information regarding transactions:

- com.ibm.ejs.jts.*
- com.ibm.ws.LocalTransaction.*

## Conclusion

In this chapter, we discussed how WebSphere Application Server supports J2EE transactions. We discussed how the WAS Transaction Manager supports both local and distributed transactions. We also discussed the J2EE transaction model and how WAS uses JTA and JTS. We then talked about some of the features of the WAS Transaction Manager. Finally, we discussed transaction recovery and optimization techniques. In the next chapter, we will focus on our next resource, JMS.

CHAPTER 12

# JMS and Message Driven Beans

In the last chapter, we talked about distributed transactions and how they are needed to coordinate transactions across various resources. Up until now, JDBC has been our only resource; in this chapter, we will talk about another very important resource: the Java Message Service (JMS). JMS is a common interface used to access an asynchronous messaging system. In this chapter, we will also talk about Message Driven Beans. We will then talk about how WebSphere Application Server (WAS) supports JMS and Message Driven Beans. We will discuss the various JMS providers supported by WAS. Finally, we will go through another automation example by deploying another version of the Personal Trade System.

## Understanding JMS and Message Driven Beans

Messaging allows applications to read and write messages from a common destination. This is a key distinction from applications that exchange information through Remote Procedure Call (RPC) mechanisms such as those provided by Session and Entity EJBs. With an RPC style of communication, clients rely on calling directly to another application and waiting until the procedure returns. On the other hand, with messaging, an application only needs to write a message to some location such as a queue and forget about it. Another application can then read the message whenever it wants. The *producer* (the sender of the message) and the *consumer* (the reader of the message) are time-independent of each other.

Much like JDBC, JMS provides a standard API to access messaging systems. In addition to the simple sending and receiving of messages, JMS applications can be configured to receive messages on an event basis (message arrival triggers the read of the message) using Message Driven Beans (MDB). An MDB is a special type of EJB meant to receive asynchronous messages from a JMS destination.[1] As with most of the concepts in this book, we will not focus heavily on the programming model. There are several resources such as [Brown 2004] and [Yusuf 2004] that cover the programming model. Understanding how J2EE applications use JMS and MDBs is essential, however, to help drive deployment and configuration.

## Understanding Messaging

As stated, application messaging is used to exchange information between different applications or between different components of the same application in an *asynchronous* way. Asynchronous means that the producer of the message does not wait for the message to be consumed. In order to accomplish this, an underlying messaging system needs to serve as an intermediary between the producer of the message and any consumer of the message. These messaging systems provide well-known *destinations* to store the messages. Figure 12-1 illustrates this concept. The producer places a message on a well-known destination and forgets about it. A consumer then reads the message from the destination. Depending on the message and destination settings, the consumer can read the message from this destination immediately or at a future point in time.

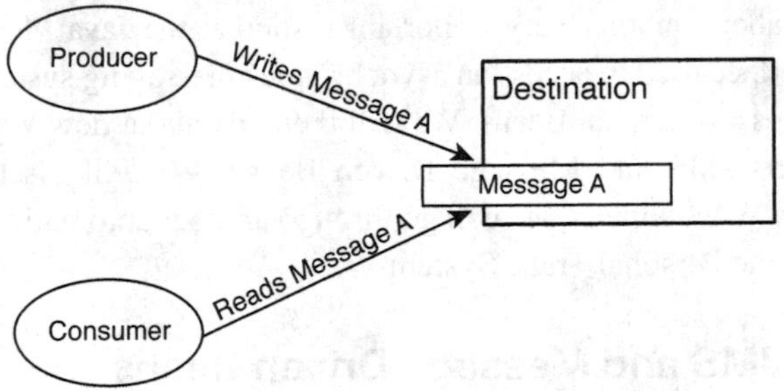


**Figure 12-1** Messaging system.

Messaging is a popular way for applications to exchange data because it allows for loose coupling between applications. This means that one process (the producer) can be operational, sending a message to a destination and not worrying about whether the consumer of the message is operational. Conversely, the consumer can read a message even after the producer has stopped running. Thus, the running states of the producer and the consumer are totally independent of each other. For example, the consumer can run on a different day than the producer, and the transaction can still succeed.

As messaging technologies have evolved, two types of messaging models have emerged: *point-to-point* messaging and *publish/subscribe* messaging. The JMS API supports both models. To understand messaging today in the J2EE world, it is important to understand the differences between the two models and the problems that each solves.

1 In J2EE 1.4, the MDB has been expanded beyond the JMS technology, allowing messages to arrive from other messaging systems that do not implement the JMS API.

## Point-to-Point

In the point-to-point model, a message written by the producer is intended for one recipient. This means one producer puts a message on the destination, and *only one* consumer reads the message from that destination. Once the consumer reads that message, the message is removed from the destination, and no other consumer can receive the message. In JMS, the destination for a point-to-point model is called a *queue*. Figure 12-2 illustrates point-to-point messaging.

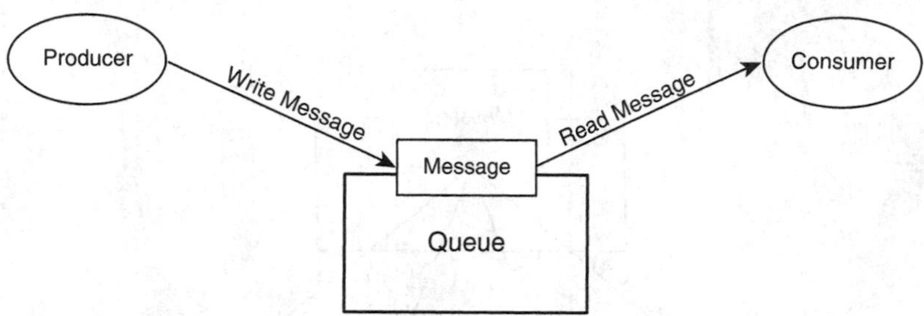


**Figure 12-2** Point-to-point messaging.

## Publish/Subscribe

Rather than writing messages on a queue for a single consumer, the publish/subscribe model implements a broadcast style of messaging. In JMS, the destination in the publish/subscribe model is called a *topic*, which represents messages that all relate to a particular subject. When a producer wishes to broadcast a message concerning that subject, it publishes the message to the topic. The message is intended for any interested consumers, which may be zero, one, or many consumers and which may change between one message publication and the next. Any consumer interested in messages concerning that subject can subscribe to the topic. Any consumer that is subscribed to a topic when a message is published to the topic will receive a copy of that message. The topic does not delete the message until every subscriber receives a copy of the message. The publish/subscribe model is illustrated in Figure 12-3.

In a publish/subscribe model, a subscription can be durable or nondurable. A nondurable subscription ends when the subscriber disconnects from the messaging system, such as when its application stops running. If the subscriber reconnects, it will not receive any messages published while it was disconnected. When a durable subscriber disconnects, the topic retains any messages published and delivers them when the subscriber reconnects. To end a subscription, a durable subscriber must explicitly unsubscribe from the topic.

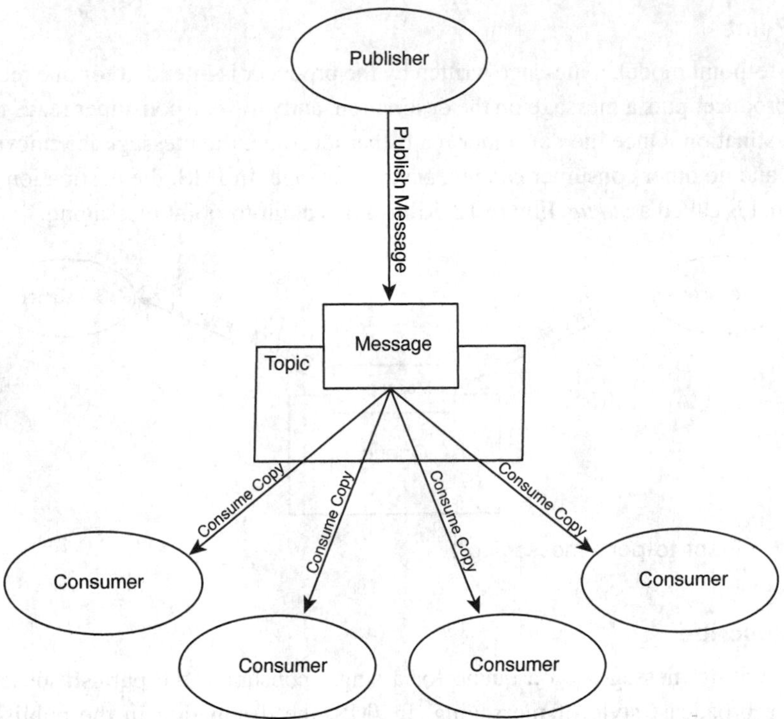


**Figure 12-3** Publish and subscribe.

## Java Messaging Service

Much like JDBC does for relational database access, JMS is a standard API for messaging systems. Any messaging vendor that pledges to support JMS can, in theory, be installed as a messaging provider on any J2EE-compliant application server.

### JMS Programming Model

We will briefly go over the programming model of a JMS program. Although there are two messaging models, the steps needed to read or write messages are similar. A JMS developer interacts with a JMS API that enables an application to read and write messages. Figure 12-4 illustrates these concepts.

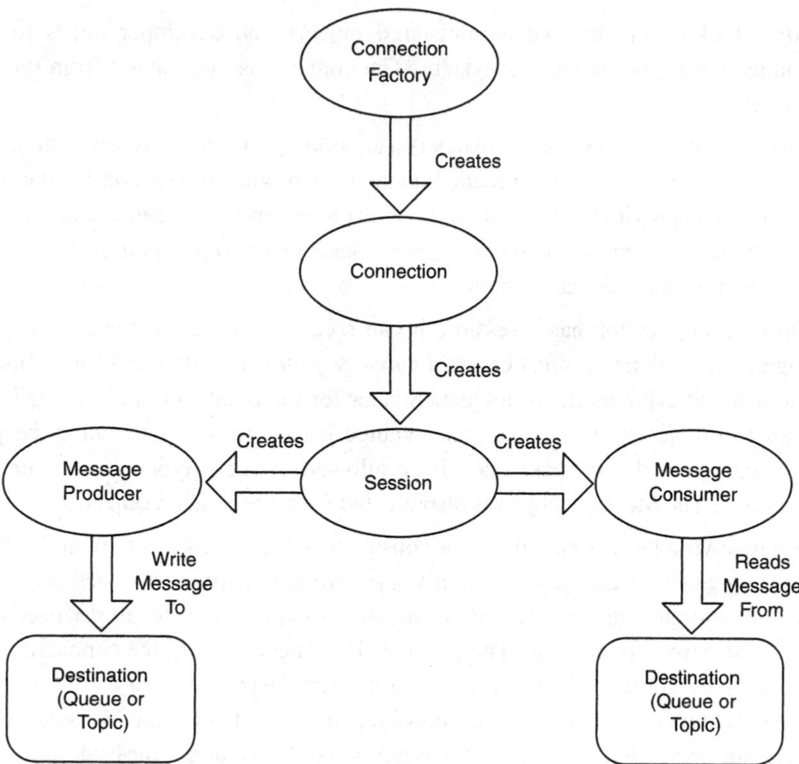


**Figure 12-4** JMS programming model.

There are several steps in using the API:

1. First, a developer accesses JMS-administered objects: *Connection Factories and Destinations*. The connection factory and destination are acquired through the JNDI API. This is similar to looking up a JDBC data source. The type of connection factory and destination used are dependent on whether publish/subscribe or point-to-point is desired. For connection factories, a QueueConnectionFactory is used for point-to-point messaging while a TopicConnectionFactory is used for publish/subscribe. For destinations, a queue is used for point-to-point, and a topic is used for publish and subscribe.

   Both connection factories and destinations are administered objects. Applications that use JMS need administrators to configure both a connection factory (*QueueConnectionFactory* or *TopicConnectionFactory*) and a destination (*queue* or *topic*). This is a bit different from JDBC, where an administrator defines only one datasource. We will elaborate on this later in the chapter.

2. After looking up the two administered objects, the developer needs to establish a connection to the messaging system. The connection is obtained from the connection factory.
3. The next object a developer creates is a *session*, not to be confused with an HTTP session. A session is a single-threaded context for producing and consuming messages. A session also provides a transactional context to group a set of sends and receives. As you may expect by now, you can have a *QueueSession* or a *TopicSession*. A Session object is obtained from the connection object.
4. Once an application has a session, it can receive or send messages. For writing messages, the application must create a *message producer*, either a TopicPublisher for the publish/subscribe model or a QueueSender for the point-to-point model. The producer uses the *topic* or *queue* that was obtained earlier from JNDI. Once the producer is created, the code can pass one of the allowed message types to send or publish the message. The Message object is also created from the Session object.

   For receiving messages, a message consumer object needs to be created. There are two ways to receive messages—explicitly (synchronously) or event-based (asynchronously) using message listeners. To receive messages explicitly, a developer needs to create a *consumer* from the Session. Then the developer needs to start the connection and explicitly call a receive method. To receive a message asynchronously, a developer needs to create a message listener object. This object must implement the MessageListener interface and override onMessage (Message message). When a message arrives, the JMS messaging system will automatically call the onMessage method and pass it in.[2]

The other important aspect in the programming model is the Message object itself. There are several message types in JMS, such as TextMessage or BytesMessage; however, we will not discuss these in detail here. [Brown 2004] is a good source for that topic. It is important to know that a message is made up of three parts: a header, properties, and a body. The JMS specification defines standard message headers and properties. In addition, a more enhanced messaging system such as WebSphere MQ will contain extra header and property information to allow communication to other consumers that may be using a different programming API.

JMS also allows for messaging filtering using a mechanism called Message Selectors. A Message Selector is a string that contains a SQL-like expression. The message consumer then receives only messages with headers and properties that match the criteria. Selectors can be defined on custom properties defined by an application or with built-in properties or header fields defined by JMS or the message provider.

2 The J2EE specification mandates that Message Driven Beans are the only allowed event-based message listener. We will cover Message Driven Beans later in this chapter. J2EE applications can still receive messages synchronously; however, they must not call setMessageListener().

> **NOTE**
> Message Selectors can be the cause of many performance problems in messaging applications. This is because some messaging systems do not implement indexing on message properties. For example, WebSphere MQ only supports indexing on mainframe platforms.

## Transactional Behavior in JMS

Until now, we have discussed how relational databases behave in transactions through a JDBC Provider. We discussed how isolation levels control application access to data being read or modified in different transactions. Messaging is usually not that sophisticated. In essence, messaging doesn't provide the same level of isolation control. In both the publish/subscribe and the point-to-point models, there are two basic operations: writing a message or reading a message.

In messaging, any message written to a destination during a transaction cannot be read by any other consumer, even a consumer within the same transaction, until the commit. This behavior is the same both in the publish/subscribe model and the point-to-point model.

Point-to-point and publish/subscribe behave differently within a transaction when reading messages. For point-to-point messaging, when a transaction reads a message, the message becomes available to the transaction but does not get removed from the destination at the time it is read; instead, the messaging system leaves the message on the destination but does not allow other transactions to see it, much like a database exclusive write lock. When the transaction commits, the message is completely removed from the destination; however, if the transaction rolls back, the message stays on the destination and is now allowed to be read by other transactions. This allows for a powerful feature called replay. Replay is the ability to retry the transaction after a rollback. The danger here is that you can get caught in an infinite loop trying to replay the transaction. However, many JMS systems are sophisticated enough to handle these situations. For example, WebSphere MQ places messages that appear stuck on a special queue.

For publish/subscribe, if the transaction is rolled back, the message is discarded. This is because the publish/subscribe engine, usually called a *broker*, only delivers a copy of the message due to its broadcasting style. So how does a failed consumer retrieve a lost message? Remember, in the publish/subscribe model, there exists the notion of a durable subscriber. If a subscriber is in durable mode and a message is rolled back, then the durable subscriber goes back to a state of never having processed the message. Because the messaging system stores missed messages for durable subscribers, it will resend the message as if the durable subscriber had never read the message. Nondurable subscribers will lose the message.

JMS is a resource inside WAS and therefore can participate in a global transaction using JTA. In addition, JMS code that is accessed under the transaction context of an EJB can be managed using Container Managed Transactions. In addition, a developer can use a JMS session to demarcate JMS transactions directly; however, this is not recommended for the same reason you should not manage JDBC transactions using the autoCommit() option (as explained in Chapter 11, "Transactions with WebSphere Application Server").

## JMS in WebSphere Application Server

WebSphere Application Server has strong support for JMS. In addition to providing its own embedded JMS server, WAS can be easily configured to support higher-end messaging systems such as WebSphere MQ or WebSphere Business Integration (WBI) Message Broker. Furthermore, any messaging provider that supports the JMS contract can be configured to work with WAS. A messaging system that implements the JMS API is known as a *JMS provider*. Once a provider is configured, JMS resources can be defined in much the same way to support applications that use JMS and Message Driven Beans. In this section, we will discuss JMS messaging providers from a WebSphere Application Server stand point; [Yusuf 2004] is a good book that's solely dedicated to using JMS with the WebSphere platform. We will also discuss Message Driven Beans and touch upon JMS security.

### JMS Providers

A J2EE 1.3-compatible application server must include a JMS provider—a complete messaging system that implements the JMS API. The application server integrates with the JMS messaging system in two main respects:

- The application server must implement support for including a JMS transaction as part of a Java Transaction API (JTA) distributed transaction.
- The application server must implement support for a Message Driven Bean that acts as JMS message listener.

To meet these requirements, WebSphere Application Server ships with a built-in embedded JMS server. As a built-in JMS provider, it has the advantage of requiring no separate installation or configuration, and it is tightly integrated into the application server management environment and uses the same security model.

Enterprise-level messaging infrastructure, however, generally requires high-end flexibility and robustness. Although embedded messaging provides a JMS server, it only supports messaging between applications that are deployed in WebSphere Application Server and that use JMS, and it does not support load balancing and failover of message routing through multiple network connections. WebSphere Application Server can be configured to support higher-end external JMS providers, such as WebSphere MQ. Furthermore, WebSphere Application Server makes it easy to plug in third-party JMS servers.

The JMS resources can be configured using any of the WAS-supported administrative tools. In the admin console web application, you will find three JMS-related items off the Resource Menu, as shown in Figure 12-5:

- **WebSphere JMS Provider**—This is the built-in embedded server that comes with WebSphere Application Server.
- **WebSphere MQ Provider**—This is used to configure resources for WebSphere MQ and WebSphere MQ-related products that extend the functionality of the base messaging server such as WBI Event Broker.
- **Generic JMS Provider**—This is used to configure any third-party JMS server.

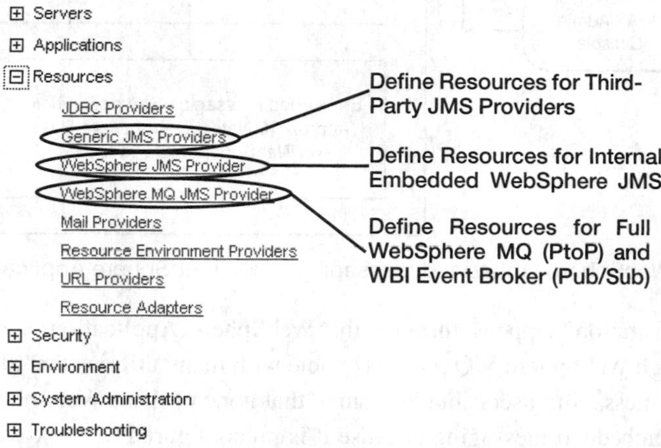


**Figure 12-5** JMS providers.

In the following two sections, we will discuss the two messaging providers from IBM: the embedded provider and WebSphere MQ.

## WebSphere Application Server Embedded Messaging

As stated, embedded messaging is the built-in JMS server that comes with WebSphere Application Server. It is a scaled down version of WebSphere MQ that is meant to hide the details of the underlying WebSphere MQ technology. Embedded JMS servers run standalone and cannot be configured to communicate with each other or interoperate with the full WebSphere MQ product. This obviously limits the topologies that can be implemented to support distributed messaging. Figure 12-6 depicts embedded messaging within the WebSphere Application Server Base product.

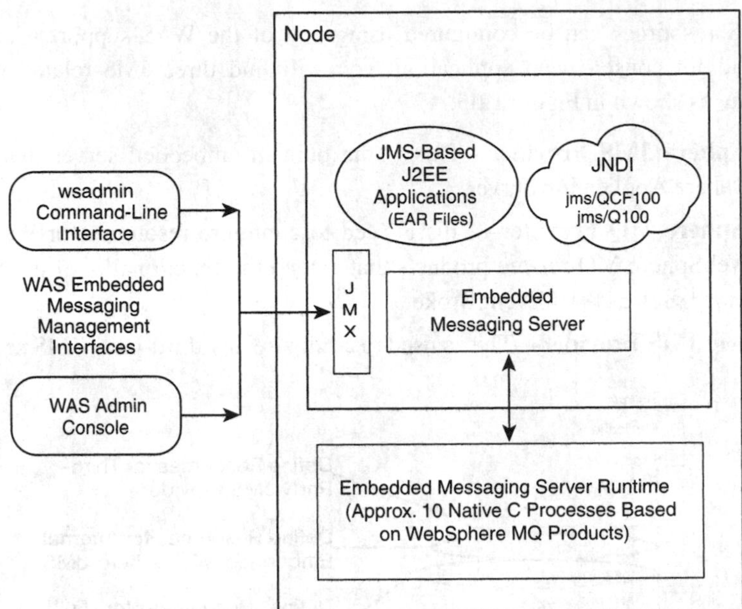


**Figure 12-6** WebSphere embedded messaging inside WebSphere Application Server Base.

All administration happens through the WebSphere Application Server administrative facilities. Although WebSphere MQ products come with many utilities that allow different functions, embedded messaging users should assume that none of these WebSphere MQ utilities are available to the embedded messaging because it is preconfigured to work with WAS. Theoretically, you can use the traditional WebSphere MQ administration utilities against queues and other resources. **If you do use these utilities, it is essential that you do not make any changes to the WebSphere administrative objects.** We will explain the WebSphere MQ administrative objects in the next section.

The WebSphere JMS provider is designed to support communication from JMS clients only. This is because the embedded messaging product does not come configured with any of the other communication protocols supported by the full WebSphere MQ product. Furthermore, it does not provide any other programming language API like the full products do.

When accessing the WebSphere JMS provider in the admin console, you can configure the four administrative objects under the additional properties, as shown in Figure 12-7. These objects can be created on any one of the WebSphere Application Server scopes: cell, node, or server.

| Additional Properties | |
|---|---|
| WebSphere Queue Connection Factories | |
| WebSphere Topic Connection Factories | |
| WebSphere Queue Destinations | |
| WebSphere Topic Destinations | |

**Figure 12-7** Accessing administrative objects.

## WebSphere MQ

WebSphere MQ is quite simply a messaging provider, the entity that provides message-based communication services to applications. First released by IBM in 1993 under the brand name MQSeries, it was re-branded in 2001 to WebSphere MQ. It is the market share leader, owning about 81 percent of the message-oriented middleware market. A major factor in its adoption is that it is available on over 35 different platforms (operating systems) and supports communication across numerous network protocols. In addition to the JMS API, WebSphere MQ also supports its own proprietary API, MQI, which is implemented in most of the major computer languages. Coupled with this is its ability to deliver mission-critical levels of service in terms of assuring the delivery of messages and providing once-and-once-only delivery semantics. It thus provides a firm foundation for enabling application connectivity between business applications that exist in the enterprise.

### WebSphere MQ Components

WebSphere MQ can be configured as an external JMS provider to WebSphere Application Server, providing point-to-point functionality. Because WebSphere MQ predates JMS, it uses different terminology for administrative objects. Part of the job of the WebSphere Application Server administrator then is to match the administrative objects of the JMS technology to the administrative objects of WebSphere MQ. In order to understand how to do this, a brief explanation of some of the core objects is in order. We will keep it brief and leave the details to [Yusuf 2004].

**Queue manager**: The queue manager is the base entity that supplies the messaging facilities used by the application. It provides access to MQ queues, which store MQ messages, and is responsible for maintaining the queues and ensuring messages are delivered to the right queue destination with the defined qualities of service. Applications interact with the queue manager using either JMS or one of a number of other APIs. The application may establish either a local or client connection to the queue manager. A *local connection* requires that the application run on the same node as the queue manager and use inter-process memory to communicate with the queue manager. A client connection allows the application to run on a remote machine from the queue manager and, in contrast, employs a protocol exchange over the network to invoke messaging facilities. The client connection uses a network abstraction called a client channel. Channels will be described shortly.

While communication between applications can be based on a single queue manager, most typical implementations involve more than one queue manager, with applications and associated queue managers potentially running on different physical machines and different operating systems. A queue manager name is unique among a network of interconnected queue managers so that a queue manager can be unambiguously identified when a message is to be sent to a queue it manages.

**Queues**: The MQ queue is the ultimate destination of the message; messages are sent to, received from, and moved between queues in fulfillment of the communication process. Hence, it defines the underlying implementation of the JMS *destination*. A queue belongs to a queue manager, which is responsible for maintaining the queue. The queue is a named entity and must be unique within the queue manager that owns it. The queue acts as a storage medium, accumulating messages that are later removed by the queue manager for transmission or by the application for processing. Queues that reside in a queue manager are referred to as *local queues*. There are other specialized queues in a queue manager as well.

Queue managers that are connected to each other (via server channels, which we will explain shortly) can have *remote queue definitions*. A remote queue definition is a definition that appears as a local queue to applications that access the queue manager, but in essence, the remote queue definition is an alias (or proxy) to queue on another queue manager. Remote queue definitions can only be written to; this makes sense since a remote queue definition is just an alias to another queue.

*Transmission queues* are special queues that are tied to a specific server channel (specifically, a sender channel—see the next section). Messages that are written to a remote queue definition are placed in a local transmission queue. Then special MQ processes send the message from the transmission queue over the channel to another queue manager. An application writing to a remote queue only waits until the message is placed on the transmission queue, not until the message is transferred over the channel. This type of interaction provides a much more powerful communication facility than using a client channel, where the application has to wait for some communication back that the message has been placed on the remote queue manager. However, using this type of communication requires that a queue manger, and thus a full WebSphere MQ installation, is co-located on the same machine with the WebSphere Application Server instance that is using the queue manager. We will explain this concept further when we explain channels.

There are other types of queues, such as model queues, dynamic queues, or system queues, that are beyond the scope of this book. [Yusuf 2004] provides more details.

**Channels**: A channel is a network abstraction that allows WebSphere MQ to support various protocols. WebSphere MQ supports both client and server channels.

A client channel allows the application to run on a machine that is remote from the queue manager and employs a protocol exchange over the network to invoke messaging facilities. A client channel (ironically called a server connection channel in WebSphere MQ) is bidirectional, being designed to pass both JMS API calls and return values defined on the JMS API.

Communication over a client channel can be optionally authenticated and secured. Figure 12-8 illustrates how a WebSphere Application Server JMS-based application communicates with queue managers that reside on a different machine using a client channel.

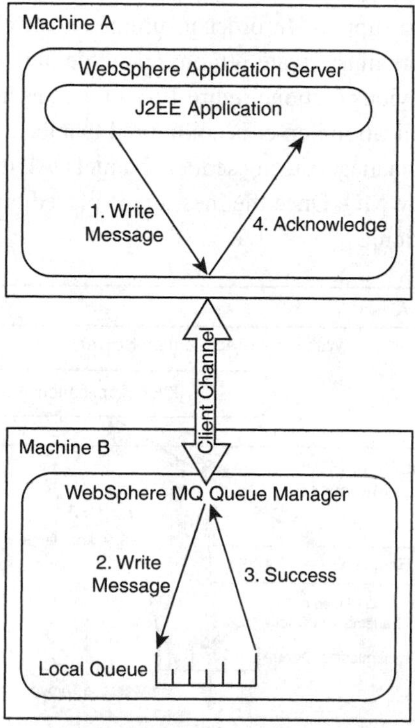


**Figure 12-8** Using client channels.

> **NOTE**
> Client channels are the only kind of channel supported by the WebSphere embedded server since it is a light-weight version of WebSphere MQ. This allows J2EE application clients to communicate to the embedded JMS server and allows different servers within a WAS ND environment to contact a single JMS server. WAS ND and JMS in a clustered environment will be explored in the ND portion of this book.

Queue managers are connected to each other by server channels, which, like client channels, are network abstractions that isolate the queue managers and, by extension, the applications from the different network protocols that may be in use in the enterprise (e.g., TCP/IP and SNA). Server channels are typed, the most common being a sender channel and a receiver channel. In contrast to client channels, server channels are unidirectional, so a sender/receiver pair are required by a given queue manager to enable bidirectional communication. Transmission and receipt of messages across channels are managed by an internal component called the Message Channel Agent (MCA), and this communication can be similarly authenticated and secured using the inbuilt SSL support. In order to utilize server channels for communication, WebSphere MQ administrators must create remote queue definitions and transmission queues, which we explained in the previous section. Figure 12-9 illustrates how a JMS-based J2EE application inside WebSphere Application Server is configured to a local queue manager, which communicates with remote queue managers using sender channels. All the communication is handled asynchronously by WebSphere MQ. Once the message is placed on the transmission queue, the control returns to the application.

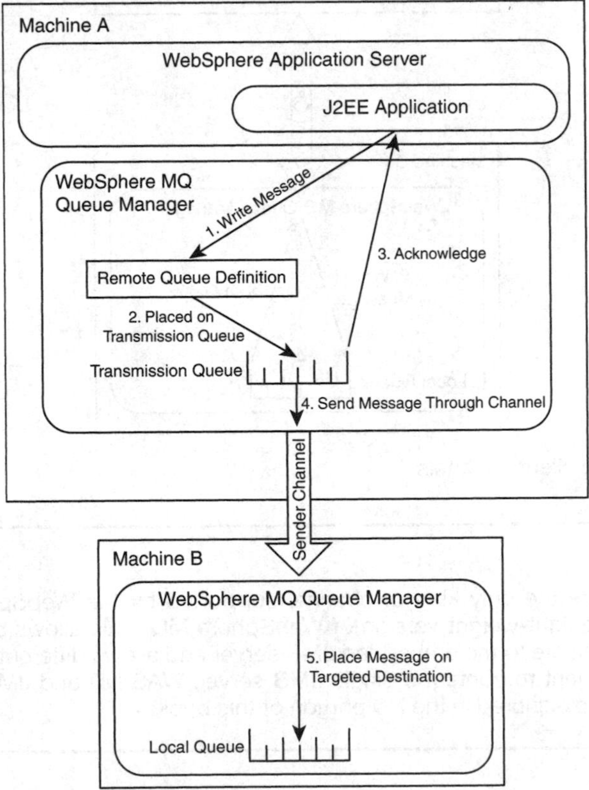


**Figure 12-9** Using server channels.

In addition to the remote queue manager capabilities, WebSphere MQ supports its own clustering, which is different from WAS ND clustering technology and which provides for higher scalability and distribution. Using a combination of WebSphere Application Server and WebSphere MQ clustering can provide a powerful combination of high availability and scalability. The network deployment portion of this book will cover clustering.

### WebSphere MQ Message Formats

Besides understanding the differences between the administered objects, some understanding about the MQ message formats may be helpful. We previously stated that a JMS message was made up of a header, properties, and a body. The WebSphere MQ message is the unit of exchange and contains the data that is to be communicated between applications. It thus defines the physical implementation of the JMS message. In its most basic form, the MQ message consists of a message header called the MQ message descriptor (MQMD) and a body that contains data. The MQMD header contains the fields that match the JMS header fields that are expected by the JMS specification. Additional headers may be used to convey specific information; for example, the rules and formatting header v2 (RFH2) can convey topic associations for publish-subscribe-based distribution. In all cases when additional headers are used, they are placed within the message body in front of the message data. In the instance when the message contains additional headers, these headers are arranged in a chain. Each header typically includes a format field that describes the format of the header that follows. The last header in the chain optionally describes the format of message data. The relevance of this to the JMS API is that it allows JMS applications to send messages that can be understood by NON-JMS programs that access queues using native MQ APIs. More details can be found in [Yusuf 2004].

The good news for a JMS developer is that the application code does not have to deal with this issue most of the time. The application uses standard JMS administrative objects. However, these properties need to be defined on the JMS destination when defined on the application server, and thus, the translation falls in the hands of the WebSphere Application Server administrator. We will look at defining MQ resources next.

### WebSphere MQ Administration

Unlike embedded messaging, configuring the queues for WebSphere MQ happens outside of WebSphere Application Server. It is usually done by an MQ administrator who knows the product well. WebSphere MQ has its own tools and administrative programs to handle this. Figure 12-10 shows the WebSphere MQ explorer used on the Windows platform, which enables administrators to create MQ objects.

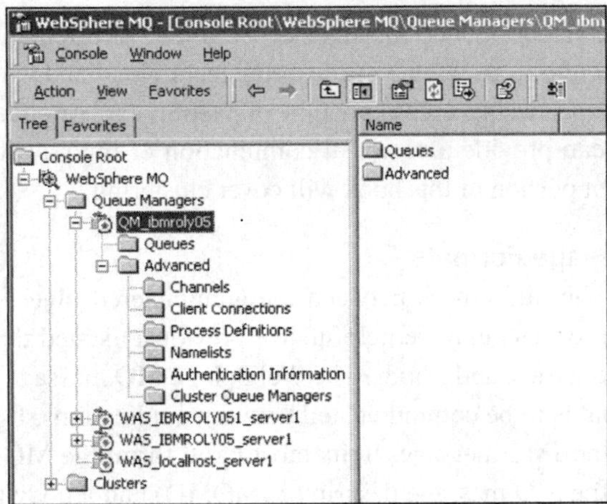


**Figure 12-10** WebSphere MQ Explorer.

When defining the JMS queue connection factories in WebSphere Application Server for WebSphere MQ, there are fields to match the MQ-administered objects to JMS terminology. Figure 12-11 illustrates the page for creating a queue connection factory for WebSphere MQ. The page is similar to the one for embedded messaging but contains extra fields for WebSphere MQ. Obviously, the queue manager is the main component. If the queue manager is on the same machine as WebSphere Application Server, then you can select the transport type to BINDINGS. If the queue manager is remote and thus needs to talk to a client channel, that information can be specified. The transport type would obviously be CLIENT.

| Scope | * cells:IBMROLY05:nodes:IBMROLY05 |
|---|---|
| Name | * |
| JNDI Name | * |
| Description | |
| Category | |
| Component-managed Authentication Alias | (none) |
| Container-managed Authentication Alias | (none) |
| Mapping-Configuration Alias | (none) |
| Queue Manager | |
| Host | |
| Port | 0 |
| Channel | |
| Transport Type | CLIENT<br>BINDINGS<br>CLIENT |

**Figure 12-11** WebSphere MQ queue connection factory.

Similarly for queue resource definition, when defining a queue JNDI resource for WebSphere MQ, the definition page contains entries for mapping to external queues created using WebSphere MQ tools. This is shown in Figure 12-12. Here, you can define the queue name that is configured in WebSphere MQ (and optionally the queue manager, but this is not necessary since the connection factory has this information). Another property highlighted at the bottom of the screen is the target client. By selecting MQ, you are allowing messages written to this queue to be mapped to an MQ type and allowing non-JMS applications to consume messages as well as allowing the JMS application to understand non-JMS messages that are produced by other WebSphere MQ applications. By selecting JMS, however, only other JMS applications can read the message, and no translations will take place.

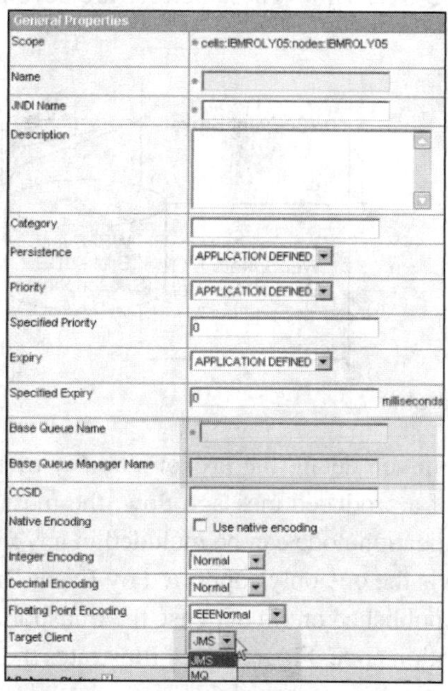


**Figure 12-12** JNDI queue definition.

## WebSphere Business Integration Event Broker

The WebSphere MQ product is the basis for many other MQ products. By default, WebSphere MQ only provides a point-to-point implementation. The WebSphere Business Integration (WBI) Event Broker performs the role of a publish-and-subscribe broker, managing subscription requests and matching publications to interested subscribers. WBI Event Broker also extends the connectivity and transport capabilities of the messaging providers by providing message brokering facilities. WBI Event Broker is available as a standalone product or as a subset of WBI Message Broker that adds message-processing services, including message transformation, message warehousing, and content-based routing.

The main component of the WBI Event Broker is the broker runtime. A broker is a named entity that provides the operating environment that hosts and runs message-processing services. From a JMS perspective, the broker provides a full and robust publish/subscribe implementation. Coupled with the queue manager, the broker provides WebSphere Application Server with a full JMS implementation that supports both the point-to-point and publish/subscribe messaging capabilities. WBI Event Broker actually uses WebSphere MQ to implement much of its functionality and thus sits on top of a queue manager, as illustrated in Figure 12-13. Subscriptions to the WBI Event Broker are done via the underlying WebSphere MQ middleware. Applications that can connect to WebSphere MQ middleware can connect to the subscription. Actually, WBI Event Broker supports more subscription types other than the Base WebSphere MQ, such as WebSphere MQ Mobile or WebSphere MQ Real Time. These options are beyond the scope of this book.

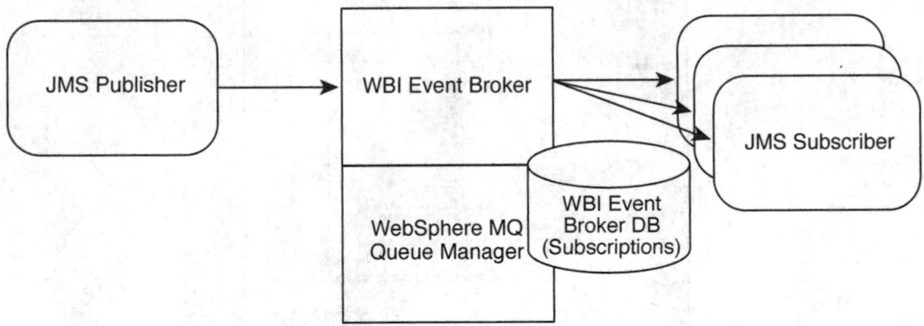


**Figure 12-13** WBI Event Broker.

Without going into too much detail, the broker's ability to publish messages is encapsulated in a *Publication* node of a produced message flow; the message flow is created using the WBI Broker toolkit. The Publication node can be included in any visual message flow. However, a simple publish flow (which is the one only supported by Event Broker) contains an input node for the transport that is being published on (in our case the transport is the underlying WebSphere MQ Provider) and the Publication node. Figure 12-14 illustrates the simple flow developed inside the Event Broker Toolkit.

Once the message flow is created, it can be deployed into the runtime. In order to get a basic understanding, let's evaluate Figure 12-15.

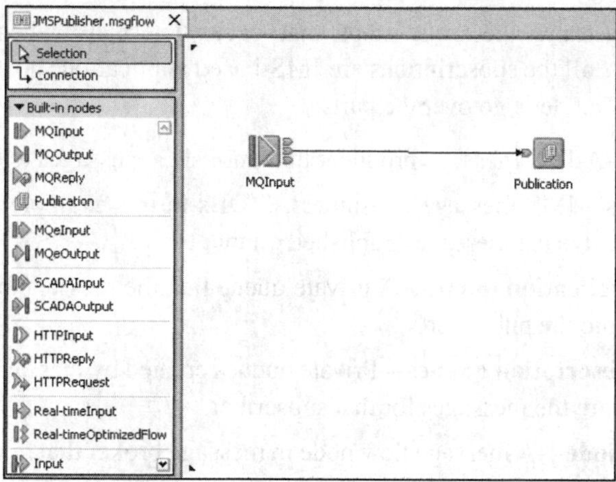


**Figure 12-14** Developing simple publication flow.

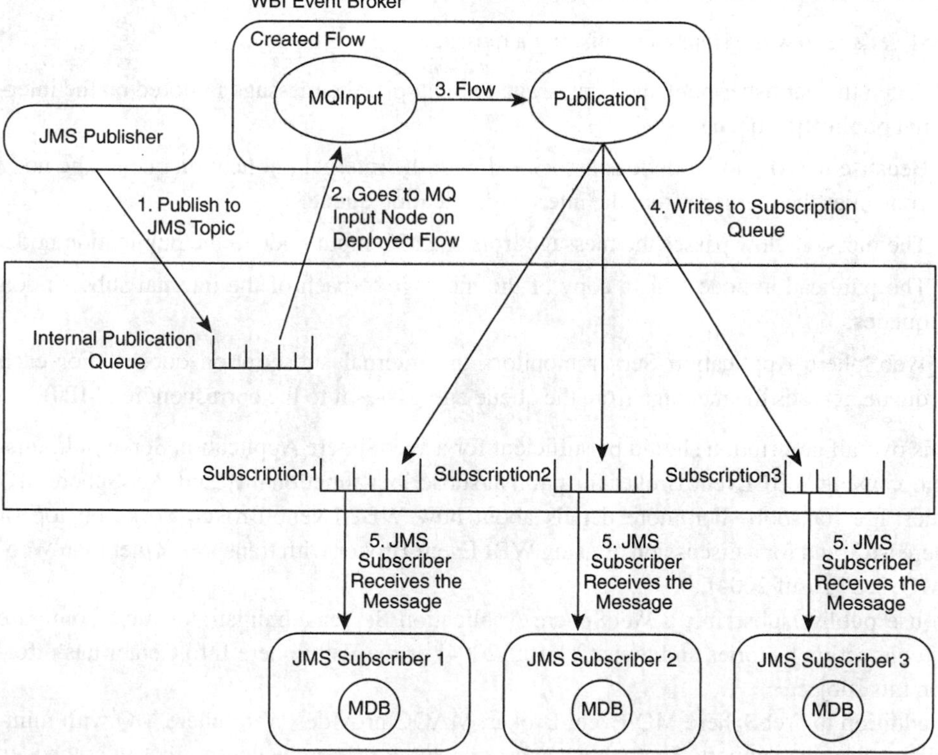


**Figure 12-15** WBI Event Broker publish and subscribe.

The figure illustrates the basic steps that occur internally when using publish-and-subscribe. In this case, all the subscriptions are JMS-based applications hosted inside WebSphere Application Server. First, let's go over the parts:

- **Publisher**—A JMS message producer that publishes messages to the topic.
- **Subscribers**—JMS message consumers, MDBs in this example, that subscribe to the topic and receive the messages published on that topic.
- **Internal publication queue**—A private queue that the message broker creates to store messages from the publisher(s).
- **Internal subscription queues**—Private queues created by message broker, one per subscriber, to store the messages for that subscriber.
- **MQ input node**—A message flow node in message broker that reads messages from the internal publication queue.
- **Publication node**—A message flow node in message broker that copies a message to each of the internal subscription queues.

Next, let's review the steps in publishing a message:

1. When the publisher publishes a message to the topic, the message is stored on the internal publication queue.
2. Because the MQ input node is associated with the internal publication queue, the node consumes the message from the internal publication queue.
3. The message flow passes the message from the MQ input node to the publication node.
4. The publication node adds a copy of the message to each of the internal subscription queues.
5. WebSphere Application Server monitors the internal subscription queues. For each queue, it reads the message from the queue and passes it to the corresponding MDB.

This overall description should be sufficient for a WebSphere Application Server administrator who is using WBI Event Broker for publish/subscriber functionality and WebSphere MQ as the message transport. For more details about how WBI Event Broker works on top of WebSphere MQ, and for a discussion of using WBI Event Broker with transports other than WebSphere MQ, see [Yusuf 2004].

To use publish/subscribe, a WebSphere Application Server administrator must configure the topic connection factories and topics. [Yusuf 2004] or the WebSphere Info Center has information on this subject.

In addition to WebSphere MQ Event Broker, MAOC provides WebSphere MQ with minimal publish/subscribe support. The publish/subscribe support is equivalent to that in embedded messaging; however, unlike MAOC, the embedded messaging provider is actually a subset of WBI Event Broker. To use this extension, you must set Version to BASIC inside the topic connection factory configuration. The MAOC site is downloadable from the WebSphere MQ product Web page on the IBM Web site.

### Third-Party Providers

It is possible to configure WAS V5.X to work with third-party generic JMS providers such as SonicMQ, Tibco, etc. To do so, you need to register the third-party provider to WebSphere Application Server in the administrative console, under Resources, Generic JMS Provider. Once you have registered the provider, the connection factories and destinations can be created. This procedure for registering a generic JMS provider and creating the necessary resources that back up the connection factories and destinations is vendor-specific. [Gang 2003] is a good example; in the article, Sonic MQ is configured as a JMS provider to WebSphere Application Server.

## Message Driven Beans

A Message Driven Bean is a special EJB type that receives JMS asynchronous messages. As we learned in Chapter 9, "Enterprise JavaBeans," an MDB does not have any client interfaces, just a bean class. The bean class implements a *MessageDrivenBean* interface and implements the *MessageListener* interface defined by the JMS specification. It is the job of the container to manage the life cycle of the bean and to interact with the JMS API.

### Message Driven Bean Programming Model

An MDB implements the ejbCreate, ejbRemove, getMessageDrivenContext and setMessageDrivenContext methods declared by the MessageDrivenBean interface. The main code, however, is in the onMessage method defined by the JMS *MessageListener* interface. Code Snippet 12-1 shows an example of an MDB onMessage method. A developer just codes an onMessage method. The container handles passing the message to the MDB.

**Code Snippet 12-1** MDB onMessage

```
//onMessage() method from Message Listener Interface
  public void onMessage(javax.jms.Message msg)
  {
    TextMessage txt = (TextMessage)msg;
    System.out.println("IN MDB, XML Order:");
    try
    {
       String textStr = txt.getText();
       System.out.println(textStr);
       ExchangeBO exchangeBO = new ExchangeBO();
       ExchangeVO exchangeVO = exchangeBO.parseMessage
       ➥(((TextMessage)msg).getText());
       exchangeBO.processOrder(exchangeVO);
    }
    catch(Exception e)
    {
```

```
        fMessageDrivenCtx.setRollbackOnly();
        e.printStackTrace(System.out);
    }
}
```

A Message Driven Bean has a similar life cycle to that of a Stateless Session Bean, as shown in Figure 12-16. Its life cycle is completely managed by the container.

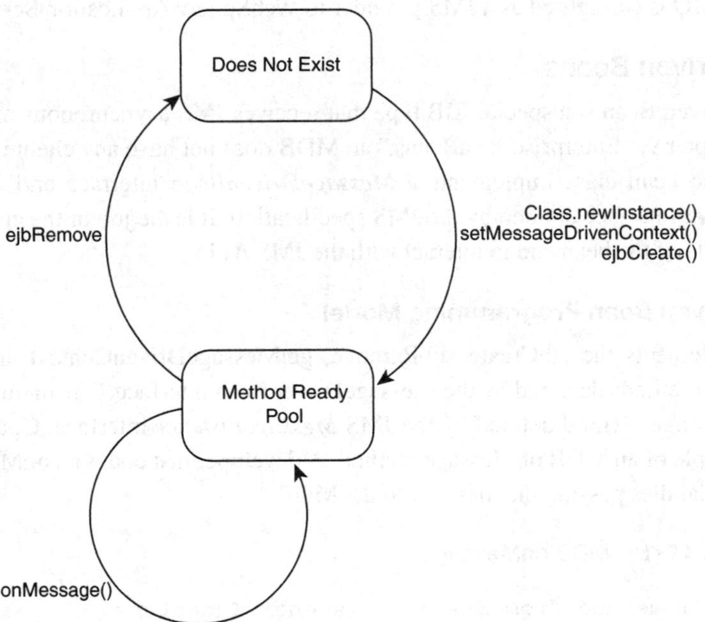


**Figure 12-16** Message Driven Bean life cycle.

Remember, unlike other EJB types, a client does not interact directly with an MDB. Instead, an MDB is tied to some type of listener and is invoked when a message arrives on a queue or topic. A client interacts with JMS or some other message API by writing messages to the queue or topic that the MDB is tied to.

### Message Driven Bean Deployment Descriptor

Much like the other EJB types, an MDB is defined in the *Bean* section of the EJB deployment descriptor. Code Snippet 12-2 illustrates the definition of the MDB we will deploy in this chapter. The only item unique to MDBs in this Code Snippet is the message-driven-destination.

**Code Snippet 12-2** MDB definition

```
<message-driven id="ExchangeMDB">
  <!--  BEAN DEFINITION -->
  <ejb-name>ExchangeMDB</ejb-name>
  <ejb-class>com.deploybook.exchange.ExchangeMDBBean</ejb-class>
  <!--  TRANSACTION DEMARCATION -->
  <transaction-type>Container</transaction-type>
  <!--  MDB TYPE - QUEUE FOR PtoP or TOPIC for Pub/Sub -->
  <message-driven-destination>
    <destination-type>javax.jms.Queue</destination-type>
  </message-driven-destination>

  <!-- RESOURCE REFERENCE to other EJB used by the MDB code -->
  <ejb-local-ref id="EJBLocalRef_1074832719459">
    <ejb-ref-name>ejb/TradeData</ejb-ref-name>
    <ejb-ref-type>Entity</ejb-ref-type>
    <local-home>
                com.deploybook.exchange.TradeDataLocalHome
      </local-home>
    <local>                    com.deploybook.exchange.TradeDataLocal
  ➥</local>
    <ejb-link>TradeData</ejb-link>
  </ejb-local-ref>
</message-driven>
```

An MDB is packaged in an EJB JAR along with other EJBs and deployed on a server. Because the container manages all the JMS code, the container needs information at deployment time in order for the container to use the correct JMS connection factory and destination. WebSphere Application Server uses a Listener Port, which is a configuration object on the server, to describe these attributes. We will talk about Listener Ports later in the chapter.

## MDB Transactional Behavior

MDBs using Container Managed Transactions can only have two possible values: REQUIRED and NOTSUPPORTED. This makes sense since no other component can call an MDB directly. Under the REQUIRED, the transaction is started by the container, and the message is removed from its destination under the newly started transaction and passed to the MDB. Any transactional code within the MDB code will be part of the same transaction that reads the message.

Message Driven Beans also support Bean Managed Transactions, but the actual read of the message by the container cannot be part of the transaction since the transaction is in the code after the message is read.

## Message Driven Bean Configuration

Once the provider and resources are defined, applications that use Message Driven Beans can be configured. The MDB configuration is independent of any provider configuration. An MDB is bound to a connection factory and destination through its JNDI names. This is done with a special configuration object called a *Listener Port*. A Listener Port is a special object that is associated with a Message Driven Bean at deployment time. This allows for deployment simplicity, as an MDB only needs to be configured with the Listener Port name. The Listener Port is configured with the JNDI name of the JMS connection factory and JMS destination.

In addition, a Listener Port is configured with properties to define the required appropriate behavior for the listener. These properties include:

- **Maximum sessions**—As we stated, a JMS session is a multi-thread context for JMS operations. This setting controls the number of sessions that are created for the Listener Port and thus controls the concurrency for reading messages. Each Listener Port has its own pool of sessions. This allows for multiple listeners and thus allows MDB to process messages concurrently. A setting of one means that the listener would have to wait for the MDB to finish before processing the next message for that MDB. If the MDB processing takes longer than usual, you can consider having more sessions.

  This setting should always be less than the connection pool size of the corresponding connection factory since a JMS connection creates JMS sessions.
- **Maximum messages**—This specifies the number of messages that a single session can process in a single transaction. This setting is only supported for WebSphere embedded messaging and WebSphere MQ; for a generic JMS provider, the Listener Port processes each message in its own transaction, so the setting is effectively ignored, and its value is always treated as "1." This setting allows for the possibility of having an MDB process a group of messages in a single transaction.
- **Maximum retries**—This setting is based on messages that are rolled back in a transaction onto its originating destination. JMS messages have a retry count that keeps track of how many times a message has been rolled back. If a message is rolled back more times than allowed by this setting, the Listener will shut itself down to avoid getting stuck in an infinite loop. The message provider may intervene before this point, as it may have its own settings to control this. For example, WebSphere MQ has a threshold count.

Listener Ports are configured on individual servers. Using the admin console, you can access the Message Listener Service under the server properties, as shown in Figure 12-17.

From there, you can select the Listener Ports link, as shown in Figure 12-18. This takes you to the Listener Port page.

Application Servers >
**server1**

An application server is a server which provides services requir

Runtime | Configuration

General Properties

Name

Application classloader policy

Application class loading mode

Apply | OK | Reset | Cancel

Additional Properties

| | |
|---|---|
| Transaction Service | Spe |
| Web Container | Spe par |
| EJB Container | Spe |
| Dynamic Cache Service | Spe |
| Logging and Tracing | Spe |
| Message Listener Service | Cor dep sett |
| ORB Service | Spe |
| Custom Properties | Add her |
| Administration Services | Spe |
| Diagnostic Trace Service | Vie |
| Debugging Service | Spe |
| IBM Service Logs | Cor |
| Custom Services | Def |
| Server Components | Add |
| Process Definition | A p |

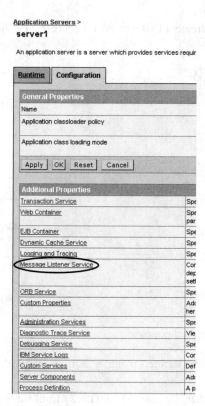

**Figure 12-17** Message Listener Service.

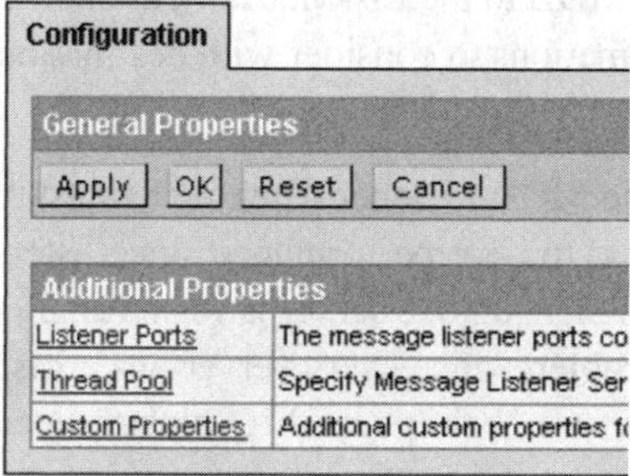


**Figure 12-18** Message Listener Service page.

You can select New to create a Listener Port. Figure 12-19 shows the Listener Port wizard in the admin console.

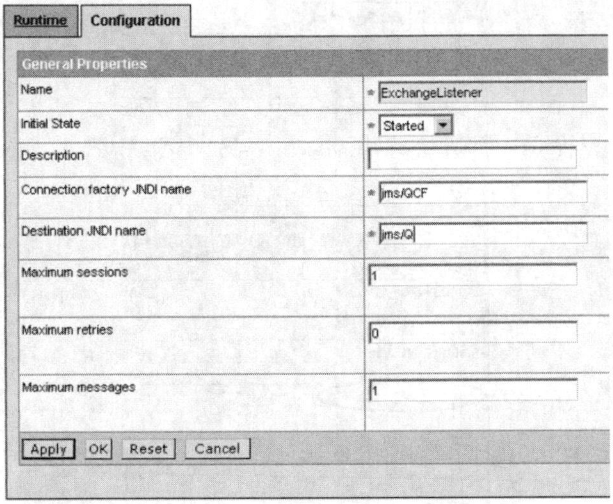

**Figure 12-19** Listener Port configuration.

Listener Ports can also be defined using wsadmin. We will do this when deploying our sample.

The Message Listener Service also has a Thread Pool Setting. All Listener Ports share a thread pool, which can be configured on the Message Listener Service. The thread pool controls the total number of threads across *all* Listener Ports. This is different from the maximum sessions option on the Listener Port, which controls the total number of threads for a single Listener Port.

The Message Driven Bean is bound to the Listener Port in the binding file of the EJB JAR file. Using WebSphere tools such as the ASTK or WebSphere Studio, you can use the deployment descriptor editor to match the MDB to the Listener Port, as shown in Figure 12-20.

There are various combinations to consider with destinations, Listener Ports, and Message Driven Beans:

- Having more than one MDB Listener listening against the same destination is possible. However, this can lead to poor performance since listeners can compete for messages. Defining multiple listeners on one server is wasteful; however, cloned WAS servers suffer from the same problem since every server has a Listener Port pointing to the same queue. It is better to use WebSphere MQ cluster queues in cloned environments to reduce contention.

- Having different MDBs configured on a Single Listener Port is also possible. In this scenario, the MDB shares the same Listener Port settings. For example, if there are two MDBs configured under the Same Listener Port with a max sessions set to 1, then only one of those two MDBs will be processing at a time. While this pattern is rarely useful, in some rare circumstances, it might be helpful to limit the rate of access to a single queue across multiple MDBs.

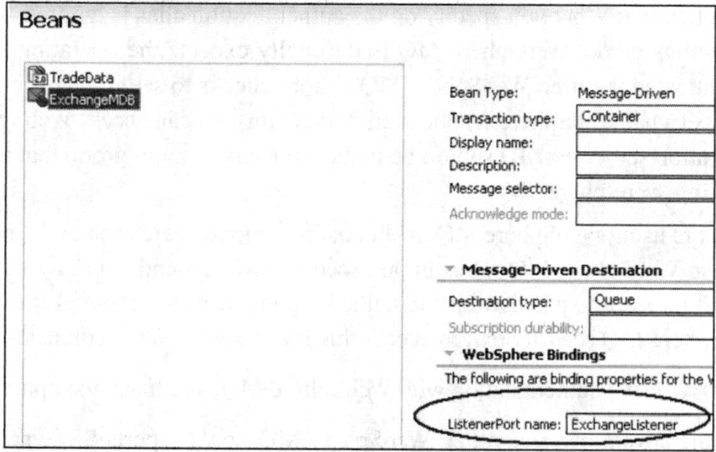


**Figure 12-20** Mapping an MDB to a Listener Port.

## JMS Security

Since JMS is a resource, you must consider the security implications. For the WebSphere embedded messaging, many of the security considerations are handled by WebSphere Application Server directly. For external providers, such as WebSphere MQ, security will require additional configuration in WebSphere Application Server and the external provider.

JMS connection factory resources are accessed underneath the covers by WAS through the J2C framework. This has several implications for JMS resources. First, when you create a JMS connection factory using the console or wsadmin, it becomes visible in the JNDI namespace. (An application can look up the resource using a global JNDI lookup, or the resource can be bound into the local namespace of an application using resource-references.) The connection factory should have an associated J2C *authentication alias* (we explained this concept with JDBC in Chapter 7, "JDBC as a Resource"). An authentication alias can be either container managed or application managed. As stated in Chapter 7, container managed authentication is strongly recommended if you wish to control access to those queues by applications running within the WAS cell. JMS resources that have component aliases cannot be protected by WAS.

When authentication is being performed, the semantics are dependent on the messaging provider:

- If you are using embedded messaging, the user ID and password specified on the connection are verified against the WAS security registry. User IDs longer than 12 characters cannot be used for authentication with the embedded JMS provider.
- If you are using WebSphere MQ, in bindings mode, there is no user ID/password authentication. What you specify on the authentication alias is ignored. This is because in bindings mode, WebSphere MQ traditionally expects the operating system to have authenticated the user. WebSphere MQ simply checks to see if the userid of the calling process (what WebSphere Application Server runs as) can access WebSphere MQ. The application server user ID should be in the appropriate mqm group that is created when installing WebSphere MQ.
- If you are using WebSphere MQ in client/server mode, there is no built-in authentication because WebSphere MQ relies upon process-level authentication by default. The user ID and password specified on the authentication alias are ignored unless you write a WebSphere MQ security exit to access this information on the connection and verify it.

In order to achieve authentication with WebSphere MQ, you have two options:

- With the advent of version 5.3, WebSphere MQ now supports SSL encryption. Therefore, you can configure its SSL support, which will provide coarse-grained process-to-process-level authentication along with encryption.
- If you need fine-grained authentication that can distinguish between different applications in a shared environment, you'll need to write a custom WMQ security exit for authentication. Security exits can provide granular, per-connection factory authentication. See [Yusuf 2004].

Once the connection is authenticated (if applicable), authorization checks are performed to make sure the user can access the queue or topic requested. For embedded JMS, authorization is controlled by the file *integral-jms-authorizations.xml*. This file can be found in the config directory of the WebSphere Application server install. For WebSphere MQ resources, authorization is configured using a utility command called *setmqaut*.

## Automation

We will now use our build process to configure our WebSphere Application Server and deploy the application. This new version of the Personal Trade System contains the actual trade use case. As part of the trade process, a message is written to a JMS queue, which sends an XML message to the stock exchange. We will also deploy a second StockExchange EAR file, which mimics the stock exchange. The StockExchange EAR contains an EJB JAR with an MDB that receives the message, parses it, and stores it in a database.

Besides the additional EAR, we have added configuration scripts for our JMS resources. This includes creating resources such as a queue connection factory and a queue as well as a Listener Port for our MDB. We will briefly examine the scripts and then run the build process.

## Defining JMS Configuration with wsadmin

As part of our build process, we have added scripts that will configure our JMS resources as well as the server. We will use the embedded JMS server for our application. Our application uses the point-to-point JMS programming model. We need to:

- Create a Security Alias for our JMS resources.
- Define our JMS resources—We will create a queue connection factory and a queue.
- Create a JMS Listener Port—We have one Message Driven Bean that will need a Listener Port to bind to.
- Add the queue to the JMS server—This is specific to the embedded server. This creates a concrete implementation of the queue. If you were using WebSphere MQ, you would not need this step.

Let's briefly look at the scripts.

### Create Security Alias

Just like we did for the JDBC resource, we need to create a J2C authentication alias for the resource. The script is shown in Code Snippet 12-3. There is not much of a difference between this script and the one for JDBC.

**Code Snippet 12-3** J2C authentication alias

```
#-------------------------------------------------------------
# Create a J2C Authentication Alias
#-------------------------------------------------------------


# Set variables for authentication alias
set defaultUser1 "jmsuser"
set defaultPassword1 "jmsuser"
set aliasName "JMSUser"
set aliasDescription "J2C alias for the JMS Server"

puts "\nGetting the name and ID of the cell we are on"
set cellName [$AdminControl getCell]
set cellID [$AdminConfig getid /Cell:$cellName/]
puts "\nInstall JDBC Provider on cell:$cellName Cell ID:$cellID"
```

```
puts "\nSearch for and remove the alias if it exists"
set secID [$AdminConfig getid /Cell:$cellName/Security:/]
set aliases [$AdminConfig list JAASAuthData $secID]
foreach al $aliases {
  set thisAlias [lindex [lindex [$AdminConfig show $al {alias}] 0] 1]
  if {($thisAlias == "$aliasName")} {
   puts "\nRemoving old JAAS Auth Alias:$thisAlias"
   $AdminConfig remove $al
   $AdminConfig save
  }
}

puts "\nCreate the J2C Authentication Alias"

set alias_attr    [list alias $aliasName]
set desc_attr     [list description $aliasDescription]
set userid_attr   [list userId $defaultUser1]
set password_attr [list password $defaultPassword1]
set attrs         [list $alias_attr $desc_attr $userid_attr
➥$password_attr]

$AdminConfig create JAASAuthData $secID $attrs

puts "\nSaving configuration"

$AdminConfig save

puts "\nDone creating J2C Alias!\n"
```

### Create JMS Resources

Next, we have two scripts for creating the resources: one for the queue connection factory and another for the queue. Code Snippet 12-4 illustrates the script for the queue connection factory. Besides creating variables, we find the cell we are on and look for the WebSphere JMS provider. We then set up the attributes and create the factory. We also set up a Mapping module, which allows us to use a container managed alias. For WebSphere MQ, you would have to change the provider name and add the additional MQ attributes to the connection factory.

**Code Snippet 12-4** Creating the queue connection factory

```
#--------------------------------
#This section sets up the cell and the node. This
#needs to be updated for your machine. Notice that the jmsprovider
#will point at the embedded provider. If you wish to use MQ Server
➥instead of embedded server then change the name to
#"WebSphere MQ JMS Provider"
#----------------------------------------

# JAAS auth alias Users and passwords..
set aliasName "JMSUser"

# Provider
set jmsprovider "WebSphere JMS Provider"

set found 0

#---------------------------------
#This Section sets up the Queue Connection Factory Name and
#retrieves the Cell ID we are on.
#----------------------------------------
set QCFname StockExchangeQCF
set JNDIName jms/StockExchangeQCF

puts "\nGetting the name and ID of the cell we are on"
set cellName [$AdminControl getCell]
set cellID [$AdminConfig getid /Cell:$cellName/]

puts "\nGetting the ID of the JMS Provider"
set jmsProviderID [$AdminConfig getid /Cell:$cellName/
➥JMSProvider:$jmsprovider/ ]


set description "This is a Description"
set category "This is a category"

#----------------------------------------
#This section sets up attributes lists
#----------------------------------------
```

```
set nattrs [list name $QCFname]
set descattrs [list description $description]
set catattrs [list category $category]

set tattrs [list $nattrs $descattrs $catattrs]

#--------------------------------------------------------------
#Create the Queue Connection Factory
#--------------------------------------------------------------
set list [$AdminConfig list WASQueueConnectionFactory]
foreach fnm $list  {if {[string compare $QCFname [$AdminConfig
➥showAttribute $fnm name]] == 0} {$AdminConfig remove $fnm}}

set qcf1 [$AdminConfig create WASQueueConnectionFactory $jmsProviderID
➥$tattrs]

#Set the auth mapping properties
set attrs4 [subst {{jndiName $JNDIName}}]
$AdminConfig modify $qcf1 $attrs4

#--------------------------------------------------------------
#Configure the Connection Factory to use container authentication
#--------------------------------------------------------------

set authDataAliasList [list authDataAlias $aliasName ]
set mappingConfigAliasList [list mappingConfigAlias
➥DefaultPrincipalMapping ]
set mappingList [list $authDataAliasList $mappingConfigAliasList]

$AdminConfig create MappingModule $qcf1 $mappingList
$AdminConfig save
puts "Created WAS Queue Connection Factory as requested"
```

Code Snippet 12-5 illustrates the script for creating the queue. Just like the other resource scripts, we look for the current cell, set up the attributes and the properties, and create the resource.

**Code Snippet 12-5** Create queue for WebSphere JMS

```
set jmsprovider "WebSphere JMS Provider"

set found 0

set Qname StockExchangeQueue
set JNDIName jms/StockExchangeQueue


set list [$AdminConfig list WASQueue]
foreach fnm $list {if {[string compare $Qname [$AdminConfig
➥showAttribute $fnm name]] == 0} {$AdminConfig remove $fnm}}

puts "\nGetting the name and ID of the cell we are on"
set cellName [$AdminControl getCell]
set cellID [$AdminConfig getid /Cell:$cellName/]

puts "\nGetting the ID of the JMS Provider"
set jmsProviderID [$AdminConfig getid /Cell:$cellName/
➥JMSProvider:$jmsprovider/ ]

set description "This is a Description"
set category "This is a category"
set persistence "PERSISTENT"
set Priority "APPLICATION_DEFINED"
set expiry "APPLICATION_DEFINED"
set specifiedPriority 9
set specifiedExpiry 9
set nattrs [list name $Qname]
set jattrs [list jndiName $JNDIName]
set descattrs [list description $description]
set catattrs [list category $category]
set perattrs [list persistence $persistence]
set priattrs [list priority $Priority]
set expattrs [list expiry $expiry]
set spriattrs [list specifiedPriority $specifiedPriority]
set sexpattrs [list specifiedExpiry $specifiedExpiry]
```

```
set tattrs [list $nattrs $jattrs $descattrs $catattrs $perattrs
➥$priattrs $expattrs $spriattrs $sexpattrs]


$AdminConfig create WASQueue $jmsProviderID $tattrs
$AdminConfig save
puts "Created WAS Queue as requested"
```

### Create JMS Listener Port

Next, we create the JMS Listener Port. We look for the MessagingListenerService within the current cell. We set up attributes and create the Listener Port. Code Snippet 12-6 illustrates the script.

**Code Snippet 12-6 Create MDB Listener Port**

```
set found 0

set portname ExchangeListener
set cfactory jms/StockExchangeQCF
set dest jms/StockExchangeQueue
set state START

puts "\nGetting the name and ID of the cell we are on"
set cellName [$AdminControl getCell]
set cellID [$AdminConfig getid /Cell:$cellName/]


set sessions 5
set retries 1
set messages 2

set nattrs [list name $portname]
set cfattrs [list connectionFactoryJNDIName $cfactory]
set dattrs [list destinationJNDIName $dest]
set stateattrs [list stateManagement $state]
set sessattrs [list maxSessions $sessions]
set retryattrs [list maxRetries $retries]
set messattrs [list maxMessages $messages]
set tattrs [list $nattrs $cfattrs $dattrs $sessattrs $retryattrs
➥$messattrs]
```

```
set list [$AdminConfig list ListenerPort $cellID]
foreach fnm $list {if {[string compare $portname [$AdminConfig
➥showAttribute $fnm name]] == 0} {$AdminConfig remove $fnm}}


set mls [$AdminConfig list MessageListenerService $cellID]

set LP [$AdminConfig create ListenerPort $mls $tattrs]
$AdminConfig create StateManageable $LP {{initialState START}}
$AdminConfig save
puts "Created LP as requested"
```

### Add the Queue to the JMS Server

The last JMS script, illustrated in Code Snippet 12-7, adds the queue to the embedded JMS server. This step is only necessary if you are using embedded messaging. For WebSphere MQ, you would have to create the queue using WebSphere MQ tools. The queues are maintained on the JMS server as a list. Note that in WAS Base, the JMS server is a component of the application server. The script looks for the JMS server as a component of server1. It then looks for the queue list to see if the queue is on the list. If not, it will add it to the existing list.

**Code Snippet 12-7** Add the queue to JMS server

```
puts "\nGetting the name and ID of the cell we are on"

set JMSServer "Internal JMS Server"
set Qname StockExchangeQueue
set qnAppend  "true"
set cellName [$AdminControl getCell]
set nodeName [$AdminControl getNode]

set server [$AdminConfig getid
/Cell:$cellName/Node:$nodeName/Server:server1]

$AdminConfig list Component $server

set components [$AdminConfig list Component $server]
foreach fnm $components {if {[string compare $JMSServer [$AdminConfig
➥showAttribute $fnm name]] == 0} {set jmsServerId $fnm}}
```

```
set queueNames [$AdminConfig showAttribute $jmsServerId queueNames]
# parse the semi-colon-separated string into a jacl list

set queueList [split $queueNames \;]
  # make sure the specified queue is added to it
  if { [lsearch $queueList $Qname]==-1 } {
     if { $qnAppend } {
       set queueList $Qname
     } else {
       lappend queueList $Qname
     }
     # join the list back together
     set queueNames [join $queueList \; ]
     set attrs "{queueNames $queueNames}"
     set newQN [$AdminConfig modify $jmsServerId $attrs]
  } else {
    # do nothing because the queue is already present
  }

puts "\nSaving configuration"

$AdminConfig save
```

## Run the Build Deployment Process

We are now ready to run the build process. We have added additional tests to test out the trade function. We will then execute a trade through the browser. Finally, we can check the logs to verify that our MDB received the message and stored it in its tables.

1. Create a new repository in CVS and call it C:/cvs_chapter12.
2. Extract C:\WASDeployBook\Chapter12\cvs_chapter12 into the new repository.
3. Next, run C:\WASDeployBook\Chapter12\CreateDBScript.bat script in a DB2 command window to create the tables needed for this exercise.
4. Let's run the build process we described previously. From the command prompt, go to the C:\WASDeployBook\Chapter12\ANTBuildScripts directory and enter **RunBuildProcess buildDeployVerifyNoStop**.

5. Once the build is complete, you can examine the verification test by going to c:\testreport and opening index.html. You will see the additional tests for the trade use cases.
6. Next, open a browser and go to http://localhost:9080/pts. Log in as bbird and use password1a as the password. Select the Trade Center link, as shown in Figure 12-21. Either buy IBM stock or sell any holdings the user has.

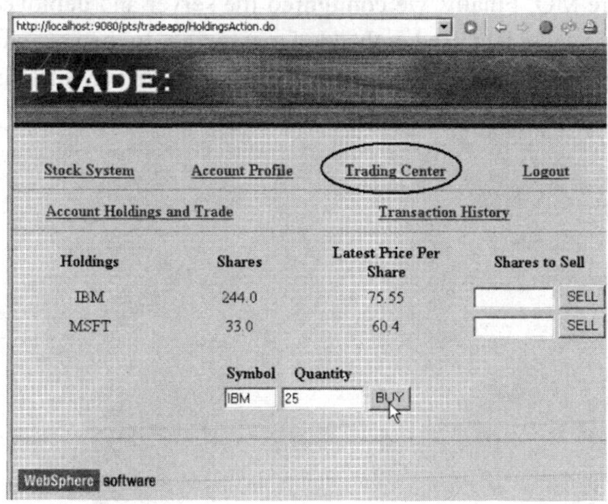


**Figure 12-21** Trade use case.

7. Now look for the System.out for the server. It should be under <WAS INSTALL ROOT>\logs\server1. It should indicate that MDB received the message and print it out, as shown in Code Snippet 12-8.

**Code Snippet 12-8 Printout of Message Driven Bean receiving message**

```
[2/12/04 23:07:08:495 EST] 262ce758 SystemOut     O IN MDB, XML Order:
[2/12/04 23:07:08:495 EST] 262ce758 SystemOut     O <trade-
order><accountId>123456789</accountId><action>BUY</action><symbol>IBM</
➥symbol><shares>25.0</shares></trade-order>
```

8. Undeploy and stop the application by running the same BAT file and passing in the UndeployStop target as shown: **RunBuildProcess UndeployStop**.

## Conclusion

In this chapter, we covered JMS in detail. We talked a bit about messaging. We also provided a brief overview of the JMS and MDB programming models. We talked about the various JMS providers supported by WAS, both internal and external. We also showed how WebSphere Application Server works with various JMS providers. Specifically, we focused on the embedded JMS server and WebSphere MQ. Finally, we configured the server and deployed the Personal Trade System with added use cases that used embedded messaging. In the next chapter, we will look at some other resources supported by WebSphere Application Server, such as JavaMail and URL Resources.

CHAPTER 13

# Other Resources

We have dedicated entire chapters in this book to the more popular types of J2EE resources—JDBC for database access in Chapter 7, J2C for enterprise connectivity in Chapter 8, and JMS for messaging in Chapter 12. While not prolific enough to earn their own chapter individually, two other types of J2EE resources are important as well. This chapter will focus on JavaMail and Uniform Resource Locator (URL) resources. We will talk a little about their function, provide some tips for their use, and show how to configure them with the wsadmin scripting facility.

## URL Resources

The URL is the most common means of accessing information on the Internet, typically through a web browser. URLs were devised as a simple way to access *any* resource across a network, not just web pages. In the early days of the Internet, when all content was static, *resource* meant "file," and URLs were used commonly to access files using various protocols. In that context, a URL has two primary components:

```
<protocol>://<protocol_info>
```

Breaking down a typical URL, such as http://www.pts.com/info/contact_us.html, we can see that it will access the file contact_us.html from the info directory on the www.pts.com server using the hypertext transfer protocol. If there were no file specified, the directory would end with a slash, in which case, the server would serve up whichever file it is configured to use as a default (typically index.html for HTTP servers). This URL is something you might enter into a web browser's address field to view the HTML file, which is just a file retrieved into the browser and parsed/rendered by the browser per the HTML specification. The protocol could be any of a number of others, such as 'ftp' for file-transfer or 'file' for other types of files located on a file system.

The URL can also have a port number appended to the host name in order to override the default port for the given protocol. For example, http://www.pts.com:81/info/contact_us.html would use port 81 on the server rather than the default HTTP port of 80.

URLs are not only useful for browsers. Programs may also need to access information using URLs. It is not unusual for a program to explicitly use an HTTP URL to access a web page and "clip" some data from it for processing or display; or to transfer a file using the file URL and parse its contents; or to provide file download capability by using an FTP URL. In the past, it was typical for programs to have these URL links hard-coded, which was not a good idea since hard-coded values are difficult to change. The second and perhaps more interesting reason for using URLs is that if the program is not concerned with the resource implementation (e.g., it just wants to read from a stream), it is better to provide a layer of abstraction. By using the URL abstraction, all information is accessed the same way, regardless of the underlying representation. Thus, if the information needed resides in a local file or on a remote FTP server, URLs provide transparent access to the information, ignoring issues like availability. As with JDBC, URL resources can be configured with JNDI names for better flexibility. Let's look at some of the WebSphere Application Server (WAS) resources for configuring URL providers. Figure 13-1 shows the WAS Default URL Provider. There isn't much interesting here, as support for this default provider is built into the JDK. The default URL provider handles the standard J2SE 1.3.1 protocols such as HTTP, file, and FTP. Users are free to invent their own protocols or use those from other vendors by creating URL providers that specify the implementation class name and protocol name in the designated fields.

URL Providers >

**Default URL Provider**

Factory used to create new URLs. Although URLs are actually created using classes in the JVM, this type hides the actual mechanism used to create the URLs

**Configuration**

| General Properties | |
|---|---|
| Scope | * cells:BILLHINEST40Cell1 |
| Name | * Default URL Provider |
| Description | |
| Classpath | |
| Stream Handler Classname | * unused |
| Protocol | * unused |

Apply | OK | Reset | Cancel

| Additional Properties | |
|---|---|
| URLs | Configurations for Uniform Resource Locators (URLs), which are used to locate resources. |
| Custom Properties | Properties that may be required for Resource Providers and Resource Factories. For example, most database vendors require additional custom properties for data sources that will access the database. |

**Figure 13-1** WAS default URL provider.

Clicking on the URLs link in Figure 13-1 takes you to a list of configured URLs. There are none configured by default, but Figure 13-2 is an example of a sample configuration.

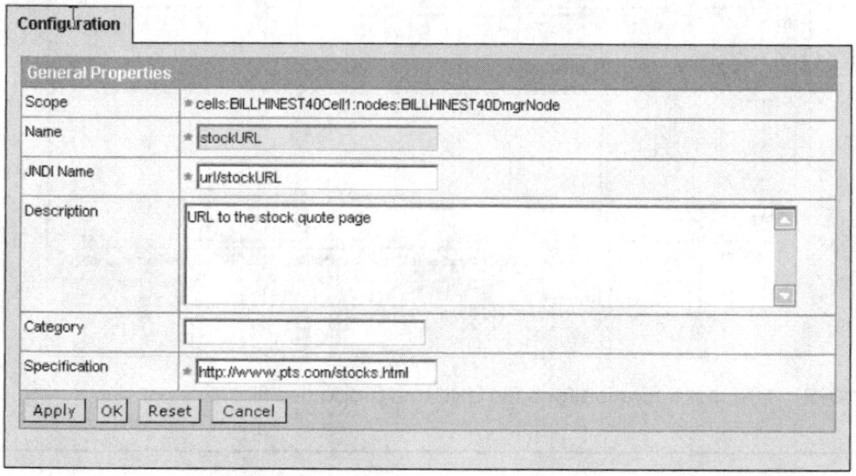

Configuration

| General Properties | |
|---|---|
| Scope | * cells:BILLHINEST40Cell1:nodes:BILLHINEST40DmgrNode |
| Name | * stockURL |
| JNDI Name | * url/stockURL |
| Description | URL to the stock quote page |
| Category | |
| Specification | * http://www.pts.com/stocks.html |

Apply OK Reset Cancel

**Figure 13-2** URL configuration for a stock page.

## URL Resources and Properties Files

One of the great challenges in developing complex, flexible systems is the need for configuration parameters that can be set by an administrator. J2EE resources provide a number of parameters that are configurable. Unfortunately, most applications have additional application-specific configuration parameters that are not directly supported by J2EE. While application teams can develop their own custom configuration framework, most use Java property files because they are more than adequate. However, there is a challenge with property files. First, technically, it is illegal for a J2EE application to read a file directly. Second, the most common work-around to the first problem is to place the property file on the classpath of the application code. Unfortunately, this usually involves placing the property file in the EAR or in a JAR within the EAR. This makes editing the properties file cumbersome after deployment (the EAR must be altered). Ideally, properties files should be easily editable files on the file system that administrators can edit directly. URL resources provide an interesting way to try to side step this problem. By configuring a URL resource that represents a file, a J2EE-compliant application can read property information from the URL resource stream without truly accessing the file system. Of course, this assumes that your J2EE container supports URL resources pointing to files, as WAS does. Figure 13-3 shows a file-based URL resource, in this case a properties file on the local C: drive of a Windows server.

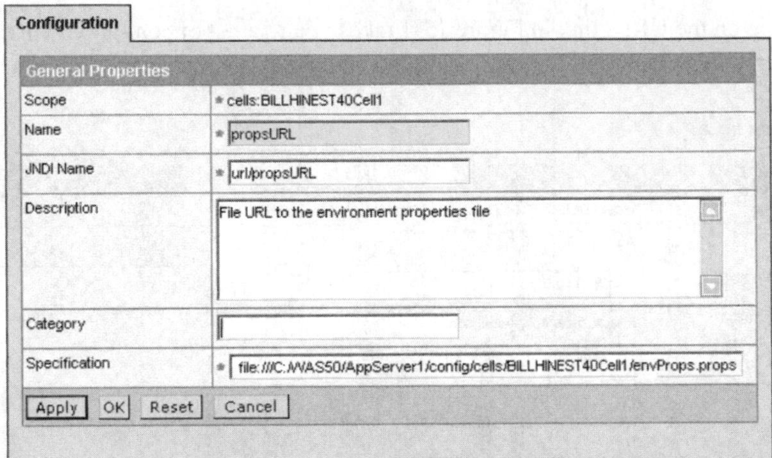


**Figure 13-3** URL configuration for a file URL to a properties file.

> **NOTE**
>
> Figure 13-3 shows a URL resource that points to a file-based properties file that is located under the application server's config/cells/<cell> directory. For WAS Network Deployment installations, placing the master copy of the property file in the same directory tree under the Deployment Manager has the advantage that it can be replicated by the Deployment Manager to all nodes in a multi-node environment. In that case, what you see here would be a copy of the file that is placed under the application server config directory after the replication. Obviously, the original copy is under the Deployment Manager config directory since that is the source for configuration files. Using this technique is preferable to the error-prone approach of manually copying the files to each node. However, because the file is not managed by the normal WAS admin tools, when the file is edited using a text editor, WAS will not realize the file has been changed. This means that the properties file will not be synced unless a full node sync is forced using either the WAS admin tools or the syncNode script.

## Creating a URL Resource with wsadmin

In keeping with our theme of showing common administrative tasks using the wsadmin WAS scripting language, Code Snippet 13-1 shows a script for creating a new URL resource under the default URL provider. This will create a URL resource configured as shown previously in Figure 13-2.

**Code Snippet 13-1** Creating a URL resource with wsadmin

```
#-------------------------------------------------------------------
# Create a URL Resource
#-------------------------------------------------------------------
```

```
set urlProviderName "Default URL Provider"
set urlAdminName "stockURL"
set urlJNDIName "url/stockURL"
set urlDescription "URL to the stock quote page"
set urlSpecification "http://www.pts.com/stocks.html"

puts "\nGetting the name and ID of the cell we are on"
set cellName [$AdminControl getCell]
set cellID [$AdminConfig getid /Cell:$cellName/]
puts "\nCreating URL resource for cell:$cellName cell ID $cellID"

puts "\nGetting the ID of the URL Provider"
set urlProviderID [$AdminConfig getid /Cell:$cellName/
➥URLProvider:$urlProviderName/ ]
puts "\nURL Provider ID: $urlProviderID"

set name [list name $urlAdminName]
set jndi [list jndiName $urlJNDIName]
set desc [list description $urlDescription]
set urlSpec [list spec $urlSpecification]
set urlAttrs [list $name $jndi $desc $urlSpec]

$AdminConfig create URL $urlProviderID $urlAttrs

puts "\nSaving configuration"
$AdminConfig save

puts "\nDone!\n"
```

## JavaMail

JavaMail provides a facility for sending email to and receiving email from mail servers in a platform- and protocol-independent way. The JavaMail APIs, as implemented by J2EE containers such as WAS, provide developers a way to write email functionality into application programs. As an administrator, you will have to create and/or configure resources. The deployer (and perhaps you wear that hat as well!) will then bind the JavaMail resource references in the application deployment descriptors to the resources defined. With JavaMail 1.1, configuration settings were placed in a properties file, but JavaMail 1.2 (as implemented by WAS5 and required in the J2EE 1.3 specification) improves on this. Just as you should never hard-code database connection information in your application or in properties files, you should not hard-code mail server connection information. As we've seen throughout this book, J2EE-compliant resources, resource references, and JNDI should be used instead. WAS ships with two Sun-licensed JAR files—mail.jar and activation.jar—to implement JavaMail runtimes. The former implements the JavaMail APIs and three included protocols (which are discussed next). The latter provides an implementation of the Java Activation Framework (JAF), which helps to handle complex mail, such as MIME (Multi-Purpose Internet Mail Extensions) or file attachments. Let's look at some of the components of JavaMail as implemented by WAS.

## Mail Providers

Mail providers differ from the JDBC Providers we discussed in Chapter 7, "JDBC as a Resource," which are implemented as physical classes in JAR or ZIP files. Mail providers exist only as a configuration "shell" around service providers called *protocol providers*, which in turn implement specific classes for sending mail to and receiving mail from mail servers. WAS has a built-in mail provider (named, reasonably enough, Built-In Mail Provider), which you can see under Resources > Mail Providers in the admin console, as shown in Figure 13-4. It is all that is typically needed by your applications, but under some circumstances, you might want to create other mail providers, as we will discuss later in this section. As you can see in Figure 13-4, the mail provider simply provides context for protocol providers and mail sessions. Custom properties can also be configured for the mail provider, but the built-in mail provider does not require any. Let's take a closer look at protocol providers and mail sessions.

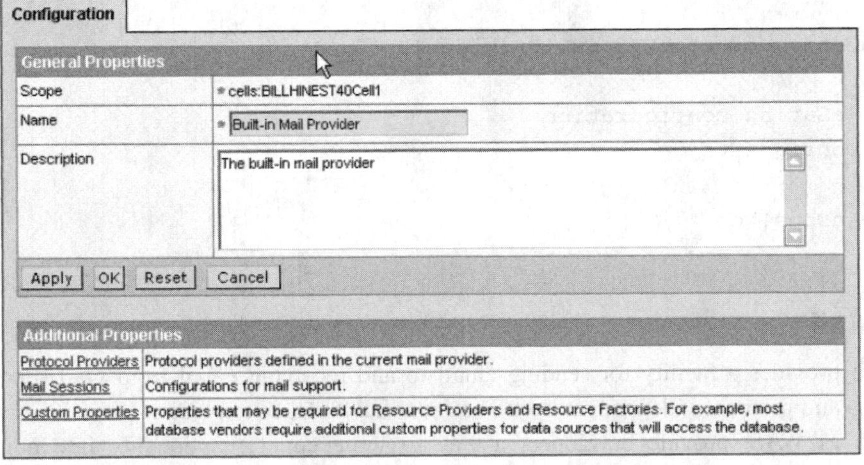


**Figure 13-4** The built-in mail provider.

### Protocol Providers

JavaMail providers incorporate protocol providers to provide a transport for mail messages to and from mail servers using specific protocols. There are three primary protocols that are used for sending and receiving mail over the Internet. You have probably dealt with these if you've ever configured your email client (i.e., Lotus Notes or Microsoft Outlook) for a mail server. They are as follows:

- **SMTP**—Simple Mail Transfer Protocol is used by most mail servers for sending email.
- **POP3**—Post Office Protocol is the most popular protocol for receiving email.
- **IMAP**—Internet Message Access Protocol is an alternative to POP3 for receiving email, although it's not as popular.

The built-in mail provider in WAS has protocol providers for each of these, as shown in Figure 13-5. If the mail servers you need to communicate with require some other protocol, you will have to install a new protocol provider in order to use it.

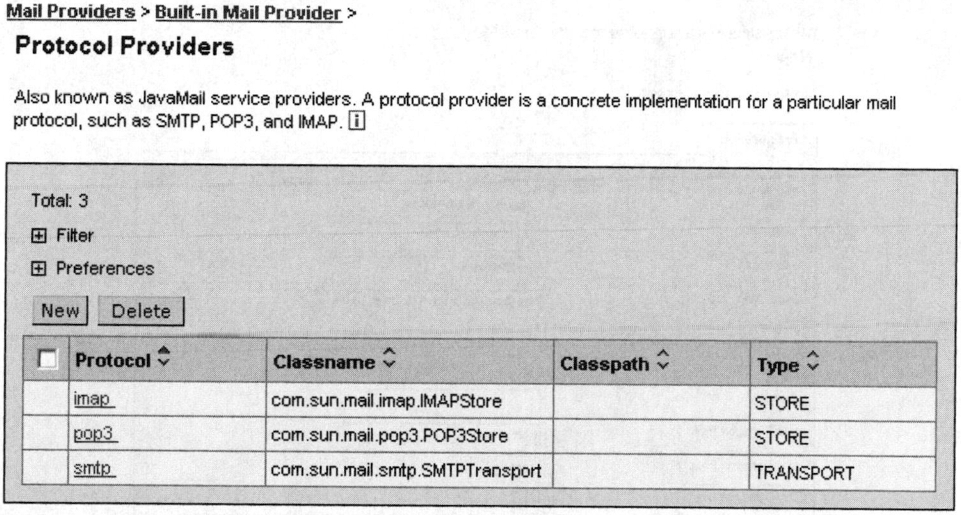

Mail Providers > Built-in Mail Provider >

**Protocol Providers**

Also known as JavaMail service providers. A protocol provider is a concrete implementation for a particular mail protocol, such as SMTP, POP3, and IMAP.

Total: 3

⊞ Filter

⊞ Preferences

New Delete

| ☐ | Protocol | Classname | Classpath | Type |
|---|---|---|---|---|
| | imap | com.sun.mail.imap.IMAPStore | | STORE |
| | pop3 | com.sun.mail.pop3.POP3Store | | STORE |
| | smtp | com.sun.mail.smtp.SMTPTransport | | TRANSPORT |

**Figure 13-5** Protocol providers for the built-in mail provider.

You can see in Figure 13-5 that each protocol provider must provide an implementation class (as the JDBC providers did in Chapter 7), and each has to be designated either for STORE (receiving) or TRANSPORT (sending) mail.

## Mail Sessions

The other link of importance on Figure 13-4 is Mail Sessions, which allows you to configure mail sessions on the mail provider. Mail sessions are more synonymous with the JDBC data sources in Chapter 7, in that they provide the information to connect and interact with a specific physical server—in this case, a mail server. Figure 13-6 shows a sample pane for adding a mail session to the built-in mail provider. As with other types of J2EE resources, we have provided an administrative name and a JNDI name, which can be bound with a resource reference in the application's deployment descriptor. Notice that there are sets of parameters for both mail transport (sending mail) and mail store (receiving mail). The transport user ID and password is optional depending on your mail server.[1] The store user ID and password are used for connecting to the mail server when receiving mail. The user ID is concatenated with the mail store host to form a valid email address (in this case, inbox@mail.pts.com). When connecting to the email server identified by this mail session for the purpose of receiving mail, this is the default email address that will be checked for any new incoming mail on the server. This could be used for any mail that you might want to check and process/route programmatically, such as corporate addresses like abuse@pts.com. There is also a default email address of javamail@pts.com for outgoing mail. This means that if no reply address is provided by the application code, this address will be used—be aware that mail recipients may choose to respond to this address! These settings are defaults and can be overridden dynamically by your application developers using the JavaMail APIs.

Mail Providers > Built-in Mail Provider > Mail Sessions >
**New**

Configurations for mail support.

**Configuration**

| General Properties | |
|---|---|
| Scope | * cells:BILLHINEST40Cell1 |
| Name | * PTSMailSession |
| JNDI Name | * mail/PTSMail |
| Description | Mail Session for the PTS Email Server |
| Category | |
| Mail Transport Host | smtp.pts.com |
| Mail Transport Protocol | smtp |
| Mail Transport User ID | |
| Mail Transport Password | |
| Mail From | javamail.pts.com |
| Mail Store Host | mail.pts.com |
| Mail Store Protocol | pop3 |
| Mail Store User ID | inbox |
| Mail Store Password | ***** |
| Debug | Enable debug mode |

Apply OK Reset Cancel

**Figure 13-6** Adding a mail session to a mail provider.

1 It's worth noting that if the mail transport user ID and password are not required, your mail servers have a security hole.

## JavaMail Tips

### Debugging

It is useful to enable debugging mode by checking the box on Figure 13-6 to see details of the conversation between the application server and mail server as well as property settings for the current session. Debug messages appear in the stdout file, typically SystemOut.log for the specified application server. See the WAS InfoCenter for a detailed section on reading and interpreting this debug output.

> **NOTE**
> For local testing where a true SMTP mail server may not be available, a free download at http://www.postcastserver.com will allow you to install a local mail server on your machine for sending mail.

### Performance

The example screen shot in Figure 13-6 shows a mail session configured to talk to two remote servers, one for sending mail and one for receiving mail. For low-volume email situations, this is probably sufficient. However, remember that a web site can generate high amounts of traffic and potentially also requires high availability. It is crucial that you work with the mail server manager to ensure that the mail servers can meet your needs. It is all too common to use existing internal mail servers without any appropriate capacity planning. This can result in catastrophic outages or performance problems that impact the entire infrastructure as thread pools grow while existing threads wait for responses from the mail servers.

If the remote mail servers do not respond in a timely fashion, application server threads can back up while waiting for the responses. While threads are stalled, additional threads will be used to service new requests, causing a downward spiral as additional server resources are consumed. Eventually, the entire application server can hang once all of the service threads are blocked from talking to the mail server. An alternative to resizing the existing mail server is to offload mail processing to a dedicated mail process on the local server, such as sendmail on Unix systems. This allows the application server to quickly resolve the mail tasks from the servlet or EJB container threads. Of course, be aware that this local mail process could represent a single point of failure if not configured for high availability. For fully robust mail services in situations that warrant them, consider a separate local highly available mail server rather than local co-located mail processes or remote servers.

### Creating a Mail Session with wsadmin

In keeping with our theme of showing common administrative tasks using the wsadmin WAS scripting language, Code Snippet 13-2 shows a script for creating a new mail session under the built-in mail provider. This creates a mail session configured as shown in Figure 13-6.

**Code Snippet 13-2 Creating a mail session with wsadmin**

```
#------------------------------------------------------------------
# Create a mail session
#------------------------------------------------------------------
set mailProviderName "Built-in Mail Provider"
set mailAdminName "PTSMailSession"
set mailJNDIName "mail/ptsMail"
set mailDescription "Mail Session to connect to the PTS mail server"
set mailFrom "javamail@pts.com"
set mailTransHost "smtp.pts.com"
set mailTransProtocol "smtp"
set mailStoreHost "mail.pts.com"
set mailStoreProtocol "pop3"
set mailStoreUser "inbox"
set mailStorePassword "secret"

puts "\nGetting the name and ID of the cell we are on"
set cellName [$AdminControl getCell]
set cellID [$AdminConfig getid /Cell:$cellName/]
puts "\nCreating mail session for cell:$cellName cell ID $cellID"

puts "\nGetting the ID of the Mail Provider"
set mailProviderID [$AdminConfig getid
/Cell:$cellName/MailProvider:$mailProviderName/ ]
puts "\nMail Provider ID: $mailProviderID"

set name [list name $mailAdminName]
set jndi [list jndiName $mailJNDIName]
set desc [list description $mailDescription]
set frm [list mailFrom $mailFrom]
set mth [list mailTransportHost $mailTransHost]
set msh [list mailStoreHost $mailTransHost]
set msu [list mailStoreUser $mailStoreUser]
set mspw [list mailStorePassword $mailStorePassword]
set msAttrs [list $name $jndi $desc $frm $mth $msh $msu $mspw]
```

```
$AdminConfig create MailSession $mailProviderID $msAttrs

puts "\nSaving configuration"
$AdminConfig save

puts "\nDone!\n"
```

## Conclusion

This chapter gave an overview of two "minor" but not unimportant types of resources—URLs and JavaMail. While not used as often as JDBC resources, they can be the source of some unnecessary and non-J2EE compliant code and performance problems if used incorrectly. We urge you to utilize the flexibility of J2EE resources, resource references, and JNDI.

CHAPTER 14

# Client Applications

Browser-based web applications account for most of today's J2EE development, but Java has its roots in thick-client GUI applications, and those applications continue to be developed today as well. When the term "client applications" is used, this type of thick GUI application, built with attractive Swing user interface components, comes to mind. However, a client application can take any of several other forms, such as standard pure Java command-line applications or applets running in browsers. While not as simple to deploy and administer as web applications, client applications offer advantages such as a richer user interface and distributed processing. J2EE client applications are full participating members of the J2EE family and are portable across J2EE environments. As such, they and their containers must adhere to the J2EE specification. In addition to the J2EE client, WebSphere Application Server (WAS) also supports four other types of clients—thin, pluggable, applet, and ActiveX. WAS comes with an Application Clients CD, which will install the runtime support code on the client workstation for each type of client application to communicate with WAS servers.

In this chapter, we will discuss all five client types (including issues regarding their packaging, deployment, and runtime use) and how to use the Application Clients CD. We will start our chapter by briefly describing the five types of Java client applications supported with WAS V5, showing a few examples of client applications, cover the Application Clients CD, and discussing the packaging, deployment, and execution of client applications. Then we will proceed throughout the chapter to discuss each client type in detail. We will not discuss security for client applications. See [IBM WAS Security Redbook] and the Info Center for additional information regarding security for client applications. This chapter is primarily a survey of client technologies and how to use them with WAS. Throughout this chapter, we will point out where to get more detailed information on each topic.

## What Is a "Client Application?"

All supported WAS client application types have the following features:

- They have the necessary runtime support to communicate to a backend WAS server.
- They support the use of the RMI-IIOP protocol.
- They can access EJB and CORBA object references. Note that only J2EE clients can use optional CORBA services (if those optional services are used, the clients are then non-portable to other J2EE environments).
- They support secure access to EJBs.
- They can use Java Naming and Directory Interface (JNDI).

From there, they vary greatly in their size and capabilities. We continue by providing a brief overview of each type.

### Types of WAS-Supported Client Applications

As we learned in Chapter 2, "J2EE Applications," full *J2EE clients* are packaged within and deployed from Enterprise ARchive (EAR) files and have access to J2EE services and resources using local naming via resource references, just like web applications. J2EE clients require a J2EE client container to run within and to provide these services, much as an application server provides them for web applications. This is the only type of client application that is portable across J2EE environments.

The *thin client* does not have to run "inside" a container, but it does require JAR files containing WAS runtime classes to be installed and some property files to be configured in order to run. Since it is not a J2EE client, it cannot use J2EE resources, although it can call EJBs using the server configured JNDI name. Startup time is faster since it does not require the full J2EE container. The thin client requires the IBM JVM, which is installable from the WAS Application Clients CD.

The *pluggable client* is the same as the thin client but runs under the Sun JVM, which must be supplied by the user (it is not on the WAS Application Clients CD). The WAS Application Clients CD will supply runtime and property files required to connect to WAS from the Sun JVM. This client is supported only on Windows.

*Applet clients* are embedded in HTML pages, and so they are run from inside a browser container. The WAS Application Clients CD will install files required for the applet to interact with WAS, as well as a configuration utility. This is the only client type where the actual client application code does not have to be distributed to client machines, as it is sent dynamically from the host server when the browser page loads. This client is supported only on Windows.

*ActiveX clients* run inside a Visual Basic application, from VBScript or from an Active Server Page (ASP) container. The ActiveX to EJB Bridge must be installed from the Application Clients CD to support ActiveX interaction with WAS. This bridge provides an environment similar to the J2EE client, which in addition to EJB access also allows ActiveX usage of J2EE resources such as JDBC and JMS through standard naming constructs.

## Client Application Examples

When "Java application" is mentioned, most people think of the "thick" GUI applications that early Java was known for. Component sets, such as Swing, allow for a richer user interface that is not possible with web applications using HTML. The need for this type of interface continues to be a good reason to use a client application. Figure 14-1 shows an example dialog box from the WAS Log Analyzer tool client application, which demonstrates the type of rich user interface that is possible with a client application.

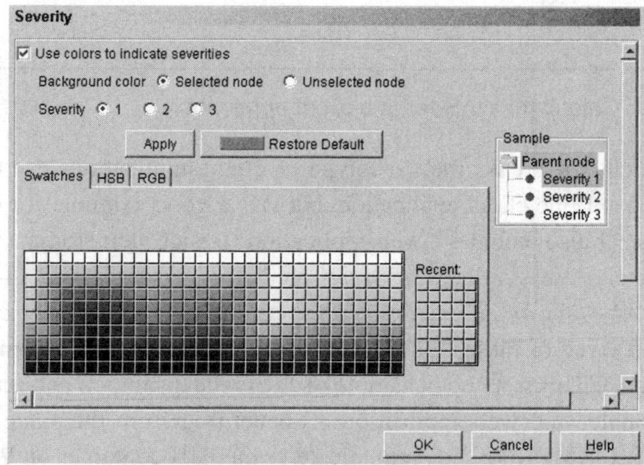


**Figure 14-1** Example of a GUI client application using Swing components.

However, client applications are not limited to this type of interface. Client applications can also be faceless command-line "utility" applications, where parameters are passed in on the command line and run batch-style. An example of this type of client application is the Basic Calculator example that comes with WAS as part of the Samples Gallery from the WAS Application Clients CD. Load the Samples Gallery page in your browser with http://***your_host***/WSsamples/en/index.html (it should also be available from the Start Menu for Windows users), and navigate to Technology Samples > J2EE Application Client. Reading the tech notes, you will find that this is a J2EE client application that functions as a calculator, with the ability to do rudimentary math operations. It runs as a command-line application, as shown in Figure 14-2. You can see the parameters "add," "1," and "2" passed in, and the result in this case is dumped to the console. Since this is a J2EE client application, it could have written its output to a backend database or message queue. In this example, the client application is in a JAR file named BasicCalculatorClient.jar, inside the TechnologySamples.ear enterprise application along with other samples. There are two other JAR files in that EAR that the calculator client uses—BasicCalculatorEJB.jar, which is an EJB JAR file that contains the stateless session EJB code that does the actual calculations, and BasicCalculatorCommonClient.jar, which has other code modules that are used in the implementation.

```
C:\>D:\WebSphere\AppServer\bin\launchClient D:\WebSphere\AppS
erver\samples\lib\TechnologySamples\TechnologySamples.ear add 1 2

IBM WebSphere Application Server, Release 5.0
J2EE Application Client Tool
Copyright IBM Corp., 1997-2002
WSCL0012I: Processing command line arguments.
WSCL0013I: Initializing the J2EE Application Client Environment.
Debugging is set to false
Loading the Security Configuration...
WSCL0035I: Initialization of the J2EE Application Client Environment has completed.
WSCL0014I: Invoking the Application Client class com.ibm.websphere.samp
les.technologysamples.basiccalcclient.BasicCalculatorClientJ2EEMain
--Creating InitialContext... Done.
--Looking-up Home... Done.
--Narrowing... Done.
--Creating Home... Done.
Result: 1.0+2.0 = 3.0

C:\>
```

**Figure 14-2** Basic Calculator WAS sample client application.

The Basic Calculator breaks the stereotype of client applications as "GUI applications" because it is a command-line client application, but it is a good example for other reasons, too. TechnologySamples.ear also includes a web application (BasicCalculator.jar) that is a web interface to the same stateless session EJB in BasicCalculatorEJB.jar. Figure 14-3 shows this web application. Figure 14-4 shows an example of the calculator as an applet client running in a browser window. All three of these front-end applications are using the same backend EJB as their calculation engine. This is a good example of J2EE encapsulation and reuse, with the J2EE client application, applet and web application all benefiting from the same backend business logic. The first two use RMI-IIOP to communicate to the EJB container on WAS, and the latter uses HTTP and the web container.

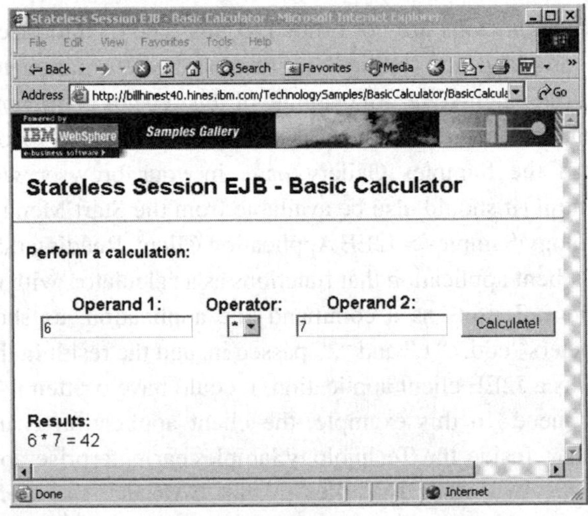


**Figure 14-3** Basic Calculator WAS sample web application.

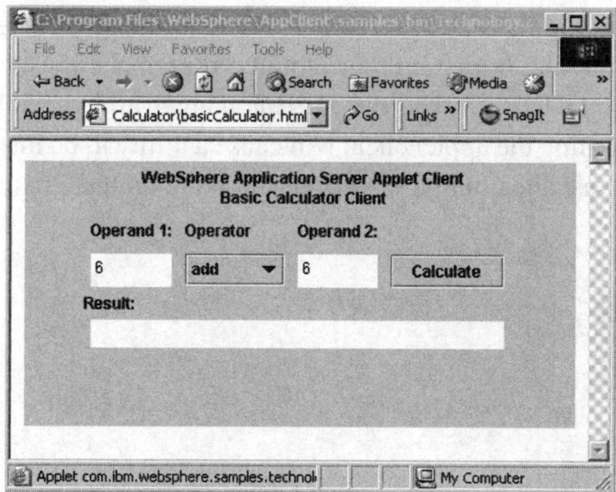


**Figure 14-4** Basic Calculator WAS sample applet.

To fully explore all client types and review information on their implementation and configuration, we recommend that you install the Application Clients CD on a workstation, configure it for a WAS server, and run its Client Samples Gallery (which is different from the WAS Samples Gallery).

## WAS Application Clients CD

Client applications are designed to run remote from the WAS server—on remote servers or user workstations. Because there is no application server on the client workstation to provide the connectivity services the client application needs to converse with WAS, the Application Clients CD needs to be installed on the client machine. This is the case not just for the J2EE client, but for *every* type of WAS client application. The use of client applications to interoperate with WAS without installing the CD on the client is not supported. This is true even for applets, which normally do not require any deployment on the client machine. Clients require the infrastructure that the Application Clients CD provides to use WAS-specific features such as security and workload management (WLM). Figure 14-5 shows the selection panel for the Application Clients CD Installation Wizard. As you can see, there is a check box here to also install the embedded messaging component, which will be discussed later in this chapter. As the interface implies by its layout, you can either select components under *J2EE and Java thin application client* or the *Pluggable Application Client*, but you cannot combine them on a single workstation or server. This is because the pluggable client uses the Sun JVM, while the others all use the IBM JVM.

The Installation Wizard will ask you the remote WAS host server name and port for the remote WAS server that the client application needs to interface to. This can be changed later by modifying the setupclient.bat (or .sh for Unix systems) file that is created, as shown in Code Snippet 14-1. Depending on which client you choose in Figure 14-5, several JAR files, property files, and other files required for the client to communicate with WAS are installed on the client machine. Selecting the J2EE client will install the full J2EE client container. Selecting the thin client will install the required IBM JVM for thin clients. For the pluggable client, which uses but does not include the Sun JVM, important files required for connectivity to WAS are installed. If you choose the ActiveX to EJB Bridge, the J2EE container and special code to facilitate the bridge are installed. Choosing the applet client will cause a utility to be installed in your Windows control panel that can be used to configure the applet to communicate with the WAS server.

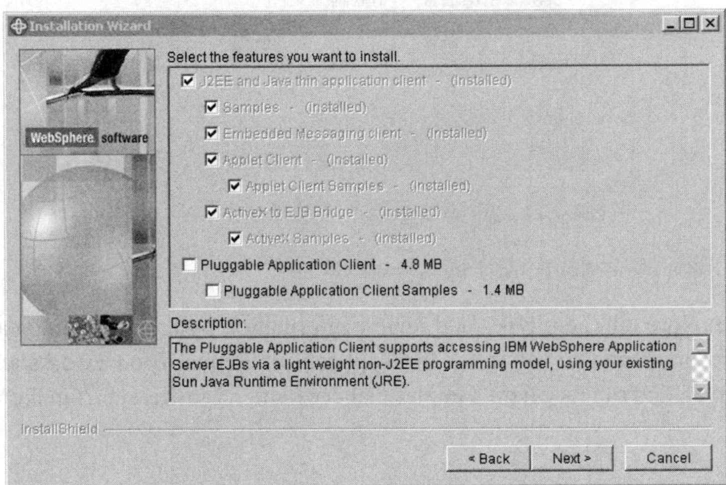


**Figure 14-5** WAS Application Clients CD Installation Wizard.

**Code Snippet 14-1 Setupclient.bat file with server config properties**

```
REM -----------------------------------
REM Install settings follow
REM -----------------------------------
REM   CLIENT_TYPE will be set by install to J2EETHIN or PLUG
set CLIENT_TYPE=J2EETHIN
set COMPUTERNAME=BILLHINES
set DEFAULTSERVERNAME=billhinest40.hines.ibm.com
set SERVERPORTNUMBER=2809
set WAS_HOME=C:\Program Files\WebSphere\AppClient
set JAVA_JRE=%WAS_HOME%\java\jre
set JAVA_JDK=%WAS_HOME%\java
set JMS_PATH=C:\Program Files\IBM\WebSphere MQ\Java\lib
```

The Application Clients CD has instructions for installing the various types of client runtimes silently—that is, from the command line without running the GUI to select options. This is useful for packaging with your applications as part of your application install. Instructions for this are in the Application Clients CD documentation and in the WAS Info Center.

As stated earlier, it is highly suggested to install the utilities and examples due to the abundance of information on building, using, and configuring each type of client application. The CD also installs some rudimentary tools for packaging, such as a command (rmic) for generating client-side bindings. As Figure 14-6 shows, there are plenty of samples and information on this topic, including ActiveX and even CORBA. Each sample in the left-hand menu is complete with technotes, JavaDoc, and instructions to configure, run, and build it yourself.

We are now going to discuss the details of using each client type in turn.

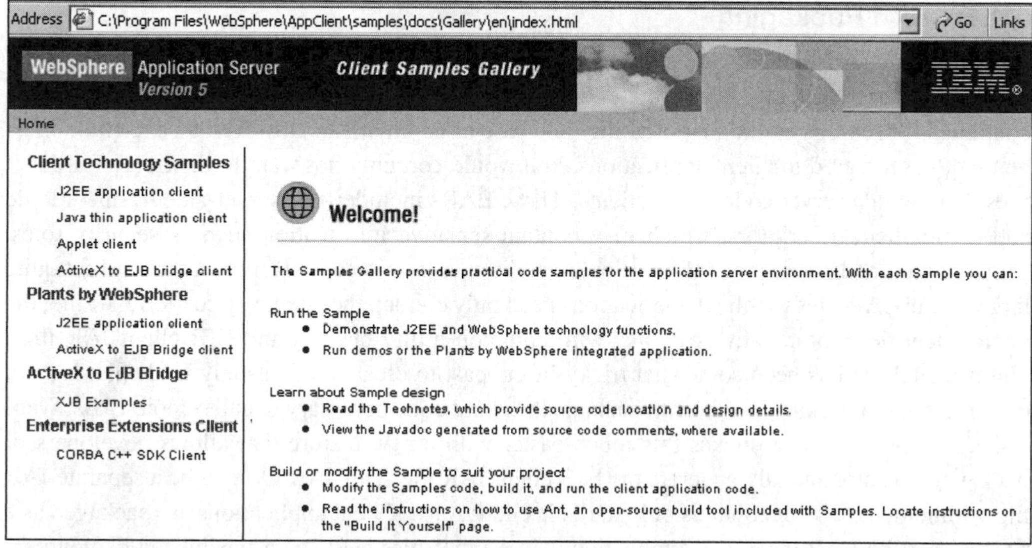


**Figure 14-6** WAS Client Applications sample gallery.

## J2EE Clients

The J2EE client application model extends some of the benefits of J2EE to client applications. A J2EE-compliant client application should be portable from one J2EE container and server to another without code changes, needing only to be redeployed in each new environment. As stated in our introduction, the J2EE client is an application that has access to J2EE services such as EJBs, backend resources via JDBC or J2EE Connector Architecture (J2C), JavaMail, or JMS message queues. It uses the standard J2EE mechanism to connect to and use these resources—that being J2EE naming (deployment descriptors, resource names, resource references, and JNDI). Accordingly, it is packaged as an enterprise application (as an EAR file) but is installed and run on the client machine, as opposed to the server, where EARs are normally deployed. We will discuss packaging in more depth shortly.

The container benefits extended to J2EE clients include not only the runtime services but also development, assembly, and deployment. The same WAS tools that you use for your other applications are just as useful for J2EE clients—WebSphere Studio Application Developer (WSAD) to develop and Application Assembly Tool (AAT) (before WAS 5.1 only) or Application Server Toolkit (ASTK) (WAS 5.0.2 and beyond) to build or package. Client bindings are done inside a tool such as the AAT or ASTK or by using client-specific tools that we will discuss later. Of course, since the client container is much lighter than the full WAS runtime, client applications aren't "deployed" as typical J2EE EAR files are—in fact, most client apps are launched directly from the EAR file, as we saw in Figure 14-2.

## J2EE Client Packaging

As with any enterprise application, you can assemble the client application EAR file using AAT or ASTK. The spirit of J2EE dictates that enterprise applications should be entirely self-contained for reasons including portability and ease of deployment. However, an exception must be made with regard to client applications. You would certainly not want to distribute full EAR files that include server code to the clients. These EARs include your server-side business logic and deployment descriptors, which may contain sensitive information such as security roles, server names, and connection information. In addition, server-side EAR files can tend to get quite large, while EAR files for client applications need only contain the client application JAR file, the deployment descriptors, any JAR files with common utility classes, and EJB client JAR files. Unfortunately, it has been somewhat tricky in the past to create a client-only EAR file. It's not obvious what to package and how to package the client code necessary to call remote EJBs. WebSphere Studio 5.11 now makes this much easier with a new feature that allows developers or packagers to automatically generate the EJB client JAR file. This JAR file will be a separate JAR file within the EAR that contains only the EJB client stubs. Client applications are packaged as a JAR within the EAR (as a web application is in a WAR file) but have a specialized deployment descriptor named application-client.xml.

Let's look at the contents of an EAR file containing a J2EE client JAR file. We have provided a StockSystemClientEAR.ear in the download materials. It is located in C:\WASDeployBook\Chapter14. The client application contacts the EJB deployed in the Chapter 9 sample. You can run the client as a self-exercise after reading this chapter. We will view this in the WAS Application Assembly Tool (AAT)[1] in order to get an idea of what the contents are and then correlate that to the descriptors that are required. AAT gets the information it displays by reading these descriptor files in the EAR and JAR files. Figure 14-7 shows a tree view of an EAR file, which is a client application for the example stock system application we are using for this book. The EAR file has four files in it—StockSystemClient.jar (the client app), StockSystemClientEJBClient.jar (the EJB client JAR file created by WebSphere Studio), the manifest file, and the application.xml

1. Note that this chapter is using the AAT tool and not the ASTK. Both tools work fine for this purpose, although you should be aware that as of WAS 5.1, the AAT is deprecated.

deployment descriptor. This figure shows the StockSystemClientEAR.ear with the client JAR section selected and expanded so we can see its contents. We can see the file name for the client app JAR, the client app display name, its classpath (other JAR files that contain classes the client needs—in this case, the EJB client JAR), and main class name, which needs to be identified because it is the one that will be called when the application is initialized.

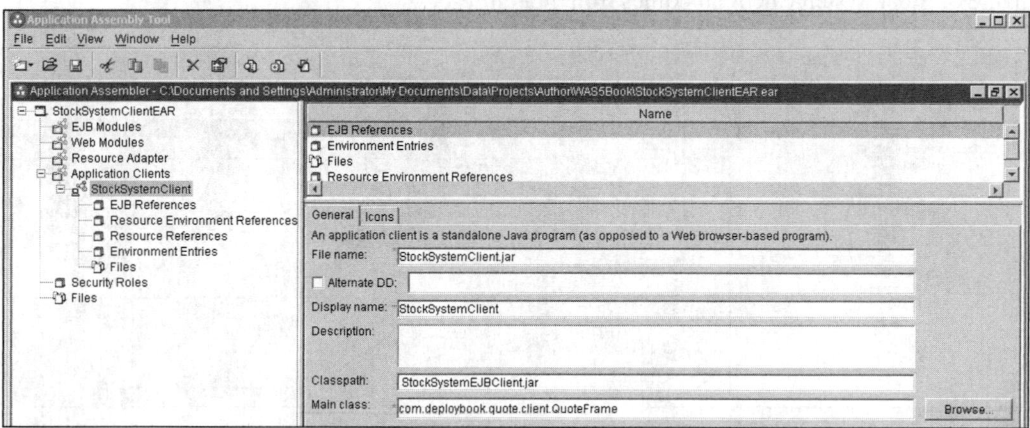


**Figure 14-7** Stock System Client Main Application Assembly tab.

Figure 14-8 shows the contents of the EJB reference tab for the Stock System client app. The EJB reference name, type, and home/remote classes are shown here. There is also a 'Link' drop-down menu that is used to link to an EJB in another module in the same enterprise application. If this is not used, a JNDI name must be specified at installation. This is the more common approach with client applications, which will likely be calling EJBs in remote containers. As you can see, there is also a **Bindings** tab in Figure 14-8, which we do not show in the interest of brevity. It contains one field, which is the JNDI name of ejb/StockFacade.

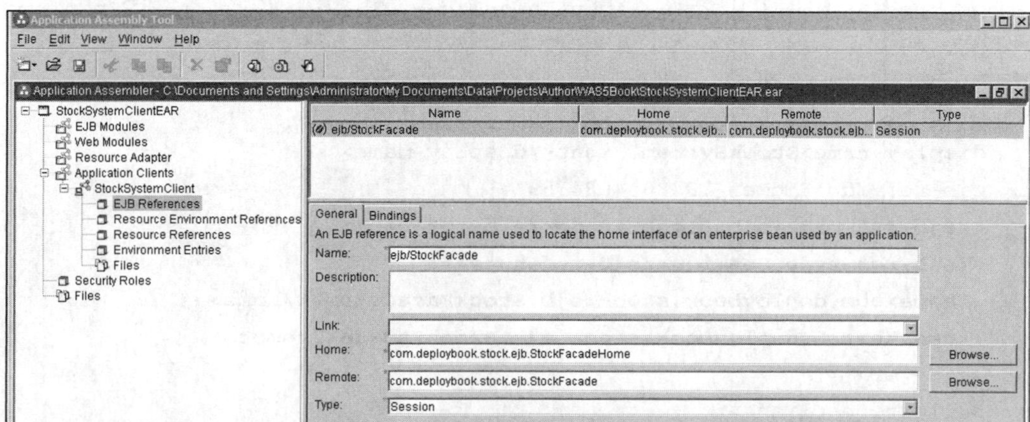


**Figure 14-8** Stock System Client EJB Reference Application Assembly tab.

Figure 14-9 shows the file list for the entire client application JAR file. As you can see, it's pretty basic—just two class files with their source code, the deployment descriptors, and the manifest file. Let's continue to look closer at the descriptors and manifest file. We have already talked about deployment descriptors earlier in this book, so we know that the StockSystemClientEAR.ear file must have an application.xml descriptor. We do not show it, but this is where the file name of StockSystemClient.jar comes from in Figure 14-7.

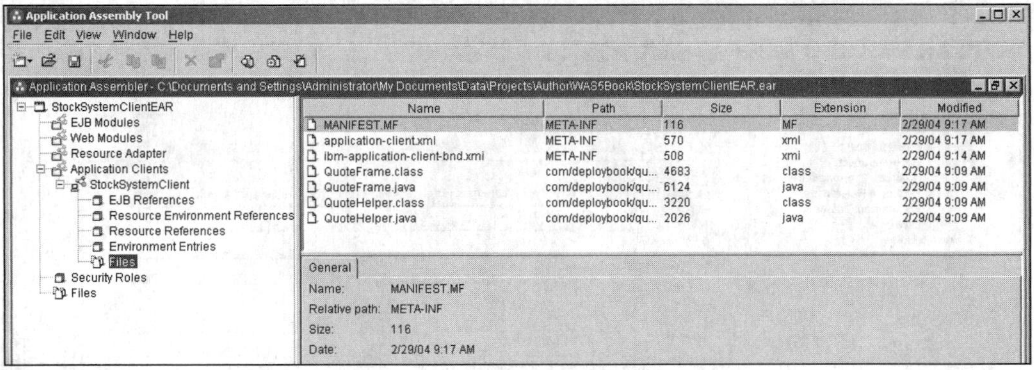

| Name | Path | Size | Extension | Modified |
|---|---|---|---|---|
| MANIFEST.MF | META-INF | 116 | MF | 2/29/04 9:17 AM |
| application-client.xml | META-INF | 570 | xml | 2/29/04 9:17 AM |
| ibm-application-client-bnd.xmi | META-INF | 508 | xmi | 2/29/04 9:14 AM |
| QuoteFrame.class | com/deploybook/qu... | 4683 | class | 2/29/04 9:09 AM |
| QuoteFrame.java | com/deploybook/qu... | 6124 | java | 2/29/04 9:09 AM |
| QuoteHelper.class | com/deploybook/qu... | 3220 | class | 2/29/04 9:09 AM |
| QuoteHelper.java | com/deploybook/qu... | 2026 | java | 2/29/04 9:09 AM |

**Figure 14-9** Stock System Client files listing.

As discussed in Chapter 2, J2EE client apps must also have a deployment descriptor named application-client.xml. An example of this for the Stock System Client is shown in Code Snippet 14-2. A review of this file shows that it defines the application display name, EJB type, reference name, and home/remote interfaces that we saw in the AAT screen shots.

**Code Snippet 14-2** Application-client.xml

```
<?xml version="1.0" encoding="UTF-8"?>
<!DOCTYPE application-client PUBLIC "-//Sun Microsystems, Inc.//DTD
➥J2EE Application Client 1.3//EN" "http://java.sun.com/dtd/
➥application-client_1_3.dtd">
<application-client id="Application-client_ID">
  <display-name>StockSystemClient</display-name>
  <ejb-ref id="EjbRef_1078064084758">
    <ejb-ref-name>ejb/StockFacade</ejb-ref-name>
    <ejb-ref-type>Session</ejb-ref-type>
    <home>com.deploybook.stock.ejb.StockFacadeHome</home>
    <remote>com.deploybook.stock.ejb.StockFacade</remote>
  </ejb-ref>
</application-client>
```

Code Snippet 14-3 shows the manifest file. In addition to the classpath, which we are used to seeing in manifest files, the main class is identified here for the client application. This needs to be identified so that the container knows which class to call to initialize the application.

**Code Snippet 14-3 MANIFEST.MF**

```
Manifest-Version: 1.0
Main-Class: com.deploybook.quote.client.QuoteFrame
Class-Path:  StockSystemEJBClient.jar
```

Code Snippet 14-4 shows the ibm-application-client-bnd.xmi file. We learned about the IBM binding files in Chapter 2, "J2EE Applications." This is a special one for client applications to specify their binding information, and you can see that this one is the source for the JNDI name for the EJB that it will be calling on the remote WAS server.

**Code Snippet 14-4 ibm-application-client-bnd.xmi**

```
<?xml version="1.0" encoding="UTF-8"?>
<clientbnd:ApplicationClientBinding xmi:version="2.0"
xmlns:xmi="http://www.omg.org/XMI" xmlns:clientbnd="clientbnd.xmi"
xmi:id="ApplicationClientBinding_1078064084758">
  <applicationClient href="META-INF/application-client.xml#Application-
  ➥client_ID"/>
  <ejbRefs xmi:id="EjbRefBinding_1078064084758"
jndiName="ejb/StockFacade">
    <bindingEjbRef href="META-INF/application-
    ➥client.xml#EjbRef_1078064084758"/>
  </ejbRefs>
</clientbnd:ApplicationClientBinding>
```

## J2EE Clients and Resources

One of the benefits of using full J2EE clients is the ability to use J2EE resources. We will not go into great detail in this area, but we will touch on a few important points. However, for reasons including simplicity of packaging and deployment, we encourage you to not use resources from client applications but rather use the model of accessing EJBs as proxies to backend resources. If clients have direct access to J2EE resources, the client footprint is typically much larger, and the complexity of the client is greatly increased. This goes against the usual principles of multi-tier architecture, where we try to push complexity to the server. That said, we will briefly discuss the use of J2EE resources from clients for those that have a clear need.

## J2EE Clients and JMS

In this section, we will touch briefly on using JMS from J2EE clients and provide references for more detail. In our section on the WAS Application Clients CD, we showed the install options in Figure 14-5, which include the Embedded Messaging Client. Client applications can use JMS resources administered by the client container or the application server. If you would like to use resources that are administered from the client container, configure the resources in the client EAR as resource references. If you want the client application to use resources administered on the server, configure the resources as resource environment references. The tabs in the AAT to do this are shown in Figure 14-7. See Chapter 12, "JMS and Message Driven Beans," in this book or the Resources topic in the WAS 5.1 Info Center for more information on developing, deploying, tuning, and troubleshooting JMS client applications. The documentation on the Application Clients CD has an extensive section on installing and configuring the Embedded Messaging Client on client application machines.

## J2EE Clients and JDBC Data Sources

J2EE clients can also access JDBC data sources directly, and just as with JMS, components must be available on the client machine. In this case, client machines must have database drivers installed if the client is to access a database using JDBC—these are not supplied with the Application Clients CD. When using JDBC from a client application, you do not have the benefit of a JDBC connection pool as you do from server-side technologies such as Servlets and EJBs. These complications are one reason why it is recommended that client applications use insulating layers such as EJB to facilitate input and output, rather than the complications of distributing and configuring drivers on remote client machines. However, if this is necessary, the Application Client Resource Configuration Tool (ACRCT) can be used to configure JDBC and other J2EE resources on the client machine or on the WAS server before deploying.

## Application Client Resource Configuration Tool

After assembling your client application EAR file, in some cases it will need to be configured for each environment it is to be deployed to. For example, client applications may need to be configured to connect to local resources, such as databases using JDBC and data sources or mail servers using JavaMail. In most cases, you will want to change the EAR before distributing it to client machines; if all client machines are identical, then you only need to do this once. However, if there are various different types of environments, you may want to configure the EAR and keep the various "flavors" to distribute to the appropriate clients. WAS provides a tool for this called the Application Client Resource Configuration Tool (ACRCT). It is installed as part of the WAS install and as part of the Application Clients CD (where you could use it to configure the EAR file directly on the client machine). This tool is used to reach inside the EAR file and change properties and settings for J2EE resources. It is used by executing the clientconfig batch or shell command in your application server bin directory. Figure 14-10 shows what the tool looks like and the type of resources you can modify with it.

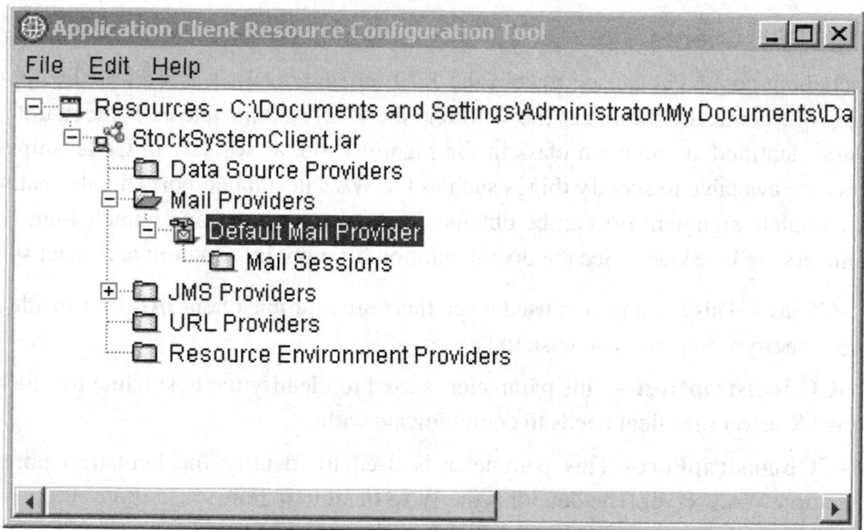


**Figure 14-10** Application Client Resource Configuration Tool.

We don't have any J2EE resources in our stock system sample client, but Figure 14-11 shows how you might change settings for the Default Mail Provider, which we discussed in Chapter 13, "Other Resources." Chapter 6 of the WAS 5.1 Info Center has extensive documentation on using this tool to configure resources.

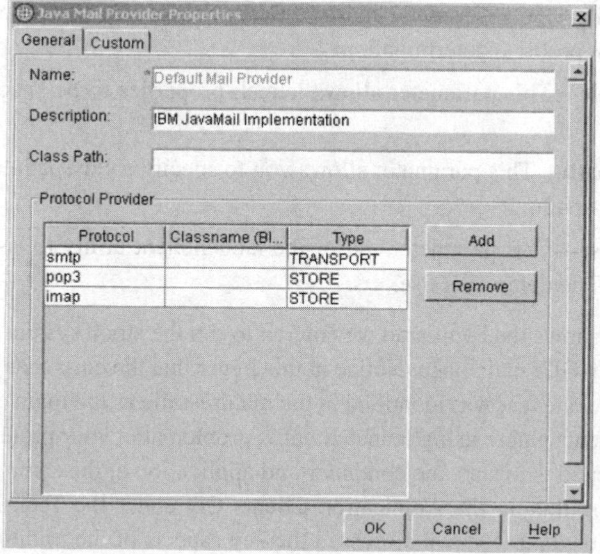


**Figure 14-11** ACRT Default Mail Provider properties.

## Running J2EE Clients

The launchclient command is used to start the J2EE client container as well as the application. Essentially, this command initializes the JVM and the WAS runtime and calls the main() method in the class identified as the main class in the manifest file, as we saw in Code Snippet 14-3. Arguments are available to specify things such as the WAS host name/port and alternative classpaths. A complete argument list can be obtained by using the command launchclient -?. A few key parameters are listed here. See the documentation for more information and exact syntax:

- **-CCjar**—This parameter is used when there are multiple client JAR files inside an EAR to specify which one you wish to launch.
- **-CCBootstrapHost**—This parameter is used to identify the host name for the backend WAS server the client needs to communicate with.
- **-CCBootstrapPort**—This parameter is used to identify the bootstrap port for the remote WAS server. The default is the WAS default of 2809.
- **-CCProviderURL**—This parameter allows you to specify a CORBA object URL or IIOP URL to allow the container's initial context factory to obtain an initial context from the remote WAS server. This is important for clustered environments, as multiple servers can be specified in the URL, such as -CCProviderURL= corbaloc:iiop:server1.pts.com:9810,:server2.pts.com:9810. This parameter overrides the use of the two previous parameters (bootstrap host and port) for naming, which is good since they don't support specifying multiple servers.
- **-CCtracefile**—This parameter causes the launchclient utility to emit a trace file, which is useful for problem determination.
- **-CCpropfile**—This parameter allows launch properties to be specified in a properties file.
- **-CCclasspath**—This parameter allows you to specify a classpath to use rather than the system classpath.
- **-CCverbose**—This parameter causes the launchclient utility to issue more descriptive messages. The default is false.

Figure 14-12 shows the command we entered to run the stock system J2EE client application and the resulting GUI main page. Notice in this figure that the class that was executed to start the application is the one that was identified in the manifest file as the main class.

For environments where using launchclient is problematic, your programmers can include APIs in your applications to start the container and application at the same time. There is documentation describing this on the Application Clients CD under the Tech Notes for the Client Samples Gallery. Now that we have discussed the key aspects of the traditional J2EE client, we are going to turn our attention to several variants known as thin clients, and then discuss ActiveX.

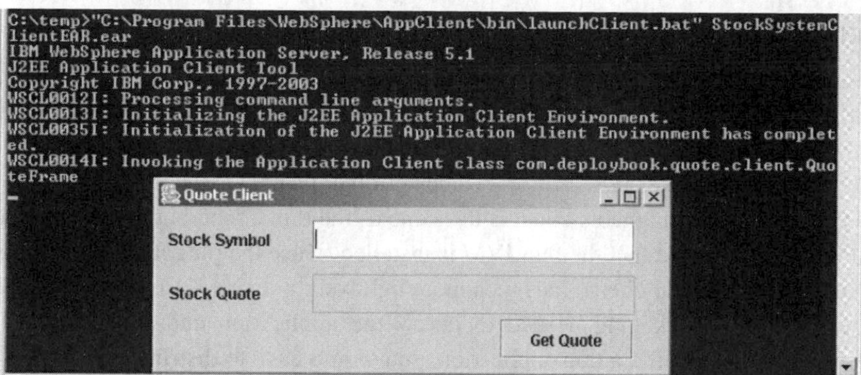


**Figure 14-12** Stock System Client launch command and main GUI page.

## Thin Clients

Thin clients are traditional Java applications that are run by the execution of a main() method. Thin clients are often launched by batch or shell commands that initialize the environment by setting variables such as CLASSPATH and JAVA_HOME. They do not run inside a container, but they do require JAR files containing WAS runtime classes to be installed in order to access WAS.

The advantage of thin clients is that they are lightweight and easier to distribute, and they run faster than thicker clients. They are also quite functional as proper clients. They can call EJBs using the fully qualified JNDI name, including the location of the name server. Some server-like things, such as various J2EE services normally provided by the application server (packaging, deployment, and access to resources such as JDBC), are not available, but this is often not a burden. If needed, the thin client can even use local services (such as JDBC or JMS) but must create connections using specific information rather than using the insulating advantages of the J2EE naming infrastructure. If you are not using J2EE resources through deployment descriptors, or if you are doing name service lookups and can go straight to the name server instead of using java:comp/env, you may want to use a thin client rather than the full J2EE container. The WAS dumpNameSpace command-line utility is actually a thin-client that accesses the WAS namespace and prints out its contents.

Just like proper J2EE clients, thin clients use RMI-IIOP to communicate with EJBs running on a WAS server. After your programmers have developed the thin client application, the client bindings are typically generated for EJB objects and packaged together for installation on remote machines. These bindings can be generated by the AAT, ASTK, or the rmic command included with the Application Clients CD.

## Pluggable Clients

The thin client is quite sufficient for most situations, but it requires the IBM-supported JDK on the client. The pluggable client is used for Windows environments only, due to issues on that platform with JVM availability. Windows has no "native" JVM as the Sun and HP platforms do. The pluggable client option gives WAS customers the option of using a JVM other than IBM's for the Windows platform. The pluggable client is the same as the thin client, but it does not come with its own JVM. It is required that the Sun JVM is installed to use the pluggable client application, which makes this particular client type much more lightweight than a J2EE or thin client application in terms of the packaging needed to install the application and supporting JVM. For example, if you were to build a thin application, you would have to distribute the IBM-provided WAS JVM along with it. On the other hand, the pluggable client allows you to use an existing Sun JVM on the client. It is worth noting that there are limitations to accessing clustered EJBs from the pluggable client, and therefore you lose the WLM benefits of J2EE or thin clients.

## Applet Clients

Applets are components that are embedded in HTML pages, and so they are run from inside a browser. The WAS Application Clients CD will install files required for the applet to interact with WAS, as well as a configuration utility. Figure 14-13 shows this utility, which is installed in the Windows Control Panel by the WAS Application Clients CD for managing WAS applets. Notice the setting that allows the applet to find the standard WAS properties files. As of this writing, WAS applet clients are supported only on the Windows platform.

Because applets run in a browser, they have restricted access to anything outside of that browser. This is a major difference in the area of security between the applet and other types of client applications. Any exceptions to this have to be configured in the client.policy file.

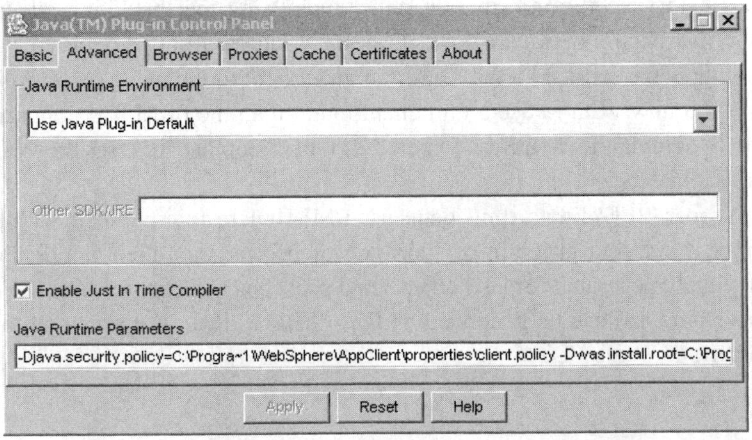

**Figure 14-13** Applet Plug-in Control Panel installed from the Application Clients CD.

## ActiveX Clients

ActiveX components run inside a Visual Basic application from VBScript or an Active Server Page (ASP) container. The ActiveX to EJB Bridge must be installed from the Application Clients CD to support ActiveX interaction with WAS. The bridge is a set of ActiveX automation objects, and it provides an environment similar to the full J2EE client, which in addition to EJB access also allows ActiveX usage of J2EE resources such as JDBC and JMS through standard naming constructs.

The bridge loads the JVM into the ActiveX container. This construct allows the ActiveX client to use Java Native Interface (JNI) to call into the WAS client container JVM to access J2EE services that allow it to interface with a remote WAS server. The use of JNI indicates that the ActiveX client and JVM must run in the same process space. The bridge ActiveX components create proxy objects in the ActiveX container that call out to the real Java objects in the JVM, much like the EJB model. Exceptions in Java are converted and rethrown as COM errors by the ActiveX component. Data type conversion between ActiveX primitives and Java primitives must occur as part of any method call or data returned from methods. As you might expect, this has implications in the area of performance, so test thoroughly.

## Conclusion

In this chapter, we reviewed the various types of client applications that are supported by IBM for access to WAS. We showed examples including the packaging and launching of a sample J2EE client application for the stock system app we are using throughout this book. We discussed the WAS Application Clients CD and the Client Samples Gallery included with it, which contains samples and useful documentation on the building, packaging, deploying, and running of each client application type. For further information, it is recommended that the reader explore this CD and the documentation contained within, as well as the usual Info Center, Redbooks, and web site WAS information resources. Chapter 6 of the WAS 5.1 Info Center has extensive information on developing, assembling, packaging, deploying, configuring resources for, running, and troubleshooting the various types of client applications.

# PART III

# Managing WebSphere Application Server Infrastructure

CHAPTER 15

# Advanced Considerations for Build

In Part II of this book, we illustrated how WebSphere Application Server (WAS) supports different aspects of J2EE technology. In the process, where applicable, we deployed the Personal Trade System using the build and deployment process illustrated in Chapter 4, "Build and Deploy Procedures." We are now going to spend a bit of time discussing several issues related to the packaging of J2EE applications. This is important because packaging issues are often overlooked and can lead to subtle problems late in the development cycle. We'll then wrap up by briefly discussing a seemingly simple yet quite helpful enhancement to the development process known as a verification workspace.

## Application Packaging

Packing J2EE applications is a surprisingly complex topic. The J2EE module is quite rich and provides quite a bit of freedom when packaging applications for deployment. As we discussed in earlier chapters, J2EE EARs contain modules that are part of the same application, and some of these modules can contain JAR files of utility classes. Application developers must choose how to package these modules and JARs into one or more EAR files. If that wasn't enough, J2EE applications can use modules and JAR files from within and outside of the EAR, depending on the classloader structure. This leaves development teams many options when it comes to application packaging. Unfortunately, many development teams do not even think about packaging code until the last minute and then make unfortunate decisions that can greatly complicate deployment. We've seen poor packaging decisions that stem from one of several factors:

- Poor code structure often leads to poor packaging structure. Following standard layered architectures and modular coding is the first step to packaging code well. We will not offer much advice on code structure because [Brown 2004] covers this area quite well.

- Many developers do not fully understand J2EE packaging, classpaths, and available options on the server. For example, one mistake we see often is developers confusing compile time classpaths with runtime classpaths.
- Developers often concentrate on making something work on their desktop or inside an IDE. For example, a developer may just point to arbitrary utility JAR files on his or her machine. The problem with this approach is that there is no real consideration for how the code will be deployed on another server.

Now we are going to discuss J2EE packaging in more detail and then offer advice on packaging in a variety of situations.

## Understanding J2EE Packaging

We'll start with perhaps the simplest J2EE packaging scenario and slowly increase its complexity to demonstrate some interesting problems. Consider a simple but common example, as illustrated in Figure 15-1: A simple EAR file with one WAR file and one EJB JAR file. If an application is packaged in such a way, it usually means that the EJB JAR contains the business logic and the data access code, while the WAR file contains the presentation layer.

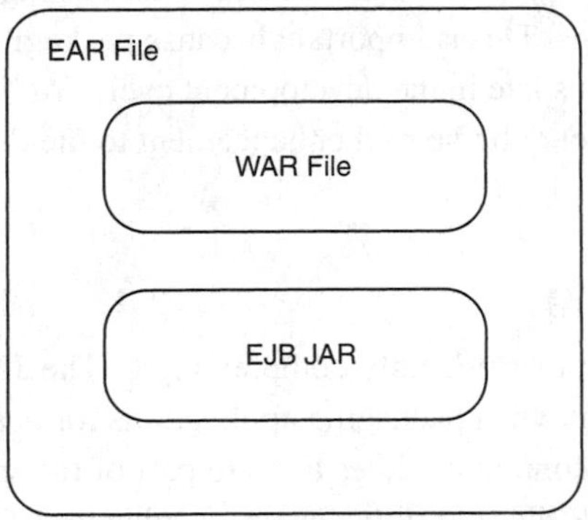


**Figure 15-1** Simple EAR file.

A good design requires that the business logic have no knowledge of the presentation logic. Thus, we expect this simple dependency as illustrated in Figure 15-2.

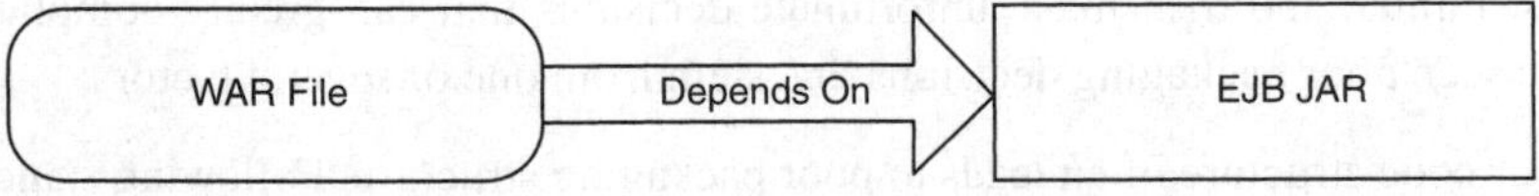


**Figure 15-2** WAR depends on EJB JAR, but not the reverse.

This means that code in the WAR file depends on code in the EJB JAR file. Therefore, the EJB JAR needs to be in the classpath of the WAR file. This is done by specifying the name of the EJB JAR file in the MANIFEST.MF of the WAR file. This allows the code in the WAR file to find the code in the EJB JAR file when the code is running in the server. We explained this in Chapter 2, "J2EE Applications."

> **NOTE**
> The MANIFEST specifies the J2EE classpath at runtime. This is different than specifying the classpath for the code to compile.

The Application Server Toolkit (ASTK) or WebSphere Studio allows you to specify module dependencies (both compile and runtime) using the properties of the J2EE projects. So for example, if you wanted to add the EJB JAR as a dependency of the WAR file, right-click the web project that corresponds to the WAR file and select Properties. Then go to the Java JAR Dependencies option. There, you will select the EJB JAR. The tool will list any JAR files in the EAR, as shown in Figure 15-3.

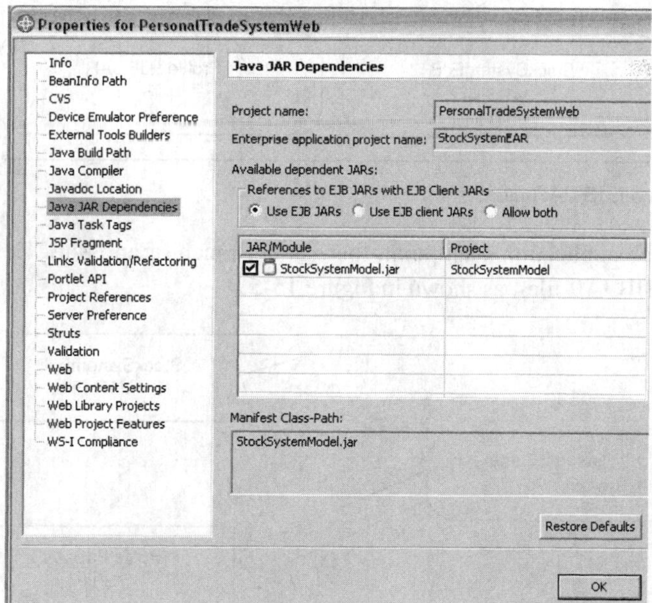


**Figure 15-3** Using ASTK or Studio to set the MANIFEST.MF.

Notice that in the Properties window, there is also a Java Build Path entry. Setting the classpath under the Java Build Path will only affect the compile time classpath, not the runtime path. Thus, when you deploy the application, the WAR file code will not be able to find the EJB JAR file code. Setting the JAR dependency actually sets both the compile time classpath for the compiler and the runtime classpath (by updating the MANIFEST.MF file) for the application. Without understanding this fundamental concept, you will not be able to package your J2EE applications correctly.

Small development efforts can get by with the simple EAR file we illustrated previously. However, most projects will have more complex requirements. Consider the following example. The Personal Trade System web application accesses information about Stock as well as Profile information for users. (We will assume that there is a single development team responsible for the StockSystem EAR application.) Let's say the business logic for each component (the Stock Data and Profile) is stored in different EJB JAR files. The EAR file will then look like Figure 15-4.

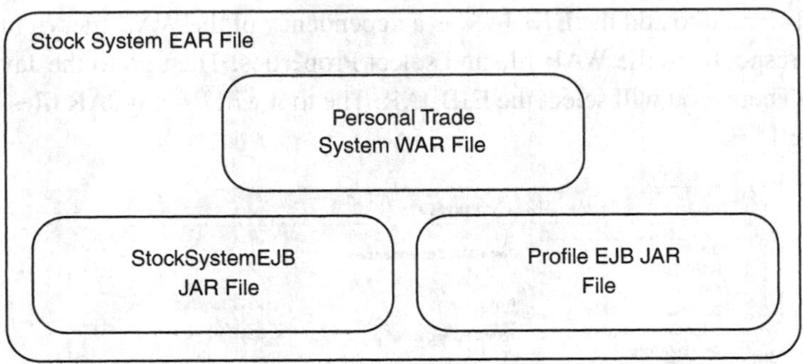


**Figure 15-4** Two EJB JAR files.

From the web application standpoint, there is not much of an issue. The web application depends on both EJB JAR files, as shown in Figure 15-5.

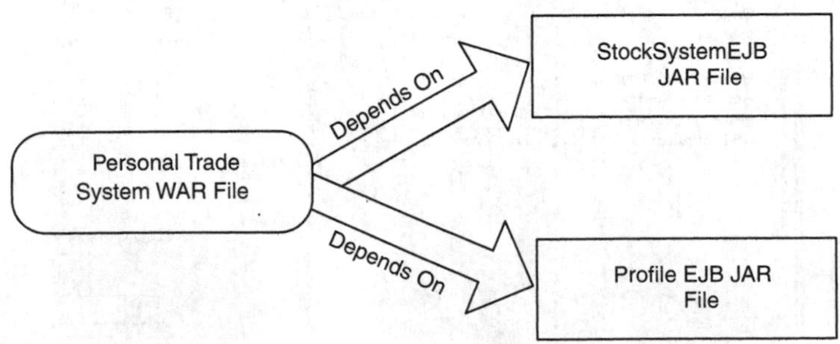


**Figure 15-5** WAR dependencies.

Now suppose as part of trading logic inside, the StockSystemEJB JAR needs to access Profile EJB JAR to access some of the user's profile. The StockSystemEJB JAR needs to see Profile EJB JAR. Therefore, the StockSystemEJB JAR file needs to define the Profile EJB JAR file in its MANIFEST. The dependencies are shown in Figure 15-6.

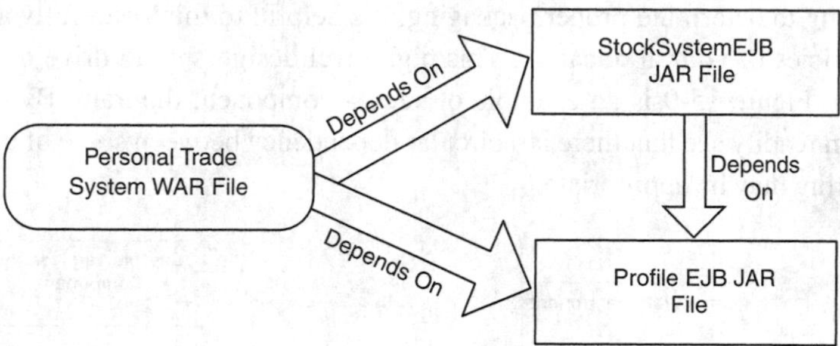


**Figure 15-6** EJB dependency.

So far, this is pretty straightforward; you just keep adding dependencies among the modules as you did in the first example. Now let's say there is new requirement where the profile balance calculations need to check the latest stock price in order to successfully calculate the trading balance. In this case, the Profile EJB JAR business logic needs to access the Stock System EJB JAR logic. Then the dependency model looks like Figure 15-7.

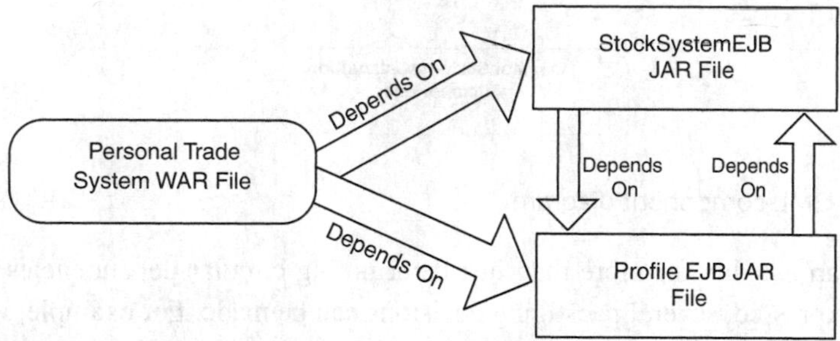


**Figure 15-7** Circular dependency.

This creates a situation called a *circular dependency*. This affects the compile time classpath because each EJB JAR file needs to see the other. When running a sequential build process, compiling each project means compiling its dependencies. If an application contains many circular dependencies, the compile time of the build process could significantly increase. Circular dependencies are a clear indication that these EJB JAR files should be refactored. The simplest approach is to create a single EJB JAR file,[1] as shown in Figure 15-8. It may also be possible to factor out the common function from the two EJB JARs into a third EJB JAR.

1 Practically speaking, combining the two EJB JAR files assumes we have a single development team that can readily repackage its code.

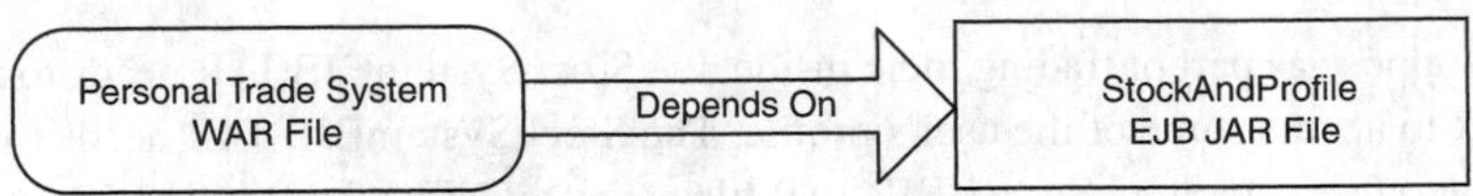


**Figure 15-8** Combined EJB JAR file.

When trying to determine proper packaging, it's helpful to think carefully about the component dependencies of your application. This high-level design should drive the packaging of your application. Figure 15-9 is an example of such a component diagram. By examining this diagram, you can readily see that there is a circular dependency between some of the components and that refactoring may be appropriate.

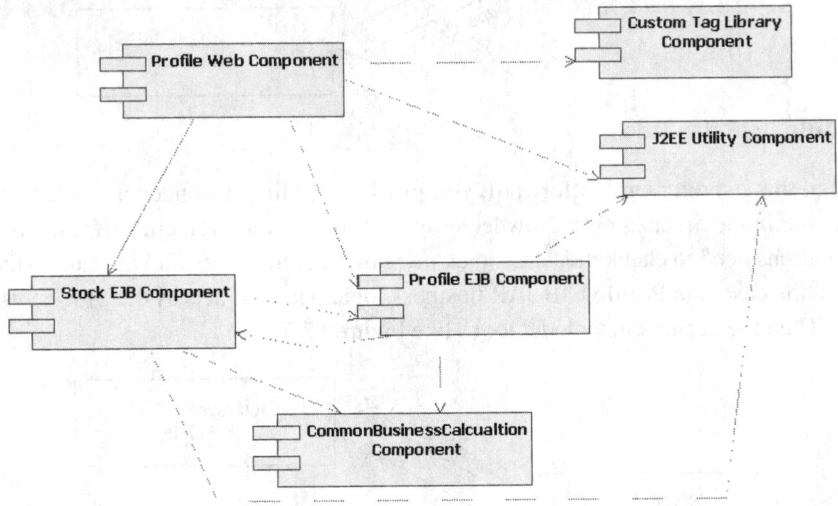


**Figure 15-9** UML component diagram.

But we can use this for more than just determining circular dependencies. Based on the dependencies expressed, several packaging decisions can be made. For example, we can see that the J2EE utility component is used by two different modules and, therefore, needs to be packaged at the EAR level. On the other hand, the Custom Tag Utility is only needed by a single web application. Thus, this utility can be stored in the lib directory of the WAR file. Figure 15-10 shows the component diagram with packaging applied.

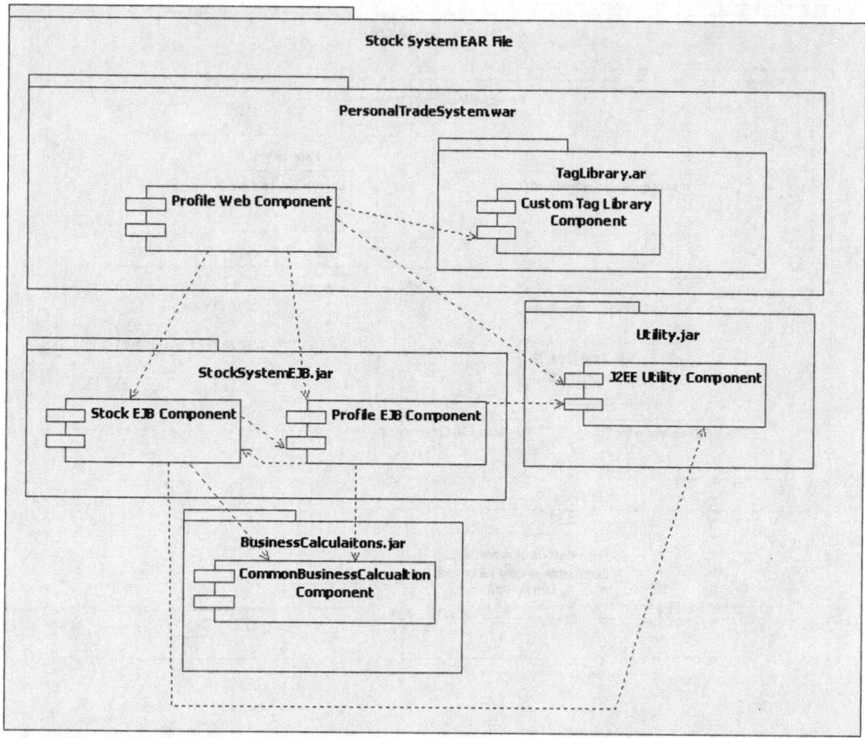


**Figure 15-10** Apply packaging.

Successfully identifying dependencies not only defines packages, but also can help clarify what needs to go into the MANIFEST within each module. It is well worth taking the time to understand these dependencies because they affect how you will package the system and structure the development teams and how the system may be deployed.

## Sharing Common EJBs

So far, we've discussed some fairly simple examples of packaging that are essentially within a single application. Sometimes, things get more complex. Consider the following example: Suppose that there is a new requirement for batch trades. As part of the requirement, a batch job runs at the end of the day, executing all the possible trades. The batch component has been added to the StockSystemEJB JAR, as illustrated in Figure 15-11.

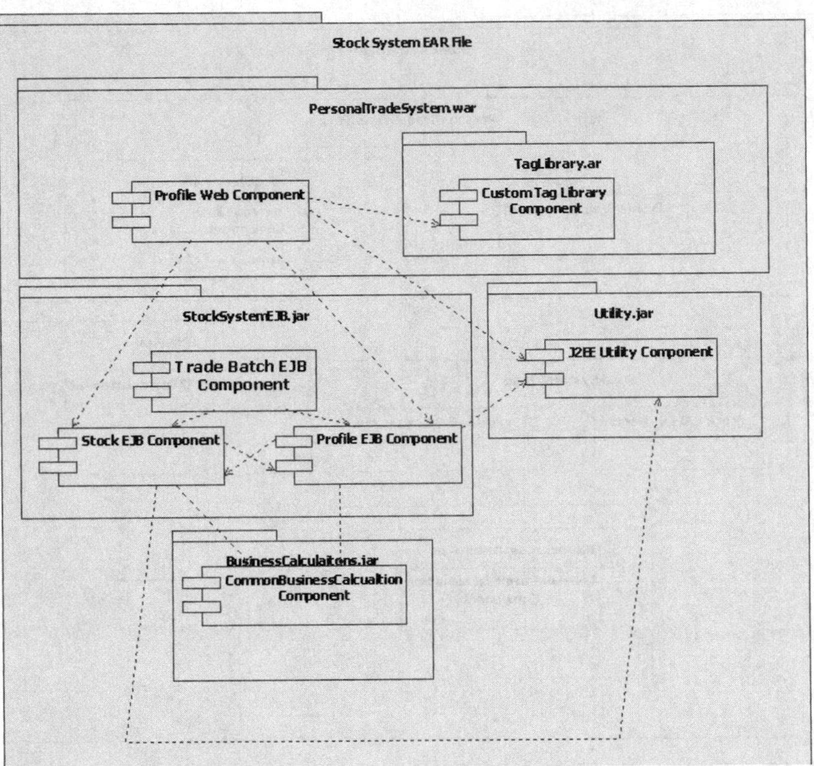


**Figure 15-11** Adding batch EJB component.

However, because the batch job was very process intensive, it was slowing down the web site. Because of this, the development team has decided to externalize the EJB batch component onto a different server. Since the components used by the batch component are EJBs, accessing them remotely is not a problem. However, this may not be the right choice. There are two approaches you can take:

- **Deploy as a shared service**—In this model, the shared EJBs are placed in one server and accessed by other applications as needed.
- **Deploy as a private internal service**—In this model, the shared EJBs are collocated with each application that uses them.

Using a shared service approach, you create two separate EARs. The EAR that depends on the other components becomes a client. Therefore, you must create an EJB client JAR and package it with the new batch EAR file. This is shown in Figure 15-12.

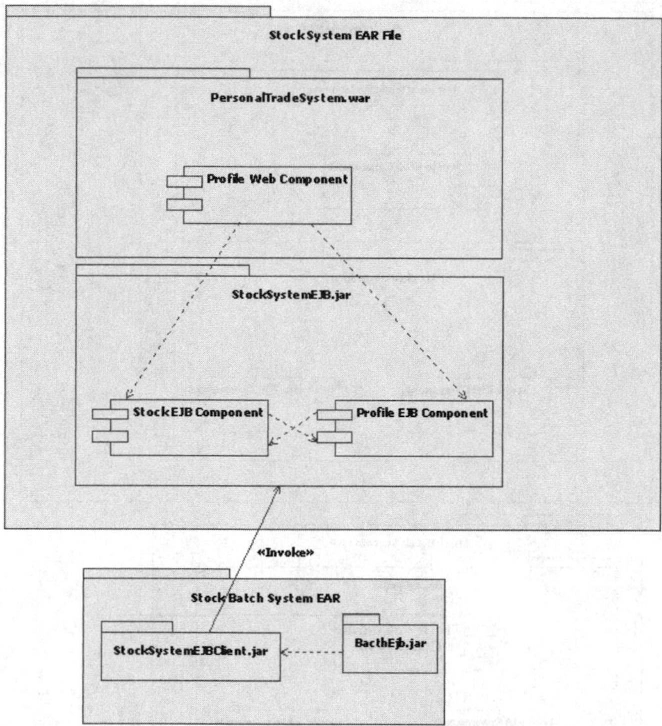


**Figure 15-12** Shared service deployment.

This helps to some degree, but the Profile web application is still competing with the Stock Batch application for resources at runtime since they both use the same EJBs.

It may make more sense to choose a private deployment with each application. This involves creating a copy of the shared components and deploying them in each application. This is shown in Figure 15-13.

Depending on your experience, either approach may seem intuitively obvious as the "right" approach. In general, we find that most people seem to prefer the shared service approach based on the false belief that "shared services" are inherently a good thing. They are not; distributed components add tremendous complexity to a system for a variety of reasons, including one obvious example we have shown here—competition for shared resources. In fact, in most situations, while deploying applications as a private service does slightly increase the complexity of builds (you must obtain and install the shared code), the provided service approach greatly simplifies runtime issues that can be very difficult to track down. That said, there are cases where shared services make sense. Rather than belabor the point here, we refer you to [Brown and Botzum 2003] for a detailed discussion of this topic.

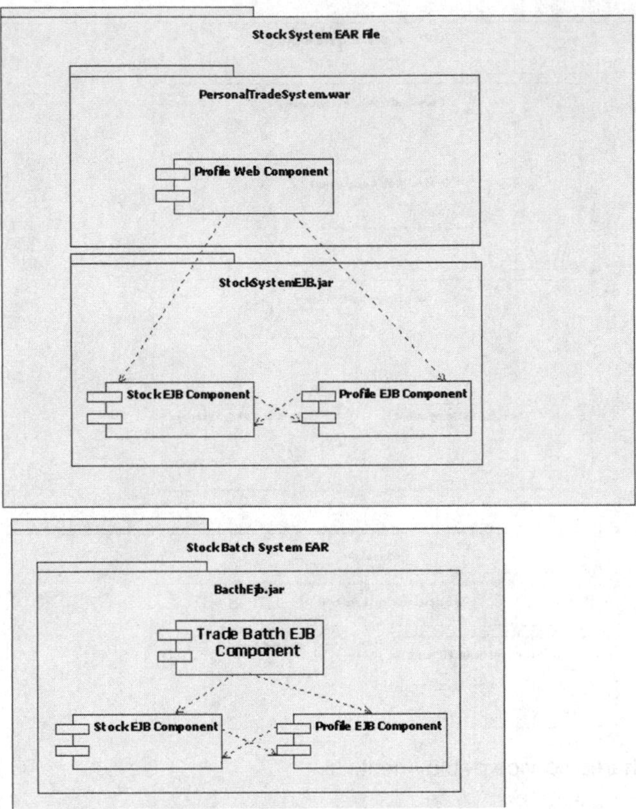


**Figure 15-13** Private service.

Now that we have discussed sharing with EJBs, it's time to consider the simpler case: sharing ordinary Java code libraries.

## Sharing Utility Code

Many applications depend on common shared Java libraries for needed utility function—internally developed code or third-party libraries. Sharing utility code across multiple modules within a single application is not much of an issue. As we've already said, the utility JARs can be placed in the WAR/lib directory if used only by a single web application or in the root of the EAR if shared by multiple modules in the EAR.

The more interesting case is common code that is used by multiple applications. These libraries can be packaged with each application or separately from the applications and shared. As we discussed in Chapter 5, "WebSphere Application Server Architecture," separate J2EE applications can share libraries through the use of the WAS library mechanism.

The J2EE specification assumes that applications are self-contained and deployable as a single unit. This way, applications can be independent of each other and are easier to deploy. In general, we strongly recommend packaging applications as self-contained units. That said, there are tradeoffs. The *benefits* of placing common code in a common location and thus sharing it across all applications are:

- The common code development team only has to support one (or possibly two) versions in production, rather than the multiple versions that could conceivably exist if applications were bundled with common code versions. However, limiting the versions that applications can use could contain this situation.
- The common code and underlying databases can change in sync. Since the common code changes in all applications at once, it is easier to force database changes.
- Fixes to the common code automatically apply to all applications. Of course, this is a mixed blessing.
- Some small amount of disk and memory space is saved by not having multiple copies of the same binary images on disk and in memory. Except for extraordinarily large libraries, this is not a significant benefit.

Frankly, we consider these benefits to be of limited value. On the other hand, the *challenges and risks* raised by sharing the code across applications are:

- Backward compatibility is paramount. Since every application uses the same version of the common API, it is nearly impossible to coordinate API changes. Thus, the API must be very stable.
- Changes desired by one application impact all applications. This makes introducing change very difficult. Application teams will have to coordinate their development and test cycles.
- Fixes required by one application impact all applications. This creates the difficult tradeoff between fixing one application quickly and the risks introduced by the change in other working applications.

The last two items are why we strongly recommend against sharing common code in production environments. This sharing of the same binaries can lead to extremely difficult-to-address cross-project interdependencies. Minor emergency fixes can become major political battles as different teams have different (and reasonable) goals.

Third-party utilities present some more challenges. Examples of this code include utilities in the Jakarta Apache Project such as Struts. The use of these third-party libraries is further complicated by the fact that WAS often makes use of popular open source libraries, such as those from the Apache project. If your application needs to use third-party utilities, follow these guidelines:

- Does WAS provide the same version of the utility needed? If so, do not place a copy in the EAR. Use the one in WAS. One such example is Apache's commons-logging.jar.
- Does WAS provide a different version of the same utility? If so, try to switch your implementation to the same version as WAS. If not, put it in the EAR file and switch the class loading policy to PARENT_LAST, as illustrated in Chapter 5.[2]
- If WAS does not provide the utility but has a similar utility, look for conflicts. For example, XML parsers often have common classes, even if they are provided by different vendors. If you can get by using one of the techniques described previously, do so.
- If WAS does not provide the utility, store it in the EAR or WAR lib based on what we discussed previously.

[Botzum 2002] covers this topic in more detail.

## Verification in Large Development Environments

We are going to close this chapter with an additional suggestion that we have found surprisingly valuable. One of the most famous phrases that we hear from almost every development group is, "Well, it worked on my machine!" This usually happens when someone is testing a new component for the first time in an integration or system test environment. One of the most insidious reasons for this is that a developer's workspace may slowly become cluttered with old code or perhaps code that he or she neglected to check in to the version management system (yes, discipline processes should prevent this, but they often don't). Rather than waiting for these problems to be found in a central Golden Workspace test or in the development integration build, it is helpful to encourage developers to test on their own desktop more rigorously. We do this using a "Verify Change Environment." This is essentially a read-only version of the application that each developer uses to test changes that have been checked in. For example, if you use WebSphere Studio for development, a developer should have two workspaces—one for development and one for the "Verify Change Environment." Figure 15-14 shows a simplified example of the process.

The verified change environment can be added to any of the build models we showed in Chapter 4. This is pictured in Figure 15-15.

2 Be aware that in some very subtle situations, this will not work. For example, if components are part of the JDK (JDK 1.4 includes many common formally open source libraries), they cannot be overridden.

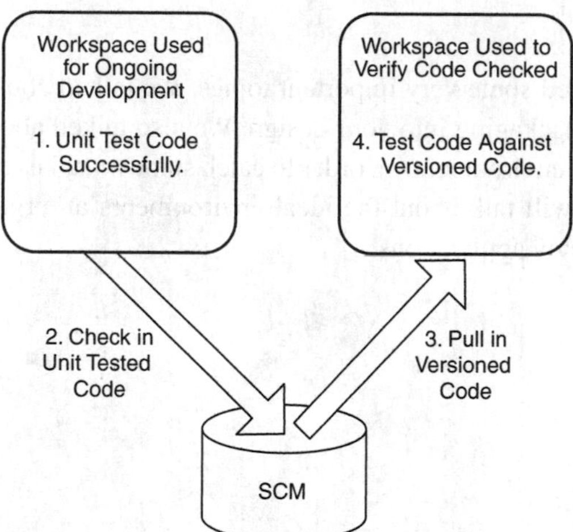


**Figure 15-14** Verifying code change in the "Change Verify Environment."

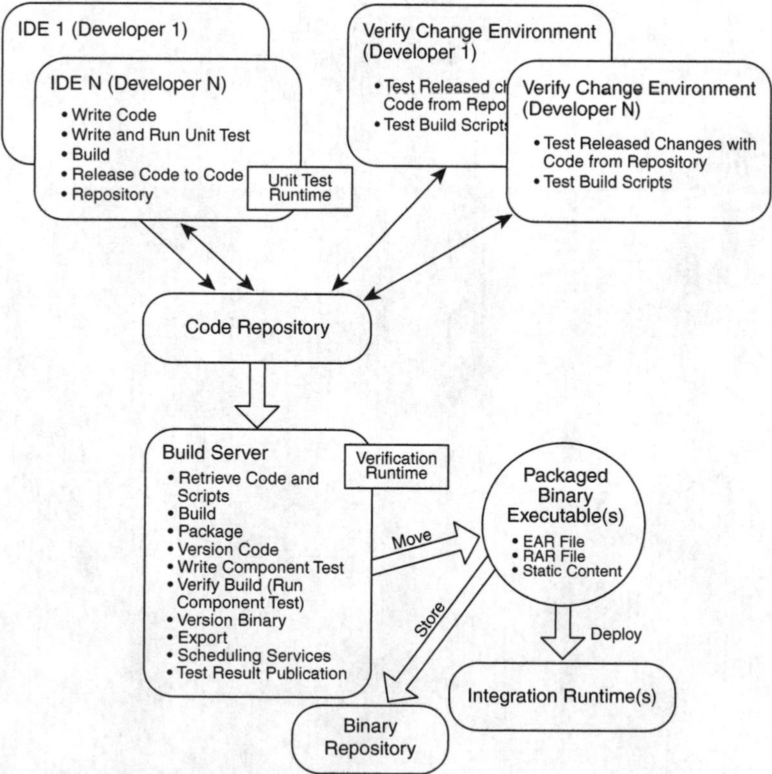


**Figure 15-15** Adding a verify change environment.

## Conclusion

In this chapter, we covered some very important topics. We talked about application packaging and how to incorporate packaging into your design. We also talked about adding more verification to your development environments in order to catch some mistakes early in the build process. In the next chapter, we will talk about the ideal environments an organization should have in order to successfully deploy applications.

CHAPTER 16

# Ideal Development and Testing Environments

> **NOTE**
> The content of this chapter is reprinted from an article originally published in the IBM WebSphere Technical Journal in December 2003 by Keys Botzum and Wayne Beaton. The article has been modified to match the formatting of this book, and some minor edits have been made for consistency with this book. The article is otherwise unchanged in content. As a result, some material here may overlap with other portions of the book, but we felt that the article provided a nice synthesis of most of the key reasons for the various environments and chose to reuse it here.

## Ideal Development Environments

This document describes the ideal environment for WebSphere Application Server and closely related WebSphere products, such as WebSphere Portal Server. The word "environment" is used in the largest sense possible—it includes virtually every aspect of enterprise application ownership starting with development and finishing with production.

When developing large and complex applications using enterprise-class infrastructure, great discipline, care, and planning is required in order to ensure the greatest likelihood of success. There are a number of aspects to creating such a disciplined environment including, but not limited to, rigorous software engineering, strong architecture, detailed design, quality staffing, careful planning, risk management, and more. This paper focuses on one aspect that is often overlooked: a set of well-designed stages where applications can be rigorously developed, tested, and deployed. These separate stages serve two purposes. First, separate stages allow you to design an environment that is optimized to its purpose (e.g., performance test needs lots of fast hardware). Secondly, by supporting multiple testing stages with rigorous processes, we are trying to find problems "earlier" in the development life cycle. Most problems will eventually be found in production, but our goal here is to find them sooner.

While this paper is naturally focused on WebSphere, it is important to remember that these issues are really not related to WebSphere, but rather to the general problem of disciplined development. As you read this paper, notice how little of it is in any way WebSphere-specific.

An overview of the ideal environment is presented in Figure 16-1. Note that this picture does not explicitly call out a "build environment." This is only because that environment is assumed to be within the "development environment" as build is considered a development activity (that doesn't actually mean developers perform the builds). Builds may be done implicitly using tools like WebSphere Studio or explicitly using tools such as ANT.

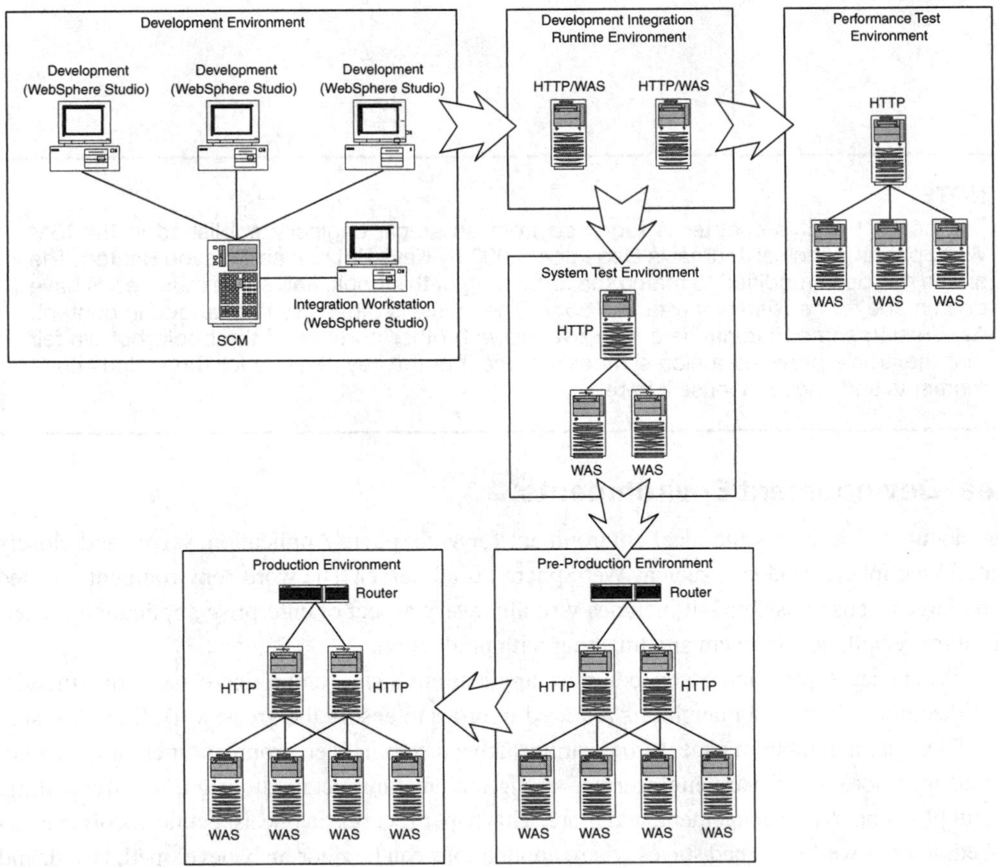


**Figure 16-1** The ideal WebSphere environment.

This figure represents an "ideal" environment that includes all of the necessary stages for a first-class rigorous environment. In this environment, each subenvironment is as complete as it needs to be to serve the intended task.

The extent to which you adopt an environment as is described here depends on the amount of risk you can accept for your applications. An environment such as what is described here does require a lot of investment, both in time and in money. Organizations developing simpler applications or that are willing to assume increased risk may scale down some aspects of this ideal environment. Later in this paper, we'll describe how this can be done and the risks involved. First, however, we will discuss each environment in more detail.

## Environment Stages

In this section, we describe in more detail the subenvironments listed earlier. We'll describe their purposes as well as describe some key aspects.

### Development Environment

The development environment is where developers live and work every day; this is where developers work hard and need to be productive. Thus, they need the best tools and the fewest barriers to progress.

The ideal development environment for WebSphere is shown in Figure 16-2. This environment is composed of a number of development workstations (one for each developer), a source code management (SCM) tool, and an integration workstation.

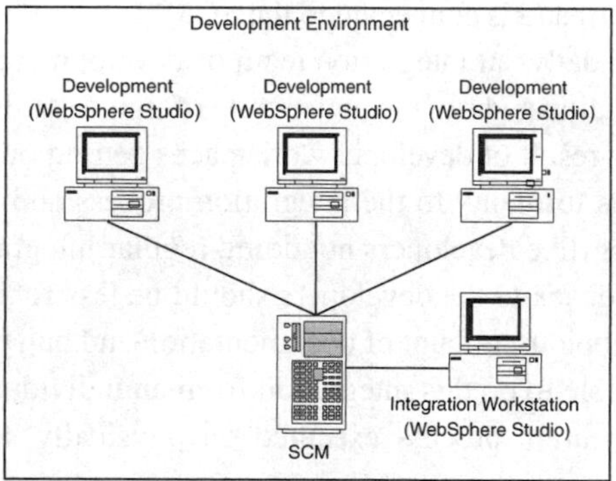


**Figure 16-2** The ideal WebSphere development environment.

Ideally, application developers use WebSphere Studio. There are many great advantages to using WebSphere Studio, including tight integration with the WebSphere product family.[1] The unit test environments, in general, have the same code base as their runtime equivalents, so developers can test their application within their IDE and have confidence that the behavior of the application in that environment will be very similar to the behavior of the application in the production environment.

1 WebSphere Application Server and WebSphere Portal Server, for example, are very tightly integrated into WebSphere Studio.

WebSphere Studio is the development tool of choice, but other tools can be used. If Studio is not used, we recommend that WebSphere Application Server be installed on the developer's desktop to support unit testing. In addition, even if developers work on, for example, a shared Unix server, it is still advisable for individual developers to run their own instance of WebSphere Application Server for testing purposes.[2] The key point here is that developers have a reasonably dedicated place to perform their own testing. If developers have to share their most basic test environment, their productivity will be greatly hindered.

The majority (90%) of all testing should occur in the unit test environment. Testing should occur on an ongoing basis—developers will typically run their application many times an hour within this environment as they incrementally develop and then test their work. In order to make repeated testing effective, we recommend that some form of automated unit testing be used.

As developers complete their work on individual features, they should immediately consolidate their changes against what is currently in the repository. Developers should be integrating their work with other changes before committing their own work to the repository. Such integration should occur frequently throughout the day.

## Integration Workstation

It is often useful to dedicate one special machine to the purpose of integration. This means that, ideally, the integration workstation runs WebSphere Studio (other configurations are possible as noted in the previous section) and is connected to the SCM.

Periodically, perhaps daily, an integration team or development lead should load the code onto the integration workstation and run the entire suite of unit tests. This sort of testing will help uncover bugs that may be a result of developer workspaces getting out of sync with the baseline. More importantly, this adds formality to the integration process and helps to uncover problems with the integration process (like developers not doing regular integrations). The process is both formal and controlled. Feedback to the developers should be less formal, however—this is not a development stage where copious amount of documentation and bug tracking is required.

It is technically possible to do this integration from an individual developer's workstation. However, having the integration process executed on physically separate hardware helps to formalize the process. Further, the use of an integration environment encourages frequent integration. By extension, this generally means that each integration involves a relatively small number of changes, which makes it generally easier to do. With a smaller number of changes, fewer things can break as part of the process and, therefore, remediation of problems is generally less difficult and time-consuming.

When the development integration machine is not being used for integration, it contains the most up-to-date version of the application (and always runs). This makes the machine a very handy tool for doing quick demos when required.

2 A single instance of WebSphere Application Server can require a lot of resources (especially memory) to run in a production scenario. For development purposes, the memory requirements are a lot smaller.

If the development organization is using automated build and validation processes, the integration workstation is less valuable. It is much more likely that the automated build and validation will be done on designated build machines rather than on a dedicated integration workstation. Both approaches are perfectly valid. The key is that there is a separate, semi-formal place where development makes an effort to validate that what they are doing is working as expected.

### Equipment

The desktop machines used by developers need to be high-caliber desktop machines. Development productivity is crucial—slow underpowered machines (lacking in CPU power, disk space, or memory) will only impede your team's success. In extreme cases, underpowered systems can trigger bugs in the underlying products that would never be seen elsewhere. This wastes precious time.

Refer to the official product documentation for the recommended (not minimum) settings and ensure that you have machines of at least that caliber. Even more is typically beneficial. This is because IDEs and other tools to improve developer productivity tend to use lots of machine resources. When you add in the needs of other standard desktop tools such as email and word-processing tools, machines that are sized conservatively often end up frustrating developers and wasting development time.

### Configuration Management Systems

The hardware running your source code management software must perform well and be highly reliable (daily backups are strongly recommended). Developers will move files to and from the version management server frequently, and any breakdown of the system will likely be very costly in terms of developer productivity.

In order to perform well, the machine must be fast and have plenty of memory and disk. Do not use some leftover PC that no one else wants. Also, avoid using a development desktop as a version management server for all but the smallest projects. Refer to your configuration management vendor for more detailed advice.

## Development Integration Runtime

The development integration runtime environment is used by developers to test their application on hardware and software that resembles the target production environment (see Figure 16-3). Testing in this environment is concerned with uncovering issues related to subtle differences between the development and production systems as well as testing the deployment procedures. This may include such things as the use of various operating system services, WebSphere Application Server security, replication testing (which often exposes subtle bugs related to reference locality), backend systems, and others.

Developers use this environment to perform integration tests among all system components. This environment is also used to test installation and operational procedures, which are often operating system-specific.

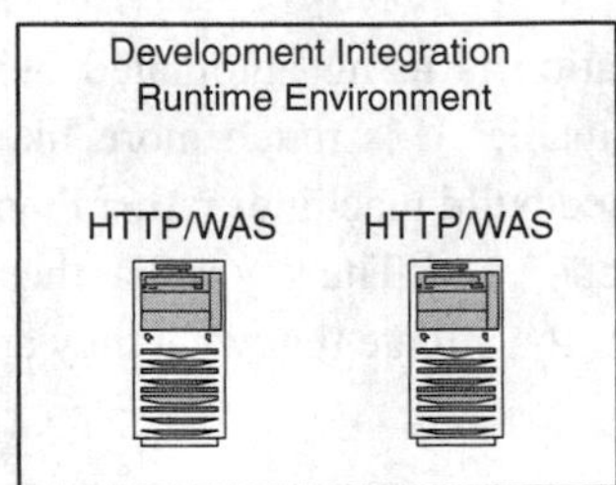


**Figure 16-3** The ideal development integration runtime environment.

The development integration runtime environment is configured to mirror the production environment at the smallest possible scale and complexity. In general, this environment does not include network devices such as load balancers, routers, or firewalls.

Systematic testing on this environment does not typically occur on a daily basis but does occur regularly, perhaps bi-weekly as a significant change is introduced into the application. It is a recommended practice that the application is run on these production-like platforms by developers on a regular basis.

This environment is controlled by the development team; it is used informally by developers and updated as often as necessary by developers while performing their tests. Periodically, this environment is refreshed using a formal build, deploy, and test procedure, thereby removing any inconsistency and testing the full build and install procedures.

In general, this environment does not include any development tools. As such, testing depends on the use of test scripts and tracing to determine correctness and identify problems.

## Motivation

The development desktop is generally different from the production platform: typically, Windows or Linux is used on development desktops, and more robust Windows, Linux, Unix, or z/OS systems are used for production. Most of the code base for WebSphere Application Server is shared across all platforms, so applications built on one platform should behave the same way on all other platforms. In general, J2EE artifacts such as Servlets, JSPs, and EJBs should all work the same way on all platforms.

However, there may be subtle differences between the unit test and production environments that can be exposed during this testing. It is best that these differences be discovered as early in the development process as possible. In general, it is easier to find and remediate a small number of bugs at key points in your development cycle than to find and remediate a much larger number of bugs as you try to move your application into production.

## Equipment

The development integration runtime environment mirrors the production environment at the smallest possible scale. For a typical project, this is a single machine running the same operating system and version of WebSphere Application Server as is used in the production environment.

### Sizing the Development Integration Runtime Environment

One topic that comes up frequently is how to properly size the development integration runtime environment. We aren't going to dwell on specifics like how many CPUs or how much memory, as these issues depend on far too many variables to enumerate. The issue here is to identify in broad strokes what is appropriate.

There is little point in spending a lot of money on hardware you don't need. But there is a catch. With a small team of developers (10 or fewer), it is feasible to have a single shared environment. Developers do most of their work on their desktop systems and only occasionally use the development integration runtime environment. When they use this environment, since it is shared, they run the risk of interfering with each other's work, but this should be manageable.

As the size of the development team grows, or if multiple projects share the same machine, a single shared integration environment becomes extremely difficult to manage. In that case, multiple environments should be created so that developers can experiment independently of each other. This is where things get tricky. For complete separation, developers need completely independent WebSphere Application Server domains or cells. Thus, a single development integration runtime environment needs to support a large number of cells, or there needs to be multiple environments.

As a rule of thumb, we recommend that no more than about 5 to 10 developers share a single "integration" environment. The right number for you might be higher or lower, but hopefully this gives you an idea. In addition, at least some of the developers may need to perform more complex experiments that may damage the cell. They may need a dedicated WebSphere Application Server instance or entire cell for their experiments. The essential point is that you should plan to create multiple cells and multiple application server instances and that there should be sufficient hardware to support this.

## System Test

The system test environment is a carefully controlled formal test environment. Development teams run their applications on this environment on a relatively infrequent basis—perhaps every six to eight weeks. A system test environment mirrors the production environment more closely than does a development integration environment, but it still does so at the smallest possible scale. Figure 16-4 shows an example system test environment.

A key aspect of the system test environment is formality. The purpose of this environment is to ensure that the application will truly deploy and run as required in production. Thus, the system test team is responsible for testing all aspects of the application, including both functional and non-functional requirements. Functional requirements are generally obvious—does the application execute the business rules as defined, does the application behave as required from the user's perspective? However, it is important to remember that testing here should also encompass non-functional requirements, including installation, backup, and failure procedures. Any failure during system test should result in a rejection of the build. This is not a place to experiment. Development experiments are executed informally in the development integration runtime environment.

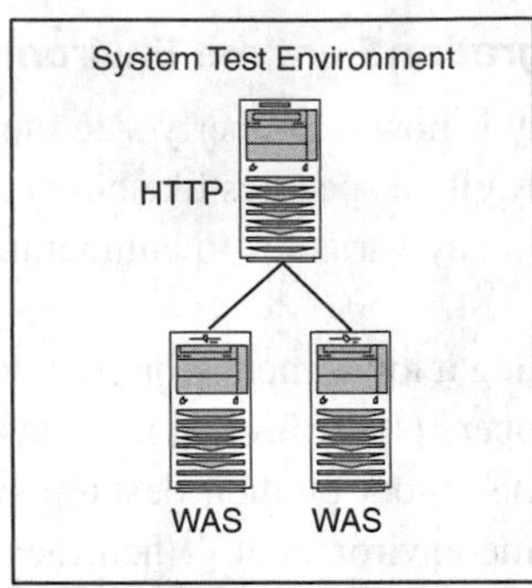


**Figure 16-4** The ideal system test environment.

A system test environment may serve multiple masters. In addition to being used formally by testers, other groups may use it as well depending on what is appropriate to your environment. For example, the administration staff may use this environment to test new patches and configuration changes before they are rolled into the pre-production and production environments. User acceptance testing, if this is a formal stage in your development processes, may also occur here.[3] A formal user acceptance process usually means that the system is left running for some well-defined period (without developers touching it), and users simply use the system to validate that it is working as they wish. In many ways, this overlaps with the concept of functional testing. However, having the end-user community actually agree that the system meets their needs is valuable. And, if those tests are done early enough, problems can be addressed.

It should be clear that a system test environment will have many different activities that need to be carefully controlled, scheduled, and managed. The reality of system test is that it is slow. Every problem found requires formal procedures for resolution; otherwise, crucial information may be lost. Ideally, system test environments should be owned and run by a separate team that is composed of people other than the development team.

### Equipment

This environment typically involves more than one application server instance running on more than one piece of physical hardware. And, the environment should use the same operating system and software versions as production. The system test team uses this environment to observe how the application works in a load-balanced environment. This testing might include, for example, testing to see how the application responds in a failover situation.

## Performance/Load Test

Performance and load testing is performed to find load-related problems in applications. This testing requires highly specialized skills and equipment to perform optimally. Hence, this is a dedicated environment and team.

3 User acceptance testing might also occur in the pre-production environment or the performance/load test environment.

Like the system test environment, the performance test environment is a carefully controlled formal test environment. Development teams run their applications on this environment on an even less frequent basis. A performance test environment mirrors the production environment in complexity, but it does so at the smallest possible scale. Figure 16-5 shows an example of an ideal performance test environment.

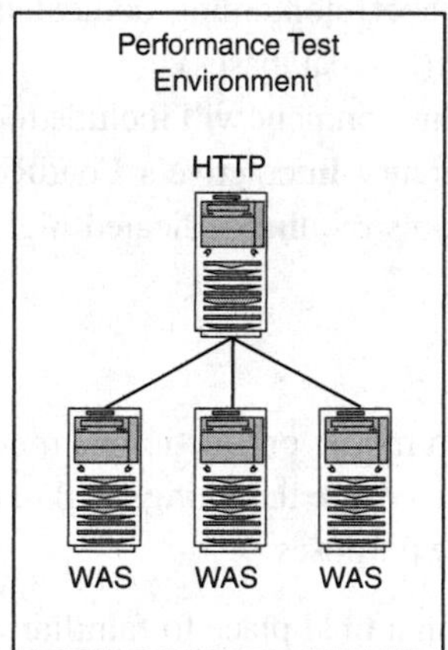


**Figure 16-5** The ideal performance test environment.

Load-related problems can be found in several areas: validation of ability to meet response and scalability criteria, determination of scaling factors, and the search for latent bugs. For more information on performance testing, see [Joines 2002].

During load testing runs, the testing team will carefully monitor various aspects of performance: CPU, memory usage, disk usage, response time, etc. They will use this information to determine if the system meets the response and scalability criteria and determine how well the system scales. This second piece of data is useful for predicting future hardware needs as the system is scaled in production. Lastly, the testing team will work to push applications as close as possible to the breaking point to find latent bugs. Sadly, many applications contain subtle bugs that either occur very rarely or are caused by concurrent access. Only through large-scale load testing can these bugs be found before your customers find them. Experience has shown that applications often behave quite differently under load than when used under lightly loaded manual testing scenarios. This is why load testing is so crucial.

Ideally, this environment is owned and operated by a dedicated performance testing group whose members have specialized load testing skills. Each development team schedules time with this group. Typically, an application is load tested less frequently than it is run on the system test environment. As with a system test environment, one application is tested at a time.

### Equipment

The performance test environment is very much like a system test environment with a specialized purpose. This environment also mirrors the production environment, but at a generally larger scale than a system test environment. This environment should use the same hardware and software configuration as the production environment (including operating system versions) and run on a dedicated network (or subnet) containing dedicated firewalls, web servers, load balancers and other required resources (like databases).

In addition, the load-testing environment will include tools for generating the needed load. High quality products such as Mercury Interactive's LoadRunner[4] or the IBM Rational load-testing tools will be used. These tools require dedicated high performance client machines for generating load.

## Pre-Production

The purpose of pre-production is to mimic production as much as possible (with **exactly** being the norm). This is the final chance to ensure that things will really work in production.

This environment serves three purposes:

1. It gives the operations team a final place to familiarize themselves with the application and its procedures.
2. It provides the opportunity to test unrelated applications running together. This is crucial with shared deployment environments. Prior to this point, the applications have been tested and built independently.
3. It provides the operations team with a chance to test their operational procedures (backup, failover, problem resolution, etc.).

As mentioned earlier, pre-production might also be used for user acceptance testing. In any case, testing on a pre-production staging environment generally coincides with an application's release schedule. Each external release of the application is tested on the pre-production system before it is finally moved into production. This environment is generally used to prove that the application works well with other applications.

This environment may be used by quality assurance testers as part of your release cycle.

### Equipment

Ideally, the pre-production environment exactly mirrors the production environment in complexity and in scale (including dedicated firewalls, web servers, load balancers, and other required resources). This environment is used to test multiple—possibly unrelated—applications running together as may be done in production.

4 http://www.mercuryinteractive.com/products/loadrunner/.

## Production

There isn't much to say here. Production is, of course, production. This is where you really run your applications. The key point is that if you have carefully followed procedures up until this point, the actual roll into production will be boring and predictable, rather than exciting and scary, since you have tested everything already.

# Process Matters

While we didn't go into every aspect of environment management, we do want to remind the reader of two important items that are often overlooked. First, it is crucial that you define a process for moving between the various environments. This includes, among other things, defining the process for moving an application from the development environment to various testing environments, and finally to the production environment. This should include entrance and exit criteria for each environment as well as defining how an application is rolled back to a prior environment to fix issues found in any particular environment.

A second key topic is environment verification. Once an environment has been built, it is worth taking the time to validate it using some simple test applications or procedure. This way, when real applications are deployed, you can have a high degree of confidence that if problems are found, they are in the application, not in the procedure used to build the environment. This will save everyone time and frustration.

# Tools

As the system test, performance test, and pre-production environments are used for testing, there is a set of tools that no ideal environment should be without. These tools provide the ability to collect data that assists in defining baseline characteristics of the application. As changes and new versions are applied in these environments, the tools are used to both re-create the scenarios and provide data showing either an improvement or not. Some of these tools are also helpful in troubleshooting and problem determination.

## Load Tools

No environment can predict how its application will perform under load without performing some load testing in the performance test environment. Load tools are the way to apply volume. There are open source tools such as Apache's JMeter[5] and high-end commercial tools such as IBM's Rational Test Suite and Mercury Interactive's LoadRunner.

The high-end tools generally provide features such as graphing, response validation,[6] and generators, which the open source tools often do not provide and leave you to have to manually correlate data.

5 http://jakarta.apache.org/jmeter/.

6 Response validation is very important. We've encountered applications that, under load, return the wrong answer perhaps 0.1% of the time. It is not feasible to scan output logs looking for such results. Thus, the automated tool must check that the response is the response that is expected.

### Application Monitoring

In order to understand how your application behaves under load, you need to be able to see into the application server environment itself. This is accomplished with application monitoring tools that provide statistics such as Servlet response time and the number of JDBC connections currently open.

A variety of tools exist in this space, from the low-end and free Resource Analyzer from IBM to the high-end like Wily's Introscope[7] and Tivoli's Performance tools. Again, the high-end tools tend to provide extensive features such as providing a view of the entire cluster, which tools like Resource Analyzer cannot provide.

### Troubleshooting

While you will be using both your load tools and application monitors in typical troubleshooting exercises, other lower-level tools also help in problem determination and root cause analysis. Some tools, such as an HTTP Proxy Tunnel,[8] allow quick analysis of HTTP traffic between a browser and the web server. For really difficult problems, sophisticated tools like Ethereal[9] can be used to provide network level packet sniffing.

## Reducing Costs

In an ideal world, all organizations would strictly follow the recommendations made in this document. However, most organizations have very real cost constraints. Besides, not all applications are "enterprise class." Thus, there are legitimate reasons for trying to reduce the costs implied by the previous sections. In this section, we'll briefly describe some suggested ways of reducing the costs and the risks involved in doing this.

### Pre-Production Staging

While certainly desirable, this is quite expensive to build and maintain. For smaller companies and environments with low complexity, it is quite common not to have a staging environment.

### System Test

While a separate system test environment should not be eliminated, there are several things that can be done to reduce the cost.

First, the system test environment can be shared by multiple teams. As described earlier, each application will probably only use the environment for a few days during each test cycle. Thus, if multiple applications are deploying to similar hardware, sharing this makes a great deal of sense. In large organizations with many concurrent development projects underway, it may

7 http://www.wilytech.com.

8 We are using this term somewhat vaguely on purpose. WebSphere Studio includes a built-in function like this as a Server Configuration of type TCP/IP monitor. There are also freeware tools that perform similar functions that can be downloaded.

9 http://www.ethereal.com.

make sense to have shared system test environments. In any case, access to these environments should be carefully managed and scheduled. However, keep in mind that sharing inevitably leads to scheduling conflicts. It is simply impossible to guarantee that applications won't have conflicting needs. As a result, while substantial money will be saved on hardware and possibly staffing, application test cycles will be longer.

Secondly, there is no need to exactly mimic production. In particular, there is no need to equip system test with large-scale high performance hardware. In fact, it is somewhat desirable to use lower powered hardware in system test in order to force load-related bug discovery earlier.

## Performance Test

First, for small applications with low performance requirements, there is no need for formal performance testing. Some simple load tests can be performed elsewhere. However, keep in mind that without at least some basic load testing, latent bugs may never be found.

Secondly, while we have recommended a dedicated performance testing environment and team, this is only practical for some organizations. Thus, in this case, performance testing could be done on system test hardware using the system test team. However, bear in mind that your system test environment then needs the hardware[10] and skills to support this type of testing. In particular, do not forget the importance of a dedicated (or at least stable) network; otherwise, performance test numbers are meaningless.

Another equally viable approach with respect to saving money on the performance test environment is to use the production or pre-production hardware for performance testing prior to the first application release. The problem with this approach is that you can use it only once. Once the application is deployed, production hardware is no longer available.

## Development Integration Test

It is quite common for a development team to be provided with a large-scale and expensive machine for development. This is often a waste of money. There is no need for development to have a top-of-the-line machine with all of the bells and whistles. An older or slower machine is quite appropriate as long as the operating system and basic features are the same. For example, if production will use a large AIX box with 20 CPUs, development should be able to get by with a smaller box with 4 CPUs (don't use a uniprocessor). Of course, bear in mind that if the development team is large, a large machine will be needed just to support all of the developers (see earlier discussion on sizing development).

Ideally, every development team has their own development integration runtime environment. If money is very tight, with appropriate scheduling, multiple development teams can share the environment. However, this can result in fairly serious conflicts if different development projects on different schedules have conflicting hardware and software requirements, conflicting versions being the most serious problem. Also, keep in mind that if sharing is taken too far, rigorous and cumbersome change control procedures will be required. This is inappropriate for

10 This means that system test will require large-scale machines mimicking production, firewalls, and load balancers.

development. Developers need to get work done...now. Later stages require formality. Earlier stages should be as loose as feasible. Where appropriate, multiple teams can share the same physical hardware but use separate WebSphere Application Server cells to alleviate this issue. But, there are limits.

Finally, and in the most extreme case, the development integration runtime and system test environments can be combined. However, doing this is extraordinarily risky and borders on reckless. It is very difficult to ensure that system test is really testing a proper build when development has access to the same machine.[11]

## Conclusion

This chapter has discussed in detail the various subenvironments or stages that are appropriate when developing complex systems using enterprise class software. We've described why each stage is necessary and have also described ways of reducing costs when appropriate. Applying these recommendations to your enterprise may cost more up front, but in the long-term we believe it will result in fewer sleepless nights and projects that suddenly fall months behind schedule without warning. Or, even worse, systems that fail in production when your customers can see the problems.

Remember the old adage: It costs far more money to fix a bug found by your customer than to fix (or prevent) one earlier.

11 We have seen instances where developers, completely innocently, modified configuration files that were being used by the System Test organization. A high degree of physical separation helps to prevent these types of errors.

CHAPTER 17

# JMX in WebSphere Application Server

The administrative runtime in WebSphere Application Server (WAS) V5 is implemented using Java Management Extensions (JMX). In this chapter, we'll briefly introduce JMX, cover how WAS implements JMX, and then discuss how to use JMX. We'll close with a discussion of how to install, configure, and secure custom JMX MBeans in WAS V5.

## An Introduction to JMX

Java Management Extensions (JMX) provides a standard way of managing Java resources with a systems management infrastructure. Java resources comprise any object in a system that needs to be controlled or monitored. Examples of objects that JMX can manage are enterprise applications, web modules, and application servers, as well as other essential application and runtime components. In short, JMX prescribes the API that allows us to manage Java applications.

JMX is comprised of three layers:

- Instrumentation layer
- Agent layer
- Distributed services layer

These layers are depicted in Figure 17-1.

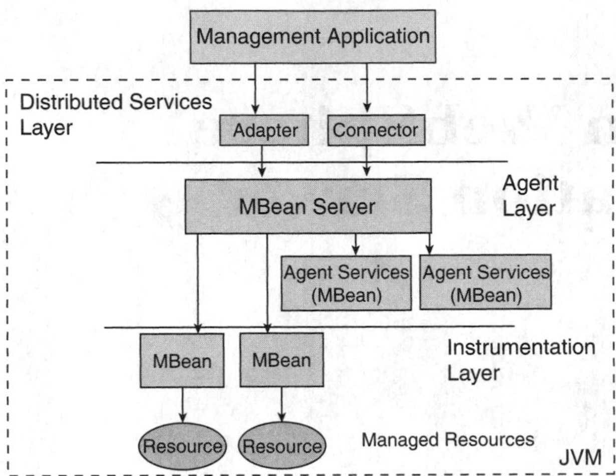


**Figure 17-1** JMX architecture.

## Instrumentation Layer

The instrumentation layer is the bottom JMX layer. This is the layer that most directly reflects individual managed resources. Each managed resource is described by an interface that specifies the attributes it has, the operations it supports, and the notifications it sends. Each resource in this layer is managed by a Managed Bean, which is also known as an MBean. An MBean is a Java class that implements one or more methods that allow you to monitor and/or control some Java runtime or application artifact.

## Agent Layer

The middle layer in the JMX architecture is the management layer. Each JMX managed process contains a JMX agent that includes an MBean server, which provides an MBean registry and entry point for MBeans. Management clients interact with an MBean server to access registered MBeans.

### Notifications and Listeners

Notifications are the mechanism employed by JMX that allows resources to notify management applications that specific administrative events have occurred.[1] Examples of these types of events are starting and stopping application servers as well as server resource utilization. Corresponding to the notion of notifications are listeners. Listeners programmatically register with an MBean server for notifications that are of interest. This concept of notification and listeners is quite powerful. WAS itself uses this internally. For example, the node agents in WAS-ND listen for interesting events on the application servers that they are managing.

1 Notifications are the JMX counterpart to SNMP traps.

## Distributed Services Layer

The top layer in the JMX architecture is the distributed services layer. This layer defines how external management applications can interact with the underlying layers in terms of protocols, APIs, and so on. Included in this layer are management applications, application connectors, and protocol adapters. These connectors and adaptors can be exposed through SNMP, HTTP, or a number of other protocols.

# JMX in WebSphere Application Server

In WAS V5, all runtime components are instrumented as MBeans, which correspond to the instrumentation layer in the JMX architecture. WAS V5 implements a JMX MBean server in each WAS process, corresponding to the JMX agent layer. At the distributed services layer, WAS V5 supports two types of connectors—RMI/IIOP and SOAP/HTTP(S)—which provide administrative client access to server resources.

WAS management function is achieved using JMX. The administrative clients that you are familiar with (wsadmin and the admin console) are simply clients of the WAS JMX infrastructure. In essence, WAS management, under the covers, boils down to using JMX MBeans. WAS V5.x implements over 70 MBeans.[2] The documentation for these MBeans is located in the <wasroot>/web/mbeanDocs directory, which is depicted on the Windows platform in Figure 17-2.

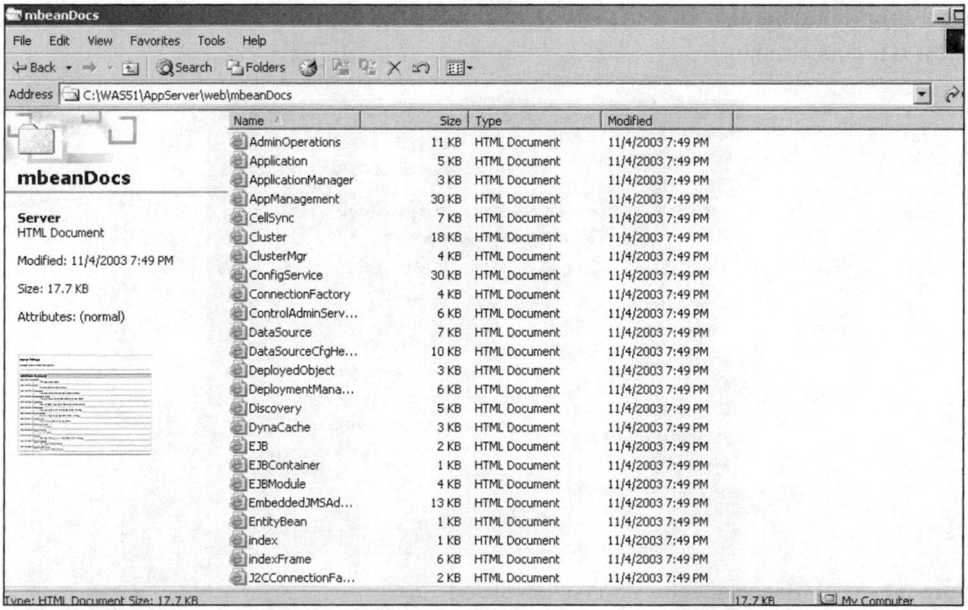

**Figure 17-2** MBean documentation.

2 Some of the MBeans are only applicable to WAS-ND; other MBeans are only applicable to WAS on z/OS.

A powerful side effect of this architecture is that it is possible to directly access WAS MBeans in a variety of ways: the MBean browser, wsadmin, and via Java clients.

## WAS MBeans via the MBeanInspector

MBeanInspector for WebSphere Application Server is a JMX-based administration program for WAS V5. MBeanInspector can connect to WAS servers and inspect the JMX MBeans that are registered with that server. This allows users to examine MBean attributes, invoke MBean operations, and listen for MBean notifications.

> **NOTE**
> The MBeanInspector doesn't ship with WebSphere Application Server but can be downloaded from the IBM alphaWorks web site (http://www.alphaworks.ibm.com/tech/mbeaninspector).

To use the MBeanInspector, you simply extract the downloaded ZIP file into the <wasroot> (e.g., C:\WebSphere\AppServer), open a command shell (DOS or Unix command window), navigate to the <wasroot>\bin directory, and type **"mbeaninspector" (bat/sh)**.

This will launch the MBeanInspector Connection dialog shown in Figure 17-3. Specify the correct host and port, and the MBeanInspector will connect to the MBean server in the WAS process it is connected to.

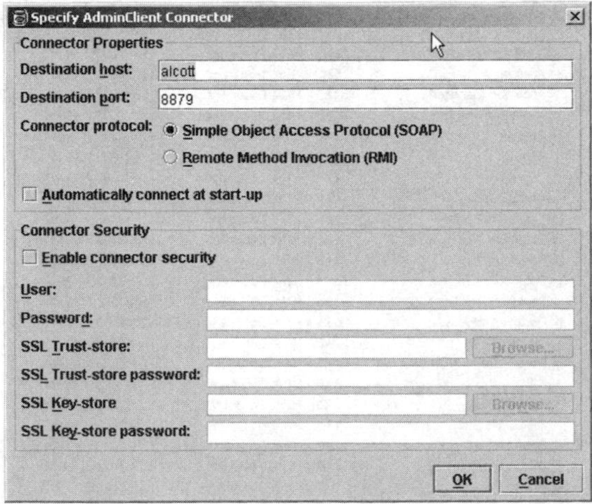


**Figure 17-3** MBeanInspector Connection dialog.

Once connected to the MBean server, the MBeanInspector will display all the MBeans running in WAS, as shown in Figure 17-4, and will allow you to query all the MBeans for the methods they expose and the signature for those methods.

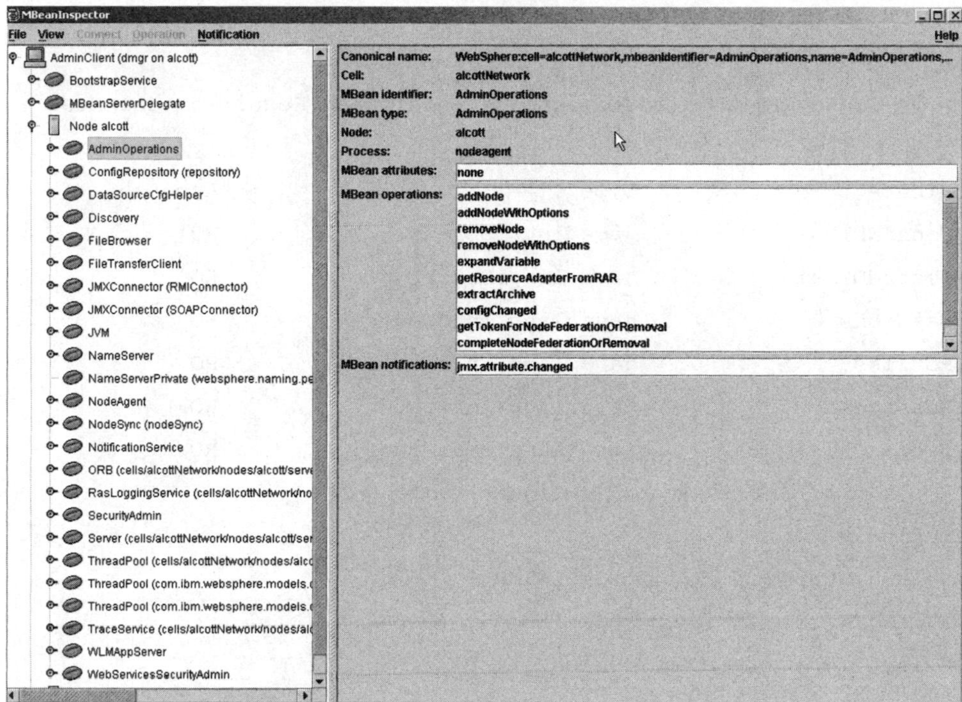


**Figure 17-4** MBeanInspector.

## wsadmin MBean Access

It is also possible to directly access the WAS MBeans using wsadmin. This gives you direct access to the internal MBeans and sometimes provides more powerful functionality than is available in the administrative clients.

Let's look at an example of using wsadmin to access an MBean. In this case, we will access the ListenerPort MBean that is used by an application server to service Message Driven Bean requests (see Code Snippet 17-1). First, we will obtain a reference to the ListenerPort for a specific application server by using queryNames. Then we'll display the methods of the MBean by invoking the wsadmin $Help MBean command.

**Code Snippet 17-1 wsadmin access of ListenerPort MBean**

```
wsadmin> set listenerport  [$AdminControl queryNames
➥*:*,node=sonoma,type=ListenerPort, process=server1]

wsadmin $Help all $listenerport

Name:WebSphere:platform=common,cell=sonomaNetwork,version=5.0,name=foo_
➥MDB_listener_port,mbeanIdentifier=cells/sonomaNetwork/nodes/sonoma/
➥servers/server1/server.xml#ListenerPort_1084845123095,type=
➥ListenerPort,node=sonoma,process=server1
```

```
Description: Management interface for JMS
➥MessageListenerService ListenerPort
Class name: javax.management.modelmbean.RequiredModelMBean
```

| Attribute | Type | Access |
|---|---|---|
| jmsConnJNDIName | java.lang.String | RO |
| jmsDestJNDIName | java.lang.String | RO |
| maxSessions | java.lang.Integer | RO |
| maxRetries | java.lang.Integer | RO |
| maxMessages | java.lang.Integer | RO |
| started | java.lang.Boolean | RO |

```
Operation
java.lang.String getJmsConnJNDIName()
java.lang.String getJmsDestJNDIName()
java.lang.Integer getMaxSessions()
java.lang.Integer getMaxRetries()
java.lang.Integer getMaxMessages()
java.lang.Boolean isStarted()
void start()
void stop()


Notifications
jmx.attribute.changed

Constructors
```

A list of all *running* MBeans can be retrieved with $AdminControl queryNames *:*, though likely you'll want to return a smaller list by providing additional arguments specific to a process such as a node agent or server. You can list all configuration MBeans with $AdminConfig types.

In any case, once you have the signature for the MBean and its methods, you can use the invoke operation to execute methods from wsadmin (see Code Snippet 17-2). This provides additional alternatives to the simple administrative commands exposed via wsadmin.

**Code Snippet 17-2** ListenerPort MBean stop, start, and status with wsadmin

```
wsadmin>$AdminControl invoke $listenerport stop

wsadmin>$AdminControl invoke $listenerport isStarted
false
wsadmin>$AdminControl invoke $listenerport start

wsadmin>$AdminControl invoke $listenerport isStarted
true
```

You should notice one difference between using the normal $AdminControl commands and invoking an MBean method to obtain the status of a process (a ListenerPort in this example). The MBean methods return a value, true in the case when the ListenerPort is started, and false when it is not started, that is not present when using $AdminControl. This can be useful in scripting by allowing the script to catch the values for additional processing or error checking.

### Writing Java Clients to Access MBeans

Last but not least, MBeans can be accessed from Java clients. These clients can be within a WAS application server or standalone Java applications. In WAS V5, the AdminClient class provides the framework for establishing a connection to a WAS server and the means to invoke methods on remote MBeans. The AdminClient provides a proxy to a remote WAS AdminService object though a WAS JMX connector. There's a complete discussion on writing a standalone application using the WAS AdminClient API in [Cundiff 2003].

## Custom MBeans in WAS

While WAS V5 has been instrumented with a large number of MBeans, and these should be more than sufficient for administering WAS itself, there may be cases where you have a new application that you wish to add custom administrative capabilities to, or you may have a requirement to integrate WAS with an existing systems management infrastructure. If so, you may need to write your own custom MBeans and deploy them in WAS. As mentioned before, we're not going to cover the MBean programming model. If you are interested that, refer to [Perry 2002] or [Kreger 2003]. Nor are we going to discuss the specifics of writing custom MBeans using the WAS-specific administrative APIs; this is discussed in [Williamson 2004]. Instead, we'll focus on installing custom MBeans in WAS.

There are two approaches for instrumenting a J2EE enterprise application with a custom MBean. The first is to add MBean code to a J2EE application artifact, such as a Servlet. The second is to write an MBean and configure it as an ExtensionMBeanProvider.

In the case of adding the MBean to a J2EE application artifact, you simply add the appropriate code to an existing application. This is depicted in Code Snippet 17-3, which obtains a reference to the MBeanFactory, creates an instance of the collab RuntimeCollaborator, then calls the activateMBean method for “MyMBean,” passing in the necessary parameters.

**Code Snippet 17-3** J2EE application MBean example code

```
try {
MBeanFactory mbfactory =AdminServiceFactory.getMBeanFactory();
RuntimeCollaborator collab = new Collab();
Mbfactory.activateMBean("MyMBean", collab,MYMBeanID, collab);
System.out.println("MyMBean Activated") ;
}
```

The downside to this approach is that the MBean won’t be available until the artifact is called by a client for the first time unless some provision is made address this. This can be readily addressed by, for example, writing a startup Servlet to specifically instantiate the MBean and then specifying that the Servlet be loaded on application startup. This is specified by selecting the **Load on startup** property for the Servlet in WebSphere Studio or the ASTK, as shown in Figure 17-5.

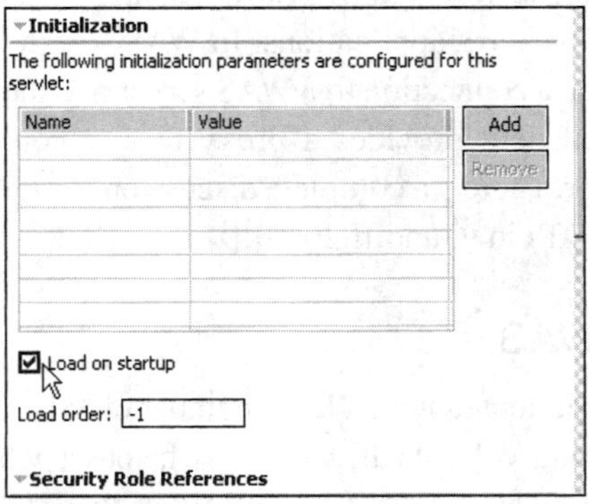

**Figure 17-5** Setting a Servlet for load at startup.

A better approach than adding the MBean to a J2EE application artifact is to configure an Extension MBean Provider. Doing so makes the MBean independent of the application. When using an Extension MBean Provider, you can still use a Servlet or startup JavaBean to instantiate the MBean, but a better approach is to use a WebSphere Custom Service to activate the MBean during server startup.

**NOTE**

A Custom Service provides the ability to add a component into the WAS application server startup and shutdown process. There are two parts to a Custom Service; first, the application will need to implement a class that implements the CustomService interface. Second, the administrator configures the Custom Service in a WAS application server. When an application server starts, any Custom Services defined for the application server are loaded, and the server runtime calls their initialize methods.

As far as configuring an MBean as an Extension MBean Provider, there are several steps. The first step is to navigate to the Extension MBean Provider, which is part of the Administration Services dialog for an application server, as shown in Figure 17-6.

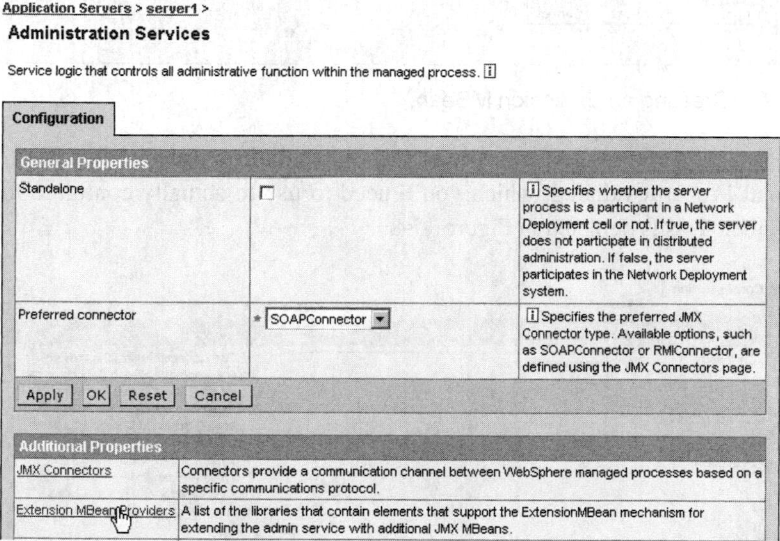


**Figure 17-6** Accessing the Extension MBean Providers.

Once in the Extension MBean Provider dialog, you'll first specify "New" to create a Extension MBean Provider and then specify the classpath for the MBean as well as a name for the Extension MBean Provider, as shown in Figure 17-7.

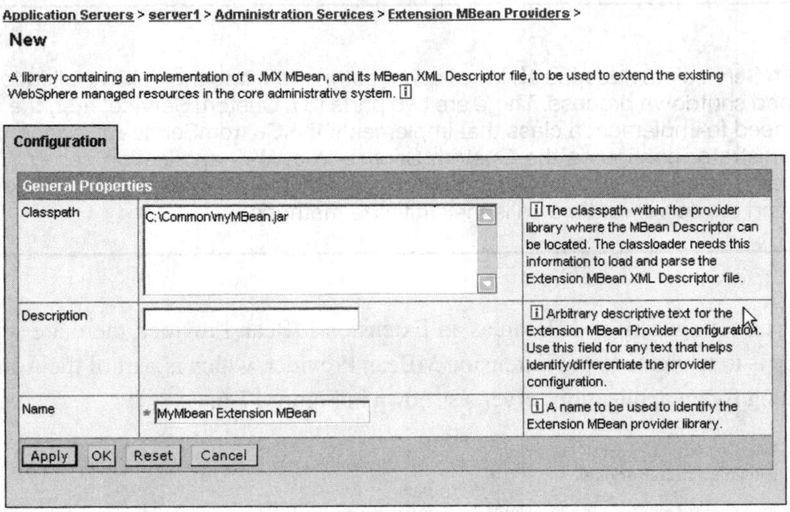

Application Servers > server1 > Administration Services > Extension MBean Providers >

New

A library containing an implementation of a JMX MBean, and its MBean XML Descriptor file, to be used to extend the existing WebSphere managed resources in the core administrative system.

Configuration

| General Properties | | |
|---|---|---|
| Classpath | C:\Common\myMBean.jar | The classpath within the provider library where the MBean Descriptor can be located. The classloader needs this information to load and parse the Extension MBean XML Descriptor file. |
| Description | | Arbitrary descriptive text for the Extension MBean Provider configuration. Use this field for any text that helps identify/differentiate the provider configuration. |
| Name | * MyMbean Extension MBean | A name to be used to identify the Extension MBean provider library. |

Apply OK Reset Cancel

**Figure 17-7** Creating an Extension MBean.

Once you have entered either **Apply** or **OK** in this dialog, you will then be presented with the Additional Properties dialog, which you'll need to use to actually configure the Extension MBean Provider. This is depicted in Figure 17-8.

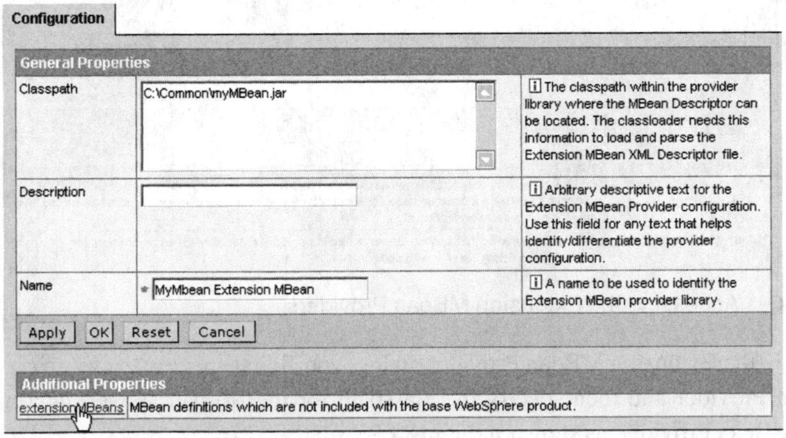

Configuration

| General Properties | | |
|---|---|---|
| Classpath | C:\Common\myMBean.jar | The classpath within the provider library where the MBean Descriptor can be located. The classloader needs this information to load and parse the Extension MBean XML Descriptor file. |
| Description | | Arbitrary descriptive text for the Extension MBean Provider configuration. Use this field for any text that helps identify/differentiate the provider configuration. |
| Name | * MyMbean Extension MBean | A name to be used to identify the Extension MBean provider library. |

Apply OK Reset Cancel

| Additional Properties | |
|---|---|
| extensionMBeans | MBean definitions which are not included with the base WebSphere product. |

**Figure 17-8** Extension MBean additional properties.

You'll then be presented with the dialog for defining an Extension MBean, which is depicted in Figure 17-9. Definition of an Extension MBean requires two pieces of information:

- **descriptorURI**—The location, relative to the provider classpath, where the MBean XML descriptor file is located. Since we will put the descriptor file in the root of our JAR file, the value in this case is the name of the file, MyMBean.xml.

- **type**—The type to be used for registering this MBean. This *must* match the type declared in the MBean descriptor file, which, in our example, is MyMBean.

Application Servers > server1 > Administration Services > Extension MBean Providers > Extension MBean Providers > ExtensionMBean >

**New**

Identifies where the metadata for the MBean is located.

**Configuration**

| General Properties | | |
|---|---|---|
| descriptorURI | * MyMBean.xml | The location of the MBean's descriptor |
| type | * MyMBean | The type of the MBean. |

Apply OK Reset Cancel

**Figure 17-9** Extension MBean additional properties specification.

Once the Extension MBean has been defined, you'll still need to configure a Custom Service if you want WAS to start the MBean for you when the server starts up. The Custom Services dialog is located on the Additional Properties panel for an application server, as shown in Figure 17-10.

| Additional Properties | |
|---|---|
| Transaction Service | Specify settings for the Transaction Service, as well as manage active transaction locks. |
| Web Container | Specify thread pool and dynamic cache settings for the container . Also, specify session manager settings such as persistence and tuning parameters, and HTTP transport settings. |
| EJB Container | Specify cache and datasource information for the container. |
| Dynamic Cache Service | Specify settings for the Dynamic Cache service of this server. |
| Logging and Tracing | Specify Logging and Trace settings for this server. |
| Message Listener Service | Configuration for the Message Listener Service.This service provides the Message Driven Bean (MDB) listening process, whereby MDBs are deployed against ListenerPorts that define the JMS destination to listen upon. These Listener Ports are defined within this service along with settings for its Thread Pool. |
| ORB Service | Specify settings for the Object Request Broker Service. |
| Custom Properties | Additional custom properties for this runtime component. Some components may make use of custom configuration properties which can be defined here. |
| Administration Services | Specify various settings for administration facility for this server, such as administrative communication protocol settings and timeouts. |
| Diagnostic Trace Service | View and modify the properties of the diagnostic trace service. |
| Debugging Service | Specify settings for the debugging service, to be used in conjunction with a workspace debugging client application. |
| IBM Service Logs | Configure the IBM service log, also known as the activity log. |
| Custom Services | Define custom service classes that will run within this server and their configuration properties. |

**Figure 17-10** Accessing Custom Services.

Once again, you'll need to select "New" to create a new Custom Service and then fill in the dialog, as shown in Figure 17-11. You'll note that "Startup" is selected so that the Custom Service is started when the application server is started. We've also configured the classname for the Custom Service, the classpath to the class that implements the WAS CustomService in our application, and a name for the Custom Service. The other two properties—External Configuration URL, which can be used for configuration data for this Custom Service, and Description, which can be any text that is useful to distinguish this Custom Service from others—are both optional.

Application Servers > server1 > Custom Services >

**New**

Provides an extension point for configuration data for plug-in services. Allows customers to add in custom code which will be executed during process initialization.

**Configuration**

| General Properties | | |
|---|---|---|
| Startup | ☑ | Specifies whether the server will attempt to start the specified service when the server starts. |
| External Configuration URL | | Specifies the URL for a custom service configuration file. |
| Classname | * MyMbean.CustomService | Specifies the class name of the service implementation. This class must implement the Custom Service interface. |
| Display Name | * MyMBean Custom Service | Specifies the name of the service. |
| Description | | Describes the custom service. |
| Classpath | * C:\Common\MyMbean.jar | Specifies the class path used to locate the classes and jars for this service. |

Apply OK Reset Cancel

**Figure 17-11** Custom Service properties specification.

At this point, your Extension MBean and associated Custom Service is ready to run, except for one *very* important aspect—security.

## MBean Security

There are two aspects to MBean Security—Java 2 Security and Resource Authorization. You'll need to consider both of these to ensure that any Extension MBeans are able to be executed appropriately by someone authorized to execute them.

### Java 2 Security

If you run WebSphere Application Server with Java 2 Security enabled, an Extension MBean will throw an exception because the embedded JMX in the WAS runtime code is protected against use by any non-privileged code base. What this means is that in order to use JMX code in a WebSphere Application Server process (indeed, in order to use any WebSphere administration APIs at all), you must grant your code the necessary permissions in a policy file read by the Java 2 Security infrastructure. The JMX code in WebSphere Application Server is protected by two layers of permissions:

- WebSphere management permissions that include com.ibm.websphere.security WebSphereRuntimePermission "AdminPermission"
- Tivoli TMX4J permissions, which include com.tivoli.jmx.MBeanServerPermission "MBeanServer.*" and "MBeanServerFactory.*"

To enable these permissions, you will need to add a policy stanza in the was.policy file for your application contains code that accesses the embedded JMX server (see Code Snippet 17-4).

**Code Snippet 17-4** was.policy file example

```
grant codeBase "file:${application}" {
permission com.ibm.websphere.security.WebSphereRuntimePermission
"AdminPermission";};
grant codeBase "file:${application}" {
permission com.tivoli.jmx.MBeanServerPermission "MBeanServer.*";
};
```

Of course, the preceding allows your JMX code to execute by granting it administrative access to the WAS runtime. This is, in itself, very dangerous. This code can now perform administrative actions. If you choose to do this, you should structure your application code such that the smallest portion is trusted. Thus, rather than granting the permissions to the entire application as in the preceding, grant them just to a JAR file that contains the JMX code. This will reduce the danger.

If instead, you choose to define your JMX code as Extension MBeans, you won't have to grant any special Java 2 permissions. But, because those MBeans are loaded by the WebSphere extensions classloader and this is considered a "trusted" classloader, code there is more trusted than normal application code.

The net here is that executing JMX MBeans have elevated permissions that can compromise the WAS internals. Use such MBeans sparingly and carefully inspect them to avoid allowing an application to compromise the entire WAS cell.

Java 2 Security is only part of the security equation, though; with Java 2 Security, the JVM system resources are protected. For example, application access to read and write to files on file systems, listen to sockets, exit the application server process, etc. is protected, but Java 2 Security can't secure a network-accessible resource. Further, Java 2 Security is process-based, relying on the code source, not the user identity. As a result, it's likely that additional steps will be required to restrict user access to the MBean methods.

## Resource Authorization

All MBeans are part of the administration program in WAS, and as part of that program, they are subject to role-based authorization to ensure the caller is mapped to one of the four administration roles for the system (Monitor, Configurator, Operator, Administrator). If the creator of the MBean does not supply a role-to-operation mapping, a default algorithm is used to set this for the MBean when it is activated. The default logic is to require Configurator or Administrator role in order to perform configuration functions and to require Operator or Administrator role in order to perform all other operations.

While optional, it's recommended that the creator of the MBean supply a <MBeanType>Security.xml file that overrides the default algorithm and explicitly maps the roles required for specific functions for that MBean.[3] An example of the format for this file is in shown in Code Snippet 17-5. This file should be located on classpath that is used to load the MBean operational descriptor XML file (and the MBean itself). You would usually do this by packaging it (along with the regular MBean descriptor file) in the JAR file used for your Extension MBean Provider that you configure for the server in which this MBean is to be executed. Recall that the Extension MBean Provider configuration includes a classpath property that should identify the path to your JAR file containing this file.

**Code Snippet 17-5** sample MBean Security.xml file

```
<?xml version="1.0" encoding="UTF-8"?>
<!DOCTYPE role-permission SYSTEM "RolePermissionDescriptor.dtd" >

<role-permission>
    <resource>
        <resource-name>sample</resource-name>
        <class-name>com.ibm.ws.security.descriptor.sample</class-name>
        <description>This is a sample for testing role permission
        ➥descriptor.</description>
    </resource>
    <security-role>
       <role>
           <role-name>monitor</role-name>
       </role>
    </security-role>
    <security-role>
       <role>
           <role-name>operator</role-name>
           <imply>
```

3 While there are no known problems related to using the WAS administration program to correctly protect MBeans, since this is custom code that is being added and protected, it's preferable to explicitly map MBean methods to administrative roles.

```
            <role-name>monitor</role-name>
         </imply>
      </role>
   </security-role>
   <security-role>
      <role>
         <role-name>configurator</role-name>
         <imply>
            <role-name>monitor</role-name>
         </imply>
      </role>
   </security-role>
   <security-role>
      <role>
         <role-name>administrator</role-name>
         <imply>
            <role-name>operator</role-name>
            <role-name>configurator</role-name>
         </imply>
      </role>
   </security-role>
   <method-permission>
      <description>Sample method permission table</description>
      <role-name>operator</role-name>
      <method>
         <description>Sample operation</description>
         <resource-name>sample</resource-name>
         <method-name>stop</method-name>
      </method>
   </method-permission>
   <method-permission>
      <description>Sample method permission table</description>
      <role-name>operator</role-name>
      <method>
         <description>Sample operation</description>
         <resource-name>sample</resource-name>
         <method-name>start</method-name>
         <method-params>
            <method-param>java.lang.String</method-param>
            <method-param>java.lang.String</method-param>
```

```
            </method-params>
        </method>
    </method-permission>
    <method-permission>
        <description>Sample method permission table</description>
        <role-name>operator</role-name>
        <method>
            <description>Sample operation</description>
            <resource-name>sample</resource-name>
            <method-name>monitor</method-name>
            <method-params>
            </method-params>
        </method>
    </method-permission>
    <method-permission>
        <description>Sample method permission table</description>
        <role-name>configurator</role-name>
        <method>
            <description>Sample operation</description>
            <resource-name>sample</resource-name>
            <method-name>setValue</method-name>
            <method-params>
               <method-param>java.lang.Boolean</method-param>
            </method-params>
        </method>
    </method-permission>
    <method-permission>
        <description>Sample method permission table</description>
        <role-name>monitor</role-name>
        <method>
            <description>Sample operation</description>
            <resource-name>sample</resource-name>
            <method-name>getValue</method-name>
        </method>
    </method-permission>
</role-permission>
```

## JMX in WAS-Network Deployment

While we've only been dealing with WebSphere Application Server base up until now, and WebSphere Network Deployment (WAS-ND) architecture won't be discussed for a few more chapters, we need to introduce a few architectural terms from WAS-ND in order to complete our discussion of JMX in WAS.

WAS-ND adds two additional runtime components that are used for systems management. First, there's the Deployment Manager (or Dmgr). The Deployment Manager manages the configuration for all servers and applications in a cell and serves as the central point of administration. There can be one or many machines in a cell; each one of these is referred to as a node. On each node, WAS uses a Node Agent to manage the local configuration and to provide process management for application servers and a JMS server (if one is configured) on the node.

This interaction between the Dmgr JMX server, Node Agent JMX server, and JMX server in each server[4] on a node is depicted in Figure 17-12.

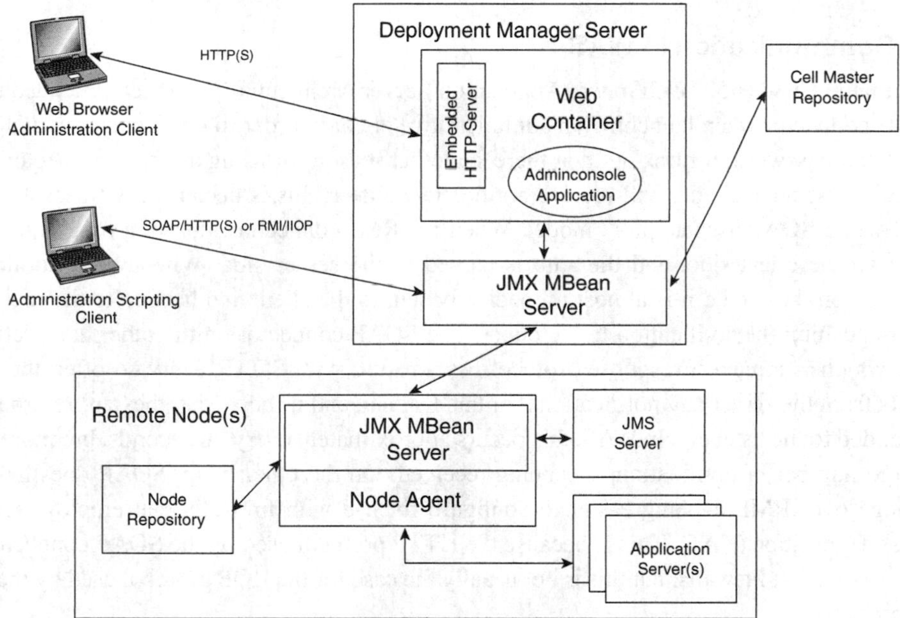


**Figure 17-12** WAS JMX architecture.

In WAS base, the administrative client programs interact directly with the application server process and send administrative requests to that process. In WAS-ND, administrative client programs can attach to any process in the topology (Dmgr, Node Agent, or server process). Normally in WAS-ND, administrative clients attach to the Dmgr because all servers can be

4 Recall that in Chapter 5, we discussed the WAS base architecture that includes a JMX server in the application server.

controlled from that process. When a request for an MBean operation is submitted to the Dmgr, it is automatically routed to the server where the target MBean and underlying runtime component exists.

The runtime and application configuration in WAS-ND are managed in a similar fashion to MBean requests. The central configuration is managed by the Deployment Manager, and then it is pushed down to each node via the Node Agent, where a local copy of the configuration is maintained.

Communication between WAS-ND processes occurs via JMX notifications. The MBean server in the Node Agent subscribes to notifications from application servers. Notifications occur when a significant event occurs, such as starting or stopping a server. In turn, the Dmgr subscribes to notifications from the Node Agents as runtime events occur. While WAS-ND uses a management hierarchy for propagation of notifications, employing the hierarchy is an implementation choice. If required, any MBean in a WAS-ND cell can subscribe to notifications from any other WAS-ND MBean.

## JMX Communication in WAS

Recall that in Chapter 5, "WebSphere Application Server Architecture," we recommended use of the RMI connector when launching an administrative client in order to receive a login dialog for user ID and password. It turns out that there's another reason for using an RMI connector. With RMI, administrative clients will receive notifications faster; this is because RMI uses a "push" model, while SOAP uses a "pull" model. When the RMI connector is used, a remote object is created on the client side, and the stub is passed to the server side. Whenever a notification is received on the server, it is almost immediately sent to the client and handed to the registered listeners pushing the notification to the client. The SOAP connector on the other hand relies on HTTP, which is a request/response protocol. As a result, with SOAP, every so often the client requests from the server any notifications for this listener, and if they exist, they are returned and then handed to the listeners. In WAS, this occurs approximately every 20 seconds, but more often if a large number of notifications are being received. On the other hand, SOAP does have the advantage over RMI of being easier to configure for use with firewalls that employ Network Address Translation (NAT). This is because the HTTP protocol used by the SOAP connector can be passed by most firewalls, but this is not usually the case for the IIOP protocol used by the RMI connector.

## Conclusion

This chapter has discussed JMX, the WAS JMX implementation, different client access methods for WAS MBeans, how to install and configure custom (or extension) MBeans, and last but not least, how to secure these MBeans.

CHAPTER 18

# Security

In this chapter, we will cover several aspects of security. We will briefly discuss why security is important and then detail the WebSphere Application Server (WAS) security architecture. We'll cover some subtle points of WAS security and then move on to detailed discussions of how to harden a WAS environment to be secure. Finally, we'll provide some tips for troubleshooting security problems. Given the limited space available, much of this material will be high level and will not delve into the details. Wherever possible, we will point you to appropriate references that show the details.

## Why Security?

Hopefully, most readers of this book realize that security is a key aspect of enterprise systems. Nonetheless, we'll briefly justify security here in order to introduce some common ways of thinking about it. The fundamental purpose of security is to keep the bad people out of your systems. More precisely, security is the process of applying various techniques to prevent unauthorized parties, known as intruders, from gaining unauthorized access to things.

There are many types of intruders out there—foreign spy agencies, corporations in competition with you, hackers, and even your own employees. Each of these intruders has different motivations, different skills and knowledge, different access, and different levels of need. For example, an employee may have a grudge against the company, and employees have tremendous levels of internal access and system knowledge but probably have limited resources and hacking skills. An external hacker is probably an expert in security attacks but may not have any particular grudge against you. A foreign spy agency, depending on your business, may have a great deal of interest in you and possess tremendous resources.

Intruders may be after your systems for one of two reasons—to gain access to information that they should not have or to alter the behavior of a system in some way. In the latter case, by changing the system behavior, they may seek to perform transactions that benefit them, or they may wish to simply cause your system to fail in some interesting way in an effort to harm your organization. As you can see, there are many different types of intruders and motivations and, as we will discuss later, many different types of attacks. As you plan your security, you need to be aware of this.

We also want to emphasize that security should not be seen as simply a gate that keeps the "outsiders" out. That is a far too simplistic view. Many organizations today focus their security efforts entirely on people outside of the organization in the mistaken belief that only outsiders are a danger. This is simply not the case. People within your organization are also very likely to attack your systems. Several recent studies have indicated that perhaps as many as half of all break-ins are caused by or involve employees or contractors within the organization. It's crucial that your security efforts protect your systems from all potential intruders. This is why this chapter is so long. Security consists of more than just some firewalls at the edge of your network protecting you from the "outside." It is a difficult and complex set of actions and procedures that strive to strengthen your systems as much as appropriate.

## Limits and Reality

It is important for you to realize that there is no such thing as a perfectly secure system. Your goal is to protect the system as well as you can within the constraints of the business. When thinking about security, you ideally should:

- Analyze the various points of attack.
- Consider the risk of an attack at each point.
- Determine the potential for damage from a successful attack that results in a security breach.
- Estimate the cost of preventing each attack.

When estimating the damage of a security breach, never forget that security breaches can cause users to lose faith in the system. Thus, the "cost of security breach" may include very high indirect costs (e.g., loss of investor confidence).

Once you have performed the steps listed previously, you can then determine appropriate tradeoffs of risk versus cost. Essentially, the goal is to make the cost to the intruder of breaking into your system exceed the value of what is gained,[1] while at the same time ensuring that the business can bear the costs of running the secure system. Ultimately, the level of security required is a business, not a technical, decision. However, as technicians, we must help all parties understand the value and importance of security.

1 This can be a problem when some hackers break into systems simply for the fun of it. What you can hope is that by creating a reasonably secure environment, intruders will move on to easier targets.

Security is a large topic, and it is impossible to completely cover all aspects of security in a single chapter. This chapter is not intended to be an introduction to security or a tutorial on how to secure WAS-based systems. Rather, it is a high-level overview or checklist of the core technical issues that need to be considered as they relate to WAS. The information in this chapter should be used in conjunction with a much larger effort that is designed to create a secure enterprise.

Readers interested in learning more should refer to the references section. In particular, the article on Enterprise Application Security ([Botzum 2000]) provides a high-level, if somewhat dated, overview of the basics of application security.

### Social Engineering

Since this is a technical book, we are focused on technical solutions to securing systems. In fact, we are focused primarily on the WAS piece of the security puzzle. Nonetheless, you should be aware that it is often easier to compromise systems using social engineering techniques. That is, by tricking the human beings that work for your organization, attackers are able to gain access to systems and information to which they should not have access. Refer to [social engineering 2003] for more. Perhaps the one conclusion of relevance to this chapter's discussion that we can learn from social engineering attack techniques is the fact that by using social engineering, your attackers may be coming from within your network. This again serves to emphasize the earlier point that security that is focused solely on keeping the intruders out of the network is foolishly insufficient. This is why the discussion here will focus on security at multiple levels. Each level tries to thwart different types of attacks and also provides more barriers to attackers.

## WAS Security Architecture

We assume that you are familiar with J2EE security and the basics of security. If you are not, refer to the J2EE specification for details on how to secure J2EE applications as well as [Botzum 2000]. Here, we are concerned with how WAS implements security. We will not delve into low-level details, as they are generally irrelevant, but it is helpful to understand at a high level how the WAS security infrastructure works. This will aid in defining a secure infrastructure and in troubleshooting.

As with any secure system, WAS provides functions for authentication, authorization, and data protection. WAS provides for three forms of authentication: user ID/password, client certificates, and identity assertion. WAS implements the required J2EE authorization methods and also provides for plugging in Tivoli Access Manager as an external authorization engine. In most cases, WAS uses SSL for data protection when transmitting information over a network connection. We now discuss each form of authentication in greater detail.

### Authentication

There are two authentication cases to consider: web client authentication and EJB client authentication. We will not be discussing web services authentication. Other than a brief mention of the JAAS client authentication APIs (for use in EJB clients), we will not be discussing JAAS either.

This is because while WAS V5 does partially support JAAS and custom login modules, JAAS is only able to supplement the WAS authentication process. The JAAS custom login modules cannot alter or replace the existing WAS authentication tokens. Thus, a JAAS login module can add custom attributes to a Subject, but the WAS login module still needs to be executed as well to achieve proper authentication. Figure 18-1 shows the basic architecture of the WAS authentication infrastructure.

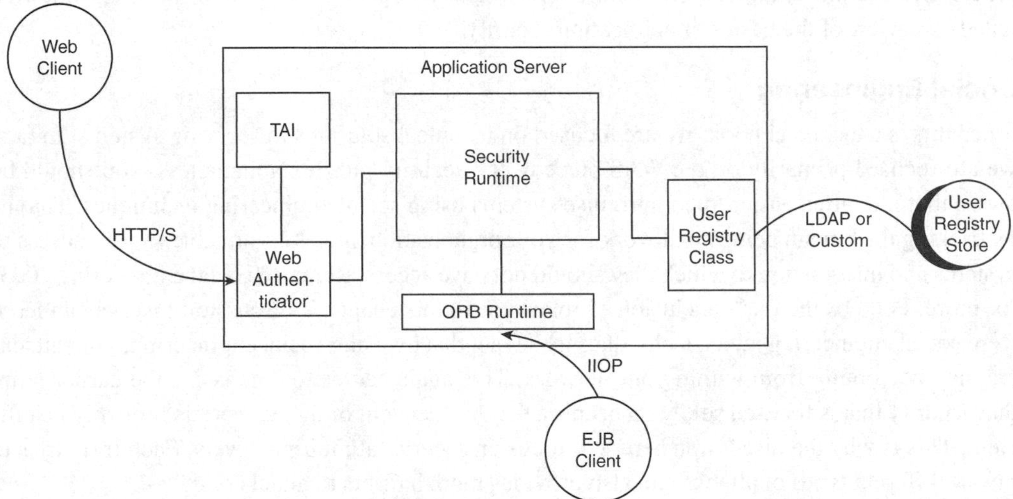


**Figure 18-1** WAS authentication architecture.

> **NOTE WAS VERSION**
> The information in this section applies to WAS 5.0.x and early versions of WAS 5.1.x. There are plans in a later versions of WAS to change the authentication process to support transmitting custom Subject attributes among application servers and increased pluggability. Once that happens, there will be more flexible ways of authenticating users. As this model evolves, it will be possible for TAIs and JAAS login modules to provide to WAS the information it needs to create WAS credentials. This will allow for much more flexible integration with existing security systems.

### Web Authentication

The most common way for web clients to authenticate is by providing a user ID and password (as HTTP basic auth or form-based). WAS takes this information, looks up the user's unique ID (e.g., a DN for LDAP) in the registry, and then verifies the password against the registry. In the case of LDAP, an ldap_bind is performed.

Web clients can also authenticate using client certificates. As with any SSL system, client certificate authentication is done at the termination of the SSL connection. Thus, the web server is responsible for performing the client certificate authentication, not WAS. Once the certificate authentication is complete, the WAS web server plug-in forwards the client certificate information to the WAS application server, and the application server then extracts information from the certificate and looks up the user in the registry. The information used for the lookup is customizable, and can be totally customized if a custom registry is developed.

### Trust Association Interceptors (TAIs)

Web clients can also authenticate by using a TAI. Essentially, by using a TAI, WAS allows an external component to authenticate the user and then assert the identity (identity assertion) to the WAS web container. You can custom develop a TAI or use one of several that are already commercially available. These TAIs are typically used in conjunction with a web authentication proxy server such as IBM's Tivoli Access Manager or Netegrity's Siteminder. These products authenticate the user and then simply inform WAS as to the end-user's identity. Typically, this is done by the proxy server sending the user's ID and some additional verifiable information to the application server. The TAI extracts this information and then returns to WAS the user's ID. WAS then queries the registry as it normally would,[2] but does not validate the user's password. This provides a powerful mechanism for allowing WAS to participate in a Single Sign On domain.

In any case, after the web authentication is complete (in the TAI or normal web authentication case), WAS creates a JAAS Subject containing the user's authentication information and an LTPA token. For web clients, WAS also creates an LTPA cookie to send to the browser. This cookie is essentially a string representation of the encrypted LTPA token.

### EJB Client Authentication

EJB clients can authenticate using passwords or certificates. In the case of password-based authentication, the client runtime is responsible for obtaining the user ID and password and sending them to the server where they are verified against the registry. In any case, if the authentication is determined to be valid, a CSIv2 session is established that contains an LTPA token and is used for future requests. As with web client authentication, a JAAS Subject is created as well.

By default, the WAS client runtime prompts for a user ID and password using a graphical dialog box if one is needed. This behavior can be controlled by editing the sas.client.props WAS property file. You can even specify a userid and password in that file. However, it is best for clients to use the JAAS login APIs to authenticate after obtaining the user ID and password in some appropriate way under application control.

### Internal Authentication

Application code, as well as WAS itself, may also authenticate from within the process, essentially creating an authenticated Subject on-the-fly. To do this, the standard JAAS login APIs are used. When this is done, the same approach is used as in other scenarios. The provided user ID

2 If the user ID is not found in the registry, authentication will, of course, fail.

and password are validated against the registry, and if validation is successful, a JAAS Subject and LTPA token are created. Though it may not be obvious, this implies that when WAS servers authenticate themselves, they use the same registry for authentication as user-level authentication.

> **NOTE JAAS Subject.doAs()**
> When a JAAS Subject is created using the JAAS LoginContext.login() method, the Subject is not associated with the current thread of execution. In order for WAS authorization to work, application code must explicitly associate the Subject with the current thread by using the WSSubject.doAs()[3] method. Refer to the Info Center for details.

## JAAS Subjects and LTPA Token

Once the authentication process is completed, WAS creates a JAAS Subject to represent the current authenticated user. This Subject contains the WAS credentials needed by the WAS runtime to authorize user access. As you might expect, the information it contains comes from the registry. Subjects are cached in a memory table by each application server.

In addition to the JAAS Subject, WAS creates an LTPA token that is essentially a key into the Subject table. For security reasons, the LTPA token has a finite lifetime and is digitally signed and encrypted. Once the token expires, the user will have to reauthenticate. The token itself contains only the user's unique identifier and a timestamp. Thus, the token itself contains little information of value (e.g., it does not contain a password). This total approach provides for a high degree of security.

Since the LTPA token uniquely identifies a user, if an LTPA token is sent (via a web request or IIOP request) to an application server that does not have a cached copy of the user's Subject, the target WAS application server can re-create the Subject by querying the registry. Once this is done, the Subject will be held in the cache to ensure high performance for future requests. This method ensures Single Sign On at both the web layer and at the EJB layer.

> **NOTE**
> You may have noticed that we have not mentioned SWAM. This is not an accident. SWAM is a second authentication mechanism in addition to LTPA. SWAM is inferior to LTPA on many levels. First, it is weaker since it relies on the HTTP Session for maintaining state. Secondly, SWAM authentication is not forwardable to remote EJBs. Thus, SWAM is of little use in a multi-node WAS-ND environment. In fact, SWAM is not even available with WAS-ND. Thus, there is no good reason to use SWAM since all editions of WAS support LTPA.

3 This is unfortunately required because the JVM standard Subject.doAs() methods don't properly associate the WAS CORBA-based credentials with the current thread.

## Registries

We've mentioned registries several times. WAS supports three types of registries: operating system, LDAP, and custom. When using an operating system registry, WAS uses native operating system commands to verify user information against the local machine. Generally speaking, operating system registries cannot be used in a multi-node WAS-ND environment because each machine has its own registry.[4] An LDAP registry is by far the preferred approach and is fully supported with a multi-node WAS-ND environment. When WAS is configured to use LDAP, it uses the standard LDAP V3 protocols to communicate with the LDAP directory and verify user information. WAS also supports a custom registry. In the event that you cannot use one of the supported registries, you are free to write your own registry by implementing the UserRegistry interface (in Java).

In any case, when WAS uses a registry, it performs the following operations as part of the authentication process. Understand that these operations are always performed regardless of other considerations:

- **Obtain full user unique identifier**—Security information is tracked based on this internal registry identifier rather than the short username that humans generally provide.
- **Verify password**—This is used if password authentication is being used.
- **Obtain user group information**[5]—This is used later as part of authorization.

Be aware that a single WAS cell can have only one registry. This means that all users, including the WAS administrators and the Security Server ID, must be in this one registry. This also means that all group information for those users must be in this same registry. If you require that users be in one of several registries (perhaps you have multiple LDAP servers), you will have to write a custom registry.

## Authorization

In compliance with the specification, WAS implements the J2EE-required authorization model. J2EE applications can use the standard J2EE APIs as well as deployment descriptors to specify authorization information.

It is also possible to externalize WAS's authorization to Tivoli Access Manager and a few other authorization vendors,[6] although we won't cover that here.

4 With Windows hosts and a common domain registry, a single WAS cell can span multiple hosts when using an operating system registry.

5 In a PTF of WAS 5.1.x, a new interface known as TAI++ will be published that will make it possible to avoid this step with TAIs. Basically, the TAI can assert to WAS the group information.

6 Because the API used for externalizing authorization is proprietary in WAS 5.x, only vendors that sign an agreement with IBM have access to this API. Once JACC is available, this will change.

> **NOTE JAVA AUTHORIZATION CONTRACT FOR CONTAINERS (JACC)—JSR 115**
> In the future, WAS will support the new Java standard for externalizing authorization from a container to an external authorization engine.

## Advanced Considerations for Security Configuration

We assume that you are familiar with the basics of WAS security configuration. If this is not the case, refer to [IBM WAS security redbook] or the WAS Info Center. Here, we will discuss a few of the more advanced and perhaps more obscure aspects of configuring WAS security.

### SSL, Keystores, and Ikeyman

SSL is a key component of the WAS security architecture. SSL is used extensively for securing communication. It is used to protect HTTP traffic, IIOP traffic, LDAP traffic, and internal SOAP traffic. SSL requires the use of public/private key pairs, and in the case of WAS, these keys are stored in keystores. In order to better understand how to properly configure SSL, we are going to briefly digress into a high-level discussion of SSL and public keys. This discussion is intentionally superficial and discusses only the key points you need in order to properly configure SSL in WAS.

Public Key Cryptography is fundamentally based upon a public/private key pair. These two keys are related cryptographically. The important point is that the keys are asymmetric—information encrypted with one key can be decrypted using the other key. The private key is, well, private. That is, when you are issued a "certificate," which sometimes includes a private key as part of the certificate creation process, you must carefully protect that private key. If you create your own public/private key pair prior to requesting that the certificate authority (CA) sign the public key, thus creating a certificate, you still must protect that private key. Possessing the private key is proof of identity. The public key is the part of the key pair that can be shared with others.

If there is a secure way to distribute public keys to trusted parties, that would be enough. However, Public Key Cryptography takes things a step further and introduces the idea of signed public keys. A signed public key has a digital signature (quite analogous to a human signature) that states that the signer vouches for the public key. The signer is assuring that the party that possesses the private key corresponding to the signed public key is the party identified by the key. These signed public keys are called certificates. Well-known signers are called certificate authorities. It is also possible to sign a public key using itself. These are known as self-signed certificates. These self-signed certificates are no less secure than certificates signed by a certificate authority. They are just harder to manage, as we'll see in a moment. Figure 18-2 shows the basic process of creating a certificate and distributing it.

When looking at this picture, take note that the client must possess the certificate that signed the generated public key. This is the crucial part of trust. Since the client trusts the CA (since it has the CA certificate), it trusts certificates that the CA has signed. It's worth noting that if you were to use self-signed certificates, you would need to distribute manually the self-signed certificate to each client rather than relying on a well-known public CA certificate. This is no less secure, but if you have many clients, it is much harder to manage.

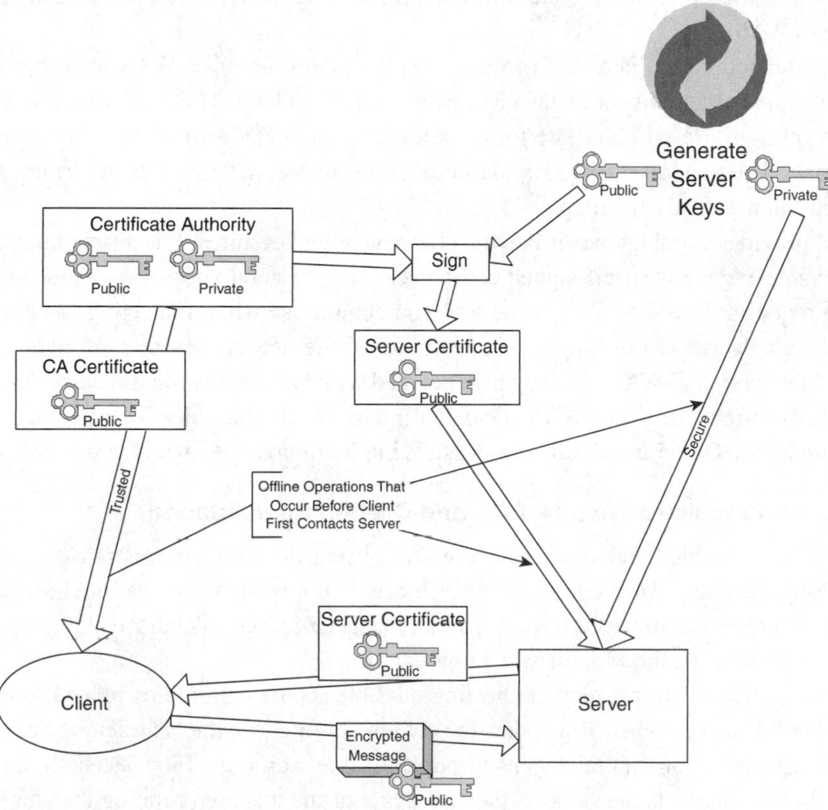


**Figure 18-2** Certificate creation and distribution.

In order for a client to authenticate a server using certificates, the server must posses its own private key and corresponding certificate. The client must posses the signing certificate that corresponds to the server's certificate. On the other hand, in order for a server to authenticate a client (this is often called client certificate authentication), the reverse is true. That is, the client must possess a private key and corresponding certificate, while the server must possess the corresponding signing certificate. That's really all there is to it. Since SSL uses certificate authentication, each side of the SSL connection must possess the appropriate keys in a keystore file. Whenever you configure SSL keystores, think about the fundamental rules about which party needs which keys. Usually, that will tell you what you need.

As we have already seen, WAS manages keys in keystore files. There are two types of keystores: keystores and truststores. A truststore is nothing more than a keystore that, by convention, contains only public information. Thus, you should place CA certificates and other signing certificates in a truststore and private information in the keystore. However, it really makes no difference to WAS.

Unfortunately, there is a catch to this simple system. Most of WAS uses the new Java-defined keystore format known as Java Key Stores (JKS).[7] The IBM HTTP server and the WAS web server plug-in use an older key format known as the KDB format (or more correctly, the CMS format). The two formats are similar in function but are incompatible in format. Thus, you must be careful not to mix them up.

IBM provides a tool known as ikeyman for managing keystores. It is a very simple tool that creates keystores, generates self-signed certificates, imports and exports keys, and can generate certificate requests for a CA. This is the tool you should use when managing keystores. As of WAS 5.1, a single version of ikeyman supports all of the needed keystore formats. If you are using an older version of WAS, the ikeyman included with WAS in the bin directory does not support the KDB format. To create KDB files, you'll have to run the older ikeyman that should be available under the GSK5 install directory[8] that is implicitly installed when you install WAS.

### Web-Based Administrative Interface and Certificate Validation

When security is enabled and you connect to WAS using the web administrative console, your web browser will likely warn you that the certificate is not trusted and that the host name does not match the host name in the certificate. You should see messages like those in Figures 18-3 and 18-4 (here, we are using the Mozilla web browser).

These messages are warnings indicating possible security problems related to the certificates that WAS is using. When you update the default keyring (see the "Hardening Security" section in this chapter), you can take steps to prevent these warnings. First, generate a certificate where the Subject name is the same as the host name of the machine running the administrative web application (the one server in base or the deployment manager in other editions). That will take care of the second browser error message. The first message can be prevented by either buying a certificate from a well-known CA for the WAS administrative console (probably a waste of money) or simply by accepting the certificate permanently. Keep in mind that if you ever see this message again, that is quite possibly a sign of a security breach. Thus, your system administration staff should be trained to recognize that this warning should only occur when the certificate is updated. If it occurs at other times, it's a red-flag warning that the system has been compromised.

7 Actually, WAS SSL configurations support three modern key database formats: JKS, JCEKS, and PKCS12.

8 On Windows, the GSK is usually under c:\program files\ibm\gsk5. On Solaris, it is usually under /opt/ibm/gsk5. Other platforms are similar.

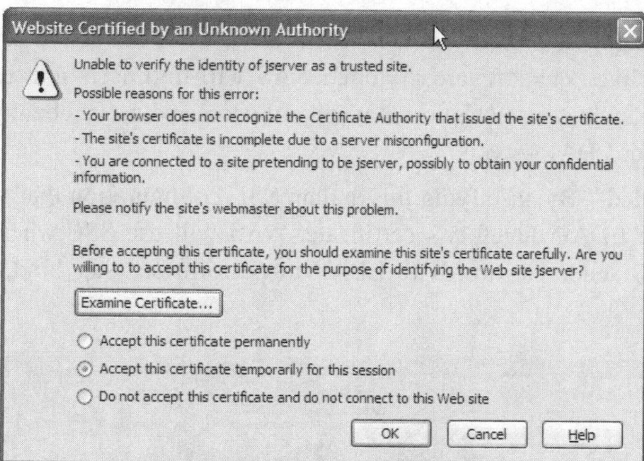


**Figure 18-3** Mozilla informing the user that the certificate is not trusted.

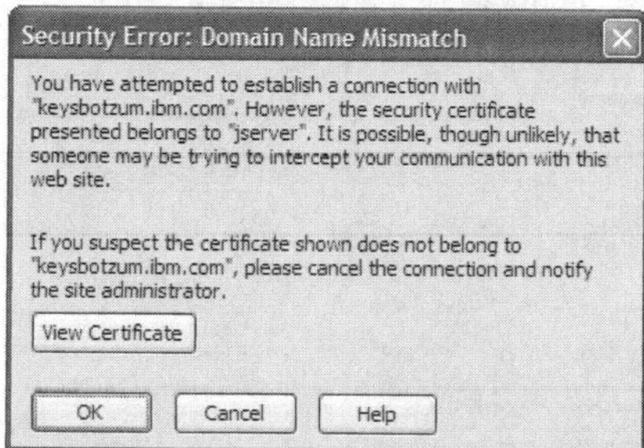


**Figure 18-4** Mozilla informing the user that the certificate is specifying a host name different from the host name that the browser is connecting to.

## Advanced LDAP Considerations

When configuring WAS to use LDAP, there are a number of issues to consider. First and foremost, recognize that WAS fully supports "standard" LDAP access. This means that in general, WAS can be configured to work with any LDAP server and any reasonable configuration that follows generally accepted LDAP techniques. WAS makes very limited use of LDAP, as we mentioned earlier, and is very flexible even in that limited use. By using the LDAP configuration page and the LDAP Advanced Settings page, you can control a great deal of WAS's behavior. We'll discuss a few points of interest here. Figure 18-5 shows the main LDAP configuration page.

Items of interest include:

- **Host**—This is the single host name that WAS will use when connecting to LDAP. If the connection to LDAP should fail, WAS will reconnect to the same host. This means that WAS does not support replicated LDAP directories unless this replication is done transparently, possibly using a load balancer (refer to Chapter 23, "WebSphere Edge Compnents," for more).

- **Base Distinguished Name (DN)**—This is the start of the LDAP search tree, generally something like "ou=software, o=ibm." WAS will find users and groups by searching under this single root. WAS does not support users and groups being in completely separate trees or LDAP servers.
- **SSL Enabled**—By specifying this and an SSL configuration that contains the signing key for the LDAP directory's certificate, WAS will use SSL when contacting LDAP. Since WAS sends passwords to LDAP to perform an ldap_bind, using SSL is very important.

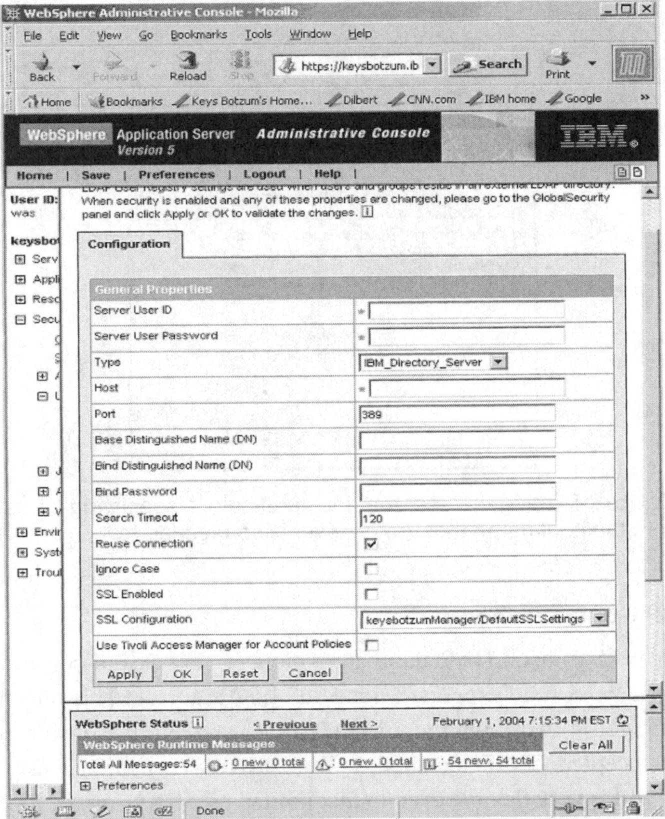


**Figure 18-5** Main LDAP configuration page.

After you have configured the basic settings, including specifying the LDAP directory type, you are typically done. However, if your LDAP directory is not one tested by IBM, or if you have configured your directory in some slightly unusual way, you can control how WAS queries your directory. To do this, click on the "Advanced LDAP Settings" link. Figure 18-6 shows what you will see.

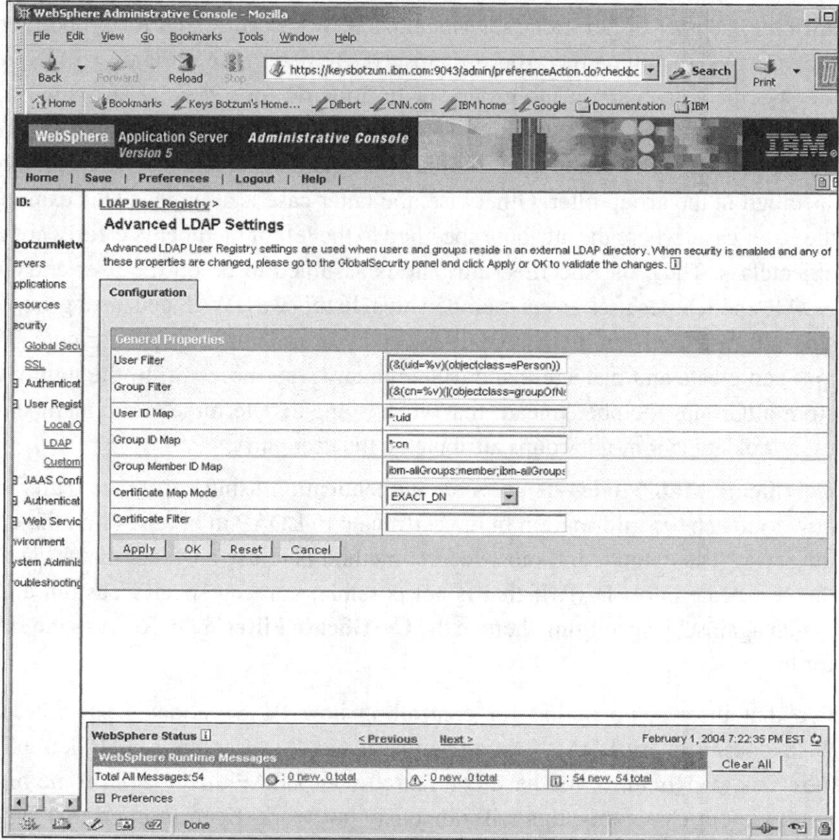


**Figure 18-6** Advanced LDAP settings.

In Figure 18-6, what you see is the filters used by WAS when querying LDAP. These filters give you the flexibility to control WAS's queries. Let's take a moment to discuss those settings:

- **User Filter**—The first filter is used when a user types in a user ID and WAS tries to find the user entry in LDAP. You'll notice that in this example, users are identified by the uid field and are of type ePerson. You can change either to meet your needs. In some registries, you might change uid to samAccountName or cn.
- **Group Filter**—This works much like the User Filter, but is used to find groups.
- **User ID Map**—This states that when WAS is looking at an LDAP entry for a user, the field that uniquely identifies the user is the uid field. Again, you can change this as needed.
- **Group ID Map**—This works much like the user id map.
- **Group Member ID Map**—This specifies how WAS will determine group memberships. This is a list of semicolon-separated pairs that are interpreted as either

attribute:member or objectclass:attribute pairs. WAS can search for group membership in two ways: searching the groups themselves to determine if the user's DN is listed in the specified attribute on the group, or by looking for a special attribute on the user object that contains that user's group memberships (this is more efficient). WAS considers the ID Map to be the first case if the objectclass value is the same as the objectclass specified in the group filter. Otherwise, the latter case is assumed. This example shows the latter case, where the attribute specified to the left of member is clearly not the group objectclass. Thus, the specified attribute is assumed to be on the user entry object in LDAP, and it holds user group memberships. In this way, WAS gets user group membership information from the LDAP directory by examining a single attribute. The directory can create and manage that attribute in any way it sees fit. In the figure, the value "ibm-allGroups:member" means that when trying to determine group membership for a user, look at the ibm-allGroups attribute on the user entry.

- **Certificate Map Mode**—If users are authenticating using certificates, this tells WAS how to match the information in the certificate to LDAP in order to find the corresponding user. The default, and most secure, method is to use an exact match on the DN in the certificate into LDAP. If that is not possible, you can specify custom attributes to match against by specifying them in the **Certificate Filter** field. Refer to the Info Center for more.

Notice that there is no option for controlling how WAS validates passwords. That is because WAS doesn't query LDAP for passwords. Instead, it uses the LDAP-defined standard method known as ldap_bind. If you have configured your LDAP directory in some highly nonstandard way without passwords, this will obviously not work. Keep in mind that WAS has no control or interest in how user passwords are stored or managed in the LDAP directory. That is entirely under the control of the LDAP administrator.

Now that we have discussed the basics of WAS security, it is time to turn our attention to the real purpose of security—creating a secure environment.

## Hardening Security

The J2EE 1.3 specification and WAS provide a powerful infrastructure for implementing secure systems. Unfortunately, many people are not aware of all of the issues surrounding creating a secure WAS-based system. There are many degrees of freedom and many different sources of this information. This tends to lead to people overlooking WAS security issues and to deploying systems that are not particularly secure. This section summarizes the key issues of greatest importance.

Security hardening is the act of configuring WAS, developing applications, and configuring various other related components in a way to maximize security—in essence, to prevent or block various forms of attack. In order to do this effectively, it is important to consider the forms of attack. There are four basic approaches to attacking a J2EE-based system:

- **Network-based attacks**—These attacks rely on low-level access to network packets and attempt to harm the system by altering this traffic or discovering information from these packets.
- **Machine-based attacks**—In this case, the intruder has access to a machine on which WAS is running. Here our goal is to limit the ability to damage the WAS configuration or to see things that shouldn't be seen.
- **Application-based external attacks**—In this scenario, an intruder uses application-level protocols to access the application, perhaps via a web browser or EJB client, and uses this access to try to circumvent the normal application usage and do inappropriate things. The key is that the attack occurs using the J2EE-defined APIs and protocols. The intruder is not necessarily outside the company but rather is executing code from outside of the application itself.
- **Application-based internal attacks**—In this case, we are concerned with the danger of a rogue application. In this scenario, multiple applications share the same WAS infrastructure, and we do not completely trust each application. While perfect security is unachievable here, there are techniques that can limit how much each application can do.

Note that we will not be considering one other form of technical attack: Denial of Service (DoS) attacks. While very important, this is beyond the scope of this book. Preventing DoS attacks requires very different techniques.

## Total System View—The Details Matter

Before delving into the specific point-by-point recommendations, we want to take a moment to outline the fundamental techniques for creating secure systems. The fundamental view is to look at every system boundary or point of sharing and examine what actors have access to those boundaries or shared components. That is, given that this boundary exists (we presume reasonable trust within a subsystem), what can an intruder do to break this boundary? Or, given that something is shared, can intruders share something inappropriately? Most boundaries are obvious and physical: network connections, process-to-process communication, file systems, operating system interfaces, etc., but some boundaries are more subtle. For example, if one application uses J2C resources within WAS, you must consider the possibility that some other application might try to access those same resources. This occurs because there is a system boundary between the first application and WAS and a second application and WAS. Perhaps both applications can access this common infrastructure (in fact, they can). This is a case of possibly inappropriate sharing.

The way we prevent these various forms of attack is to apply a number of well-known techniques. For lower-level network-based attacks, we apply encryption and network filtering. We essentially deny the intruder the ability to see or access things they should not see. We also rely on operating systems to provide mechanisms to protect operating system resources from abuse.

For example, we wouldn't want ordinary user-level code to be able to gain access to the system bus and directly read internal communication. We also leverage the fact that most modern operating systems possess fairly robust protections for system APIs.[9] At a high level, we apply authentication and authorization rigorously. Every API, every method, and every resource potentially needs to require some form of authorization. That is, access to these things must be restricted based upon need. And, of course, authorization is of little value without robust authentication. Authentication is concerned with knowing the identity of the caller. We add the word robust because authentication that can be easily forged is of little value.

Where appropriate authentication and authorization are not available, we frankly have to resort to clever design and procedures to prevent potential problems. This is how we protect J2C resources. Since WAS does not provide for authorization of access to J2C resources, we instead apply other techniques to limit (based on configuration) the ability of applications to reference J2C resources inappropriately.

As you might imagine, examining all of the system boundaries and shared components is a difficult task. And, in fact, securing a system leads to thinking deeply about complexity. Perhaps the hardest truth about security is that creating a secure system works against abstraction. That is, one of the core principles of good abstraction is the hiding of concerns from higher-level components. That is a highly desirable and good thing. Unfortunately, intruders aren't kind to us. They don't care about our abstractions or our good designs. Their goal is to break into our systems any way they can. And, in doing so, they will look for holes in our wonderful designs. Thus, in order to validate a system's security, you have to think about it at every level of abstraction: at the highest architectural level but also as the lowest level of detail. Rigorous reviews of everything are required.

The smallest mistake can undermine the integrity of an entire system. This is best exemplified by the technique of taking control of C/C++-based systems by using buffer overrun techniques. Essentially, an intruder passes in a string that is too large for some existing buffer. The extra information then overlays a part of the running program and causes the runtime to execute instructions that it should not execute. With care, one can cause a program to do almost anything. As a security architect, to even identify this attack, you have to deeply understand how the C/C++ runtime manages memory and executes running programs. Refer to [buffer overflow] for more details. You also have to review every line of code to find this particular hole, assuming you understood that it existed. Today, we know about the attack, yet it continues to be successful because individual programmers make very small bad decisions that compromise entire systems. Thankfully, this particular attack seems to be infeasible in Java. But, do not believe for an instant that there aren't other small errors out there that lead to compromise. Think hard about security; it *is* hard.

9 Unfortunately, in a WAS environment, these operating system protections are of limited value since they are based on process identity, which is a very coarse-grained concept when you consider application servers servicing requests from thousands of users at once.

We are now going to identify the various known[10] steps one should take to protect the WAS infrastructure and applications from these four forms of attack. Ideally, we would organize the information into four buckets—one for each form of attack. Unfortunately, attacks don't neatly divide along those lines. Several different techniques of protection help with multiple forms of attack. And, sometimes a single attack may leverage multiple forms of intrusion in order to achieve the end goal. For example, in the simplest case, network sniffing can be used to obtain passwords, and those passwords can then be used to mount an application-level attack. Instead, we organize the hardening techniques into a logical structure based on when the activity occurs or the role of the person concerned with these issues:

- **Infrastructure**—Actions that can be taken to configure the WAS infrastructure for maximum security. These are typically done once when the infrastructure is built out and involve only the system administrators.
- **Application Configuration**—Actions that can be taken by application developers and administrators and are visible during the deployment process. Essentially, these are application design and implementation decisions that are visible to the WAS administrator and are verifiable (possibly with some difficulty) as part of the deployment process. This section will have a large number of techniques, further reinforcing the point that security is not a bolt-on—security is the responsibility of every person involved in the application design, development, and deployment.
- **Application Design and Implementation**—Actions that are taken by developers and designers during development that are crucial to security but may be difficult to detect as part of the deployment process.

Within each section, we order the various techniques by priority. In order to help the reader tie these techniques back to the classes of attack just presented, for each technique we will use the following graphic:

The four squares will be filled in as appropriate to represent the type of attack this technique helps to prevent. Keep in mind that internal applications can always take advantage of "external" methods of attack. Thus, we don't explicitly list I when E is already present. We do however list I when the vulnerability is uniquely exploitable by internal applications.

## Infrastructure-Based Preventative Measures

When securing the infrastructure, we focus first on encrypting the WAS traffic among the various components as well as ensuring that the WAS administrative function is secured. Before delving into the details, it's useful to review a standard WAS topology and see all of the network links and

10 It is likely, perhaps even certain, that there are other weaknesses that we have not identified.

protocols. As someone concerned about security, you need to know about all of these links and focus on securing those links. These links represent the coarsest grained system boundaries we mentioned earlier (see Figure 18-7).

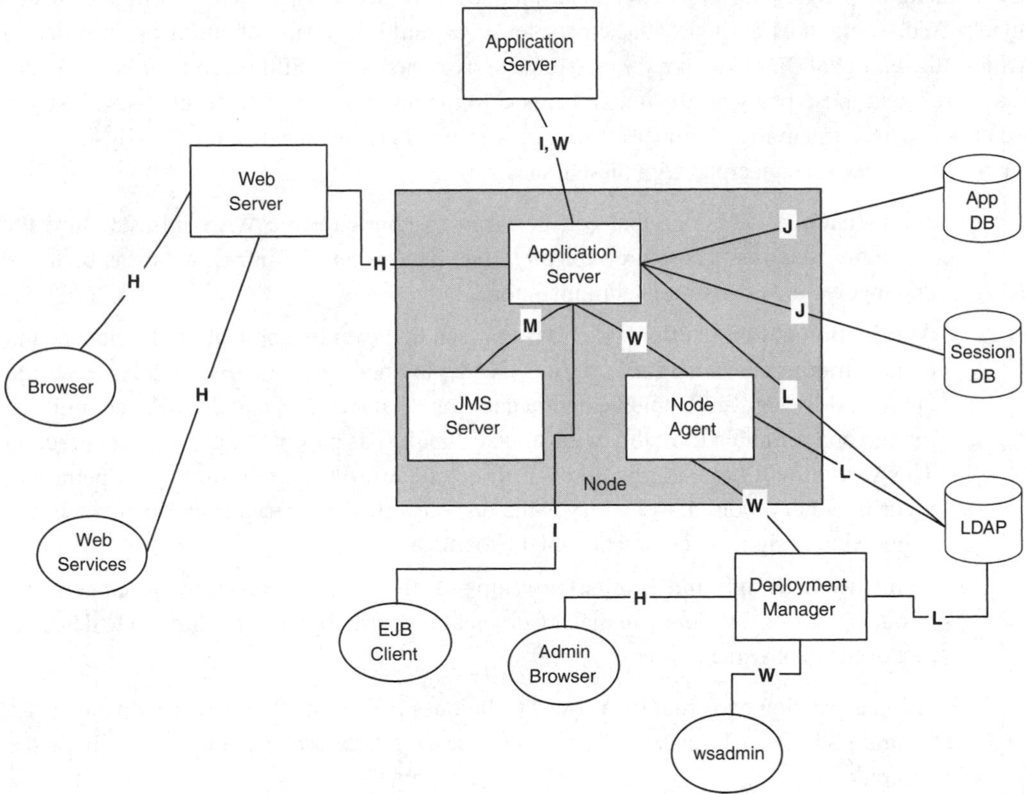


**Figure 18-7** Network link picture.

The letters on the links indicate the protocols used across those communication links. For each protocol, we list the usage and also provide some information on firewalls. They are:

- **H = HTTP traffic**
  - Usage: Browser to web server, web server to app server, and admin web client
  - Firewall friendly
- **W = WAS internal communication**
  - Usage: Admin clients and WAS internal server admin traffic. Note that WAS internal communication uses one of several protocols:
    - RMI/IIOP or SOAP/HTTP: Admin client protocol is configurable.

        - File transfer service (dmgr to node agent): Uses HTTP(S)
        - DRS (memory to memory replication): Uses private protocol
    - Firewall friendly if using SOAP/HTTP
- **I = RMI/IIOP communication**
    - Usage: EJB clients (standalone and web container)
    - Generally, firewall hostile because of dynamic ports and embedded IP addresses (which can interfere with firewalls that perform Network Address Translation)
- **M = MQ protocol**
    - Usage: MQ clients (true clients and application servers)
    - Protocol: Proprietary
    - Firewall feasible (there are a number of ports to consider). Refer to MQ support pac MA86.
- **L = LDAP communication**
    - Usage: WAS verification of user information in registry
    - Protocol: TCP stream formatted as defined in LDAP RFC
    - Firewall friendly
- **J = JDBC database communication via vendor JDBC drivers**
    - Usage: Application JDBC access and WAS session DB access
    - Protocol: Network protocol is proprietary to each DB.
    - Firewall aspects depend on database (generally firewall friendly)
- **S = SOAP**
    - Usage: SOAP clients
    - Protocol: Generally SOAP/HTTP
    - Firewall friendly when SOAP/HTTP

In the remainder of this section, we will discuss the steps required to secure the infrastructure.

## Use HTTPS from the Browser (N M E I)

If your site performs any authentication or has any activities that should be protected, use HTTPS from the browser to the web server. If HTTPS is not used, information such as passwords, user activities, WAS session IDs, and LTPA[11] security tokens can potentially be seen by intruders.

11 While these tokens can be safely transmitted over an unencrypted channel, for maximum security, it is best that they be protected.

### Put the Web Server in the DMZ Without WAS (N M E I)

One of the key principles of a demilitarized zone (DMZ) is to put as little function as possible in it to reduce the risks associated with an intruder breaking through the outer firewall.[12] Thus, it is normal to place the web server in the DMZ and the WAS application servers inside the inner firewall. This is ideal, as the web server machine then can have a very simple configuration and require very little software. Additionally, the only port that must be opened on the inner firewall is the HTTP(S) port for the target application servers. These steps make the DMZ a very hostile place for an attacker. If you place WAS on a machine in the DMZ, far more software must be installed on those machines (e.g., a JDK, X libraries, etc.), and more ports must be opened on the inner firewall so WAS can access the production network. This largely undermines the value of the DMZ.

In Chapter 20, "WAS Network Deployment Architecture," a basic WAS topology will be discussed that includes a DMZ. Those firewalls provide your first level of defense and are your first priority. However, those firewalls are insufficient. All they do is block certain types of traffic. It is important to have additional layers of defense to supplement what the firewalls provide.

### Separate Your Production Network from Your Intranet (N M E I)

Most organizations today understand the value of a DMZ that separates the outsiders on the Internet from the Intranet. However, far too many organizations fail to realize that many intruders are on the inside. For a large corporation, there are literally thousands of people, many of which are not employees but have access to the internal network. The people are all possible intruders. And, since they are on the inside, they have better access to the network. It is often a simple matter of plugging a laptop into a network connection. Just as you protect yourself against the large untrusted Internet, you should also protect your production systems from the large and untrustworthy Intranet. Separate your production networks from your internal network using firewalls. These firewalls, while likely more permissive than the Internet-facing firewalls, can still block numerous forms of attack.

### Enable Global Security (N M E I)

By default, WAS uses no security. This means that all network links are insecure and that any user with access to the Deployment Manager (HTTP to the web admin console or SOAP/IIOP to the JMX management ports) can use the WAS administrative tools to perform any administrative operation, up to and including removing existing servers. Needless to say, this presents a great security risk.

Therefore, at a minimum, you should enable WAS security in a production environment to prevent these trivial forms of attack. Once WAS security is enabled globally, the WAS internal links between the Deployment Manager and the application servers and traffic from the

12 In a typical DMZ configuration, there is an outer firewall, the DMZ network containing as little as possible, and an inner firewall protecting the production network.

administrative clients (web and command line) to the Deployment Manager are encrypted and authenticated (refer to Figure 18-7). Among other things, this means that administrators will be required to authenticate when running the administrative tools.

Be aware that enabling global security does not encrypt all network links but rather a number of key internal links. We'll discuss securing additional network links later in this chapter. We will also discuss securing applications by leveraging WAS security now that it has been enabled.

> **NOTE ENABLE SINGLE SIGN ON**
>
> When enabling WAS global security with LTPA, always enable Single Sign On (SSO). This tells WAS to create LTPA cookies and send them back to the browser. It makes it possible for WAS to remember the user's identity across requests. If you do not enable SSO, WAS will not create a cookie and must reauthenticate the user on every request. In many cases, this will not work.[13] More importantly, it is inefficient. Since every request results in a reauthentication of the user, the performance of the system will be quite poor.

## Change the Default Key File (N M E I)

As stated earlier, enabling WAS security causes most internal traffic to use SSL to protect it from various forms of network attack. However, in order to establish an SSL connection, the server must posses a certificate and corresponding private key. To simplify the initial installation process, WAS is delivered with a sample key file containing a sample private key. This "private" key is included in every copy of WAS sold. As such, it is not very private. The name of the key file—DummyServerKeyFile—makes this clear.

To protect your environment, you should create your own private key and certificate for WAS communication. All of this is done using the ikeyman tool. Refer to the Info Center and [IBM WAS Security Redbook] for more details on how to do this.

While we are talking about certificates, we want to digress briefly on a crucial point—certificates expire. Should the WAS certificates expire, WAS will stop working. No communication will be possible. Thus, when you create new certificates as we recommend, ensure that you mark the expiration date on a calendar. If, against our advice, you use the default keys, remember that they expire as well. You must actively plan for certificate expiration and obtain or generate new certificates prior to their expiration.

A typical WAS configuration has a number of network links (refer to Figure 18-7). It is important to protect traffic on each of those links as much as possible to stop intruders. As should be apparent, various pieces of confidential information may be transmitted by an application, and it should be protected. We have already discussed the securing of many of the links by enabling WAS security as well as securing the web browser to web server link. Now we will discuss the remaining links.

13 With form-based login without SSO, every login results in the user being returned to the login page since the redirect to the page after login never succeeds, as WAS has forgotten the user's identity immediately after login.

> **NOTE BE CAREFUL WHEN CHANGING THE DEFAULT KEYRING**
> When changing the default certificates, there is one important thing to keep in mind. As with any SSL-based system, the client must be able to verify the certificate presented by the server. This requires that the client hold the CA certificate for the CA that signed the certificate presented by the server.
>
> When WAS ships, all of this is taken care of for WAS Java clients (IBM provided tools such as wsadmin and Tivoli Performance Viewer, as well as custom-written clients). However, when you update the server key file to use a new private key and certificate signed by some signer, you must ensure that the Java clients can verify those certificates. You will need to update the client trust file to contain the signer certificate for the party that issued your new server certificates. This means that any Java clients, such as the WAS admin clients, may need new client key files. If you use certificates issued from a well-known CA, such as Verisign, this will not be necessary since the default WAS client key rings include signing certificates from the most common public CAs already.[14]
>
> This issue also affects the web server to application server communication. Since the web server plug-in supports HTTPS by default, the web server plug-in keyring contains a copy of the WAS sample signing certificate. If you change the default keyring, do not forget to update the web server plug-in keyring to include the new certificate.

## Use SSL for Web Server to WAS HTTP Link (N M E I)

The WAS web server plug-in forwards requests from the web server to the target WAS application server. With WAS 5.0, if the traffic to the web server is over HTTPS, then the plug-in will automatically use HTTPS when forwarding the request to an application server, thus protecting its confidentiality.

Furthermore, with some care, you can configure the WAS application server (which contains a small embedded HTTP listener) to only accept requests from known web servers. This prevents various sneak attacks that bypass any security that might be in front of or in the web server. To do this, you configure the application server web container SSL configuration to use client authentication. Once you have ensured that client authentication is in use, you need to ensure that only trusted web servers can contact the web container. To do this, you must limit the parties that have access to the appropriate keys as follows:

- Create two keyrings using ikeyman, one for the web container and one for the web server plug-in.
- Delete from each keyring all of the existing signing certificates. At this point, neither keyring can be used to validate any certificates. That's intentional.
- Create a self-signed certificate in each keyring and export just the certificate (not the private key).

14 This is not a recommendation to buy certificates from a CA for WAS internal communication. If you have few Java clients, it is usually easier and cheaper to simply generate a self-signed certificate and update the small number of client keyrings manually.

- Import into each keyring the certificate exported from the other keyring. Now each keyring contains only a single signing certificate. This means that each keyring can be used to verify exactly one certificate—the self-signed certificate created for the peer.
- Install the newly created keyrings into the web container and web server plug-in.

### Encrypt WAS to LDAP Link

When WAS is using an LDAP registry, WAS verifies a user's password using the standard ldap_bind. This requires that WAS send the user's password to the LDAP server. If that request is not protected, a hacker could use a network sniffer to steal the passwords of users authenticating to WAS. Most LDAP directories support LDAP over SSL, and WAS can be configured to use this. If you use a custom registry, you'll obviously want to secure this traffic using whatever mechanism is available.

### Protect WAS to Database Link

Just as with any other network link, confidential information may be written to or read from the database. Although most databases support some form of authentication, many do not support encrypting JDBC traffic between the client (WAS applications in this case) and the database. Thus, you must recognize this weakness and take appropriate steps. Some form of network-level encryption such as a Virtual Private Network (VPN), perhaps using IP Security Protocol (IPSEC), is the most obvious solution, although there are other reasonable choices. If you can place your database near WAS (in the network sense), various forms of firewalls and simple routing tricks can greatly limit the access to the network traffic going to the database. The key here is to identify this risk and then address it as appropriate.

### Encrypt Distributed Replication Service (DRS) Network Links

As stated in Chapter 20, do not forget to turn on DRS encryption as a separate manual step. DRS traffic is not encrypted by default even when global security is enabled.

### Configure and Use Trust Association Interceptors Carefully

TAIs are often used to allow WAS to recognize existing authentication information from a web SSO proxy server, such as Tivoli Access Manager (TAM). Generally, this is fine. However, be careful when developing, selecting, and configuring TAIs. A TAI extends the WAS trust domain. WAS is now trusting the TAI and whatever the TAI trusts. If the TAI is improperly developed or configured, it is possible to completely compromise the security of WAS. For example, IBM provides a secure TAI for integrating TAM with WAS. When configured properly, this is a highly secure setup. However, there is a property known as com.ibm.websphere.security.WebSEAL.mutualSSL that indicates to the TAM TAI that the link from the web server to the application server is securely authenticated, as described earlier in the section, "Use SSL for Web Server to WAS HTTP Link." When used properly, that's fine. However, if you set this property to true but do not ensure the web server to application server link is secure, then you have opened WAS to trivial forms of attack since the TAI does not validate the connection.

If you custom-develop a TAI, ensure that the TAI carefully validates the parameters passed in the request and that the validation is done in a secure way. We've seen TAIs that perform foolish things such as verifying the IP address in the HTTP headers. That's useless since HTTP headers can be forged.

## Create Separate Administrative User IDs (N M E I)

When WAS security is configured, a single security ID is initially configured as the Security Server ID. This ID is effectively the equivalent of root in WAS and can perform any WAS administrative operation. Because of the importance of this ID, it is best not to widely share the password.

As with most systems, WAS does allow multiple principals to act as administrators. Simply use the WAS administrative application and go to the System Administration/Console Users (or Groups) section to specify additional users or groups that should be granted administrative authority. When you do this, each individual person can authenticate as himself or herself when administering WAS.[15] As of WAS 5.0.2, all administrative actions that result in changes to the configuration of WAS are audited by the Deployment Manager, including the identity of the principal that made the change. Obviously, these audit records are more useful if each administrator has a separate identity. Audit records are treated as serious messages and sent, by default, to SystemOut.log from the Deployment Manager.

The approach of giving individual administrators their own separate administrative access can be particularly handy in an environment where central administrators administer multiple WAS cells. You can configure all of these WAS cells to share a common registry, and thus the administrators can use the same ID and password to administer each cell, while each cell has its own local "root" ID and password.

## Take Advantage of Administrative Roles (N M E I)

WAS V5 allows for four administrative roles: Administrator, Operator, Monitor, and Configurator. These roles make it possible to give individuals (and automated systems) access appropriate to their level of need. The most interesting role is the Monitor role. By giving a user or system this access level, you are giving only the ability to monitor the system state. The state cannot be changed, nor can the configuration be altered. We strongly recommend taking advantage of those roles whenever possible. For example, if you develop monitoring scripts that check for system health and have to store the userid and password locally with the script, use an ID with the monitor role. Even if the ID is compromised, little serious harm can result.

15 All administrators have the same authority throughout the cell. WAS does not support instance-based administrative authorization.

## Don't Run Samples in Production (N M E I)

WAS ships with several excellent examples to demonstrate various parts of WAS. These samples are not intended for use in a production environment. Do not run them there, as they create significant security risks. In particular, the showCfg and snoop Servlets can provide an outsider with tremendous amounts of information about your system. This is precisely the type of information you do not want to give a potential intruder. This is easily addressed by not running server1 (that contains the samples) in production. If you are using WAS base, you'll actually want to remove the examples from server1.

## Enable Java 2 Security (N M E I)

At this point, we have done a pretty good job of protecting the WAS infrastructure from external attacks. We are now encrypting network traffic and thus preventing snooping and traffic alteration. We are also authorizing all administrative traffic, which will prevent external intruders from damaging the infrastructure. However, the infrastructure is still fairly vulnerable to attack from applications *within* the cell. As we discussed earlier, in WAS V5, all application servers contain the WAS administrative infrastructure and thus the APIs for performing most administrative operations. An application programmer that learns the APIs can thus write an application that can call any of these APIs and potentially cause serious problems.

WAS V5 includes support for Java 2 security as provided by the standard JDK. IBM has enhanced the Java 2 support to enforce the J2EE specifications as well as to protect the WAS internal APIs from unauthorized access. Simply by enabling Java 2 security, these rules are automatically enforced. Thus, by enabling Java 2 security, substantial additional protections are added to the runtime to prevent illegal application access. We'll discuss Java 2 security restrictions more a bit later.

**NOTE**

Be aware that Java 2 security is not a panacea. Neither WAS nor any J2EE application server to our knowledge is built as a hardened, compartmentalized security system. Thus, while Java 2 security can greatly strengthen the security of WAS, do not assume that this will provide complete isolation and protection of applications. If you can't trust the code you are running on the WAS application servers, you should be very cautious.

Concerns about "rogue" programmers are better addressed via secure configuration management systems that track every code change and rigorous code inspections to validate that code development meets your security guidelines.

## Choose Appropriate WAS Process Identity (N M E I)

The WAS processes run on an operating system and must therefore run under some operating system identity. There are three ways to run WAS with respect to operating system identities:

- Run everything as root.

- Run everything as a single user identity, such as "was."
- Run the node agents as root and individual application servers under their own identities.

IBM tests for and fully supports the first two approaches. The third approach may seem tempting since you can then leverage operating system permissions, but it isn't very effective in practice for the following reasons:

- It is very difficult to configure, and there are no documented procedures. Many WAS processes need read access to numerous files and write access to the log and transaction directories.
- By running the node agent as root, you effectively give the WAS administrator root authority.
- The primary value of this approach is to control file system access. This can be achieved just as well using Java 2 permissions.
- This approach creates the false impression that applications are isolated from each other. They are not. The WAS internal security model is based on J2EE and Java 2 security and is unaffected by operating system permissions. Thus, if you choose this approach to protect yourself from "rogue" applications, your approach is misguided.

The first approach is obviously undesirable since, as a general best practice, it is best to avoid running any process as root if it can be avoided. This leaves the second approach, which is fully supported, easy to implement, and provides good security when used in conjunction with Java 2 security. We therefore recommend that approach.

Obviously, once you have chosen a WAS process identity, you should limit file system access to WAS's files by leveraging operating system file permissions. WAS, like any complex system, uses and maintains a great deal of sensitive information. In general, no one should have read or write access to most of the WAS information.[16] In particular, the WAS configuration files (<root>/config) contain configuration information as well as passwords.

## Protect Private Keys (N M E I)

WAS maintains several sets of private keys. The two most important examples include the primary keystore for internal communication and the keystore used for communication between the web server and the application server. These private keys should be kept private and not shared. Since they are stored on computer file systems, those file systems must be carefully protected, as we discussed earlier. However, also be careful to avoid incidental sharing. For example, do not use the same keys in production as in other environments. Many people will have access to development and test machines and their private keys. Guard the production keys carefully.

16 Do not take this too far. We've seen far too many cases where during development, developers aren't allowed to even see the WAS log files. Such paranoia is unwarranted. During development, maximal security is not productive. During production, you should lock down WAS as much as possible. During development, be more lenient.

### Never Set Web Server Doc Root to WAR (N M E I)

WARs contain application code and lots of sensitive information. Only some of that information is web-servable content. Thus, it is inappropriate to set the web server document root to the WAR root. If you do this, the web server will serve up all the content of the WAR without interpretation. This will result in code, raw JSPs, and more being served up to end users.

### Certificates Are Not a Panacea (N M E I)

When using client certificate authentication, realize that the web server is now part of your trust domain. Compromise of the web server will compromise WAS security completely. Further, when you are using client certificate authentication, since WAS now completely trusts the web server, you should configure authenticated HTTPS between the web server and the application server. Otherwise, it is possible to spoof users by bypassing the web server.

### Keep Up to Date with Patches and Fixes (N M E I)

As with any complex product, IBM occasionally finds and fixes security bugs in WAS, IBM HTTP server, and other products. It is crucial that you keep up to date on these fixes. At a minimum you should make an effort to use recent PTF levels that usually include all of the recent security fixes. In addition, it is advisable that you subscribe to support bulletins for the products you use. Those bulletins often contain notices for recently discovered security bugs and the fixes. You can be certain that potential intruders learn of those security holes quickly. The sooner you act, the better.

## Application-Based Preventative Measures—Configuration

At this point, we have focused on the basic steps that a WAS architect and the administration team can take to ensure that they create a secure WAS infrastructure. That's obviously an important step, but it is not sufficient. Now that the infrastructure has been configured to be secure, we must examine things that applications need to do in order to be secure. Obviously, applications will need to take advantage of the infrastructure provided by WAS, but there are also numerous other actions that application developers need to take. We'll detail many of those issues here.

### Carefully Verify That Every Servlet Alias Is Secure (N M E I)

WAS secures Servlets by URL. Each URL that is to be secured must be specified in the web.xml file describing the application. If a Servlet has more than one alias (that is, multiple URLs access the same Servlet class) or there are many Servlets, it is easy to accidentally forget to secure an alias. Be cautious. Since WAS secures URLs, not the underlying classes, if just one Servlet URL is insecure, an intruder might be able to bypass your security. In order to alleviate this, whenever possible, use wildcards to secure Servlets. If that is not appropriate, carefully double-check your web.xml file before deployment.

The alias problem is further aggravated by the feature known as *serve servlets by classname*, which brings us to our next recommendation.

### Don't Serve Servlets by Classname (N M E I)

Servlets can be served by classname or via a normal URL alias. Normally, applications choose the latter. That is, developers define a precise mapping from each URL to each Servlet class in the web.xml file by hand or using one of the various WAS development tools.

However, WAS also lets you serve Servlets by classname. Instead of defining a mapping for each Servlet, a single generic URL (such as /servlet) serves all Servlets. The component of the path after the base is assumed by WAS to be the classname for the Servlet. For example, "/servlet/com.ibm.sample.MyServlet" refers to the Servlet class "com.ibm.sample.MyServlet."

Serving Servlets by classname is accomplished by setting the serveServletsByClassnameEnabled property to true in the ibm-web-ext.xmi file or by using the ASTK and checking **serve servlets by classname** in the WAR editor. Do not enable this WAS feature. This feature makes it possible for anyone who knows the classname of any Servlet to invoke it directly. Even if your Servlet URLs are secured, an attacker may be able to bypass the normal WAS URL-based security. Further, depending on the classloader structure, an attacker may be able to invoke Servlets outside of your web application.

### Do Not Place Sensitive Information in WAR Root (N M E I)

WAR files contain web-servable content. The WAS web container will serve HTML and JSP files found in the root of the WAR file. This is fine as long as you place only servable content in the root. Thus, you should never place content that shouldn't be shown to end users in the root of the WAR. For example, don't put property files, class files, or other important information there. If you must place information in the WAR, place it within the WEB-INF directory, as allowed for in the Servlet specification. Information there is never served by the web container.

### Consider Disabling File Serving and Directory Browsing (N M E I)

You can further limit the risk of inappropriate serving of content by disabling file serving and directory browsing. Obviously, if the WAR contains servable static content, file serving will have to be enabled.

### Use Container Managed Aliases on J2EE Resources (N M E I)

Any J2EE application that runs within the cell can access any J2EE resource. This is because the resources have JNDI names that can be looked up by any application. There is no authorization on resource access. Thus, if application A uses an enterprise database, simply by defining the database as a data source, it is possible that application B in the same cell can access this database.

When an application tries to access a resource by calling getConnection() on the resource factory (e.g., a data source or a JMS connection factory), WAS will automatically provide authentication information to the underlying resource if it is available. The decision of what authentication information to provide depends upon the authentication mode and the available J2C authentication aliases. The details are quite complex, but in brief, any application can look up any resource in the JNDI namespace. When this is done, the authentication mode of "application" is used implicitly. This in turn means that WAS will use a component authentication alias if one is available. Thus, any resource defined with a component alias is accessible to *any* application in the cell.

On the other hand, if only a container alias is defined on a resource, then rogue application will not be able to access the resource since they can only steal access to resources via global JNDI access, which always uses component aliases.

If you choose to use this approach, define all resources with container managed aliases. Then require that applications use local references to access the resource and specify container managed authentication on the reference as part of the development process. Some pictures may help to make this clear. Figure 18-8 is a picture of the WebSphere Studio reference editor where we are specifying container managed authentication on a database reference.

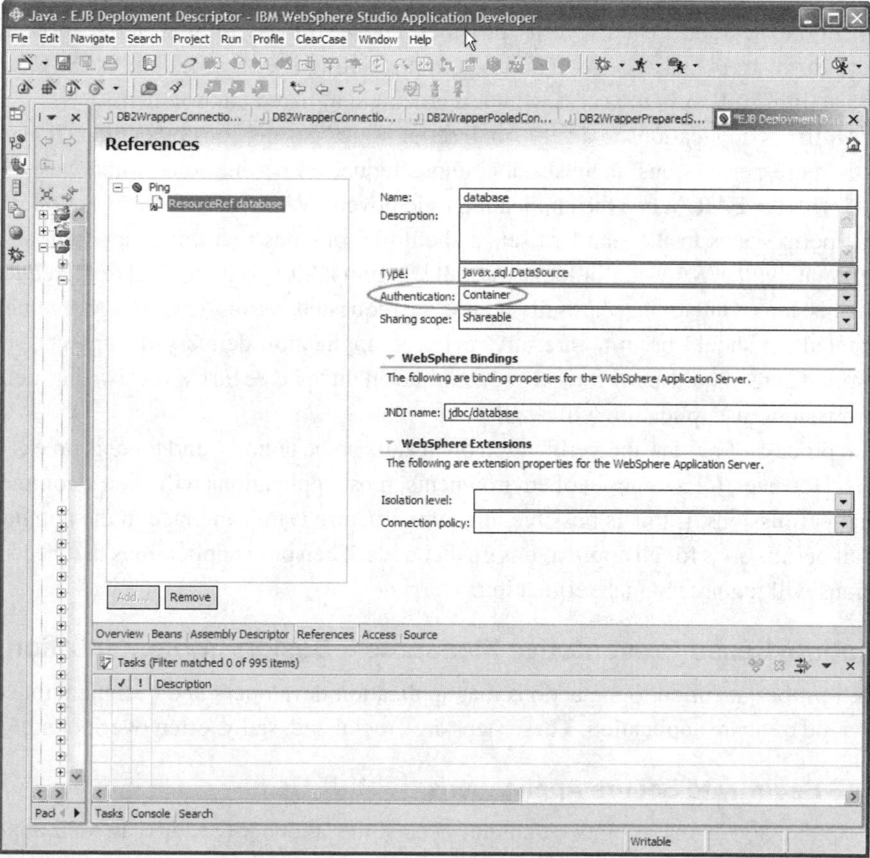


**Figure 18-8** Database resource reference using container managed authentication.

### Do Not Define a Default User ID and Password on a Resource (N M E I)

A corollary of the previous item is that you should not define a default user ID and password on a resource. If you do so, then any application within the cell can look up the resource and then implicitly use the provided user ID and password. Instead, always specify only container managed aliases.

### Be Cautious with J2C Resources (N M E I)

The careful reader may realize that some resources do not support container managed aliases. Perhaps they only support a default user ID and password being provided in the resource definition. If this is the case, use great caution and, if at all possible, don't supply the default user ID and password. In many cases, there will be other programmatic ways of providing authentication information.

### Configure Java 2 Security Properly (N M E I)

As we mentioned earlier, Java 2 security provides a powerful way to limit applications and prevent many forms of illegal access. In addition to preventing illegal access to WAS APIs, Java 2 security also limits file system access, which is crucial in a shared environment.

WAS limits applications to a very small set of "safe" permissions by default. If an application needs more permissions, it must define those requested permissions in the was.policy file contained with the EAR. When the application is deployed, WAS will read the was.policy file and add those permissions to the standard set. It should be obvious that this is a potential security hole. Fortunately, the WAS admin tools warn the administrator when applications request additional permissions. Our advice: carefully review the requested permissions. If any are unexpected (the expected set should be in a carefully reviewed application delivery document), reject the application. There should be a formal process that includes a security review that determines what permissions an application will be allowed.

The process of review and verification on install can be tedious, and there is no easy way to avoid this. However, for a large set of environments, most applications will need a common set of additional permissions. If this is possible, the infrastructure team can place in the app.policy file the default permissions for all applications on that node. Then only applications that need unusual permissions will require manual verification.

## Application-Based Preventative Measures—Design/Implementation

Here, we turn our attention to the actions that application developers and designers must take in order to build a secure application. These steps are crucial and, sadly, often overlooked.

### Use WAS Security to Secure Applications (N M E I)

Usually, application teams recognize that they need some amount of security in their application. This is often a business requirement. Unfortunately, many teams develop their own security infrastructure. While this is possible to do well, it is very difficult, and most teams do not succeed.

Instead, there is the illusion of strong security, but in fact, the system security is quite weak. Security is simply a hard problem. There are subtle issues of cryptography, replay attacks, and various other forms of attack that are easily overlooked. The message here is that WAS security should be used unless it truly does not meet your needs. This is rarely the case.

Perhaps the most common complaint about the J2EE-defined declarative security model is that it is not sufficiently granular. For example, you can only perform authorization at the method level of an EJB or Servlet,[17] not at the instance level. Thus, for example, all bank accounts have the same security restrictions, but you would prefer that certain users have special permissions on their own accounts.

This problem is addressed by the J2EE security APIs (isCallerInRole and getCallerPrincipal). By using these APIs, applications can develop their own powerful and flexible authorization rules but still drive those rules from information that is known to be accurate—the security attributes from the WAS runtime.

### An Example of Weak Security

Here is one quick example of a weak security system. Applications that don't use WAS security tend to create their own security tokens and pass them within the application. These tokens typically contain the user's name and some security attributes, such as their group memberships. It is not at all uncommon for these security tokens to have no cryptographically verifiable information. The presumption is that security decisions can be made based on the information in these tokens. This is false. The tokens simply assert user privileges. The problem here is that any Java program can forge one of these security objects and then possibly sneak into the system through a back door. The best example of this is when the application creates these tokens in the Servlet layer and then passes them to an EJB layer. If the EJB layer is not secured (see the next section), intruders can call an EJB directly with forged credentials, rendering the application's security meaningless. Thus, without substantial engineering efforts, the only reliable secure source of user information is the WAS infrastructure.[18]

### Secure Every Layer of the Application (Particularly EJBs) N M E I

All too often, web applications are deployed with some degree of security (home-grown or WAS-based) at the Servlet layer, but the other layers that are part of the application are left unsecured. This is done under the false assumption that only Servlets need to be secured in the application since they are the front door to the application. But, as any police officer will tell you, you have to lock the back door and windows to your home as well. There are many ways for this to occur, but this is most commonly seen when EJBs are used as part of a multi-tier architecture when Java clients aren't part of the application. In this case, developers often assume that the EJBs do not

17 In this context, a method on a Servlet is one of the HTTP methods: GET, POST, PUT, etc.

18 It should be noted that the WAS security infrastructure can be integrated with other authentication or authorization products. For example, Tivoli Access Manager can provide authentication and authorization support to WAS. This does not weaken WAS security; rather, it extends the WAS trust domain to include those products.

need to be secured since they are not "user-accessible" in their application design, but this assumption is dangerously wrong. An intruder can bypass the Servlet interfaces, go directly to the EJB layer, and wreak havoc if you have no security enforcement at that layer. This is easy to do with available Java IDEs that can inspect running EJBs, obtain their metadata, and dynamically create test clients. WebSphere Studio is capable of this, and developers see this every day when they use the integrated test client.

Often, the first reaction to this problem is to secure the EJBs via some trivial means—perhaps by marking them accessible to all authenticated users. But, depending on the registry, "all authenticated users" might be every employee in a company. Some take this a step further and restrict access to members of a certain group that means roughly "anyone that can access this application." That's better, but it's usually not sufficient, as everyone that can access the application shouldn't necessarily be able to perform all the operations in the application. Refer to the previous section to see how this can be addressed.

### Do Not Rely on HTTP Session IDs for Security (N M E I)

Unfortunately, some applications that use their own security track the user's authentication session through the use of the WAS HTTP Session. This is dangerous. The WAS session is tracked via a session ID (on the URL or in a cookie). While the ID is cryptographically generated, it is still subject to replay attacks, does not timeout (except when idle), and can be stolen via network sniffing attacks. The WAS LTPA token, which is created when WAS security is used by the application, is designed to make these types of attack much more difficult. In particular, LTPA tokens have limited lifetimes and use strong encryption, and the WAS security subsystem audits the receipt of invalid LTPA tokens.

In any case, if HTTP Sessions are used for tracking users, all traffic should be sent over HTTPS to prevent network sniffing.

### Prevent Cross-Site Scripting (N M E I)

Cross-site scripting is a fairly insidious attack that takes advantage of the flexibility and power of web browsers. Most web browsers can interpret various scripting languages, such as JavaScript. The browser knows it is looking at something executable based upon a special sequence of escape characters. There lies the power, and dangerous flaw, of the web browser security model.

Intruders take advantage of this hole by tricking a web site into displaying in the browser a script that the intruder wants the site to execute. This is accomplished fairly easily on sites that allow for arbitrary user input. For example, if a site includes a form for inputting an address, a user can instead input JavaScript. When the site displays the address later, the web browser will execute the script. That script, since it is running inside the web browser from the site, has access to secure information, such as the user's cookies.

So far, this doesn't seem terribly dangerous, but intruders take this one step further. They trick a user into going to a web site and inputting the "evil script" perhaps by sending the user an innocent URL in an email. Now the intruder can use the user's identity to do harm. Refer to

[XSS] for more information.

This problem is actually a special case of a much larger class of problems related to user input validation. Whenever you allow a user to type in free text, you must ensure that the text doesn't contain special characters that could cause harm. For example, if a user were to type in a string that is used to search some index, it may be important to filter the string for improper wildcard characters that might cause unbounded searches. In the case of cross-site scripting prevention, you need to filter out the escape characters for the scripting language.

### Store Information Securely (N M E I)

To create a secure system, you must consider where information is stored or displayed. Sometimes, fairly serious security leaks can be introduced by accident. For example, be cautious about storing highly confidential information in the HTTP Session object, as this object is serialized to the database. Thus, that information could be read from there. If an intruder has access to your database or even raw machine-level access to the database volumes, he or she might be able to see information in the session. Needless to say, such an attack would take a high degree of skill. Unfortunately, the next two attacks are not nearly as difficult.

An even subtler problem occurs with Stateful Session Beans. These beans are serialized to the file system by WAS when memory is short. Here again, confidential information could be inadvertently written to disk.

Logging is probably the most dangerous area of security compromise. Developers often put highly informative messages in log files to aid with debugging. Unfortunately, sometimes this information is confidential. Remember, you never know who will have to look at a log file. Some applications have been known to log Social Security Numbers to files. Needless to say, this raises all sorts of disturbing possibilities. The key message here is to carefully review all logs and other forms of output for security-sensitive information.

### Invalidate Idle Users (N M E I)

Invalidate user HTTP Sessions and authentication sessions as soon as you are done with them. Doing so reduces the possibility of idle sessions being hijacked by another user. It also frees up resources within WAS for other work.

HTTP Sessions are destroyed by using the HTTPSession.invalidate() method. WAS authentication information is destroyed by directing the user to the ibm_security_logout URL. Refer to the Info Center for details. It's worth noting that the most reliable way to eliminate session cookies is to simply exit the web browser. Many web sites now recommend this explicitly; perhaps yours should as well.

We are now done with the bulk of this chapter. We've discussed the numerous steps required for hardening a WAS environment. As should be obvious, there are many difficult and complex steps that must be taken to ensure that your systems are secure. When you are building complex J2EE systems, ensure that sufficient time is allowed for security in the schedule. Adding it "after-the-fact" is unlikely to work. We now turn our attention to the final topic of this chapter.

## Troubleshooting

Like the rest of WAS, the security subsystem is fully traced. To trace WAS security, enable tracing of these packages: com.ibm.ws.security.* and com.ibm.websphere.security.*.

Generally speaking, unless the security problem you are experiencing is related to server startup, it is best to start an application server, let it stabilize, and then enable dynamic tracing of security. Then run your test and observe the trace output.

It is also often useful to determine how WAS is managing the LTPA cookie or token. You should enable your web browser to "warn me about cookies." Once you do this, your browser will inform you when WAS sends back an LTPA token. If you don't get such a warning after a seemingly successful authentication, that usually means that the browser or some intermediate proxy has swallowed the cookie. It could be that the DNS domain setting in the LTPA SSO page is wrong or that a proxy server is configured improperly. It is often helpful to turn on the web server plug-in tracing and possibly the WAS web container tracing (com.ibm.ws.webcontainer.*) to see if the LTPA token is being generated by WAS and then perhaps lost.

## Conclusion

This chapter has covered a great deal of ground. We've discussed numerous aspects of security, although we've focused on the core theme of hardening a WAS environment. Hopefully, you now have the basic information you need to secure your J2EE systems.

CHAPTER 19

# WebSphere Caching

Caching is a well-known technique for improving application performance. Developers have been hand-building caches for decades in numerous technologies. J2EE applications can benefit from caching just like any other application. WebSphere Application Server (WAS) recognizes this by including a powerful caching mechanism known as dynamic caching (dynacache).

When considering caching opportunities in a J2EE application, it is helpful to consider the basic structure of a typical application. J2EE application developers often build their applications to the Model View Controller (MVC) paradigm, where "layers" of code handle the user interface (View), business logic (Controller), and data access (Model). Similarly, the physical topology of the hardware that serves the application is often split into tiers—an "edge" tier that might have load balancers and caching proxy servers, a "web" tier that would have web servers, an "application" tier that would have application servers such as WAS, and a "data" tier that might have database servers or Enterprise Information Systems (EIS). In these types of distributed architectures, caching can be used to maximize the performance and minimize the workload of each tier, resulting in substantial performance improvements.

Caching is generally spoken of in two groups—static caching, which means the caching of static or unchanging content, such as HTML, graphics, and JavaScript files; and dynamic caching, which is the caching of runtime program execution results. In this chapter, we will start by exploring a basic multi-tier application and discussing the various points at which caching can be applied. We will then move on to detailed discussions of the various caching options and how to identify potential uses of caching in your application.

## Caching Opportunities

Figure 19-1 shows the path of a typical J2EE request/response without caching. In order to clearly show the benefit of caching and what is happening to a request/response with various caching configurations, we will use this diagram throughout this chapter. A dynamic request, such as one to a Servlet or JSP, would likely traverse the entire path each time it is executed.

Even a simple static request with file serving enabled would still continue through to the application server. Clearly, there are many network hops taking place to various servers and resources utilized on those servers in order to complete these requests. The network hops introduce latency into the system. More importantly, the processing within each tier has a real cost in time and resources. For example, in the application server, many layers are affected by each hop, such as the web container, EJB container, and other services, such as JDBC and JNDI. You can imagine that just to generate a single page (perhaps via a JSP), a Servlet must be executed, EJBs called, backend databases accessed, and then the entire result rendered into a final page for presentation. It doesn't take much imagination to see that doing this repeatedly when the same results are returned (such as for each of hundreds of users to view the same product catalog page) results in extra work and use of resources that could potentially be avoided. Caching is a key technique for improving performance.

Figure 19-1 is a simplified diagram. Typically, there are many servers at each tier for failover and scalability. For example, the web tier might consist of several web servers being fronted by a set of load balancers feeding a set of proxy servers. We include a proxy server in this figure in order to show the "worst-case" scenario, which includes a maximum number of hops, and to feed our later discussion; however, few environments use proxy servers. It should be noted that if the proxy server is actually a caching proxy server, it can dramatically improve performance rather than reducing it, as we will see in our later discussion on the WAS caching proxy.[1] There would also be redundancy at the application server and possibly user directory servers.

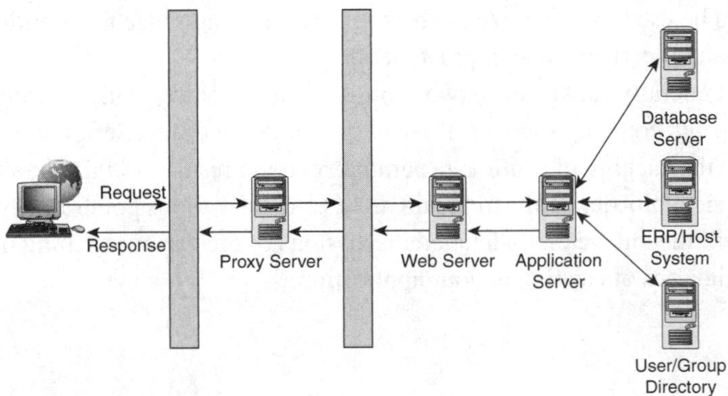


**Figure 19-1** J2EE request/response with no caching.

1 The function of proxy servers related to caching will be discussed later in this chapter. The role of load balancers and proxy servers in general will be discussed in Chapter 23, "WebSphere Edge Components."

## Caching Implications on Performance

In considering Figure 19-1 in a scenario where the user requests a product catalog view, it is not hard to imagine the sorts of resources that are invoked to satisfy the request. To build the list of products, complex SQL joins might be executed to pull in data from the manufacturing and marketing databases, as well as calls to ERP systems, such as Siebel, for customer pricing and information. Consider now the difference in performance if this request was resolved not by invoking and taxing all of these backend servers, but simply returned as HTML results from a front-end cache on the proxy server. Additionally, consider now that all of these backend servers experience significantly less load when a majority of the requests are resolved from cache, as opposed to consuming their resources. The result is much more throughput, as many more users can be serviced by the existing hardware and software investment. It is not hard to understand that caching is a major performance-tuning knob. In some cases, it can result in triple-digit performance improvements.

It has often been said that you cannot tune your way out of a badly written application. The impact of bad code on performance can be reduced by available WAS performance optimizations such as tuning the queuing network of threads and connection pools, and sizing JVM heaps. But, ultimately, one of the most effective ways to improve application performance is to avoid performing any work at all. Dynamic caching can offer some relief in this situation, particularly to those applications that misbehave only under heavy load. Dynamic caching is supported directly by WAS, so applications can now use the IBM-provided infrastructure instead of going to great lengths to build their own "home-grown" caching subsystems. **It is our recommendation that programmers avoid developing custom caching or any other type of "system" code (such as that for security, connection pooling, and persistence) and instead use the built-in features they have paid for, and focus on writing only the logic to solve the business problem at hand.**

## Caching Static Files

The simplest form of caching is the caching of static file content. In this section, we will explain how static files are served in WAS as well as the opportunities for caching them.

### Static File Handling

To understand static file handling in WAS, let's set the stage by describing how things are laid out in a typical J2EE application. Recall that a J2EE application is packaged as a single file known as an EAR. The EAR in turn contains a variety of J2EE modules—in particular, a WAR file. The WAR file of course contains web-related components, including static elements such as HTML files and graphics, plus Servlets, JSPs, and other Java classes. In the most simple deployment scenario, the EAR file is deployed to an application server, and the entire application is served from there. This includes the application's static content, which is handled by a WAS facility called the File Serving Enabler.

The File Serving Enabler is a component of the application server's web container, which listens for HTTP requests that appear to be file requests. The File Serving Enabler acts as a web server and serves up these static files. Essentially, any request that does not match a Servlet or JSP URL is assumed to be a file name, and the file serving component will serve up a file by that name from the WAR. When an application is deployed to WAS, one of the steps is to regenerate the plug-in file and copy it to the web server. When the plug-in is regenerated, entries are created that act as "pass" rules, which tell the web server to always forward certain requests to WAS and not try to serve them up itself. When the File Serving Enabler is turned on, the entry in the plug-in file is wild-carded from the context root, as shown in Code Snippet 19-1. This results in the web server forwarding everything under that context root (both static and dynamic requests) to WAS.

**Code Snippet 19-1** plugin-cfg.xml entry with file serving enabled

```
<Uri Name="/pts/*"/>
```

The File Serving Enabler can be turned off by unchecking this option for the web module in the Application Server Toolkit (ASTK) or by changing the ibm-web-ext.xmi file. When this is done, the plug-in entry for this web module would appear quite differently; it would include pass rules for only the non-static content, as shown in Code Snippet 19-2.

**Code Snippet 19-2** plugin-cfg.xml entry with file serving disabled

```
<Uri Name="/pts/PTSMainServlet"/>
<Uri Name="/pts/*.jsp"/>
<Uri Name="/pts/*.jsv"/>
<Uri Name="/pts/*.jsw"/>
<Uri Name="/pts/j_security_check"/>
```

Consider a web request sent from a browser for a simple HTML page with a few embedded graphics from our J2EE application, which has been deployed as described previously with WAS file serving enabled. The web server will see the request, find the pass rule in the plug-in file, and correspondingly forward the request to WAS. At the web container, the File Serving Enabler will read the file from the directory where the application has been deployed and send the response back. When the user's browser receives the HTML file, it will parse and display it. During this process, it will see that it needs a few graphics files to render the page and will send requests for those, which will be handled similarly by the File Serving Enabler.

As you can probably guess, this is the simplest deployment scenario but not the most efficient in terms of performance. Prior to WAS 5, deployers would often separate static content out to the web server and disable the WAS File Serving Enabler for performance. After all, web servers were designed to serve static content and can certainly do this faster than an application server. Obviously, the greater the amount of static content, the more benefit gained from this technique. However, this creates complications for deployment since content must now be deployed to both a web server and an application server. It also complicates the packaging process because we can no longer simply deploy a single EAR file. The techniques and tradeoffs for this approach are discussed in [Brown 2002]. In essence, there is a trade-off to be made between packaging simplicity and the need for performance improvements via caching. Fortunately, the WAS V5 web server plug-in can remedy this situation. As we will discuss later in this chapter, the WAS V5 web server plug-in can be configured to cache static content in the web server while allowing it to remain in the WAR. This provides performance benefits similar to serving statics from the web server, while keeping the simpler deployment process.

## Browser Caching

The most familiar form of cache to most web users is the browser cache. Web browsers will typically retrieve files from web requests (such as graphic files), cache them as temporary Internet files on the user's local hard drive, and then serve them from there upon the next request. There are two benefits to this—the user gets the file much faster since it is on his/her local hard drive, and the web server is free to do more work for other users. However, this "cached" copy of the file is useful to only one person—the one on whose hard drive it is cached. For caching that benefits many users, we have to cache files at the other tiers of the architecture. For example, consider 1,000 requests for a page with a 100K graphic image. With browser caching alone, the first 1,000 users to hit this page will cause an end-to-end request-response from the browser to the file serving process on the application server and back to the user, amounting in WAS serving a total of 100Mb of redundant data. However, as we will see in the balance of this chapter, with other forms of caching, the first user's request will result in the file's placement in a cache that is closer to the users and less expensive to retrieve for the remaining 999 requests, resulting in WAS serving a total of 100K in a single request for the same amount of load.

## Web Server Caching

Most web servers can cache static files. The IBM HTTP Server (IHS) that comes with WAS has a facility called the Fast Response Cache Accelerator (FRCA) on AIX and Adaptive Fast-Path Architecture (AFPA) on Windows that can cache static and dynamic content.[2] This is a kernel-based cache and is by far the fastest cache of any discussed here. However, the static cache is limited to caching files that are served by the HTTP server itself and not for those that are invoked via pass rules that forward the request to the application server. In order to use this cache for our scenario, we would have to split the static files out separately after deployment and place them on the web server instead of using the simple deployment and built-in WAS file serving facility. Figure 19-2 shows the routing for a request that is served up from the web server cache.

2 This feature is not available on all platforms. As of this writing, AFPA/FRCA is supported on Windows and AIX for caching static files and on Windows only for caching dynamic data. Check the IHS public web site at http://www-3.ibm.com/software/webservers/httpservers/ for up-to-date information.

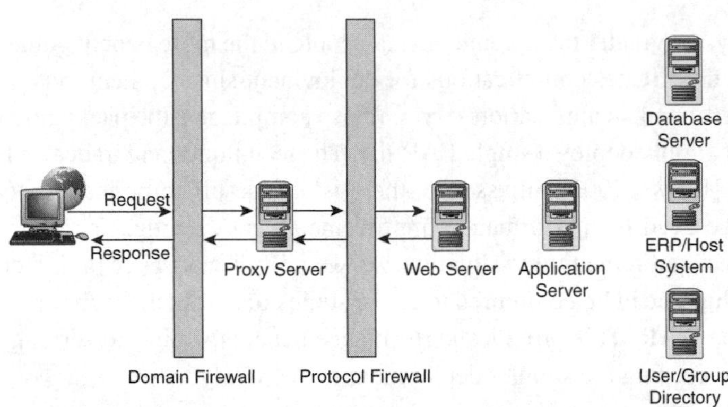


**Figure 19-2** Request/response routing for files served from a web server's static cache.

## WAS Plug-In Static Caching

Another possibility for caching at the web tier is to cache static files with the WAS plug-in. The WAS 5 plug-in incorporates the Edge Side Includes (ESI) feature for caching and assembly of pages and page fragments (both static and dynamic). ESI is an open standard written by IBM, Akamai, and others for page/fragment caching and assembly. Fragments written with standard ESI markup language can be assembled together at the edge, and no special markup is needed for caching. Products such as IBM's WebSphere Edge Server, WAS V5 Network Deployment (ND), and Akamai EdgeSuite are ESI-aware. More information on ESI can be found at http://www.esi.org.

For the purposes of this discussion, we will focus on the ability of the plug-in to use ESI to cache static content at the web server, where the plug-in is installed. Referring to our network topology diagram, this means that the flow of network hops for retrieving a static file cached with ESI would be as shown previously in Figure 19-2, essentially the same as if it was served from the web server's static cache. However, the benefits to using the plug-in are that static content can be left in the WAR, thereby simplifying packaging and deployment, and the ESI cache can also cache dynamic requests, which will be discussed later in this chapter. Caching at the plug-in reduces the burden on the file-serving facility back at the application server. This does not perform as well as splitting the static content off separately to the web server, but it is less administrative work for shops unwilling to take on the additional deployment steps.

Shown in Code Snippet 19-3 are the entries in the plugin-cfg.xml file for configuring the ESI. By default, ESI is enabled, and the cache size is set to 1024 kilobytes (1 megabyte) of memory space in the web server in which the plug-in is running. When this space is filled, entries will be purged from the cache based on their pending expiration (those closest to expiration will be purged first). The invalidation monitor setting is used for communication with WAS—it monitors messages from WAS that say when a given entry or group of entries is now invalid and should be purged from the cache. It also monitors what entries are in the static cache and accumulates other statistics.

**Code Snippet 19-3** plugin-cfg.xml entries for the ESI processor

```
<Property Name="ESIEnable" Value="true"/>
<Property Name="ESIMaxCacheSize" Value="1024"/>
<Property Name="ESIInvalidationMonitor" Value="false"/>
```

Static cache entries in the ESI time out every 300 seconds (5 minutes) by default. This can be changed by placing the property shown in Code Snippet 19-4 on the application server's JVM command-line parameters. The value provided is in seconds, so the value in Code Snippet 19-4 specifies a 2-minute timeout.

**Code Snippet 19-4** Property to place on the plug-in's JVM command-line parameters to change static expiry

```
-Dcom.ibm.servlet.file.esi.timeOut=120
```

WAS comes with two applications that are used for caching. They are both found in the installableApps directory:

- **Cachemonitor.ear**—This application allows an administrator to monitor both the ESI cache at the plug-in and the dynamic cache in the application server, and offers some basic operations, such as clearing the cache contents.
- **DynaCacheESI.ear**—This application consists of a single Servlet, which acts as an external cache adapter to the ESI cache at the plug-in when it is installed at the application server. This enables the application server cache engine to gather cache statistics to display in the cache monitor application and to send cache entries and information related to them to the ESI cache at the plug-in.

It should be noted that the plug-in will cache static files by default, but the DynaCacheESI adapter is not installed. That means that the static cache entries will only expire after their configured timeout. By installing the DynaCacheESI adapter, WAS can send invalidation messages to the plug-in when the static files are updated, as well as provide the interface required for the Cachemonitor application to gather statistics and clear caches.

To use these applications, set the ESIInvalidationMonitor property on the plugin-cfg.xml file (shown in Code Snippet 19-3) to true and install both applications; then regenerate your plug-in and restart the application server. Running one of the sample applications should result in cache entries. Figure 19-3 shows some ESI cache statistics from the cache monitor application, and Figure 19-4 shows some sample cache contents. Notice that there is a mix of graphics and JavaScript files in the cache from the monitor application itself, as well as the PetStore demo application. Static files are cached with no additional configuration.

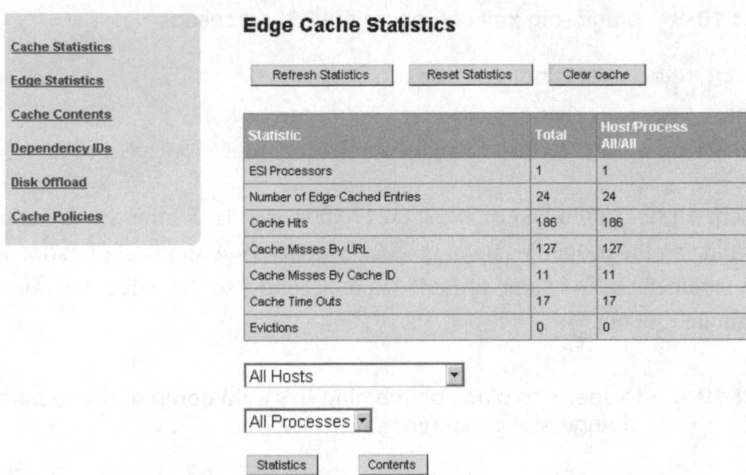


| Statistic | Total | Host/Process All/All |
|---|---|---|
| ESI Processors | 1 | 1 |
| Number of Edge Cached Entries | 24 | 24 |
| Cache Hits | 186 | 186 |
| Cache Misses By URL | 127 | 127 |
| Cache Misses By Cache ID | 11 | 11 |
| Cache Time Outs | 17 | 17 |
| Evictions | 0 | 0 |

**Figure 19-3** ESI statistics from the WAS CacheMonitor application.

| Cache ID | Host | Process |
|---|---|---|
| /cachemonitor/images/background.jpg | billhinest40.hines.ibm.com | 972 |
| /cachemonitor/images/cachemon_bottom.gif | billhinest40.hines.ibm.com | 972 |
| /cachemonitor/images/cachemon_top.gif | billhinest40.hines.ibm.com | 972 |
| /cachemonitor/images/cache_monitor_logo.jpg | billhinest40.hines.ibm.com | 972 |
| /cachemonitor/images/IBM-logo.jpg | billhinest40.hines.ibm.com | 972 |
| /cachemonitor/menu.js | billhinest40.hines.ibm.com | 972 |
| /petstore/images/banner_logo.gif | billhinest40.hines.ibm.com | 972 |
| /petstore/images/ja_flag.gif | billhinest40.hines.ibm.com | 972 |
| /petstore/images/splash.gif | billhinest40.hines.ibm.com | 972 |
| /petstore/images/us_flag.gif | billhinest40.hines.ibm.com | 972 |

**Figure 19-4** ESI cache contents from the WAS CacheMonitor application.

> **NOTE**
> Under certain circumstances in WAS V5.0 and 5.1, unauthorized users may be able to access the secured static content from the ESI cache without authenticating through the WebSphere security infrastructure. An interim fix PQ81192 is available from the IBM WAS support web site.

## Dynamic Caching

As described previously, static caching is a valuable benefit, increasingly so with the amount and size of static elements in an application. However, with the current trend toward more personalized, portalized, and dynamic sites, dynamic caching is much more useful. In addition to the reasons cited previously, dynamic requests tend to use far more enterprise resources in order to build a response. Dynamic content often requires the most resource-intensive work in an enterprise system, so dynamic caching can dramatically enhance performance. Revisit Figure 19-1 at the beginning of this chapter and consider the amount of computing power required at each tier to build these requests. CPU utilization, memory, and connections are expensive at each tier, particularly in the application server's web and EJB containers. Hitting backend database, host, EIS, and other servers tends to be expensive. With every request served from dynamic cache, usage of these resources is spared, and they are freed up to handle many more concurrent requests. This is very much preferred to buying additional servers to handle peak load!

Dynamic caching is more complex than static caching and requires detailed knowledge of the application. You must consider the candidates for dynamic caching carefully since, by its very nature, dynamically generated content can be different based on the state of the application. Therefore, it is important to consider under what conditions dynamically generated content can be cached to always return the correct response. This requires knowledge of the application, its possible states, and other data, such as parameters, that ensure that the dynamic data is generated in a deterministic manner.

Dynamic caching in WAS 5 can be administered via the administrative console. Navigating through the admin console menu from Servers > Application Servers > server1, you will see Dynamic Cache Service under Additional Properties. Clicking on this will present a page similar to Figure 19-5.

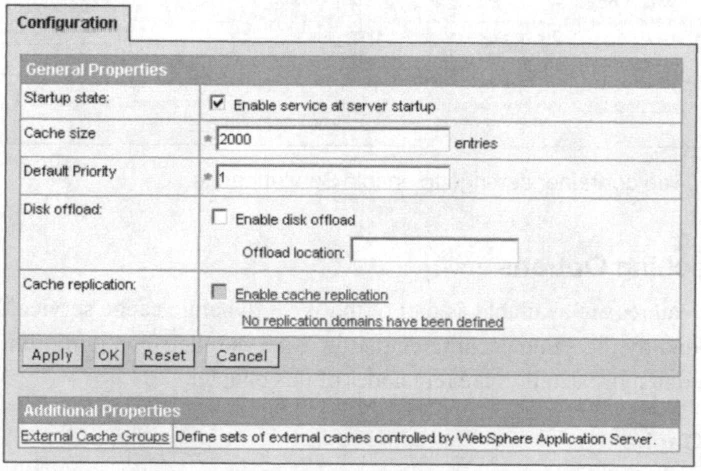

Configuration

| General Properties | |
|---|---|
| Startup state: | ☑ Enable service at server startup |
| Cache size | * 2000 entries |
| Default Priority | * 1 |
| Disk offload: | ☐ Enable disk offload<br>Offload location: |
| Cache replication: | ☐ Enable cache replication<br>No replication domains have been defined |

Apply | OK | Reset | Cancel

| Additional Properties | |
|---|---|
| External Cache Groups | Define sets of external caches controlled by WebSphere Application Server. |

**Figure 19-5** Dynamic cache service settings in the WAS admin console.

Several of the available dynamic cache options can be seen here. Notice in particular that the cache size is in entries, as opposed to a physical memory size as we saw when we discussed the ESI caching facility of the plug-in. This makes sizing the cache tricky—it can be done by monitoring the cache statistics to watch for cache evictions during load testing and peak production periods. The Default Priority field shown here is related to eviction. Evictions are determined by a Least Recently Used (LRU) algorithm. The "Priority" is essentially the number of free passes an entry can have to stay in the cache once its number comes up from the LRU algorithm. This setting is rarely changed here, but you might keep this in mind when setting priorities on individual cache entries when you configure them. Giving them higher numbers will keep them in the cache longer, so you might want to do that for entries that are expensive to build. You might also notice here that there is a facility to offload cache entries to disk when the cache becomes full instead of purging them from the cache completely. While the pages will serve more slowly from the disk offload area, this is still generally better than invalidation, in which case, the page results would have to be completely rebuilt by running the transactions again.

To use dynacache for Servlets and JSPs, Servlet caching also needs to be enabled for the web container. Navigating through the admin console menu from Servers > Application Servers > server1 >Web Container will present a page with the options shown in Figure 19-6. Notice that the **Enable servlet caching** box is checked.

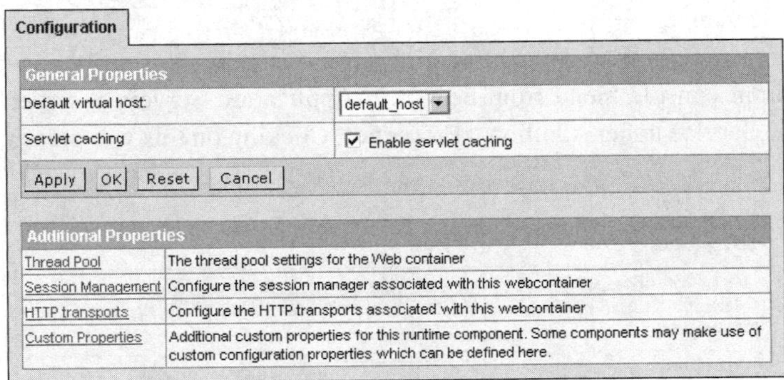


**Figure 19-6** Web container settings to enable Servlet cache.

## Dynamic Caching Options

The following features are available as part of the WAS dynamic cache service. All of these services are provided by the same caching engine in WAS, so their configuration is similar. Each will be discussed in more detail in the remainder of this chapter.

### Servlet/JSP Cache

The Servlet/JSP caching facility will catch the response from Servlet/JSP invocation and cache the HTML results. Servlets and JSPs are configured for caching via entries in the cachespec.xml file (described later). They can be designated by their URI path or by classname. The latter option is more inclusive since it will catch any invocation of the Servlet, regardless of the aliases. Usually, the Servlet is cached by its alias since different aliases often imply different actions. Determining whether to cache on URI or classname depends entirely on the application.

In most cases, the cache entry for the Servlet needs to be further qualified by additional inputs, such as the request parameters or values from the user session information. We will explain this further in our section on specifying cache entries.

When preparing to execute a Servlet, the dynacache engine filters the service() method of each Servlet that is about to be executed and determines if this matches any cache ID entries based on the parameters present. If a match is found, the cached results are returned rather than executing the service() method and all of the work that would have been done beyond it. This avoids all of the processing that would have been done by the Servlet, resulting in a substantial performance boost. If there isn't a cache entry for this ID, the service() method is executed as normal, and the results are caught and placed in the cache before they are returned to the user.

### Command Cache

The command cache can cache the results of the invocation of server-side commands, which implement the WebSphere command pattern interfaces. This is useful for caching intensive operations such as complex SQL joins or host requests. The results here are typically an object or container of objects rather than the HTML results that are held in the Servlet/JSP cache. The command pattern is widely used and relatively simply to retrofit to an existing application if you feel it could benefit from this type of caching. Retrofitting involves writing thin command wrappers around the existing code. Similar to how the caching engine filters on a Servlet or JSP's service() method, the command cache filters on a command's execute() method to determine if the command is cacheable and if there are already results in the cache.

### Web Services Cache

This cache holds the result of web services SOAP invocations. Web services SOAP calls can be expensive, primarily due to the extensive parsing of XML files that must happen on both ends. Cache identifiers can be built from both HTTP headers and the SOAP envelope—in fact, the entire SOAP envelope could be hashed and used as a cache ID. Refer to the WAS5 Info Center for more information.

### Distributed Object Cache

This cache holds Java objects for use in a distributed environment. For example, objects may be stored by one application server and then retrieved by other application servers in the same Data Replication Service (DRS) cluster. This cache is only available in the Enterprise Edition of WAS, however. These cache instances are retrieved by a JNDI name that is configured on the Cache Instance resource (which is similar to a JDBC resource). This cache can even be configured so that objects are persistent—that is, they are flushed to disk when the server is stopped and loaded again upon restart. Individual entries can be designated as non-shared, push (sent to all servers when they are cached), or pull (only their names are sent, and values are retrieved only when "pulled" from other servers). Refer to the WAS5 Enterprise Info Center for more information under "Using the DistributedMap interface for the dynamic cache."

> **NOTE**
> Dynacache is not architected for maintaining security-sensitive information. While the use of DRS encryption can protect information from attack from processes outside of a WAS environment, there are no provisions for protecting information within the application server. Thus, any information that is cached (Servlet cache, object cache, web services cache, or command cache) can be accessed by any application within the same application server. If you are unable to trust applications within the same application server, do not place sensitive information in the cache. Fortunately, since caching is generally used to cache shared information, this restriction is generally not a major problem.

## Dynamic Caching Concepts

### Invalidation

We saw that with static files, invalidation is pretty easy. HTML files often have expiration tags in their headers, and other types of files have a simple timeout configured for them. However, with dynamic caching, invalidation is more complex. Dynamic caches have the following types of invalidation:

- **Simple timeout**—On the cache specification for a particular cache entry, you can specify a default timeout value. This could be short term (seconds) or long term (years). It could also specify infinity.
- **Dynamic invalidation**—Suppose you are caching long-term data, such as a baseball team's schedule for the current season. In this case, a reasonable timeout value could be the end of the season, before playoffs start. However, a rainout can easily change that. For situations like this, dynamic invalidation can be used. This can be done by virtue of cache entries that are designated as Invalidate Only (as we will see in the following section on creating cache specifications) or via a programming API that is provided with the dynacache engine. In the former case, you might configure an invalidation cache entry for the Servlet that is executed to update the baseball team's schedule so that when the dynacache engine sees this Servlet executed, it knows to invalidate any cache entries that hold schedule data for this team. Your developers might choose instead to execute an invalidation API directly in their code, which is probably less desirable. For portability, applications should execute with little or no knowledge about their environment.
- **Cache eviction**—Cache entries are invalidated when the cache is full and they are purged to make way for new entries. For a static cache, this is simply which entry is closest to timing out. For a dynamic cache, a Least Recently Used algorithm is executed to determine which entries should be purged, as well as the priority assigned to each cache entry (see the previous discussion for how this works).

## Specifying Cache Entries

Cache entries are specified in the cachespec.xml file. This is a file that holds cache specification and invalidation policies. It can be placed in the <was-root>/properties directory for global cache specifications (there is a sample file already there that will cache the snoop sample Servlet if it is renamed to cachespec.xml), but more likely, you will want to define these files per application module and place them in the WEB-INF directory of each web module or META-INF of the Enterprise Bean directory. These files are reloaded by the application server based on the configured time interval. The following Code Snippets are example cachespec.xml files for a JSP (Code Snippet 19-5), command (Code Snippet 19-6), and web service call (Code Snippet 19-7). Each of these will be discussed in turn, following a general description of the entries in cachespec.xml. See the WAS Info Center for more detailed instructions on configuring cache policies or review the cachespec.dtd file in the application server properties directory.

The following lists the components of the cachespec.xml file:

- **<cache>**—This is the root element of the cachespec.xml file, appearing only once. It holds multiple <cache-entry> stanzas.
- **<cache-entry>**—There is one of these for each item to be cached. Cache entries can describe items to be cached, items that will invalidate other cache entries, and dependencies between cache entries. We will see examples of each later.
- **<class>**—This identifies the type of entry. Possible values are command, servlet, and webservice. 'servlet' is used for both Servlets and JSPs.
- **<name>**—This is the name of the item to be cached. For commands, it should be the fully qualified package and classname, including the .class suffix. For Servlets or JSPs, it should be the URI path relative to the application's context root. For example, if the full URL to the JSP is http://www.myco.com/myapp/products/catalogList.JSP, the value here would be /products/catalogList.JSP. If you were using the cachespec.xml file from the application server properties directory (global), the entire URL would be necessary. If you have multiple Servlet aliases, multiple <name> stanzas could be included here to list each alias that you intend to cache.
- **<property>**—This is used to set optional properties on a cache entry, such as whether it can be cached outside of WAS and whether this entry can be persisted to disk. There is a list of definable properties in the WAS5 Info Center. There can be multiple properties per cache entry.
- **<sharing-policy>**—This entry determines whether a cache entry should be shared between distributed caches, and if so, how that should occur. Distributed caches will be discussed later in this chapter.
- **<cache-id>**—These are where the cache identifiers for each cache entry are configured. This is a "key," similar to a database key structure, that identifies a particular cache entry as unique. Caching is generally not as simple as specifying a particular Servlet, JSP, or

command to cache. These must be qualified with attributes that distinguish one cache entry from another. For example, caching a Servlet that returns a weather forecast by the URI /weather/forecast would not be desirable—think of what would happen if one user asked for the forecast in Miami and that result was cached, and the following user invoked this URI to get the forecast in Anchorage. In this case, there is probably a request parameter that is sent along with the Servlet invocation that has the city name or zip code for the forecast. This is the piece of data that would ensure that the cached results are unique and match the request, so for example, Miami forecasts are always returned to other users asking for Miami weather. This parameter should be designated as required because the cache entry is meaningless without it. Code Snippet 19-5 shows a similar cache specification. There may also be other parameters as part of the cache ID, such as whether the user is asking for a short-range or long-range forecast. Each component of the cache ID is specified in a <component> tag, as shown in the following examples.

Not surprisingly, how the cache ID is computed depends upon the technology. Servlet/JSP cache IDs can be composed of request parameters/attributes, path information, header values, request locale, cookie values, and even HTTP Session values. It is best to avoid using server-side values, such as HTTP session data, since the use of those would negate moving the cache entry out past the application server's cache (hence, it could not be marked "edge cacheable"). We will discuss edge caching later in this chapter. Using path information is useful for applications based on the Struts programming model since Servlet names/aliases can be dynamic, only having the .do suffix to identify them. For applications that use controller Servlets, the same Servlet may be marked as cacheable when its "action" parameter has the value of "list" and may be marked as "invalidate" when the action parameter has the value of "update." The cache ID for a command can be based on a method in the command object, while web services cache IDs are based on information from the SOAP request. While not shown here, when using the Distributed Object Map, cache IDs are specified programmatically. There can be multiple cache IDs for each cache entry. Now that we are familiar with the basic structure of the cachespec.xml file, let's examine a few sample entries.

**Code Snippet 19-5** Sample cachespec.xml file for a JSP

```
<cache>
   <cache-entry>
      <class>servlet</class>
      <name>/displayForecast.jsp</name>
      <property name="EdgeCacheable">true</property>
      <cache-id>
         <component id="zip" type="parameter">
```

```
                <required>true</required>
            </component>
            <priority>3</priority>
            <timeout>20</timeout>
        </cache-id>
    </cache-entry>
</cache>
```

Code Snippet 19-5 shows a simple cachespec.xml file with a single cache entry for a JSP. You might notice in the Code Snippet that the <class> is servlet, while the <name> clearly identifies a JSP. This is because JSPs are compiled into Servlets on the backend, so from the application server's perspective, they are essentially the same thing. This JSP has a property that states that it is "edge cacheable." We will discuss caching on the edge later in this chapter. Notice that the cache ID is composed of a single request parameter, the zip code for the forecast. This means that if seven users request forecasts for seven different zip codes, there will be seven cache entries in the cache with the zip code serving as their "key." Subsequent users requesting forecasts for any of these seven zip codes will be served up the forecast for the appropriate area. This cache entry has been configured with a priority of three, meaning it gets three "free passes" to stick around if it is designated as ready to be invalidated by the LRU algorithm mentioned earlier in our discussion on invalidation. The entry is set to a default timeout of 20 seconds; however, it could be invalidated earlier by means of a program API, another cache entry that is designated to invalidate it, or purging due to a full cache.

**Code Snippet 19-6** Sample cachespec.xml file for a command

```
<cache>
    <cache-entry>
        <class>command</class>
        <sharing-policy>not-shared</sharing-policy>
        <name>com.myco.productapp.ProductListCommand.class</name>
        <sharing-policy>not-shared</sharing-policy>
        <cache-id>
            <component type="method" id="getProductCategory">
                <required>true</required>
            </component>
            <priority>1</priority>
            <timeout>3600</timeout>
        </cache-id>
    </cache-entry>
</cache>
```

Code Snippet 19-6 shows a simple cachespec.xml file with a single cache entry for a command. The <class> is appropriately enough "command," and the <name> is the fully qualified package and classname. This entry is not to be shared between distributed caches, as indicated by the <sharing-policy>. The cache ID is obtained this time from the result of calling the getProductCategory() method on the ProductListCommand object. This indicates that product list entries are cached by some sort of category, such as sporting goods, clothing, or hardware. As you might expect for something like a product list, this cache has a longer timeout value of one hour (3,600 seconds), as product catalog entries aren't likely to change very rapidly.

Code Snippet 19-7 shows a simple cachespec.xml file with a single cache entry for a web service call. The class designation is obvious, and the name is the URI path to the soaprouter Servlet familiar to those who work with web services. There are two cache IDs configured for this entry. The first is a combination of a stock quote lookup request and the SOAP envelope, and the second is a combination of a getQuote service operation and a hash of the SOAP envelope. With two cache IDs, the caching engine will parse from the top down and use the first one that fits the particular entry that it is working with at runtime for either inserting a new entry into cache or returning a cache entry for a request.

**Code Snippet 19-7** Sample cachespec.xml file for a web service call

```
<cache>
   <cache-entry>
      <class>webservice</class>
      <name>/soap/servlet/soaprouter</name>
      <cache-id>
         <component id="" type=SOAPAction>
            <value>urn:stockquote-lookup</value>
         </component>
         <component id="Hash" type="SOAPEnvelope"/>
         <timeout>600</timeout>
         <priority>1<priority>
      </cache-id>
      <cache-id>
         <component id="" type="serviceOperation">
            <value>urn:stockquote:getQuote</value>
         </component>
         <component id="Hash" type="SOAPEnvelope"/>
         <timeout>600</timeout>
         <priority>1</priority>
      </cache-id>
   </cache-entry>
</cache>
```

Let's look at a more complex example of a cachespec.xml file, shown in Code Snippet 19-8.

**Code Snippet 19-8** Sample cachespec.xml file for a web service call

```
<cache>
  <cache-entry>
    <class>servlet</class>
    <name>/ProductControllerServlet</name>
    <cache-id>
      <component id="action" type="parameter">
        <value>view</value>
        <required>true</required>
      </component>
      <component id="productID" type="parameter">
        <required>true</required>
      </component>
      <priority>3</priority>
      <timeout>20</timeout>
    </cache-id>
    <cache-id>
      <component id="action" type="parameter">
        <value>view</value>
        <required>true</required>
      </component>
      <component id="category" type="parameter">
        <required>true</required>
      </component>
      <priority>3</priority>
      <timeout>20</timeout>
    </cache-id>
    <dependency-id>category
      <component id="category" type="parameter">
        <required>true</required>
      </component>
    </dependency-id>
    <invalidation>category
      <component id="action" type="parameter" ignore-value="true">
        <value>update</value>
```

```
            <required>true</required>
        </component>
        <component id="category" type="parameter">
            <required>true</required>
        </component>
    </invalidation>
  </cache-entry>
</cache>
```

Code Snippet 19-8 shows a cachespec.xml file with a single cache entry for a controller Servlet such as you might find in an MVC-type application. From the top down, you see:

- A cache ID for when the product controller Servlet is run with a parameter named 'action' with a value of 'view,' using the product ID. This probably indicates a view for a single product's information. Notice that not only is the parameter name of 'action' provided as part of the cache ID but also a required value of 'view' for that parameter as well.
- A cache ID for when the product controller Servlet is run with parameter 'action' with value 'view' and a 'category' parameter is provided. This would be an example of when a page of products in a certain category is requested.
- A dependency ID named 'category' using the parameter name 'category' and its value as the cache ID. This and other cache entries can have the same dependency ID and will be invalidated as a group if certain events occur (such as an invalidation rule firing).
- An invalidation rule named 'category,' which causes it to be linked to the category dependency ID. It requires that the 'action' parameter of this Servlet have the value 'update.' Based on the linkage, when the Servlet is run in update mode for this category, all cache entries for both the individual product view and the list for that category will be invalidated.

## Planning for Caching

Caching is best done as a planned activity, not as something that is retrofitted on an existing application. The latter is quite possible but not as easy or fruitful. Obviously, the best candidates for caching are operations (or files) that are large, slow, or expensive to produce. They should also be public—the more users that can take advantage of a given cache entry, the better. Therefore, private data is not a good candidate for caching. Pages that have been "personalized" to include information specific to a particular user make poor candidates for caching, but there are ways around that if you have a good design. Consider an airline frequent flyer page that presents:

- The user's name, status, and point total in a welcome message

- Promotions, messages, and news based on status
- Other generic promotions and messages for the general population

If this were all one JSP file, it would not be very useful for caching since it has data specific to one user. However, if the page were to be broken into individual JSP fragments, as shown in Figure 19-7, there would be much greater potential, particularly if those fragments were cached and assembled at the edge with ESI.

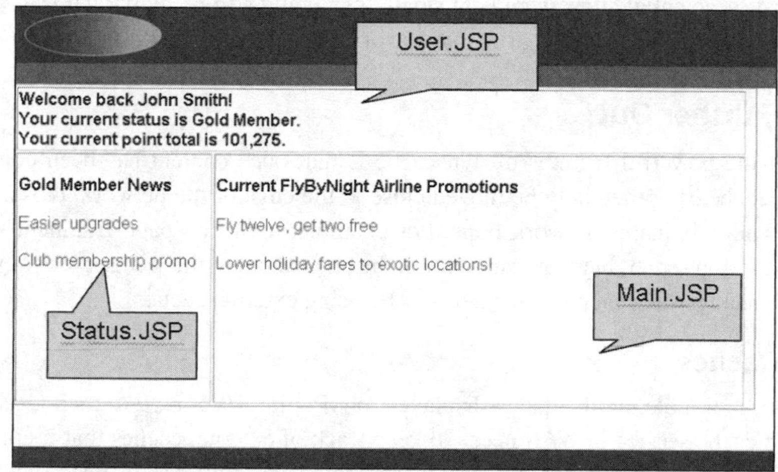


**Figure 19-7** Sample page broken into cacheable fragments.

- **User.jsp**—This fragment has the user's name, status, current points, and other personal info. It would probably not be cached because only one user could benefit from the cache entry.
- **Status.jsp**—This fragment would hold the status (i.e., Platinum, Gold, Silver) and special promotions and messages specific to that status. The cache ID would likely be the StatusName, and there would likely be one entry in the cache for each one, shared by all users of that particular status.
- **Main.jsp**—This fragment would contain the generic portions of the page—perhaps general news, promotions, and links for contact info or searching. This one is an excellent candidate for caching!

To introduce another common dilemma with caching, let's assume that there is also a fragment that would hold the weather forecasts for five cities. As a personalization feature, each user could designate which cities to show the forecast for (perhaps the ones they visit most often), and those would display in the fragment each time they visited the page. The forecast is slow to retrieve—it must contact a backend computer. At first glance, this seems like a good cache candidate—after all, the forecast is public, shared data. However, not too many users are likely to have the same five cities on their fragment, and the possible permutations would mean a potentially huge number of entries in the cache. A possible solution here is to not use the Servlet/JSP cache but rather to cache the forecasts for all major cities using the command cache. Then, no matter which cities the user has designated, they are likely to come from cache and not the slow transaction. If the list of potential cities were kept small, they could still be individual fragments themselves, pulled into the larger fragment of five "favorites."

## Caching Further Out

One of the powerful features of dynacache is that once content has been configured for caching, the cache can potentially be moved close to the edge of the network, closer to the user population. This eliminates network hops. For example, a cached page fragment is normally served from the app server, but that fragment can be pushed out to the web server or even a proxy server. WAS manages this caching "further out" by using external caches.

### External Caches

The final item of note in the page displayed on Figure 19-5 is External Cache Groups. The dynamic cache service in WAS needs to keep track of external caches that it communicates with. In the section on the ESI processor, it was noted that you had to install an application called DynaCacheESI as the external cache adapter for the ESI cache at the plug-in. If you have done that, clicking on External Cache Groups shows the ESIInvalidator Servlet that was installed as a result. Essentially, any external cache, such as the ESI cache at the plug-in, the WAS5 ND Caching Proxy, or the AFPA/FRCA cache in IHS, must have an external cache adapter and group defined here. Cache entries in external caches can be grouped together for easier invalidation of related entries—they can be invalidated as a group rather than one by one.

### Web Tier Dynamic Caching

Earlier in this chapter, we configured the WAS plug-in at the web server for static file caching. These steps (changing a parameter in the plugin-cfg.xml file and installing the DynaCacheESI application on the application server) also set the plug-in up for dynamic caching. When the DynaCacheESI application was installed, it defined to the application server an external cache residing at the ESI plug-in on the web server. If a particular cache entry has the property EdgeCacheable set to true, as shown in Code Snippet 19-3, when it is requested, it will be pushed out to and served from the cache at the plug-in, further lightening the application server's load on future requests. The application server will notify the plug-in cache when the entry is invalidated. As mentioned earlier, for cache entries to be edge cacheable, they should avoid using server-side values such as the data from the user's HTTP Session as part of their cache identifiers.

## Caching at the Edge

Proxy servers, such as the one included with WAS 5 Network Deployment Edge Components, can cache content before the web server, removing even more network hops.

In the simplest case, the proxy server can cache just static files. Proxy servers are typically dedicated to serving content from backend servers such as web servers and rarely serve their own content. A caching proxy can cache static content from these backend servers. The proxy server included with WAS 5 ND can cache static and dynamic content. These features will be covered more thoroughly in Chapter 23. To demonstrate the effect of caching at the proxy server tier, see to Figure 19-8, an updated version of the network diagram we are using for this chapter. You can see how this would have a profound impact on response time, performance, and resource utilization when static and dynamic requests are served from caches this far on the edge. Figure 19-8 shows a reverse proxy configuration in the DMZ. For even more efficiency, some companies will implement a forward proxy configuration, with proxy servers placed at remote offices to cut down on Internet/intranet traffic. Chapter 23 will cover proxy configurations in further detail.

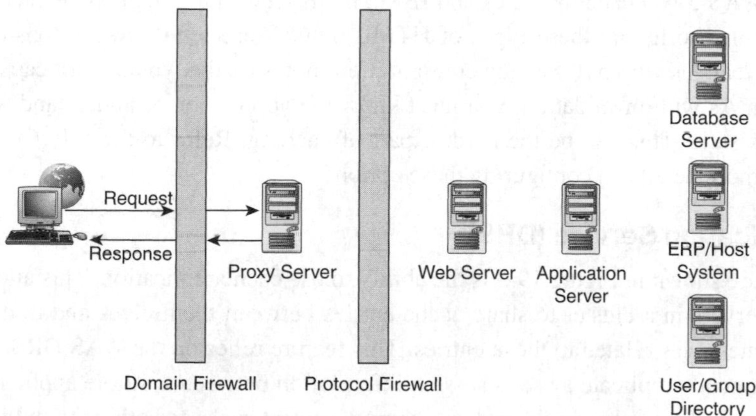


**Figure 19-8** Proxy server serving requests from its cache.

There are a few differences between the WAS, plug-in, and caching proxy caches. The caching proxy dynamic cache can only cache full pages, not fragments, and it can only be configured for either memory or disk cache, not memory cache with a disk overflow as WAS and the plug-in can. If a disk cache is used, it must be configured for a specially formatted partition on the hard drive. While it is slower than the in-memory cache, the benefits to the disk cache are that it can be much larger and that it is persistent, thereby surviving proxy server crashes or restarts.

In most cases, these factors tend to lean in the favor of the using the plug-in for static and dynamic caching, particularly since it is easier to use and avoids the extra tier for proxy servers. So, unless specific requirements mandate their use, you might not want to use the Edge Components caching proxy for caching purposes alone. A good example of when to use the caching proxy might be when the forward proxy configuration is desired to position the cache at the front of the network, closer to the users, to save network bandwidth.

## Advanced Caching Topics

Adequately covering the breadth of caching and all advanced topics would require a dedicated book on the subject, but we did want to draw your attention to two items of importance.

First, while all of our examples have focused on caching using configuration options, it is also possible to have your developers write code for dynamic cache "hooks" that can make caching, cache ID, and invalidation decisions on-the-fly. For example, certain entries may only be cached at certain times of the day or only after a certain number of repeated 'hits' and perhaps invalidated more often as resources become scarcer. This is covered in more detail in the WAS5 JavaDoc at http://publib7b.boulder.ibm.com/wasinfo1/en/info/ae/javadoc/ae/index.html. See the JavaDoc at that site for packages com.ibm.websphere.cache and com.ibm.websphere.servlet.cache.

Second, when trying to cache content, it is important to know that HTML pages often have header tags to thwart caching. Thus, you may think you are caching content when you are in fact not caching it because the HTML says the content should not be cached. Caching engines such as those in the WAS 5 ND caching proxy and IBM HTTP server have aggressive caching features that can be tuned to ignore these types of HTML hints. You should always consult with your development team as with any caching configuration to ensure that you are not causing undesirable behavior. As with invalidation, you must know the application to understand when cached data becomes stale. This can be the hardest part of caching. Refer to the Info Center for both products for more details on configuring these options.

### Data Replication Service (DRS)

Another feature shown in Figure 19-5 is the ability to use cache replication. This allows multiple application servers in a cluster to share cache entries between themselves and to communicate invalidation messages related to those entries. This feature relies on the WAS DRS. DRS is also used to dynamically replicate a user's session information between multiple application servers. The replicated cache can be configured as a shared, central cache for others to pull from or as a cache that is replicated to all servers. Code Snippet 19-4 illustrated the `<sharing-policy>` tag that specifies whether a cache entry should be excluded from cache sharing or how it should be shared if it is included. There are options to specify whether the entry should be pushed out to other caches automatically or pulled on demand. This is an advanced configuration, requiring some understanding of configuring DRS and the creation of replication domains, which is discussed in Chapter 20, "WAS Network Deployment Architecture," and Chapter 22, "Session Management," as well as in the WAS Info Center.

> **NOTE**
> DRS communication is insecure by default. This yields the maximum performance, but if you are concerned about others seeing or altering the cache replication between servers, you should enable DES encryption. This will be explained in Chapter 20.

## Troubleshooting Caching Problems

Several tools are useful for troubleshooting caching problems. At the application server, detailed traces can be obtained by using the powerful WAS trace facility. This can be enabled by selecting any of the cache groups under the trace configuration page or by using the generic trace string com.ibm.ws.cache=all=enabled. In analyzing a trace file, you can view the decision process for placing and serving cache entries and often the reasons that they are not behaving as expected. Remember that a trace facility also exists at the plug-in so tracing can be done there as well by changing LogLevel to "trace" in the plugin-cfg.xml file. The CacheMonitor application mentioned earlier in this chapter is also quite useful. Drilling down into the links provided will show details on cache identifiers and other valuable information. If you are not seeing a Servlet cached, make sure that all aliases for that Servlet have been configured for caching. In general, anything that can be served up from the browser address bar can be served up by the Servlet/JSP cache.

In troubleshooting static file caching, the log files are quite useful. The IBM HTTP Server and WAS5 ND caching proxy have separate log files to show cache "hits" and the standard access logs to show cache "misses." Remember that if you do not see entries in these logs, your request may well have been served up right from the browser's temporary Internet files. For this reason, it is often useful to test caching from different workstations and to delete temporary Internet files between requests. The administrative console for the WAS5 ND caching proxy has a proxy access page where entries returned from cache are shown in blue, but it is only the last few dozen requests—the log must be viewed for a complete list.

Remember, with any caching, it may take a few "hits" to load the cache—don't expect to see the entry there on the first request!

## Conclusion

In this chapter, we covered the many caching options available with WAS. Now that we have covered these, Figure 19-9, which shows the WAS caching architecture, might be useful and interesting.

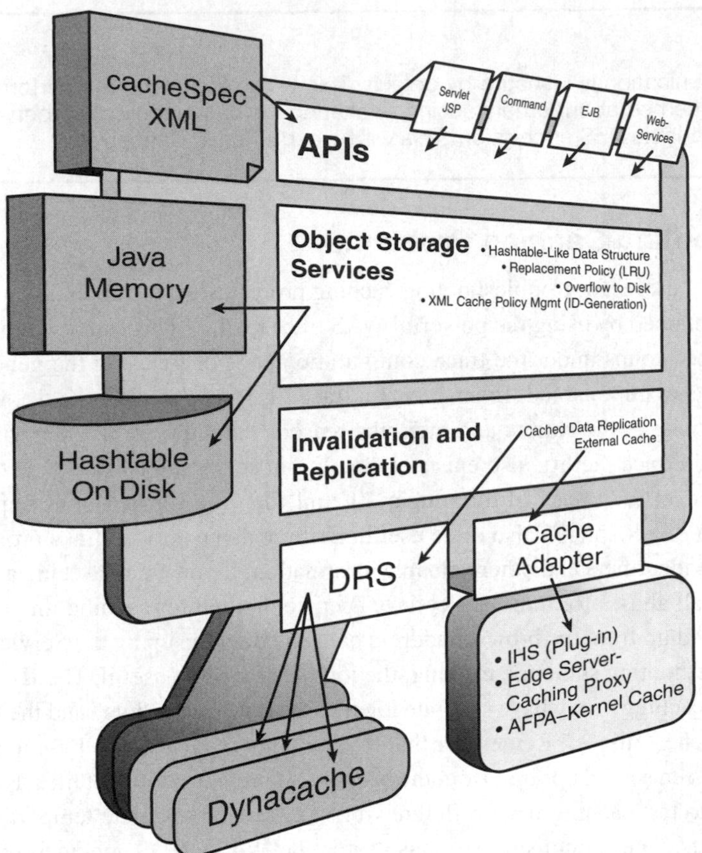


**Figure 19-9** WAS dynamic caching architecture.

Caching is an advanced topic, well worth further investigation considering the tremendous performance improvements that are possible. Further information can be found in the WAS Info Center.

# PART IV

# WebSphere Application Server Network Deployment

CHAPTER 20

# WAS Network Deployment Architecture

In an earlier chapter, we discussed the WebSphere Application Server (WAS) V5 architecture. In this chapter, we'll examine the additional functions that are available in the WebSphere Application Server-Network Deployment (WAS-ND) edition, and we'll also expand on some features previously covered in order to point out the differences between the single server runtime in WAS V5 and the multi-server runtime in WAS-ND V5.

## WebSphere Architecture Terms

The definition of a server, node, and cell are the same in WAS-ND as in WAS, but before discussing the additional terms that apply to WAS-ND, let's briefly review the definitions for these three constructs.

### Server

As noted before, an application server is a Java Virtual Machine that hosts user-written J2EE applications.

### Node

A node is generally a single physical computer system on which an application server resides. A node is usually a single machine, but some hardware can use partitions or regions that mimic multiple machines. WAS allows for more than one application server to be configured on a given node, but in WAS base, each of these servers is "standalone" and is managed independently, while in WAS-ND, multiple servers can be configured and managed centrally. In WAS, a node name is normally the same as the host name for the computer.

### Cell

A cell is an administrative configuration notion construct. In WAS base, the cell is composed of one node and a single application server, which differs from WAS-ND, where the cell can consist of one or more nodes, each with one or more application servers.

### Cluster

A cluster is multiple application servers running the same application(s) that have been logically combined for purposes of work load management (WLM), which can be centrally administered in WAS-ND. In a cluster, there can be multiple application servers on a single node (vertical clustering), an application server running on all or some nodes in a cell (horizontal clustering), or a combination of vertical and horizontal clustering. For those readers familiar with prior versions of WAS, a V5 WAS-ND cluster is analogous to a WAS V4 Server Group or a WAS V3.x Model from which application server clones were created. Since WLM and clustering are such a significant portion of what is provided by WAS-ND over WAS base, we've devoted an entire chapter to the WAS-ND WLM architecture and cluster management later in this book.

### Managed Processes

The last architectural term with WAS-ND V5 is "managed processes." Briefly, all WAS processes are called managed servers or managed processes, meaning that all are part of a single administrative domain (cell) and as a result can be centrally managed and monitored. In WAS-ND, the following are managed processes:

- Deployment manager
- Node agent
- Application server
- JMS server

## Runtime Architecture

### Deployment Manager

In WAS-ND, the deployment manager (Dmgr) process provides a centralized administration mechanism for all nodes in a cell, including all WAS processes on each node as well as the cell configuration repository for both WAS and installed applications. The Dmgr works in conjunction with each node agent to control processes on each node and to maintain the configuration for each node. By providing a central point for management, the Dmgr allows you to control cells consisting of numerous nodes and, in turn, nodes running one or more servers. The Dmgr and the administration clients are depicted in Figure 20-1.

The same administration clients (the admin console browser client and the wsadmin command-line client) that are used to administer an application server in WAS base are used to administer a WAS cell via the Dmgr. Unlike an application server, the deployment manager is only intended to be used for administration purposes, and not for hosting user applications.

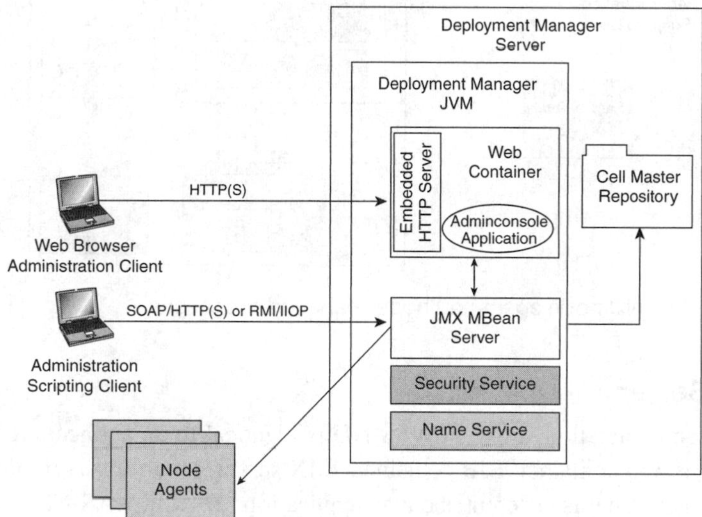


**Figure 20-1** WAS-ND deployment manager and clients.

## Node Agent

As implied by its name, a node agent is a local administrative agent process running on every node in a WAS-ND cell. The node agent serves as the local proxy for deployment manager, providing the ability to operationally manage servers and the configuration for servers defined on a node. As is the case with all WAS V5 managed processes, the node agent contains a name service, a security server, and a JMX server. While the wsadmin command-line client can connect directly to a node agent,[1] as shown in Figure 20-2, only the AdminControl functions are available. This is to guard against configuration changes being made local to a node with either AdminConfig or AdminApp that differ from the master configuration maintained by the deployment manager. Intended solely as an administrative process, the node agent does not provide a J2EE application runtime.

1 This is accomplished by specifying the host name and port for the node agent as command-line arguments when invoking wsadmin.

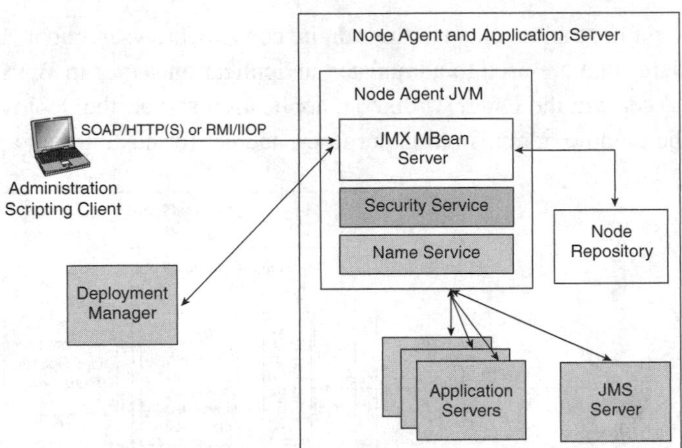


**Figure 20-2** WAS-ND node agent and node-managed processes.

## Application Server

Architecturally, an application server in WAS-ND is identical to an application server in WAS base, containing a web container, EJB container, JMX server, security server, name server, and transaction manager. What is different about an application server in WAS-ND is the removal of the admin console application, this application runs instead in the deployment manager, and the delegation of some of the administrative MBeans to the node agent and deployment manager. As is the case with a node agent, if you choose to connect the wsadmin client directly to the JMX server in an application server, only the AdminControl functions are available.

## JMS Server

This is the server that hosts the WebSphere Embedded Messaging Service on a node. In WAS-ND, there can be one JMS server per node.[2] As with the other runtime components described previously, the JMS server is managed via JMX.

## Administration Clients

WAS-ND utilizes the same administration clients that are available in WAS base—a web browser-based administration client or the wsadmin command-line scripting client, both of which interact with the JMX server running inside the deployment manager[3] as opposed to the application server in WAS. As is the case with WAS base, the admin console is available on port 9090 on the server running the Dmgr (or 9443 when running secured) and is invoked from a browser with the URL http://hostname:9090/admin.

2 In WAS base, the JMS server runs as part of the application server process.

3 Recall from earlier in the chapter that wsadmin can also be directed to the JMX server running in any specific managed process by specifying the host and port number for the process as command-line arguments when invoking wsadmin.

What differs in the admin console and wsadmin in WAS-ND is the exposure of additional functions that are required to manage an entire cell topology. The additional functions in the admin console are highlighted in Figure 20-3.

As with WAS base, when logging in to the admin console application in WAS-ND, a workspace is created for the user ID supplied, and all configuration changes are made in the workspace until the changes are saved to the configuration repository.

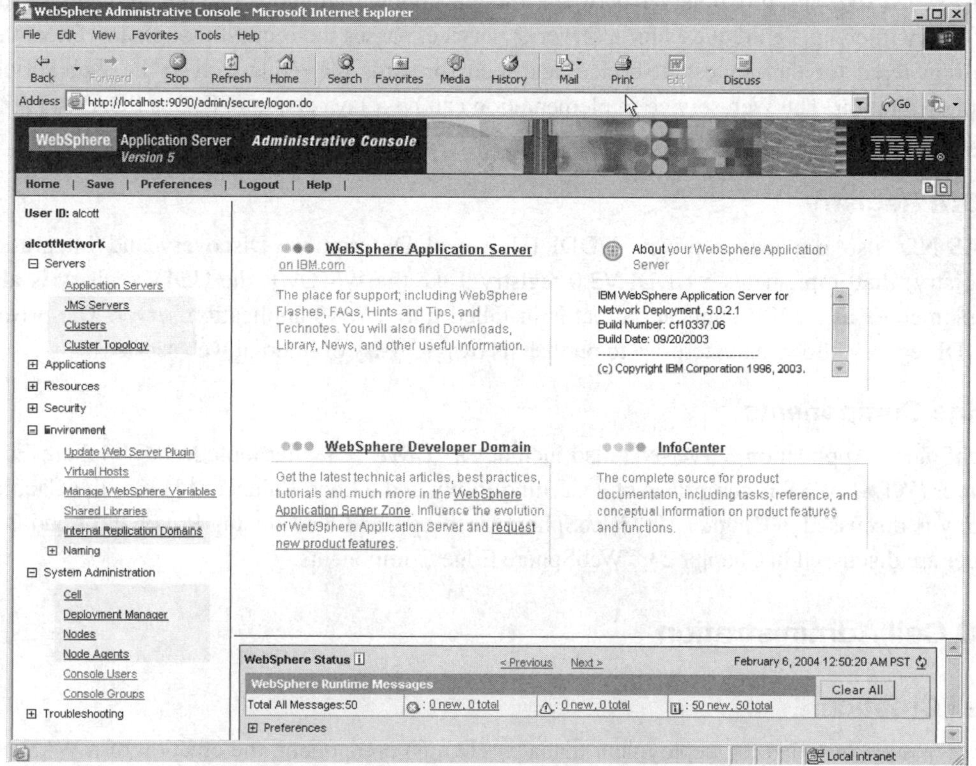


**Figure 20-3** WAS-ND admin console.

The creation of a workspace per user ID, which occurs with both the browser console and wsadmin, allows for multiple users to make changes to a function that is useful in a WAS-ND cell with multiple servers and applications. WAS relies on an optimistic concurrency mode, so if changes are made by multiple users to the same configuration artifact, say, the configuration for a given application server, the admin console application will provide a warning of a save conflict. This was previously depicted in Chapter 5, "WebSphere Application Server Architecture." In this same situation, wsadmin will throw a com.ibm.websphere.management.exception.ConfigServiceException. In a large environment, manual procedures likely need to be employed to ensure the separation of work by multiple administrators so that the changes made by one administrator do not conflict with simultaneous changes being made by another administrator.

## Web Services in WAS-ND

### Web Services Gateway

The Web services gateway (WS-Gwy) is a J2EE application included with WAS-ND that serves as a proxy for Web service requests by providing a mechanism to configure a mapping for a WSDL (Web Services Definition Language) service request to another service request and transport. Much like any proxy server between a client application and the application server, the WS-Gwy intercepts all requests for a server or service, passes the request though any filters that are registered for the requested service, and then forwards the request on to the Web service implementation. The Web service implementation can be a Java class, an EJB, a SOAP server, a SOAP/JMS server, or even another gateway.

### UDDI Registry

WAS-ND also provides a private UDDI (Universal Description, Discovery and Integration Registry) that implements a UDDI V2.0 registry. Like the WS-Gwy, the UDDI registry is also implemented as a J2EE application that is installed into a WAS application server. The private UDDI registry allows an enterprise to publish its own registry of internal web services.

### Edge Components

WebSphere Application Server-ND also includes a "DMZ" CD that includes WebSphere Edge Server (WES). WES is comprised of a Caching Proxy and a Load Balancer.[4] Use of the Caching Proxy is discussed in Chapter 19, "WebSphere Caching," and the Caching Proxy and Load Balancer are discussed in Chapter 23, "WebSphere Edge Components."

## ND Cell Administration

### Cell Creation

Once you've installed the deployment manager (Dmgr) component, the creation of a WAS-ND cell is basically a two-step operation. The first step is to start the Dmgr, which is accomplished by opening an OS shell, navigating to the bin directory under the installation root for the deployment manager (e.g., /opt/WebSphere/DeploymentManger/bin), and running the startManager (bat/sh) command,[5] which is depicted in Figure 20-4.

4 The Load Balancer component was known in prior versions of WES as the Network Dispatcher.

5 On Windows, the deployment manager or any WAS-managed process can also be configured to run as a Windows Service.

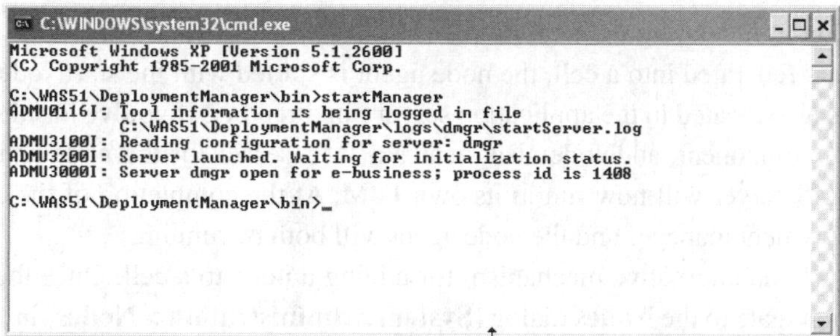


**Figure 20-4** Starting the deployment manager.

Once the Dmgr is running, you'll need to open an OS shell and navigate to the bin directory under the installation root on a node where WAS base (the application server) is installed (e.g., /opt/WebSphere/ApplicationServer/bin) and run the addNode command. The addNode utility adds a standalone node to an existing cell. The command syntax is: addNode <deployment manager host> <deployment manager port>, though the port argument is not required if you are using the default port of 8879. This is depicted in Figure 20-5.[6]

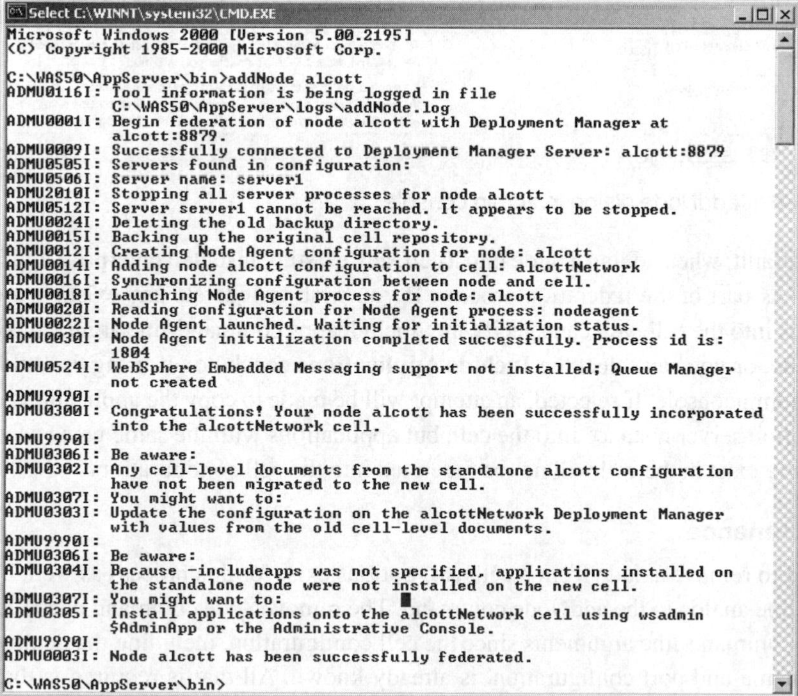


**Figure 20-5** Node Federation via the addNode command.

6 Since all nodes are equally trusted, you shouldn't add a node unless you trust the people that own the machine; otherwise, you could compromise the WAS security domain.

In addition to federating the node to the cell, addNode also starts the node agent process. After the node is federated into a cell, the node agent is started with the startNode (bat/sh) command, which is also located in the application server bin directory. If you've installed the Embedded Messaging component, addNode also creates a JMS server for the node and configures it. The internal JMS server will now run in its own JVM. At the completion of the addNode command, the deployment manager and the node agent will both be running.

There's also an alternative mechanism for adding a node to a cell. Once the Dmgr is running, you can navigate to the **Nodes** dialog (**System Administration > Nodes**) in the admin console and invoke the **addNode** dialog, which is depicted in Figure 20-6. To use this dialog, the application server process must be running on the target node in order to have a local agent[7] that can run the commands required to federate a node into a cell and create and start the node agent. As can be seen, this dialog requires that you enter the host name of the node to be added into the cell.

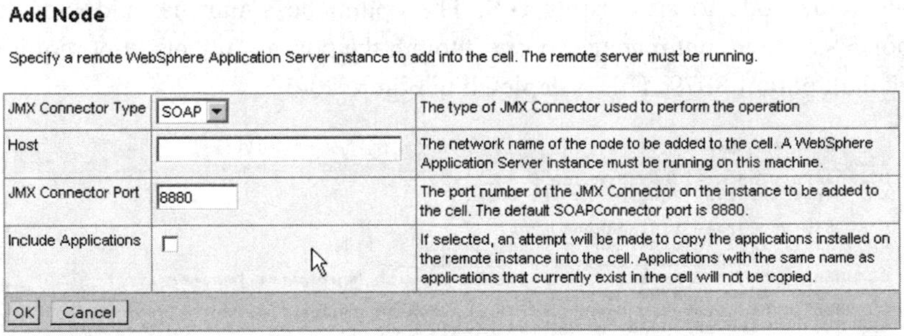

**Add Node**

Specify a remote WebSphere Application Server instance to add into the cell. The remote server must be running.

| | | |
|---|---|---|
| JMX Connector Type | SOAP | The type of JMX Connector used to perform the operation |
| Host | | The network name of the node to be added to the cell. A WebSphere Application Server instance must be running on this machine. |
| JMX Connector Port | 8880 | The port number of the JMX Connector on the instance to be added to the cell. The default SOAPConnector port is 8880. |
| Include Applications | ☐ | If selected, an attempt will be made to copy the applications installed on the remote instance into the cell. Applications with the same name as applications that currently exist in the cell will not be copied. |

OK Cancel

**Figure 20-6** addNode dialog in admin console.

By default, when adding a node into a cell, any existing installed enterprise applications are uninstalled as part of the federation process. If you wish to federate any existing user-installed applications into the cell, you can specify the -includeapps command-line argument when invoking addNode, or you can select the **Include Applications** check box if using the **Add Node** dialog in the adminconsole. If selected, an attempt will be made to copy the applications installed on the application server instance into the cell, but applications with the same name as applications that currently exist in the cell will not be federated into the cell configuration.

## Cell Maintenance

If you need to remove a node from a cell, two options exist for this process as well. The first is a command line analog to the addNode command. The removeNode command doesn't require any additional command-line arguments since the cell configuration, including the deployment manager host name and port configuration, is already known. All that is required is that the Dmgr process be running. The second option is to use the **Remove Node** dialog in the admin console

7 The addNode command starts a process to serve as the local agent in the first procedure described for node federation.

(**System Administration > Nodes**). This second option requires that the node agent be running on the node to be removed.

## Namespace

In WAS-ND V5, there is a single logical namespace across a cell, which is implemented as a distributed namespace with a CORBA CosNaming server running in the deployment manager, node agent, and Server processes. As a result, most applications read from an application server image[8] of the namespace, which consists of persistent elements that are read upon server startup from the local XML document-based configuration repository, as well as transient namespace elements that are programmatically bound. Since lookup operations are performed locally by the name server running in an application server, no support is required from the deployment manager or the node agent.

While this provides for a robust and fault-tolerant name service, since there is no single point of failure for the name service, there is one significant implication resulting from the specifics of the name service implementation. Named objects running in a server are bound to the server root context for that particular server. The result is that the qualified names for objects registered in the namespace, which are automatically generated by the system, are topology-based names, meaning the names have elements of the server topology embedded within them. The result is that the lookup names will change if you move the target object to a different location in the topology, such as to a different server or to a different cluster. The result of this is depicted in Figure 20-7.

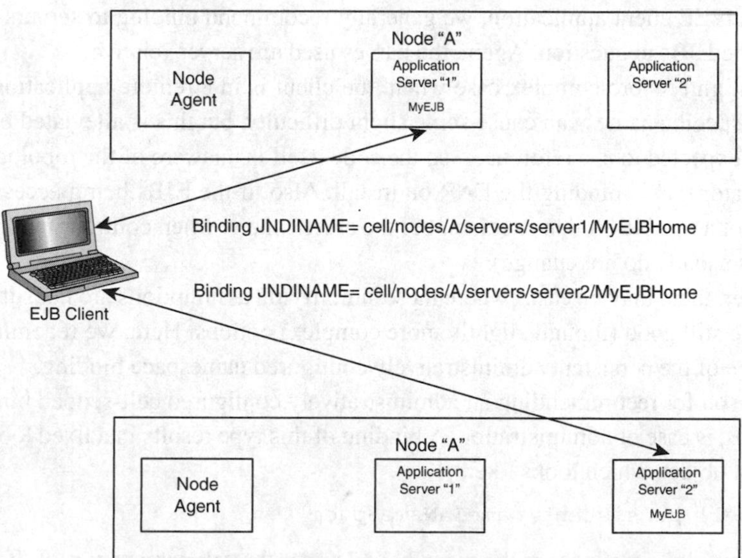


**Figure 20-7** Topology-dependent JNDI names in WAS-ND.

8 In fact, binding a client to an application server and reading from the local namespace is the preferred method.

The lookup names for server objects can be either JNDI names corresponding to EJB-refs and resource-refs or the lookup names in thin clients and can take the form of:

- A relative name (name relative to server root), such as "ejb/myEjb," which is usable only when the client is in the same server or when the client is bootstrapped to the specific server containing that object.
- A server-qualified CORBA Object URL, such as "corbaname::myhost1:9812/NameServiceServerRoot#myEjb," which will always work but is typically only used for interoperability with namespaces.
- A topology-qualified name such as "cell/nodes/myNode/servers/myServer/myEjb" for a single server or "cell/clusters/myCluster/myEjb" for a cluster, both of which are created by the system when registering objects.
- A fixed name, such as "cell/persistent/myEjb," which is a cell-scoped configured name binding created by an administrator, usable from anywhere in the cell.

At first glance, this would seem to negate all of the advantages that a distributed namespace provides since, for purposes of fault tolerance and scalability, most applications are deployed to a WAS cluster of application servers, and the multiple JNDI bindings that result from a context root-specific naming implementation would seem to preclude a single common binding for an object deployed in a cluster.

Fortunately, the situation is not as bleak as it appears at first glance. First, in most situations, the client of an EJB is in the same application server and thus uses server-relative names. If the client is a J2EE client application, we generally recommend binding to servers in the cluster that contain the EJBs in question. Again, the names used are server-relative.

In the slightly more complex case where the client is in a remote application server, then the topology-specific names can cause some slight difficulty, but this is alleviated by a few facts. First, code is expected to use references, so the code itself is unaware of the topology issues, just the administrator that is binding the EAR on install. Also, if the EJBs being accessed are in the cluster, it is not a terrible burden to remember the cluster name when configuring the clients (and cluster names usually do not change).

However, there may be cases where these simplifying assumptions are not sufficient. If that is so, there are still good (though slightly more complex) options. Here, we recommend that you take advantage of the persistent administratively configured namespace binding.

The reason for recommending an administratively configured cell-scoped binding, such as one for an EJB, is ease of administration. A binding of this type results in a fixed lookup name for an application object, which looks like:

```
cell/persistent/nameInNameSpace
```

Here, nameInNameSpace is the name bound under the cell persistent root. If you move the target object to a different location in the topology, then you must update the configured binding, but all applications that reference the configured binding name remain unaffected. As a result, the change only requires one administrative action instead of possibly several corresponding to each application that uses the object. The value of this should become clear in the following example.

## Persistent Namespace Bindings

The fixed bindings mentioned previously make it possible to administratively configure a cell-scoped binding. These bindings can represent an

- EJB in a server in the cell
- A CORBA object that can be identified with a corbaname URL
- Any object bound in WebSphere namespace accessible with JNDI
- A string constant

These configured name bindings can be relative to:

- The server root
- The node-persistent root
- The cell-persistent root

To configure a binding in the administrative console, navigate to **Environment > Name Space > Name Space Bindings** and then be sure to specify cell scope for the binding, as shown in Figure 20-8.

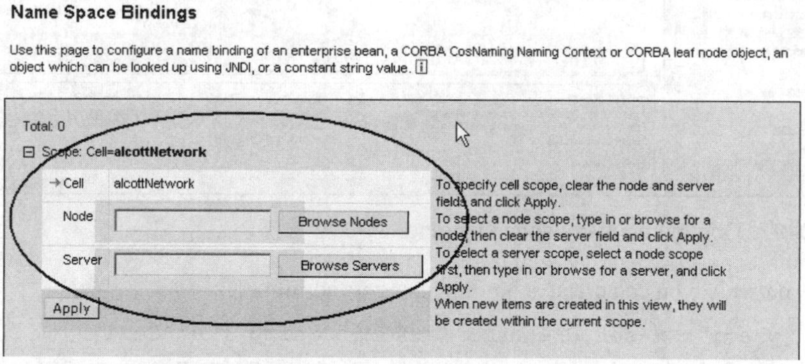

**Name Space Bindings**

Use this page to configure a name binding of an enterprise bean, a CORBA CosNaming Naming Context or CORBA leaf node object, an object which can be looked up using JNDI, or a constant string value.

Total: 0

Scope: Cell=**alcottNetwork**

Cell alcottNetwork

Node Browse Nodes

Server Browse Servers

Apply

To specify cell scope, clear the node and server fields and click Apply.
To select a node scope, type in or browse for a node, then clear the server field and click Apply.
To select a server scope, select a node scope first, then type in or browse for a server, and click Apply.
When new items are created in this view, they will be created within the current scope.

**Figure 20-8** Name Space Bindings configuration dialog.

To create a new binding, click **New** and then select the appropriate type. We'll assume that, for purposes of discussion, it's an **EJB**. Click **Next** and then enter following information:

- Binding Identifier (a unique name used as a label)
- Name in the Namespace (JNDI name of EJB expected by legacy clients)
- Enterprise Bean location (server's node name if single server)

- Server (server name or cluster name)
- JNDI name (JNDI name of EJB as bound in V5)

Click on **Next**, then **Finish**, and then save your configuration. The result is depicted in Figure 20-9.

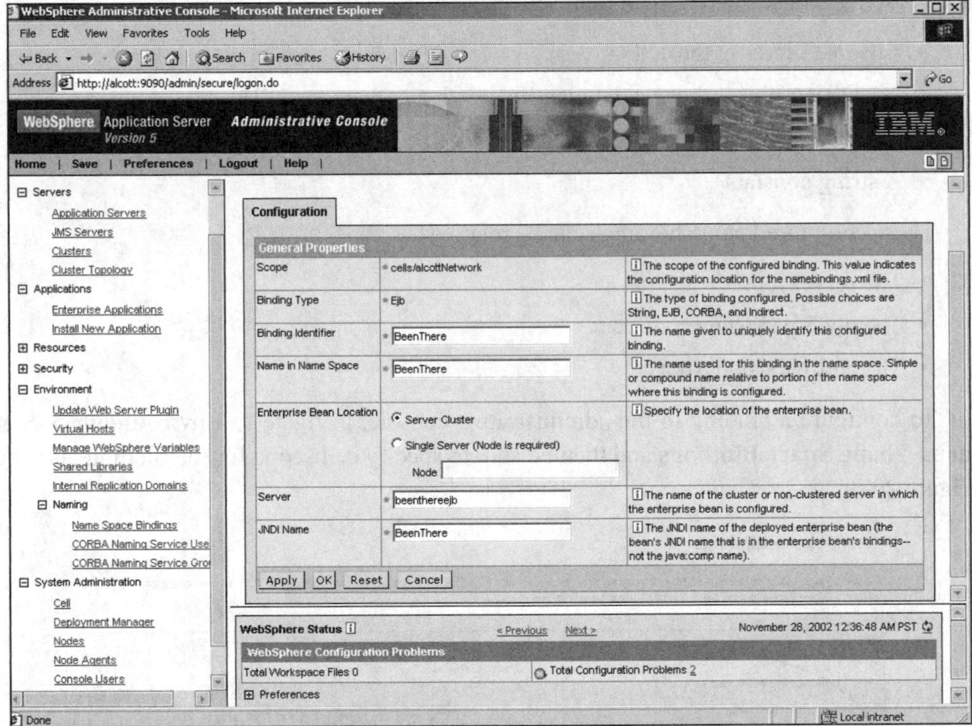

**Figure 20-9** Configured Namespace binding.

Alternatively, you can create a binding using wsadmin:

```
wsadmin > set CELLNAME [ $AdminConfig list Cell]
wsadmin. $AdminConfig create EjbNameSpaceBinding CELLNAME
➥{{name UNIQUENAME} {nameInNameSpace EJBNAME}
➥{bindingLocation SINGLESERVER} {applicationServerName
➥SERVERNAME} {applicationNodeName NODENAME} {ejbJndiName
➥EJBNAME}}
```

## Distributed Replication Service

As implied by its name, the Distributed Replication Service (DRS)[9] is a runtime component in WAS-ND that is used to replicate data among distributed processes in a WAS cell. In WAS-ND V5, DRS can either be used as a failover mechanism for HTTP Session objects, as discussed in Chapter 22, "Session Management," or to replicate dynacache entries, as described in Chapter 19.

### DRS Concepts

Before we discuss configuring DRS and topology options, we need to outline the various components that comprise DRS as well as some terms relating to its use.

The first term is *replica*. A replica is nothing more than an in-memory copy of data. If one server updates a piece of cached data, it will be replicated to other replicas on other servers. Servers maintain their own data as well as replicas depending on the configuration.

The second term is *replicator*. A replicator is a WAS-ND runtime component that is responsible for data transfers between members of a replication domain. That is, it copies data to replicas. By default, a replicator is associated with each application server, but as we'll see, it's not required that an application server have a replicator defined in order for it use DRS.

The last term is *replication domain*, which is a grouping of application servers that are associated with each other for the purpose of sharing replicated data. When application servers are configured as members of a replication domain for purposes of sharing data, they serve as a "client" of other servers in terms of receiving replicated data from another server (or servers), a "server" where they send out replicated data to client application servers in the domain, or both. By default, all members of a domain are both a client and a server ("both" mode), meaning they both send and receive data from other members of the domain (this is also know as peer-to-peer).[10] Aside from the default, we can also configure a server to be only a client or only a server.

When dealing with HTTP session, there is also the notion of *partitions*. A partition is a group within a replication domain to which an HTTP session object can be assigned. The number of groups is inclusive for the entire replication domain and all session managers connected to the replication domain via any of the replicators in that domain. By default, there are ten partitions,[11] and when an HTTP session is created, the session manager does round-robin assignment of the session to one of the groups. At the session manager level, the session manager can be configured when in either "server" or "both" mode to listen to a subset of the groups. By default, it listens to all of them, which allows you to "partition" where an HTTP session is replicated.

9 DRS is sometimes also referred to as WebSphere Internal Messaging.

10 When using DRS with distributed sessions, the runtime mode can be "both," "client," or "server," while the corresponding modes for DRS with the Dynamic Cache Service (Dynacache) are "Both push and pull," "pull only," and "push only." By default, with dynacache, the mode is "not shared," meaning no replication.

11 Ten partitions is the recommended minimum for performance reasons.

## DRS Topologies

DRS can be configured into many different and complex topologies based upon configuration values for the replication domains. Here, we will discuss the four basic topologies. These topologies can be combined in various ways to create even more complex topologies, although we do not recommend this, as increasing system complexity is generally not a good idea. After we discuss the topologies and their configuration, we'll discuss some tradeoffs to help you select an appropriate topology.

As mentioned, there are two modes for servers in a DRS domain, one in which a server is both a client and a server ("both" or "peer-to-peer") and one in which a server is either a client or a server. We'll start our discussion of DRS configurations with "peer-to-peer," in which each application server in a replication domain holds a copy of the replicated data for all other application servers in the same replication domain. In addition, each server also has a replicator; this is shown in Figure 20-10.[12]

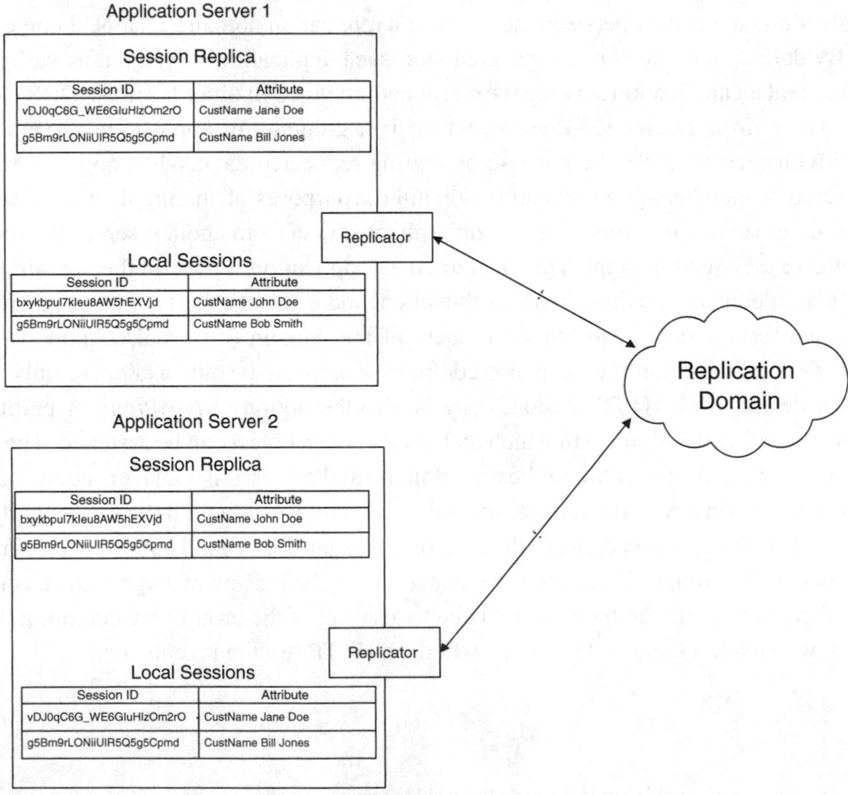


**Figure 20-10** DRS peer-to-peer configuration.

12 We've chosen to depict HTTP Session objects as being replicated, but the replicated data could also be dynacache entries.

The second option is a variant of peer-to-peer, where the replicator process is running in another application server (or servers for redundancy). This is depicted in Figure 20-11.

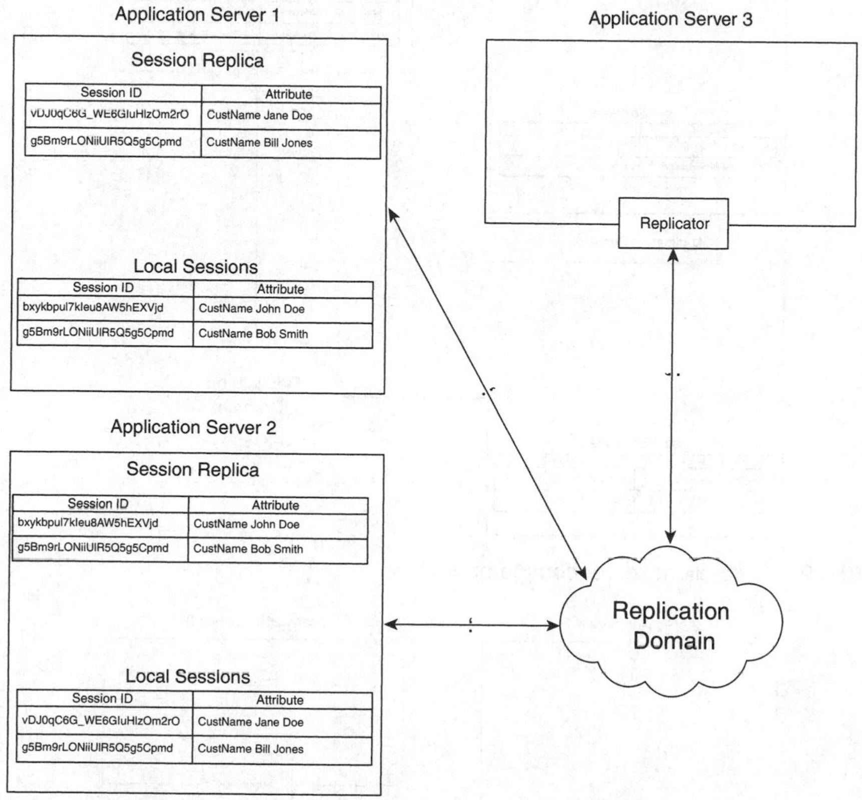


**Figure 20-11** DRS peer-to-peer configuration with separate replicator server.

The third option for memory-to-memory replication is a "client server" configuration, in which some servers are configured as clients (these are typically the application servers where applications are running) and some application servers run as dedicated replication servers, as shown in Figure 20-12.

The last configuration is client server with dedicated replicators and dedicated replicas, where each application server maintains just the session object for requests to that application server, with application servers running the replicator process and additional application servers storing copies of the session objects for the replication domain. This is depicted in Figure 20-13.

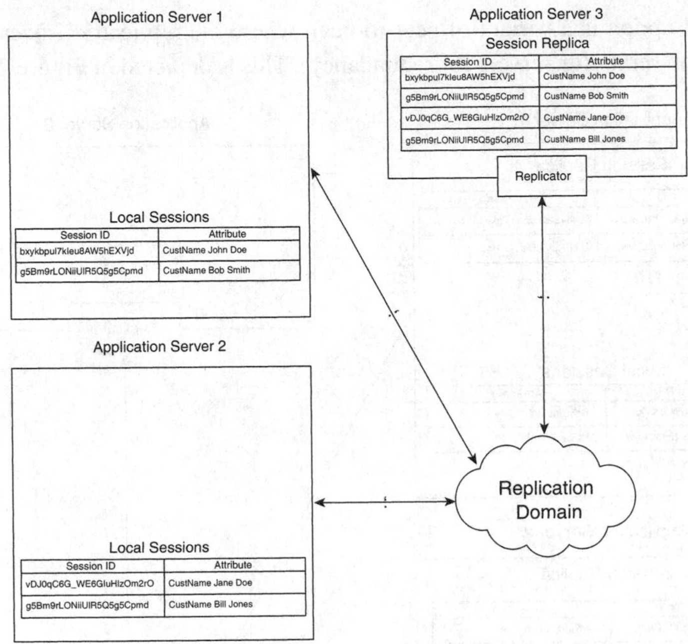


**Figure 20-12** DRS client server configuration.

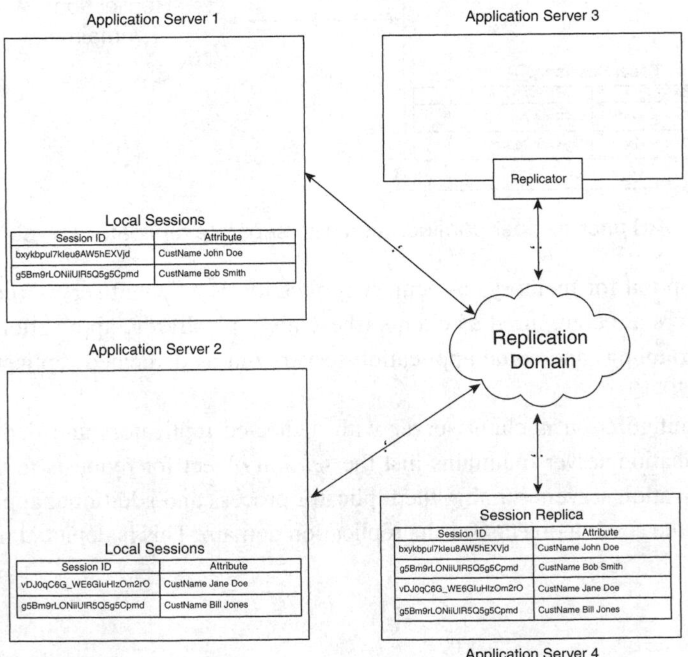


**Figure 20-13** DRS client server configuration with separate replication server.

## DRS Configuration

The first step in configuring DRS is the definition of a replication domain. There are two mechanisms for creating a replication domain, though the specifics of doing so will vary based on which of the four DRS deployment options you choose. Starting with peer-to-peer, the first and easiest option is to select the check box specifying that a replication domain be created when creating a server cluster. This is depicted in Figure 20-14.

**Create New Cluster**

Create New Cluster

| → Step 1 : Enter Basic Cluster Information | | |
|---|---|---|
| Cluster name: | * SessionCluster | The name of this cluster. |
| Prefer local: | ☑ Prefer local enabled | Enable or disable Node scoped routing optimization. |
| Internal replication domain: | ☑ Create Replication Domain for this cluster | If this option is selected, a Replication Domain will be created and the name will be set as the Cluster name |

**Figure 20-14** Replication domain when creating a server cluster.

You'll then need to specify **Create Replication Entry in this Server** for each of the servers you create in the cluster as you create application servers in the cluster, as shown in Figure 20-15.

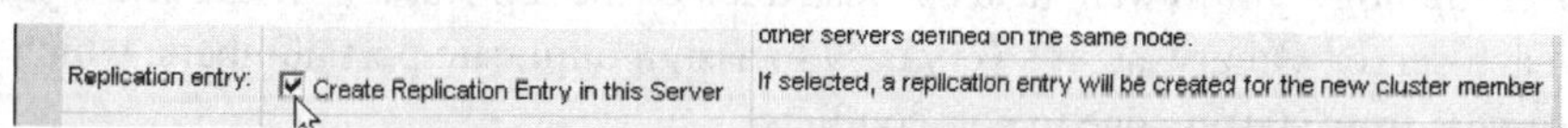
other servers defined on the same node.
Replication entry:
Create Replication Entry in this Server
If selected, a replication entry will be created for the new cluster member

**Figure 20-15** Application Server Replicator Entry.

Understanding the two attributes just discussed are essential for the deploying more advanced DRS configurations. As noted previously, an application server can be a member of a replication domain but does not necessarily have to serve as a replicator. So in some of the more advanced topologies, you'll configure application servers that are part of the replication domain that are not replicators, while other application servers will be replicators.

The second mechanism for configuring a replication domain is a bit more involved, so you're encouraged to create a replication domain as part of the server cluster definition process, at least when you're first learning this technology. In the event you're unable to plan for the eventuality in advance, you'll first need to create a replication domain. This is performed by navigating to the **Internal Replication Domains** dialog located under **Environment** in the web administration console, as shown in Figure 20-16, and then selecting **New**.

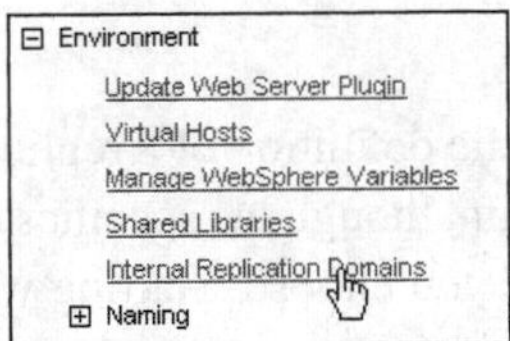


**Figure 20-16** WAS internal replication domains in admin console.

This launches the configuration dialog for the replication domain. You'll need to specify the name for your domain and select **apply**. The **Replicator Entries** will appear as an **Additional Property** at the bottom of the configuration dialog, as illustrated in Figure 20-17.

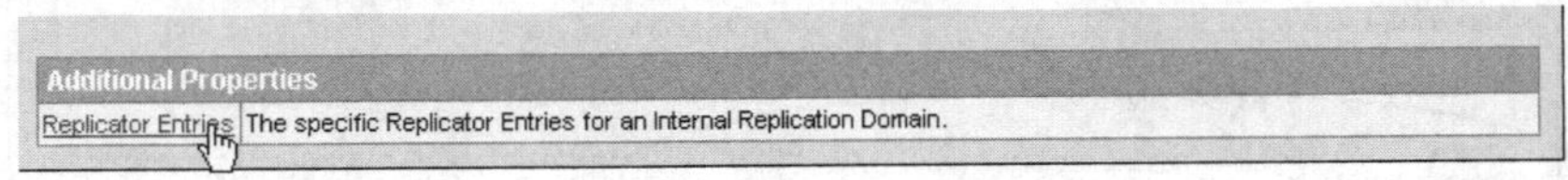


**Figure 20-17** Adding Replicator Entries.

After selecting **Replicator Entries**, you'll then need to specify **New** on the resulting dialog and proceed to add existing servers to the replication domain, as shown in Figure 20-18. When configuring a server to be a replicator, a word of caution is in order. If you're configuring more than one server to act as a replicator on a single node, which is not uncommon for the default peer-to-peer topology, you'll want to keep close track of the replicator port and client port assignment for each server. Otherwise, it's very easy to assign duplicate port numbers, which will prevent the servers from starting due to port conflicts.

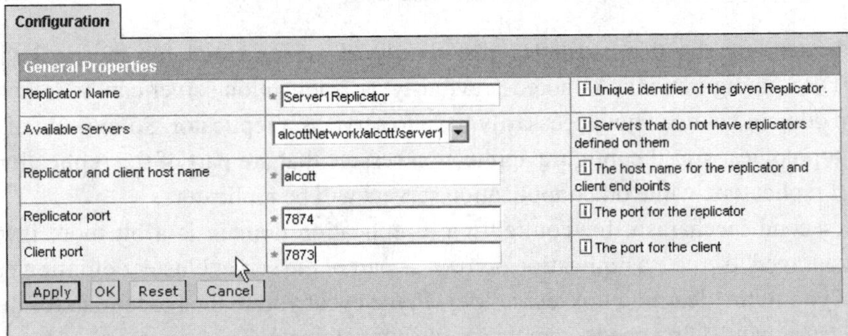


**Figure 20-18** Replicator Configuration.

By simply walking though the dialogs depicted in Figures 20-16 through 20-18 and taking the options indicated for all the servers in a cluster, you will end up with peer-to-peer configuration. The end result is a configuration like that depicted in Figure 20-10. In this configuration, the default is for the local replicator (the one on the same server) to be used for replication if it exists.

You'll note that a peer-to-peer configuration is the most redundant since every server in the cluster replicates data to every member of the replication domain. The downside to this is that as the number of servers in the domain increases, scalability and performance will tend to decrease. This is because additional memory is needed in each server to maintain the copies of the replicated data from all the other domain members, and additional CPU is required to replicate the data. As might be expected, the number and size of the replicated data objects have a direct correlation to the performance impact.

The second configuration option is to separate the replication server from the application server(s). This option requires the definition of an application server to function as the replication server and a cluster for running the application. The replication server will handle the replication between servers in the "application cluster." This will result in the configuration depicted in Figure 20-11. As with peer-to-peer, this configuration is easiest to construct during the cluster definition process. Unlike peer-to-peer, you do not define a replication domain for the "application cluster" (refer to Figure 20-14), nor do you define a replicator for each server (refer to Figure 20-15) in this cluster. Instead, you'll create a cluster without these attributes and deploy your application to that cluster. You'll then create a "replicator server," where you define the replication domain and replicator for that server.

The last step in this process is to configure either the session manager to use memory-to-memory replication (**Application Servers > "servername" > Web Container > Session Management** >) or the enable cache replication for the Dynamic Cache Service (**Application Servers > "servername" > Dynamic Cache Service**) in the admin console. Either of these will invoke the Internal Messaging dialog, as shown in Figure 20-19. As described previously, the administration server process in the deployment manager will automatically pick the first replication domain and the first replicator under that domain for the server to use.

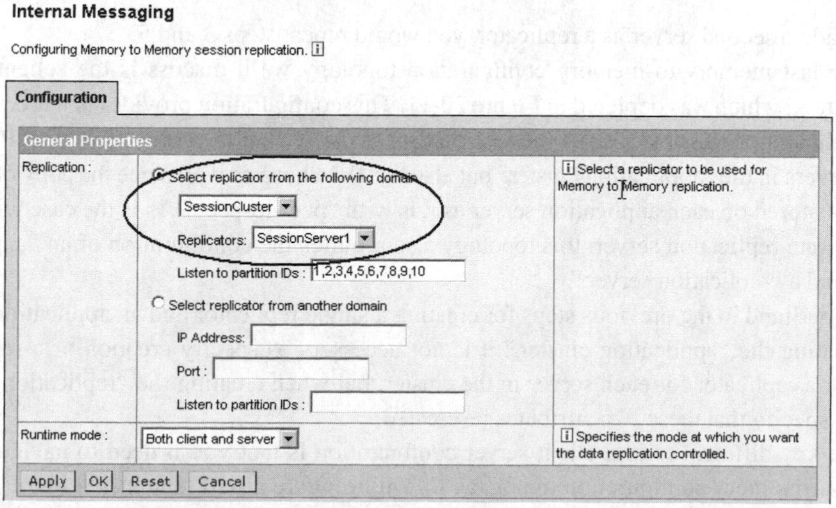

**Figure 20-19** DRS/Internal Messaging configuration for Session Manager.

In order to make the steps clearer when choosing to configure an application cluster and a replication server, let's walk through the steps as you would in the administration console:

1. Define an application server called **DRSSessionServer** with the attributes **Generate Unique HTTP ports**. This application server will be the session replication server.
2. Define a cluster called **DRSAppCluster** with the attributes **Prefer local enabled**. This cluster is where the application will run. When creating the cluster, add two application servers, **AppServerA** and **AppServerB**, with the attribute **Generate Unique HTTP ports**.
3. Navigate to **Environment > Internal Replication Domains** and create a new replication domain called **DRSAppDomain**. Then add a new replicator called **DRSSession-Replicator**, select **DRSSessionServer** as the server, enter your host name, and then enter two ports not in use for the replicator (default is 7874) and client (default is 7873).
4. Navigate to **Application Servers > AppServerA > Web Container > Session Management > Distributed Environment Settings**, choose **Memory-to-memory Replication**, and select **DRSAppDomain** for the domain and **DRSSessionReplicator** as the replicator and **Both client and server** for the runtime mode. Repeat these steps for **AppServerB**.
5. Navigate to **Application Servers > DRSSessionServer > Web Container > Session Management > Distributed Environment Settings**, choose **Memory-to-memory Replication**, and select **DRSAppDomain** as the domain and **DRSSessionServer** as the replicator.
6. Install an application to **DRSAppCluster**, update the Web server Plug-in, and then start the **DRSReplicationServer** and the **DRSAppCluster**.

To add a second server as a replicator, you would repeat steps 3 and 5.

The last memory-to-memory configuration topology we'll discuss is the "client server" configuration, which was depicted in Figure 20-11. This configuration provides isolation not only of the replicator process but also of the session data as well, which not only frees up CPU cycles for the servers in the "application cluster" but also the JVM heap as well since the copy of the session is not stored on each application server as it is with "peer-to-peer." As is the case with creating a separate replication server, this topology also requires the configuration of an "application cluster" and a "replication server."

As outlined in the previous steps for creating a single replicator and an application cluster, when creating the "application cluster," it is not necessary to specify creation of a replication domain or a replicator for each server in the cluster, but when creating the "replication cluster," you must specify that these two attributes be created.

The key differences in a client server configuration is that you'll need to navigate to the Memory-to-memory configuration dialog, as shown in Figure 20-20 (and step 4 in the previous example), and specify a Runtime Mode of Client only for the servers in the application cluster and a Runtime Mode of Server only for the replication server.[13]

If you have defined multiple replication domains, you will also need to specify the replication domain to be used by each of the servers in the "application cluster," and optionally, you can specify an explicit server to be used in the replication domain. Again, this is depicted in Figure 20-20. Since you'll likely want to provide for failover of the replication server in this scenario, it's recommended that you do the following:

- Create multiple application servers for replication. You can do this either by adding servers to your replication domain or by creating a server cluster of replication servers (you would create this cluster as you would any other application server cluster).
- Assuming you create multiple replication servers, then you should distribute the replication clients (application servers in the "application cluster") equally across the replicators (application servers in the "replication cluster"). Otherwise by default, the clients will select the first replicator in the domain since both replication servers are doing work anyway (and not acting as a hot standby).

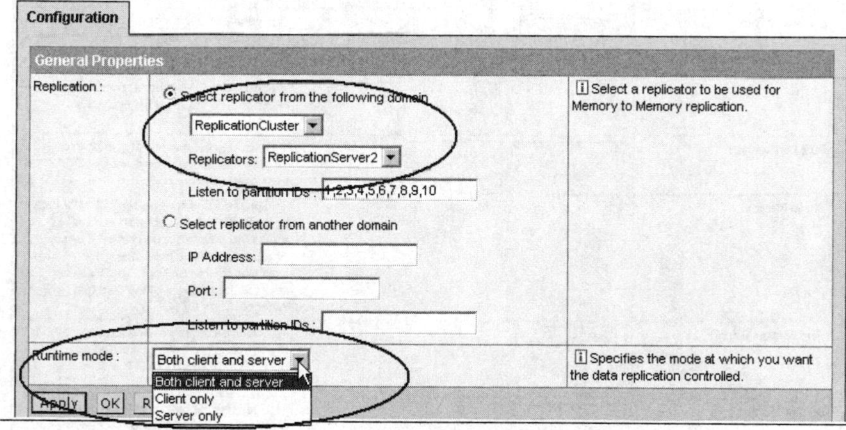


**Figure 20-20** Explicit replication server definition.

## Tuning DRS

Before leaving the subject of memory-to-memory replication, there are some tuning and configuration options that are specific to this mechanism that need to be covered, which were depicted in Figure 20-18. The dialog shown is specific to each replication domain you've defined and can be reached by navigating to **Environment > Internal Replication Domains** in the admin console and then selecting the domain of interest.

13 The options mentioned are for distributed sessions; recall that with the Dynamic Cache Service, the options are "Both push and pull," "pull only," and "push only."

First, there's an option to change the request timeout between domain members, which defaults to 5 seconds. It's not likely that you'll need to tune this, but if you choose to do so, you'll want to do so with care; otherwise, you'll be adding additional latency into requests between replication domain members, which will translate into application performance latency. The reason increasing the timeout translates into increased latency is because this increases the amount of time that will occur before a domain member stops trying to contact another member. As an example, if you increase the timeout to 60 seconds from the default of 5, then requests can stall for 60 seconds, not just 5.

The next parameter is the encryption type, which defaults to none, with options for DES and Triple DES. Unless the information being saved in session is of absolutely no value, you'll likely want to specify DES encryption, which should suffice for most cases unless the information is extremely sensitive, in which case Triple DES should be specified.

| Name | * ReplicationCluster | Specifies a name for the replication domain. |
|---|---|---|
| Request Timeout | * 5 | Specifies the number of seconds that a replicator will wait when requesting information from another replicator before giving up and assuming the information does not exist. The default is 5 seconds. |
| Encryption Type | * NONE | Specifies the type of encryption used before transfer. The options include\: NONE, DES, TRIPLE_DES. The default is NONE. The DES and TRIPLE_DES options encrypt data sent between WebSphere processes and better secure the network joining the processes. |
| DRS partition size | * | Specifies the number of groups into which a replication domain will be partitioned. |
| Single Replica | ☐ | Specifies that a single replication of data be made. Enable this option if you are replicating data to support retrieval of an HttpSession should the process that maintains the HttpSession fail. This option restricts the recipient of the data to a single instance. |
| Serialization Method | * BYTES | Specifies the object serialization method to use when replicating data. The options are\: OBJECT and BYTES. The default is BYTES. |
| DRS pool size | * | Specifies the maximum number of items allowed in a pool of replication resources. The default is 10. |
| DRS Pool Connections | ☐ | Specifies whether the data replication |

**Figure 20-21** DRS parameters dialog.

The DRS partition size is the next parameter. By default, each replication domain has 10 partitions, but this can be changed to provide some additional tuning. For example, let's take a peer-to-peer topology with three application servers. In order to evenly distribute the sessions across these servers, let's increase the number of groups to 15 and then split up which servers listen to which groups into thirds. To do so, you would specify 15 on this dialog and then go into each application server Memory-to-memory configuration dialog (refer to Figure 20-17) and configure the "listen to partition IDs" to be 1–5 for the first server, 6–10 for the second server, and 11–15 for the third server. As a result, the replica table in each application server will hold one third of the sessions from the other two servers.

You can think of "single replica" as a second type of partitioning, which is enabled by selecting the check box for this option. When this option is specified, every application server session manager connected to a replication domain will use single replica replication. This means that clients send out changes to one and only one other application server session manager (not in the same JVM), while servers only receive; those in "both" mode do both. If you choose this option, give careful consideration to how you configure your replicators as well as replication clients and servers. If you configure these to be on the same node, then the loss of one node, for either planned or unplanned reasons, will result in the loss of the session object. If you configure these to be on different nodes, then you'll need to make sure that you don't stop the node with the client and the node with the server on it at the same time during system maintenance.

As its name implies, the serialization method specifies the method of serialization used for replicating data. Two options are provided; session data can be replicated as an object or as bytes. In general, object replication is generally faster than byte replication, but it requires that class definitions be available on the receiving side. This means that all class types of the objects in the session must be defined in the classpath[14] of all application servers that use and/or store the session. On the other hand, storing session data as byte data is convenient because there is no classpath definition required on the receiving side. This option is preferred since it avoids the complexity and management challenges associated with ensuring that every application's session objects are visible on the common shared classloader for every application server. Doing so is difficult to manage (the session objects can't just be in a utility JAR file that is part of the application EAR) and can cause unexpected naming conflicts between applications since these objects are now visible to all applications.

The last two parameters on this dialog deal with pooling for connections within a replication domain. By default, pooling of connections is not enabled because with the current default topology for memory-to-memory replication is "peer-to-peer," in which every member listens to every partition in the domain. As a result, pooling connections is not beneficial. Specifying that connections be pooled is of benefit in a "client server" configuration as well as "peer-to-peer" with a single replica. This is because in peer-to-peer mode, a DRS instance both publishes and subscribes to the same set of topics on a JMS connection, and there is a flag to prevent receiving a message you send. However, if a DRS instance has multiple connections, there is nothing to prevent a message sent on a topic from one connection to be retrieved by a subscriber from another connection. As a result, we would in effect be replicating the HTTP session object to ourselves in peer-to-peer mode without specifying a single replica. In contrast with client server, you either subscribe to a topic (server) or publish (client), not both.

14 The classloader visible to the WAS runtime; e.g., lib or lib/ext.

In terms of configuration and tuning of memory-to-memory replication, the following "rules of thumb" seem to help the most:

- Once the size of all the replicated objects (the result of the object size multiplied by the number of objects) exceeds the JVM heap size, performance will degrade. At this point, the best options, aside from reducing the size of the replicated object, are either to add additional replication servers or to partition the data into specific servers, though a specific formula is not possible since performance is also somewhat dependent on the capacity of the server and client nodes.
- Pooling connections in the DRS clients and removing the replicators from the replication client JVMs helps performance.
- Tests by the WebSphere performance lab have shown that a single replicator (server) can likely handle multiple application servers, with a good ratio of about 6 or 7 to 1. Thus, in cases where you have more than 6 servers in your "application cluster," you may wish to specify the replication domain and the replicator to be used by each server in the "application cluster" in the "Internal Messaging" dialog shown in Figure 20-19. If you have fewer than 7 servers in your "application cluster," you probably won't need to perform any additional configuration. On the other hand, if you have more than 7 servers in the "application cluster," you'll likely want to use the dialog depicted in Figure 20-19 to configure explicit replicator servers for your application servers. By removing the replicator component from the application servers, this configuration frees up CPU cycles in the "application cluster" servers. However, it does require additional dedicated processes for replication in the "replication cluster," so this is likely a "zero sum game" from total CPU requirements, but it may help with performance for the "application cluster" servers. One more point from a high-availability perspective—assuming that you've specified at least two servers in your "replication cluster," if one of the replicator servers fails, the session manager will automatically switch to the next replicator in the domain.

## Conclusion

In this chapter, we introduced the architectural components that make WAS-ND different from WAS base and outlined the differences between WAS and WAS-ND implementation for a number of components that exist in both WAS versions.

CHAPTER 21

# WAS Network Deployment Clustering

The ability to cluster applications and the application servers hosting them is essential in providing a scalable and fault-tolerant infrastructure that is not constrained by a Single Point of Failure (SPOF). In Chapter 20, "WAS Network Deployment Architecture," we made brief mention of clustering and WAS-ND workload management (WLM). In this chapter, we'll delve into the underlying architecture used for clustering in WAS-ND as well as other technologies that may be required to build a truly fault-tolerant and scalable infrastructure. We'll also discuss possible deployment topologies as well as how and why you might choose one topology over another.

## WebSphere Clustering Architecture

### Hardware Clustering

Later in this chapter, we'll walk through the mechanics of creating a WAS-ND cluster as well as some maintenance for a cluster and applications installed in a cluster. First, let's discuss the underlying technologies for WAS-ND clustering and WLM. Most likely, many of you are acquainted—at least in passing—with hardware clustering. Some examples of hardware clustering products are HACMP, Veritas Cluster Server, SunCluster, HP MC/Serviceguard, and Microsoft Cluster Server. All of these are examples of high availability (HA) products that provide "process recovery" or "process failover," meaning that all the products mentioned monitor a process (or server), detect a failure, and then restart (or recover) the process on an alternate machine.

## WAS-ND Clustering

As noted in Chapter 20, a WAS-ND cluster[1] is composed of multiple application servers running the same application(s) that have been logically combined for purposes of workload management (WLM), which can be centrally administered in WAS-ND. In a cluster, there can be multiple application servers on a single node (vertical clustering) or an application server running on all or some nodes in a cell (horizontal clustering), or a combination of vertical and horizontal clustering.

In contrast to hardware clustering, WAS-ND relies on client request redirection for failover.[2] With client request redirection, a client attempts to contact a server to make a request, and when the connection to the server fails, the request is redirected to another server that is defined to the WAS-ND cluster. Since a WAS-ND cluster consists of multiple identical application servers, all able to satisfy a given client request, the expectation in the event of an outage is that at least one cluster member is available to respond to client requests. It's also worth noting that by working with multiple server instances, WAS-ND clustering provides for scalability while hardware clustering is specific to one processs instance; hence, there's no provision for scalability with hardware clustering.

WAS-ND relies on two different technologies to provide client request redirection-based WLM, both employing a plug-in. The first, and likely the most widely used technology, since most WAS applications use web clients, is in the HTTP server plug-in. An instance of the plug-in is installed with and loaded by each HTTP server. The plug-in definition of the cluster is contained in the plug-in configuration file (plugin-cfg.xml) and uses that information when dispatching requests from the HTTP server to one of the application servers in the cluster. In addition to providing for distribution of requests, the plug-in also provides for failover of requests once an application server is determined to be unavailable or not responding to requests. The second technology is a plug-in that is part of an EJB client ORB, whether the client is a standalone Java client, another EJB, or a Servlet (or JSP) in a web application that is running in an application server process remote from the application server in which the EJBs are running. As with the HTTP server plug-in, the EJB client ORB eliminates any one point of failure by dispatching requests among 1 to n application servers residing on multiple nodes. The ORB plug-in functions in a manner similar to HTTP server plug-in and will redirect requests across the cluster once a server is unavailable or not responding to requests.

## Web Container Failover

Chapter 23, "WebSphere Edge Components," details how to eliminate the HTTP server as a single point of failure by using WebSphere Edge Server to spray incoming web requests across multiple HTTP servers. Once an HTTP request has reached the HTTP server, it is necessary for a decision to be made regarding where to route the request. Whether the request should be handled

1 Recall that clusters and WLM are only available in WAS-ND and not in WAS base.

2 The deployment manager and node agent in WAS-ND provide for server process monitoring when the server is started via an administration client and will attempt a server restart but cannot restore a process that was running on one node to another node.

or passed to the WAS web container is decided by the HTTP server plug-in. Some requests for static content may be handled by the HTTP server, while requests for dynamic content and some static content will be passed to a web container running in WAS. The request flow from a web client to the web container running in an application server is outlined in Figure 21-1.

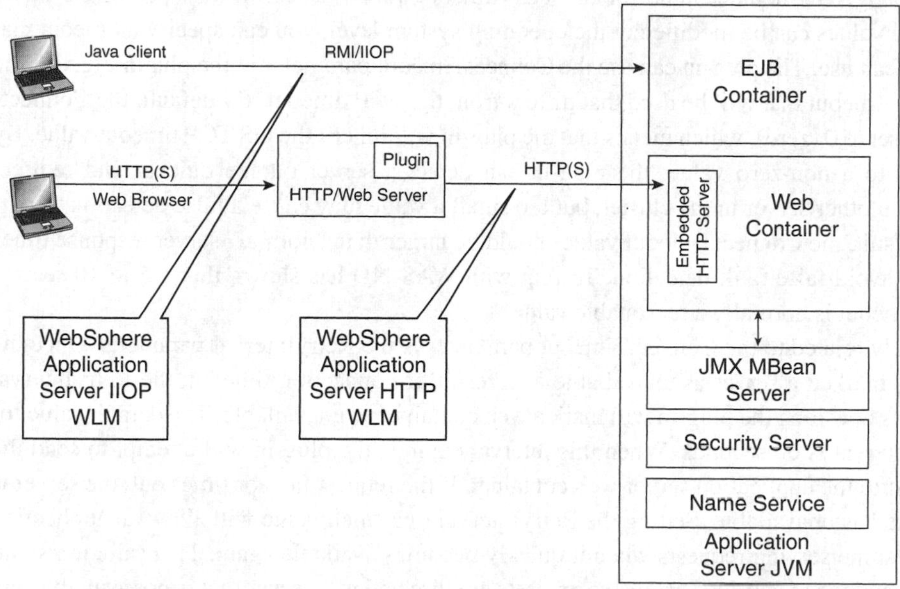


**Figure 21-1** WAS-ND client WLM types.

When a web container fails, it is the responsibility of the HTTP server plug-in to detect this failure and mark the web container unavailable. Web container failures are detected based on the TCP response values or lack of response to a plug-in request. There are four types of failover scenarios for web containers:

- **Expected outage of the application server**—The application server containing the web application is stopped from one of the administrative interfaces (admin console, wsadmin).
- **Unexpected outage of the application server**—The application server crashes for an unknown reason.
- **Expected outage of the machine**—WAS is stopped, and the machine is shut down.
- **Unexpected outage of the machine**—The machine is removed from the network due to shutdown, network failure, hardware failure, etc.

In the first two cases, the physical machine where the web container is supposed to be running will still be available, although the web container port will not be available. When this happens, the plug-in attempts to connect to the web container to process a request for a web resource, and the result is that the machine refuses to open a connection. Consequently, the plug-in quickly marks the server as unavailable. In the second two cases, however, the physical machine is no longer available to provide any kind of response. In these cases, by default, the plug-in must wait for the local operating system to timeout the TCP request before marking the server unavailable. While the plug-in is waiting for this connection to timeout, requests routed to the failed server appear to hang. The default value for the TCP timeout varies based on the operating system. While these values can be modified at the operating system level, you can specify a timeout that the plug-in can use. The plug-in can use the ConnectTimeout parameter in the plugin-cfg.xml file to specify a timeout that will be used that differs from the TCP timeout. By default, the ConnectTimeout is set to 0 (zero), which means that the plug-in will inherit the OS TCP timeout value. By setting this to a non-zero value, the plug-in can detect a server outage quicker and redirect requests to another server in the cluster, but too small a value may cause a false detection of outage. As a result, the ConnectTimeout value should be larger than "normal" server response times in order to avoid false fault detection. Testing with WAS-ND has shown that a 5 to 10 second ConnectTimeout is normally a reasonable value.

Closely related to the ConnectTimeout parameter is the RetryInterval parameter. Once the plug-in has marked a server as unavailable as a result of connection timeout, the RetryInterval then governs how long the plug-in will mark a web container as unavailable. The default value for the RetryInterval is 60 seconds. When this interval expires, the plug-in will attempt to send the next request to the application server web container. If the request fails or times out, the server is again marked as unavailable. Setting the RetryInterval to a small value will allow an application server to resume serving requests when it quickly becomes available again. That said, too small of a value can lead to spurious errors, as requests are directed to a server that is not available and the client request waits for the ConnectTimeout to elapse before redirecting the request. A reasonable value for this parameter is minimally several minutes in length. This allows sufficient time for corrective action to affect a node or application server restart. The exact value will likely depend on the automated monitoring and recovery mechanisms in place. Certainly, a value of several minutes should be adequate for an enterprise that provides on-site 24-7 operations coverage, while an enterprise that relies on paging and remote access will likely want to specify a higher value to reflect the amount of time required for corrective action.

> **NOTE**
> The RetryInterval and ConnectTimeout are process-based; thus, each process in a multi-process HTTP server, such as Apache 1.3.x or IHS 1.3.x, will block one request for ConnectTimeout seconds every RetryInterval. Better failover behavior is likely in a multi-threaded HTTP server running one (or a small number) of processes, such as Apache 2.x or IHS 2.x.

Another HTTP server plug-in parameter that has failover implications is MaxConnections,[3] which governs how many connections the plug-in will open to each web

3 MaxConnections is available in WAS V5.02 and above.

container. This is important in cases of failover. If several web containers were to fail or be taken offline, the plug-in would redirect requests to the surviving web containers. However, without a limit to the requests, the number of connections to a given web container could overwhelm the thread pool in the web container, resulting in a decrease in throughput as the web container spends more time performing process management than servicing requests. A reasonable value for MaxConnections is 20–25% greater than the maximum threads in the web container.

> **NOTE**
> The parameters just discussed are set by hand-editing the plugin-cfg.xml file for the HTTP server plug-in. If you choose to edit these parameters, be aware that those changes will be lost when the plug-in configuration file is regenerated. The next parameter, LoadBalanceWeight, can be set via the WAS admin tools and therefore does not suffer from this issue.

The last HTTP server plug-in parameter with failover and WLM implications is LoadBalanceWeight, which is specified via the weight parameter for each server in a server cluster, as depicted in Figure 21-2. This is also a new parameter in WAS V5.x, and it allows specification of request weighting so that more requests may be directed to one server in a cluster.

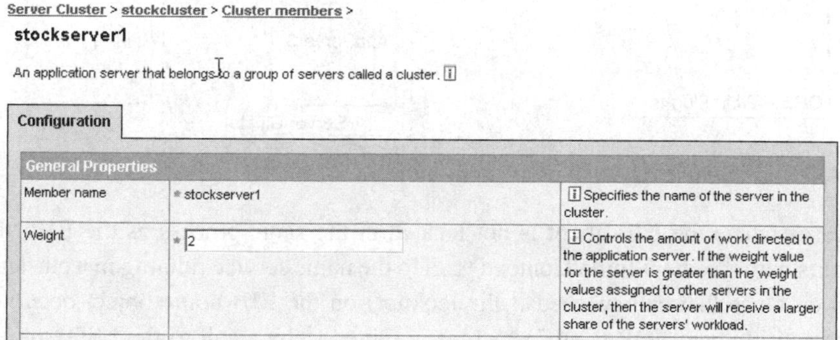


**Figure 21-2** Server Weight dialog.

Specifying that more requests, via a higher weight, be directed to one server over another (or others) in a cluster can result in performance improvements when some of the nodes in a cell have more CPUs (or faster CPUs) than other nodes in a cell. As we'll see later in this chapter, this parameter is also of use when performing application or other cell maintenance.

## EJB Container Failover

WAS also provides for failover of EJB client requests. The EJB client can be either a standalone EJB client[4] or web application components, such as Servlets or JSPs running in a web container

4 Sometimes referred to as a "fat Java client."

in another application server or EJBs[5] running in another application server.[6] Refer to Figure 21-1 for a depiction of the request flow from an EJB client to an EJB container that is covered by WAS IIOP WLM.

Although EJB container failover relies on a plug-in just as with the web container, since we're dealing with IIOP clients instead of HTTP clients, a different technology is employed. In the case of an IIOP client, the plug-in is part of the client ORB. The interaction of the client ORB plug-in and the WAS-ND runtime is depicted in Figure 21-3.

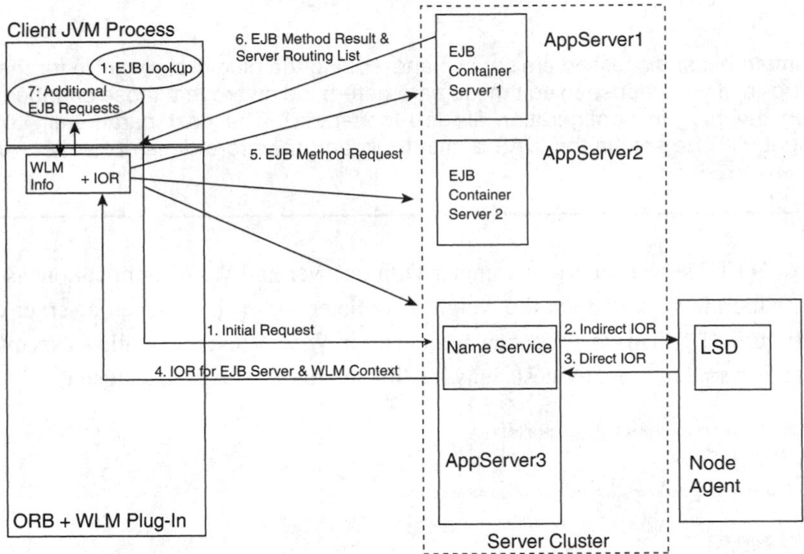


**Figure 21-3** ORB/IIOP WLM.

In cases where the EJB client is not located in the same process as the EJB, the WLM process starts with the client InitialContext() call to the name service running in a clustered application server. Once that call succeeds,[7] the lookup() on the EJB home object occurs (step 1), which returns in Indirect IOR (step 2),[8] which is routed to by a call to the LSD running in the

5 EJB – IIOP WLM in WAS-ND applies to Stateless Session EJBs and Entity EJBs. For Stateful Session EJBs, the creation of EJB home objects across the cluster is WLM'd, but once a client has affinity to a specific Stateful Session EJB, all subsequent requests are directed to that specific instance.

6 When the EJB client and EJB are located in the same process (application server JVM), WAS always selects an EJB in the local application server. WAS will never direct an EJB client request to a remote application server when a local EJB instance is available.

7 Usually, the EJB client is running within an application server in the same cell. In this case, the InitialContext creation will always succeed since this is a local in-memory call. This is not the case for standalone EJB clients. If WAS cannot contact the first server in the list, it will try the other servers, though to avoid overloading servers, the server order in this list should be varied.

8 As of WAS V5.1, if the ORB_LISTENER_ADDRESS for an application server is assigned a static (non-zero) value, then a direct Interoperable Object Reference (IOR) is returned bypassing the indirect IOR and the LSD in the node agent.

node agent[9] (this is known as "location forwarding" by the CORBA standard), which returns a direct IOR (step 3) to one of the application servers running in the cluster, which is returned to the client (step 4) along with a "WLM context" (a flag stating this EJB is WLM'd). The client gets the EJB home reference and makes his business request (step 5). On the response to the client request (step 6), WAS will return a "cluster description," which is a list of the running servers in the cluster and their direct IORs. Subsequent client requests are then distributed (assuming no affinity) to other servers running in the cluster, based on the WLM policy and WLM weights in effect. If, for some reason, step 5 fails, the ORB goes back to the LSD and gets another IOR and will continue to do so until it exhausts the cluster description list that the LSD has.

**NOTE**

To provide for failover of the bootstrap call from a client accessing a remote name service, a CORBA Object URL should be coded in the application client to specify multiple provider URLs corresponding to clustered application servers. An example of this is

```
env.put(Context.PROVIDER_URL, "corbaloc::myhost1:9810,:
➥myhost2:9810");
   Context initialContext = new InitialContext(env);
```

The EJB client ORB plug-in also has provisions for marking an EJB container as unavailable, should a request fail or timeout. At the time of this writing, the timeout is governed by OS TCP timeout. This is a result of the java.net.Socket implementation prior to J2SE (JDK) 1.4, which made no provisions for specifying how long a thread would wait when attempting to create a socket. The result is that an EJB client timeout depends on the operating system's TCP settings (e.g., for AIX, it is the tcp_keep_init parameter). While JDK 1.4 provides a mechanism for a connection timeout parameter that can be passed to a new "connect" method on the socket, WAS V5.1 made no provision for use of this feature. Fortunately, this feature is planned for a maintenance release of V5.1 in mid-2004. Until that time, the ORB plug-in will have no equivalent to the HTTP plug-in ConnectTimeout parameter. As a result, EJB clients will remain dependent on the OS TCP timeout as the limit before a connection failure occurs marking the EJB container as unavailable. As a result, careful modification of the TCP timeout using the same guidelines described previously for the ConnectTimeout is probably desirable.

If a connection is already established to a server when a machine fails (resulting in a loss of a network endpoint), then the com.ibm.CORBA.requestTimeout parameter governs (the default value is 180 seconds) how long a client will wait this length of time before a failure is detected. The default value should only be modified if an application is experiencing timeouts repeatedly, and great care must be taken to tune it properly. Too high a value will result in slow failover, while

9 The node agent LSD is clustered from a WLM perspective (for clusters only) in order to remove the node agent as a Single Point of Failure (SPOF) when dealing with indirect IORs (and cluster failover). The name servers in the node agents are not clustered; therefore, bootstrapping into a node agent would still be a SPOF, where bootstrapping to an application server cluster, as described previously, provides full failover capabilities.

with too low a value, requests will time out before the server has a chance to respond. The two most critical factors affecting the choice of a timeout value are the amount of time to process a request and the network latency between the client and server. The time to process a request in turn depends on the application and the load on the server. The network latency depends on the location of the client. For example, those clients running within the same LAN as a server may use a smaller timeout value to provide faster failover. If the client is a process inside of a WebSphere Application Server (i.e. the client is a Servlet), this property can be modified by editing the request timeout field on the Object Request Broker property sheet. If the client is a Java client, the property can be specified as a runtime option on the Java command line:

```
java -Dcom.ibm.CORBA.requestTimeout=<seconds> MyJavaClient
```

When a client request times out, new client requests will not be routed to a cluster member until new cluster information is received (for example, after the server process is restarted) or until the expiration of the com.ibm.ejs.wlm.unusable.interval, which defaults to 300 seconds. This property can be set by specifying -Dcom.ibm.ejs.wlm.unusable.interval=<seconds> on the command-line arguments for the client process. As with setting the timeout parameters noted previously, care should be taken when setting the unusable.interval parameter. If this value is set too low, meaning before corrective action can occur to restart a server, then client performance will be degraded as they attempt to direct requests to a server every unusable.interval and wait for the OS connect timeout before trying another server in the cluster. Assuming that the deployment manager and node agent remain running, the client should only mark a server as unavailable once before the cluster description is updated on the client as part of the EJB method request and response flow.

While the WAS-ND EJB WLM implementation is for the most part transparent to the application programmer, there is one notable case where application code is affected. WAS will automatically reroute requests destined for downed servers if it can accurately determine the server state, and the client won't even know it. If WAS is unable to determine the status of the request, it instead returns an exception to the caller indicating that the request failed. It must do this because the request may have been partially completed, and it is therefore inappropriate for WAS to automatically reroute the request. As a result, the application code for the client should make provisions to catch CORBA errors as described later as part of the remote method invocations and decide whether to retry the request. If the same EJB is used again, the WAS runtime will automatically reroute the request to a working server. There is no need to destroy the client handle.

For those that are interested, the state of the request is determined based upon CORBA error codes. In the cases where a client request results in an org.omg.CORBA.COMM_FAILURE or org.omg.CORBA.NO_RESPONSE, the return value of the COMPLETION_STATUS determines whether the WLM runtime can transparently redirect a request to another server. In the case of a COMPLETED_NO, the request can be rerouted since it did not succeed. If the completed status is COMPLETED_YES, no failover is required since the request was successful. If, however, a communication error was encountered during the marshalling of the response, a value of COMPLETED_MAYBE may be returned. In this case, WAS-ND cannot verify whether the request was completed successfully and cannot automatically redirect the request.

## Weighted WLM

WAS-ND V5 introduced a server weight parameter as part of the WLM mechanism for application servers in a cluster. The server weight controls the amount of work directed to the application server. If the weight value for the server is greater than the weight values assigned to other servers in the cluster, then the server receives a larger share of the server workload.

Not surprisingly, the fact that there are two plug-in technologies used for failover and WLM by WAS-ND—one for the HTTP server and another for the ORB client—has resulted in two slightly different implementations for the weighted WLM algorithms used for distributing requests.

We'll start by describing the HTTP server plug-in, where the server weights are reduced to a Least Common Denominator (LCD) and the LCD values are the basis for maintenance to the values in the routing table. This starts with the first successful browser request being routed to a cluster member and then its weight is decremented by 1. New browser requests, meaning those requests without affinity to a specific server, are then sent round robin to the other application servers and, subsequently, the weight for each application server is decremented by 1. The spreading of the load is equal between application servers until one application server reaches a weight of 0. From then on, only application servers without a weight of 0 will receive new requests, although servers will continue to receive requests for which session affinity exists.[10] Once all servers reach a value of zero or less, the minimum multiple of the LCD weight required to reset the weights for all servers to a positive number is added to the routing table, allowing all servers to accept new requests in addition to requests from clients with session affinity. This is depicted in Figure 21-4 where a multiple of two times the LCD weight is added to the server routing table.

The IIOP WLM plug-in has a different approach. First, it does not normalize the weights as the HTTP plug-in does. While it starts out as standard weighted round robin (decrementing the weights as it goes), once there are several outstanding requests to multiple cluster members, an outstanding request weight algorithm is employed. This algorithm compares each cluster member's weight to the number of outstanding requests that have been sent to that cluster member and ensure it has the correct proportion relative to its weight and the weight of the other cluster members. Using the example depicted in Figure 21-5, if the weights were 3 and 3 and the number of outstanding requests to the first server was higher than the second server, as occurs at the 5$^{th}$ request shown in Figure 21-5, the next request will go to the second server, even though it was the first server's turn (based on weighted round robin). This approach ensures the servers are balanced based on their weight.[11]

10 The decrementing in the server routing table to negative numbers shown in Figure 21-4 occurs in V5.01 and above. In WAS V5.0, the values would never decrement below zero.

11 IIOP WLM actually uses two tables, one for local objects where the client and EJB are in the same application server and one for remote clients. For simplicity, only a single table is depicted.

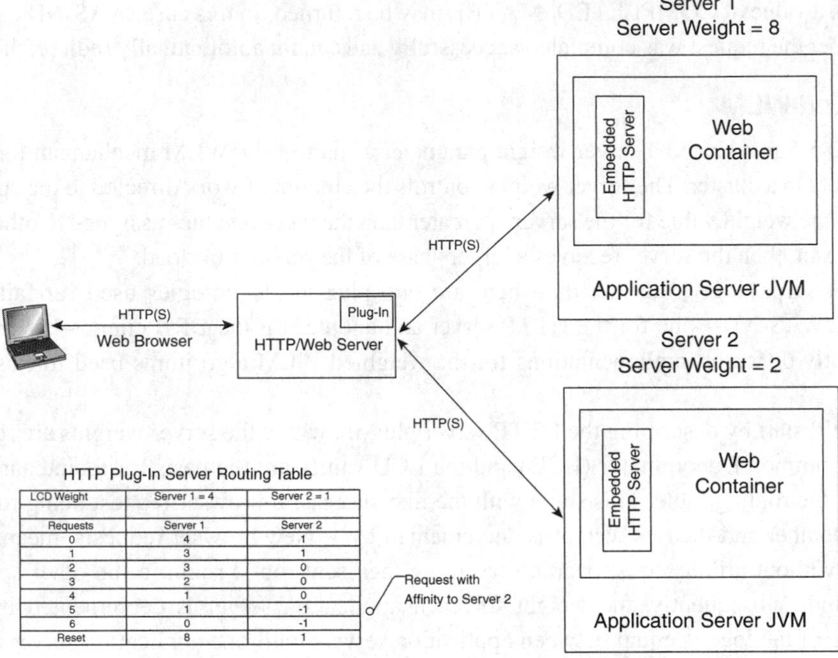


HTTP Plug-In Server Routing Table

| LCD Weight | Server 1 = 4 | Server 2 = 1 |
|---|---|---|
| | | |
| Requests | Server 1 | Server 2 |
| 0 | 4 | 1 |
| 1 | 3 | 1 |
| 2 | 3 | 0 |
| 3 | 2 | 0 |
| 4 | 1 | 0 |
| 5 | 1 | -1 |
| 6 | 0 | -1 |
| Reset | 8 | 1 |

**Figure 21-4** HTTP server plug-in WLM example.

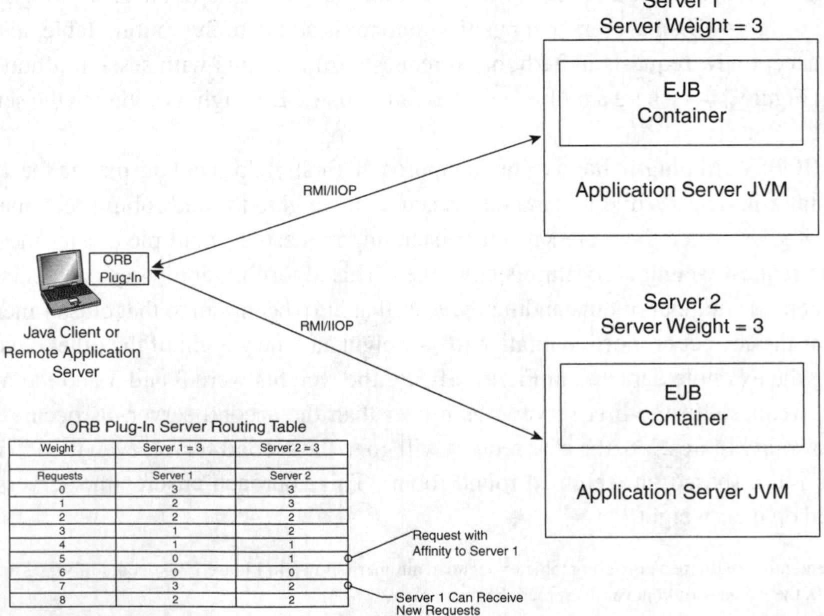


ORB Plug-In Server Routing Table

| Weight | Server 1 = 3 | Server 2 = 3 |
|---|---|---|
| | | |
| Requests | Server 1 | Server 2 |
| 0 | 3 | 3 |
| 1 | 2 | 3 |
| 2 | 2 | 2 |
| 3 | 1 | 2 |
| 4 | 1 | 1 |
| 5 | 0 | 1 |
| 6 | 0 | 0 |
| 7 | 3 | 2 |
| 8 | 2 | 2 |

**Figure 21-5** IIOP WLM example.

## Creating WebSphere Application Server-ND Clusters

There are a number of alternatives for creating a WAS-ND cluster. Not only can you use either the adminconsole or wsadmin, but for each of these administration tools, multiple options exist as well. We'll focus here on using wsadmin scripting, as that is a key focus of this book.

Probably the easiest way to configure a cluster is to start with a server that will serve as a template for the other servers in the cluster. By creating a template server and using that for cluster creation, you only have to apply configuration changes to one application server instead of to all servers in the cluster. The template should have the application installed that will be run in the cluster and should also be tuned (JVM heap size, thread pools, etc.) as the result of performance testing for the application and application server. Additionally, initial test and performance tuning with a single application server greatly simplifies multiple issues. Once you have that done, you can then take this single tuned server, make it into a cluster, and repeat your tests.

> **NOTE**
> Templates are available in WAS V5.02 and above and are analogous to a model in earlier versions of WebSphere Application Server. Unlike a model in earlier versions of WAS, a change to a template server after cluster creation does not update the application servers in the cluster. Updates to application servers after cluster creation must be performed to each application server in the cluster.

Let's walk through cluster creation using wsadmin, assuming that we've already created an application server, installed our application, and tuned the application server that will serve as the template server for our cluster (see Code Snippet 21-1).

**Code Snippet 21-1** Cluster creation with wsadmin using a template server

```
# set a server to serve as the template server

set serverId [$AdminConfig getid /Server:stockserver1/]

# create the cluster and convert the server to the cluster

$AdminConfig convertToCluster $serverId stockcluster

$AdminConfig save
```

At this point, we've taken an existing server, stockserver1, created a cluster, stockcluster, and added the existing server, stockserver1, to our cluster. Now that we've created a cluster, we will add an additional server to the cluster (see Code Snippet 21-2).

**Code Snippet 21-2 Adding cluster members with wsadmin using a template server**

```
# set the cluster ID

set clusterId [$AdminConfig getid /ServerCluster:stockcluster/]


# set the node that the new server will be added to

set nodeId [$AdminConfig getid /Node:alcott/]


#specify the template server

set templateId [$AdminConfig getid /Server:stockserver1/]


#add the cluster member on the node with the name stockserver2 using
➥stock
# server1 as a template

$AdminConfig createClusterMember $clusterId $nodeId {{memberName
➥stockserver2}} $templateId

#last save our changes

AdminConfig save
```

After specifying the cluster we want to work with, we then specified the node where the cluster member (server) was created, as well as the server to be used as a template. Finally, we created a new cluster member—stockserver2. The result of these commands is a two-server cluster with one server of two nodes, which can be seen in the cluster topology dialog in the admin-console (Servers > Cluster Topology), depicted in Figure 21-6.

If required to meet scalability requirements, and if adequate resources (memory and CPU) exist on the two nodes depicted, then additional application servers could be created on those nodes. Additionally, if more nodes existed in the cell, then servers could be created on each of these as well.

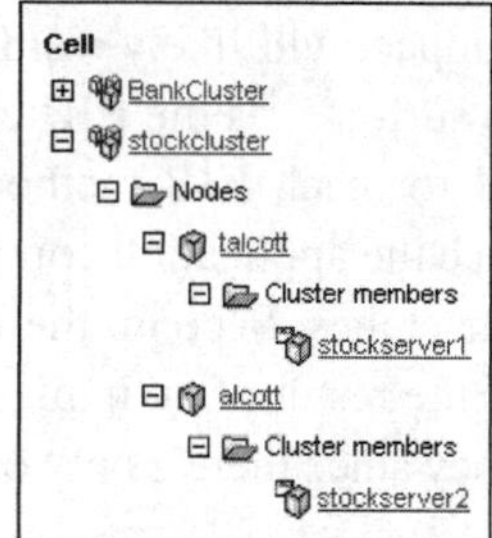


**Figure 21-6** Cluster topology in WAS-ND adminconsole.

# Application Installation and Maintenance

## Application Deployment Considerations

Before discussing the mechanics of application installation and maintenance in WAS-ND, let's take a step back and look at some of the options available for application deployment. While WAS allows you to deploy a single enterprise application across multiple tiers with the web application in a one application server (or cluster) and the EJB components in another application server (or cluster), doing so is not recommended. Let's look at why this is the case by looking at such a deployment (illustrated in Figure 21-7).

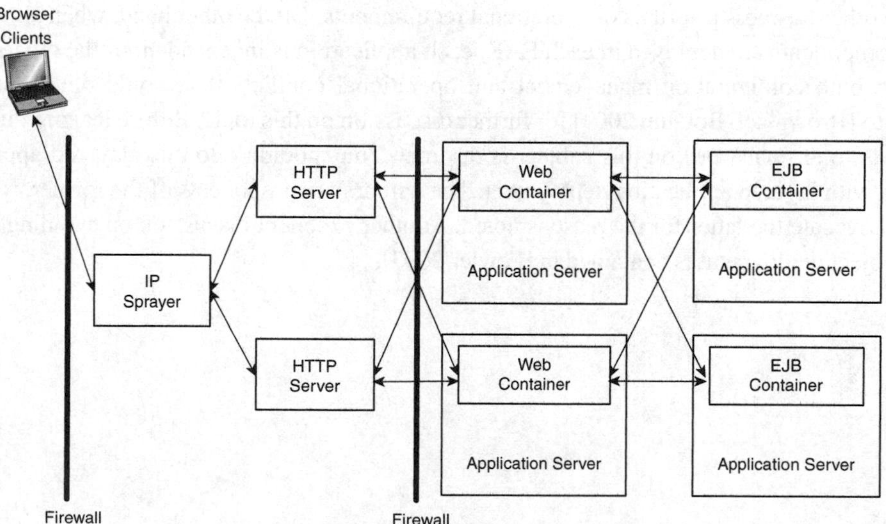


**Figure 21-7** Enterprise application (EAR) deployed across multiple tiers.

First, a negative performance impact will likely result when an application is deployed in this fashion. This should come as no surprise, as the EJB clients (the web application) not only have to make an out-of-process call for each EJB method request, but in this case, network latency also impacts performance since the application components are running not only in separate processes but also on separate machines. Second, the loss of any single application server, either for planned maintenance or as the result of an unplanned outage, results in a 50% loss of capacity and a loss in server redundancy since there's only one server left running in the web container or EJB container tier.

Contrast this to the same number of servers with all the application components running in a single application server, as depicted in Figure 21-8. In this case, the outage of a single machine results in a 25% loss in capacity, and the topology is still redundant. Moreover, performance will be significantly better[12] because the EJB clients in the web applications in the same process (JVM) can leverage either the EJB 2.0 local interface or the WAS "noLocalCopies"[13] optimization to avoid marshalling of method requests and results.

The benefit of deploying all application components in a single application server isn't limited to performance; maintenance is also easier. Let's consider the case where EJBs are deployed in an application server (or cluster) as a shared service for many applications. The illustration in Figure 21-7 depicts this reasonably well. Initially, everything is fine, as several applications are able to use the common business components that the EJBs provide. This breaks down when a change to one or more EJBs is required. By not packaging and deploying the EJBs with each application, version drift will result when one (or more) of the client applications can't change due to other business priorities or operational requirements. On the other hand, when all application components are deployed in each EAR, each application is independent of the others, minimizing both configuration management and operational conflicts that would otherwise arise. Refer to [Brown and Botzum 2003] for further discussion on this topic. Before leaving this topic, however, one final word on this subject is in order. You shouldn't confuse layered application design with layered application deployment. The authors are proponents of the former, while we don't advocate the latter for the reasons noted. Another excellent discussion on avoiding distributed object deployment is contained in [Fowler 2003].

12 Typically 20% or more.

13 noLocalCopies is also known as the "Pass by Reference" setting for the ORB service for an application server. This setting specifies that the ORB is to pass parameters by reference instead of by value, which bypasses a copy operation.

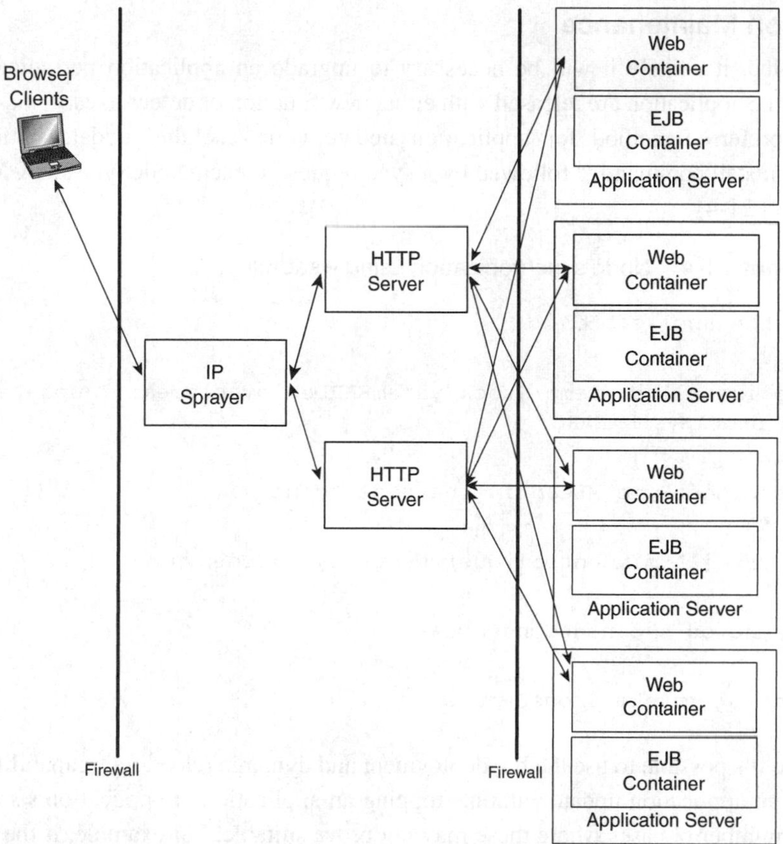


**Figure 21-8** Enterprise application (EAR) deployed to a single tier.

## Application Installation

While the preceding discussion on cluster creation assumed that the application had already been installed in the server being used as a template for the cluster, the wsadmin commands shown in Code Snippet 21-3 install an application into the cluster.

**Code Snippet 21-3** Application install in a cluster using wsadmin

```
$AdminApp install c:/temp/StockSystemEARDeployable.ear "-cluster
➥stockcluster"

#save the change to the configuration

$AdminConfig save
```

## Application Maintenance

Once installed, it's likely it will be necessary to upgrade an application periodically as new versions of the application are released with either new function or defect fixes.

The preferred method for application update is to use the -update option for the AdminApp install command,[14] followed by a sync request to each NodeSync JMX MBean (see Code Snippet 21-4).

**Code Snippet 21-4** Node synchronization using wsadmin

```
# update the application

$AdminApp install c:/temp/StockSystemEARDeployable.ear "-update -
➥appname StockSystemEAR"

#access the nodeSync MBean in the node agent

set nodeSync [$AdminControl queryNames type=NodeSync,*]

#invoke sync on the nodeSync MBean

$AdminControl invoke $nodeSync sync
```

While it's possible to use the hot deployment and dynamic reloading[15] capabilities in WAS to perform an application update without stopping an application or application server process, there are a number of cases where these may not prove suitable. For example, if the application you are updating is deployed on a server that has its application classloader policy set to SINGLE, you might not be able to dynamically reload your application. At a minimum, you must restart the server after updating your application. Another case where hot deployment is dangerous is when updating an application that is not backward compatible with the current release running in production. In this case, multiple requests from the same user could potentially fall across two different versions of the application during the upgrade if there is user session state in the browser and the application server tier is stateless.

14 The "update" option for an application is also available in the admin console. The "update" operation is preferred to attempting to devise a script composed of several commands to stop, uninstall, install, and start an application because a script of this sort does not include registration of several events that are critical to the timing of this operation in a distributed multi-node configuration. The "update" operation, on the other hand, does receive various notifications as an EAR file is stored, expanded, and distributed (via node synchronization). As a result, the application server is able to load and execute the new code correctly.

15 Hot deployment is the process of adding new components (such as WAR files, EJB JAR files, Enterprise JavaBeans, Servlets, and JSP files) to a running server without having to stop the application server process and start it again. Dynamic reloading is the ability to change an existing component without needing to restart the server in order for the change to take effect. Dynamic reloading involves changes to the implementation of a component of an application, such as changing the implementation of a Servlet or changes to the settings of the application, such as changing the deployment descriptor for a web module.

> **NOTE**
> The NodeSync MBean exposes two forms of sync operation: blocking and non-blocking. The requestSync operation is non-blocking. It returns immediately, and the actual synchronization of the node's configuration occurs over some amount of time after the operation returns. Code that employs the non-blocking requestSync operation can be notified when the sync operation actually completes by registering to receive the websphere.nodesync.complete event notification generated by the NodeSync MBean after each sync operation completes. The sync operation of the NodeSync MBean blocks and does not return to the caller until the sync operation completes.

In general, the easiest way to update an application is to force all users off the system for some small period of time (say an hour or so). However, in some cases, this may not be acceptable for business reasons. If the application is completely forward and backward compatible, there is a relatively straightforward procedure that can be used to perform an upgrade while keeping the site running.[16] If the application does not satisfy these criteria, then you will likely need to consider multiple cells, which will be discussed later. You may recall the earlier mention of making use of the server weight parameter for application maintenance. By setting this value to zero, a server can be drained of requests, thereby allowing application maintenance. Once the application upgrade is complete, the weight can be reset to its original value to bring it back into service. This is a better process than simply stopping the application server because even though the HTTP and ORB plug-ins will fail to make new connections, mark the server as down, and redirect the requests, the plug-ins will continue to periodically retry the server,[17] which can increase response time as the client waits for a timeout before redirecting the request.

The basic procedure for this is:

1. Turn off node sync.
2. Update the application in Dmgr.
3. Mark all the application server instances in a cluster on a single node as down by setting the server weight to zero and regenerate the HTTP server plug-in.[18]
4. Monitor the number of requests in the server(s) using PMI (Performance Monitoring Infrastructure) with wsadmin or in the IBM Tivoli Performance Viewer[19] until no more requests are being processed.
5. Synchronize the chosen node.
6. Reset the server weight for that node.
7. Repeat for each node in the cell.

16 Assuming adequate capacity exists to run the site on a reduced number of servers.

17 After the RetryInterval has elapsed for the HTTP server plug-in or the unusable.interval has elapsed for the ORB plug-in.

18 Or directly manipulate the LoadBalanceWeight in the plugin-cfg.xml.

19 The Tivoli Performance Viewer is covered in Chapter 25, "Performance Tuning Tools."

You can combine the wsadmin commands for application updates depicted previously in this chapter with the commands shown in Code Snippet 21-5 to create a script appropriate from your environment.

**Code Snippet 21-5 Changing server weight and regenerating the plugin-cfg.xml file using wsadmin**

```
# Get the id of the clusterServer to change the weight of
set clusterServer [$AdminConfig getid /ClusterMember:
➥$clusterServerName/]


# Set the weight of the server to the value of newWeight so plugin/WLM
➥will direct traffic accordingly

$AdminConfig modify $clusterServer [list [list weight $newWeight]]

# Save the config

$AdminConfig save

# Regen the plugin

set pluginGen [$AdminControl completeObjectName
➥type=PluginCfgGenerator,*]

$AdminControl invoke $pluginGen generate "c:/WebSphere/DeploymentManager
➥c:/WebSphere/DeploymentManager/config mycell null null plugin-cfg.xml"
```

## Hardware Clustering and WAS-ND

While the clustering provided by WAS-ND is sufficient for many high-availability deployment requirements, there are cases where hardware clustering can be complementary to WAS-ND clustering. The cases when you may want to consider hardware clustering are:

- Application servers that coordinate distributed transactions. As stated earlier in Chapter 11, "Transactions with WebSphere Application Server," the transactional state is written persistently to disk by WAS. If the machine should fail, that state would be lost, resulting in the transactions being hung in an undefined state. While you can manually recover transaction logs and restart a server process on another node (and there are directions for this in the WAS Info Center), if you desire automatic recovery from an outage, then hardware clustering is an appropriate solution. In this case, you'll also need to ensure that the resource managers (e.g., the JMS and DB servers) are clustered, and the transaction logs will need to be highly available as well.

- An application server that is not clustered. It may be possible in some cases that only one application server is used to run an application due to processing order dependencies or other application-related constraints. If high availability is also required, then hardware clustering can be employed for this use case.
- The WAS Embedded Messaging Server. While you deploy an embedded JMS server per WAS-ND node, only one JMS server can service a specific queue per cell; hence, that JMS server is a single point of failure within the cell. When the JMS (queue manager) server fails, all application servers using those queues will lose their messaging service. The impact of this can be mitigated by using hardware clustering, as depicted in Figure 21-9. This also applies to the use of WebSphere MQ as the JMS provider for WebSphere Application Server. WebSphere MQ also provides a queue manager and queue distribution as a mechanism for eliminating single points of failure, and while this provides a robust solution, there are cases where there are queue order processing dependencies. If this applies to your application, then distribution of the queues will not be an appropriate solution since some number of records could become locked in a queue during an outage while other records are processed. In such a case, you will need to deploy a single highly available queue with hardware clustering. A comprehensive discussion of JMS server configuration and clustering is available; see [Barcia 2003].

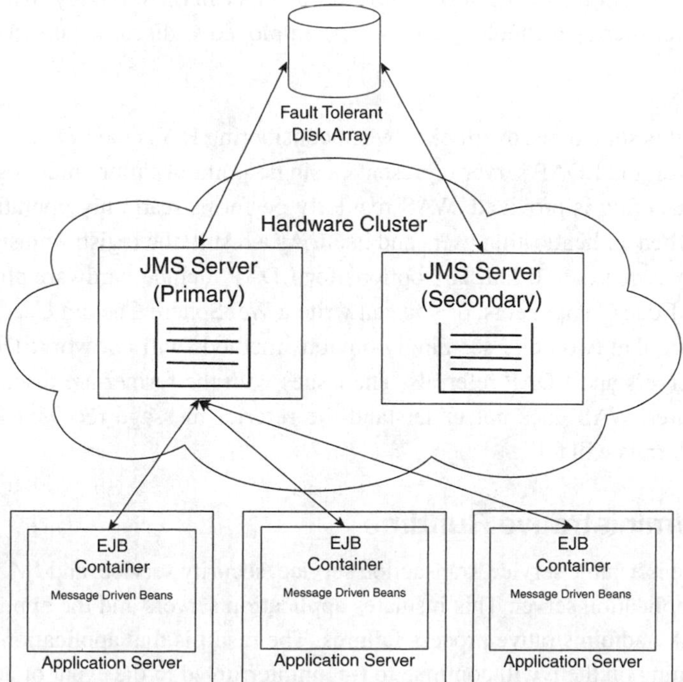


**Figure 21-9** JMS server HA with hardware clustering.

## Other Components

Chapter 23 describes how to configure WAS-ND Edge Components to distribute IP requests across multiple HTTP servers and also describes the issues associated with the use of non-robust request distribution mechanisms such as DNS round-robin, so we'll not repeat that here, but you'll want to refer to that chapter to ensure you've made adequate provisions to make certain this portion of your topology is highly available. There are other components that need to be highly available in addition to WebSphere Application Server.

### Firewall

Firewalls are another major component of a WebSphere environment. Much like the network itself, failure of a firewall can result in catastrophic consequences. Some provisions need to be made to make your firewalls highly available. Normally, this is accomplished using hardware clustering, but WebSphere Edge Server can also be employed to make firewalls highly available.

### Database Server

Another tier that needs to be made highly available is the database server. Without highly available application data, your web applications cannot provide dynamic and personalized data to your customer, and order processing and transactions are not possible. In short, a web site could only serve static content for the most part. It is at this layer in the topology that either the hardware or software clustering technology needs to be employed as discussed previously.

### LDAP Server

A component that is sometimes overlooked when considering HA is the LDAP server. Much like the database server, the LDAP server represents a single point of failure unless some manner of replication or clustering is provided. WAS regularly performs read-only operations against the LDAP registry when authenticating users and itself. As a result, the registry must be available, or else new security requests will fail. HA options for LDAP include hardware clustering and the use of WAS-ND Edge Components, or you can write a WebSphere Custom User registry for this purpose. Be aware that two other seemingly obvious methods will not work: DNS round-robin lists of LDAP servers and LDAP referrals. The issues with the former are discussed in Chapter 23. As to the latter, WAS does not understand the referral message received from the LDAP server, so any referrals will fail.

## WAS-ND Administrative Runtime

In WAS V5, there is a name service, transaction service, security service, and JMX administrative server in each application server. This insulates application servers and the applications running in them from WAS administrative process failures. The result is that application servers and the applications running on them will continue to run uninterrupted in the event of an administrative process failure. The preceding point is a key difference between WAS V5 and prior versions of WebSphere Application Server, and it's an important point to consider when determining how and what you make highly available in your WAS-ND cell. If the WAS-ND deployment manager or a node agent fails to run, then you might not have a means to administer your Network Deployment cell or one of the nodes in the cell, but since application servers (and applications) will continue to run uninterrupted, high availability for the deployment manager and the node agent is less critical than for other components in your infrastructure.

## Node Agent High Availability

The node agent provides local process and configuration management for each node in a WAS-ND cell. As a result, if a node agent is not running, the local configuration may not reflect the global configuration until restart of the node agent (when synchronization occurs by default). Since the node agent serves as the bootstrap server for all application servers on a node, when a node agent is not running, application servers on the node cannot be started.[20] Given the relatively minor impact of a node agent failure, it's hard to justify an investment in hardware clustering for the node agent since any outage in which hardware clustering would be of value would likely be an entire node failure, in which case it would be the application servers that might require hardware clustering for the reasons described previously. Realistically, it should be sufficient to monitor, or "nanny," the node agent via a Unix inittab entry or creation of a Windows Service.

## Deployment Manager High Availability

As the central controller of administration and configuration for the administrative domain (or cell), the deployment manager represents a single point of failure within the cell. The deployment manager works with node agents to carry out all administrative and configuration tasks. It does not participate directly in distributing requests to cluster members; however, the application server's runtime depends on the data distributed by the deployment manager. When the deployment manager is unavailable, it impacts several items:

- The ability to make configuration changes
- The ability for changes to be propagated to the application servers (including the stopping and starting of application servers)
- Optimal propagation of up-to-date cluster information regarding server state (could affect the quality of EJB WLM)

While application servers will continue to run and respond to client requests in the event of a node agent or deployment manager failure, the cell cannot be administered effectively in such a case. You can choose to manually modify the local XML files that make up the configuration repository, but this entails additional manual effort and would likely be subject to errors so is not recommended. You can also stop and start individual server processes using startServer and stopServer scripts or using wsadmin. You therefore need to make some provision to ensure that the deployment manager can be made quickly available so that even in the event of a catastrophic server failure, you would still be able to effectively administer your WebSphere Application Server cell.

20 In the case of a node agent outage, application servers can be stopped via the stopServer command-line script and can also be administered directly via the wsadmin AdminControl MBean.

While you could configure the deployment manager in a high-availability cluster using the clustering software appropriate for your chosen operating system, such as HACMP for AIX, Sun-Cluster for Solaris, MC/Serviceguard for HP-UX, and MS Cluster for Windows 2000, this is likely not required. Such a configuration would provide for automatic failover and recovery of the deployment manager and the configuration of such a cluster is described in detail by [Branson and Hao 2003] but it's not clear that the cost and complexity of doing so provides sufficient benefit to be justified.

Fortunately, other options can be employed to provide for recovery of a deployment manager in the event of a failure. While the approach described here does not provide for fully automatic failover and recovery, it is relatively inexpensive and can be easily implemented, and given its simplicity and the minimal impact of a deployment manager outage, it's likely more than sufficient. Additionally, the approach outlined here is the one recommended by a number of IBM Software Services for WebSphere consultants over the use of hardware clustering for deployment manager HA; among them are the authors of this book. The steps consist of:

1. Making regular backups of the cell configuration using the backupConfig script.
2. Installing Network Deployment on a backup or alternate server.
3. Restoring the configuration on a backup server using the restoreConfig script.
4. Changing the IP address on the backup server to match the IP address of the original server.
5. Starting deployment manager on the backup server.

First, you must make backups of your cell on a regular basis (in case you were to experience an outage). WAS V5 provides a command-line tool for this purpose: backupConfig.sh/bat. This tool is located in the bin directories for both WebSphere Application Server and the Network Deployment runtime. For the purpose described here, which is specific to cell configuration, you should run the batch file provided with Network Deployment. Figure 21-10 depicts the execution of this script.

Notice that the default execution stops the deployment manager. While it is a good idea to do this (this prevents changes from being made while the backup is running), this action is not necessary. If you execute backupConfig using the -nostop option, the deployment manager will not be stopped. Once you have the backup, place a copy of it in a highly available file system; otherwise, a disk outage on your deployment manager server could make the file unavailable to you. As you can see, backupConfig creates a file with the name WebSphereConfig_<date>.zip. A single backup per day is sufficient for most production environments, but note that subsequent backups on a given day have a number appended to the file name; for example, WebSphereConfig_2004-05-13.zip.

Before you continue to the next step, wait for a deployment manager failure and then remove the machine from the network. This will then free up its IP address.

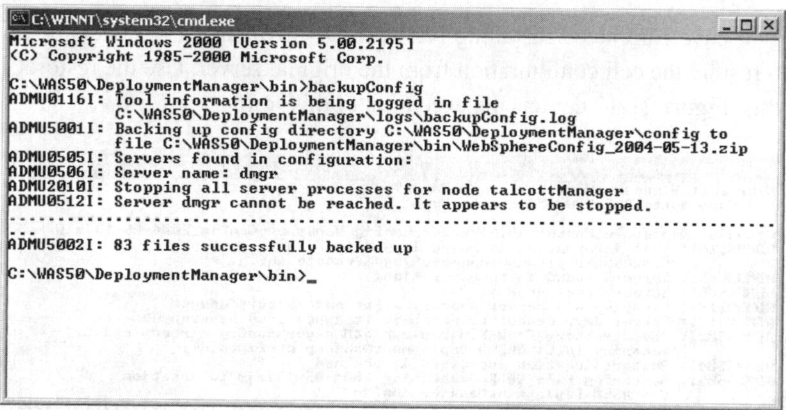


**Figure 21-10** Command-line execution of backupConfig script.

Next, you must install Network Deployment on your backup server. The important part of this step is that you specify the Node Name, IP Address or Host Name, and Cell Name from the original server. In Figure 21-11, the installation takes place on the server "alcott," but it is being used as a backup for the server "talcott." Consequently, you override the values that were populated by the installation with the ones for the original server. You need to specify the values for the original server because your cell configuration makes use of the server name when constructing the cell configuration. As part of this process, you will also need to copy the keyrings from the <was deployment manager root>/etc directory (e.g., /opt/WebSphere/DeploymentManager/etc) to the new machine. This should be done in advance of the machine failure.

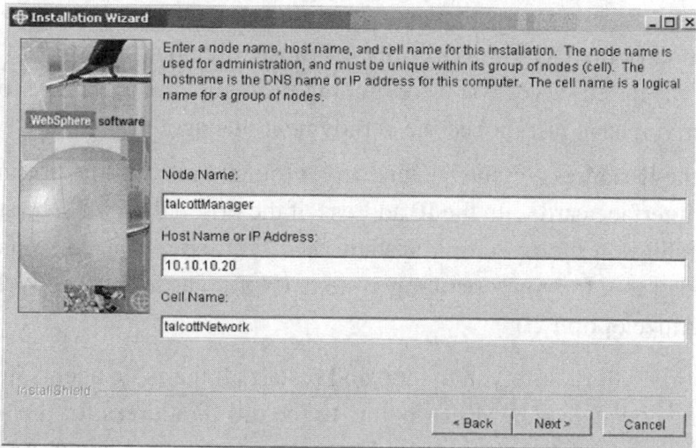


**Figure 21-11** Installation dialog specifying node, host, and cell names.

Once you have completed installing Network Deployment on the backup server, you are now ready to restore the cell configuration from the original server. Use the restoreConfig.sh/bat script to do this. Figure 21-12 depicts the execution of this script.

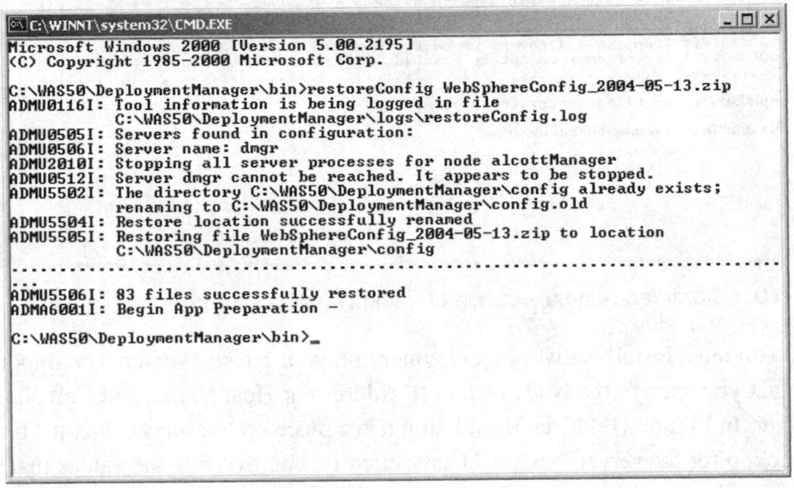

```
C:\WINNT\system32\CMD.EXE
Microsoft Windows 2000 [Version 5.00.2195]
(C) Copyright 1985-2000 Microsoft Corp.

C:\WAS50\DeploymentManager\bin>restoreConfig WebSphereConfig_2004-05-13.zip
ADMU0116I: Tool information is being logged in file
           C:\WAS50\DeploymentManager\logs\restoreConfig.log
ADMU0505I: Servers found in configuration:
ADMU0506I: Server name: dmgr
ADMU2010I: Stopping all server processes for node alcottManager
ADMU0512I: Server dmgr cannot be reached. It appears to be stopped.
ADMU5502I: The directory C:\WAS50\DeploymentManager\config already exists;
           renaming to C:\WAS50\DeploymentManager\config.old
ADMU5504I: Restore location successfully renamed
ADMU5505I: Restoring file WebSphereConfig_2004-05-13.zip to location
           C:\WAS50\DeploymentManager\config
..............................................................................
...
ADMU5506I: 83 files successfully restored
ADMA6001I: Begin App Preparation -

C:\WAS50\DeploymentManager\bin>_
```

**Figure 21-12** Command-line execution of restoreConfig script.

Although the deployment manager is not running in the example depicted here, restoreConfig has a -nostop option that you could specify if the deployment manager were running.

At this point, if you're running WebSphere V5.01 (or later), you have two options. You can do the following:

1. Add or modify the DNS entry (or the /etc/hosts file on all machines) so that the server name for the failed server you were running the deployment manager on now resolves to the server you have just moved the deployment manager to.
2. Change the IP address on the backup server to match that of the original server or add a network interface card with the IP address of the original server. The steps to do this differ depending on the operating system used; you simply need to use the appropriate command or tool for your operating system. (Note: Those running WebSphere V5.0 will need to utilize option 2.)

The first option will require you to stop and restart all the node agents in order to clear the "stale" cache in the node agent JVM that points to the old IP address for the server. The "stale" cache occurs because Java "remembers" the IP resolution of a host name. As a result, all of the running node agent JVMs have cached the IP address for the original server that the deployment manager was running on once a connection has been made. Alternatively, you can configure a command-line argument for each node agent that will force a DNS cache refresh on a periodic basis. The property is:

```
-Dsun.net.inetaddr.ttl=<time in seconds>
```

A reasonable value for this property is 60 seconds. Stopping and starting the node agents ensures that this occurs in a timely manner and is preferred by the authors in small cells (<10 nodes).

The second option does not require you to stop and restart the node agents because you have added or changed the IP address to the new server. Note also that during the installation of the deployment manager, when using the first option, you *must* specify the host name for the server (refer to Figure 21-11), while the second option *requires* that you specify the IP address.

Lastly, start the deployment manager by running the startManager script. Once you receive the "ADMU3000I: Server dmgr open for e-business; process id is xxxx" message, as shown in Figure 21-13, you're ready to administer your cell using the Administrative Console or wsadmin. You can continue to do this until your original server is repaired. A reminder—you may need to stop and restart all the node agents at this point, depending upon how you have chosen to change the IP address as described previously.

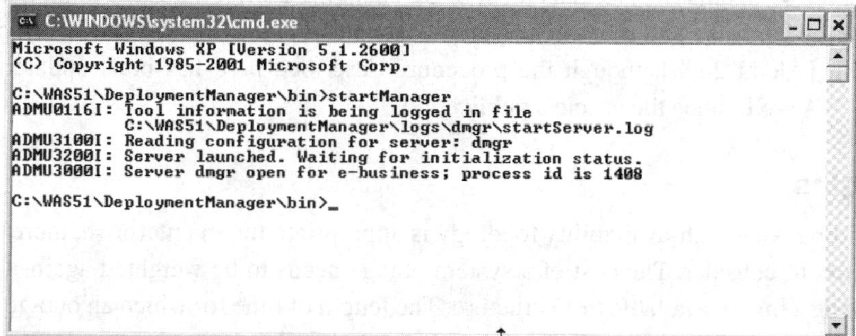


**Figure 21-13** Deployment manager start.

You can accomplish the steps relatively quickly, as depicted in Table 21-1.

**Table 21-1** Approximate Deployment Manager Backup, Install, and Restore Timings

| Task | Time |
|---|---|
| Installing Network Deployment | 10 minutes |
| Backing up the cell configuration | 1 minute |
| Restoring the configuration | 2 minutes |
| Changing the IP address | 1 minute |
| Starting the deployment manager | 1 minute |
| Total time (approximate) | 15 minutes |

Of course, the amount of time required to perform these tasks in your environment will vary somewhat, depending on your server CPU speed, network speed, and size of the configuration backup file. The installation time can also vary based on the number of fix packs and versions that need to be installed. In the case of a WAS-Enterprise deployment manager that is managing a WAS-ND and WAS-Enterprise cell, this could actually require several installations (e.g., WAS-ND, WAS-Enterprise, PTFs), so installation on a backup server in advance of a failure will speed up the recovery time in the event of a Dmgr failure. If you should choose not to perform the installation in advance of a failure, you should practice this procedure repeatedly or, even better, script it to ensure that there will be no surprises in the event of a serious outage.

If you follow the steps outlined, you will be prepared in the event of a prolonged outage of a deployment manager that might occur from a CPU or disk failure. By simply backing up on a regular basis, ensuring that the backups are highly available, and scripting some of the process to ensure repeatability, you can guard against an extended outage. Best of all, you can use an existing server by adding a DNS alias for it or by changing its IP address or adding a NIC to it, minimizing the hardware and software required to accomplish these tasks. The steps here are also described in [Alcott 2003], though the procedure described here has been updated to reflect changes in WAS-ND since the article's publication.

## Topologies

When deciding what high-availability topology is appropriate for an enterprise, there are a number of factors to consider. The cost of a system outage needs to be weighted against the cost of implementing a highly available infrastructure. The length of time for which an outage can be tolerated also needs to be considered. The following definitions are used by the authors when discussing HA and are the basis for the remainder of this discussion:

- **Low availability**—Anything less than high availability (HA).
- **High availability**—Application cannot undergo an unplanned outage for more than a few minutes/seconds at a time, but may do so as often as necessary or may be down for a few hours for scheduled maintenance. This is likely achievable in WAS V5 without the "gold standard," although prior versions of WAS may have required the "gold standard."[21]
- **Continuous availability**—Application cannot go down at all. This is essentially the "five 9's" (or 99.999% availability). The level of availability will likely require a "gold standard" topology.

Figure 21-14 depicts a minimal topology for HA, with two physical servers deployed in each layer of the topology, for a total of 12 servers, assuming two servers for each clustered component, from the edge of the network to the database and LDAP server (also required but not depicted are firewall servers). This topology assumes some co-location of data servers to reduce

21 The "gold standard" is a multi-cell topology that we'll discuss shortly for this service level.

hardware costs. While the number of servers could be reduced further by compressing the various layers (e.g., WAS-ND Edge Components Network Dispatcher could be co-located on each of the HTTP server machines, though this is not recommended), in practice, administration issues as well as security considerations (firewalls) probably preclude much more reduction in servers in practice.

For many enterprises, a single hardware redundant domain such as that depicted will prove more than sufficient for their HA requirements, with "four 9s" (99.99 %)[22] or better availability possible, so unless you really require "Non-Stop" service, the additional hardware and software required to improve upon this is likely not cost-justified, though a third server in each layer will provide additional capacity and redundancy.

Any configuration with only two servers does have one glaring weakness. During planned maintenance where one server is offline, an unexpected outage of the other server results in a site outage. As a result, you need to consider your availability requirements when determining the number of redundant servers in each tier of your deployment.

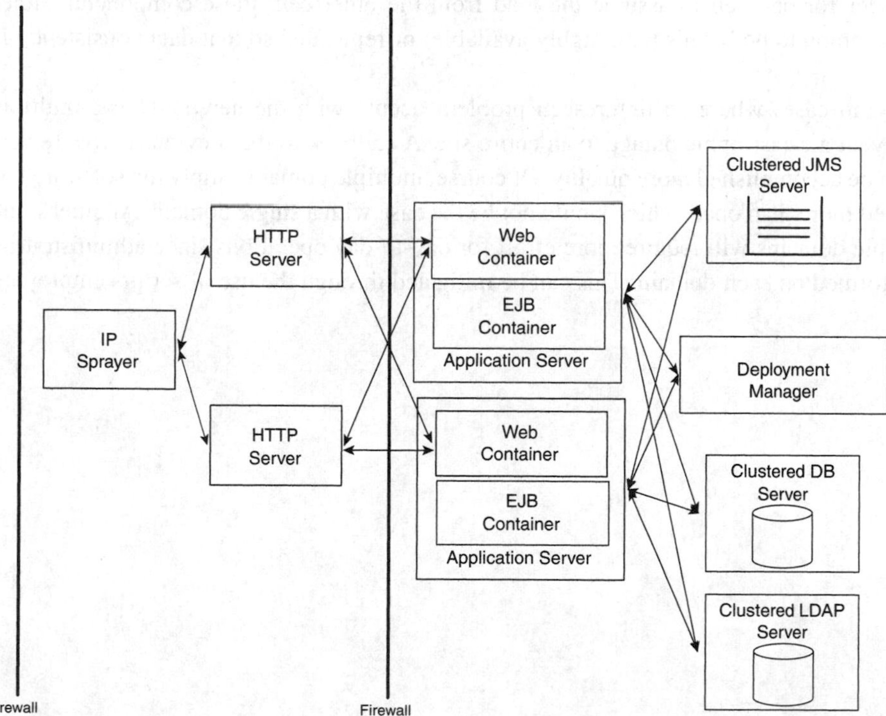


**Figure 21-14** Sample high-availability topology.

22 99.99% availability implies about 52 minutes per year in downtime, while 99.999% ("five nines") results in just over 5 minutes of downtime.

## More Cells Increase Availability

An even more robust infrastructure is depicted in Figure 21-15. In this case, two separate WAS-ND cells (sometimes referred to as domains) are created to provide what is often referred to as the "gold standard" in high availability.

While the application maintenance procedures described previously in this chapter should allow you to perform maintenance while applications continue to run, you may want to consider creating multiple WAS-ND domains for a variety of reasons.

Two (or more) domains can be employed to provide not only hardware failure isolation but also software failure isolation as well. This can come into play in a variety of situations, such as planned maintenance, when deploying a new version of WAS or when applying an e-fix or patch. Multiple domains are also of use when rolling out a new application or revision of an existing application that is not backward compatible.

You'll notice in looking at Figure 21-15 that some of the components are labeled "shared infrastructure": the application database, the session database,[23] the JMS server, and the LDAP server. In order for one cell to assume the load from the other cell, these components either need to be common to both cells (and highly available) or replicated so that data consistency is maintained

Finally, in cases where an unforeseen problem occurs with the new software, multiple domains prevent a catastrophic outage to an entire site. A rollback to the previous software version can also be accomplished more quickly. Of course, multiple domains imply the software has to be deployed more than once, which would not be the case with a single domain. Another issue is that multiple domains will require more effort for day-to-day operations since administration must be performed on each domain. This can be mitigated through the use of scripts employing wsadmin.

23 We'll discuss why a highly available database server is the preferred alternative for HTTP session failover in Chapter 22.

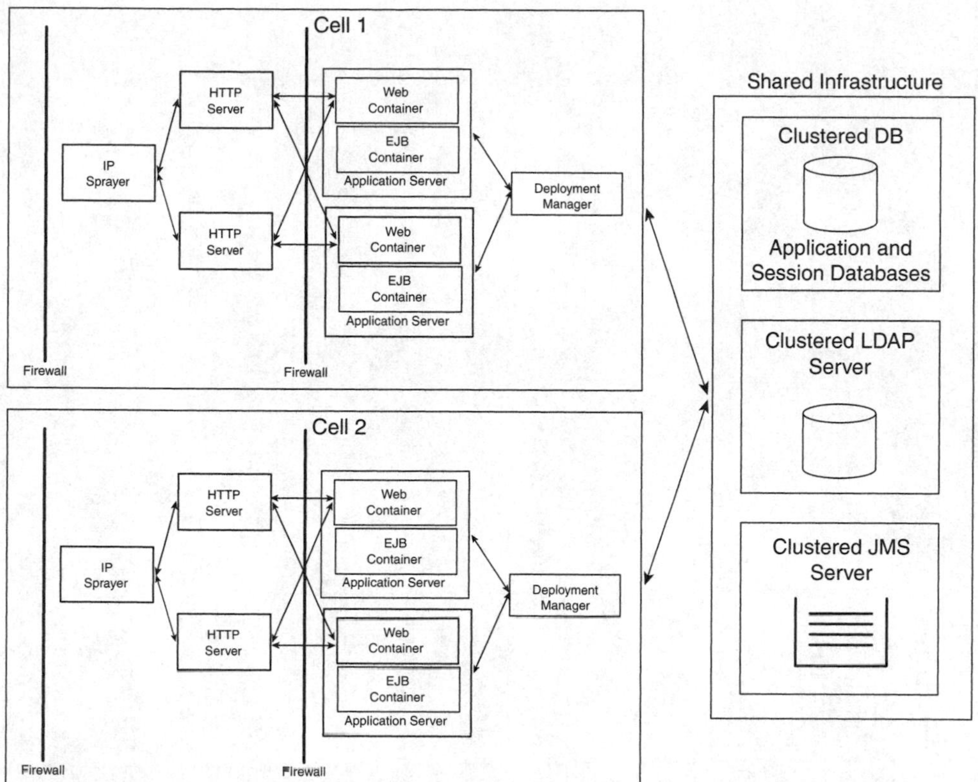


**Figure 21-15** "Gold Standard" topology with multiple cells.

## Conclusion

In this chapter, we discussed the technologies that WAS-ND provides that can be used for a scalable and highly available infrastructure. We also discussed how complementary technologies such as hardware clustering may be of use in certain cases and provided alternatives to hardware clustering for some WAS-ND components. Application installation and maintenance procedures that can be used to ensure minimal or no disruption of service were covered, and last, we outlined possible deployment topologies.

CHAPTER 22

# Session Management

The HTTP session API is an essential component in constructing interactive web sites. The session API of the Java Servlet specification provides a mechanism for associating a series of requests with a specific browser or user. This is required because the Hypertext Transfer Protocol (HTTP) employed for web browser to web server requests is a stateless protocol. As a result, a web server has no means of associating a series of requests with a specific browser or user. This chapter will expand on the coverage of HTTP session from Chapter 4, "Build and Deploy Procedures," by providing a brief overview of HTTP session and will then discuss the WebSphere Application Server (WAS) session management implementation, as well as the specifics of configuring the various session management options that exist in WAS.

## Introduction to HTTP Session

It's almost impossible to visit any interactive web site today that does not make use of the HTTP session API. By providing multiple options for tracking a series of requests and associating those requests with a specific user, HTTP session allows applications to appear dynamic to application users. The most often cited example of HTTP session is the creation of a "shopping cart" for shoppers on a web site. In this example, information associating the user and their prior navigation through the web site and their selections are stored as objects in HTTP session. Once the users are ready to check out from the web site and purchase their selections, the application typically constructs a page composed of all the selected items stored in the "shopping cart."[1] By maintaining application state between browser requests, HTTP session overcomes the default stateless behavior for HTTP requests.

1 It's worth noting that this is actually a poor use of a session. Sessions are not designed for robust "permanent" storage. By storing the shopping cart in a session, if there were a client failure (perhaps the browser crashed), the user would lose his or her entire shopping cart. That's a great way to lose a sale. Important information is better stored in a database directly.

The HTTP session API component of the Java Servlet specification provides a mechanism for web applications to maintain a user's state information, and this mechanism addresses some of the problems with other options for maintaining state, such as those based solely on cookies. This mechanism, known as a session, allows a web-application developer to maintain user state information on the server, while passing minimal information back to the user to track the session via one of three options: cookies, URL encoding, and SSL sessions.

## Session Tracking

In order to associate the user's session with a particular browser, WAS needs to maintain some form of association with the client browser. There are several techniques available, and we'll detail them here. It is important to note that while WAS allows for great flexibility in choosing the tracking mechanism, cookies are by far the best approach.

### Cookies

The use of a cookie for tracking session state is the default in WAS. This option differs from a pure cookie-based solution in that the HTTP session uses a single cookie named JSESSIONID that contains the session ID, which is used to associate the request with information stored on the server for that session ID, while an entirely cookie-based solution would employ multiple cookies, each containing possibly sensitive user state information (account number, user ID, etc.). With HTTP session, all attributes associated with the user's request are stored on the server. Since the only information transmitted between the server and the browser is the session ID cookie, which has a limited lifetime, HTTP session can provide a much more secure mechanism than cookies for tracking application state when configured in conjunction with SSL.

The mechanics of using a cookie for tracking session are depicted in Figure 22-1. A request arrives at the server requiring that a session be created as the result of a getSession() method call. The server creates a session object, associating a session ID with it. The session ID is transmitted back to the browser as part of the response header and stored with the rest of the cookies in the browser. On subsequent requests from the browser, the session ID is transmitted as part of the request header, allowing the application to associate each request for a given session ID with prior requests from that user.

The interaction between browser, application server, and application are all handled transparently to the end user and the application program, aside from the getSession() method call inside the application. The application and the user need not be, nor are they likely aware of the session ID provided by the server.

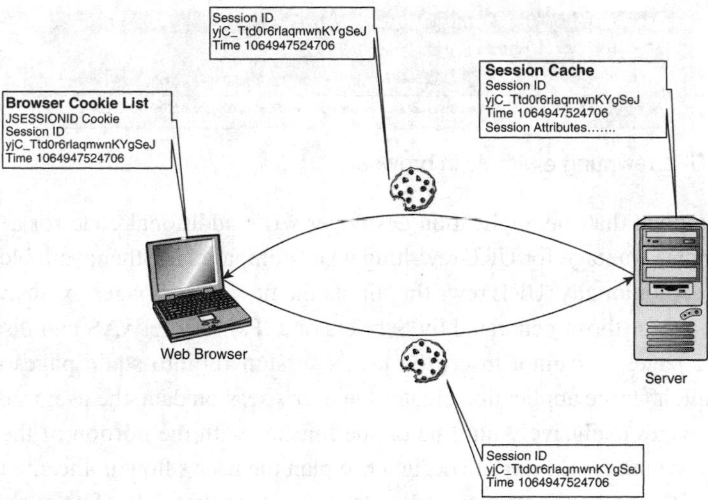


**Figure 22-1** Browser-session manager cookie interaction.

Unfortunately, not all users configure their browsers to accept cookies. Often, this is related to security concerns over accepting a cookie into the browser. Most often the restrictions on accepting a cookie into the browser are the result of concerns about persistent cookies. Persistent cookies remain in the browser after the browser is closed and allow a web site to "remember" you on ensuing visits. Most important in terms of presenting a risk, persistent cookies may contain personal information about you, which is then accessible to any application that has access to the cookie folder in your browser. However, WAS generates a session cookie that exists only until the browser has been closed and is used only to ensure that you are "recognized" as you move from page to page within the web site. This technique is not generally considered to be a security or privacy concern. In fact, most modern browsers can be configured to accept all session cookies while still blocking persistent cookies.

Finally, in a WAS environment with security enabled, disabling all cookies is actually counterproductive since the most often used authentication mechanism is LTPA (Lightweight Third Party Authentication), and LTPA relies on creating a token (cookie) that is used to represent the identity of the authenticated user to the browser. In any event, other options exist for maintaining an application state such as URL rewriting, although they are not recommended.

## URL Rewriting

Most often, URL rewriting is employed when a browser is configured not to accept cookies. URL rewriting stores the session identifier in the page returned to the user. WAS encodes the session identifier as a parameter on any link or form the user submits from a web page. This option requires that the Servlet code be modified to include either an encodeURL() or encodeRedirectURL() method. When a browser user clicks on a link that utilizes one of these methods, the session identifier passes into the request as a parameter, with the result shown in Figure 22-2, where the session ID is appended to the URL for the web page.

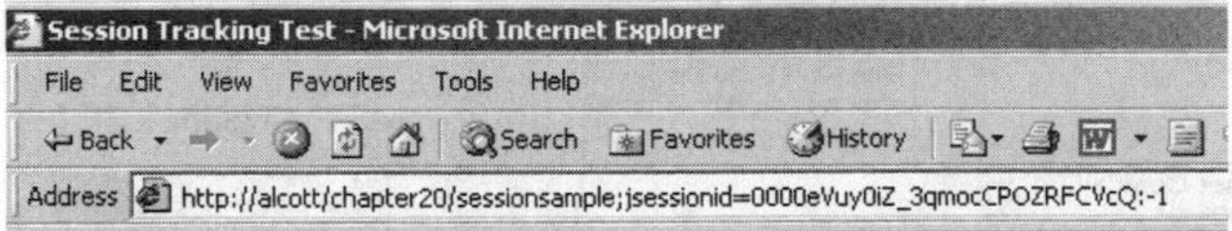


**Figure 22-2** URL rewriting example in browser.

The requirement that the application developer write additional code for a Servlet or JSP presents a major disadvantage for URL rewriting when compared to other available session tracking mechanisms. Additionally, URL rewriting limits the flow of site pages exclusively to dynamically generated pages (those generated by Servlets or JSPs). While WAS can insert the session ID into dynamic pages, it cannot insert the user's session ID into static pages (.htm or .html pages). As a result, after the application creates the user's session data, the user must visit dynamically generated pages exclusively until he or she finishes with the portion of the site requiring sessions. URL rewriting forces the site designer to plan the user's flow in the site to avoid losing his or her session ID. Lastly, the system administrator must configure WAS to enable URL rewriting by checking the box shown in Figure 22-3.

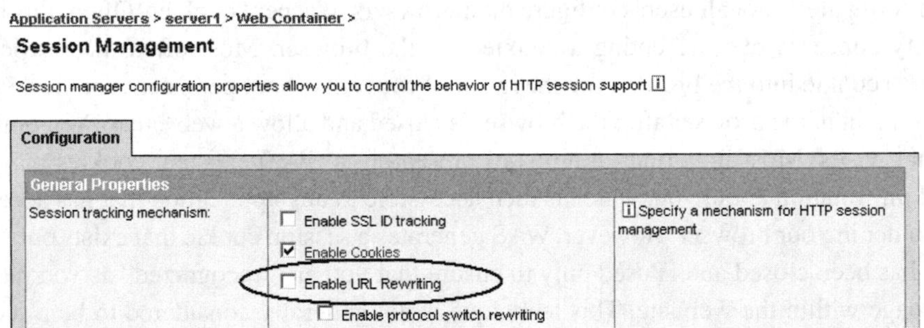


**Figure 22-3** Session tracking mechanism dialog.

Fortunately, the WAS session management implementation can recognize when a browser is configured to accept cookies and will use this option instead of URL rewriting in cases when both cookies and URL rewriting are enabled.

## SSL ID Tracking

Another alternative tracking mechanism is the Secure Socket Layer (SSL) ID that is negotiated between the web browser and the HTTP server. While secure, this alternative presents a number of disadvantages. Since this ID is negotiated between the browser and the HTTP server, the failure of the HTTP server results in the loss of this ID. In a clustered environment, the IP sprayer used to direct requests to the HTTP servers must provide some sort of affinity mechanism so that browser requests return to the HTTP server that negotiated the ID with the browser. Additionally, in a clustered environment with multiple application servers, either cookies or URL rewriting must be enabled for affinity between the HTTP server and application server. Lastly, in a fashion similar to URL rewriting, the administrator must also explicitly configure WAS to employ this option by selecting this option on the configuration dialog (refer to Figure 22-3).

## The Session API

The interface declaration of HttpSession contains over a dozen methods in all. Minimally, an application will likely call three of these methods. The first of these is the getSession() method, which is used to either create a session object if one does not already exist or to associate a request with an existing session. In order to store information in the session object, the setAttribute() method is called, and the application retrieves information that is stored via a call to the getAttribute() method. Often overlooked in an application is the invalidate() method call. There should also be some provision in the application to invalidate the session object once the application no longer requires the session:

```
session.invalidate() ;
```

Unless configured to never do so, the web container will eventually invalidate the session object once the inactive interval for the session is reached. When the application explicitly invalidates the session, it reduces the overhead on the runtime of tracking sessions that are no longer required. You can also minimize the size of session objects prior to invalidation by removing attributes no longer required by explicitly calling the removeAttribute() method in the application.

Another constraint exists for applications that implement distributable sessions, which are sessions that can be handled by more than one web container, typically in order to provide for failover. In this case, all objects placed into HttpSession via the `setAttribute()` method must be serializable. WebSphere Application Server does provide for exceptions to this requirement for some J2EE objects that are not serializable:

- javax.ejb.EJBObject
- javax.ejb.EJBHome
- javax.naming.Context
- javax.transaction.UserTransaction

The specifics on how WAS overcomes this restriction vary for each of these objects. Except for UserTransaction, which requires a WebSphere specific public wrapper object, the mechanism employed is transparent to the application.

It is best if all objects placed into HTTP session are serializable or you'll experience a java.io.NotSerializable Exception, as shown in Code Snippet 22-1. This provision ensures transparent deployment in both non-clustered and clustered environments, without requiring application changes for the latter. It's also important to note that it's not sufficient that the application simply implement the java.io.Serializable interface; the objects must actually be serializable, which is an important but subtle distinction that we'll return to later.

## WAS Session Management Configuration

WebSphere Application Server V5 provides a large number of options for configuring the behavior of the session manager portion of the runtime. The default is for these options to apply to all applications running inside a given application server, but they can also be configured on a case-by-case basis for each enterprise application running on an application server or web applications within an enterprise application. By tuning at the application level, you ensure that the application behaves in the same fashion, regardless of the configuration of the application server. Customization of the session manager for a web application or enterprise application is performed by selecting the **Overwrite Session Management** check box for the enterprise application or web application, as shown in Figure 22-4.

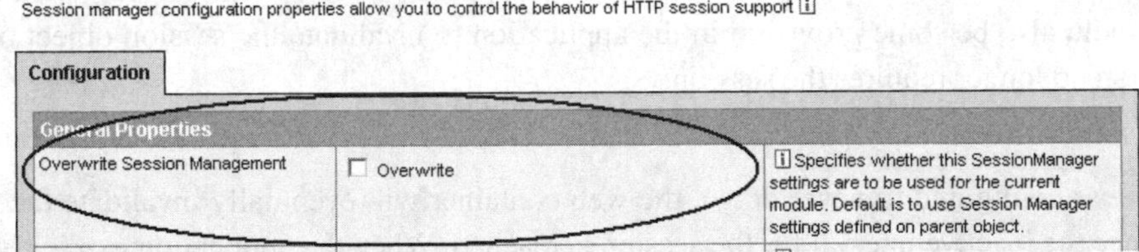


**Figure 22-4** Overwriting session management for an EAR or web application.

The Configuration tab depicting the Overwrite property is located on the Session Manager dialog for both the enterprise application and web applications, which is reached from the administration console by navigating to **Applications > Enterprise Applications > Additional Properties > Session Management**. In cases where you want to overwrite the properties for a web application, the dialog is reached by selecting the **Web Modules > Session Management** for a specific enterprise application. All of the options described here can be configured specifically to a web application or enterprise application, so as an example, one application in an application server could persist session to a database, while other applications could use memory-to-memory replication.

### Local and Distributed Session Options

The default with WAS V5 is to store the HTTP session object locally as part of the application server JVM. WAS also provides for distributed sessions that can be replicated in memory to other application servers or persisted to a database. Distributed sessions provide for failover of the session object to a surviving application server in the case of an application server outage. Through the use of cookies or URL rewriting, WAS provides affinity so that requests from a specific browser return to the application server where the session object was initially created. The configuration options common to both local and distributed sessions are depicted in Figure 22-5, though the meaning for some of these varies on whether local or distributed sessions are in use.

This dialog is reached by navigating to **Application Servers** > *application server name* > **Web Container > Session Management** in the administration browser client.

Configuration

| General Properties | | |
|---|---|---|
| Session tracking mechanism: | ☐ Enable SSL ID tracking<br>☑ Enable Cookies<br>☐ Enable URL Rewriting<br>☐ Enable protocol switch rewriting | Specify a mechanism for HTTP session management. |
| Maximum in-memory session count: | 1000 sessions | Specifies the maximum number of sessions to maintain in memory. |
| Overflow: | ☑ Allow overflow | Whether to allow the number of sessions in memory to exceed the value specified by Max In Memory Session Count property. This is valid only in non-persistent sessions mode. |
| Session timeout: | ○ No timeout<br>◉ Set timeout<br>30 minutes | Specifies how long a session is allowed to go unused before it will be considered valid no longer. Specify either "Set timeout" or "No timeout." If you select to set the timeout, the value must be at least two minutes, specified in minutes. |
| Security integration | ☐ Enable | When security integration is enabled, the Session Manager will associate the identity of users with their HTTP sessions. |
| Serialize session access: | ☐ Allow serial access<br>Maximum wait time : 5 seconds<br>☑ Allow access on timeout | Serialize session access indicates whether to disallow concurrent session access in a given server (JVM). |

**Figure 22-5** Session management configuration.

## Maximum Session Count and Allow Overflow

The next two parameters on this dialog are for the maximum number of session objects stored in memory and whether the maximum can be exceeded. This allows you to limit the memory footprint of sessions stored locally or in local cache when distributed sessions are in use. When local sessions are in use, the session count specifies the number of sessions that are stored in memory, assuming that you do not specify "Allow Overflow." When Allow Overflow is specified and local sessions are in use, a second session memory table is constructed, and all sessions greater than the specified maximum are stored there, up to the available memory for the JVM. For distributed sessions, when Allow Overflow is specified, the session manager employs a Least Recently Used (LRU) algorithm so that only the most recently used sessions, up to the maximum count, are kept in the local cache, with the remainder of the session objects either replicated in memory to a remote application server or persisted to a database depending on your configuration. Specifying Allow Overflow should probably never be configured. Doing so removes the limiting mechanism that it provides. As a result, the number of session objects could grow to consume the entire application server JVM, either as the result of a spike in load or as the result of a denial of service attack.

## Session Timeout

As its name implies, the Session Timeout parameter specifies how long an unused session exists before it times out and is removed from the memory table for local sessions or the cache for distributed sessions. This setting is an important one from a performance perspective because of the memory impact that unused sessions can have on the application server JVM until they are removed. In the same vein, specifying "No Timeout" can result in a memory leak since the session objects are never eligible for garbage collection by the JVM, unless the application explicitly calls session.invalidate(). As a result, No Timeout is generally not recommended, though it might be appropriate for a small percentage of applications where the user population is very small and stable. In order to minimize the memory impact of session objects, this setting should be set as low as practical in order to satisfy application requirements and use patterns. For applications with a large number of short-lived visits of perhaps a few minutes, a timeout of 5–10 minutes would likely be appropriate. Some web sites even provide a timer to show when the current session will expire and a logout function that invalidates the session.

## Session Security Integration

When "Security Integration" is enabled, WAS checks the user ID of the HTTP request against the user ID for the session object as part of the processing of the request.getSession() method. If the check fails, an UnauthorizedSessionRequestException is thrown. When used in conjunction with SSL, Security Integration can be used to prevent "man in the middle" intrusions. Thus, when architecting a secure infrastructure, it's recommended that this option be employed.

## Serialize Session Access

This option is somewhat misnamed since, when specified, the session manager actually synchronizes access to a session inside a JVM in order to provide thread-safe access to the session object. Prior to WAS V3.5.3, this was the default for session access, but in order to improve performance, the responsibility for thread safety was shifted from the runtime to the application developer. For best performance, it's recommended that applications continue to take appropriate measures inside the application to ensure thread safety rather than relying on this option. This means that application code must be careful when modifying a session to ensure that multiple threads don't simultaneously modify the same session object in conflicting ways. This is most likely to occur in web applications that use frames where multiple Servlets are executing on behalf of the same client simultaneously. This is fairly easy to prevent by ensuring that only one of the Servlets in the frame modifies the session and the others only read from it.

## Shared Session Context

Before leaving the session management options, there is one additional option that can be configured in the Application Server Toolkit (ASTK), WebSphere Studio, or the Application Assembly Tool (AAT). This is a J2EE extension that allows for the session object to be shared across the multiple Servlet contexts inside a single enterprise application. While this is a useful option when migrating pre-J2EE applications (Servlet 2.1) to J2EE compliance, we recommend that this be avoided if at all possible. Sharing session in this fashion tends to lead to large session objects that in turn are usually detrimental to application performance. This option is enabled in the ASTK or Studio by selecting the check box indicated in Figure 22-6.

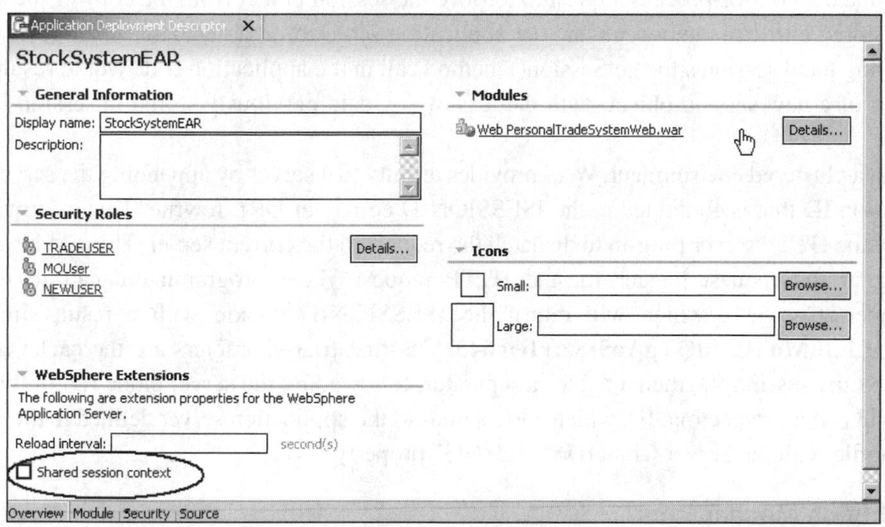


**Figure 22-6** Session sharing option in ASTK.

## Distributed Sessions

As previously noted, distributed sessions provide for failover in case of application server outage, allowing an end user to continue using a web site without any loss of an application state that could require a re-login or navigation through previously viewed pages. While local sessions only provide for a single copy of the session object, distributed sessions provide at least one copy of the session object in addition to the local copy that is cached in the application server JVM. It's worth mentioning that aside from ensuring that the information placed into the HTTP session is serializable, there's no impact to application development when choosing to use this option.

### Session Affinity

Strictly speaking, session affinity isn't an option; it's the default behavior for WAS, but before discussing the other session-management settings in WAS, it's important to have some understanding of how WebSphere Application Server implements this feature. Session affinity allows WAS to return requests associated with a given browser and session object back to the same application server instance in a clustered environment. This in turn aids performance by allowing sessions to be accessed from the cache in the application server when distributed sessions are in use and allows local sessions to be utilized in cases where session failover is not a requirement. Without affinity, browser requests would be distributed across all application servers in a cluster. The impact of requests being distributed in this fashion would depend on whether distributed or local sessions were in use. In an environment using distributed sessions, the application server would make an out-of-process request to retrieve the session object from the copy of the session object stored either in memory in another application server or in a database. In an environment employing local sessions, the getSession() method call in the application code would result in the creation of a new session object, with the loss of any data previously stored in session for that client.

In a clustered environment, WAS provides affinity to a server by appending the server ID to the session ID that is contained in the JSESSIONID cookie or URL rewrite. This information is used by the HTTP server plug-in to dispatch the request to the correct server. This can be seen by looking at the request header for the HTTP request via a programmatic call to request. getHeader("Cookie"), which will return the JSESSIONID cookie with a result similar to **0001kJLEJhMoitCnI0QTgAo5z8z:v1efc643**. The first four characters are the cache ID, followed by the session ID, then a ":" for a separator, followed by the server clone ID. In this case, **v1efc643** is the server clone ID, which corresponds to the application server defined in the plugin-cfg.xml file with the Server CloneID="v1efc643" property.

## Distribution Mechanisms

In order to maintain session state across multiple application servers, some mechanism for distribution of the session object is required. That way, if one application server should fail, when the request is routed to another application server, that server can obtain the state from a remote persistent store. In looking at the link to the Distributed Environment Settings dialog (see Figure 22-7), you'll note the word "persistence," which is probably not the best term for this, but it has been used historically, so we continue to use it here, even though only one of the options provides persistence. Keep in mind that sessions are not intended for long-term stable storage. The lifetime of their "persistence" is essentially the lifetime of the client browser. In any case, WAS provides two persistence mechanisms for maintaining session state: database and memory to memory. The dialog for configuration of Distributed Sessions is accessed from Distributed Environment Settings under the Additional Properties heading at the bottom of the session configuration dialog, as shown in Figure 22-7.

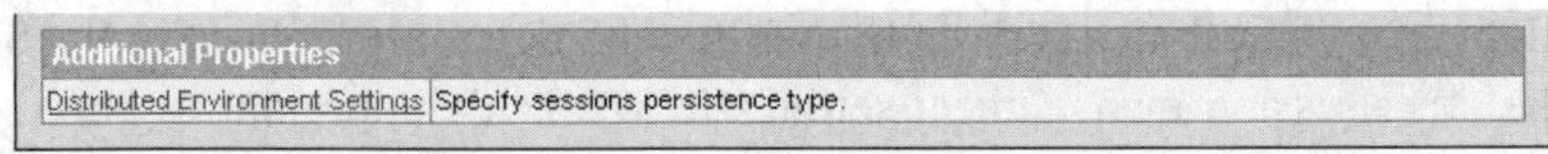


**Figure 22-7** Link to Distributed Environment Settings dialog.

This in turn leads to the dialog depicted in Figure 22-8, where the options for Distributed Sessions are specified.

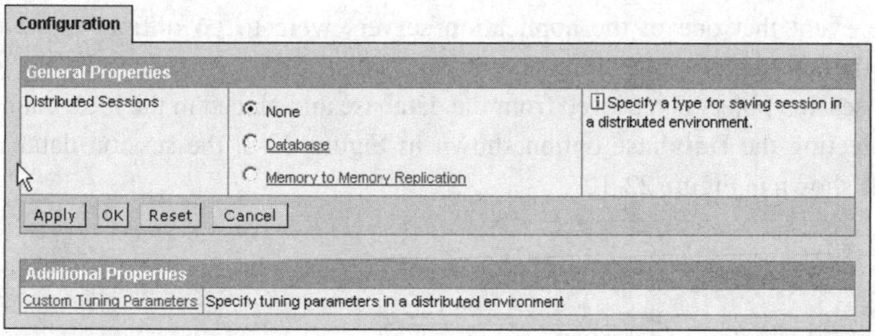

Configuration

General Properties

Distributed Sessions | None / Database / Memory to Memory Replication | Specify a type for saving session in a distributed environment.

Apply | OK | Reset | Cancel

Additional Properties

Custom Tuning Parameters | Specify tuning parameters in a distributed environment

**Figure 22-8** Session distribution options.

The default of "None" is depicted, with options for "Database" and "Memory to Memory Replication." If your web site requires that application state be maintained in the event of a server outage, you will want to provide for failover by selecting one of the two options. The decision on which option is appropriate for your environment will depend on several factors, which we'll explore, but first let's discuss how each of these options is implemented and configured.

## Database Session Persistence

When a database is used for session failover, the WAS session manager uses a database table to store a copy of the session object. This is depicted in Figure 22-9. Each application server maintains a local cache of the session object with a copy maintained in the database.

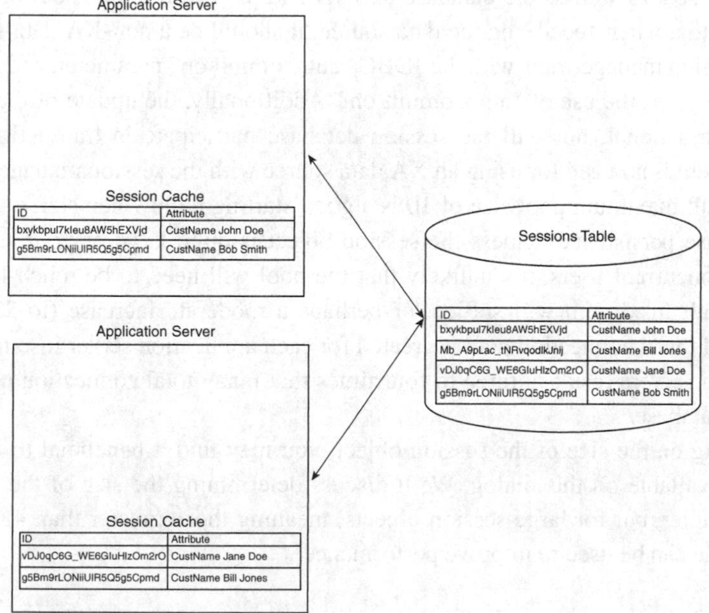


**Figure 22-9** Database session persistence.

In the event that one of the application servers were to go offline, requests would be directed to the surviving application servers, and when the application calls the getSession() method, the session object is retrieved from the database and placed in the local cache.

By selecting the **Database** option shown in Figure 22-8, the session database dialog is displayed, as shown in Figure 22-10.

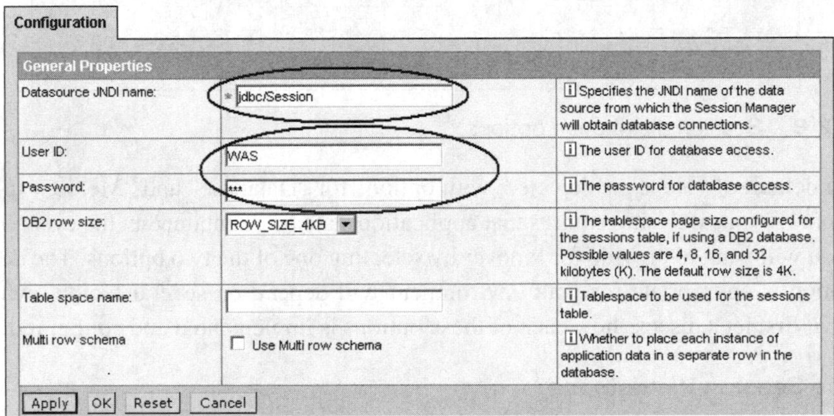


**Figure 20-10** Configuring a database for session persistence.

At a minimum, you need to supply a JNDI name for a data source that corresponds to a database to be used, as well as the database user ID and password to be used for accessing the database. Note that when specifying the data source, it should be a non-XA data source. This is because the session manager runs with the JDBC "autocommit on" parameter, and some XA data sources don't support the use of "autocommit on." Additionally, the update of the session database is not transactional, nor will the session database participate in transactions with other resources, so there is no need for using an XA data source with the session manager.

The default maximum pool size of 10 is a good starting point when sizing the connection pool for database persistence. Unless the session object is quite large or your site is handling thousands of concurrent users, it's unlikely that the pool will need to be much larger. In most cases, the default maximum will suffice, or perhaps a moderate increase (to 22–30) may be required. Recall that a connection pool is created for each application server instance, so three or four application servers result in three to four times that many total connection objects that are accessing the database.

Depending on the size of the session object, you may find it beneficial to use one of the other options available on this dialog. We'll discuss determining the size of the session object later in this chapter, but for large session objects, meaning those greater than 4KB in size, the options available can be used to improve performance.

When DB2 is used as the database, the page size can be adjusted from the default of 4KB to 8KB, 16KB, and 32KB. This allows the **varchar** database column used for the session object to fit onto a single database page. The result is faster performance for session objects that are approximately 7KB, 15KB, and 31KB in size.

The multi-row schema option can be employed to improve performance in some cases for large session objects, regardless of the database in use. With multi-row sessions, each attribute in the session object is stored in its own row in the database, instead of the default of storing all attributes in one column in a single row. This can be used to improve performance in two ways. The first is for non-DB2 databases, where WAS makes no provision to adjust the table page size. If each attribute stored in session is smaller than the page or block size for the database, specifying multi-row allows each row to be contained in a single database block. This can be combined with the optional write setting "only updated attributes" so that only the rows corresponding to each updated attribute are written to, instead of a write to all rows.

The other advantage to using multi-row sessions is that they allow you to have a session object larger than 2MB in size. Such extremely large session objects are most definitely not recommended from a performance and failover perspective, but WAS does provide a mechanism for dealing with objects of this size.

### Memory-to-Memory Replication

As implied by the name, memory-to-memory replication stores a copy of the session object in the memory of one or more application server processes. In this mode, the WAS Distributed Replication Service (DRS) is used to replicate session information among application servers. Since DRS is used by multiple WAS runtime components, there's a discussion of the DRS architecture and configuration options in Chapter 20, "WAS Network Deployment Architecture," including instructions that walk through configuring DRS as a failover mechanism for HTTP session. As a result, if you plan to use DRS/Internal Messaging for an HTTP session failover, you should refer to that chapter. In order not to duplicate content, all we'll provide here is a brief review of the components in DRS and their role in HTTP session management:

- **Replicator**—The data transfer component of DRS running in an application server.
- **Replication domain**—The set of replicators that are connected together to share data.
- **Session manager**—The web container component that manages HTTP session objects.
- **Replication mode**—A server is a "client" if it only forwards changes to other session managers, while it is considered a "server" if it only receives changes from other session managers, and "both" (or peer to peer) if it does both.
- **Group**—A session object is assigned to a group; by default, all session managers listen to all groups, but you can partition where a session object is replicated to.
- **Single replica**—An alternative to groups in which, as the name implies, the session object is only replicated once.

There are four configuration options for memory to memory replication:

- Peer-to-peer, where each application server has a "replicator" process and stores a copy of the session object for all other application servers in the domain.
- Peer-to-peer with standalone replicators, where each application server stores a copy of the session object for all other application servers in the domain, but additional dedicated application servers run the replicator process.
- Client-server, where the application servers running the application have just a local copy of the session object for requests to that application server, and dedicated application servers store session copies and run the replicator process.
- Client-server with dedicated replicators and dedicated stores, where each application server maintains just the session object for requests to that application server, with application servers running the replicator process and additional application servers storing copies of the session objects for the replication domain.

Memory-to-memory replication provides failover in much the same manner as with database persistence. When a request arrives at an application server and the session object is not in the local cache, the session manager component of the runtime will attempt to retrieve it from the local or remote replica.

In order to configure the session manager to use memory-to-memory replication, a replication domain must be defined. This is somewhat analogous to creating a database when database persistence is to be employed and must be performed prior to specifying "Memory to Memory Replication" in the Distributed Session dialog shown in Figure 22-8.

Once you specify memory to memory as the mechanism for distributing sessions, the steps for configuring and tuning DRS are the same as those described in Chapter 20.

Before leaving the topic of distribution mechanisms, let's give some consideration to what might lead you to choose one option over the other. Performance will not be a factor since 95% of the cost of replicating session is serialization/deserialization of the session object, which must occur regardless of how the session is distributed (memory to memory or database). Additionally, as the size of the session object increases, performance degrades, again about equally for both session distribution options. Instead, the decision will be based partially on how the two technologies differ:

- With a database, you actually persist the data (to disk), so a highly available database server can survive a cascading failure, while using application servers as session stores and replicators for this purpose may not.

- In the case of a "gold standard" (two identical cells/domains), a highly available database can pretty much assure session failover between domains, while with memory to memory, there can only be a single replicator common to the two cells; hence, it becomes a single point of failure (SPOF).[2]

Thus, for configurations where cross-cell session failover is a requirement, a highly available database is the only option for eliminating a SPOF. Note that while sharing sessions across cells is supported, this is not generally recommended. By sharing state between cells, it makes it significantly more difficult to independently upgrade components (application and WAS) in the two cells.

In the end, the decision then becomes based on what technology you are most comfortable with and which delivers the required quality of service for your availability requirements.

### Custom Tuning Parameters for HTTP Session

The Custom Tuning Options dialog controls the frequency and type of updates that the session manager makes to either the database or to memory-to-memory replicas. This dialog is reached by selecting **Custom Tuning Parameters** on the bottom of the **Distributed Environment Settings** dialog (Figure 22-8) and is depicted in Figure 22-11. In prior versions of WebSphere Application Server, the default was to update the session object at the end of the Servlet service method, and while this remains an option in V5 ("medium tuning" in the Tuning dialog), the default in WAS V5 is for a time-based write of the session updates. As of V5.02 (and above), the default time interval is every 10 seconds; earlier WAS V5 releases defaulted to 120 seconds.[3]

While time-based writes offer better performance than writing at the end of the Servlet service method, they also introduce the possibility of inconsistent application state. By deferring updates to the end of the specified time interval, an application could appear to move "backward" in state in the event of an application server failure during the specified update interval. Session changes made between updates will be lost while the end user will continue to use the web site. It is possible that the application's session state could move backward in time while the web page being viewed does not reflect this, potentially resulting in problems. Tests by the WebSphere performance lab have shown that a 10-second interval provides essentially all of the performance benefit of longer intervals, while limiting the vulnerability of inconsistent session state.

While requiring more resources (CPU, I/O), the update of the session object at the end of each Servlet service method ensures data consistency in the event of the failover of requests from one application server to another.

2 This is because all the application servers (in both cells) must be defined as "clients" to that server, and the admin console only gives you the ability to provide one replicator IP address and port at a time on a server, so if that replicator were to go down, then it would amount to a SPOF (single point of failure). This differs from the default behavior in a single cell, where the multiple application servers in a replication domain can be configured in a "client server" configuration.

3 The longer default interval was simply the result of limited testing and development resources that were available prior to the V5.0 release. The 10-second interval is a recommended starting point in V5.0 and V5.01, though you may want to tune it for your application and environment.

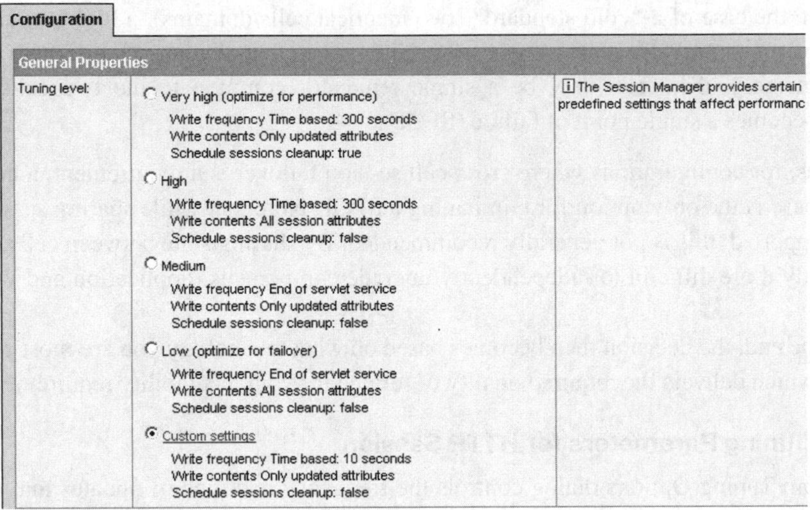


**Figure 22-11** Session Write Frequency Tuning dialog.

In order to avoid possible application state inconsistencies, the authors favor the **Medium** tuning setting shown in Figure 22-11 since it minimizes the cost of writing updates by only writing the session attributes that have been updated.

You can further refine the tuning levels depicted by selecting **Custom Settings**, which invokes the dialog shown in Figure 22-12.

Configuration

General Properties

| | | |
|---|---|---|
| Write frequency | End of servlet service<br>Manual update<br>Time based:<br>10 seconds | This option controls when the session will be written to the persistent store. |
| Write contents | Only updated attributes<br>All session attributes | Whether only updated attributes should be written to the persistent store or all of the session attributes should be written to the persistent store, whether or not they have changed. If you specify only updated attributes, only the updated attributes will be written to the persistent store If you specify all session attributes, all attributes will be written to the persistent store. |
| Schedule sessions cleanup: | Specify distributed sessions cleanup schedule<br>First time of day (0-23):<br>Second time of day (0-23): | Specifies when to clean the invalid sessions from external location. |

**Figure 22-12** Session Tuning Custom Settings.

The primary options of interest here are the ability to specify a manual update, though this requires that the application code use the IBMSession class, which is an extension to the HTTP session API, for managing sessions. With a manual update, the session manager only writes the session data and last access time to the session replica when the application invokes the sync() method in the IBMSession class. The session data that is written out to the replica is controlled by the write contents option selected. If the Servlet or JSP terminates without invoking the sync() method, the session manager saves the contents of the session object into the session cache (if caching is enabled) but does not update the modified session data in the session replica. The session manager will only update the last access time in the replica asynchronously at a later time. While this option requires using a non-J2EE extension and, as a result, is not portable to other application servers, it does provide the most control over writing updates of the session object. Use of this option is most beneficial for applications that only read or update the session object rarely. If changes in the session object don't occur on every browser interaction, the manual update will likely outperform the use of end-of-service method updates.

The other setting of interest is the ability to schedule session cleanup at certain times of day instead of when the session times out. While in some cases, such as where sessions are extremely long-lived, this option might be of value, however it's best to remove unneeded sessions as soon as they are no longer needed in order to minimize the impact of managing and tracking the sessions that are no longer needed.

## Session Tuning and Troubleshooting

### Session Object Size

As noted previously, the information contained in HTTP session is stored in the application server JVM, which is a limited resource that is shared by all applications and users. As a result, the more information that is stored in session, the greater the memory footprint for HTTP session, with a proportional decrease in JVM memory available for creation and execution of application objects. In turn, performance can degrade as the decreased heap memory leads to frequent garbage collection (GC). Another factor is the amount of time it takes to serialize and deserialize HTTP session as it is being written to a remote copy—the authors know of cases where the write of the updated session objects from the application server to the database server could not complete due to the size of the session object as the application server was failing, thus negating any failover. Keeping these factors in mind, as well as the primary purpose of HTTP session, which is simply to maintain state between browser invocations, you should strive to keep session objects small so that HTTP session serves as a bookmark and not as a library. How small, you ask? Ideally, the session object should be less than 4KB in size, which coincidentally is also the size limit for a cookie. Of course, it's not always possible to architect an "ideal application," so with this in mind, you should strive to maintain an upper size limit in the 30–60KB in range. In this range, there will be performance degradation, but it will not be as severe as with much larger sessions.

With the size of the session object serving as a primary contributor to application performance, it's fortunate that WAS V5 provides a mechanism for determining session size via the WAS Performance Monitoring Infrastructure (PMI). By configuring the maximum monitoring level in the Tivoli Performance Viewer, as shown in Figure 22-13, you can monitor the size of the session object, as shown in Figure 22-14. The size is shown in bytes. Those of you not familiar with PMI and the Tivoli Performance Viewer will want to see Chapter 25, "Performance Tuning Tools," for a more comprehensive discussion of these two subjects.

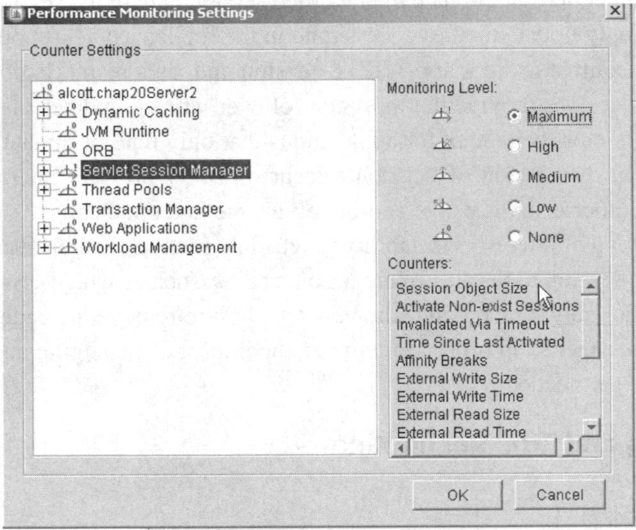


**Figure 22-13** Session Manager PMI Monitoring Level Settings.

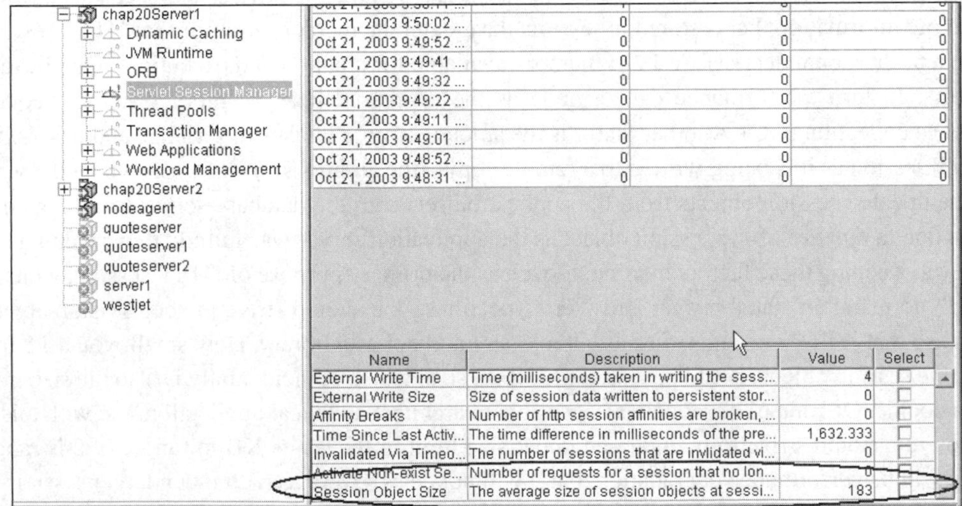


**Figure 22-14** Session object size in the Tivoli Performance Viewer.

### Non-Serializable Objects in Session

Another common issue deals with the application placing an object in HTTP session that's not serializable. This typically shows up in an application server SystemErr file, as shown in Code Snippet 22-1.

**Code Snippet 22-1** Session exception example from logs

```
[3/17/02 10:16:44:253 PST] 61602dc6 SessionContex X SESN0058E:
➥BackedHashtableMR: a problem occurred inserting a new session into
➥the database. If a SQLException has occurred then refer to the
➥appropriate database documentation for your environment. Also, assure
➥that you have properly configured a datasource for Session Manager.
java.io.NotSerializableException:
➥com.ibm.servlet.engine.webapp.WebApp...
```

In most cases, you can turn on session trace to determine the non-serializable session object, but in some cases such as Code Snippet 22-2, this still is not definitive (you can see that the "non-serializable stanza" is empty).

**Code Snippet 22-2** Non-serializable stanza from logs

```
[3/17/03 10:16:55:940 PST] 61602dc6 SessionContex >
SessionContext:getIHttpSession - leaving and returning session of

Session Object Internals: id : LE0W4B1E0SPCR2TT4AI1BZA

<omitted for brevity>

non-serializable app specific session data : {}

serializable app specific session data :

{webControler=com.sun.j2ee.blueprints.petstore.control.web.
➥ShoppingClientControllerWebImpl@69246dcc, currentScreen=MAIN,

profilemgr=com.sun.j2ee.blueprints.petstore.control.web.
➥ProfileMgrWebImpl@1e272dcc,

customer=com.sun.j2ee.blueprints.petstore.control.web.CustomerWebImpl@
➥2d572dcc,

cart=com.sun.j2ee.blueprints.petstore.control.web.ShoppingCartWebImpl@
➥33292dcc,

mm=com.sun.j2ee.blueprints.petstore.control.web.ModelManager@20bbedcc,
➥language=en_US}
<omitted for brevity
```

This is because the object implements serializable but isn't actually serializable.

Code Snippet 22-3 contains the source code for a JSP, SessionObjects.jsp, which iterates through all the attributes in the session object, actually tries to write/read all the objects out as a "true" test of serialization, and then displays the results, as shown in Figure 22-15. The JSP displays, left to right:

- The attribute name
- The attribute value
- The results of reading the object after serialization/deserialization

Any attribute that displays "read object null" is in fact not serializable and should not be placed into session if you intend to use distributed sessions.

You simply can drop the JSP into the installedApps directory for the application, *<wasinstallroot/installedApps\installedapp.ear\installed app.war*, along with the rest of the JSPs. Next, create a session object in the application though normal application flow and then invoke the JSP by invoking the appropriate URL: <webapp URL>/SessionObjects.jsp. This will show the offending object(s). You'll also note that this shows the size of each session attribute, so this can be helpful in determining if multi-row sessions would be of value. Please note that the JSP uses a large amount of Java scriptlet and, as a result, is not necessarily representative of "application best practices." Instead, it was developed rather quickly as a debugging aid.

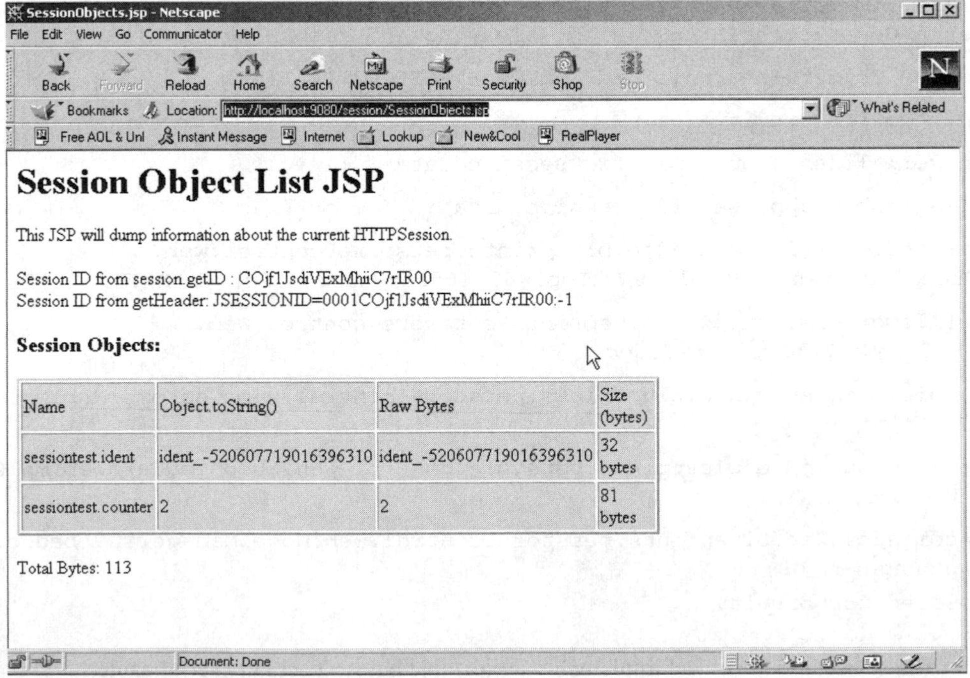


**Figure 22-15** Session Object JSP.

**Code Snippet 22-3** Session Object List JSP

```
<!DOCTYPE HTML PUBLIC "-//W3C//DTD HTML 4.01 Transitional//EN">
<HTML>
<HEAD>
<%@ page
language="java"
contentType="text/html; charset=ISO-8859-1"
pageEncoding="ISO-8859-1"
%>
<META http-equiv="Content-Type" content="text/html; charset=ISO-8859-1">
<META name="GENERATOR" content="IBM WebSphere Studio">
<TITLE>SessionObjects.jsp</TITLE>
</HEAD>
<BODY>
<H1>Session Object List JSP</H1>
This JSP will dump information about the current HTTPSession.<br><br>
<%@ page import="java.io.*,java.util.*,javax.servlet.*" session="false" %>
<%! public void dumpSession(HttpServletRequest request, JspWriter out)
➥throws IOException {
    HttpSession session = request.getSession(false);
        Object ro = null ;


    out.println("Session ID from session.getID : "
          + session.getId() + "<br>");

    out.println("Session ID from getHeader: "
          + request.getHeader("Cookie") + "<br>");


     Enumeration enum = session.getAttributeNames();
        if ( enum.hasMoreElements() )
        {
```

```
            int totalSize = 0;

            out.println("<h3>Session Objects:</h3>");
            out.println("<TABLE Border=\"2\" WIDTH=\"65%\" BGCOLOR=\
            ➥"#DDDDFF\">");
out.println("<tr><td>Name</td><td>Object.toString()</td>");
out.println("<td>Raw Bytes</td><td>Size (bytes)</td></tr>");
            while ( enum.hasMoreElements() )
            {
        String name = (String)enum.nextElement();

        Object sesobj = session.getAttribute(name) ;



        ObjectOutputStream oos = null;
                ByteArrayOutputStream bstream = new
                ➥ByteArrayOutputStream();
        try {

            oos = new ObjectOutputStream(bstream);
            oos.writeObject(sesobj);
            }
        catch (Exception e) {
            e.printStackTrace();
        }
            finally {
                if (oos != null) {
                try {oos.flush();}
                catch (IOException ioe) {}
                try {oos.close();}
                catch (IOException ioe) {}
            }
        }
```

```
        ObjectInputStream ois = null;
        ro = null ;

        try {
            ois = new ObjectInputStream(new
            ➥ByteArrayInputStream(bstream.toByteArray()));
        ro = ois.readObject();
                }
        catch (Exception e) {
        e.printStackTrace();
        }
            finally {
                if (ois != null) {
                try {ois.close();}
                catch (IOException ioe) {}
            }
        }

          totalSize += bstream.size();
                out.println("<tr><td>" + name + "</td><td>" +
                ➥session.getAttribute(name) +
    "</td><td>" + ro + "</td>");
          out.println("<td>" + bstream.size() + " bytes </td></tr>");
            }
            out.println("</table><BR>");
    out.println("Total Bytes: " + totalSize + "<br><br>");
        } else {
        out.println("No objects in session");
}
  }
  %>

<%
```

```
    response.setHeader("Pragma", "No-cache");
    response.setHeader("Cache-Control", "no-cache");
    response.setDateHeader("Expires",0);

    HttpSession session = request.getSession(false);
    if (session == null) {
          out.println("No session");
    }  else {
          dumpSession(request, out);
    }

%>
</BODY>
</HTML>
```

## Conclusion

In this chapter, we have examined the basics of HTTP session management and outlined some options for maintaining application state with HTTP session. We've seen how WAS implements HTTP session and covered the two approaches for persisting session data to a database and memory to memory. We also covered some of the performance implications of the session management configuration options and discussed some troubleshooting approaches.

CHAPTER 23

# WebSphere Edge Components

In several places in this book thus far, we have discussed and shown examples of WebSphere Application Server (WAS) topology in order to focus on features specific to WAS, such as the HTTP server plug-in for workload management (WLM) and caching to application servers on the backend. However, for most corporate applications, HTTP servers alone on the front end will not suffice for reasons related to scalability, reliability, performance, and security. Many web sites receive far too much traffic for a single web server to handle. In addition, having a single web server for each web site or application(s) is not a practical idea in terms of risk—it represents a single point of failure. When this server goes down or becomes overloaded, the entire site and all hosted applications are affected. An array of identical web servers sounds like a good solution to these problems, but then we must have some way of distributing web requests to these servers.

Included with WAS 5 Network Deployment are two software products bundled under the name "Edge Components." These two components are the Load Balancer and Caching Proxy. In addition to their primary functions, they also provide many other features such as content-based routing. We will begin this chapter by describing in general what is meant by the "edge" of the network and "edge" devices and then describe the specific features, usage, and functionality of the Edge Components. The Edge Components are a large and complex topic. Therefore, we can only cover the essential information in the space we have for this chapter. For further information, review the Edge Components Info Center for WAS ND Version 5.1. The 5.1 Info Center in particular has a greatly expanded and clarified discussion of the Edge Components over V5.0 and prior version documentation.

## Edge Topology

Let's begin by reviewing basic network topology and components. A basic topology, as shown in Figure 23-1, consists of the following (we have left out devices such as routers and switches because they are not relevant to our discussion):

- **Firewalls**—There are normally two firewalls—an Internet-facing firewall, sometimes referred to as the domain firewall, and a rear firewall, referred to as the protocol firewall. The former generally only permits HTTP traffic on ports 80 and 443 (SSL) to come into the DMZ, and the latter ideally only permits traffic coming from the WAS HTTP plug-in (or other designated devices in the DMZ) on known ports/protocols to flow through to the backend "secure" zone.
- **DMZ**—The area in between the domain and protocol firewalls is referred to as the "demilitarized zone." As it sounds, this is not considered to be a completely safe environment. In fact, you should operate under the assumption that it will at some point be breached by an attack. For this reason, it is a good practice to keep only hardened devices here and avoid any business logic or complex processes such as application/portal servers, which will also help keep the number of open ports in the firewalls to a minimum.
- **HTTP server**—This could be any type of HTTP server supported by WAS, such as IBM HTTP Server, Apache, or Microsoft IIS. As we have discussed earlier in this book, the WAS plug-in must be installed here to provide connectivity to the backend WAS servers.
- **WAS servers**—These could be multiple nodes in a WAS cell, configured as a cluster for redundancy. It doesn't make much sense to have redundancy in this tier and not in the DMZ!

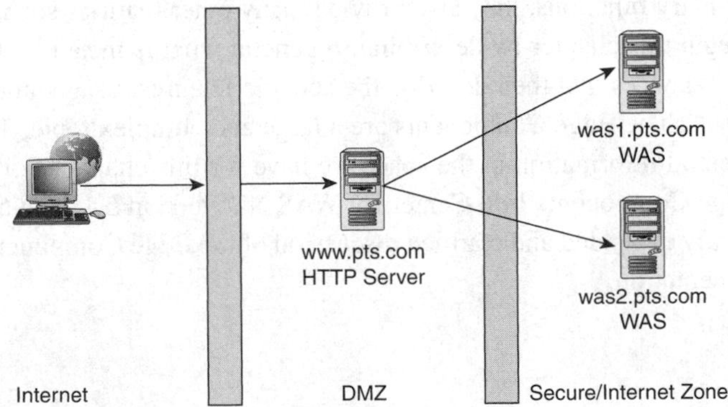


**Figure 23-1** Simple WAS topology.

In referring to the "edge" of the network, we are talking about the area from the DMZ out toward the Internet. Many corporate networks are wide-area networks that span data centers and geographies. In such cases, edge devices may be utilized—the edge of your network may be the DMZ, or it may be satellite offices or data centers. In any case, at these edge boundaries, load balancers can distribute traffic evenly to multiple servers, and proxy servers can front and hide the identity and content of web servers, filter or cache the results of static and dynamic requests, and cut back on network hops by being placed at edge locations. We will explore the usage of the Edge Components to realize all of these goals by expanding on the topology shown in Figure 23-1 throughout this chapter.

## Edge Devices

### Load Balancers

Load balancers do pretty much what the name implies. They forward traffic following some load balancing algorithm from a source to multiple destination servers over various protocols. Typically, the load balancer is acting as a single point of presence to multiple backend servers, distributing the request load among them to optimize the performance of the infrastructure. They can use simple, round-robin type algorithms or preset "weights" to determine which server each request should go to. In a more advanced configuration, they can use sophisticated mechanisms that determine which of the group of servers they are balancing is most able to handle the next request. If you are assigning static weights, and some of the backend servers are more powerful than others, these would likely be assigned a higher weight. Dynamic weighting can be used to assign more load to servers that are better able to handle it at that moment. A load balancer can be a hardware device or a software product that can be installed on some supported operating system. Referring to Figure 23-1, the following may be legitimate concerns about the single web server in the DMZ:

1. It represents a single point of failure—should it fail, the servers it is fronting become useless until it is recovered.
2. During periods of peak demand, it may not be sufficient on its own to handle load for the application servers it is servicing.
3. In order to maintain it (for example, to do operating system updates), it must be stopped, which would require some sort of outage or "maintenance window."

The solution may then be to use multiple web servers. This presents a problem in that the web sites hosted are usually tied to a single host name, such as www.pts.com, as shown in Figure 23-1. So you might ask, how can we have multiple servers under a single host name? A load balancer can solve this problem. Consider Figure 23-2, where a load balancer has been inserted into the topology in front of the web servers in the DMZ. Another advantage is that intelligent load balancers can detect failed servers and will remove them from their routing lists until they have been recovered, preventing failed user transactions.

> **NOTE**
> This usage described here is the most common usage of load balancers; however, they can actually load balance almost any TCP or UDP protocol or service. For example, a cluster of LDAP servers could be fronted by a load balancer.

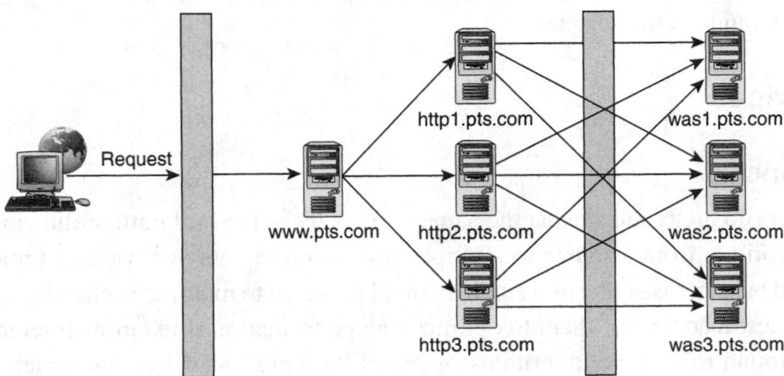


**Figure 23-2** Load-balanced web servers.

Comparing Figure 23-1 to Figure 23-2, you can see that in addition to implementing the load balancer, we have added a second and third web server and moved the host name www.pts.com from the first web server to the load balancer. This is essential so that links to the web site from the applications (as well as bookmarks to the site that users may have saved) do not have to be changed. Later, we will discuss in more detail the changes necessary to make this happen, but first let's review the benefits of this new configuration:

1. We now have multiple web servers so that if one fails, we no longer have a total outage. Keep in mind that, in this case, the "Rule of Threes" applies—if two of any resource is necessary to handle your peak load, you really need to have three of them so that if one fails, the remaining two can handle the load without becoming overwhelmed. In this example, should one web server fail, the remaining web servers will need to be powerful enough to handle peak load.
2. If we wanted to upgrade the web servers, we could now do this by quiescing traffic through the load balancer so that traffic drains from one of the servers that is then shut down for upgrade. When the upgrade is complete, the load balancer can be told to start sending traffic to the upgraded server, and the same process can be done on the other servers.

## MAC Forwarding

MAC forwarding is the most common method used for WAS Edge Components load balancing, so we will use it here for our discussion. Let's take a closer look at the configuration to better understand how this might all work. As we said, the host name www.pts.com has been shifted from the HTTP server to the load balancer. This is necessary so that all of the users out there who have the URL to our sites bookmarked do not experience disruption. The load balancer is now where we want their traffic to go, so we need to make this DNS change to assign www.pts.com to the load balancer's cluster IP address.

Referring to Figure 23-3, we have zoomed in to focus on the changes in the DMZ. You can assume that the HTTP servers are still using the WAS plug-in to communicate to backend WAS servers, which are omitted because they are not relevant to this discussion. The www.pts.com domain name has been assigned to a new "cluster address" IP of 192.168.1.110. This new IP address must be aliased to the adapter on the load balancer in addition to the native non-forwarding address (NFA) IP of 192.168.1.102. The cluster address is used to represent the "cluster" of servers to be load balanced and is the only address users see to represent the site (typically through its assigned domain name, www.pts.com). The NFA is not publicized—it is used only for maintenance and other "native" operations on the load-balancing server. The load balancer is using MAC forwarding to send the request IP packets off to the selected load-balanced server, meaning it will change the destination field of the MAC header of the packet so that it goes to the correct server. The TCP/IP packet is unchanged, so each server on the backend must have this cluster IP configured on its adapter as well so that they will accept the packets as their own. On these backend servers, the cluster IP is aliased to the loop-back adapter rather than the primary network adapter. This is an important and often overlooked part of the configuration; it allows the TCP/IP stack on the backend server to accept a packet with the cluster address in the TCP/IP packet header.

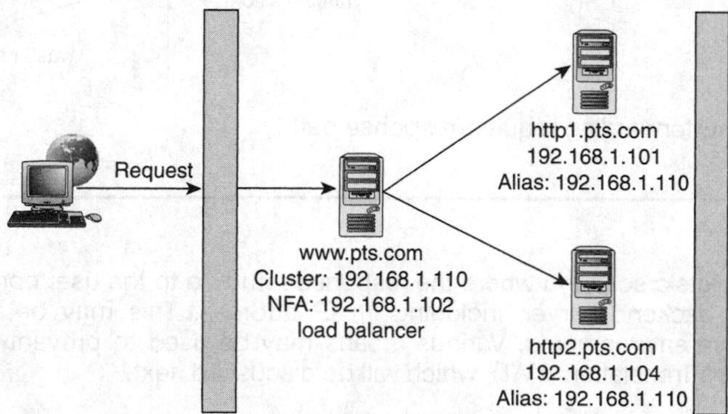


**Figure 23-3** Load-balanced web servers with IP configuration.

> **NOTE DNS ROUND-ROBIN—A POOR ALTERNATIVE**
> DNS has a feature that can select from multiple IP addresses for a single domain name in round-robin fashion. While this might be tempting as a simple and inexpensive form of load balancing, it has drawbacks because the DNS server is merely serving up IP addresses and is not actively involved in the traffic. In addition, client machines typically cache host name to IP address translations. Because of these two factors, the DNS server is not able to rapidly influence the host name to IP mappings, rendering this approach very primitive. In particular, it cannot detect failure of one of the backend servers as a true load balancer can, and it also cannot balance intelligently to distribute load among more lightly used servers.

In MAC forwarding mode, when the packet reaches the backend server, it still has the client's IP address in the source field. This means that the response will go back from the load-balanced server directly to the client, and not back through the load balancer. By taking this approach, the scalability of the load balancer is dramatically increased since the load balancer is involved only with inbound traffic, which is typically much smaller than outbound traffic. Figure 23-4 demonstrates this path.

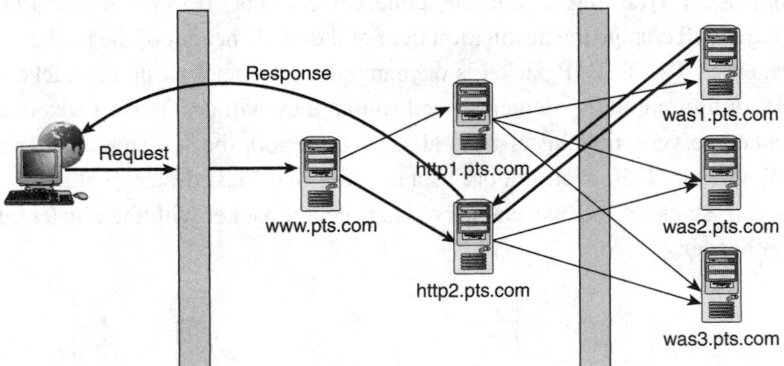


**Figure 23-4** MAC forwarding request/response path.

> **NOTE**
> Figure 23-4 depicts a scenario where the response returned to the user contains information about the backend server, including its IP address. This may be undesirable in security-sensitive environments. Various means may be used to prevent this, including Network Address Translation (NAT), which will be discussed next.

## NAT Forwarding

An important fact about MAC forwarding is that it is only good for load balancing to servers on the same local network (subnet), as the HTTP servers in Figure 23-4 are. Figure 23-5 shows a load balancer serving two servers on a different subnet from itself. You would need to use NAT forwarding to accomplish this.

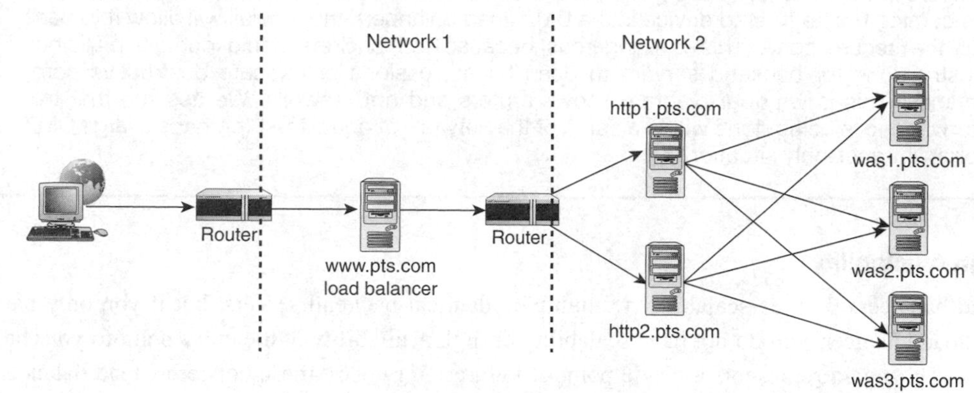


**Figure 23-5** NAT forwarding to servers on a separate subnet within a WAN.

With NAT forwarding, the load balancer will modify the packet to swap the source IP address with its own, and it saves off the client source IP address in a table. Since the load balancer IP address is now in the source field of the packet, the backend server will send the response back to the load balancer, which will do a table lookup to find the client's source IP and replace it, causing the packet to go merrily on its way back to the unknowing client. While this resolves security concerns with MAC forwarding related to clients discovering information such as the IP addresses and host names of the backend servers, it does introduce more overhead on the load balancer, which now must handle both incoming and outgoing traffic. This is a performance concern. MAC forwarding performs much better because it doesn't handle the returning traffic from the server to the client. As an alternative, load balancers could be placed on both the local and non-local networks and could forward traffic to each other, with each responsible for load balancing to their own subnets.

NAPT (Network Address Port Translation) is a variation on NAT forwarding, where the port can be modified as well as the source IP address, which is effective in hiding open port assignments for backend servers. Using NAPT, you can configure your backend servers to listen on ports other than the well-known defaults, such as port 80 for web traffic, to thwart some types of attacks. The client machines would still send requests to the load balancer on port 80, but NAPT could be configured to switch them to the second port when forwarding.

**NOTE**

As we have stated, NAT and NATP are more secure because they obscure information about backend servers and do not allow client connections directly to servers. However, it must be understood that a load balancer blindly forwards *any* user packets along to the load-balanced servers, as opposed to web or proxy servers that only accept HTTP traffic for URLs they are specifically configured for. Therefore, it is not advisable to have load balancers in the DMZ (even using NAT) forward to servers in the secure zone. Because traffic is coming from a trusted device in the DMZ (load balancer), the firewall will allow it to pass to the secure zone. This is dangerous because the packets could contain malicious instructions for backend servers to open telnet sessions or execute destructive commands. This is why our diagram shows routers and not firewalls. We assume that this forwarding is being done within an area of the network of equal trust (perhaps a large DMZ or an intranet-only situation).

### High Availability

Load balancers provide scalability to multiple, identical backend servers, but if you only have one load balancer, you do not have scalability or high availability at the entry point to your network. This again represents a single point of failure. To remedy these concerns, load balancers are often run as tandem active/standby servers. The active server does the load balancing, while the identical standby server continuously monitors its heartbeat. If the standby detects a failure of the active balancer, it immediately does an IP takeover and resumes the active server's responsibility. Another option is an active-active configuration, where two load balancers each serve up separate sets of cluster addresses but monitor each other to take over their partner's set if it should fail. Since there are typically only two load-balancing boxes, each must be able to handle the network traffic alone. This is one reason that the MAC-based forwarding approach is preferred since it reduces load on the load balancer.

As we discussed, NAT is a more secure configuration because responses do not travel directly from the backend servers to the clients. This prevents clients from learning information about the backend servers, such as their IP addresses or host names. Another way to achieve this without using NAT forwarding on the load balancer is to use a proxy server, which we will discuss in the next section.

## Proxy Server

A proxy server performs the same basic duties as a web server plus a whole lot more. Like a web server, the proxy server handles incoming requests to servers behind it and connects to those backend servers from its own pool of connections, thus hiding the backend servers. This means that the response will need to flow back through the proxy server, which will in return forward it to the requesting client. Being the "middle-man" in these transactions gives the proxy server the chance to do a number of helpful things. The following are a few of the services that proxy servers traditionally provide:

- **Proxy**—Accepts requests from clients on behalf of backend servers and performs basic web-server duties but allows for logic to be performed on a selection of backend servers. At the same time, it hides information about such servers while enabling clients to take advantage of their services. The proxy accepts the request from a client, connects to the backend server to retrieve the response, and then forwards the response on to the client.
- **Content filtering**—Proxy servers are often used to filter access to the Internet. Most corporate employees have at some point been asked to configure their browser for the company proxy server to be able to get access to the Internet. The proxy can be configured with rules to reject access to sites that contain objectionable material, preventing users from gaining access to such sites.
- **Caching**—Proxy servers often can cache the results of common user requests and serve them up directly from their cache, which results in a faster response time for the user and a lighter load on the backend servers. Caching can be done for static content for most proxy servers, for some dynamic HTTP requests (such as those for Servlets and JSPs), and even for heavy-lifting protocols, like FTP.
- **Security**—Proxy servers provide several advantages in this area. In addition to terminating the user connection in the DMZ, they can hide server identities by providing their own domain names in the URL instead of the backend server name. Some leading security tools for authentication and authorization proxying, such as Tivoli Access Manager, provide plug-ins for proxy servers so users can be authenticated before their requests are sent to any backend servers. Also, if the proxy does cache to memory, it could be considered a security benefit in that any intruders to the DMZ no longer have static content on the web server to deface with undesirable messages (a very common type of hack) since there are no longer any static files in the DMZ.

Many of the large public Internet web sites use huge arrays of proxy servers for performance and to handle these functions. Let's look at some specific proxy server configurations. Recall in Figure 23-5 that we used NAT to load balance to web servers. If the load balancer must be in the DMZ and the web servers have to be in the trusted zone, as we have stated, that topology is very dangerous.[1] Instead, let's look at another solution using proxy servers.

Figure 23-6 now shows the load balancer fronting two identical proxy servers that are proxying for our two web servers back in the secure zone. Notice how this approach provides load balancing and terminates connections in the DMZ—good security and scalability, a much better choice. In the next section of this chapter, we will show how to configure something similar using the WebSphere Edge Components, so don't worry too much about the specifics right now. We are trying to understand this from the architectural view.

1 See the related Note earlier in this chapter.

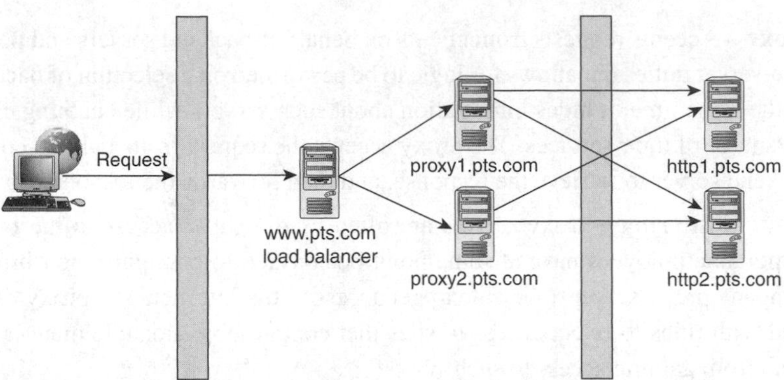


**Figure 23-6** Proxy servers in the DMZ.

> **NOTE**
>
> Since proxy servers provide "web server-like" functions, it may be tempting to always replace a web server with a proxy server. In some situations, this makes sense, but it often does not. Although replacing the web server and its WAS plug-in with a proxy server is a supported configuration, this doesn't make it the obvious best choice in all situations. Most importantly, the WAS web server plug-in, as noted in the chapter on caching, provides more sophisticated caching capabilities than WAS' Caching Proxy. In addition, the WAS web server plug-in provides workload management capabilities to the WAS servers behind it. If this is supplanted by a proxy server, some other approach to provide this (including affinity) must be configured. Finally, proxy servers are also more complex to configure than web servers, particularly compared with the ease of automatic and manual plug-in generation capabilities provided with WAS. An HTTP server is a well understood and fairly lightweight mechanism that is likely (there are no guarantees) to have fewer security issues than a more complex proxy server that provides higher function. The net is fairly simple. If you are architecting your system and find specific value in the use of a proxy server (this being any proxy server you might consider) in your configuration, then use it. Once that decision is made, it may make sense to eliminate the web server and go directly from the proxy server to WAS. Doing so eliminates a hop in your network traffic and may improve latency. However, do not simply replace the web server with a proxy server in all cases under the misguided notion that this is inherently more secure or even better. As we've stated already, the WAS plug-in provides sophisticated caching function and work-load management out of the box that is actually superior in most situations to what the WAS Caching Proxy server provides today (this may change with time).

Proxy servers have two types of common configurations—forward proxy and reverse proxy. What we have used for our examples so far is a typical reverse proxy setup; however, let's review each of these from the architectural perspective.

### Reverse Proxy

Figure 23-6 is a good example of a reverse proxy setup—proxying from server to server. The proxy server sits in the DMZ, and the host names for the web sites it is serving are configured on the proxy. Users can use the proxy server without being aware that it is even there. This is the most common form of proxy server configuration.

### Forward Proxy

Figure 23-7 depicts a simple forward proxy—proxying from user to server (as opposed to the reverse proxy, which was server to server). Imagine that the clients and the forward proxy server are in a remote branch office thousands of miles from the corporate data center. Given this scenario, consider the huge advantages in performance if the forward proxy server is now caching static and dynamic requests directly from the same location, rather than having to traverse the distance to the corporate data center. Also consider the savings if the company is paying for traffic over the network pipe from the branch office to the data center and Internet!

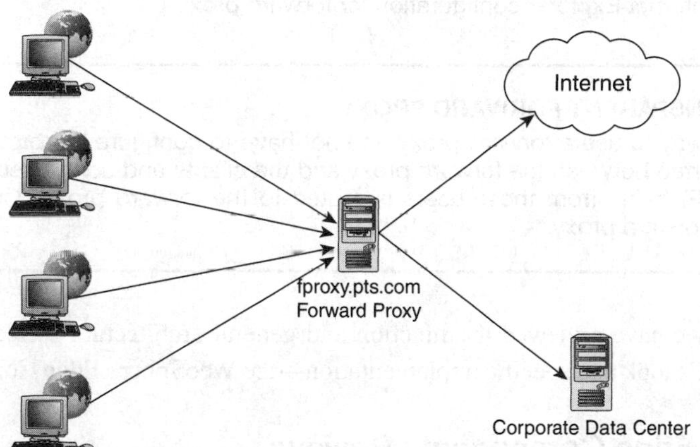


**Figure 23-7** Forward proxy.

In this configuration, the clients are connecting directly to the proxy server, which is proxying all requests from those users to the Internet, corporate data center, and anywhere else. So unlike our reverse proxy setup, the forward proxy cannot know or be assigned the host names for all possible sites to which it is proxying. Because of this, the clients must be "directed" to the proxy server for each request by having their browsers configured to use the proxy. Figure 23-8 shows Internet Explorer configured for a forward proxy via Tools > Internet Options > Connections > LAN Settings.

Because they must be configured on the client browser, forward proxies are usually only used for controlled environments, such as a company's branch office. Obviously, it would not be useful for the general public, whom you would have a hard time convincing to alter their browser settings!

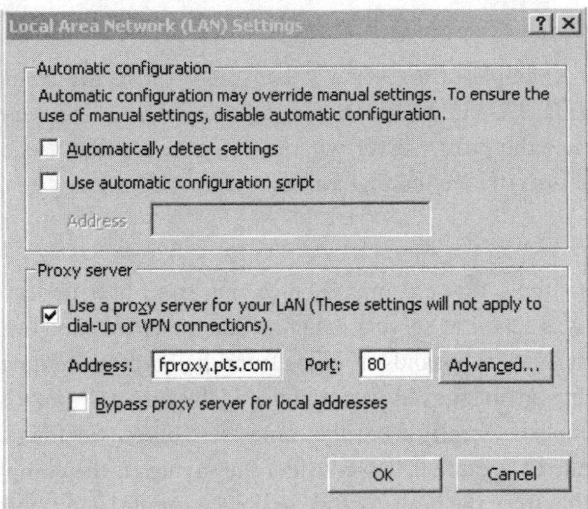


**Figure 23-8** Internet Explorer configuration for forward proxy.

> **NOTE TRANSPARENT FORWARD PROXY**
> There is one way to use a forward proxy and not have to configure the browser. A router could be inserted between the forward proxy and the clients and configured such that all port 80 (HTTP) traffic from those users is routed to the forward proxy. This is called a "transparent forward proxy."

Now that we have reviewed the function and general architecture of load balancers and proxy servers, let's look at a specific implementation—the WebSphere Edge Components.

## WebSphere Edge Components Review

### Load Balancer

Load Balancer (formerly known as Network Dispatcher) is the load-balancing piece of the Edge Components. It has the capability to do everything covered in our earlier generic load-balancing discussion, as well as a number of enhancements. For example, you can configure Advisors on the backend servers that report system metrics, such as memory and CPU utilization, and application information, such as whether an application server or data source is unavailable, to be used in load-balancing decisions. Load balancing can also be done by factoring in external data, such as the time of day, client IP address and/or port, rate of incoming connections, and total active connections.

## Load Balancer Components

Load Balancer is composed of the following components:

- **Dispatcher**—This is the load-balancing core component. It can balance most TCP or UDP protocols, such as HTTP, HTTPS, FTP, NNTP, IMAP, POP3, SMTP, and telnet traffic across a LAN or WAN. It runs in the operating system's kernel for maximum speed and examines each packet header to determine if the request is for a new or existing connection. The dispatcher itself has several components. The **executor** is actually the "brains" of the Load Balancer and does the work of routing TCP/UDP packets to the various servers. The **manager** keeps track of incoming data from advisors to set weights for the servers and provide those to the executor. The manager is optional—if the manager is not used, static weights can be assigned using the administrative facilities. If there are no weights set, round-robin load balancing occurs. **Advisors** are protocol-specific and monitor backend server health by means such as pinging and sending HTTP HEAD commands. Ping is used for all advisors to see if the server is reachable. If it is reachable, then a protocol-specific request is sent, such as an HTTP HEAD request. If the ping fails or there is no response to the protocol specific request, the server is marked down. This information is sent to the manager to determine server weighting (for example, servers that are slow to respond will be given lower weights so that less traffic is forwarded to them until things even out). Load Balancer also comes with non-protocol advisors, such as those that can monitor DB2 or WAS servers. Users can even write their own custom advisors using a supplied interface to monitor and advise on just about anything.
- **Kernel content-based routing (CBR)**—This is actually a "forwarding" alternative to MAC and NAT forwarding. This is a feature that can do more intelligent routing based on data in the HTTP request packet, such as pieces of the URI. It cannot decipher SSL, however, so it can only balance HTTPS traffic based on the SSL session ID, not the content of the request. It is much faster than the traditional web CBR. Be aware, however, that CBR is more expensive than MAC- or NAT-based forwarding because of the additional processing required. Thus, it is more intelligent but also more expensive.
- **Web content-based routing**—This is another form of CBR that is available as a Load Balancer plug-in to the Caching Proxy piece of the Edge Components. It isn't as fast as the kernel-based CBR, but it has the advantage that it can operate on contents of SSL requests. Of course, this involves decrypting and then re-encrypting the requests, which will incur overhead.
- **Cisco CSS/Nortel Alteon Controller**—The Load Balancer can also send some of the information it uses for load-balancing decisions to intelligent third-party devices—specifically, the Cisco CSS and Nortel Alteon Controller hardware controllers that provide information to their corresponding switches to facilitate intelligent switching

decisions. Load Balancer includes interfaces, which are smart hooks to send server-weighting data to each of these two third-party controllers to help them make smarter choices in routing traffic.

- **Metric Server**—This component runs as a daemon on backend servers to monitor utilization of resources such as CPU and memory and communicate that information to the Load Balancer Manager. Metric Server is used to calculate weighting metrics and detect failed server components (even for resources further back in the network, such as a database), which are passed to the Load Balancer process to assist even more with dynamic balancing decisions.
- **Site Selector**—This component acts as a DNS server in cases where load balancing needs to be augmented by dynamic mapping of IP addresses to host names. It works in conjunction with the Metric Server component to determine failed backend servers and server loads. This achieves the same effect as round-robin DNS, but with the advantages of being able to assign the host name to an IP address based on which servers are up and of being able to handle the incoming requests.

### Administration

The Load Balancer can be configured by means of a Java application GUI (**lbadmin** command), wizards (**dswizard** for general Dispatcher config, **cbrwizard** for web CBR, **sswizard** for Site Selector), a web-based administrative console, and command line/scripting. For remote administration on a machine other than the Load Balancer, the web-based console has advantages in that it can be secured with a userid/password and uses HTTP rather than Remote Method Invocation (RMI) calls. In keeping with the script-based theme of this book, we will use the command line and scripting for our configuration.

## Caching Proxy

The Caching Proxy component implements the basic proxy functions discussed in the first half of this chapter, as well as other advanced features. In addition to functioning as a proxy for HTTP and HTTPS requests, the Caching Proxy can also be configured for other protocols such as FTP and Gopher. Caching Proxy includes the following plug-ins for added functionality, or users can write their own custom-developed plug-ins with a supplied interface:

- **Internet Caching Protocol (ICP)**—This plug-in allows Caching Proxy to query other caching devices on the network that comply with the standard ICP protocol.
- **Tivoli Access Manager (TAM)**—This plug-in allows the authentication and authorization functions of TAM to be performed on the edge of the network, before the user request is sent to the backend server.
- **PAC-LDAP Authentication**—This plug-in facilitates Caching Proxy communication with LDAP servers to authenticate users. Caching Proxy has directives that can be used to secure URLs that are not configured as protected on the backend server. When the

Caching Proxy detects that a protected URL has been requested, it can authenticate and authorize the user based on the local password file or an LDAP directory using this plug-in.

- **Transcoding Publisher**—This plug-in enables caching of content that has been transcoded for various types of devices, including mobile phones and PDAs.

### Caching

Caching is such an important part of the Caching Proxy's functionality that it earned a place in the product name. This component can cache static as well as dynamic (Servlet and JSP) responses from backend WAS servers. The cache can be configured to use memory or a specially formatted disk partition and can be configured as a shareable cache in clusters of proxy servers via the Remote Cache Array feature. The caching subsystem in Caching Proxy also provides tight integration with WAS dynacache. The Caching Proxy can be identified to WAS as an external cache via the remote cache adapter that comes with Caching Proxy and is installed on WAS. The general steps to accomplish this are as follows (see the Edge Components and WAS Info Center for specific details):

1. Configure dynacache on WAS.
2. Install the Caching Proxy External Cache Adapter on WAS.
3. Identify the Caching Proxy as an external cache to WAS with an external cache name.
4. Enable the dynamic caching plug-in on the Caching Proxy.
5. Assign the Caching Proxy external cache the same cache name that was identified in WAS.
6. Specify the Servlets and JSPs that are to be cached on WAS.

At runtime, WAS and Caching Proxy will maintain an ongoing conversation regarding which entries should be cached and when those entries should be invalidated. Caching Proxy will capture full-page HTML responses for Servlets and JSPs that have specifically been configured for caching. These pages are also stored in the WAS dynacache engine, often as multiple page fragments that compose the entire page cached in Caching Proxy.

## WebSphere Edge Components Implementation

### Load Balancer

Let's move on to solving a specific, representative problem with the WAS5 ND Edge Components. Figure 23-9 shows a very simplified topology with Load Balancer distributing load to two HTTP servers. Obviously, a real WAS environment would include WAS application servers, but we have left them out to simplify this example. We will create this configuration and then insert a proxy server.

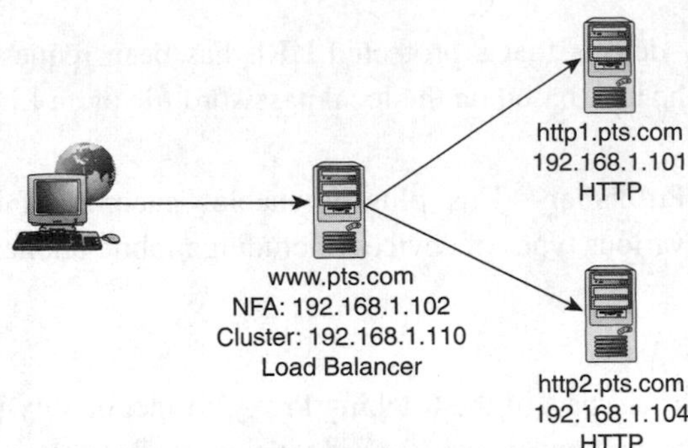


**Figure 23-9** Simple Load Balancer implementation topology.

## Network Setup

To get started implementing this topology, obtain three computers on the same subnet and install an HTTP server on two of them. You'll also need a fourth computer as a client, but it will not need any modification since you'll just be using it to run a web browser. Before starting, make sure that the machines can all ping each other. Now, proceed with the following configuration steps:

1. Create a test HTML file named test.html and place it in a new folder called "edgetest" off the document root of each web server. Ours is shown in Code Snippet 23-1. We included a sample graphic file. Modify the file contents slightly on each server to indicate the server identity so we can tell where our request is being served from, but do not change the file name.
2. From your third (client) machine, open a web browser and enter the URL to get to the test file. You should see something similar to Figure 23-10. Open the URL to the edgetest/test.html file on the other HTTP server and ensure that the two page results are identical except for the server name embedded in the text.

**Code Snippet 23-1** Test HTML file

```
<html>
<head>
</head>
<body>

Hello!(This is the HTTP1 machine)<br><br>

<img src="http_graphic5.jpg"><br>

</body>
</html>
```

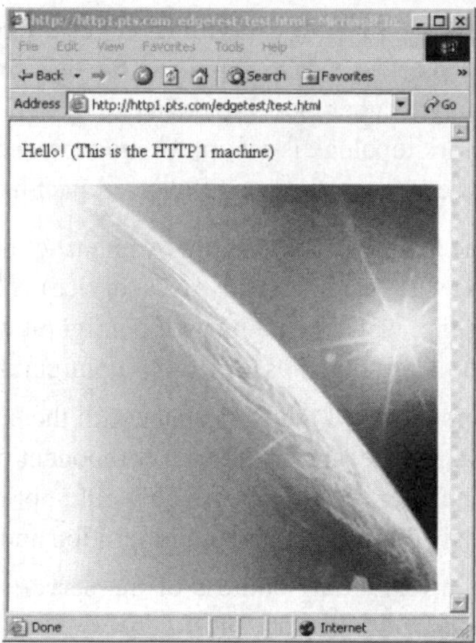


**Figure 23-10** Test file loaded into browser.

## Load Balancer Configuration

Next, we will prep the machines for the Load Balancer configuration. Some steps in this process are long and operating-system dependent, so in the interest of space, we will not cover it here. Refer instead to the Load Balancer Administration Guide section of the Edge Components Info Center for detailed instructions for all of these steps, including the configuration process using commands, scripts, GUI, or wizards. The Concepts, Planning, and Installation section also has these instructions. However, they are more conceptual and not as detailed. Keep in mind that since the Edge Components operate at a low level of the protocol stack, configuration and especially troubleshooting are difficult without an experienced network administrator and an accurate, up-to-date topology diagram of your network.

First, as we said earlier in this chapter, to load balance, we must come up with a new IP address and corresponding host name to represent our "cluster" of web servers. We will use 192.168.1.110 and assign www.pts.com to it. This is known as the *cluster address*. You can do this on your network's DNS server, or if you are able, simply modify your local "hosts" file on every machine. Similarly, you will need entries for the http1.pts.com and http2.pts.com servers. Secondly, the new IP address must now be assigned to the loopback adapter for each HTTP server. The loopback adapter is not visible to other devices, so the result is that these servers will not respond to requests for the IP address, but when the Load Balancer MAC forwards them here, they will still be accepted because they are on the loopback adapter, which is visible internally to the IP stack. At this point, it would be good to go through the verification steps in the Load

Balancer Administration Guide to be sure everything is set up correctly network-wise. This involves a series of **ping** and **arp** commands to make sure the three machines are properly configured. If they are not, things can get rather messy to debug!

Now that the basic network topology is set up, we must proceed with the steps to configure the Load Balancer. Follow these steps on the Load Balancer machine (www.pts.com):

1. Make sure the Dispatcher service is running by entering the **dsserver** command (if you are on Windows, this starts automatically as a service). This starts the Dispatcher and loads the default.cfg file, which contains your configuration. You are free to create and load files under other names to represent various configurations.
2. Start the executor component of the Dispatcher with the command **dscontrol executor start**. Remember that the executor is the core component or "brains" of the Dispatcher. Since the default.cfg config file is loaded, you would not have to do anything past this point if you had already done your initial configuration and saved it as default.cfg.
3. Configure for the non-forwarding address of the server's adapter with the command **dscontrol set nfa *ip-address***. In place of ***ip-address***, supply the primary or "native" IP address for this server, not the cluster address.
4. Define the cluster with **dscontrol cluster add www.pts.com**. Various options can be added with **dscontrol cluster set**, but they will not be necessary for our basic configuration.
5. Configure the network adapter with the cluster address using **dscontrol executor configure *cluster_ip*** (you could use the domain name for the cluster IP here as well, such as www.pts.com). This executes the operating system's command to configure the cluster IP address onto the primary network adapter so it will respond to external requests for that IP address. Note that this is different than when we configured the backend HTTP servers—in that case, we created an alias on the loopback adapter and assigned the cluster address there. The effect of this is that the backend machines will not respond to an external request for that IP address (because the loopback is not visible to other machines), but the IP stack on this server will accept the packets once they are forwarded there via the MAC header because it sees the cluster address on the loopback.
6. Add the ports to be used with the cluster. In our case, we are only responding to port 80 requests, so we will use **dscontrol port add www.pts.com:80**.
7. Add the servers to the cluster. Since we have two servers, we will execute **dscontrol server add www.pts.com:80:http1.pts.com** and **dscontrol server add www.pts.com:80:http2.pts.com**. Note that you would have to add the server multiple times if it were to respond to multiple ports (for example, 443 for SSL).
8. Start the manager component with **dscontrol manager start**. Remember that this is the component that sends server weightings to the executor.

9. Start an advisor on port 80 with **dscontrol advisor start http 80**. This is the component that monitors the servers and helps the manager to set the dynamic weights based on their responsiveness.
10. You should now save your file with **dscontrol file save default.cfg**. You can use this command to save files with various configurations, but you must specify the file you want after dsserver starts with **dscontrol file newload** filename (if you want a file other than default.cfg). Note that this will replace the entire configuration. To "append" configuration settings onto the current configuration, you can use **dscontrol file appendload** filename.

You now should be able to open a browser on another computer and use the URL http://www.pts.com/edgetest/test.html and see the response page from either the http1 or http2 backend server. Wait a moment until any port affinity times out and then reload the page, and you should see the response to the same URL, but you can tell it has come from the other backend server because the server name embedded in the text should have changed. You can continue this process and see the load balancing happen evenly, and for kicks you can shut down one of the HTTP servers and watch the Load Balancer handle this nicely by only serving up the page from the remaining healthy server. Scalability and reliability achieved! You should load the GUI admin console on the Load Balancer machine and explore the configuration tree to fully understand all of the options and settings available.

### Network/Load Balancer Configuration Caveats and Troubleshooting

As we said earlier, working with the Edge Components, particularly the Load Balancer, requires a fairly high degree of network and protocol-level savvy. If you have problems, refer first to the troubleshooting areas of the Load Balancer Guide. The following are a few items to keep in mind:

- **Network Tools**—Your best friends for troubleshooting Load Balancer problems are not the ones contained with the product. They are the network commands for your operating system, such as **arp**, **netstat**, **tracert**, **ping**, **hostname**, and **nslookup**. A very effective tool for diagnosing problems is Ethereal, which is a free protocol analyzer for Unix and Windows available at www.ethereal.com. Always do a careful review of the log files early in the troubleshooting process.

> **NOTE**
> Always be sure to check with your network group before using a packet-level tool such as Ethereal or Sniffer. Due to privacy and security standards, some companies have very strict rules and consequences for putting these on the network.

- **Save your license file**—When installing fixpacks for the Load Balancer, it is sometimes possible that the product license file (edge/lb/servers/conf/ND50Full.LIC) will be lost, so always remember to copy it somewhere and restore it after the fixpack has been applied. Regardless of this, a good backup strategy is always a good thing.
- **Extra routes**—The Load Balancer documentation has historically stated that after adding the cluster address to the loopback adapter on the backend server, extra routes in the routing table may be created and need to be deleted. The advice says "The extra route to be deleted will be the one whose network address begins with the first digit of the cluster address, followed by three zeroes." This is only the case in their example, which has a netmask of 255.0.0.0. In reality, you should check for an extra route with a network address that matches any non-zero portions of the cluster address netmask. For our example cluster address of 192.168.1.110 and netmask of 255.255.255.0, the extra route to be deleted had a network address of 192.168.1.0 and an interface address of 192.168.1.110. Remember, these extra routes will be created on each server startup, so it is best to put them in some script that will be executed then. The **route print** and **route delete** commands can be used to view and alter the route.
- **Fixpacks**—As of this writing, PTF 2 is the most current fixpack for Edge Components. Always keep up with the fixpacks available from the WAS support web site and do not hesitate to call the support team with problems. The Edge Components team in particular is very sharp.
- **Avoid DHCP**—Always ensure that DHCP is not enabled when installing Edge Components. Edge devices use IP addresses a great deal in their configuration and hence are very sensitive to changes in their own IP address, so these should be static rather than dynamic.
- **Debugging**—You can increase the logging level to very verbose with the command **dscontrol set loglevel 5**. Use this only for re-creating error scenarios and capturing debug output, as the logs can become quite large, and there is some overhead to logging at this level. It is also a good idea to archive and then delete log files before re-creating problem scenarios so that you have a more concise and clean picture of what is occurring.

## Caching Proxy Configuration

Again keeping our configuration simple, we will now modify our three-machine example to show the insertion of a proxy server into an existing configuration. Figure 23-11 shows this simple configuration. Note that it is a bit unrealistic because the Load Balancer is balancing to only one machine, but this section is intended to demonstrate the proxy server, not an entire topology.

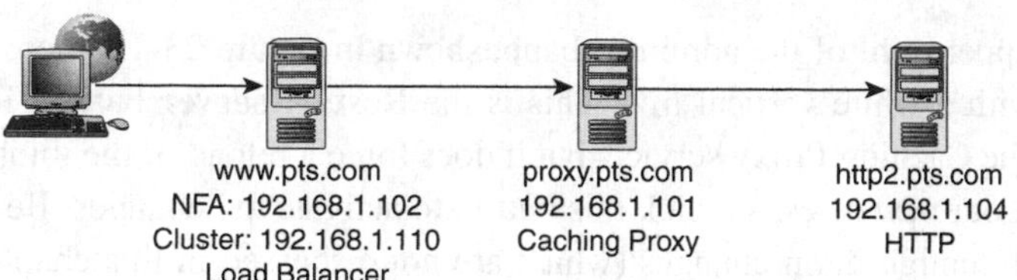


**Figure 23-11** Simple proxy server topology.

The goal for this example will be to proxy the requests for the www.pts.com/edgetest/test.html file to the web server and then to cache those requests to enhance performance. We will assume that the Caching Proxy has been installed. Since there is no command line or scripting interface for the caching proxy, we will configure it with its web administrative console, although the ibmproxy.conf file could be hand-edited to achieve the same result since the web admin console writes its updates to this file. Note that if you are using MAC forwarding in this configuration, since the proxy is being fronted by the Load Balancer, it will need to have the cluster address aliased on its loopback adapter as we discussed earlier in this chapter. Since the HTTP servers are no longer being directly fronted by the Load Balancer in this configuration, they no longer have to have the cluster address aliased to their loopback adapter:

1. Open the proxy admin webapp from any machine on the network with a URL similar to ours, which is http://proxy.pts.com/.
2. Authenticate to the user ID/password prompt with the administrator ID and password that were configured on the Caching Proxy install. If you haven't done this yet, the command to set the user ID and password is in the Caching Proxy Info Center (Admin Guide).
3. Navigate to Server Configuration > Request Processing > Request Routing in the menu on the left side of the page and scroll to the bottom of the right pane, which shows numbered, preconfigured rules as displayed in Figure 23-12. It is important to remember that this file is parsed from top to bottom by the Caching Proxy, and it will use the first rule that matches its current request. You will notice that the last rule at the bottom is the catch-all "/*" rule, which will be used for anything that is not caught above it. There are several types of rules that can be used here, the primary two being Proxy and Pass. Proxy is used to proxy the request to another server, and Pass is used to serve a request from the proxy server itself. Most of the preconfigured rules are there to allow the admin webapp to be served from the proxy server, and thus they are Pass rules.
4. We have filled out the new rule template at the bottom of the page, as shown in Figure 23-12. Notice that we have set the rules to be inserted before the wildcard catch-all. Our new Proxy rule simply states that for any request coming in matching the URI of /edgetest/*, send that request forward to the URL provided in the replacement file path, which is in this case http://http2.pts.com/edgetest/*. We did not use the optional field, which can allow us to filter requests that come in from a certain host name or IP address. After pressing the Submit button, our rule is inserted into the ibmproxy.conf file.

5. In the upper right of the admin webapp, shown in Figure 23-12, there is a round black circle with a white vertical line. This is the **Restart server** button. It does not really restart the Caching Proxy service, but it does force a reload of the ibmproxy.conf file to bring in our new rules, so click this button to activate the changes. Be aware that some types of configuration changes (which are not discussed in this chapter) require a full restart of the Caching Proxy service to activate. These are listed in the Info Center.
6. Using the URL http://www.pts.com/edgetest/test.html from any browser on the network should now yield our page from the backend HTTP2 server via the proxy.

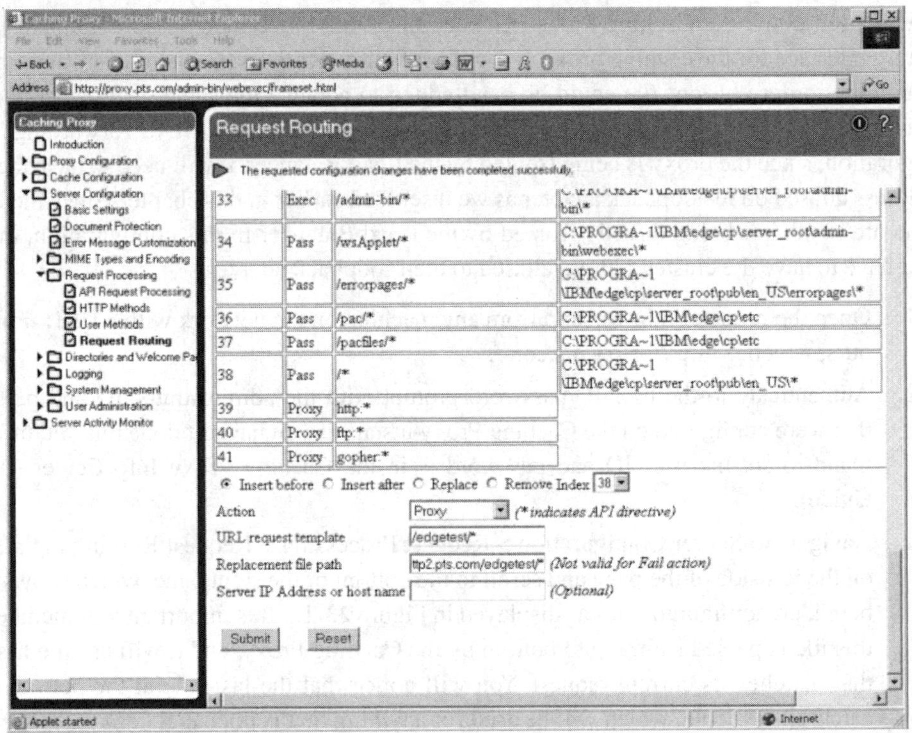


**Figure 23-12** Caching Proxy webapp.

Let's now review what has happened at each stage of this transaction so that we can fully understand how the Edge Components have made it successful. Figure 23-13 shows the path of our transaction with numbered arrows.

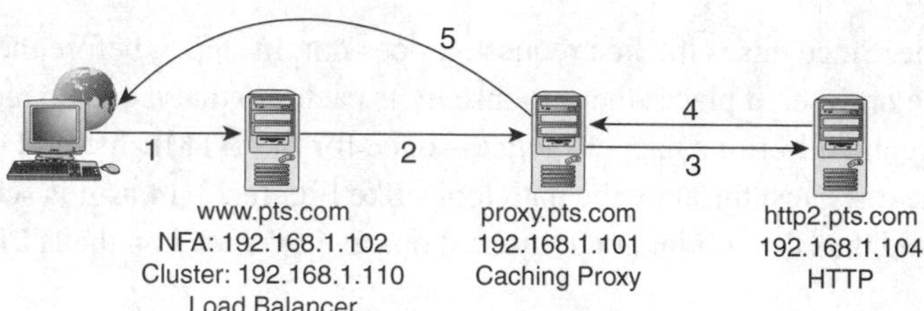


**Figure 23-13** End-to-end Edge Components transaction.

1. The user enters http://www.pts.com/edgetest/test.html into his or her browser address field and submits the request. The domain name is resolved to our cluster address of 192.168.1.110, which is aliased on the primary network adapter of the Load Balancer.
2. The Load Balancer receives the request and uses the weighting algorithm from the manager and advisors to select the next "best" backend server to receive the request out of those configured for this cluster. Since we only have one server in the cluster, proxy.pts.com is selected. The request is forwarded to that server as we described earlier in our section on MAC forwarding.
3. The request arrives at the proxy server, which looks at the 192.168.1.110 destination address and accepts the packet after seeing that address is assigned to its loopback adapter. The proxy server then begins to go through its rules to see if any match the source IP (remember, we didn't configure this in the rule) or the URL request template. It gets to our rule with /edgetest/* in the request template and sees that this is a match. It stashes the request's source IP (this is the client browser's IP address) in a table and creates a new request on one of its own connections to the backend HTTP server. This new request has the proxy server's address as the source IP and the HTTP server as the destination IP and goes off to the HTTP server.
4. The HTTP server resolves the request by loading the test.html page from its /edgetest/ directory, creates the response, and switches the source and destination IP addresses, which causes the response to be sent back to the proxy server.
5. The proxy server sees the response coming back in, grabs the browser's IP address from its table, inserts it as the destination and its own IP as the source, and forwards the response back to the user.
6. Of course, the browser then sees that this page contains a link to a graphic, and the entire process happens again to retrieve the graphic file from the HTTP server.

## Proxy Caching

This simplified scenario demonstrates the path of the request/response. However, a little bit of magic also happens during this transaction. At step 3, before the proxy server uses a connection to send a request to the HTTP server, it first checks to see if it has the response for this particular request in its cache. Since this is the first request, it does not. In step 5, before the proxy sends the response off to the browser, it places the response in its cache so that it can be returned for subsequent requests. Again, all of this happens twice—once for the HTML file and once for the JPG graphic. On the next request through, the path looks like Figure 23-14 as it is served from cache, out on the edge, and thus doesn't incur additional hops and overhead on the HTTP server.

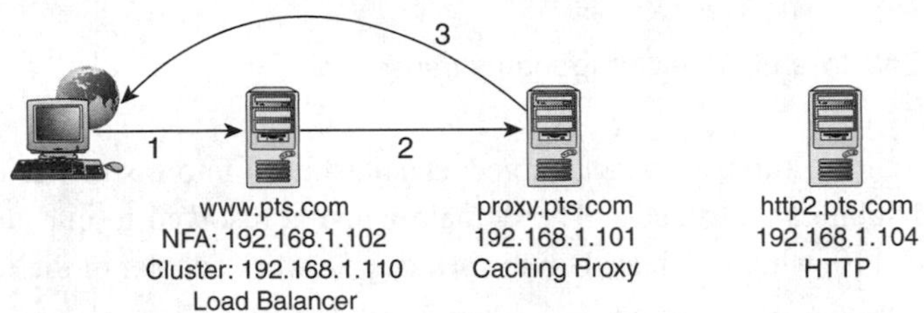


**Figure 23-14** Cached transaction with fewer hops.

To verify that the Caching Proxy is behaving as we expect, we can check the admin webapp under the Server Activity Monitor > Proxy Access Statistics as shown in Figure 23-15 and see the last two entries in blue, which indicates they were served from cache. This diagram shows that the first requests came from the HTTP server, whereas the last requests for the HTML and JPG file were returned from the proxy's cache. The administrative webapp has a great many configuration settings and logs that should be investigated, as these are good tools for enhancing performance and troubleshooting problems. It also has pages to show summary statistics on cache hits and misses and network bandwidth savings due to cache hits.

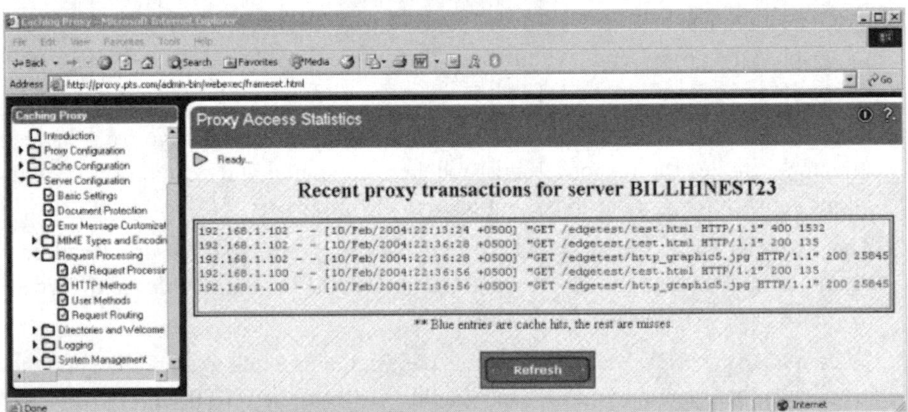


**Figure 23-15** Admin webapp showing cache hits.

## Caching Proxy Hints and Tips

- **Page verification**—When you configure each rule, make sure that you can actually reach the destination page from the proxy server using a web browser on that machine. If you cannot, the proxy will fail.
- **HTTP 1.1 browser setting**—Microsoft Internet Explorer, a popular browser, has a setting on its Tools > Internet Options > Advanced page labeled "Use HTTP 1.1 through proxy connections." To take advantage of all features of the Caching Proxy, such as caching, this option should be checked. If you are having problems, check this setting on the source browser.
- **Testing**—Applications often respond poorly to being proxied, generally due to having the host names they are familiar with being reassigned to the proxy server. Test each application to be proxied carefully and in a representative environment. For example, in a real production system, the end user's computer will likely not have any visibility to the backend content server. Make sure that this is the case in your testing. Otherwise, there may be undetected situations where the backend server does an end-run around the proxy and responds directly to the user, or the user requests begin going directly to the backend server instead of the proxy. This can happen if applications have code that composes URLs based on what they determine to be their host server name (usually by a dynamic call), or if they have hard-coded URLs. Another possibility is if the application pulls the host name from the request to build the response URL. The Caching Proxy by default will place the back-end content server's host name or IP address (whichever you provided when you configured the rule) in the request it sends to that server. If that server uses this to build its response URL, future requests will attempt to go around the proxy to directly to the content host. To prevent this, edit the ibmproxy.conf file to change the SendRevProxyName directive to "true." This will cause the proxy server to always put its own host name in the source field of the request. This change requires a true restart of the proxy server to take effect—pressing the **Restart** button in the web administrative console will not work.
- **SSL**—The proxy server can have a certificate installed on it and serve over the HTTPS protocol with SSL just like a web server. You can use the included IBM GSKIT and ikeyman tool to create the key database per the instructions in the Admin Guide. It can also be configured to use SSL for the backend servers and even to make a "best attempt" to cache those responses. Be careful though; typically these responses carry sensitive data that is best not cached. You can configure cross-port affinity to ensure that users who start a session to a server over regular HTTP and then switch to HTTPS (for example, to pay for the contents of their shopping basket) retain affinity to the same server they've been working on.

- **Debugging/logging/tracing**—To enable logging, open the ibmproxy.conf file and find the logging directives section. There will be entries for log file names and locations. To enable tracing, add this line (with your preferred path, of course) **TraceLog C:\Progra~1\IBM\edge\cp\server_root\logs\trace**. This will write out a trace log with very good debugging info. You should use this only when having problems, as it will affect performance. Turn it on, re-create your problem, and then turn it off and analyze the logs. You can also start the proxy service from the command line with the command **ibmproxy –debug –mtv**, which will cause a very verbose trace of proxy startup and operations to occur. As with tracing, use this only to capture data when re-creating problem scenarios and then turn it off. It is also a good idea to archive and then delete log files before re-creating problem scenarios so that you have a more concise and clean picture of what is occurring.

## Topology Patterns on the Edge

Now that we have discussed the Load Balancer and Caching Proxy separately in simple scenarios, let's conclude by looking at a more typical configuration. Figure 23-16 shows Edge Components in the DMZ, with scalability and failover now at each tier, as opposed to the simple, non-Edge topology we saw at the start of this chapter. We have a pair of active/standby load balancers in the DMZ serving to a pair of proxy servers. The proxy servers then send requests through to the backend "secure" zone, to our HTTP servers. Those HTTP servers are using the WAS plug-in file, which has workload management features to balance load across a tier of WAS application servers. We have redundancy at each layer of the system. However, it must be stated again that performance testing should be done using expected peak load metrics to ensure that should any component fail, the remaining components can handle the load, and the failing unit can be brought back online quickly. We can now leverage all of the static and dynamic caching benefits discussed in the chapter on caching throughout this infrastructure, from the edge to WAS.

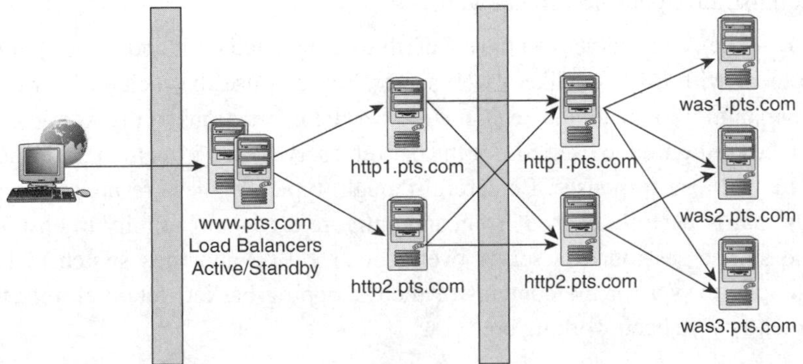


**Figure 23-16** Edge Components in a more realistic scenario.

**NOTE**

It should be noted that in Figure 23-16, we could actually eliminate the web server tier completely and have the proxy servers forward traffic directly to the WAS web container. This would simplify deployment as well, removing the need to continuously regenerate and copy the WAS plugin-cfg.xml file to the web servers. Of course, if you choose to do so, you should make sure that the proxy server provides for authentication as well as request affinity, both of which the HTTP server plug-in provides. See the Note on this topic earlier in the chapter for additional concerns about this approach.

## Conclusion

In this chapter, we have explored the use of the Edge Components, which are included in the WAS Network Deployment package. We reviewed the function of load balancers and proxy servers, the base features of the Load Balancer and Caching Proxy included with the Edge Components, and then applied that to a few simple configuration scenarios. In truth, we have only scratched the surface of the features and possibilities for these useful products. Readers are again encouraged to read the Info Center documentation to explore the entire breadth of functionality available to them.

# PART V

# Problem Determination and Server Tools

CHAPTER 24

# Problem Determination

We've all been there. It's the weekend, the production system is experiencing problems, or the imminent deployment is not functioning properly in system test, and it seems that everyone else is out enjoying life. Often, at times like this, it takes much longer than it should to resolve problems. Our organizational and problem-solving skills are not at their best due to stress and fatigue. In this chapter, we will talk about some general problem-solving skills, specific techniques by topology layer, and useful tools for problem determination. We will not discuss problem determination in relation to performance testing (see Chapter 25, "Performance Tuning Tools" for related information) or install/migration problems. The Info Center has thorough sections on troubleshooting installation and migration problems and sections for problem determination by task and by component. In fact, the Info Center Problem Determination PDF alone approaches 200 pages. The following procedures are discussed in general terms and of course should be tailored to the specific problem you are experiencing.

## Problem-Solving First Steps

In this section, we will talk about some steps that you should take at the beginning of problem determination. Often, changes or other external activities going on in the infrastructure are the root cause of WAS problems. For that reason, it is important for the WAS administrator to have a working relationship with administrators from other areas of the overall environment.

### Problem Definition

The essential first step is to make sure you clearly understand the problem. Gather all "external" data such as the exact error message, the full URLs being attempted, versions of all related software (on both the client and servers), and comments from users who are being affected (some have better observational and descriptive skills than others, so don't limit yourself to just one). Assemble this data into a coherent package. Be careful not to make assumptions at this stage, but at the same time consider possible "quick" answers. We can't overstate the importance of getting a precise problem description. If a user says, "My account doesn't work," that tells you almost nothing. Ask them to describe precisely what they saw. Here are some good and bad example problem descriptions:

- **Poor description:** I can't log in; my account is locked.

  **Good description:** I typed in the URL for the web site at 11:35 am and got the login page. I typed in my user ID and password, and in response, I got the following error message: "Your account is locked." I tried the same thing again at 11:44 am and saw the same response. I've attached a screen shot of what I saw.
- **Poor description:** The system is crashing when I look at accounts payable.

  **Good description:** I logged into the system as user "user27" just fine at 3:32 pm and saw the welcome page. Then I clicked on the "accounts" URL. At this point, I saw the accounts listed. But when I clicked on any particular account, I saw only a blank page in response. I tried several accounts and always saw the same blank page.
- **Poor description:** The system is really slow.

  **Good description:** I use this application every day, and normally it is very fast, but since noon today it is taking almost a minute to respond. Here is the URL I am using and the data I am entering.
- **Poor description:** I type in the URL for the web site and my browser crashes.

  **Good description:** I type in the URL http://foo.bigcorp.com/abcapp and I see nothing. My browser just hangs. Eventually it says, "Can't contact server." Here's a screen snapshot.

We've learned from painful experience that a clear problem description expressed in terms of what the user observes is by far the best description. Do not allow the initial problem description to include a diagnosis. Users often guess incorrectly and lead you down paths that can be dead ends. Notice also that the problem description includes timestamps. That's important since you now know where to look in the various system logs that we'll describe later.

Keep in mind the general reasons that problems occur:

1. **Application bugs**—This includes things like poor looping constructs, bad threading code (any application that does its own threading code should be suspect), or memory leaks (yes, this is possible even in Java with poor coding practices). Was a new deployment of any applications done about the same time this problem surfaced?
2. **Infrastructure saturation**—Resources in the environment are being saturated (network bandwidth, CPU, memory, connections on any of the servers). Have resources been removed from the infrastructure, or did the load increase around the same time the

problem started to occur? Has someone changed the configuration to cause saturation? Often, administrators will crank up the number of threads or connections, thinking this will "improve" performance, yet the result is quite the opposite when the infrastructure cannot handle the additional capacity. Have you checked with the company help or operations center? Perhaps there were known problems in the infrastructure around the time this error was occurring.

3. **Configuration**—Something in the environment is not configured properly. This could be at any layer of the infrastructure—HTTP servers, WAS, or databases, for example. Hopefully, these changes are controlled, and there is some audit trail to review who made the change and when it was made (there are many excellent change management/change control products on the market). If there is, seek it out and review entries that occurred about the time the problem started to surface.
4. **Product bugs**—You could be experiencing a bug in one of the software or hardware products in the infrastructure. Once you have taken realistic measures to solve the problem, if you have a reasonable suspicion that you are dealing with a product bug, you should contact vendor support and open a problem incident immediately. Often, it will take time for them to get back to you after opening an incident, so by doing this early in the game, you will have multiple problem-solving threads of attack. If you have resolved the problem by the time they call back, you can simply cancel the support record.

   Before opening a trouble ticket, you may want to browse vendor support sites and search on the error messages or symptoms you are seeing. There may already be fixes available. Visit any discussion forums (either web-based or usenet/newsgroups), search for problems similar to yours, and post a message while you are there. Often, you can get excellent support from the community of users around the world who are using the same products. Many a problem has been quickly solved by simply entering the error message into a search engine such as Google and reviewing the contents of both the "Web" and "Groups" tabs for search hits. Keep in mind that usenet postings on Google Groups are generally not as current as the actual usenet discussion threads on the hosting servers.

**SECURITY NOTE**

Be very cautious when posting questions on any public forum. In particular, avoid giving specific information about the products you use and their versions and configuration. This information is quite useful to hackers. Even when using an "anonymous" identity, messages can be traced by their source IP address.

## Understand the Problem

Now that you have an accurate problem description, take some time to consider it. Think about the information you have been given. Does it seem like an issue that might be unique to that user?

Does the problem description seem to imply a network issue? Are other users reporting the same problem? Has this user ever been able to access the application from that particular workstation, and when was he last successful? Is he authorized for what he is trying to do, and is the workstation in a part of the network that should have access to the system? Does the problem only occur for certain users? If so, it is possible those users belongs to some role or group that triggers a different path of the application code to be executed, and there is a bug in that area? Is the URL a legitimate one? For example, if the user chose the URL from his bookmarked sites, it may no longer be valid, or he may have typed it incorrectly. It is important to look at these simple solutions before engaging in deep problem solving.

This thinking is crucial. For example, the last example problem description seems to indicate that the user's web browser can't even reach the login page. If the URL that the user typed is correct, you should try the same thing yourself. If it works for you but not that user, perhaps there is a network or DNS problem affecting only that user or the network that the user is on. You want to try to work out some general hypotheses before jumping head first into problem solving. This initial consideration will help you identify the class of issues that might be causing the problem.

Continuing with our discussion of the last problem description, it's probably worth talking to the end user and asking him to try other internal web sites to see the response. You might also want to ask him to try the same request from another computer nearby. That might provide some significant information.

## Problem Validation

Once a good problem description exists, a logical next step is to validate the problem yourself. Attempt the same sequence of events as the user. The first tool you should employ is a simple one—the browser. Web browsers can be helpful in solving certain types of problems, as well as to give you some idea at which layer of the infrastructure the problem exists. Of course, by employing the browser in this section, we are limiting the scope of this discussion to web applications. We have troubleshooting tips specific to client applications in Chapter 14, "Client Applications."

### HTTP Response Codes

If the user is experiencing a problem that yields some sort of error display in his or her browser, this error could provide valuable clues. Table 24-1 shows some common HTTP response codes. Some of these, such as 403, 404, and 500, will appear in the browser response page, while others will be seen in the HTTP server or proxy logs.

**Table 24-1 Common HTTP Response Codes**

| Code | Name | Description |
|---|---|---|
| 200 | Success | The request was received and successfully completed. |
| 301 | Moved Permanently | The requested resource has been assigned a new permanent URI, which is included in the 301 page. |
| 302 | Found | The requested resource resides at a new temporary URI, which is included in the 302 page. |
| 304 | Not Modified | The requested resource has not been modified and is the same as the client's version (usually a temporary file in the browser's cache). Often, you will receive this when you were expecting to see "cache hits" on a caching proxy server because you did not delete your browser's temporary Internet files before testing. |
| 400 | Bad Request | The request could not be understood due to malformed syntax. |
| 401 | Unauthorized | The request requires user authentication. |
| 403 | Forbidden | The server refuses to fulfill the request. Sometimes this is due to the request being restricted, and sometimes because the specified resource does not exist. The server will often purposely not specify why the error occurred for security reasons. |
| 404 | Not Found | The server could not find anything matching the request URI. |
| 410 | Gone | The requested resource is permanently not available and no forwarding information is available. |
| 500 | Internal Server Error | This indicates some error condition on the server that the HTTP server is trying to reach. This often means that the backend (WAS) server that the HTTP server is trying to communicate with is down or an exception has been thrown. If it is down, before you restart it, be sure to find out how or why this state occurred, or it will likely come back at the worst time! |

**NOTE**

If you are using Internet Explorer, disable "Show friendly HTTP error messages" using the check box on the Advanced pane of the Internet Options window. This will provide more complete error information in the browser response.

### Browser Cookie Tracking

For cookie-related problems, a very effective technique is to turn on cookie prompting. Figure 24-1 shows how to get to this option in Internet Explorer. This will show you information about cookies being sent and received that could be quite useful in debugging, as shown in Figure 24-2. Many cookie-related problems are tied directly to incorrect domain/path names or expiration, all of which are shown here for the incoming cookie. In clustered environments, the WAS server ID that the user has established affinity to will be shown appended to the cookie data, which could be useful for troubleshooting. For example, this would tell you what server this session and affinity are established to, and that this is where you would put your troubleshooting tools to use. If you are using Lightweight Third-Party Authentication (LTPA) cookies for WAS authentication and single sign-on (SSO), problems such as repeated authentication can often be tracked to incorrectly specifying the cookie domain for SSO. The LTPA cookie is described in Chapter 18, and the session affinity (JSESSIONID) cookie is described in Chapter 22.

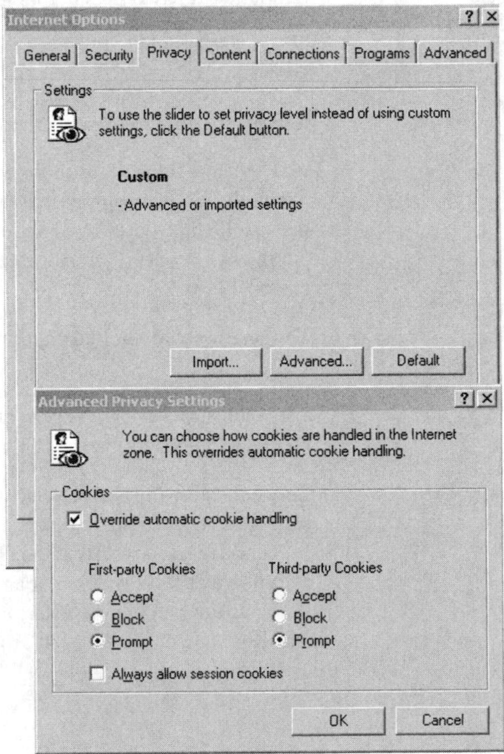


**Figure 24-1** Turn on Internet Explorer cookie prompting.

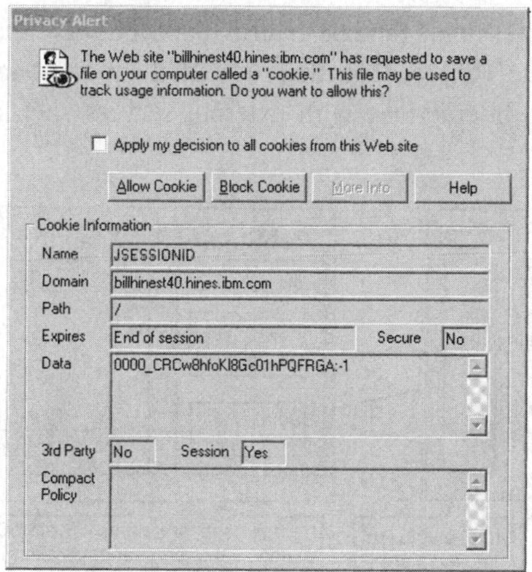


**Figure 24-2** Information shown on the cookie prompt.

> **NOTE**
> Browsers will only send cookies along with subsequent requests to the domain that established them. For example, a cookie created by a site at pts.com will only be sent along with further requests to pts.com. If you configured WAS LTPA security to use a cookie domain of sales.pts.com, users going to mfg.pts.com will not have the cookie containing their security credential sent with the request and will be reauthenticated. In this case, specifying an LTPA cookie domain of pts.com would give Single Sign On to both sites. See Chapter 18, "Security," for more information on LTPA and WAS Single Sign On.

## J2EE Request Paths

Again consider the flow of the request now from a J2EE perspective. Figure 24-3 shows the paths of three different common types of requests—for a static file from the HTTP server, for a static file served by the WAS File Serving Enabler, and for a WAS Servlet/JSP request. We won't go into detail about what is happening at each stage, as that is thoroughly covered in other places of this book. However, it is important to think about what happens at each stage of the transaction and what tools we have for troubleshooting problems there. For example, as Figure 24-3 shows, the WAS plug-in is consulted first before the HTTP server will serve up a static file from its own doc root. Knowing this may make it easy to determine that these static requests are not being resolved properly due to incorrect rules in the WAS plug-in. If the problem can be isolated and is repeatable, archive the log files at each layer of the topology, re-create the problem, capture these new "clean" log files, and then piece them together to tell the story. Correlate the log files from each component by their timestamps (and be careful that each server has not only the correct time but also the correct time zone!) to piece together the path the request has taken. Look for any hints that the problem is due to interactions with external servers such as the database or EIS in Figure 24-3.

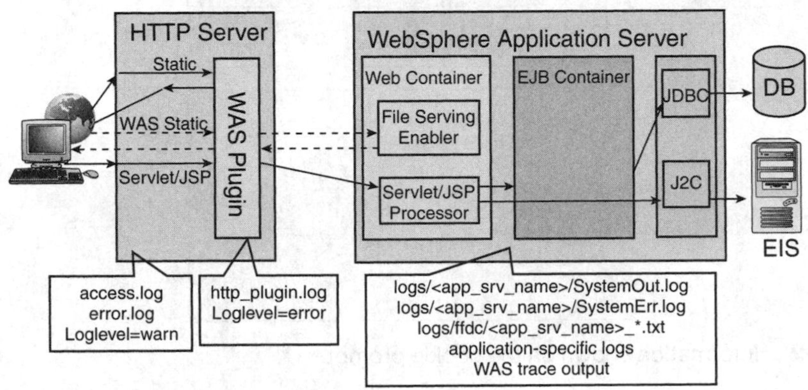


**Figure 24-3** J2EE/WAS request flow paths.

While still using the browser as a problem determination tool, it will be helpful if you know of URLs that access resources on the HTTP server directly or that access a static file on WAS, a Servlet or JSP that does no backend access, and a Servlet or JSP that does do backend access. The success or failure of these could help to narrow down the scope of the problem.

At the end of the problem validation phase, you should have some suspicions as to where the problem is occurring. If you see a generic error such as "page not found" or "page could not be displayed" or believe the request is not reaching the HTTP server, continue your troubleshooting with the Environment Validation and HTTP Server Problem Determination sections that follow. The 300 and 400 series errors could be from either the HTTP server or WAS since both are capable of serving HTTP requests. If you see these, proceed to the HTTP Server Problem Determination section and then move on to the WAS layer. The 500 series errors generally indicate a problem with the WAS server; in most cases, it is down or not responding, so proceed to the WAS troubleshooting section for these errors.

## Environment Validation

If you feel that your problem is related to something in the infrastructure, validate the environment before proceeding. Use some simple operating system network commands to validate your understanding of the network and to make sure servers all have the necessary visibility to each other. The **ping** command will tell you if a particular network resource is "visible" from the machine from which you issue it. You might use this to ensure that the browser can see the HTTP server, the HTTP server can see the WAS server, and so forth. If **ping** results in an error, the

**tracert** command can show the path that network traffic is taking from one resource to another and where it stops. Using this, you may find that traffic stops at an IP address that belongs to a firewall, perhaps indicating that some firewall rule is not permitting traffic to pass. If you don't have an understanding of these core network commands, be resourceful. Use people skills to get assistance from someone who does, or simply use the popular Internet search utilities to gain a better understanding of the topic. There are a plethora of articles out there on problem determination and troubleshooting for your particular environment. At this stage of problem determination, step through the topology and verify that each involved component is running and actively servicing requests.

Another diagram that might be useful for brainstorming is one that shows the life cycle of a request from the client browser through to the backend and back to the client as a response. This can be overlaid on the network topology diagram from your first steps. Include any protocols and ports that might be used from server to server, again thinking in terms of firewall rules or network changes that might not permit these network conversations. You might validate this by using expensive network protocol analyzers or free tools available on the Internet such as Ethereal or the TCP Header plug-in for the Mozilla Firebird browser. It is also useful to compare connection and other timeout values across the topology—stale connection exceptions are often caused by database or firewall admins lowering their connection timeout values and not informing WAS admins.

**NOTE**

Before using any network packet-sniffing type of device or software, particularly in production, check your corporate standards. Some organizations consider this a serious offense with harsh penalties due to the potential to eavesdrop on private information. It is always best to use these tools in cooperation with network specialists.

## HTTP Server Problem Determination

At the HTTP server, first ensure the obvious—is the HTTP service running, and is it able to ping the servers it needs to interact with and resolve their host names via DNS? Can you get to the HTTP server administrative facilities? Can you serve up other files from the same server? After these rudimentary health checks, begin a thorough review of the log files, starting at the end and scrolling backward.

**NOTE**

IBM Redbook SG24-6717 (available for free from the IBM Redbooks site) is focused on an older version of IBM HTTP Server (IHS) running on OS/400, but it does have a good problem solving section for IHS specifically and HTTP servers in general.

## WAS Plug-In

Once you are satisfied that the HTTP server itself is not the problem, move on to the WAS plug-in file. This file is often the source of problems in that after certain changes are made to the WAS config, particularly the deployment or redeployment of applications, someone must remember to regenerate the plug-in file, copy it to the web server(s), and restart the web server(s). One of the primary causes of trouble is an out-of-date or incorrect plug-in file. The plug-in writes its own log file. Code Snippet 24-1 shows the top section of the plugin-cfg.xml file. On the last line shown, you can see where the logging level is set, as well as the log file name and location. Valid log levels are Trace, Warn, and Error. Trace emits the most output, and it also includes warning and error messages. Warn gives you warning and error messages, while Error will give only error messages. Be cautious with Trace, as it will emit very large log files. Use this only for selective, short tests where you are reproducing the problem, and don't forget to change this back when you are done because the log file can quickly consume disk space.

**Code Snippet 24-1** First few lines of plugin-cfg.xml

```
<?xml version="1.0" encoding="ISO-8859-1"?>
<Config ASDisableNagle="false" AcceptAllContent="false"
    IISDisableNagle="false" IgnoreDNSFailures="false"
    RefreshInterval="60" ResponseChunkSize="64">
    <Log LogLevel="Trace" Name="C:\WAS50\Dmgr\logs\http_plugin.log"/>
```

> **NOTE**
> Be aware that when the plug-in file is regenerated, the logging level will be set back to its default of Error.

Code Snippet 24-2 shows sample trace output from the http_plugin.log with the LogLevel set to Trace. These few lines show the detailed logging messages as a URL comes in as http://billhinest40.hines.ibm.com/PlantsByWebSphere/ and is broken down and compared to the plug-in's configuration rules until a match is found for the virtual host and port.

**Code Snippet 24-2** Plug-in log with LogLevel set to Trace

```
[Mon Feb 23 22:54:37 2004] 000009dc 00000a20 - TRACE: lib_util:
➥parseHostHeader: Defaulting port for scheme 'http'
[Mon Feb 23 22:54:37 2004] 000009dc 00000a20 - TRACE: lib_util:
➥parseHostHeader: Host: 'billhinest40.hines.ibm.com', port 80
[Mon Feb 23 22:54:37 2004] 000009dc 00000a20 - TRACE: ws_common:
➥websphereCheckConfig: Current time is 1077594877, next stat time is
➥1077594605
```

```
[Mon Feb 23 22:54:37 2004] 000009dc 00000a20 - TRACE: ws_common:
➥websphereCheckConfig: Latest config time is 1077594385, lastModTime
➥is 1077594385
[Mon Feb 23 22:54:37 2004] 000009dc 00000a20 - TRACE: ws_common:
➥websphereShouldHandleRequest: trying to match a route for:
➥vhost='billhinest40.hines.ibm.com'; uri='/PlantsByWebSphere/'
[Mon Feb 23 22:54:37 2004] 000009dc 00000a20 - TRACE: ws_common:
➥websphereVhostMatch: Comparing '*:9080' to 'billhinest40.hines.
➥ibm.com:80' in VhostGroup: default_host
[Mon Feb 23 22:54:37 2004] 000009dc 00000a20 - TRACE: ws_common:
➥websphereVhostMatch: Comparing '*:80' to
'billhinest40.hines.ibm.com:80' in VhostGroup: default_host
[Mon Feb 23 22:54:37 2004] 000009dc 00000a20 - TRACE: ws_common:
➥websphereVhostMatch: Found a match '*:80' to 'billhinest40.
➥hines.ibm.com:80' in VhostGroup: default_host with score 1
```

## Elsewhere Around the Infrastructure

If at any time during these preliminary or later WAS-specific steps you see good evidence that the problem may be related to other infrastructural components such as proxy servers, load balancers, or database, host, Enterprise Information Service (EIS) or LDAP servers, you should then make contact with administrators from those areas. They will generally have advanced skills and troubleshooting tools at their disposal. Ask them to turn on their own tracing or monitoring tools while the error condition is present and review the results with you. Even if they don't uncover the problem, these sessions generally lead to some type of tuning possibilities and start fruitful conversations. See the Building a Team section later in this chapter for more advice on interrelating with other teams.

> **NOTE**
> If you are using the WAS Network Deployment Edge Components and suspect a proxy server or load balancer may be at fault, we have several troubleshooting hints in Chapter 23, "WebSphere Edge Components."

## WAS General Problem Determination

Since the WAS layer of the infrastructure is inherently complex, of course there are many potential things to go wrong there. Fortunately, there are also a great many more places to look for clues and a number of excellent tools (which we will discuss in the next section). In this section, we will talk about some general WAS problems and their symptoms.

As a first investigative step, if global security is on, you might check to see if the problem still occurs with it off. Certainly you wouldn't do this in production, and certainly this is not a legitimate solution to the problem, but trying things like this may help to quickly narrow the scope of where the root cause may lie. Let's move forward now to a more concrete discussion of problem determination in WAS.

## Console Messages

Often, the first indication you will get that there is a problem will be from the console messages that are always at the bottom of the administrative console, as shown in Figure 24-4. If your first indication is a phone call from a distressed user, then this is the first place you should go. The console messages area by default will cycle between two panes—one showing runtime messages, as shown in Figure 24-4, and the other showing configuration problems, as shown in Figure 24-5. You can see in Figure 24-5 that the refresh interval and automatic cycling can be configured. You can manually cycle through using the <Previous and Next> links shown in both examples. Learn to always keep an eye on these and do not disregard an indication of a problem in either of these simply because everything "seems" to be running correctly! Many times, when catastrophe strikes, we analyze logs only to find there were hints that a storm was brewing all along, only to be told, "That error has always been there." Keeping a clean house and clean logs is good for problem detection and prevention. Never let any error or warning condition become commonplace.

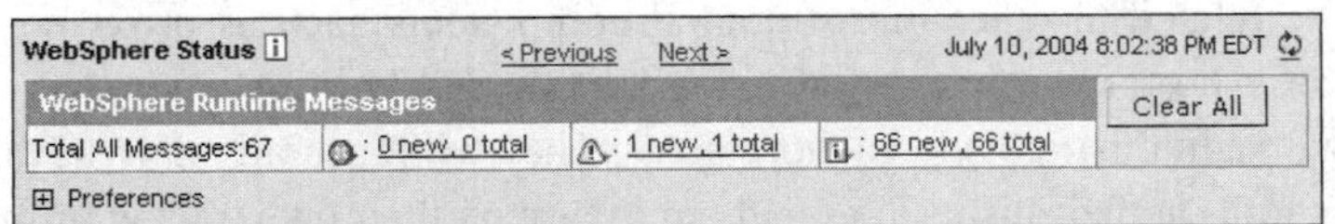


**Figure 24-4** Runtime console messages.

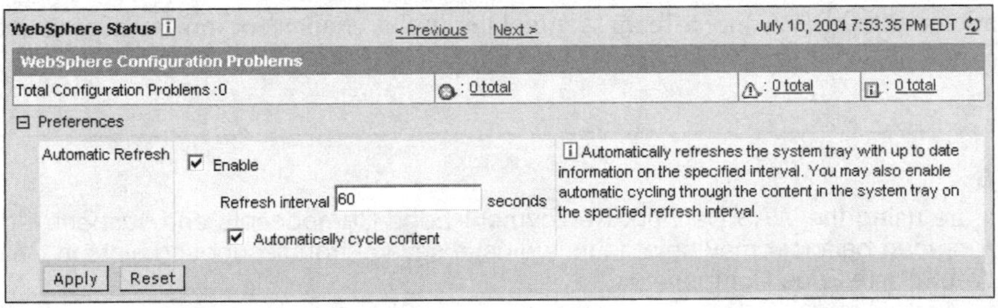

**Figure 24-5** Configuration console messages.

The messages are categorized by red (errors), yellow (warnings), and green (informational messages). Clicking on the links to each will take you to a list of messages, and you can click on individual entries in this list for details on the specific message.

You can clear the runtime messages with the Clear All button. If you can reproduce problems, it is sometimes a good idea to clear the messages and reproduce the problem to see if errors reappear here. Clearing the messages in this manner does not remove the messages from the underlying log files, which we will look at next.

The Configuration Problems list in particular can be tuned from the Troubleshooting > Configuration Problems link in the administrative console. This is shown in Figure 24-6. As you can see, the level of document validation is set low by default. Each managed process in WAS has a built-in validator that checks the XML configuration files for validation problems. When it finds them, they will be displayed here. This validation occurs on server startup and upon saving changes through the admin console. In newly configured environments, you may want to initially set this high, but turn it down in stabilized environments for performance savings. As we stated at the beginning of this chapter, configuration problems are often the cause of new problems. If you suspect such, you may want to turn this setting up and restart the server.

> **NOTE**
> Since the validator will not be executed when WAS config files are changed by hand for a running server, changing configuration files by hand is strongly discouraged. If errors are introduced, the managed process may not be able to start, meaning the validator will never have the opportunity to tell you what is wrong.

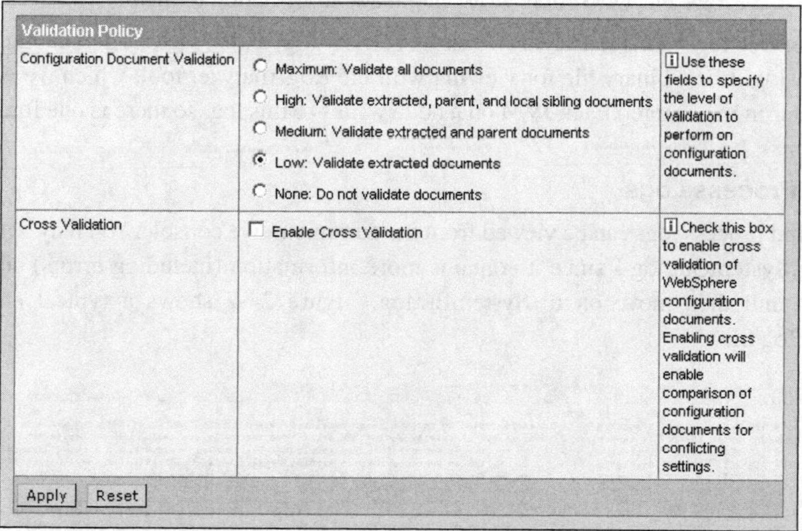


**Figure 24-6** Configuration validation settings.

> **NOTE INSTALL VERIFICATION TEST UTILITY**
> You can also use the Install Verification Test utility to check for configuration problems related to installed components. It is very simple—you execute the ivt command, and it returns a message that the install is valid or that some error condition has been found.

## WAS Logs

In troubleshooting WAS problems, you don't want to waste too much time before getting to the logs. After a cursory look around to get a general sense of any configuration or runtime problems that are occurring with the console messages, you next should have a look around the log files because this is where you are likely to get the bulk of information about any problems. There are three primary types of log WAS files. These can all be configured and viewed in the admin console from Troubleshooting > Logs and Trace > *servername*.

- **JVM logs**—These are the SystemOut.log and SystemErr.log log files, and there are a set of these for each JVM. Keep in mind that if there are multiple applications running under one application server, they will all write to these logs. WAS will generally write serious messages to these files, so they are a good place to look first. In addition to WAS messages, applications may also write to these logs with methods such as print(), println(), and printStackTrace().[1] A final note—the Deployment Manager and Node Manager also write to their SystemOut.log and SystemErr.log files.
- **Process logs**—Native code may write directly to stdout or stderr. Normally, these files are empty since there is little native code in most WAS applications. WAS does not write to these logs, but JVMs may write diagnostic information to them.
- **Service log**—This is also known as the activity log, and in fact, its default name is activity.log. It is a binary file for viewing with the LogAnalyzer tool, which we will discuss later in the chapter. Each JVM on a node writes to this log, so there is one for each node.

### JVM and Process Logs

The JVM and process logs can be viewed from the administrative console. You may want to begin by reading SystemOut.log—since it contains more information (including errors) and is better formatted—and then move on to SystemErr.log. Figure 24-7 shows a typical entry in the SystemErr.log file.

```
Log File
[7/2/04 12:17:28:330 EDT]  5067227 SystemErr     R InsertTag:doEndTag caught: javax.servlet.ServletException: An error occurred while evaluating cu
[7/2/04 12:17:28:330 EDT]  5067227 SystemErr     R javax.servlet.ServletException: An error occurred while evaluating custom action attribute "valu
[7/2/04 12:17:28:330 EDT]  5067227 SystemErr     R     at com.ibm.ws.webcontainer.jsp.servlet.JspServlet$JspServletWrapper.service(JspServlet.java:
[7/2/04 12:17:28:330 EDT]  5067227 SystemErr     R     at com.ibm.ws.webcontainer.jsp.servlet.JspServlet.serviceJspFile(JspServlet.java:692)
[7/2/04 12:17:28:330 EDT]  5067227 SystemErr     R     at com.ibm.ws.webcontainer.jsp.servlet.JspServlet.service(JspServlet.java:790)
[7/2/04 12:17:28:330 EDT]  5067227 SystemErr     R     at javax.servlet.http.HttpServlet.service(HttpServlet.java:853)
[7/2/04 12:17:28:330 EDT]  5067227 SystemErr     R     at com.ibm.ws.webcontainer.servlet.StrictServletInstance.doService(StrictServletInstance.java
[7/2/04 12:17:28:330 EDT]  5067227 SystemErr     R     at com.ibm.ws.webcontainer.servlet.StrictLifecycleServlet._service(StrictLifecycleServlet.ja
[7/2/04 12:17:28:330 EDT]  5067227 SystemErr     R     at com.ibm.ws.webcontainer.servlet.ServicingServletState.service(StrictLifecycleServlet.java:
[7/2/04 12:17:28:330 EDT]  5067227 SystemErr     R     at com.ibm.ws.webcontainer.servlet.StrictLifecycleServlet.service(StrictLifecycleServlet.java
[7/2/04 12:17:28:330 EDT]  5067227 SystemErr     R     at com.ibm.ws.webcontainer.servlet.ServletInstance.service(ServletInstance.java:283)
[7/2/04 12:17:28:330 EDT]  5067227 SystemErr     R     at com.ibm.ws.webcontainer.servlet.ValidServletReferenceState.dispatch(ValidServletReference
[7/2/04 12:17:28:330 EDT]  5067227 SystemErr     R     at com.ibm.ws.webcontainer.servlet.ServletInstanceReference.dispatch(ServletInstanceReferenc
[7/2/04 12:17:28:330 EDT]  5067227 SystemErr     R     at com.ibm.ws.webcontainer.webapp.WebAppRequestDispatcher.handleWebAppDispatch(WebAppRequest
[7/2/04 12:17:28:330 EDT]  5067227 SystemErr     R     at com.ibm.ws.webcontainer.webapp.WebAppRequestDispatcher.dispatch(WebAppRequestDispatcher.j
[7/2/04 12:17:28:330 EDT]  5067227 SystemErr     R     at com.ibm.ws.webcontainer.webapp.WebAppRequestDispatcher.include(WebAppRequestDispatcher.ja
[7/2/04 12:17:28:330 EDT]  5067227 SystemErr     R     at com.sun.j2ee.blueprints.waf.view.template.tags.InsertTag.doEndTag(InsertTag.java:99)
[7/2/04 12:17:28:330 EDT]  5067227 SystemErr     R     at org.apache.jsp._template._jspService(_template.java:172)
[7/2/04 12:17:28:330 EDT]  5067227 SystemErr     R     at com.ibm.ws.webcontainer.jsp.runtime.HttpJspBase.service(HttpJspBase.java:89)
[7/2/04 12:17:28:330 EDT]  5067227 SystemErr     R     at javax.servlet.http.HttpServlet.service(HttpServlet.java:853)
[7/2/04 12:17:28:330 EDT]  5067227 SystemErr     R     at com.ibm.ws.cache.servlet.ServletWrapper.serviceProxied(ServletWrapper.java:267)
[7/2/04 12:17:28:330 EDT]  5067227 SystemErr     R     at com.ibm.ws.cache.servlet.CacheHook.handleFragment(CacheHook.java:229)
```

**Figure 24-7** SystemErr.log file entry.

1 This is not an endorsement of applications writing to the JVM log files. In fact, we strongly discourage this. Applications should use a proper tracing system, such as Log4J or the built-in WAS JRAS facility.

The default basic format for these log files is as follows:

```
Timestamp ThreadID ShortName EventType ClassName MethodName
➥Message
```

The ShortName is the name of the WAS component that wrote the message to the log. The class and method names are optional and may not always appear. The event type will be one of the values shown in Table 24-2.

**Table 24-2 Event Type Categories**

| Code | Description |
|---|---|
| A | Audit messages |
| I | Informational messages |
| W | Warning messages |
| F | Fatal messages |
| E | Error messages |
| O | A message written to systemOut by an application or other internal component |
| R | A message written to systemErr by an application or other internal component |
| u | A special message written to the log by the WAS runtime |
| Z | Any other message that was not recognized as one of the above |

When reviewing the logs, pay particular attention to the timestamps and the thread IDs. These two key pieces of information can help you determine causality. The best way to read a log file is backwards. That is, read the most recent events first, scanning backwards in time until you find the error you are looking for. Once you've done this, note the thread ID. Now, continue your scan. Any event that occurs before that error with the same thread ID preceded the error in question and might have caused the error. That's how you can quickly determine causality in complex multi-threaded applications.

### Service Log and Log Analyzer

The service log is best viewed with the Log Analyzer tool that is provided with WAS and the Application Server Toolkit (ASTK). It can also be dumped to your standard out (console) or a file using the showlog command as documented in the Info Center. However, the Log Analyzer provides the benefit of matching records in the log to a database of known problems and solutions (called the symptom database) that is kept on your machine and that can be dynamically updated. For this reason, you may want to use this tool when obscure or cryptic errors show up in the SystemOut.log and SystemErr.log.

If using the Analyzer from the server is problematic, the service log file can be FTPed to another machine where the WAS admin tools or ASTK are installed (be sure to use binary transfer mode). You can load the Log Analyzer with the **waslogbr** command or from your menu if you are running Windows. The first action, if you have an Internet connection, should be to update the symptom database with any new records from IBM support. You use File > Update Database > WebSphere Application Server symptom database.

> **NOTE**
>
> You can actually create your own service log symptom databases using WebSphere Studio Application Developer if your developers use this tool. This may be useful for any specialized errors that occur from your application or third-party tools.

Figure 24-8 shows a service log loaded into the Log Analyzer. Warning messages are shown in yellow, while error messages are shown in pink. The currently highlighted message, Rec_2, is in red. This example shows the output after a record has been highlighted and Record > Analyze has been chosen from the menu. This has caused the symptom for this particular exception to be loaded from the symptom database and displayed in the Symptom pane. The checkmarks next to records zero through three indicate that a symptom has been found in the database, while none was found for Rec_4 when we analyzed it.

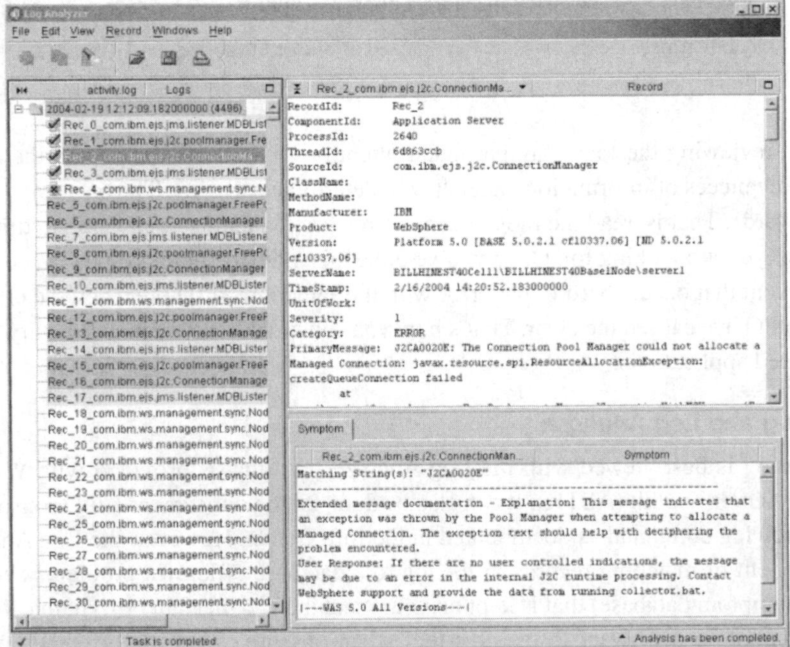


**Figure 24-8** Log Analyzer output.

While many Log Analyzer messages may appear to state the obvious, there are also occasions where direct and important feedback is given, such as notification that a specific fix is available from the WAS support site for this problem. For this reason, it is important to always consider Log Analyzer as part of the early problem-solving process, and keep its database up to date.

Before closing our discussion on the primary WAS log files, we should mention that there are many other logs under the /logs directory and its subdirectories. There are logs created when fixes are applied to WAS and when administrative tasks are performed such as startServer.log. Become familiar with these logs and review their content when there are problems, particularly if they have recent timestamps.

## Active WAS Problem Determination

Having gotten this far, if you are still experiencing the problem, you should have a very good feel for what is going on and should have collected an abundance of information. It is time to take a more active role in finding a solution.

### WebSphere Support and Related Utilities

If you have spent good money on a support contract, at this point it would be a very good idea to open a Problem Management Record (PMR) with the WAS support team. The information necessary to do this, primarily the customer number you were assigned with the support contract and the phone number to call, should always be readily available to WAS admins. In the past, the initial steps in working with support were quite frustrating. A cycle of calls would ensue where support would ask for certain logs and then call back for more logs in a seemingly endless cycle. With WAS5, there is a much better solution for this called the Collector.

#### Collector Utility

The Collector is a utility for gathering up all of the logs, configuration files, and environment information that WAS support normally asks for in one fell swoop. It is very easy to run—you just need to move to a temp directory (not in the WAS install path) and issue the collector command. You should be logged on as root or Administrator, as this tool will query information about your operating system, and Java runtime 1.2.2 or higher should be on the path. Many messages will scroll through the console window too quickly to read, but you will have access to them in the log files that the Collector creates in this directory and also to the collector.log that gets inserted into the JAR file. The final result is a large JAR file with a very complete set of logs, config files, and environmental information. You can also run a lightweight version of this command using the -Summary parameter, which will give basic information such as the install path and version of things like the JDK, WAS, and operating system. If you are feeling adventurous, have time on your hands, and want one-stop shopping, you can unzip this file to another machine or directory and use it for your troubleshooting sessions.

If you have WAS Network Deployment as well as the WAS Base product on the same server, keep in mind that you should run the Collector once in each environment, as they are considered separate installs. Run the setupcmdline command from each environment's bin directory before executing the command for that environment so that it receives the proper environment variables for the install directory, JDK, etc. Pay attention to the final return code at the end to ensure that it ran successfully. If not, inspect the collector.log file that is inside the resulting JAR file. Some interim error codes are normal; for example, if you don't have MQ installed, a bad return code will result when it tries to gather the MQ information.

### First Failure Data Capture

Each WAS-managed process has a utility running in it that captures exception information and logs it into special log files in the logs/ffdc directory. These log files are intended primarily for WAS support, and they are included in what the Collector captures. However, you may also want to keep an eye on them and become familiar with the summary information they provide. FFDC is a "preemptive" tool that is always running and capturing data; you should not attempt to turn it off or on or configure it.

### Update Installer

Invariably, one of the first questions support will ask is whether you are current on fixes for your WAS products, and if not, they may recommend installing these as a first step. Before calling them, you might go to the web site and make sure there aren't any new interim fixes, fix packs, or cumulative fixes specific to your problem area. Each fix contains a list of problems resolved, and you should check this if the fix description sounds like it could be related to your specific issue. If you have been able to reproduce the problem in a non-production area, this may afford you the ability to try any such fixes to see if they relieve the problem. You certainly don't want to do this haphazardly in production. Each fix now comes with an installation utility called the Update Installer, which makes installing and uninstalling these updates easier than in the past.

> **NOTE**
>
> **Interim Fix**—A single published emergency fix for a specific, known problem. These have names such as PQ23456.
>
> **Cumulative Fix**—A package of interim fixes, which will raise the version number in the fourth segment; for example, you would install Cumulative Fix 3 to WAS 5.0.2 in order to bring the version to 5.0.2.3.
>
> **Fix Pack**—A package of interim fixes that could also contain new functionality; for example, Fix Pack 2, which updates WAS 5.0 to version 5.0.2.

### WAS Trace

In Chapter 5, we briefly touched on the WAS tracing facility and even showed some wsadmin scripts for using it. We will expand the discussion further here. Support will usually want a trace log for a specific set of WAS components, taken while the error condition is occurring. These are also pulled in by the Collector utility. WAS trace is covered in detail in the next section.

Before we move off the topic of WAS support, a few words of advice. Be sure to never overstate or understate the priority of your call when you are asked. Even though you may be in a stressed state, be under control when discussing the problem with the support tech. It may be frustrating, but as with any support center, they have a predetermined set of questions to ask and procedures to follow. If you feel that the individual you are working with is not making progress, you should ask to escalate the problem to a higher-level support tech or to speak to a duty manager. Again, you want to do this only with justification so that you don't abuse these types of actions.

## When All Else Fails

When you've done your best using the above tactics and still cannot find a reasonable explanation, or the problem appears to be difficult or complex, you may want to employ more drastic problem solving alternatives. These are saved for the last stage of the process because they typically incur far more effort and personnel than the prior troubleshooting techniques.

### Reproducing the Problem

We have talked in this book about the importance of available environments for unit, integration, pre-production, and system testing. If your problem is occurring in production and you can reproduce the problem in one of these other environments, you have won a major battle. This is particularly important if you believe the problem looks like an application problem. Moving your efforts away from the production environment allows the use of better tools (such as debuggers, profilers, load testing, and monitoring products) and inspection without further disruption to other applications and infrastructure. You will be better able to work with support and apply their suggestions more easily in these environments. It might be best to attempt to reproduce in the environments closest to production first, where you are more likely to have success due to the similarity. From there, move back toward the development environments where more troubleshooting "power tools" are available and where developers can more easily introduce potential code fixes if the problem is application-related. If you reproduce the problem on the developer workstation/unit test environment, something has gone very wrong with the testing/acceptance process when the application moved thorough those stages initially—how this happened should be assessed after the smoke has cleared. This is another good reason why these environments are so important and eventually pay for themselves when the chips are down. For mission-critical applications, it just doesn't pay to skimp by omitting these crucial areas.

> **NOTE**
>
> Having "build" scripts for your production environment is another good practice that pays well in this situation—you can apply these scripts to servers away from production to duplicate the production configuration, increasing your chances of success in duplicating the problem.

## Building a Team

As mentioned in the introductory paragraph to this chapter, a sound mental state and good organization go a long way toward problem solving. In most cases, it is fairly evident from the initial problem-solving steps whether the problem is related to the application or some area of the infrastructure. Examples are when all database calls are failing or some area of the network suddenly appears unreachable. When this happens, a good way to begin is to step away and look at the big picture with a few stakeholders from other areas of the infrastructure (db or network admins, or application specialists). Large whiteboards with those hard-to find (working) dry-erase markers and a few good people to bounce ideas off are a good start. It is surprising how often problems are quickly resolved in these sessions when someone suddenly realizes that a recent patch or maintenance cycle coincides directly with the timeframes when the problems are occurring or started to occur.

Of course, you do not want to take others' time without first making initial attempts to solve the problem and having good cause to believe it may be related to something outside of WAS. Ensure that you have made some serious attempts to resolve the problem and that you have solid evidence that points to these areas, or your attendees will be unlikely to respond in the future. Open your meeting by passing out your problem definition package and discussing the problem in general terms, being careful not to come off as pointing to any particular group as the source of the problem. Diplomacy is an important skill for team problem solving! Get this group to think outside the (WAS) box and let them brainstorm. If there is evidence in the package or discussion that points in a particular direction, they will see it.

As an example, if the problem appears to be network-related, start with your team by drawing the topology up on the board so that changes and annotations can be viewed and discussed by all. Include all components—load balancers, proxies, firewalls, routers, and switches. Often, slight changes, such as those to firewall rules, can be the impetus for hard-to-debug problems in the backend. Get the stakeholders to acknowledge the accuracy of this diagram and begin the discussion about any recent changes. Even if it does not lead to the problem resolution, it is quite beneficial for everyone to review this information occasionally. Progress by talking about any recent changes to any of these areas and move forward with some open-ended brainstorming about what could be causing the problem. Like any good television detective (or forensic investigator in today's parlance), develop theories and prove or disprove them throughout the process. Even if these infrastructure team members come up empty at this session, they may be useful later when you have more information. For example, an operating system admin could help you create and analyze dump files from the JVM, or an application architect or developer could employ some remote debugging tools to help you.

# Problem Determination Tools

## Power Tools

### WAS Trace

The tracing facility in WAS could have been covered in our section on WAS logs. However, it is such an important tool that it deserves classification here with the other "Power Tools." In fact, if you cannot find anything useful in the log files, tracing should be your next step. By enabling WAS trace and providing trace specifications targeted at specific components, you can get a detailed narrative on exactly what WAS is doing each step of the way while processing transactions. WAS trace has two key features that make it a bit unusual but also extremely powerful. First, trace messages can be written to a circular in-memory buffer rather than to a file. This conserves disk space and performs much better than traditional file logging. Secondly, WAS trace is dynamically configurable using several administrative tools. Thus, you can easily change the trace level of a running system without restarting anything. This makes it very convenient to collect diagnostics and troubleshoot problems. WAS trace is typically used for internal WAS components; however, your programmers are free to use the JRAS API (or the Log4J wrapper) to gain these same advantages for your application logging and tracing. In addition, the Apache Jakarta Commons Logging APIs can be used and configured to direct their output to the JRAS trace-stream. There is an extensive section in the Info Center that details instructions for your programmers on how to do this and the advantages compared to standard logging practices. Let's have a look at how trace works and how to use it.

Trace configuration can be found in the administrative console under Troubleshooting > Logs and Trace >*servername* > Diagnostic Trace. This is the same area we visited when learning about the primary WAS logs. You will notice two tabs—one for Configuration and one for Runtime. The former is for setting trace levels that will take effect the next time the application server is started, and the latter is to change tracing dynamically on running application servers. In most cases you'll want to change tracing using the Runtime tab unless you think the problem you are seeing occurs during startup. Figure 24-9 shows the pane to set up Runtime tracing.

To use this, enter a trace specification, specify whether to trace to a file or memory, and press the Apply button to begin tracing the selected server. Take note that the memory buffer size is in thousands of lines, while the file size is specified in megabytes. As traces can get quite large, it is more common to trace to memory. This allows you to wait until the error condition occurs and press the Dump button to dump the buffer to a file name and path (which you must specify). Specifying a trace specification string can seem a bit cryptic. Fortunately, there are aids for configuring the trace specification that make this easier. Figure 24-10 shows our example of pressing the Modify button and selecting two component groups for tracing. You can also see the legend of available trace levels.

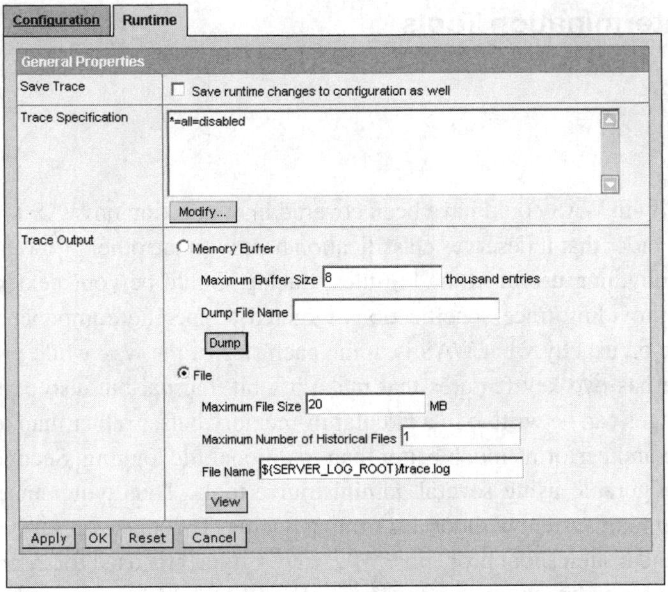

**Figure 24-9** Configuring for Runtime tracing.

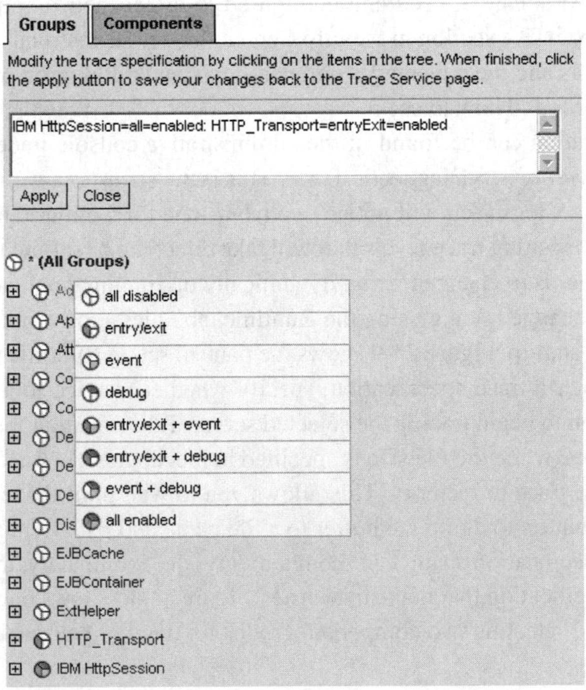

**Figure 24-10** Configuring a trace specification.

In Figure 24-10, HTTP Transport has been configured for entry/exit tracing, and HTTP Session has been selected for all tracing. As you can see, you can select either by the type of component group or switch over to the Components tab to select components by package and class. The former is useful if you only have a general idea of what functional area you want to look at, while the latter is useful if you want to trace specific, known packages and classes that you may have seen in a stack trace in one of the logs, for example. You can also visit the Info Center Troubleshooting guide, which has a listing of very useful trace specifications. If you have opened a problem incident with WAS support, they will often give you specific trace strings to use for what they would like you to capture and send to them. The intuition of what specifically to choose as the trace string and which components to trace grows with time and experience. You may want to keep your own library of common trace strings to copy and paste in, particularly if you use the trace facility from within your applications. This is much faster than clicking through the GUI to select components.

> **NOTE**
> Be selective about how much to trace. For example, if you traced everything, your eight thousand lines of trace memory buffer would only represent a very short snapshot of time, whereas a more specific trace specification could give you data from a much longer period of time in the resulting log.

Code Snippet 24-3 shows an example of trace output. It has the same basic format as the logs we looked at earlier. Notice that in this code listing, many EventTypes are "d" for debug. You will see the other EventTypes in a "real" trace, however, as well as the ">" and "<" symbols denoting entry and exit into a particular method. This trace begins with some summary environmental information, followed by the trace output. You can see our trace specification in the summary information—we have traced all of the HTTPSession component, and this is evident by looking at the trace output.

**Code Snippet 24-3** Sample trace output

```
************ Start Display Current Environment ************
WebSphere Platform 5.0 [BASE 5.0.2.3 cf30403.04] [ND 5.0.2.1
➥cf10337.06]  running with process name BILLHINEST40Cell1\
➥BILLHINEST40Base1Node\server1 and process id 840
Host Operating System is Windows 2000, version 5.0
Java version = J2RE 1.3.1 IBM Windows 32 build cn131-20030618 (JIT
➥enabled: jitc), Java Compiler = jitc, Java VM name = Classic VM
was.install.root = C:\WAS50\AppServer1
user.install.root = C:\WAS50\AppServer1
Java Home = C:\WAS50\AppServer1\java\jre
```

```
ws.ext.dirs =
C:\WAS50\AppServer1\java/lib;C:\WAS50\AppServer1/classes;C:\WAS50\
➥AppServer1/classes;C:\WAS50\AppServer1/lib;C:\WAS50\AppServer1/lib/
➥ext;C:\WAS50\AppServer1/web/help;C:\WAS50\AppServer1/deploytool/itp/
➥plugins/com.ibm.etools.ejbdeploy/runtime
Classpath = C:\WAS50\AppServer1/properties;C:\WAS50\AppServer1/
➥properties;C:\WAS50\AppServer1/lib/bootstrap.jar;C:\WAS50\AppServer1/
➥lib/j2ee.jar;C:\WAS50\AppServer1/lib/lmproxy.jar;C:\WAS50\AppServer1/
➥lib/urlprotocols.jar
Java Library path = C:\WAS50\AppServer1\java\bin;.;C:\WINNT\system32;
➥C:\WINNT;C:\WAS50\AppServer1\bin;C:\WAS50\AppServer1\java\bin;C:\
➥WAS50\AppServer1\java\jre\bin;C:\Program
Files\IBM\LDAP\bin;C:\WAS50\Messaging\Java\lib;C:\WINNT\system32;C:\
➥WINNT;C:\WINNT\System32\Wbem;C:\Notes;C:\Utilities;C:\Program Files\
➥IBM\Trace Facility\;C:\Program Files\IBM\Personal Communications\;
➥C:\Program
Files\cvsnt;C:\PROGRA~1\IBM\SQLLIB\BIN;C:\PROGRA~1\IBM\SQLLIB\FUNCTION;
➥C:\PROGRA~1\IBM\SQLLIB\SAMPLES\REPL;C:\WAS50\Messaging\bin;C:\WAS50\
➥Messaging\WEMPS\bin;C:\Infoprint;;C:\WAS50\Messaging\bin;C:\WAS50\
➥Messaging\java\bin;C:/WAS50/Messaging/WEMPS\bin
Current trace specification = IBM HttpSession=all=enabled
************* End Display Current Environment *************
[2/20/04 1:09:36:187 EST] 19d11257 SessionContex >
➥SessionContext.sessionPreInvoke
[2/20/04 1:09:36:197 EST] 30be5253 SessionContex >
➥SessionContext.sessionPreInvoke
[2/20/04 1:09:36:197 EST] 30be5253 SessionContex >
➥SessionContext.getIHttpSession(req,res,boolean):  true
[2/20/04 1:09:36:197 EST] 30be5253 SessionContex d
➥SessionContext.getRequestedSessionId
[2/20/04 1:09:36:197 EST] 30be5253 SessionContex d
➥SessionContext.getRequestedSessionIdFromCookie
[2/20/04 1:09:36:197 EST] 30be5253 SessionContex >
➥SessionContext.getIHttpSession:  0000-5MaAqhwoDI8A1k4o3f9D80:-1
➥isSSL false
[2/20/04 1:09:36:197 EST] 30be5253 SessionContex >
➥SessionContext.lockAndReturn
[2/20/04 1:09:36:197 EST] 30be5253 SessionContex >
➥SessionContext.tableGet
[2/20/04 1:09:36:197 EST] 30be5253 SessionContex >
➥SessionSimpleHashMap.get() - key=-5MaAqhwoDI8A1k4o3f9D80
[2/20/04 1:09:36:197 EST] 30be5253 SessionContex d
➥SessionSimpleHashMap.get() - key found in HashMap
```

```
[2/20/04 1:09:36:197 EST] 30be5253 SessionContex d
➥SessionContext.saveCloneInfo - input cloneInfo= :-1
[2/20/04 1:09:36:197 EST] 30be5253 SessionContex >
➥SessionContext.notifySessionAccessed
[2/20/04 1:09:36:197 EST] 30be5253 SessionContex <
➥SessionContext.notifySessionAccessed
[2/20/04 1:09:36:197 EST] 30be5253 SessionContex d increment
➥In ServiceMethodCount is now 1
```

> **NOTE**
> As you read through your trace, pay particular attention to the time span between events in the same thread. For example, if you were tracing JDBC and saw that after WAS issues a request for a connection to the backend database, it does not get a response for many seconds, it may be that the database is maxing out its available connections or is down and your thread is stalled while waiting for the database to open a free one for you.

You may also have noticed in Figure 24-9 that there is a check box to save your Runtime trace specification to the Configuration tab, which is shown in Figure 24-11. As stated earlier, the Configuration pane is different from Runtime in that changes made here are persistent—they stay set until you change them.

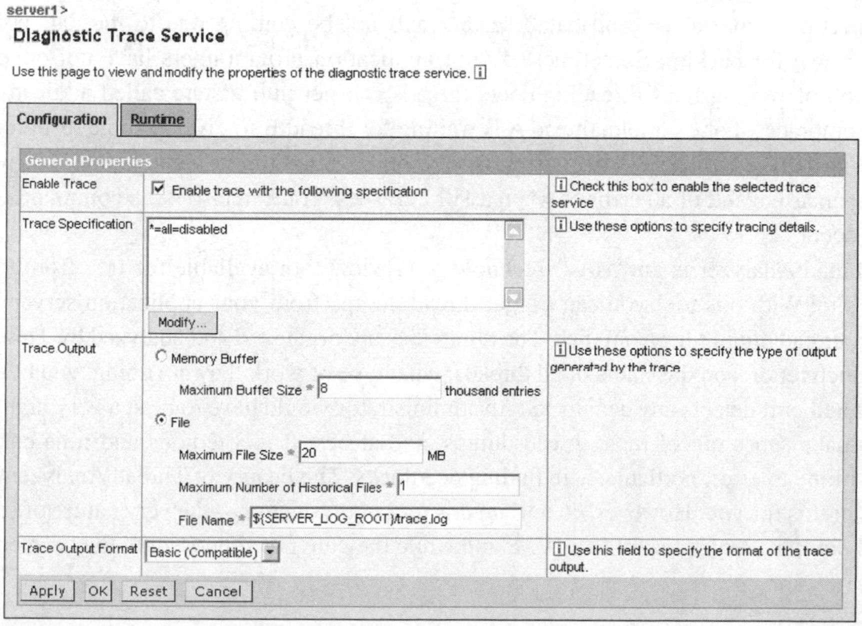

server1 >
**Diagnostic Trace Service**
Use this page to view and modify the properties of the diagnostic trace service.
Configuration | Runtime

| General Properties | | |
|---|---|---|
| Enable Trace | ☑ Enable trace with the following specification | Check this box to enable the selected trace service |
| Trace Specification | *=all=disabled<br>Modify... | Use these options to specify tracing details. |
| Trace Output | ○ Memory Buffer<br>Maximum Buffer Size * 8 thousand entries<br>◉ File<br>Maximum File Size * 20 MB<br>Maximum Number of Historical Files * 1<br>File Name * ${SERVER_LOG_ROOT}/trace.log | Use these options to specify the type of output generated by the trace |
| Trace Output Format | Basic (Compatible) | Use this field to specify the format of the trace output. |

Apply | OK | Reset | Cancel

**Figure 24-11** Diagnostic Trace Configuration panel.

You do not need to check the Enable trace check box in order to use the Runtime dynamic trace on a running server. This is only to designate that persistent trace should be started when the application server is initialized.

> **NOTE**
>
> If you are using the Configuration pane to configure persistent tracing, you want to be very careful to turn tracing off when you are done. WAS support will tell you that a very common source of calls is from administrators who have unwittingly left trace on, which will slow performance and perhaps fill the disk volume if tracing to a file.
>
> Runtime (dynamic) traces will stay in effect until you restart the application server or change the trace string back to *=all=disabled and apply the change.

## Thread Analyzer

At any given point in an application server, there are many threads executing, carrying out work for WAS and your applications. A thread dump is a way to dump out a "snapshot" of the current state of all threads running in the JVM. This tool is most useful, for example, when a JVM is perceived as "hung" or non-responsive and you need to see what is going on inside. Often, JVMs in this state are described as "frozen," but they really are not. Those threads are always doing something. The JVM may appear to be "frozen" because threads are caught in an endless loop of application code and sucking up all CPU cycles and other resources, or they may all simply be waiting for connections from a backend database that will not be coming due to the database being brought down for backup. Sometimes, if your application programmers have not done a very careful job of writing their threading code, threads can get into a state called a "deadlock" or "deadly embrace." For example, thread A is waiting for thread B to give up some resource, while thread B is waiting for thread A to give up some resource. Sometimes thread dumps (or javacores) will happen as a result of an error or when a JVM crashes. You can also issue commands to force them to occur.

Thread Analyzer is an "as-is" Technology Preview tool available for free from the WAS support site. With this tool you can trigger thread dumps from your application server[2] or load previous thread dump files from disk. The dump files are organized and analyzed by Thread Analyzer, which reports on the status of all threads, what type of work they are doing, what their state is, and whether it detects any deadlocks. An administrator would have to be at a very high level of skill to make sense out of most thread dumps, and at best it is a tedious and time-consuming process prone to error, particularly in finding deadlocks. The beauty of Thread Analyzer is that it does all of this for you. However, do not run this tool in production—the very nature of capturing a thread dump is very stressful to a JVM, and while they are not supposed to, they can crash as a result.

2 The Thread Analyzer documentation states that it is not to be used to dump threads in the WAS-ND Deployment Manager or Node Manager processes.

There are other ways to trigger a thread dump.

From Unix, kill -3 <process ID> will do this. Make sure to get the process ID right so you don't kill the wrong process!

On any platform, using wsadmin, you can use the following:

```
wsadmin>set jvm [$AdminControl completeObjectName type=JVM,
➥process=server1,*]
wsadmin>$AdminControl invoke $jvm dumpThreads
```

After triggering the dump, look for a file named javacore-<timestamp>.txt. This file can appear in various locations, from the current directory to the operating system's install path.

Figure 24-12 shows a summary screen with counts for the types of threads found after loading a thread dump with Thread Analzyer. It shows what type of work they were doing at the moment when the dump was created.

> **SECURITY NOTE**
>
> Thread Analyzer uses the SOAP port, so you cannot do a dynamic thread dump from Thread Analyzer if global security is on. In this case, it might be better to use one of the previously mentioned command-line techniques to do the thread dump and then load the file into Thread Analyzer using the menu options.

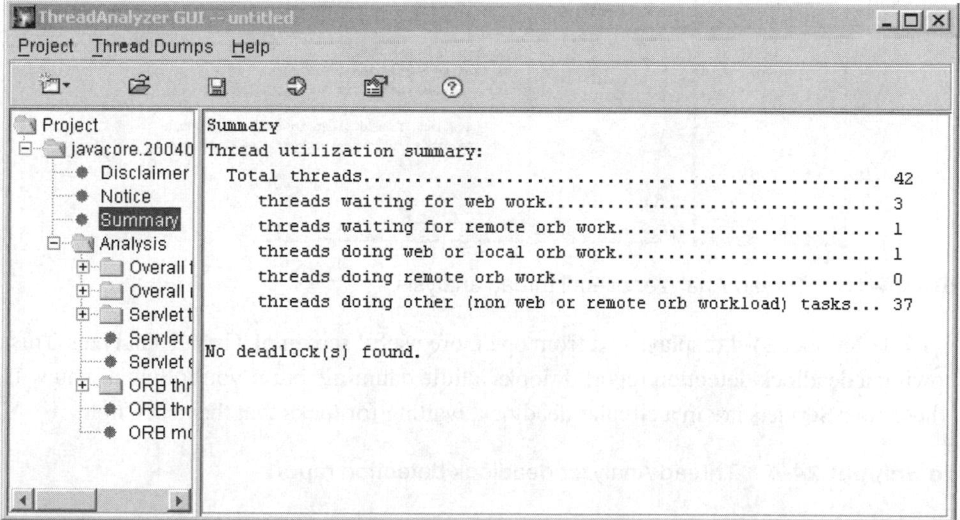


**Figure 24-12** Thread Analyzer summary page.

Figure 24-13 displays a very useful page of each package/class/method executing on a thread by count in descending order. This tells you what type of work the majority of threads were doing. This is the page where you might see, for instance, that ninety percent of your available threads were in a socket_wait() method, indicating that perhaps some backend server is not responding. You will generally see some types of sentry threads here that occasionally awake to perform maintenance tasks.

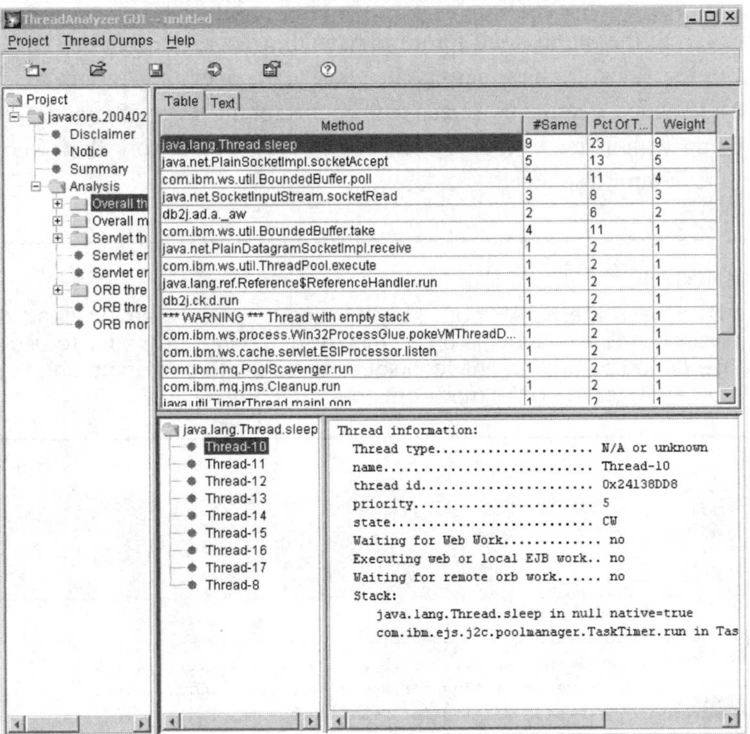


**Figure 24-13** Thread Analyzer overall thread analysis.

Code Snippet 24-4 displays text from one more useful screen of Thread Analyzer. This one is showing a deadlock detection report. It looks a little daunting, but if you follow it, you will see that these four Servlets are in a circular deadlock, waiting for locks that they each hold.

**Code Snippet 24-4** Thread Analyzer deadlock detection report

```
FOUND A JAVA LEVEL DEADLOCK:
----------------------------
"Servlet.Engine.Transports : 3":
waiting to lock monitor 0xbc360 (object 0xea3383c8, a
➥java.lang.Object),
```

```
which is locked by "Servlet.Engine.Transports : 0"
"Servlet.Engine.Transports : 0":
waiting to lock monitor 0xbc328 (object 0xea3383d0, a
➥java.lang.Object),
which is locked by "Servlet.Engine.Transports : 1"
"Servlet.Engine.Transports : 1":
waiting to lock monitor 0xbc2b8 (object 0xea3383d8, a
➥java.lang.Object),
which is locked by "Servlet.Engine.Transports : 2"
"Servlet.Engine.Transports : 2":
waiting to lock monitor 0xbc2f0 (object 0xea3383e0, a
➥java.lang.Object),
which is locked by "Servlet.Engine.Transports : 3"
```

Thread Analyzer has capabilities too extensive to cover here, such as the ability to group thread dumps into "projects." See the documentation included with the utility for further information. This documentation includes a tutorial and has detailed information about how to interpret the data to detect deadlocks or other dangerous conditions.

## HeapWizard

Like Thread Analyzer, HeapWizard is another "as-is" free download from the WAS support site. You use it by setting the environment variable IBM_HEAPDUMP=true and then starting your application server. After reproducing some test scenario, you use the same operating system or wsadmin commands as we did to get the thread dumps for Thread Analyzer. This creates a filename beginning with "heapdump." You can then pull it into the HeapWizard GUI or use the command line to generate an XML file. There are further instructions included with the package. It is most likely going to be of benefit when reviewed with someone from the application development team who is familiar with the classes in use by the application. This utility will allow you to see a view of the heap in two ways:

- **Classes by size**—This view, as shown in Figure 24-14, is a list of class names with the number of objects of that class type, the cumulative sizes of all objects of that type, and the cumulative sizes of objects of that type that have a (non-parent) root-level status. This view provides a quick summary of class utilization and can be used for problem determination and tuning. A large root-level size could mean memory leaks, and this should be reviewed with your application development staff. Be wary of high object count values. High root size values could indicate an object that is being created over and over excessively in some sort of loop. You might expect to see these for commonly used classes such as String, but perhaps not for your application classes. This view can help determine where caching may be most effective based on object usage.

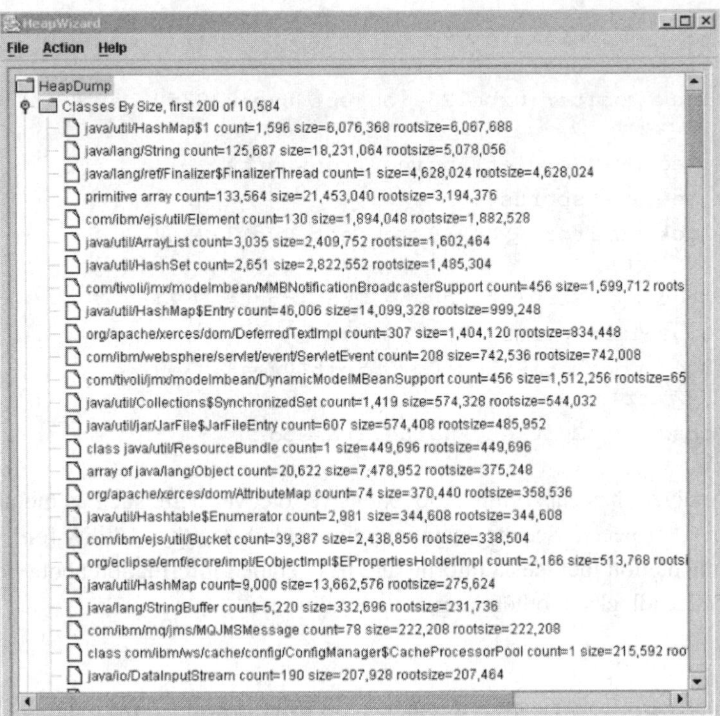

**Figure 24-14** HeapWizard Classes by size view.

- **Objects by Size**—This view, as shown in Figure 24-15, shows the objects in the heap by object types, object size, and object references. This is a simple view of heap object relationships. The real heap consists of objects with multiple, redundant, and recursive references to other objects. HeapWizard filters the object references to create a simplified parent-child object relationship that results in a simple tree structure, where an object can reference multiple child objects, but each object has no more than one parent object. This view, while eliminating a lot of information about object interconnections, tends to provide the most useful image for determining excessive object allocation.

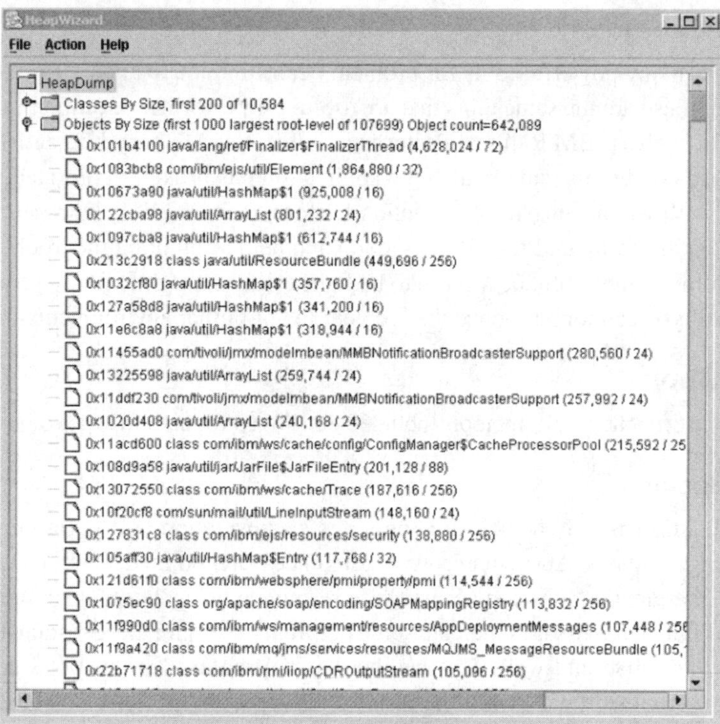


**Figure 24-15** HeapWizard Objects by size view.

### Tivoli Performance Viewer

The Tivoli Performance Viewer (TPV), formerly known as Resource Analyzer, is primarily used for performance tuning, as you can tell by its name. However, do not discount its utility in problem determination. Particularly, you could use this tool to monitor patterns in heap allocation that might indicate memory leaks or to look for resource saturation in the number of web container threads or database connections. If you can reproduce the problem in TPV, you can save this as a "recording" to send to WAS support for playback, helping them to better understand the problem. There's further discussion and some examples of using the TPV in Chapter 25.

### Developer Power Tools

Both the WebSphere Studio Application Developer (WSAD) and the Application Server Tool Kit (ASTK) have tools that could be useful in certain problem determination scenarios. If you aren't familiar with these tools, enlist the help of those who are if you suspect application code problems could be the root cause. These tools can profile applications to determine "hot spots," do remote debugging directly into the JVM where the error is occurring (of course, don't hit your production box!), and statically analyze program source code, looking for common errors like logic that loops endlessly or does not close connections to resources.

### Third-Party Power Tools

There are a great many powerful tools for problem determination available from IBM and third parties. Some of these are the same tools that are useful for performance tuning. Load-generating simulation tools, such as IBM Rational Performance Tester or Mercury Interactive LoadRunner, can simulate load conditions under which the application has broken in production. Monitoring tools such as Tivoli Monitoring for Transaction Performance and Wily Introscope can provide deep feedback on the entire end-to-end transaction and help to pinpoint the troublesome component quickly. Some of these products claim to be lightweight enough to run in production, which could be useful if you cannot reproduce the problem in your other environments.

## WAS Minor Tools

There are a few useful but not flashy tools included with WAS for certain types of problem solving.

### dumpNameSpace

As we learned earlier in this book, J2EE provides encapsulation and portability of resources using its naming features. Abstract resource references are pointed to real resources during deployment so that applications can access these resources using JNDI at runtime. Sometimes, the applications fail, and messages indicate some problem accessing these resources, even though they apparently are alive and well. This can be due to problems in the WAS namespace. The dumpnamespace command will dump the contents of the namespace to the console (as always, you can pipe this to a file for easier viewing). Since the namespace is built dynamically on JVM startup and only exists in memory, this command is useful for examining the contents to look for discrepancies. dumpNameSpace cannot provide information on local interfaces. See Chapter 5 for more information on global and local namespaces and how to dump them with wsadmin.

### Verbose Garbage Collection

A common cause of problems is excessive object usage and poor coding practices that cause memory leaks in Java. The Java heap must be occasionally inspected, and unused objects must be discarded to free up more memory by a process called "garbage collection." The faster an application in a JVM uses memory, the more often garbage collection must occur. For objects that leak memory, this can cause a death-spiral effect, where garbage collection has to happen more and more frequently, and the system can eventually choke if it cannot keep up with application object usage. Administrators may try to counter this by allocating more JVM heap size to applications, which also has an adverse effect—when the garbage collector runs, it now has a much greater space to inspect, causing it to take much longer to run. When garbage collection is running, certain threads and areas of JVM heap must be "frozen," which harms performance. Adding the verbose garbage collection option to the JVM runtime properties will result in detailed information about garbage collection cycles being added to log files, which can later be analyzed to determine how frequently garbage collection is occurring, how long each cycle is taking to complete, and how much memory was reaped. Figure 24-16 shows the verbose garbage collection flag set from Servers > Application Servers > *servername* > Process Definition in the administrative console.

**Configuration**

| General Properties | |
|---|---|
| Classpath | |
| Boot Classpath | |
| Verbose class loading | ☐ |
| Verbose garbage collection | ☑ |
| Verbose JNI | ☐ |
| Initial Heap Size | * 0 |
| Maximum Heap Size | 256 |

**Figure 24-16** Enabling verbose garbage collection for a JVM.

Code Snippet 24-5 shows a sample of verbose garbage collection output from the native_stderr.log file. It begins by stating that it needs 32 bytes of memory and cannot allocate them, triggering a garbage collection so that unused memory can be reaped. The first line also states that it has been almost a second and a half since the prior GC cycle. Reading down further, you can see that 26 megabytes of memory were freed in 91 milliseconds. GC typically occurs in two separate passes through memory—a "mark" pass where unused objects are marked for removal, and a "sweep" pass where the memory is actually freed.

**Code Snippet 24-5** Verbose garbage collection output in native_stderr.log

```
<AF[8]: Allocation Failure. need 32 bytes, 1413 ms since last AF>
<AF[8]: managing allocation failure, action=1 (0/49805904)
➥(2497544/2621360)>
<GC(48): GC cycle started Tue Feb 24 07:26:13 2004
<GC(48): freed 26207248 bytes, 54% free (28704792/52427264), in 91 ms>
  <GC(48): mark: 81 ms, sweep: 10 ms, compact: 0 ms>
  <GC(48): refs: soft 0 (age >= 32), weak 1, final 214, phantom 0>
<AF[8]: completed in 97 ms>
```

In doing garbage collection analysis, it is important to look for excessively long cycles (perhaps meaning the JVM is too large or your applications are not using objects efficiently), or those that result in increasingly less memory being reallocated (indicating a memory leak). In addition to reviewing these log entries, GC trends can be viewed graphically at runtime using the Tivoli Performance Viewer, which is covered in Chapter 25.

### Connection Manager Diagnostics

A very common source of JDBC data source connection pool problems is application code that does not release connections back to the pool when finished with them. This results in connections being left to timeout, and their unavailability during that time causes new connections to be allocated unnecessarily. These "orphaned connections" cause excess resource utilization on the application server and database and result in ConnectionWaitTimeoutExceptions when the pool is saturated. WAS 5 uses database connections based on the J2EE Connector Architecture (J2C), which forces connections to be used in the scope of a local transaction and closes them at the end of the transaction. However, as we discussed in Chapter 7, "JDBC as a Resource," you can still create WAS4-type data sources in WAS5.

If your application code uses WAS4-type data sources and does not close connections properly, you may see the ConnectionWaitTimeoutExceptions, which provide little information as to the source of the problem. Even if you do not see this exception, you may have many orphaned connections that are affecting your performance. IBM support now provides the Connection Manager Diagnostics utility in versions 5.021 and later. For earlier versions, it is downloadable from the support web site by searching on "Connection Manager Diagnostics." This utility is used by setting a custom property on the WAS4 data source. It is quite useful in that it will insert a stack trace into the SystemOut.log file when an orphaned connection times out or the ConnectionWaitTimeoutException occurs. This will show the package, class, and method in your application code where the connection was allocated (and likely not returned properly). For further details on the usage of this utility, search the IBM support web site for "Connection Manager Diagnostics" and see the TechNote there.

### IBMTrackerDebug Servlet

A very common cause of bloated JVM heaps and related problems is runaway session size. Because thin-client J2EE transactions are stateless, programmers often use the HTTP session for a general-purpose dumping ground. This is particularly troublesome in environments that are using WAS features to persist sessions to DRS memory or a database. Average user session size should be checked when it is suspected that this could be occurring or when JVM sizes grow too large. You can use the Tivoli Performance Viewer, which can now display average session size. Another way to get an abundance of session-related information is to use the built-in IBMTrackerDebug Servlet. You can get to this with the URL http://localhost:9080/servlet/com.ibm.ws.webcontainer.httpsession.IBMTrackerDebug. This Servlet is installed with the default application that comes with WAS and is not intended to be installed in production environments, so like some of our other tools, this would be useful only in non-production environments. Sample output is shown in Code Snippet 24-6.

**Code Snippet 24-6** Sample IBMTrackerDebug output

```
J2EE NAME(AppName#WebModuleName):: petstore#petstore.war
cloneId : -1

Number of sessions in memory: (for this webapp) : 2
use overflow : true
overflow size (for this webapp) :
Invalidation alarm poll interval (for this webapp) : 316
Max invalidation timeout (for this webapp) : 900
Using Cookies : true
Using URL Rewriting : false
use SSLId : false
URL Protocol Switch Rewriting : false
Session Cookie Name : JSESSIONID
Session Cookie Comment : SessionManagement
Session Cookie Domain : null
Session Cookie Path : /
Session Cookie MaxAge : -1
Session Cookie Secure : false
Maximum in memory table size : 1000
current time : Thu Feb 19 22:16:15 EST 2004
integrateWASSec :false
Session locking : false
Session locking timeout: 5
Allow access on lock timeout:true
Sessions Created:3
Active Count:0
Session Access Count:36
Invalidated Sessions Count:1
Invalidated By SessionManager:0
Garbage Collected count:0
SessionAffinity Breaks:0
Number of times invalidation alarm has run:558
Rejected Session creation requests(overflow off):0
Cache Discards:0
Attempts to access non-existent sessions:8
Number of binary reads from external store:0
Total time spent in reading from external store(ms):0
Total number of bytes read:0
```

```
Number of binary writes to external store:0
Total time spent in writing to external store(ms):0
Total number of bytes wriiten out:0
Session count 2
Total size of serializable objects in memory :0
Total number objects in memory :1
Min size session object size:0
Max size session object size :0
```

## Problem Prevention

While troubleshooting problems, think about steps that can be taken in the future to prevent these situations from happening. Practice good problem *prevention* by always using good discipline in the shop, particularly in areas of testing and change control. Keep the education level of all parties at the highest level possible. This does not have to mean sending the staff off to class every month. There are plenty of excellent materials available for free on the WAS public site, the developerworks site, and the RedBooks site. Be active in the global community on the public discussion forums on Usenet. IBM hosts Usenet servers at nntp://news.software.ibm.com, with WebSphere groups starting with ibm.software.websphere.* By maintaining a presence here and perhaps helping others, you learn from their mistakes and garner good will such that they may rush to your assistance when your time comes. Look around for user groups that may operate in your area, and if there are none, consider starting one. If you work in a large corporation, consider starting an internal user group. This is a great way to foster that all-important channel of communication and information sharing that rarely exists in huge companies, and maybe get free pizza and soft drinks.

## Conclusion

In this chapter, we have given an overview of problem determination for WAS admins. Along the way, we have provided some useful tips and introduced many tools that are useful in troubleshooting. As with other areas of this book, this subject alone could be easily expanded to a book of its own. Administrators are encouraged to read the generous Info Center section on troubleshooting, as well as the section in the [IBM WAS 5 Handbook] and [IBM WAS AIX PD]. There are also white papers on the WAS Library site, and even though they may be for prior versions, they still contain useful general information. When the chips are down and you're stuck with a problem of seemingly huge proportions while everyone else is out to play, you cannot have too much information or tools at your disposal.

CHAPTER 25

# Performance Tuning Tools

As with many of the subjects in this book, performance tuning is a topic that you could write an entire book on. In fact, many excellent books have been written on this topic. The focus of this chapter will not be performance-tuning techniques; you should refer to books such as [Joines 2002] for that. After a brief introduction to the performance monitoring portion of the WebSphere Application Server (WAS) runtime, this chapter will focus on using the tools that WebSphere Application Server provides for performance analysis and tuning.

## WAS Performance Monitoring Infrastructure

Underlying the performance monitoring capabilities in WAS is the Performance Monitoring Infrastructure (PMI), which collects performance information from a number of WAS runtime components. PMI in WAS V5 is implemented as a series of JMX (Java Management Extensions) MBeans (Management Beans), leveraging the JMX infrastructure available in WAS V5. The use of MBeans for the PMI implementation adds an additional PMI client type to WAS V5 from prior versions. Not only are the Performance Servlet HTTP client, PMI API Java Client,[1] and Tivoli Performance Viewer (TPV)[2] available, but a JMX Java client is also supported. The interaction between the clients and the WAS runtime is depicted in Figure 25-1.

1 The PMI API interface is changed for WAS V5, but the V4 PMI API remains supported as well.

2 The Tivoli Performance Viewer (TPV) is included with WAS V5. In prior versions of WAS, the TPV was known as the Resource Analyzer.

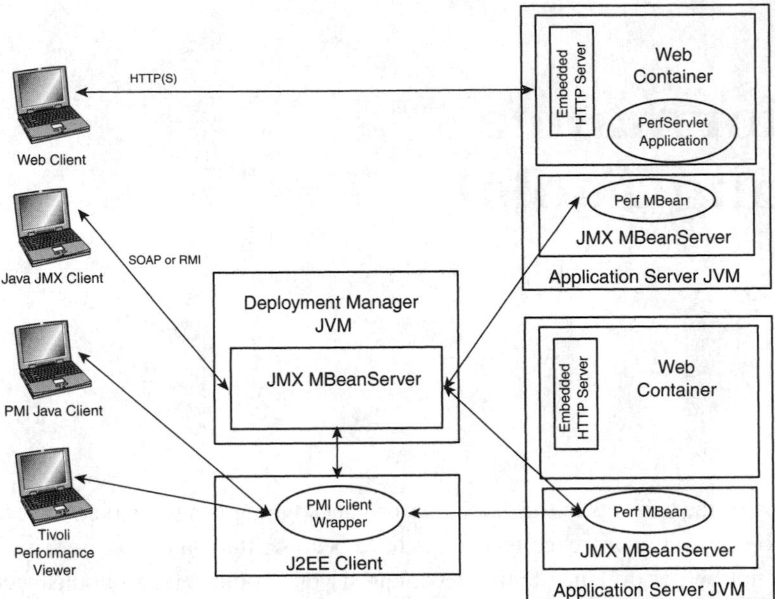


**Figure 25-1** WAS V5 PMI clients and runtime.

The preceding figure depicts a WAS-ND topology where the PMI client typically connects to the Deployment Manager in order to retrieve a list of nodes, application servers, and performance MBeans in a cell. In a WAS base installation, the performance client connects directly to an individual application server for performance data.

Each of the PMI clients' access performance data is collected from the following WAS V5 runtime components:

- Enterprise JavaBeans
- JDBC connection pools
- J2C connection pools
- Java Virtual Machine (JVM) runtime
- Servlet session manager
- Web and EJB container thread pools
- Transaction manager
- Web applications components (e.g., Servlets and JSPs)
- Object Request Broker (ORB)
- ORB/IIOP Workload Management (WLM)
- Web Services Gateway (WSGW)
- WAS dynacache (dynamic cache)

Within each of the aforementioned runtime components, a number of metrics are collected for application artifacts, such as the average response time for Servlets in a web application, HTTP session object size, and runtime process settings such as connection pool size and JVM heap utilization. For a complete list of the settings, you should refer to [WAS], specifically the discussion "Performance monitoring service settings."

## Enabling PMI

PMI is not enabled by default, so before you can monitor an application server and the applications running in it, you need to enable the Performance Monitoring Service for the application server. Minimally, this requires navigating to the Performance Monitoring Service tab in the adminconsole (Servers > Application Servers > *servername* > Performance Monitoring Service) and selecting the Startup check box, as depicted in Figure 25-2.

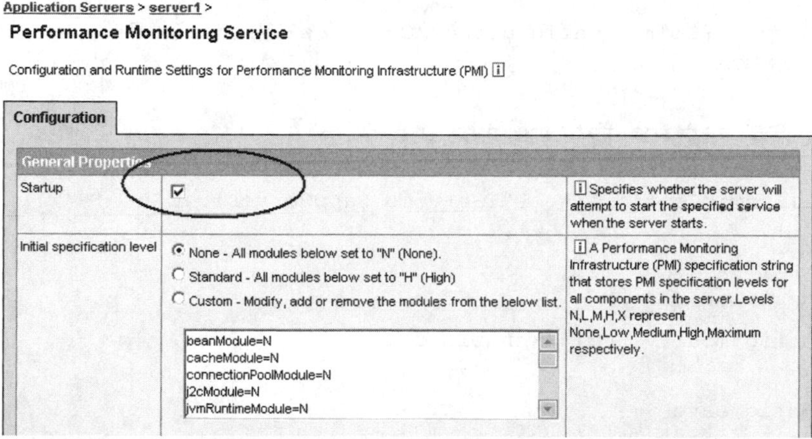


**Figure 25-2** Enabling PMI for an application server.

You can also configure the performance specification level, which selects the modules to be monitored as well as the monitoring level at this time, but that's not required since you can also specify it from the Tivoli Performance Viewer.

> **NOTE**
> In general, PMI provides information efficiently, without a significant performance impact. Selecting "standard" monitoring results in ~3% performance degradation. "Maximum" monitoring without JVMPI results in ~6% impact. Enabling JVMPI reporting results in a rather significant 55% performance degradation. As a result, you'll want to specify the highest settings only in extreme situations and for a very limited time. Do not forget to turn these settings "down" after your testing is complete!

Since enabling PMI at server startup using the administrative console for more than a single server can be a time-consuming task, you'll likely want to use wsadmin for this purpose.

The commands in Code Snippet 25-1 only enable PMI for a given application server. You'll likely also want to specify the PMI modules to monitor, as well as the monitoring level. This is accomplished by executing the commands shown in Code Snippet 25-2. In this case, monitoring for the data source connection pool, HTTP session, and JVM modules are enabled, each with a high ("H") level.

**Code Snippet 25-1 Enabling PMI for an application server with wsadmin**

```
#assume that cell, node and server are variables

#specify the server

set appServer [$AdminConfig getid /Cell:$cell/Node:$node/
➥Server:$server/]

#specify PMI service for app server

set pmi [$AdminConfig list PMIService $appServer]

#enable PMI

$AdminConfig modify $pmi {{enable true}}

$AdminConfig save
```

**Code Snippet 25-2 Enabling PMI and specifying monitoring levels using wsadmin**

```
$AdminConfig modify $pmi {{enable true} {initialSpecLevel connectionP
PoolModule=H:servletSessionModule=H:jvmRuntimeModule=H}}
```

The syntax to set monitoring levels for the example modules, assuming that PMI was already enabled, would be as shown in Code Snippet 25-3.

**Code Snippet 25-3 Specifying monitoring levels using wsadmin**

```
$AdminConfig modify $pmi {{initialSpecLevel connectionPoolModule=H:ser
vletSessionModule=H:jvmRuntimeModule=H} }
```

## WebSphere-Supplied PMI Clients

As described earlier, WAS V5 supports several different PMI clients, and provides two that are ready to use—the Performance Servlet application and the Tivoli Performance Viewer. Since the focus of this book is application deployment and administration, we won't be dealing with developing PMI clients. Instead, we'll focus our discussion on the usage of these two clients.

### Performance Monitoring Servlet

The Performance Monitoring Servlet is a web application that can be installed for use in either WAS base or WAS-ND. The specifics of using this PMI client vary based on WAS edition, but it basically functions by providing PMI data in XML format that can be viewed in a browser or captured by an application. The output of the Performance Monitoring Servlet is divided into three leaves in an XML data structure:[3]

- PerfNumericInfo
- PerfStatInfo
- PerfLoadInfo

The leaves of the structure provide the actual observations of the performance data, and the paths to the leaves provide the context.[4] An example of the XML output for JVM statistics from the Performance Monitoring Servlet is shown in Figure 25-3. The information display limits the usefulness of this client mainly to applications[5] that may expect information in this format or deployments where firewall or client constraints preclude the use of more robust performance clients. The use of the SOAP connector, which runs over HTTP(S), with the Tivoli Performance Viewer negates many firewall constraints that were present in prior WAS releases where an RMI connector was the only option. As a result, you'll likely choose to use some other client than the Performance Monitoring Servlet.

As far as configuration and use of the Performance Monitoring Servlet, if you are using WebSphere Application Server base, then you can only monitor PMI data from one application server at a time. This is because each application server is a standalone application server. As a result, you will need to install the PerfServletApp.ear (in the wasroot/installableApps directory) in each application server you wish to monitor. Once the application server (and application) is started, assuming you have enabled the PMI service, you can open a browser and use the application server host and connector port to contact the Servlet. The URL for this is:

http://perfServlet_Host:port/wasPerfTool/servlet/perfservlet?host=<host>&port=<port>&connector=<connector>&username=<username>&password=<password

3 The XML data structure precludes the use of Netscape Navigator 4.x as a client browser since Netscape does not support XML in its 4.x versions.

4 The DTD for the XML is provided in the perfServletApp.ear file.

5 The Performance Monitoring Servlet was developed for a third-party performance monitoring product.

where:

- <perfServlet_Host:port> could either be a standalone HTTP server or the web container HTTP transport. This is the host and port of the server web container that runs the servlet.
- <host> is the server host name. This is the host that should be connected for obtaining performance information.
- <port> is the connector port, the default for SOAP in 8880 in WAS base and 2809 for RMI.
- <connector> is either RMI or SOAP.
- <username> is an administrative user, when security is enabled.
- <password> is the password for the administrative user.

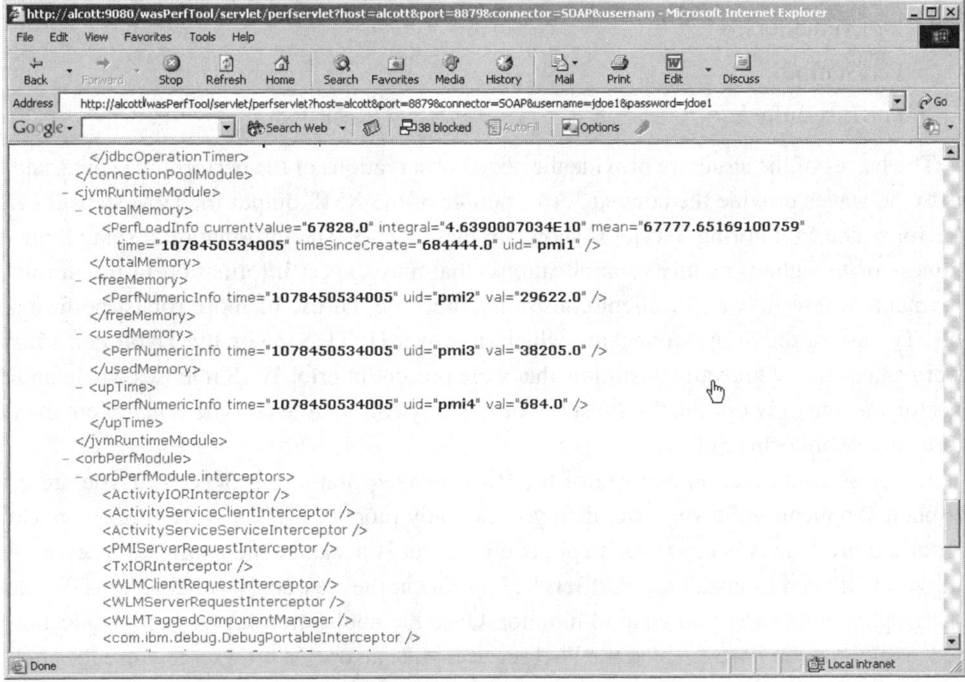


**Figure 25-3** Example output from the Performance Monitoring Servlet.

So, an example for server1 in WAS base would be:

http://myhost/wasPerfTool/servlet/perfservlet?host=myhost&port=8880&connector=SOAP&username=jdoe1&password=jdoe1

If additional WAS base standalone servers have been created, then you would use the appropriate server port[6] for the connector type for each of the application servers.

6 The port numbers for SOAP/RMI connector can be configured in the Administrative Console under Servers > Application Servers > *servername* > End Points.

If you are using WAS-ND, then you would specify the Deployment Manager host and connector port (RMI defaults to 9809 and SOAP defaults to 8879). In WAS-ND, the Performance Monitoring Servlet will display information from all application servers that have PMI enabled in the cell. An example URI for WAS-ND would be:

http://myhost/wasPerfTool/servlet/perfservlet?host=myhostt&port=8879&connector=SOAP&username=jdoe1&password=jdoe1

> **NOTE**
> The Performance Monitoring Servlet cannot connect to an individual server in a WAS-ND cell.

When deploying the Performance Monitoring Servlet in a WAS-ND cell, it is recommended that you deploy it in its own application server. Otherwise, you will have maintenance dependencies on the other application(s) that are running in that application server, and when the server is stopped for application maintenance, you will lose the performance monitoring that is provided via this Servlet.

## Tivoli Performance Viewer

The most often used WAS PMI client is Tivoli Performance Viewer (TPV). TPV is a Java client that is included with WAS V5. The client runs on Windows, Unix, and Linux platforms and can be used remotely across platforms (e.g., TPV can be launched from a workstation running Windows 2000 and monitor WAS running on Unix). The ability to specify a SOAP or RMI connection also mitigates firewall connection restrictions that may exist. TPV can log the information it collects and replay that information without a connection to WAS.

The TPV is launched from the <application server install root>/bin directory with the command tperfviewer <hostname> <port> <connector>, with the defaults of localhost, 8880 (on WAS and 8879 on WAS-ND) and SOAP for the host name, port, and connector type, respectively. If WAS is configured to use global security and SOAP is used, you will need to specify the user ID and password in the <application server install root>\properties\soap.client.props file. If the RMI connector is used,[7] you will be prompted for the user ID and password, as depicted in Figure 25-4.

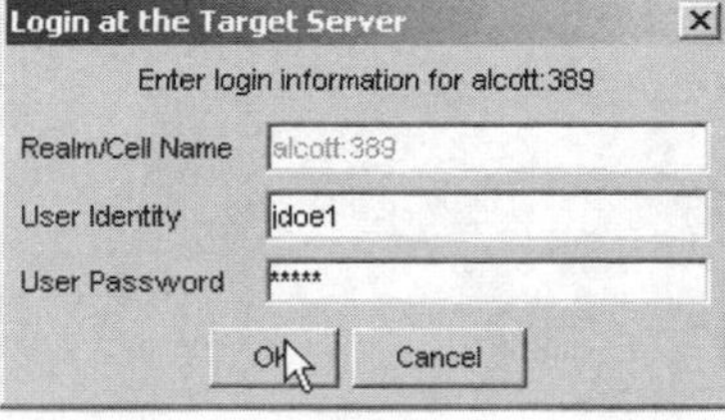


**Figure 25-4** TPV login dialog.

7 In Chapter 5, "WebSphere Application Server Architecture," we recommend use of the RMI connector for administrative clients in order to provide for the client authentication dialog.

Earlier in this chapter, we discussed how to specify modules to be monitored, as well as setting monitoring levels with the administrative console and wsadmin. The TPV also provides a mechanism for specifying the modules and monitoring levels. This allows you to change these on a running application server if you need to adjust the settings to either start or stop monitoring a given module or change the amount of information that is collected. This is depicted in Figures 25-5 and 25-6. In Figure 25-5, the Data Collection object is highlighted, which allows you to specify the server on which you wish to adjust the modules and or monitoring level. In Figure 25-6, the modules to be monitored as well as the monitoring level for each module is specified.

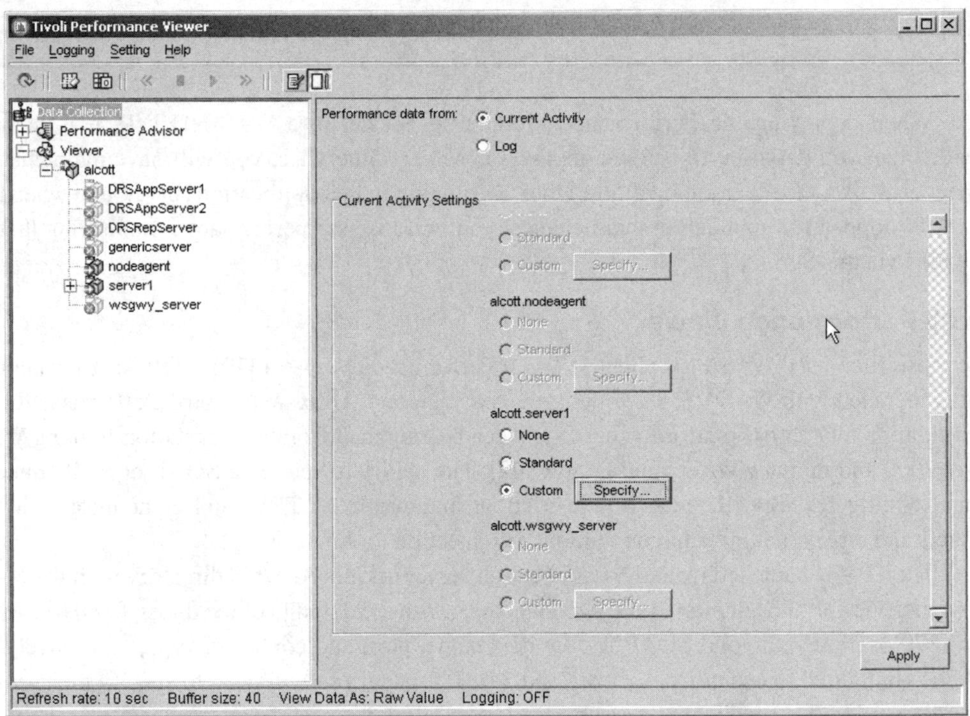


**Figure 25-5** TPV server data collection dialog.

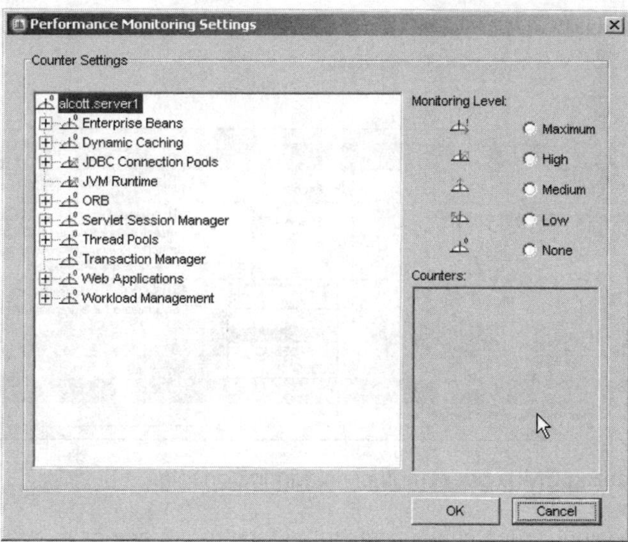


**Figure 25-6** TPV monitoring levels dialog.

## PMI Request Metrics

PMI Request Metrics (PMIRM) is another new feature in WAS V5 that allows for the tracking of requests across application server process boundaries. This enables you to follow the thread of execution for a specific request through multiple processes. PMI Request Metrics writes a record (records actually) to a text file (System.out) or sends the information to an Application Response Measurement (ARM 2.0)[8]-compliant agent, or both. Every web container and EJB container stores the timestamp of all requests entering that specific container and writes a record with response time and other metrics when an application response is provided.

Enabling Request Metrics in WAS is accomplished by navigating to the PMI Request Metrics dialog in the admin console (Troubleshooting > PMI Request Metrics) and enabling Request Metrics, as shown in Figure 25-7, and specifying the Trace Level. A setting of "Hops" (the default) is normally sufficient.

8 The Application Response Measurement (ARM) is an Open Group standard that describes a common method for end-to-end application monitoring of application performance, availability, usage, and end-to-end response time (http://www.opengroup.org/tech/management/arm/).

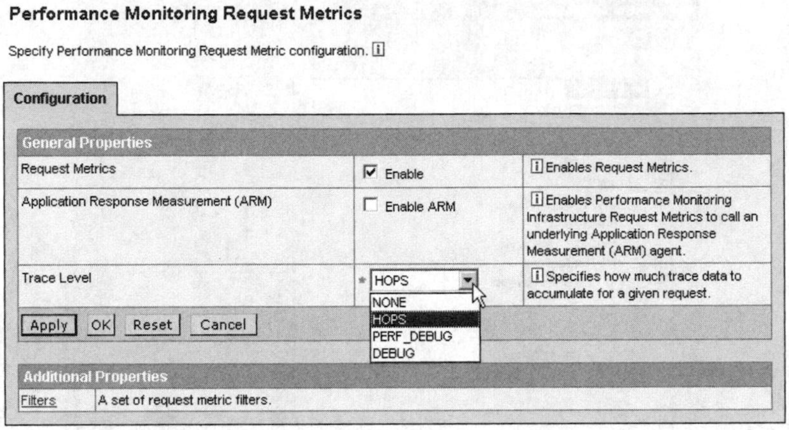

**Performance Monitoring Request Metrics**

Specify Performance Monitoring Request Metric configuration.

Configuration

| General Properties | | |
|---|---|---|
| Request Metrics | ☑ Enable | Enables Request Metrics. |
| Application Response Measurement (ARM) | ☐ Enable ARM | Enables Performance Monitoring Infrastructure Request Metrics to call an underlying Application Response Measurement (ARM) agent. |
| Trace Level | * HOPS (NONE, HOPS, PERF_DEBUG, DEBUG) | Specifies how much trace data to accumulate for a given request. |

Apply OK Reset Cancel

| Additional Properties | |
|---|---|
| Filters | A set of request metric filters. |

**Figure 25-7** Enabling PMI request metrics in admin console.

To specify the application components to be monitored, one or more PMIRM filters also need to be configured. The filter can specify a URI, as depicted in Figure 25-8, an EJB, or a source IP.

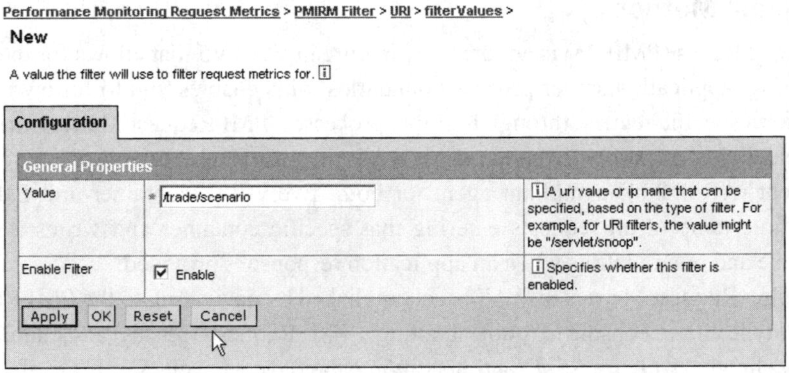

Performance Monitoring Request Metrics > PMIRM Filter > URI > filterValues >

**New**

A value the filter will use to filter request metrics for.

Configuration

| General Properties | | |
|---|---|---|
| Value | * /trade/scenario | A uri value or ip name that can be specified, based on the type of filter. For example, for URI filters, the value might be "/servlet/snoop". |
| Enable Filter | ☑ Enable | Specifies whether this filter is enabled. |

Apply OK Reset Cancel

**Figure 25-8** PMI request metrics URI filter specification in admin console.

As requests in a WebSphere environment often fan out to different processes on several physical nodes, request metrics can be scattered across different log files. As you can imagine, manual correlation of this information from several log files can quickly become complex (see example output in Code Snippet 25-4). You'll likely want to invest in a ARM agent, should you wish to utilize this feature, though it is possible to track a small number of requests manually and to determine what portions of the application are taking the longest by examining each application component's elapsed time (at the end of each record). Using an ARM agent greatly simplifies this task by correlating all the data and constructing a detailed sequence diagram of request response times and allows you to construct an end-to-end view of a request.

**Code Snippet 25-4** Example ARM output from logs

```
[3/12/04 21:03:47:489 PST] 4c65bb21 PmiRmArmWrapp I PMRM0003I:  parent:
➥ver=1,ip=127.0.0.1,time=1079154178729,pid=344,reqid=4096,event=1 -
➥current:ver=1,ip=127.0.0.1,time=1079154178729,pid=344,reqid=4097,
➥event=1 type=JDBC detail=select  q1."ADDRESS",  q1."PASSWORD",
➥q1."USERID",  q1."EMAIL",  q1."CREDITCARD",  q1."FULLNAME" from
➥ACCOUNTPROFILEEJB q1 where  ( q1."USERID" = CAST(? AS
➥VARCHAR(32672)))  for update of "ADDRESS" elapsed=2193
[3/12/04 21:03:47:879 PST] 4c65bb21 PmiRmArmWrapp I PMRM0003I:  parent:
➥ver=1,ip=127.0.0.1,time=1079154178729,pid=344,reqid=4096,event=1 -
➥current:ver=1,ip=127.0.0.1,time=1079154178729,pid=344,reqid=4098,
➥event=1 type=JDBC detail=SELECT T1.CREATIONDATE, T1.OPENBALANCE,
➥T1.LOGOUTCOUNT, T1.BALANCE, T1.ACCOUNTID, T1.LASTLOGIN,
➥T1.LOGINCOUNT, T1.PROFILE_USERID FROM ACCOUNTEJB  T1 WHERE
➥T1.PROFILE_USERID = ? FOR UPDATE  OF CREATIONDATE elapsed=130
```

## Performance Advisor

In WAS V5, there are two new mechanisms that actually provide performance tuning advice. The Performance Advisor in the Tivoli Performance Viewer is the first; the Runtime Performance Advisor is the second.

The Performance Advisor object in the Tivoli Performance Viewer can be seen in both Figures 25-9 and 25-10. Using the Performance Advisor is very easy:

1. Enable the Performance Monitoring Service in the application server and the Node Agent if running ND.[9]
2. Set the monitoring level to standard (though some JVM rules require monitoring level MAX and JVMPI).
3. Start Tivoli Performance Viewer.
4. Simulate production level load.[10]
5. Ensure application runs without exceptions/errors.
6. Apply advice, restart app server, and retest.

The display and advice from the Performance Advisor is depicted in Figures 25-9 through 25-11 and is obtained by clicking on a specific message in the Performance Advisor and following the links. In this case, the advisor is suggesting that a change be made to the size of the prepared statement cache for the data source.

9 If PMI is not enabled in the Node Agent, not all the metrics for the node the application server is running on are captured.

10 Tools for load generation were mentioned briefly in Chapter 16, "Ideal Development and Testing Environments." We'll mention some other tools at the end of this chapter. There's also a discussion of tools for this purpose in [Joines 2002] and the WAS Info Center.

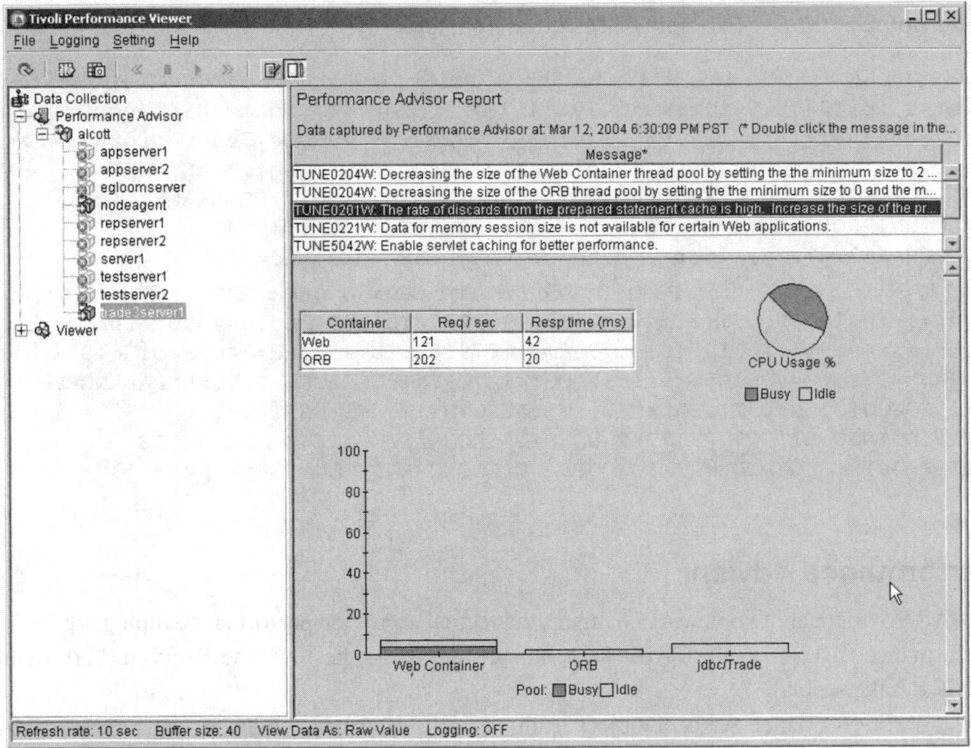


**Figure 25-9** Performance Advisor Report in TPV.

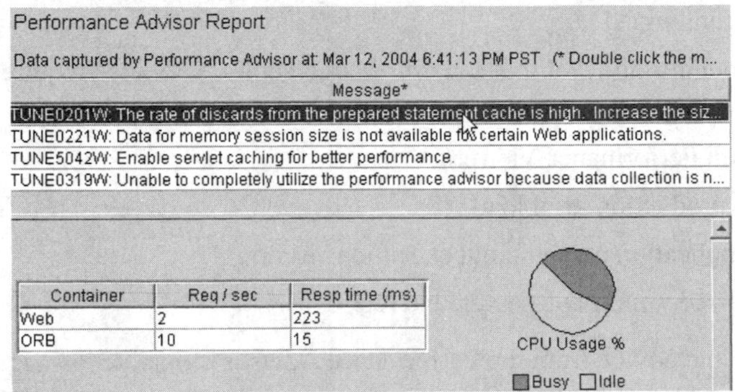


**Figure 25-10** Performance Advisor messages in TPV.

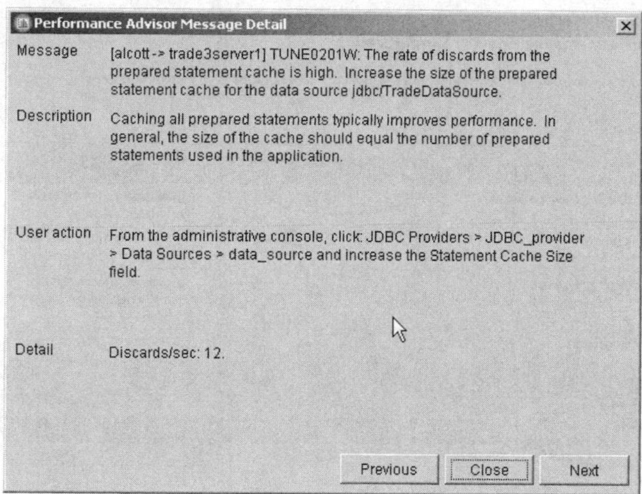


**Figure 25-11** Performance Advisor advice in TPV.

## Runtime Performance Advisor

The Runtime Performance Advisor provides advice in the same manner that the Performance Advisor does in the Tivoli Performance Viewer, but the information is displayed as messages in the admin console. As with using the TPV Performance Advisor, you first need to enable the PMI service in an application server and Node Agent and then restart them both. Then enable the Runtime Performance Advisor by navigating to the Runtime Performance Advisor dialog in the admin console (Servers > *servername* >Runtime Performance Advisor Configuration).

The navigation path is depicted in Figure 25-12. Note not only the check box that enables the Runtime Performance Advisor but also the additional properties dialog at the bottom for Advice Configuration. The Advice Configuration dialog specifies which modules (e.g., Connection Pool Size) advice will be provided for. Once this is enabled, the same steps apply for gathering advice as with the Performance Advisor in the TPV:

- Simulate production level load.
- Ensure application runs without exceptions/errors.
- Apply advice, restart app server, and retest.

The output from the Runtime Performance Advisor is available by selecting the "Warning" messages in the WebSphere Runtime Messages at the bottom on the admin console, as depicted in Figure 25-13.

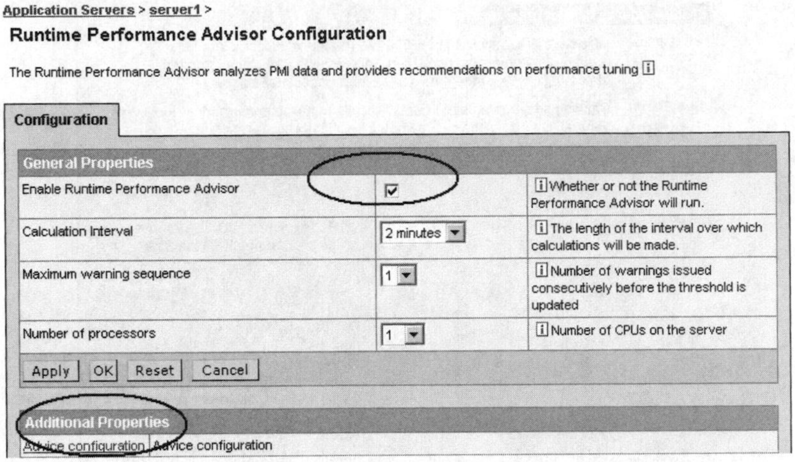


**Figure 25-12** Runtime performance advisor dialog in admin console.

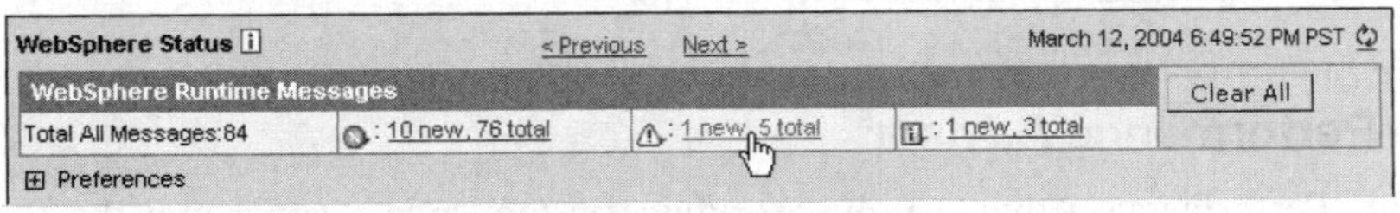


**Figure 25-13** Selecting runtime warning messages in admin console.

The messages that contain performance advice have a "message originator" of "com.ibm.ws.performance.tuning.serverAlert.TraceReponse," as depicted in Figure 25-14.

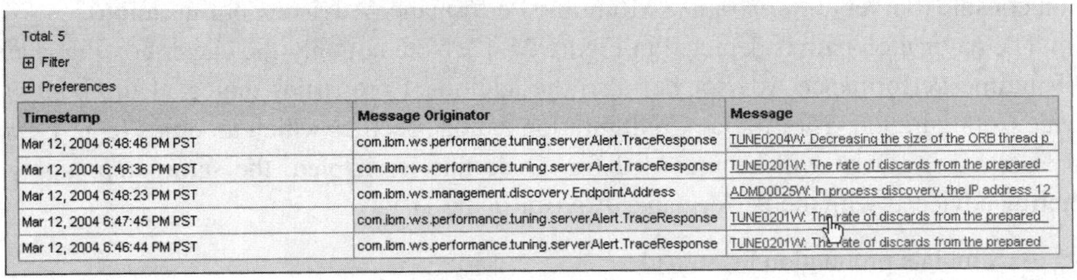
Total: 5
Filter
Preferences

| Timestamp | Message Originator | Message |
|---|---|---|
| Mar 12, 2004 6:48:46 PM PST | com.ibm.ws.performance.tuning.serverAlert.TraceResponse | TUNE0204W: Decreasing the size of the ORB thread p |
| Mar 12, 2004 6:48:36 PM PST | com.ibm.ws.performance.tuning.serverAlert.TraceResponse | TUNE0201W: The rate of discards from the prepared |
| Mar 12, 2004 6:48:23 PM PST | com.ibm.ws.management.discovery.EndpointAddress | ADMD0025W: In process discovery, the IP address 12 |
| Mar 12, 2004 6:47:45 PM PST | com.ibm.ws.performance.tuning.serverAlert.TraceResponse | TUNE0201W: The rate of discards from the prepared |
| Mar 12, 2004 6:46:44 PM PST | com.ibm.ws.performance.tuning.serverAlert.TraceResponse | TUNE0201W: The rate of discards from the prepared |

**Figure 25-14** Warning messages list dialog in admin console.

Example performance advice from the Runtime Performance Advisor is depicted in Figure 25-15, which suggests a change to the prepared statement cache for a data source.

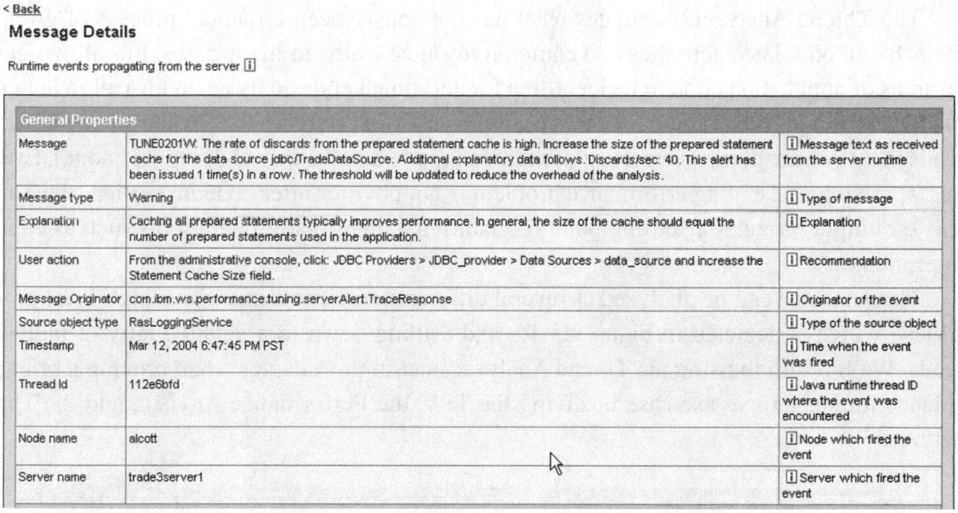

< Back

**Message Details**

Runtime events propagating from the server

| General Properties | | |
|---|---|---|
| Message | TUNE0201W: The rate of discards from the prepared statement cache is high. Increase the size of the prepared statement cache for the data source jdbc/TradeDataSource. Additional explanatory data follows. Discards/sec: 40. This alert has been issued 1 time(s) in a row. The threshold will be updated to reduce the overhead of the analysis. | Message text as received from the server runtime |
| Message type | Warning | Type of message |
| Explanation | Caching all prepared statements typically improves performance. In general, the size of the cache should equal the number of prepared statements used in the application. | Explanation |
| User action | From the administrative console, click: JDBC Providers > JDBC_provider > Data Sources > data_source and increase the Statement Cache Size field. | Recommendation |
| Message Originator | com.ibm.ws.performance.tuning.serverAlert.TraceResponse | Originator of the event |
| Source object type | RasLoggingService | Type of the source object |
| Timestamp | Mar 12, 2004 6:47:45 PM PST | Time when the event was fired |
| Thread Id | 112e6bfd | Java runtime thread ID where the event was encountered |
| Node name | alcott | Node which fired the event |
| Server name | trade3server1 | Server which fired the event |

**Figure 25-15** Runtime performance advisor advice in admin console.

> **NOTE**
> While the Performance Advisor in the Tivoli Performance Viewer and the Runtime Performance Advisor provide suggestions on a number of WAS runtime settings that can impact performance, there are many additional settings specific to the HTTP/web server, operating system, and network and database server that can impact performance. A list of settings and discussion of setting them is contained in [WAS] in the article titled "Performance Tuning Hot List."

## Other Performance Tools

### WebSphere Thread Analyzer

WebSphere Thread Analyzer is a graphical tool that provides an analysis of the thread activity (or inactivity) inside an application server JVM at a given point in time. The Thread Analyzer complements the other WebSphere performance tools mentioned previously by providing additional information that can assist in identifying the cause of system hangs and various performance bottlenecks.

> **NOTE**
> The Thread Analyzer doesn't come with the WebSphere Application Server. It is available as a separate download at http://www14.software.ibm.com/webapp/download/search.jsp?go=y&rs=thread.

The Thread Analyzer automates what has previously been a manual process of grouping threads based on related activities and common resource waits. In many cases, this allows candidate areas of application code to be identified for additional code analysis, in turn allowing quick remediation for problem code. Thread Analyzer essentially shows you what all of the active threads in a JVM are doing at a particular point in time (when the thread dump was done). Even in cases where the cause of a performance problem is not obvious after code inspection, the Thread Analyzer output provides a starting point for additional investigation with tools such as application profilers.

Thread usage can be analyzed at several different levels, starting with a high-level graphical view, which is depicted in Figure 25-16, and drilling down to a detailed tally of individual threads. We'll return to using the Thread Analyzer later in this chapter when proving a brief performance tuning sample use case involving the TPV, the Performance Advisor, and the Thread Analyzer.

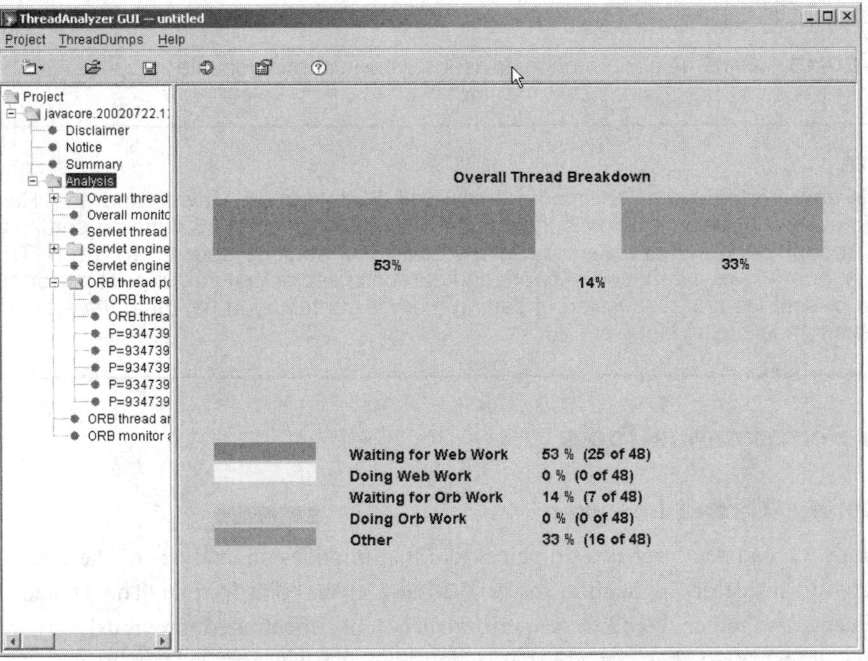


**Figure 25-16** Thread Analyzer thread summary dialog.

## WebSphere Request Queues

If you're at all familiar with WAS (or other application servers), you're apt to recognize that there are typically several different WAS components involved in constructing and providing a client response, as well as one or more external components that are part of the client request-response cycle." All of these components construct a *queuing network*, which is a network of interconnected queues that represent the various components of the application serving platform. These queues include the network, web server, Servlet engine, Enterprise JavaBean (EJB) component container, data source, and possibly a connection manager to a custom backend system. Each of these WebSphere resources represents a *queue* of requests waiting to use that resource" [Cuomo 2000]. A queuing network is depicted in Figure 25-17. In order to correctly tune WAS and the related components in your deployment topology, it is essential to recognize this. Lacking this understanding, a tuning action applied to one runtime component will likely be "hit or miss" proposition in terms of its effectiveness and will likely miss due to not coordinating and testing the change with the rest of the queuing network.

In order to better understand the notion of queues in a WAS topology, let's look closely at Figure 25-17. Requests arrive at the HTTP server from web clients, and some of these requests are for static content, so the HTTP server can satisfy them. A smaller number of requests are sent on to the WAS web container where some dynamic content is generated and returned. Of the requests arriving at the web container, a small number will require access to either the EJB container or a database to construct a response. Of the requests sent on the EJB container, only some lesser number requires access to the database server to create a response. Between each of these layers, a queue exists whenever the number of "upstream" (from the left) requests exceeds the capacity of the next component in the chain.[11] The capacity of each component is determined by their settings—the number of processes defined in the HTTP server,[12] threads for web container and EJB container, and number of connections for the database connection pool.

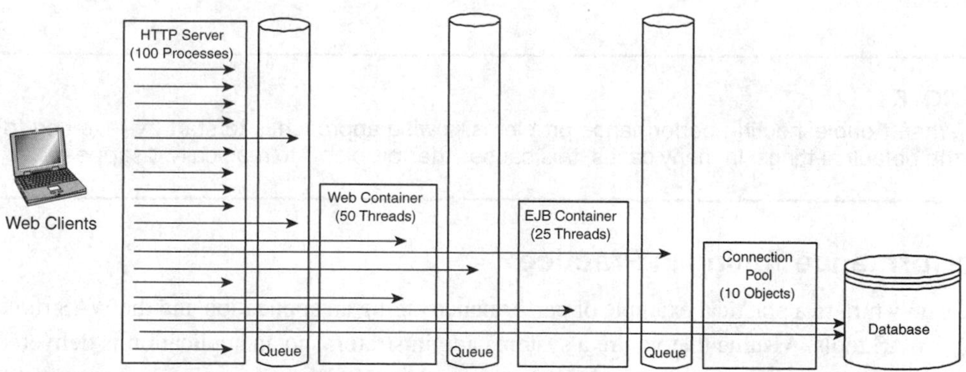


**Figure 25-17** Example WAS queuing network.

What's depicted in Figure 25-17 as we move from left to right is the funneling of the requests into a component on the right with a smaller capacity than the one(s) to the left of it. It turns out that funneling requests in this manner provides the best performance, though at first

11 Though not depicted, if the number of browser clients exceeds the processes in the HTTP server, there is a request queue in the network between the browser clients and HTTP server.

12 Some HTTP servers are process-based; some others are thread-based.

glance, this might not make sense. You don't want to have the same number of threads, processes, or objects across all layers in your topology. Let's examine why this is the case. As we move from left to right, the amount of resources (e.g., CPU and memory) required to handle a request increases; for example, a dynamic response in the web container requires more work than a static page served from the HTTP server, and this holds true as we move through the additional layers to the right of the topology. Additionally, since we want each component to be serving requests, we want to minimize the amount of process management being performed by that component. If we were to set all of the capacities to be equal for all the components, what we'd start seeing is context switching between the processes and/or threads in one or more of the layers. When a container completes its current work and requests the next unit, it is more efficient to have that unit of work nearby as a "waiter" in the same container than to have to request it from the component that feeds it. Since we have limited CPU and memory at each layer, it's better to dedicate these resources to serving requests than to managing the requests. We'll return to this subject later in this chapter when discussing some items that can be characterized as "What's wrong with this picture" using Tivoli Performance Viewer graphs. One last thought to take away from this discussion—if you find yourself *significantly* increasing the default settings for any component in the queuing network, chances are, that's the sign of a problem. The WAS Performance Lab has put a great deal of effort into specifying appropriate defaults for most applications and configurations. This isn't to say that you won't need to perform some minor tuning, but large-scale changes are unlikely. In the case of setting the thread pools, connection pools, and JVM heap, (much) bigger is usually not better! If in doubt, rely on the defaults or use the suggestions for the Performance Advisor.

> **NOTE**
> When troubleshooting performance problems, a wise approach is to start by reverting to the default settings. In many cases, this causes the "problem" to magically disappear.

## Performance Tuning in Practice

Let's now turn to a practical example of performance tuning an application and the WAS runtime using WAS tools. Assume that you're a systems administrator, and an application is delivered to your performance-testing environment. What steps do you follow in testing and tuning it? As noted at the beginning of this chapter, there are entire books written on this subject, so the coverage provided here will be brief. For detail, we recommend [Joines 2002], but here is the basic process the authors would follow. We provide a set of summarized steps and then expand in individual sections here. The application used for this example is simple for purposes of demonstration, but it is architected like many J2EE applications and is composed of JSPs comprising the view, a Servlet as the controller, and EJBs for the model. Refer to [Brown 2004] for a comprehensive discussion of J2EE application architectures:

1. Run a series of tests increasing the client load in order to establish a baseline and plot a "throughput curve" in order to determine the appropriate client load for subsequent tests with the application and hardware configuration.
2. Once an appropriate client load has been determined in Step 1, run a test using the Performance Advisor in order to fine-tune the runtime performance settings.
3. Run an additional test to validate that the suggestions from Step 2 actually improved performance, monitoring values in the TPV for anything that might appear out of the ordinary.
4. Drill down into any possible areas of concern identified in Step 3, using either the WAS supplied tools or third-party tools.
5. Tune runtime and/or correct application as required based on results from Step 4.
6. Repeat Steps 3–5 as required.

## Step 1—Construct a Throughput Curve

Figure 25-18 depicts the results from running a series of performance tests where the client load[13] (concurrent requests) is increased from 5 to 10 and so on. The purpose of this exercise is to determine how scalable the application is (it turns out that this application isn't) and to determine the appropriate number of clients to be used for further tests.

> **NOTE**
>
> Don't make the mistake of confusing performance tuning with scalability. Too often, someone will say, "I need to run x client load" and then run tests with that client load. Typically, this approach leads to a variety of overloaded conditions in one or more components either in WAS or in other infrastructure components (network, database, etc). A more productive approach is to determine what is achievable in terms of client load and throughput with a single application server and then proceed with runtime and application tuning based on this. Once tuning is complete, you can then turn your attention to determining how many application server processes and physical servers are required to satisfy scalability requirements.

In looking at the throughput curve in Figure 25-18, we can see that as we add clients, the requests per second processed increases slightly from 6.3 requests/sec to just under 6.8 requests/sec as the client load grows from 5 to 40. At that point, throughput levels off.

13 Depending on the load generation tool being used, the term used may be "concurrent clients," "virtual users," or a similar term. For the purposes of this exercise, we'll use the term "clients" or "concurrent users" interchangeably.

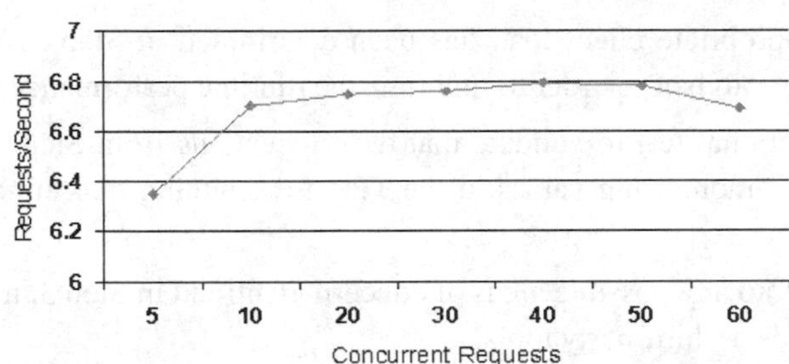


**Figure 25-18** Example throughput curve.

In fact, throughput actually decreases as the load increases from 50 to 60 clients.[14] This is often referred to as the "buckle zone." At this point, knowing that the application doesn't scale well, we're ready to proceed to our second step. What we have seen is indicative of a bottleneck. In deciding how many clients we should run our tests with, we'd normally choose the number of clients that achieved the greatest throughput, which is 40 in this case. However, since the difference in throughput with 40 clients and 50 clients is so miniscule, we're going to choose 50. We also decided to choose the higher number of clients because we're optimistic that tuning will improve the scalability, thus increasing the throughput along all the points on the curve. Normally, the difference is much more pronounced, making the choice of the number of clients more clear-cut.

## Step 2—Test with the Performance Advisor

At this point, we proceed to configure the application server and Node Agent to run the PMI service (as outlined earlier in the "Performance Advisor" section). After restarting both of these processes, launching the TPV client, and walking through the application manually a couple of times for "warm up,"[15] we're ready to start our tests.

Figure 25-19 depicts the Performance Advisor view in the TPV during our testing with 50 clients. One item that stands out is the low CPU utilization in the node running the application server. This is another hint of a bottleneck somewhere in the runtime or the application. While we don't know the source of the bottleneck, we can rule out CPU capacity as the culprit.

14 The throughput decrease observed is consistent with the increase in context switching, as described earlier in this chapter.

15 Most load generation tools make some provision for warm up at the start of each test. While many applications are too large and complex to walk through manually, some minimal manual client testing is always a good idea to ensure that all the components from end-to-end are running before starting automated load generation.

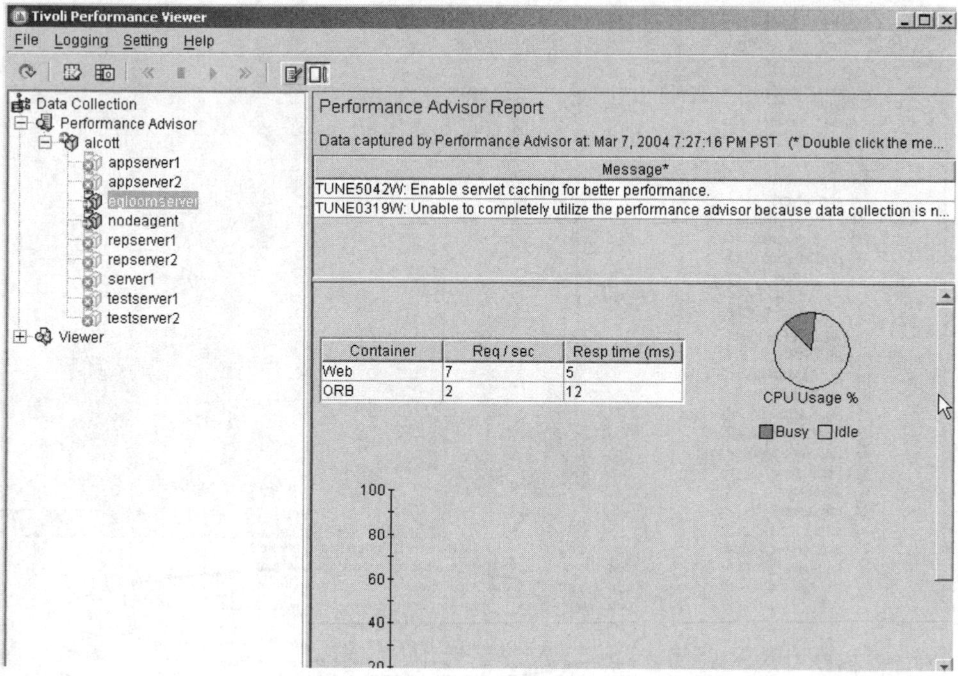


**Figure 25-19** Performance advisor during performance testing.

Once the test is complete, next we walk through the suggestions provided by the Performance Advisor. In this case, the suggestions deal with increasing the JVM heap minimum and maximum as well as downward adjustment of the web container and ORB thread pools. After applying the changes to the application server and restarting the application server, we're ready to test once again.

## Step 3—Validating the TPV Suggested Changes

The results from the performance test using the configuration changes suggested by the Performance Advisor are mixed; throughput has improved by about 11%, from just fewer than 6.8 requests/sec to just over 7.5 requests/sec, but during the tests, we looked at all the various runtime components in the Tivoli Performance Viewer, and one component stands out—the size of the connection pool. Even though we're running tests with 50 clients, only one connection object is ever in use. This is depicted in Figure 25-20.

It should be clear that something is amiss here. For some reason, only one connection object is ever in use. Since we're running a load with 50 clients, we'd expect to see the connection pool fully utilized or nearly so since at this point we haven't changed the default min/max for the connection pool from 1/10.

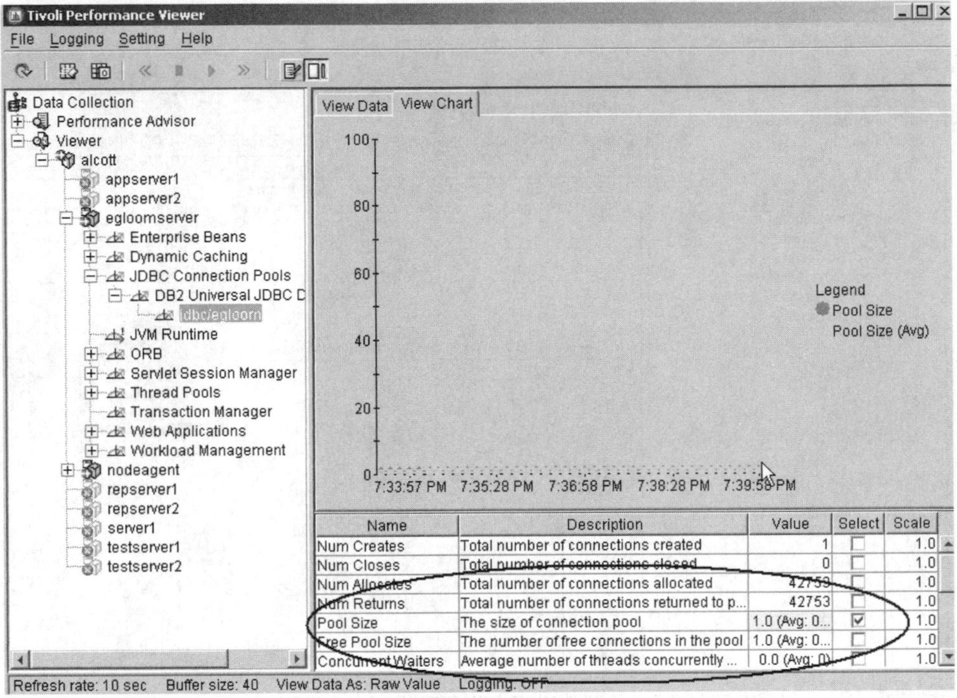


**Figure 25-20** Connection pool statistics in TPV.

> **NOTE**
>
> The 11% performance improvement achieved by applying the Performance Advisor suggestions is at the low end of "the norm" for runtime performance tuning. Normally, the improvement ranges from between 15-25%, but this depends on a variety of factors, such as the application and workload. The Performance Advisor is a great timesaver though. Prior to the Performance Advisor, runtime tuning would have taken several test runs, not the one that was run in this case.

## Step 4—Drill Down into Problem Components

As noted previously, there are a number of tools that can be used to further examine possible problem areas, but since this is a WebSphere-specific book, we're going to stick to using WebSphere-provided tools, or at least tools that can be obtained from the WebSphere support site. In this case, the tool is the Thread Analyzer. Once again, we run a test with a 50-client load and use the Thread Analyzer to force a javacore and then analyze the threads for us. The output from the Thread Analyzer points to one particular method inside the application. This is depicted in Figure 25-21, where 49 of the 50 threads running in the web container are executing in one method SalaryAdjustmentServlet.performTask and more precisely are blocked from executing.

This starts to shed some light on why only one connection object was being used and why there's only one thread executing in the method, when we should likely see many. Clearly, it's time to go talk to the application developer responsible for this code.

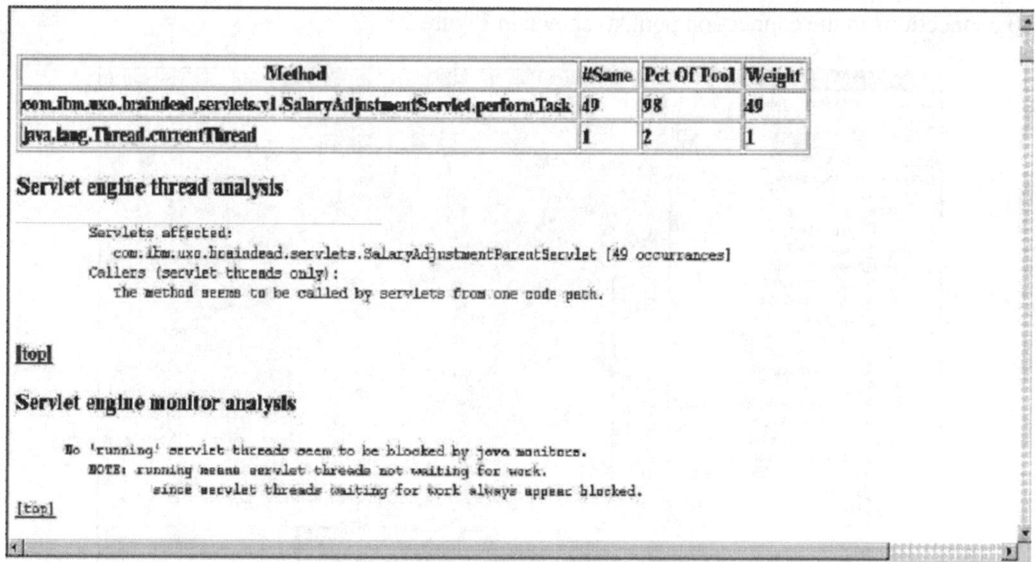

Method
#Same
Pct Of Pool
Weight
com.ibm.uxo.braindead.servlets.v1.SalaryAdjustmentServlet.performTask 49 98 49
java.lang.Thread.currentThread 1 2 1
Servlet engine thread analysis
Servlets affected:
com.ibm.uxo.braindead.servlets.SalaryAdjustmentParentServlet [49 occurrances]
Callers (servlet threads only):
The method seems to be called by servlets from one code path.
[top]
Servlet engine monitor analysis
No 'running' servlet threads seem to be blocked by java monitors.
NOTE: running means servlet threads not waiting for work.
since servlet threads waiting for work always appear blocked.
[top]


**Figure 25-21** Application thread analysis in Thread Analyzer.

## Step 5—Tune the Runtime or Change the Application

A visit with the application developer reveals that during integration and user acceptance testing, a data consistency problem was discovered. Two different users were seeing each other's data as the result of multiple threads simultaneously accessing variables that were defined as Servlet instance variables.[16] The development staff quickly fixed the problem by synchronizing the method SalaryAdjustmentServlet.performTask. Unfortunately, this synchronized and single-threaded the major code path of the application.

Since requests could only be processed one at a time instead of in parallel, this quick fix accounted for the application's inability to gain maximum CPU utilization from a multi-CPU system. A better fix, and the one the development staff now needs to make, is to modify the application code so that the Servlet avoids using Servlet instance variables.

16 Instance variables are global to the entire Servlet.

Once the application code was modified to minimize the amount of code that was synchronized, application performance almost doubled to 13 requests/sec, as multiple threads were able to simultaneously execute instead of waiting for work, and the CPU utilization is now at over 90%. In looking at the connection pool in the TPV, we can also see that we're now fully using the 10 connections in the connection pool, as shown in Figure 25-22.

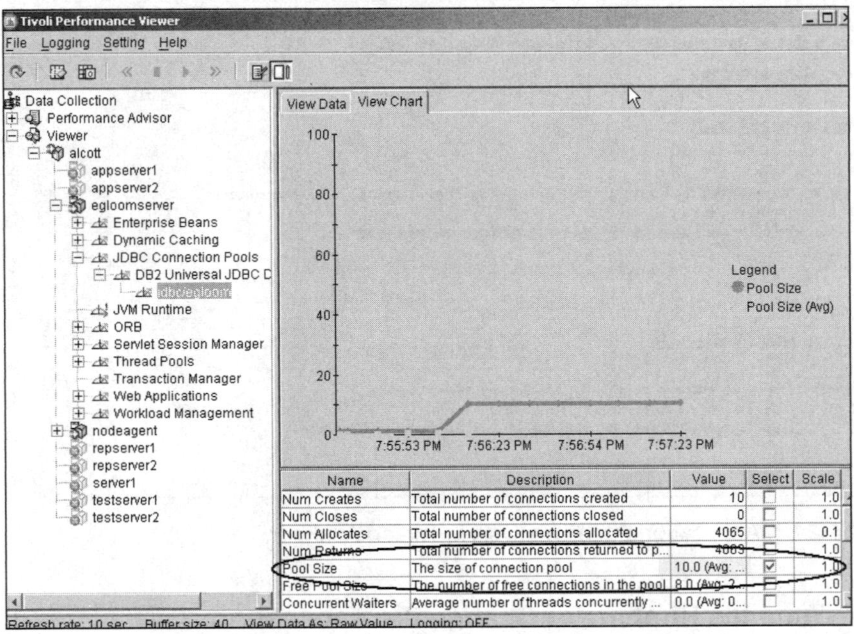


**Figure 25-22** Connection pool statistics in TPV after application changes.

## Step 6—Repeat as Required

Now it's time to rerun our test using the Performance Advisor. It's likely that we'll now receive some advice about modifying the size of the connection pool and possibly the prepared statement cache. We'll also likely receive advice to increase the threads in the web and EJB container; recall that the TPV suggested decreasing these when we were only running a single thread in the application.[17] We're not going to actually walk through these steps at this point since it should be clear what the procedure is by now.

17 Recall that there is a cost to spawning multiple threads, even if they're unused. As a result, the Performance Advisor will recommend decreasing a setting if a resource is not being used, as well as increasing a setting if a resource is always fully used.

> **NOTE**
> It should be clear that application design and implementation is a far more significant contributor to application performance than runtime tuning. By necessity, the example above was fairly simple, but the better than 70% performance improvement (from 7.5 requests/sec to 13 requests/sec, in this case) is typical of correcting application performance problems. In many cases, the performance improvement from application changes far exceeds even the sizeable improvement demonstrated here.

## Other Performance-Tuning Scenarios

As noted at the beginning of this chapter, there are a large number of excellent texts that are devoted to performance tuning. Quite simply, there isn't sufficient space in this book to cover everything you can and should look at with the tools provided by WebSphere Application Server. Additional volumes would also be required for all the third-party tools that can be used for this purpose. As a result, we would like to provide a couple of examples of what we'll term "what's wrong with this picture" when looking at runtime settings and performance monitoring results.

### JVM Heap

A common problem is an application memory leak, usually the result of the application code not releasing references to objects. When this occurs, the objects cannot be garbage collected, and as a result the heap grows over time. Figure 25-23 depicts a "healthy" JVM.

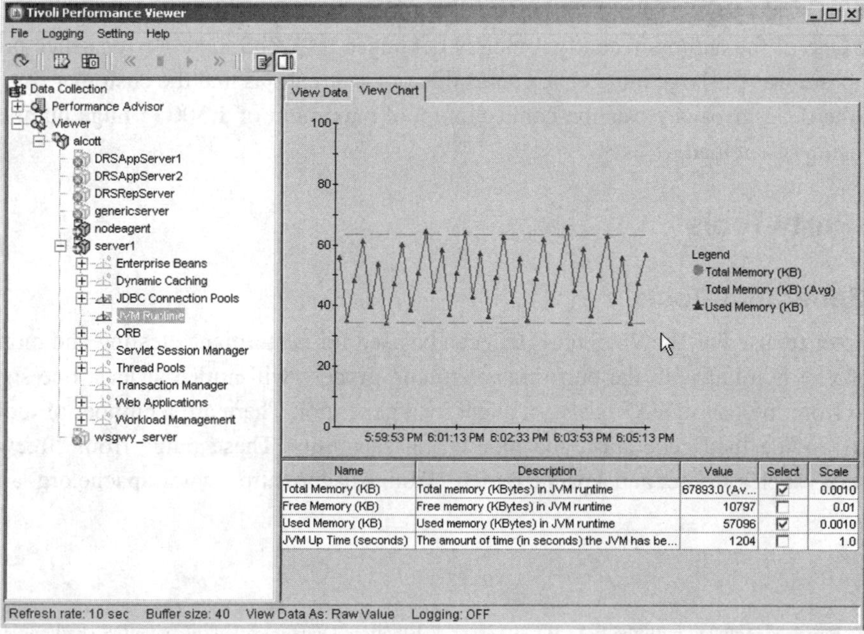


| Name | Description | Value | Select | Scale |
|---|---|---|---|---|
| Total Memory (KB) | Total memory (KBytes) in JVM runtime | 67893.0 (Av... | ☑ | 0.0010 |
| Free Memory (KB) | Free memory (KBytes) in JVM runtime | 10797 | ☐ | 0.01 |
| Used Memory (KB) | Used memory (KBytes) in JVM runtime | 57096 | ☑ | 0.0010 |
| JVM Up Time (seconds) | The amount of time (in seconds) the JVM has be... | 1204 | ☐ | 1.0 |

**Figure 25-23** JVM monitoring in TPV.

OK, so this isn't really a case of "what's wrong with this picture," but we can learn to recognize a problem by observing the correct behavior. You'll note the peaks and valleys (a saw tooth pattern) for the used memory as memory use grows, garbage collection runs, and memory is freed. While the highs and lows vary some from cycle to cycle, what's important to note is that over time, the highs never go above or below the dashed lines (inserted by the authors). The dashed lines are parallel to each other, and more importantly, they are parallel to the bottom axis. If there was a memory leak, the lows in the cycle would increase over time, as would the highs, and as a result, the two red lines would likely still be parallel to each other, *but* they would no longer be parallel to the bottom axis. Instead, they would slope from left to right, moving slightly higher as time progressed. A memory leak is evidenced by our saw tooth pattern changing into what looks like an upwardly rising staircase.

### Pools

In this example, there's no picture at all to look at! Instead, consider the following scenario. You're running a performance test, and you start noticing that the connection pool is always maxed. As a result, you increase the connection pool size and rerun your test. The connection pool fills up again. After several such cycles, you've made rather significant adjustments to the pool, and as a result, it no longer maxes out, or at least not quickly. This is another example of a leak; in this case, the likely culprit is application code that doesn't release the data source connection when finished, which likely is the result of uncaught exceptions. This type of problem should become apparent pretty quickly by simply applying a reasonability test as you adjust settings—"If the server side pool is greater than your client load, something is wrong." Think it couldn't happen? One of the authors recently remotely debugged a "WebSphere Performance problem." The symptom was the large number of connection object creations that the customer was observing, but the dead giveaway was the connection pool maximum of 1,300 (a huge number) for a much smaller client load.

## Third-Party Tools

### Load Generation Tools

This chapter focused on the WAS tools that can be used for performance testing and monitoring. Those of you familiar with the performance tuning process will notice at least one significant omission from the list of WAS tools—a client load generator. There are a number of tools available that provide load generation and monitoring capability. These range from "freeware" or "shareware," such a JMeter and Apache Bench[18] from Apache (http://www.apache.org) and Siege

18 Apache Bench is included with the IBM HTTP server distribution. Once installed, open an OS shell and navigate to the IHS bin directory and type "ab." This will launch Apache Bench and describe its use.

(http://bob.joedog.org/siege/index.php), to commercially available tools, such as Rational Suite Performance Studio (http://www-306.ibm.com/software/rational/) and LoadRunner from Mercury Interactive (http://www.mercuryinteractive.com/products/loadrunner/).

If you're not using a load generation tool today, this is one area that you'll want to investigate further. One word of warning in this area—don't write your own. While it may seem simple and easy to do so, in reality, it's far more difficult than it appears to do correctly. Certainly, it's easy to write a program or script to generate a load, but this rapidly becomes complex as error conditions and return codes need to be handled.

### Monitoring Tools

A number of tools exist for this purpose. Popular tools include Wily's Introscope[19] and Tivoli's Performance Monitoring for Web Infrastructure[20] and WebSphere Studio Application Monitor.[21] These high-end tools tend to provide extensive features such as a view of multiple components in your infrastructure, not just monitoring of the WAS runtime provided by the Tivoli Performance Viewer, which ships with WAS.

## Conclusion

This chapter described the performance monitoring architecture employed by WAS V5, as well as the tools WAS provides that are built on this architecture. Use of these tools was covered, including a brief example outlining performance tuning and application remediation.

19 Wily Introscope: http://www.wilytech.com.

20 http://www-306.ibm.com/software/tivoli/products/monitor-web/.

21 http://www-306.ibm.com/software/awdtools/studioapplicationmonitor/.

# PART VI

# Appendixes

APPENDIX A

# ANT with WebSphere Application Server

## ANT Overview

ANT is a Java-based build tool. ANT build scripts are written in XML and designed to be simple and extensible. The ANT scripting language is very robust and has many features that are beyond the scope of this book. [Hatcher 2003] is a good source for learning to use ANT. Because this book uses ANT in many places, we will provide a brief overview. The ANT language revolves around three constructs: *task*, *targets*, and *projects*:

- An ANT task is the actual construct that does the work specified. For example, there is an ANT task called <javac>, which is responsible for compiling Java Source. Code Snippet A-1 illustrates an example of how you would use the <javac> task. In the example, the <javac> task takes in several inputs in the form of XML attributes. In addition, tasks can be embedded within tasks. Each task is actually backed by a Java class. Any developer can extend ANT by writing his or her own tasks and adding them to the build scripts. WAS provides several custom tasks, which we will define in this Appendix.

**Code Snippet A-1 Example of an ANT task**

```
<javac srcdir="${srcdir}" includes="**/*.java"  destdir="${classesdir}" >
<classpath>
            <fileset dir="${wasroot}/lib"  casesensitive="no">
                  <include name="*.jar" />
            </fileset>
</classpath>
</javac>
```

- The next ANT construct is a *target*. A target represents a callable element of an ANT build script. A target is made of one or more ANT tasks. When someone executes a build script, he or she can specify a specific target. The ANT interpreter will then execute all the tasks within the target. Code Snippet A-2 illustrates an example of a target. In the example, there is a target called buildjar. The buildjar task uses the <zip> ANT task to create a JAR file.

  Targets can also have dependencies on other targets. In Code Snippet A-2, you should notice the *depends* attribute on the target tag. Dependencies force the ANT interpreter to call the target listed in the depends attribute value. The target that is a dependency must be part of the same project. A target can have several dependencies separated by commas.

**NOTE**

Dependencies are one way to force workflow of ANT tasks. We could also use the <ant> and <antcall> tasks to have targets execute other targets. We illustrated this in Chapter 4, "Build and Deploy Procedures," and throughout the samples in this book.

Generally, dependencies are good to model multiple flows of many targets within a single ANT script (called an ANT project, as we will see next). For example, we used dependencies to model the different orders of stopping and starting the WAS server. However, the *depends* attribute will only call a target once so you have to sometimes create redundant targets if you want to repeat tasks.

The <ant> task is better at creating the flow of several ANT scripts (or projects). This technique is used throughout this book to implement controller scripts.

<antcall> is best used to reduce repetition in your ANT scripts. For example, we used the <antcall> task to call the <wsadmin> tasks while passing in different JACL scripts throughout the examples in this book.

**Code Snippet A-2** Example of an ANT target

```
<target name="buildjar" depends="compile">
        <zip zipfile="${output}/${jarname}" basedir=
        ➥"${classesdir}">
              <fileset dir="${srcdir}" includes="**/*.properties"/>
              <fileset dir="${srcdir}" includes="META-INF/*.* "/>
        </zip>
    </target>
```

- The last ANT construct we are going to talk about is *project*. Every build file contains one project. For all intents and purposes, a project is the ANT script. A project is a collection of targets. Code Snippet A-3 shows an example of a project. The project has a name and a default target. The default target is the target executed when the build script is executed without specifying a target as input. In addition, a project can have several properties defined with default values. These values can be overridden depending on who calls the build script.

> **NOTE**
> Properties are a powerful way to make your build scripts behave dynamically. ANT properties are immutable; once set, they cannot be overridden. However, when using <ant> and <antcall> tasks, properties can be input by the caller. Because the calling ANT script sets the properties, the behavior of an ANT script can change. We use this technique to change the directory structures of build scripts so that the build scripts can be moved from one environment to another.

**Code Snippet A-3** Sample project

```
<?xml version="1.0" encoding="UTF-8"?>
<project name="buildejb" default="allejb">

<property name="earroot" value="StockSystem" />
<property name="wasroot" value="C:/WebSphere5_1Base/AppServer" />
<property name="buildhome" value="C:\build"/>
<property name="srcdir" value="." />
<property name="classesdir" value="${buildhome}/${earroot}/ejb/
➥classes" />
<property name="ejbjardir" value="${buildhome}/${earroot}/ejbjar" />
<property name="ejbjarname" value="StockSystemEJB.jar" />

<target name="init">
      <mkdir dir="${classesdir}" />
      <mkdir dir="${ejbjardir}" />
      <tstamp/>
</target>

<target name="compile" depends="init">
      <javac srcdir="${srcdir}" includes="**/*.java" destdir=
      ➥"${classesdir}" >
            <classpath>
                  <fileset dir="${wasroot}/lib"  casesensitive="no">
                        <include name="*j2ee.jar" />
                  </fileset>
            </classpath>
      </javac>
</target>

<target name="buildejb" depends="compile">
      <jar destfile="${ejbjardir}/${ejbjarname}" basedir=
      ➥"${classesdir}" manifest="${srcdir}/META-INF/MANIFEST.MF" >
```

```
            <fileset dir="${srcdir}" includes="META-INF/*"/>
        </jar>
</target>

<target name="clean" >
        <delete dir="${classesdir}" />
</target>

<target name="allejb" depends="clean,buildejb,clean" />
</project>
```

The ANT language comes with many predefined tasks. Tasks include integration with most popular source code managers, compiling, packaging (ZIP, JAR, WAR, EAR), copying (FTP, etc…), and a slew of very useful tasks. We will not go over that here. We do use many of the common ones throughout this book.

As stated, ANT can be extended very simply by extending a Java class. We will not cover this here. You can use custom tasks by defining them in the ANT script that uses them. WAS provides several custom tasks we will cover in this Appendix. You can use the <taskdef> task to add custom tasks to an ANT script. We will see <taskdef> examples when describing the different WAS tasks.

To run ANT scripts, you can use the ANT processor simply by calling ant in the command line. The ANT processor will look for a file called build.xml in the current directory. If you name your file something else, you can use the -buildfile option, as shown in Code Snippet A-4.

**Code Snippet A-4 Executing an ANT script**

```
C:\BuildDirectory\ant -buildfile myBuildFile.xml
```

In order to use custom tasks, the custom class as well as any classes it needs must be placed in the classpath of the ANT engine. Because the WebSphere Application Server ANT tasks use many administrative classes within WebSphere, there is a special ANT processor in the bin directory of WAS called *ws_ant*.[1] The ws_ant processor takes all the same arguments the standard ANT processor does. If you need to add additional classes, you may choose to write your own shell script using the ws_ant file as a model. We used this approach throughout this book.

## WebSphere Application Server ANT Tasks

WebSphere Application Server ships with several ANT tasks that aid in common deployment and configuration tasks. The goal is to provide the ability to have a more complete build process. In this section, we will define the available ANT tasks in WebSphere Application Server.

1 The ws_ant file will have a BAT extension on Windows and an SH extension on Unix platforms.

We have divided the scripts into five sections:

- **Assembly tasks**—Tasks that help in the assembling of applications into an EAR. The majority of these tasks wrap other utilities such as the EJBDeploy utility that generates the EJB deployment code.
- **Deployment tasks**—Tasks that aid in the deployment of an application. The majority of the WebSphere ANT tasks are wrappers to the wsadmin scripting language. When one of the WAS ANT tasks executes, it will start wsadmin and run the desired administrative tasks.
- **Administrative tasks**—Tasks that aid in some common administrative tasks that you may want to execute during deployment, such as starting a server. These tasks are also wrappers to the wsadmin scripting language.
- **Web Services tasks**—Tasks that help in the deployment of Web services.
- **WebSphere Studio tasks**—Tasks that help automate the build and deployment of applications developed inside WebSphere Studio.

## Common Attributes

Before listing all of the ANT tasks, we are going to first list some common parameters that have the same meaning in the ANT tasks. Many of these parameters are available in all of the tasks, but others are available in only some tasks. We'll list the parameter definitions here and then, with each task, indicate if the parameter is available:

- **wasHome**—Contains the location of the WAS installation directory. Optional when available.
- **classpath**—Is optional and specifies the classpath for the specified task.
- **classpathref**—Does the same thing as the classpath attribute, but allows the use of the ANT reference mechanism for the specification of the path. Optional when available.
- **properties**—Contains a Java properties file containing attributes to set in the JVM system properties. Optional when available.
- **conntype**—Specifies the type of connection to be used. The default type is SOAP. The valid values are SOAP, RMI, JMS, and NONE. NONE means that no server connection is made. Optional when available.
- **host**—Only specified if the conntype is specified. It contains the host name of the machine to connect to.
- **port**—Only specified if the conntype is specified. It contains the port on the host to connect to.
- **user**—Contains the user ID to authenticate with. Optional when available.
- **password**—Contains the password to authenticate with. Optional when available.

- **profile**—Contains a script file to be executed before the main command or file. Optional when available. A profile script is a JACL script that allows you to change the behavior of the main script. For example, you may have a script meant to run in several environments. Depending on the environment, you may want the script to behave differently. The profile script can be used to customize the environment to give the main script dynamic behavior.

## Assembly Tasks

### JspC

The JspC task compiles a directory full of JSP files into .class files. Normally, JSP files are converted into Servlets the first time they are invoked. This is because a Servlet is generated and then compiled into a .class file. Although this occurs only once, some applications may not accept the first-time invocation overhead. Pre-compiling JSPs can remove the cost of initially invoking JSP files. The JspC ANT task can make it easy to automate this as part of your build process. The structure of the JspC task is shown in Code Snippet A-5.

**Code Snippet A-5** JspC ANT task

```
<wsjspc wasHome="websphere install directory"
                    src="directory containing JSP files"
                    toDir="temporary working directory"
                    classpath="ear classes"
                    classpathref="ear classes reference element name"/>
```

- Common attributes: **wasHome**, **classpath**.
- The **src** attribute is required and specifies the directory containing JSP files to process. This directory may be the root of a WAR file or a plain directory.
- The **toDir** attribute is required and specifies the output directory for the JSP compiler to place the generated class files.
- The **classpath** attribute is optional and specifies extra EAR classes that are needed to compile the JSPs.
- The **classpathref** attribute is optional and does the same thing as the **classpath** attribute, but is specified as an ANT path reference.

> **NOTE**
> Keep in mind that the JSP files are usually dependent on other pieces of the application. If the JSP files (or any files used by a JSP) depend on other classes outside the WAR file, they must be added to the classpath or classpathref element of the ANT script. This includes EAR-level and server-level classes.

In order to add the JspC task to a build script, you can use the taskdef definition shown in Code Snippet A-6.

**Code Snippet A-6** JspC taskdef

```
<taskdef name="wsjspc" classname="com.ibm.websphere.ant.tasks.JspC"/>
```

## wsValidateModule

The wsValidateModule task performs validation of the deployment descriptor, extensions, and bindings documents of an EAR, WAR, EJB JAR, or application client JAR. Being able to validate your application modules can help catch certain errors before you deploy the application.

Given the source JAR file, it will execute the WAS validation logic against the JAR and emit messages indicating errors, warnings, or information about the configuration and structure of your application. It looks at the standard J2EE deployment descriptors and the IBM WAS-specific bindings and extensions documents, if present. The structure of the wsValidateModule task is shown in Code Snippet A-7.

**Code Snippet A-7** Validate Module ANT task

```
<wsValidateModule src="path to the ear/war/ejb-jar/client to
➥validate"/>
```

- The **src** attribute is required and specifies the path, full or relative, to the EAR/WAR/EJB-JAR/client JAR module you wish to validate.

To use the task, include the following taskdef in your build.xml file, as shown in Code Snippet A-8 and run ANT with the ws_ant script.

**Code Snippet A-8** wsValidateModule taskdef

```
<taskdef name="wsValidateModule" classname=
➥"com.ibm.websphere.ant.tasks.ModuleValidator"/>
```

## wsejbdeploy

The wsejbdeploy task[2] executes the WAS EJB deploy tool on the specified JAR file with the specified options. EJB deployment requires a certain amount of code to be generated in order to run correctly. We use this task throughout the samples in this book that contain EJB. The structure of the wsejbdeploy task is shown in Code Snippet A-9.

2 There is also another EJB deploy ANT task within WebSphere Studio's ANT task set. Please see the WebSphere Studio ANT tasks section of this Appendix for information.

**Code Snippet A-9 EJBDeploy ANT task**

```
<wsejbdeploy inputJar="jarfile"
       wasHome="WebSphere Installation Directory"
       workingDirectory="temp directory"
       outputJar="out jarfile"
       classpath="ear classes"
       classpathref="ear classes element reference"
       codegen="true | false"
       dbname="Database name"
       dbschema="Database Schema Name"
       dbvendor="Database Vendor"
       dynamic="Enable Dynamic Query Support"
       keepGenerated="true | false"
       quiet="true | false"
       noValidate="true | false"
       noWarnings="true | false"
       noInform="true | false"
       rmicOptions="rmic options"
       compatible35="true | false"
       sqlj="true | false"
       failonerror="true | false"
       trace="true | false"/>
```

- Common attributes: **wasHome**. **classpathref**. **classpath**.
- The **inputJar** attribute is required and contains the undeployed EJB JAR file you wish to deploy.
- The **workingDirectory** attribute is optional. It normally contains a temporary directory for the deploy tool to use. If not set, the Java System Property *user.home* is used.
- The **outputJar** attribute is required and specifies the name of the deployed EJB JAR to create.
- The **codegen** attribute is optional and is set to true to keep the generated Java files.
- The **dbname** attribute is optional and specifies the name of the database to create.
- The **dbschema** attribute is optional and specifies the name of the database schema to create.
- The **dbvendor** attribute is optional and specifies the type of database the EJBs will use.
- The **dynamic** attribute is optional and specifies to enable dynamic query support. This option is currently only available in WBI Server Foundations version 5.1.

- The **keepGenerated** attribute is optional and is set to true to prevent the workingDirectory from being deleted.
- The **quiet** attribute is optional and is set to true to only output error messages, surpressing informational messages.
- The **noValidate** attribute is optional and is set to true to disable validation messages.
- The **noWarnings** attribute is optional and is set to true to disable warning and informational messages.
- The **noInform** attribute is optional and is set to true to disable informational messages.
- The **rmicOptions** attribute is optional and allows additional arguments to be passed to the rmic command.
- The **compatible35** attribute is optional and is set to true to use WAS 3.5 compatible mapping rules.
- The **sqlj** attribute is optional and is set to true to generate SQL/J persistor code.
- The **trace** attribute is optional and is set to true to enable internal deploy tool tracing.
- The **failonerror** attribute is optional and is set to true to cause your build to stop on deploy errors.

To use this task, add the taskdef shown in Code Snippet A-10 to your ANT build.xml.

**Code Snippet A-10** EJB Deploy ANT task

```
<taskdef name="wsejbdeploy" classname="com.ibm.websphere.ant.tasks.
➥WsEjbDeploy"/>
```

## Deployment Tasks

### wsDefaultBindings

The wsDefaultBindings task enables you to generate default IBM WAS bindings for the specified EAR file. This task provides options to control how the bindings are generated and mimics the options provided by the WebSphere Application Install wizards inside the admin console. The structure of the wsDefaultBindings task is shown in Code Snippet A-11.

**Code Snippet A-11** wsDefaultBindings ANT task

```
<wsDefaultBindings
        ear="the ear file you wish to install"
        outputFile="output ear to generate"
        defaultDataSource="JNDI Name of the default datasource to use
        ➥for the application"
        dbUser="Database user id"
```

```
dbPassword="Datebase password"
defaultConnectionFactory="JNDI name of the default connection
➥factory to be used by the application"
resAuth="PerConnFact | Container"
ejbJndiPrefix="String to prefix to the front of all generated
➥EJB JNDI Names"
virtualHost="Virtual Host name for the application to
➥execute on"
forceBindings="true | false"
strategy="Generation Strategy"
exportFile="exported strategy file"/>
```

- The **ear** attribute is required and contains the path of the EAR for which you wish to generate bindings.
- The **outputFile** attribute is required and contains the path of the new ear with the bindings inside.
- The **defaultDataSource** attribute is optional. It specifies a default data source JNDI name to be used for all EJB 1.x CMPs.
- The **dbUser** attribute is optional. It specifies the user associated with the default data source.
- The **dbPassword** attribute is optional. It specifies the password associated with the default data source.
- The **defaultConnectionFactory** attribute is optional. It specifies the default connection factory to be used for all EJB 2.x CMPs.
- The **resAuth** attribute is optional. It specifies the resource authorization on the connection factory for EJB 2.x CMPs.
- The **ejbJndiPrefix** attribute is optional. It specifies a prefix that is prepended to any generated EJB JNDI names. The default is "ejb."
- The **virtualHost** attribute is optional. It specifies the virtual host for all WARs in the application.
- The **forceBindings** attribute is optional. When false, any pre-existing bindings will not be altered. When true, new bindings are completely generated. The default is false.
- The **strategy** attribute is optional. When specified, this attribute points to a custom strategy file that further affects the bindings. See the properties/dfltbndngs.dtd of your WebSphere installation for more details.
- The **exportFile** attribute is optional. When specified, it points to a file that will be generated containing the bindings information. This file is in the custom strategy format.

To use this inside your build script, you can use the taskdef shown in Code Snippet A-12.

**Code Snippet A-12 taskdef for wsDefaultBinding**

```
<taskdef name="wsDefaultBindings" classname="com.ibm.websphere.ant.
➥tasks.DefaultBindings"/>
```

## wsInstallApp

The wsInstallApp task enables you to install a new application into a WAS server or cell. This task is a wrapper for the AdminApp.install() command of the wsadmin tool. Refer to the wsadmin documentation for information on the valid options available during application installation. The structure of the wsInstallApp task is shown in Code Snippet A-13.

**Code Snippet A-13 wsInstallApp**

```
<wsInstallApp
        wasHome="location of websphere installation"
        ear="the ear file you wish to install"
        options="the options to pass to the installation process"
        properties="java properties file containing attributes to set in
        ➥the JVM System properties"
        profile="a script file to be executed before the main command or
        ➥file"
        conntype="specifies the type of connection to be used."
        host="the host to connect to"
        port="the port on the host to connect to"
        user="user ID to authenticate with"
        password="password to authenticate with"/>
```

- Common attributes: **wasHome**, **properties**, **conntype**, **host**, **port**, **user**, **password**, **profile**.
- The **ear** attribute is required and contains the path of the ear that you wish to install.
- The **options** attribute is optional and contains the set of options you wish to pass to the installation process.

To use this task, add the taskdef in Code Snippet A-14 to your ANT build.xml.

**Code Snippet A-14 taskdef**

```
<taskdef name="wsInstallApp" classname="com.ibm.websphere.ant.tasks.
➥InstallApplication"/>
```

## wsUninstallApp

The wsUninstallApp task enables you to uninstall an existing application from a WAS server or cell. This task is a subclass of the wsadmin task and shares many of the same attributes. This task is a wrapper for the AdminApp.uninstall() command of the wsadmin tool. Refer to the wsadmin documentation for information on the valid options available during application uninstallation. The structure of the wsUninstallApp task is shown in Code Snippet A-15.

**Code Snippet A-15 wsUninstallApp**

```
<wsUninstallApp
      wasHome="location of websphere installation"
      application="the name of the application you wish to uninstall"
      options="the options to pass to the installation process"
      properties="java properties file containing attributes to set in
      ➥the JVM System properties"
      profile="a script file to be executed before the main command or
      ➥file"
      conntype="specifies the type of connection to be used."
      host="the host to connect to"
      port="the port on the host to connect to"
      user="user ID to authenticate with"
      password="password to authenticate with"/>
```

- Common attributes: **wasHome**. **properties**, **conntype**, **host**, **port**, **user**, **password**, *profile*.
- The **application** attribute is required and contains the name of the application that you wish to uninstall.
- The **options** attribute is optional and contains the set of options you wish to pass to the uninstall process.

To use this task, add the taskdef in Code Snippet A-16 to your ANT build.xml.

**Code Snippet A-16 wsUninstallApp taskdef**

```
<taskdef name="wsUninstallApp" classname="com.ibm.websphere.ant.
➥tasks.UninstallApplication"/>
```

## Administrative ANT Tasks

### wsListApps

The wsListApps task lists all the applications installed on a WAS server or cell. This task is a wrapper for the AdminApp.list() command of the wsadmin tool. Refer to the wsadmin documentation for information on this operation. The structure of the wsListApps task is shown in Code Snippet A-17.

**Code Snippet A-17** wsListApps

```
<wsListApps
        wasHome="location of websphere installation"
        properties="java properties file containing attributes to set in
        ➥the JVM System properties"
        profile="a script file to be executed before the main command or
        ➥file"
        conntype="specifies the type of connection to be used."
        host="the host to connect to"
        port="the port on the host to connect to"
        user="user ID to authenticate with"
        password="password to authenticate with"/>
```

- Common attributes: **wasHome**, **properties**, **conntype**, **host**, **port**, **user**, **password**, **profile**.

The taskdef for the wsListApps task is shown in Code Snippet A-18.

**Code Snippet A-18** taskdef for wsListApps

```
<taskdef name="wsListApps" classname="com.ibm.websphere.ant.
➥tasks.ListApplications"/>
```

### wsServerStatus

The wsServerStatus task enables you to get the status (started or stopped) on a server instance or all server instances of a cell. The wsServerStatus calls the serverStatus execution file in the bin directory of WebSphere Application Server. It needs to be executed on the same node as WebSphere Application Server or the Deployment Manager. From the Deployment Manager, you can find the status of server that is part of the cell. The structure of the wsServerStatus task is shown in Code Snippet A-19.

**Code Snippet A-19** Server status

```
<wsServerStatus
      server="name of the server to get status on"
      quiet="true | <b>false</b>"
      trace="true | <b>false</b>"
      all="true | <b>false</b>"
      cell="name of the WebSphere Cell containing the server"
      node="name of the WebSphere Node containing the server"
      timeout="amount of time to wait for the server status"
      statusPort="port for the server to send status messages to"
      wasHome="WebSphere Installation directory"
      failonerror="true | <b>false</b>"/
      >
```

- Common attributes: **wasHome**, **properties**.
- The **server** attribute is required and contains the name of the server you want to get status on.
- The **quiet** attribute is optional. If true, the task will not print any status information.
- The **trace** attribute is optional. If true, the task will print trace information.
- The **all** attribute is optional. If true, the task will print the status of all servers.
- The **cell** attribute is optional and contains the name of the cell containing the server. If not set, the default cell is used.
- The **node** attribute is optional and contains the name of the node containing the server. If not set, the default node is used.
- The **timeout** attribute is optional and specified the amount of time to wait for the server to successfully retrieve status.
- The **statusPort** attribute is optional and specifies the TCP port the server should send status messages to.
- The **failonerror** attribute is optional and if set to true causes the build to stop if the task has an error.

To use this task, add the taskdef shown in Code Snippet A-20 to your ANT build.xml.

**Code Snippet A-20** taskdef for wsServerStatus

```
<taskdef name="wsServerStatus" classname="com.ibm.websphere.ant.
➥tasks.ServerStatus"/>
```

## wsStartApp

The wsStartApp task enables you to start an existing or newly installed application on a WebSphere server or in a WebSphere cell. The structure of the wsStartApp task is shown in Code Snippet A-21.

**Code Snippet A-21** wsStartApp

```
<wsStartApp
        wasHome="location of websphere installation"
        server="the name of the server containing the application to
        ➥start"
        node="the name of the node containing the application to start"
        application="the name of the application to start"
        properties="java properties file containing attributes to set in
        ➥the JVM System properties"
        profile="a script file to be executed before the main command or
        ➥file"
        conntype="specifies the type of connection to be used."
        host="the host to connect to"
        port="the port on the host to connect to"
        user="user ID to authenticate with"
        password="password to authenticate with"/>
```

- Common attributes: **wasHome**, **properties**, **conntype**, **host**, **port**, **user**, **password**, **profile**.
- The **server** attribute is optional and specifies the name of the server containing the application you wish to start.
- The **node** attribute is optional and specifies the name of the node containing the application you wish to start.
- The **application** attribute is required and specifies the name of the application you want to start.

To use this task, add the taskdef shown in Code Snippet A-22 to your ANT build.xml.

**Code Snippet A-22** taskdef for wsStartApp

```
<taskdef name="wsStartApp" classname="com.ibm.websphere.ant.
➥tasks.StartApplication"/>
```

## wsStartServer

The wsStartServer task enables you to start a standalone server instance. This is not used to start a server controlled by the Deployment Manager. Therefore, this task is useful for the Base Application Server and to start the Node Agent and/or Deployment Manager. If you wish to start a server managed by the Deployment Manager, use the wsadmin task to execute a scripting command. The structure of the wsStartServer task is shown Code Snippet A-23.

**Code Snippet A-23** wsStartServer

```
<wsStartServer
      server="name of the server to start"
      noWait="true | <b>false</b>"
      quiet="true | <b>false</b>"
      logFile="name of the file to log to"
      replaceLog="true | <b>false</b>"
      trace="true | <b>false</b>"
      script="the name of a script file to execute during server
      ➥startup"
      timeout="amount of time to wait for the server to start"
      statusPort="port for the server to send status messages to"
      username="name of the admin userid id to authenticate with"
      password="password of the admin user to authenticate with"
      wasHome="WebSphere Installation directory"
      failonerror="true | <b>false</b>"/>
```

- Common attributes: **wasHome**, **properties**, **conntype**, **host**, **port**, **user**, **password**, **profile**.
- The **server** attribute is required and contains the name of the server you wish to start.
- The **noWait** attribute is optional. If true, the task will return immediately without waiting for the server to start.
- The **quiet** attribute is optional. If true, the task will not print any status information.
- The **logFile** attribute is optional and specifies the name of the file to log the server start information to.
- The **replaceLog** attribute is optional. If true, the task will erase an existing log file instead of appending.
- The **trace** attribute is optional. If true, the task will print trace information.
- The **script** attribute is optional and specifies the name of a script file to execute during server startup.

- The **timeout** attribute is optional and specifies the amount of time to wait for the server to successfully start.
- The **statusPort** attribute is optional and specifies the TCP Port the server should send status messages to.
- The **failonerror** attribute is optional and if set to true causes the build to stop if the task has an error.

To use this task, add the taskdef in Code Snippet A-24 to your ANT build.xml.

**Code Snippet A-24** taskdef for wsStartServer

```
<taskdef name="wsStartServer" classname="com.ibm.websphere.ant.
➥tasks.StartServer"/>
```

## wsStopApp

The wsStopApp task enables you to stop an existing or newly installed application on a WebSphere server or in a WebSphere cell. The structure of the wsStopApp task is shown in Code Snippet A-25.

**Code Snippet A-25** wsStopApp

```
<wsStopApp
    wasHome="location of websphere installation"
    server="the name of the server containing the application to
    ➥start"
    node="the name of the node containing the application to start"
    application="the name of the application to stop"
    properties="java properties file containing attributes to set in
    ➥the JVM System properties"
    profile="a script file to be executed before the main command or
    ➥file"
    conntype="specifies the type of connection to be used."
    host="the host to connect to"
    port="the port on the host to connect to"
    user="user ID to authenticate with"
    password="password to authenticate with"/>
```

- Common attributes: **wasHome**, **properties**, **conntype**, **host**, **port**, **user**, **password**, **profile**.
- The **server** attribute is optional and specifies the name of the server containing the application you wish to start.

- The **node** attribute is optional and specifies the name of the node containing the application you wish to start.
- The **application** attribute is required and specifies the name of the application you wish to stop.

To use this task, add the taskdef in Code Snippet A-26 to your ANT build.xml.

**Code Snippet A-26 taskdef for wsStopApp**

```
<taskdef name="wsStopApp" classname="com.ibm.websphere.ant.tasks.
➥StopApplication"/>
```

## wsStopServer

The wsStopServer task enables you to stop a standalone server instance. This is not used to stop a server controlled by the Deployment Manager. Therefore, this task is useful for the Base Application Server and to stop the Node Agent and/or Deployment Manager. If you wish to stop a server managed by the Deployment Manager, use the wsadmin task to execute a scripting command. The structure of the wsStopServer task is shown in Code Snippet A-27.

**Code Snippet A-27 wsStopServer**

```
<wsStopServer
      server="name of the server to stop"
      noWait="true | <b>false</b>"
      quiet="true | <b>false</b>"
      logFile="name of the file to log to"
      replaceLog="true | <b>false</b>"
      trace="true | <b>false</b>"
      timeout="amount of time to wait for the server to stop"
      statusPort="port for the server to send status messages to"
      conntype="SOAP | RMI"
      host="hostname of the machine running the server you wish to
      ➥stop"
      port="admin port of the server you wish to stop"
      username="name of the admin userid id to authenticate with"
      password="password of the admin user to authenticate with"
      wasHome="WebSphere Installation directory"
      failonerror="true | <b>false</b>"/>
```

- Common attributes: **wasHome**, **properties**, **conntype**, **host**, **port**, **password**, **profile**.
- The **server** attribute is required and contains the name of the server you wish to stop.

- The **username** contains the user ID to authenticate with. Optional when available. (It does not use the common parameter user like the other ANT tasks.)
- The **noWait** attribute is optional. If true, the task will return immediately without waiting for the server to stop.
- The **quiet** attribute is optional. If true, the task will not print any status information.
- The **logFile** attribute is optional and specifies the name of the file to log the server start information to.
- The **replaceLog** attribute is optional. If true, the task will erase an existing log file instead of appending.
- The **trace** attribute is optional. If true, the task will print trace information.
- The **timeout** attribute is optional and specifies the amount of time to wait for the server to successfully stop.
- The **statusPort** attribute is optional and specifies the TCP port the server should send status messages to.
- The **failonerror** attribute is optional and if set to true causes the build to stop if the task has an error.

To use this task, add the taskdef in Code Snippet A-28 to your ANT build.xml.

**Code Snippet A-28** taskdef for wsStopServer

```
<taskdef name="wsStopServer" classname="com.ibm.websphere.ant.tasks.
➥StopServer"/>
```

## wsadmin

The wsadmin task executes the WebSphere command-line administration tool with the specified arguments. This task can be used to execute any wsadmin command or wsadmin script. The structure of the wsadmin task is shown in Code Snippet A-29.

**Code Snippet A-29** wsadmin ANT task

```
<wsadmin
     wasHome="location of websphere installation"
     command="command to be passed to the script processor"
     properties="java properties file containing attributes to set in
     ➥the JVM System properties"
     profile="a script file to be executed before the main command or
     ➥file"
     script="a set of commands in a file to be passed to the script
     ➥processor"
```

```
        lang="the language to be used to interpret scripts."
        conntype="specifies the type of connection to be used."
        host="the host to connect to"
        port="the port on the host to connect to"
        user="user ID to authenticate with"
        password="password to authenticate with">
        <arg value=""/>
        .
        .
        .
        <arg value=""/>
</wsadmin>
```

- Common attributes: **wasHome**, **properties**, **conntype**, **host**, **port**, **user**, **password**, **profile**.
- The **command** attribute is required, unless script is specified, and it contains the command to be passed to the script processor.
- The **script** attribute is required, unless command is specified, and it contains a set of commands in a file to be passed to the script processor.
- The **lang** attribute is optional, and it contains the language to be used to interpret scripts. The supported values are jacl, javascript, and jpython.
- The **arg** task can contain 0 or more nested arg elements that contain arguments that are passed to the script.

To use this task, add the taskdef in Code Snippet A-30 to your ANT build.xml.

**Code Snippet A-30** taskdef for wsadmin

```
<taskdef name="wsadmin" classname="com.ibm.websphere.ant.
➥tasks.WsAdmin"/>
```

## Web Service ANT Tasks

These ANT tasks help developers generate some of the Web services plumbing classes at assembly or deployment time. Using these tasks requires knowledge of Web services. [Brown 2003] provides information on building Web services.

## endptEnabler

The endptEnabler task enables a set of Web services within an Enterprise Application Archive (EAR) file. For each Web service–enabled EJB JAR in the EAR file, it adds one or more router modules to the EAR. The structure of the endptEnabler task is shown in Code Snippet A-31.

**Code Snippet A-31** Endpoint enabler

```
<EndpointEnablerTask earfile="location of input EAR file">
   <property key="property name" value="property value"/>
   <property key="another property name" value="another property
   ➥value"/>
</EndpointEnablerTask>
```

- The **earfile** attribute shows the location of the EAR file that will host the Web service.

To use this task, add the taskdef in Code Snippet A-32 to your ANT build.xml.

**Code Snippet A-32** taskdef for Endpoint enabler

```
<taskdef name="EndpointEnablerTask"
         classname="com.ibm.websphere.ant.tasks.endptEnabler">
         classpath="location of installed websphere classes">
</taskdef>
```

## Java2WSDL

The Java2WSDL task maps a Java class to a Web Services Description Language (WSDL) file. The structure of the Java2WSDL task is shown in Code Snippet A-33.

**Code Snippet A-33** Java2WSDLTask ANT task

```
<Java2WSDLTask output="pathname of wsdl file to create"
className="name of Java class to be mapped"
implClass="name of Java class implementation to be mapped"
namespace="target namespace for the WSDL file being generated"
location="location or URL of the service">
<mapping namespace="namespace to map to"
        package="Java package to map"/>
</Java2WSDLTask>
```

- The **output** attribute defines where the WSDL file should be stored.
- The **classname** attribute represents the fully qualified name of one of the following Java classes:
  - Stateless Session EJB remote interface that extends the javax.ejb.EJBObject class
  - Service endpoint interface that extends the java.rmi.Remote class
  - JavaBean
- The **implClass** attribute is used for a special purpose. The Java2WSDL command uses method parameter names to construct the WSDL file message part names. The command automatically obtains the message names from the debug information in the class. If the class is compiled without debug information, or if the class is an interface, the method parameter names are not available. In this case, you can use the implClass argument to provide an alternative class from which to obtain method parameter names. The implClass does not need to implement the class if the class is an interface, but it must implement the same methods as the class.
- The **namespace** attribute defines the XML schema namespace for the WSDL file.
- The **location** attribute defines the URL that Web service clients will use to invoke the Web service.
- The **mapping** attribute defines the namespace for the Java package that implements the Web service.

To use this task, add the ANT task shown in Code Snippet A-34 to your build script.

**Code Snippet A-34 taskdef for Java2WSDLTask**

```
<taskdef name="Java2WSDLTask"
classname="com.ibm.websphere.ant.tasks.Java2WSDL">
<classpath>
  <pathelement path="location of installed websphere classes"/>
  <pathelement path="location of Java class to be mapped"/>
</classpath>
</taskdef>
```

## WSDL2Java

The WSDL2Java task creates Java classes and deployment descriptor templates from a WSDL file. It is a wrapper for the WSDL2Java execution file in the WebSphere Application Server bin directory. The structure of the WSDL2Java task is shown in Code Snippet A-35.

**Code Snippet A-35** WSDL2JavaTask

```
<WSDL2JavaTask url="location of input WSDL document"
         output="root directory for emitted files"
         role="J2EE development role"
         container="J2EE container"
         genjava="generate java files">
</WSDL2JavaTask>
```

- The **output** sets the root directory for emitted files.
- The **role** specifies the J2EE development role that identifies which files (Web service deployment descriptors) to generate. It is used in conjunction with the container attribute. Valid arguments are:
  - **client**—Combination of develop-client and deploy-client
  - **deploy-client**—Generates binding files for client deployment
  - **deploy-server**—Generates binding files for server deployment
  - **develop-client** (default)—Generates files for client development
  - **develop-server**—Generates files for server development
  - **server**—Combination of develop-server and deploy-server
- The **container** attribute determines the J2EE container to be used to generate the appropriate Web service descriptors. The valid values are *ejb*, *web*, *client*, or *none*.

  This flag works in conjunction with the role flag. For example, when the role is a server role, the container argument specifies which J2EE container the implementation uses.
  - When the ***-role develop-server -container ejb*** arguments are specified, the webservices.xml, ibm-webservices-bnd.xmi, ibm-webservicesclient-ext.xmi and the mapping file are generated into the META-INF subdirectory of your EJB module. These are the server-side Web service descriptors for the module hosting the Web service.
  - When the ***-role develop-server -container web arguments*** are specified, the files are generated into the WEB-INF directory of your web module. These are the server-side Web service descriptors for the module hosting the Web service.

  If you specify one of the containers with the role as deploy-client, then it will generate the appropriate descriptors for your application to be a Web service client.
- The **genjava** attribute determines whether to keep the source files for the Java class.

**Code Snippet A-36** taskdef for WSDL2JavaTask

```
<taskdef name="WSDL2JavaTask"
              classname="com.ibm.websphere.ant.tasks.WSDL2Java">
              classpath="location of installed websphere classes">
</taskdef>
```

## WebSphere Studio ANT

Throughout this book, we tried not to base the build process on a particular IDE. However, using a set of custom ANT tasks from an IDE can really increase productivity. Such ANT tasks provide a level of consistency between the developers and assemblers.

WebSphere Studio provides a set of ANT tasks that use the existing metadata within WebSphere Studio. By basing the build on WebSphere Studio projects, you can quickly produce ANT build scripts without compromising the efficiency of an IDE.

> **NOTE**
> When using these WebSphere Studio ANT tasks, you must have a good plan for maintaining the IDE workspace. This means understanding early in the build process what your J2EE packaging plan will be. This includes the number of J2EE modules and where utility JARs will be placed in the final deployment.

The controller build script can be as easy as:

- **compileWorkspace**—Compile the development workspace.
- **ejbDeploy**—For applications that use EJB, generate the EJB deployment code.
- **exportEAR**—Export the final EAR file.

This greatly simplifies the build process and provides consistency between the development environments and build environments.

### AppClientExport

This task performs the same operation as the Application Client export wizard for exporting an application client project to an application client JAR file. The ANT task is shown in Code Snippet A-37.

**Code Snippet A-37** appClientExport ANT task

```
<appClientExport
      AppClientProjectName="ProjectClient"
      AppClientExportFile="C:\ProjectClient.jar"
      ExportSource="true"
      Overwrite="true"/>
```

- The **AppClientProjectName** task is the name of the application client project. The project name is case-sensitive. This task is mandatory.
- The **AppClientExportFile** task is the absolute path of the application client JAR file.
- The **ExportSource** is a flag to determine whether to include the Java source file into the application client JAR.
- The **Overwrite** flag determines if you want to override an existing application client JAR in the same directory.

To use this ANT task, use the taskdef in Code Snippet A-38.

**Code Snippet A-38** taskdef for appClientExport

```
<taskdef name="appClientExport "
      classname="com.ibm.etools.j2ee.ant.ApplicationClientExport">
      classpath="location of installed websphere and websphere studio
      ➥classes">
</taskdef>
```

## compileWorkspace

This task compiles the entire workspace. It performs the same action as javac. While this task is running, all the validation and other builders are turned off. Notice that rather than having to compile individual projects, compileWorkspace assumes you have setup a WebSphere Studio workspace to properly represent the J2EE packaging structure. See Code Snippet A-39.

**Code Snippet A-39** compileWorkspace task

```
<compileWorkspace BuildType="Full"
                Quiet="false" />
```

- The **BuildType** attribute identifies the type of build: Incremental or Full. This is not a required field, and the default is Incremental.
- The **Quiet** attribute determines whether or not to print out messages. (The quiet mode can give you a substantial performance gain when running this ANT task in the workbench.)

To use this ANT task, use the taskdef in Code Snippet A-40.

**Code Snippet A-40** taskdef for compileWorkspace

```
<taskdef name="compileWorkspace"
     classname="com.ibm.etools.ant.extras.RebuildWorkspace">
     classpath="location of installed websphere and websphere studio
     ➥classes">
</taskdef>
```

## EARExport

This task performs the same operation as the EAR export wizard for exporting an Enterprise Application Project to an EAR file. Because the EAR export wizard handles all the modules configured in the workspace, this task may be the only one needed to produce the EAR. Although there are ANT tasks for exporting modules, they exist for convenience. See Code Snippet A-41.

**Code Snippet A-41** EARExport task

```
<earExport EARProjectName="EARProject"
           EARExportFile="C:\EARProject.ear"
           ExportSource="true"
           IncludeProjectMetaFiles="false"/>
```

- The **EARProjectName** attribute is the name of the EAR. This is a required field.
- The **EARExportFile** is the absolute path of the EAR file. This is the EAR file that is created. This is a required field.
- The **ExportSource** attribute determines whether to include the actual source files as part of the EAR. This is not a required field, and the default is No.
- The **IncludeProjectMetaFiles** attribute determines whether to include the IDE metadata files. This is useful if you want to re-import the built EAR back into the IDE. This is not a required filed, and the default is No.
- The **Overwrite** option will overwrite the EAR file if it already exists. This is not a required field, and the default is No.

To use this ANT task, use the taskdef in Code Snippet A-42.

**Code Snippet A-42** taskdef for EARExport

```
<taskdef name="earExport "
      classname="com.ibm.etools.j2ee.ant.EarExport">
      classpath="location of installed websphere and websphere studio
      ➥classes">
</taskdef>
```

## EJBExport

This task performs the same operation as the EJB JAR file export wizard for exporting an EJB project to an EJB JAR file. This task is not available in version 5.x of WebSphere Studio Site Developer or WebSphere Application Server Express. This task is useful when you only want to build the EJB JAR. Such a scenario may exist if different development groups are developing different pieces of the same EAR. See Code Snippet A-43.

**Code Snippet A-43** EJBExport task

```
<ejbExport
      EJBProjectName="EJBProject"
      EJBExportFile="C:\EJBProject.jar"
      ExportSource="true"
      Overwrite="true"/>
```

- The **EJBProjectName** is the name of the EJB project. This is a required field, and the project name is case-sensitive.
- The **EJBExportFile** is the absolute path of the EJB JAR. This is the EJB JAR produced. This is a required field.
- The **ExportSource** attribute determines whether to include the source files. This is not a required field, and the default is No.
- The **Overwrite** attribute determines whether to overwrite an existing EJB JAR file. This is not a required field, and the default is No.

To use this ANT task, use the taskdef in Code Snippet A-44.

**Code Snippet A-44** taskdef for EJBExport

```
<taskdef name="ejbExport "
      classname="com.ibm.etools.ejb.ant.EJBExport">
      classpath="location of installed websphere and websphere studio
      ➥classes">
</taskdef>
```

## EJBDeploy

This task generates deployment code and RMIC code for an EJB project. This is not available in version 5.x of WebSphere Studio Site Developer or WAS Express. See Code Snippet A-45.

> **NOTE**
>
> As you may have noticed, there are two EJBDeploy ANT tasks: one that is part of the WebSphere Application Server ANT tasks and one that is part of WebSphere Studio ANT tasks. They both call the same EJBDeploy.bat file.
>
> The **WebSphere Studio version of EJBDeploy** is used for WebSphere Studio EJB projects within a WebSphere Studio project. This will generate the EJBDeploy code before packaging the EAR, much the same way the wizard-driven approach inside WebSphere Studio does.
>
> The **WebSphere Application Server version of EJBDeploy** takes in an already-packaged EJB JAR or EAR file that contains an EJB JAR. It will then generate the EJB deployment code and produce a new EJB-JAR file or EAR file.

**Code Snippet A-45** EJBDeploy ANT task

```
<ejbDeploy EJBProject="EJBProject" NoValidate="true"/>
```

- The **EJBProject** attribute is the name of the EJB project. This is a required field, and it is case-sensitive.
- The **IgnoreErrors** attribute determines whether to stop the EJB deployment generation if it detects a compilation error. This is not a required field, and the default is No.
- The **NoValidate** attribute determines whether you want to run a validation on the EJB project before running the EJB deployment generation. The default is No.
- The **Quiet** attribute determines whether to display only error messages. This is a required field, and the default is No.
- The **Use35Rules** attribute determines to generate CMP mappings based on WebSphere 3.5 Application Server Rules. This is a deprecated field and has been replaced with the Compatible35 attribute. It is not a required field, and the default is No.
- The **Compatible35** attribute determines to generate CMP mappings based on WebSphere 3.5 Application Server Rules. It is not a required field, and the default is No.
- The **CodeGen** flag says only generate the deployment code, do not run RMIC or javac. This is not a required field, and the default is No.

To use this ANT task, use the taskdef in Code Snippet A-46.

**Code Snippet A-46 taskdef for EJBDeploy**

```
<taskdef name="ejbDeploy"
     classname="com.ibm.etools.ejb.ant.EJBDeploy">
     classpath="location of installed websphere and websphere studio
     ➥classes">
</taskdef>
```

## getJavacErrorCount

This task gets the error count for the last internal javac compilation of the specified project. This task can be used to get the errors for every project. This can then be used in the build report. See Code Snippet A-47.

**Code Snippet A-47 getJavacErrorCount ANT task**

```
<getJavacErrorCount
   ProjectName="MyProject"
   PropertyName="MyJavacErrorCount" />
<echo message="MyJavacErrorCount=${MyJavacErrorCount}" />
```

- The **ProjectName** is the name of the project for which you want to get the errorCount. This is a required field.
- The **PropertyName** attribute is the name of the property with the count result. It can then be used later in the ANT script. This is not a required field, and the default is JavacErrorCount.

To use this ANT task, use the taskdef in Code Snippet A-48.

**Code Snippet A-48 taskdef for getJavacErrorCount**

```
<taskdef name="getJavacErrorCount"
     classname="com.ibm.etools.ant.extras.GetJavaErrorCount">
     classpath="location of installed websphere and websphere studio
     ➥classes">
</taskdef>
```

## getProjectData

This is an internal (utility) task that gets the current project information. This can be used to display specific information about the projects during a build. This task is also used internally by other WebSphere Studio ANT tasks. See Code Snippet A-49.

**Code Snippet A-49 getProjectData task**

```
<getProjectData  Basedir="${basedir}" />
<echo message="getProjectData: projectName=${projectName}
nature=${natureName}
workspace=${workspaceName}
basedir=${basedir}" />
```

- The **basedir** is the fully qualified name of where the project is located. This is a required field.
- The **projectName** attribute will be populated with the project name after running the task. It can then be used later in the build to display the project name. This is not a required field, and the default is *projectName*.
- The **workspace** attribute will be populated with the workspace path. This is not a required field, and the default is *workspaceName*.
- The **nature** attribute will be populated with the Eclipse nature of the project. For example, the property will tell you if the project is an EJB project. This is not a required field, and the default is *natureName*.

To use this ANT task, use the taskdef in Code Snippet A-50.

**Code Snippet A-50 taskdef for getProjectData**

```
<taskdef name="getProjectData"
    classname="com.ibm.etools.ant.extras.GetProjectData">
    classpath="location of installed websphere and websphere studio
    ➥classes">
</taskdef>
```

## projectBuild

This task builds the specified project. Rather than compiling the whole workspace, you may choose to just compile the projects individually. This is usually used when the workspace contains projects that may not have to be built during the build. See Code Snippet A-51.

**Code Snippet A-51 projectBuild task**

```
<projectBuild
    ProjectName="myProject"
    failonerror="true"
    DebugCompilation="false"
    BuildType="full" />
```

- The **ProjectName** attribute is the name of the project to be built. This is a required field.
- The **BuildType** attribute determines the type of build: Incremental or Full Build. This is not a required field, and the default is Incremental.
- The **failonerror** attribute determines whether or not builds should fail on errors. This is not a required field, and the default is true.
- The **DebugCompilation** determines whether to include debug information. This is not a required field, and the default is true.

To use this ANT task, use the taskdef in Code Snippet A-52.

**Code Snippet A-52** taskdef for projectBuild

```
<taskdef name="projectBuild"
     classname="com.ibm.etools.ant.extras.ProjectBuild">
     classpath="location of installed websphere and websphere studio
     ➥classes">
</taskdef>
```

## setDebugInfo

This task sets the internal Java compilation debug level and returns the current settings. See Code Snippet A-53.

**Code Snippet A-53** setDebugInfo task

```
<setDebugInfo
   LineNumber="false"
   LocalVariable="false"
   sourceFile="false"
   DebugInfo="false"
   PropertyName="DebugInfo"/>
<echo message="current settings: ${DebugInfo}" />
```

- The **DebugInfo** attribute changes the three possible settings in one place. This is not a required field, and the value is dependent on the settings set in WebSphere Studio. The value can be true or false.
- The **LineNumber** attribute specifies the line number attribute of Java compilation. If set to true, stack traces may display the line number of a particular error. This is not a required field, and the value may be true or false depending on the workbench settings.
- The **LocalVariable** attribute sets the compilation option of the symbol table. This is not a required field, and the default may be true or false.

- The **SourceFile** attribute sets the compile option for the source file name. This is not a required field, and the value may be true or false.
- The **PropertyName** field determines where to hold the results of the DebugInfo. This is not a required field, and the default is *DebugInfo*.

To use this ANT task, use the taskdef in Code Snippet A-54.

**Code Snippet A-54 taskdef for setDebugInfo**

```
<taskdef name=" setDebugInfo"
     classname="com.ibm.etools.ant.extras.SetDebugInfo">
     classpath="location of installed websphere and websphere studio
     ➥classes">
</taskdef>
```

### UtilJar

This task is DEPRECATED. The task was not removed in order to maintain compatibility with previous versions, but it will be removed in the future. It should no longer be required; the recommended approach is to use the application deployment descriptor editor to map Java projects to utility JARs. This task JARs up source and/or build output of a Java project and places the JAR file in an Enterprise Application Project.

### WARExport

This task performs the same operation as the WAR file export wizard for exporting a web project to a WAR file. This task is useful when you need to produce just a standalone module. For example, in WebSphere Portal, you only need to deploy WAR files. See Code Snippet A-55.

**Code Snippet A-55 WARExport task**

```
<warExport WARProjectName="ProjectWeb"
           WARExportFile="C:\ProjectWeb.war"
           ExportSource="true"
           Overwrite="true"/>
```

- The **WARProjectName** attribute is the name of the WebSphere Studio web project. This is a required field.
- The **WARExport** attribute is the absolute path of the WAR file produced. This is a required field.
- The **ExportSource** attribute determines if you want to export the Java source files inside the WAR as well. This is not a required field, and the default is No.

- The **Overwrite** attribute determines if you want to override an existing WAR file with the one produced. This is not a required field, and the default is false.

To use this ANT task, use the taskdef in Code Snippet A-56.

**Code Snippet A-56** taskdef for WARExport

```
<taskdef name="warExport "
     classname="com.ibm.etools.j2ee.ant.WARExport">
     classpath="location of installed websphere and websphere studio
     ➥classes">
</taskdef>
```

## Conclusion

This Appendix provides a quick reference to using ANT with WebSphere Application Server. As an open source “standard,” ANT is an accepted mechanism to automation of the assembly, deployment, and configuration process. Having a basic understanding of ANT is important to process automation with WAS. In addition, knowing the available ANT tasks can also increase productivity. We also provided a brief overview of ANT and provided the available ANT options when using the WebSphere Application Server platform.

# APPENDIX B

# Deployment Checklist

Often, the best-laid deployment plans go awry due to haste or miscommunication. It only takes one missed step to thwart the careful planning and hard work of an entire team, and backing out a botched deployment isn't pleasant. Deployment is something that is best done quickly and efficiently, particularly since, in many cases, systems are down or applications are unavailable during this time. We have provided a checklist of things to think about before the actual process starts. This can (and should) be augmented with environment-specific items or others found in this book.

## Testing

**T1**. Have unit, integrated, performance, functional, and acceptance testing been completed satisfactorily? What are the detailed, reproducible, and carefully reviewed results of these tests? Can all service-level agreements, such as response time under a peak-simulated load, be met, including the overhead of authentication/authorization if they are required? Is this also the case when failover is occurring during some reasonable failure scenarios?

**T2**. Has failover been verified by "disconnecting" components to simulate runtime failures? Do any single points of failure exist, and has the "Rule of Threes" been taken into account? Has this testing been done while load testing is under way to test the behavior under load?

**T3**. Was testing done with security on?

**T4**. Was final pre-production or staging testing done in an environment identical to production (or if not, are the deltas and associated risks well documented)?

**T5**. Have other infrastructure areas (network, database, operating system) been involved in testing, and have tuning changes been made to accommodate the new deployment?

**T6**. Have HTTP Session sizes been verified for the new application under typical use cases and load?

**T7**. Have all functional and non-functional requirements been signed off?

## Security

**S1**. Have security requirements been carefully defined and the system implementation evaluated against those requirements? Has a security expert reviewed the system design and implementation? Have all system components been hardened?

**S2**. Is WAS global security on? Have WAS sample certificates been replaced with self-signed certificates or certificates from a legitimate Certificate Authority?

**S3**. If you are concerned about the trustworthiness of your application code in the infrastructure, have you turned Java2 security on? Has testing been done, and are all necessary policy files intact and accurate?

**S4**. Has any form of ethical hacking been done, at a minimum turning some of the more "creative" employees loose on the system?

**S5**. Have expire dates been checked and documented on all certificates and passwords? Is there a clear plan for updating these when needed?

**S6**. Has it been verified that all identities used for connecting to backend resources such as databases are valid and have the correct privileges?

## Environment

**E1**. Will all necessary user IDs/password (including root) be available for the deployment?

**E2**. Has it been verified that all infrastructure components are fully operational, with no errors occurring in the logs?

**E3**. Is all the necessary information (for example, server names and port numbers) available for resources, such has databases or legacy systems? Has connectivity to these resources from the target environment been verified?

**E4**. Have all network traffic routes through firewalls, switches, and routers been verified? Are documents showing the topology, firewall rules, etc., up to date and available for troubleshooting?

**E5**. Is there plenty of space on volumes used for logging? Has capacity planning been done for all system components?

**E6**. Has configuration data for both pre-deploy and post-deploy been checked into change management?

**E7**. Has it been verified that there is appropriate monitoring and that alerts go to the appropriate places?

**E8**. Are all commercial-software infrastructure components at the appropriate version/fixpack levels? Are all vendor prerequisites in place?

**E9**. Have all "test harnesses" or test-only configurations been removed?

**E10**. Have configurations for logging been turned down to production levels?

## Deployment Process

**D1**. Have all team member responsibilities and their status for the deploy date been verified?

**D2**. Is there a well-defined, reproducible deployment process? There should be a clear document describing the process. Is the deployment process automated?

**D3**. Have deployment scripts (where used) been verified prior to deployment in production-like environments?

**D4**. Has the build been verified to include all components at the correct version level?

**D5**. Have all team members reviewed the rollout plan (downtime, rolling servers, etc.)?

**D6**. Have arrangements been made to have representatives of various infrastructure areas such as network, operating system, legacy system, and database admins available in case there are problems? Have those persons been briefed on how the new application interacts with their areas?

**D7**. Will the application architect and key developers be available for troubleshooting in case there are problems?

**D8**. Are initialization scripts (such as those to "prime" the application after it has been deployed, or pre-compile JSPs) in place and tested?

**D9**. Is there a back-out plan, and has it been tested?

**D10**. Are all team members in agreement that the deployment should proceed?

## Administration

**A1**. Are all WAS administrative IDs/roles in place?

**A2**. Is there a process for log file review and archiving?

**A3**. Have all operational procedures (such as backup and disaster recovery) been tested?

**A4**. Are all product licenses and support agreements up to date for the intended environment?

**A5**. Has the help desk received proper training and documentation on the new deployment? Is there a well-defined process for fixing production problems? This includes well-defined phone numbers, pager access numbers, call lists, and escalation procedures.

**A6**. Have the users been prepared and trained? Will they have the opportunity to use the prior version for some period of time?

**A7**. Is a system monitoring process in place? How will the system be monitored to ensure that it is running? How will its logs and errors be monitored to capture potential problems before they become serious?

**A8**. Does the monitoring process including monitoring load and other resource usage? Is that information being used to predict future load and system needs? Have you taken into account load spikes that might be based on calendar events or perhaps special marketing events?

APPENDIX C

# Setup Instructions for Samples

In this book, we have included a number of examples to help you understand the concepts introduced. In order to run these examples, you need to obtain and install a number of products. This Appendix lists those products and how to obtain sample or free versions of them. We also briefly outline how they were installed to support the examples. You are, of course, free to use purchased versions of these products if you have them available.

## Getting Products and Samples

Here, we list the web download sites for obtaining the software used in this book. We list the URL and the version of the product that we used when testing the book samples. Many of these products regularly undergo enhancements. As a result, these sites may contain newer minor versions of these products. In general, you should use the exact version we listed if available or the most recent minor update of each product:

- Materials for this book:
  - http://www.phptr.com/title/0131468626
- WebSphere Application Server 5.1.0.3 or 5.1.04
  - http://www-106.ibm.com/developerworks/websphere/downloads/WASsupport.html—Download both the server and the messaging provider.
  - The latest cumulative fixes for WebSphere Application Server (ensure you obtain at least 5.1.0.3)—http://www-306.ibm.com/software/webservers/appserv/was/support/

- Application Server Toolkit 5.0.2 (Use this version of the ASTK if you are using WAS 5.0.2. If you are using WAS 5.1 and above, the install of ASTK version 5.1 is shipped with a licensed copy of WAS 5.1. If you are using the trial edition of WAS 5.1, you can use the trial version of WebSphere Studio Application Developer instead of the ASTK to run the samples.)
    - http://www-1.ibm.com/support/docview.wss?rs=180&context=SSEQTP&q1=Application+Server+Toolkit&uid=swg24005125&loc=en_US&cs=utf-8&lang=en+en
- WebSphere Studio Application Developer 5.1.1
    - http://www-106.ibm.com/developerworks/websphere/downloads/WSsupport.html
- DB2 Universal Database Enterprise Server Edition 8.1.5
    - Download the server—http://www14.software.ibm.com/webapp/download/search.jsp?rs=db2udbdl
    - Download the patches for DB2—http://www-306.ibm.com/software/data/db2/udb/we_downloadv8.html
    - CVSNT 2.0.41a (We also tested the examples using version 2.0.12.)
    - http://www.cvsnt.org/wiki/—We suggest downloading the executable installer.

## Installing Software

In this section, we briefly outline the key steps for installing the software in the Windows environment. The wizards are pretty straightforward, so we will not go over the individual steps. For specific installation issues, see the WebSphere Application Server InfoCenter.

### WebSphere Application Server

To install WAS, you extract the installation files and then run setup. You then apply the cumulative fix and finally verify the installation. The steps are described here:

1. Unzip the two ZIP files: **ibmwas5_trial_for_nt.zip** and **messaging_trial_for_nt.zip** into the same directory.
2. Go the directory where you extracted the ZIP files into and run the BAT file called **launchpad.bat**.
3. Follow the wizards and do a full installation. (Uncheck the option to run as a Windows service.)
4. Once you have installed WebSphere Application Server version 5.1, unzip the cumulative fix file **was510_cf3_win.zip** (if you are using a more recent cumulative fix, the name will differ slightly) into a different directory than that used for the WAS install.

5. Be sure to set the **JAVA_HOME** variable on your system to the root of your JDK. WebSphere Application Server comes with a JDK. The Java JDK is located in <WAS_ROOT>/java.
6. In the directory where you unzipped the cumulative fixes, run the BAT file called **updateWizard.bat**.
7. Follow the prompts. The update wizard should detect your WebSphere Application Server installation. Make sure it is selected. The cumulative fix directory textbox should default to the cumulative fixes location.
8. Once the cumulative fixes are installed, open a command prompt and go to the bin directory of your WebSphere Application Server install. Run the command **startserver server1**. Wait for the server to start. The last message should be *Server server1 open for e-business; process id is <pid>*.
9. Open a browser to http://localhost:9090/admin. This should render the login page for the administrative console. Close the browser.
10. In order for the samples to run smoothly, we have provided a clean-up script that will remove some predefined variables that may overlap with ones we create in our samples. This is a WebSphere wsadmin script. Back in the command prompt, run the following command: **wsadmin -fC:\WASDeployBook\wassetupscript\wascleanup.jacl**.
11. Back in the command prompt, issue the command stopserver server1. Wait for the server to stop and close the command prompt.

## Application Server Toolkit

The Application Server Toolkit (ASTK) is used in this book to help with manual packaging and deployment preparation. Remember that the ASTK replaces the AAT and is included as a separate install with WAS 5.1 and beyond and that the ASTK is a separate download from WAS 5.0.2. To install it, follow these three steps:

1. Extract the **ASTK_windows.zip** file into a temporary directory.
2. In the folder you extracted the ZIP file in, run **setup.exe**.
3. Follow the install wizard through a typical installation.

## WebSphere Studio Application Developer

For this book, you can use WebSphere Studio instead of the ASTK for the manual assembly examples. WebSphere Studio Application Developer is a multi-part download. The installation process is fairly simple. The steps are given here:

1. After downloading the required and optional pieces, run **wsextract.exe** to assemble the install. Any of the optional features should be automatically selected.

2. Once wsextract.exe finishes, it will launch the WebSphere Studio Application Developer LaunchPad. Select **Install IBM WebSphere Studio Application Developer**.
3. Follow the wizard instructions and select the default options.

## DB2 Universal Database

In this section, we are going to go over installing DB2 Universal database Enterprise Server Edition.

1. Run the self-extractor file **DB2_V81_ESE_WIN32_NLV.exe** file. Choose a temporary directory to store the temp files.
2. Under the temp directory, traverse to the root and run **setup.exe**. On the welcome page, select **Install Products**.
3. Be sure that you are installing DB2 UDB Enterprise Server Edition and press **Next**.
4. Follow the wizard and do a typical installation. Select the following options when prompted. Select the default options for everything else:
   - Do not add any extra features.
   - Use **db2admin** for both user and password.
   - Do not install SMTP.
   - Create the default DB2 instance.
   - Defer any contact information.
5. Once the install finishes, exit the First Steps wizard.
6. Next, you need to install the latest fixpack. Here, we assume fixpack 5. Run the file called **FP5_WR21334_ESE.exe**. This will extract the install and start the installation of the fixpack.
   - Select the **Install Products** link. Make sure that you are installing the DB2 UDB Enterprise Server.
   - Click **Yes** to shut down any DB2 running processes.
   - Restart your machine when the installation completes.

## Installing CVSNT

To mimic a true development environment, we used CVSNT as a team repository. The choice to use CVS for this book was based on it being easily obtainable. Also, we chose CVS on the Windows platform so people can try the samples on their desktop. In your real environment, you should use CVS on a Unix platform or a higher-end team repository such as IBM Rational Clearcase:

1. Run the cvsnt-2.0.41a.exe.
2. Follow the install wizard and select the default options.

## Setting Up Examples

Now that you have installed the products needed for the examples, we'll briefly cover the steps for setting up the examples that go with this book. In brief, we will extract the download materials for this book, set up our WSTRADE database (which is used throughout the book), and then show you how to load a CVS repository into WebSphere Studio or the ASTK. This is not necessary to run the samples; however, we assume most of you will want to look at the scripts and source code we wrote.

### Extracting WASDeployBook.zip

The materials for this book are located in a file called **WASDeployBook.zip**. Included are the artifacts needed to run the different exercises in this book:

1. Extract the file **WASDeployBook.zip** to the root of the C:\ drive. If you extract the materials to a different directory, you may need to modify certain commands or path information yourself when doing an exercise.
2. This will create a directory in the root of the C: drive called **WASDeployBook**.

### Setting Up WSTRADE Database

In the samples throughout this book, we use the same database. We have provided a script that will create the initial database:

1. Open a DB2 Command window. On the Windows platform, you can launch the DB2 Command window by going to **Start > All Programs > IBM DB2 > Command Line Tools > Command Window**.
2. In the DB2 Command window, switch the directory to **C:\WASDeployBook\DBInfo** (assuming you extracted the book download materials to the C: drive).
3. Type **CreateWSTrade WSTRADE db2admin db2admin.**
   - This will create the WSTRADE database using the db2admin user and password. If you used a different user or password, you must use them at the command line.

### Viewing Source Code and Model Scripts in WebSphere Studio/ASTK

Since some of the scripts and the Java Source files are located in the CVS repository, you may want to load a version of the code into a WebSphere Studio/ASTK workspace to view, modify, correct, or experiment. We will show you how to load a repository using one of the CVS repositories we ship. We assume basic knowledge of the Eclipse platform to accomplish this task. If you are unfamiliar with this, refer to [Brown 2004]:

1. Throughout this book, we have you create various CVS repositories. Refer to the first automation sample for learning how to do this (Chapter 6).

2. Start WebSphere Studio by going to **All Programs > IBM WebSphere Studio > Application Developer 5.1.X** or the ASTK by going to **All Programs > IBM > ASTK > ASTK**.
3. Enter a directory where you want your workspace to be when prompted.
4. Once the workbench starts, go to the CVS Repository Explorer Perspective. This can be done by going to the Main Menu and selecting **Window > Open Perspective > Other > CVS Repository Explorer**.
5. In the CVS Repository Perspective, you should see a view called CVS Repositories. Right-click in that view and select **New > Repository Location**.
6. This will bring up the Add a New CVS Repository wizard. Enter the following:
   - **Host**—localhost
   - **Repository Path**—Location of directory where CVS Repository was extracted, for example: C:\cvs_chapter06. See chapter 6 for more details.
   - **User**—A valid CVS user. The CVS documentation shows how to configure a user for CVS.
   - **Password**—<password>
   - **Leave the defaults for the rest.**
7. Once the repository is loaded, expand the tree as follows: **<tree root> >HEAD**. You will see a folder called CVSROOT followed by the other folders. Each folder, except for CVSROOT, is a project. Select each project and right-click it. Select **Check Out As Project**, as shown in Figure C-1. (Make sure you repeat for each project.)

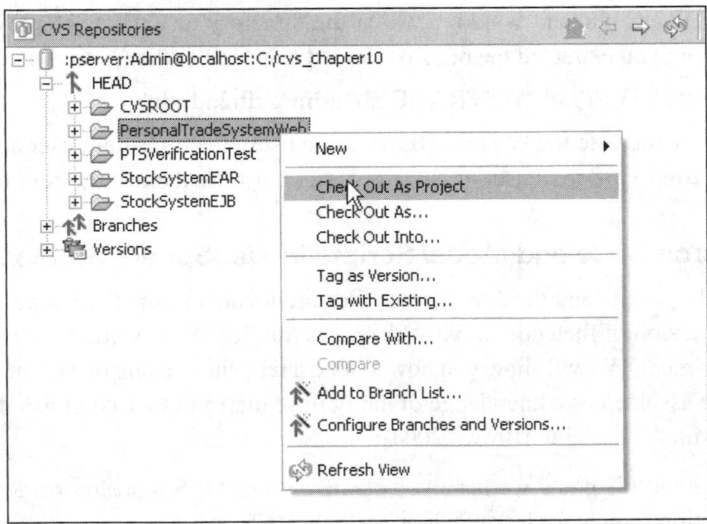


**Figure C-1** Check Out As Project.

## Conclusion

This Appendix provides the necessary information to download and install the products you need for the examples and then explains the steps needed to prepare the examples.

APPENDIX D

# Web Services Gateway Clustering

## Web Services Gateway Overview

WebSphere Application Server V5 - Network Deployment (WAS-ND) provides a Web Services Gateway (WSGW), which serves as an intermediary between Web service clients and Web service deployments. The WSGW provides valuable functions for WAS installations running Web service applications; WAS administrators, therefore, must be familiar with WSGW. Unfortunately, clustering of the gateway, while very important, is not well documented elsewhere. We've chosen to provide this documentation here, even though this book otherwise spends very little time on Web services. In order to understand this Appendix, you must be familiar with Web services and WSGW. If you are not, refer first to the official Info Center documentation. [Brown 2004] is a good resource for developing Web Services.

The WSGW serves as a mediator between a Web service requestor and a Web service provider. Serving as an intermediary, the WSGW can provide a common transport endpoint, typically HTTP, for Web service requests and then forward the request using a different transport, say, JMS. The WSGW also provides filters and handlers[1] that can be used to transform and log incoming requests. WebSphere dynacache is also available for Web services using the WSGW and can provide a substantial performance improvement. Last, by not directly exposing the target Web service and its associated end points, the WSGW allows a company to safely and securely expose internal business processes as Web services to both internal and external users. The interaction between Web service clients, the WSGW, and target Web services is depicted in Figure D-1. The WSGW is implemented as a J2EE enterprise application that is installed into a WebSphere Application Server. Once installed, the application is then configured to point to Web service

1 JAX-RPC–compliant handlers are provided in WAS V5.1 and above.

providers, called target services. All target services associated with a gateway service must be described by a Web Services Description Language (WSDL) document with identical WSDL portTypes. A gateway service thus logically represents a real service provider of a specific portType.

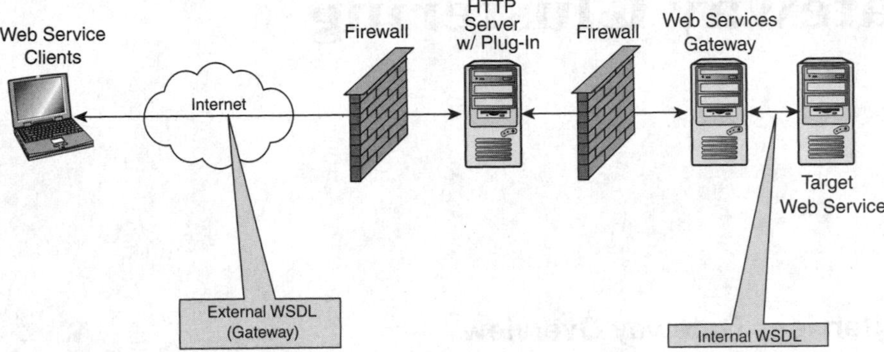


**Figure D-1** Web service client, gateway, and target service interaction.

In Chapter 21, "WAS Network Deployment Clustering," we discussed the WAS clustering implementation and other high availability aspects required for an enterprise-capable deployment. Unfortunately, the WSGW is not integrated with WAS clustering in WAS-ND V5. This is the result of the relative newness of Web services when compared to other J2EE APIs, such as Servlets and EJBs, for which WAS clustering does provide failover and workload management (WLM).[2] Fortunately, the WSGW can be clustered in WAS V5, but some additional assembly is required on the part of the system administrator. The steps of creating a WSGW cluster and using the WAS HTTP server plug-in for WLM of Web service requests, as depicted in Figure D-2, are described in the remainder of this Appendix.[3]

We've chosen this approach, using the WAS-supplied HTTP server plug-in for distributing Web service requests across multiple WSGW servers, because it's likely the most familiar WAS workload management technology, but other options also exist. An IP sprayer such as the Network Dispatcher component in WebSphere Edge Server could also be used to distribute requests but would not provide the termination point that the HTTP server provides, so this factor also contributed to the decision to proceed with the approach indicated.

2 In fact, Web services are not part of J2EE 1.3, the J2EE standard implemented in WAS V5. Support for the J2EE Web service Java Specification Requests (JSR 101 and JSR 109), as well as the WSGW, are part of WAS V5.02 (and above).

3 The steps outlined were performed with WAS V5.1.04. Some of the steps outlined for the backup and restore of the WSGW do not function correctly in earlier versions of WAS V5.1.

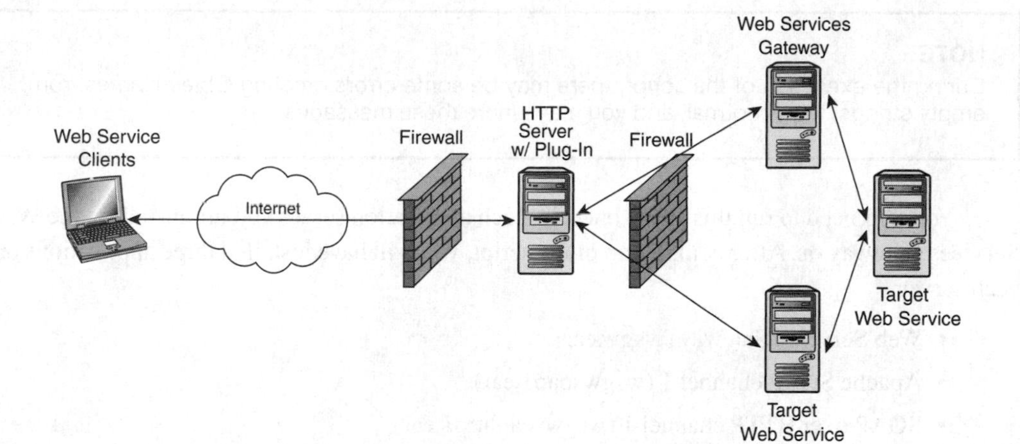


**Figure D-2** Web Services Gateway cluster.

## Web Services Gateway and Channel Installation

Installation of the J2EE enterprise applications that implement the Web Services Gateway as well as the associated channel(s)[4] is easiest to perform using a wsadmin script, setupWSGW.jacl, that comes with WAS-ND, though it can also be accomplished using the admin console. Assuming that you included the Web Services Gateway as part of your WAS-ND install,[5] that you've created the application servers on which you intend to deploy the WSGW, and that the WAS deployment manager and node agent(s) are running, you would navigate to the deploymentmanagerroot\WSGW\scripts\install directory, set the OS shell PATH variable to include the deploymentmanagerroot\bin directory, allowing execution of wsadmin, and then execute the code shown in Code Snippet D-1 from the OS command shell.

**Code Snippet D-1** Web Services Gateway install using wsadmin

```
wsadmin -f setupWSGW.jacl deploymentmanagerroot servername nodename
# example on Windows
# "wsadmin -f setupWSGW.jacl C:/WAS51/DeploymentManager server1 node1
# note you MUST use forward slashes "/" even on Windows
```

Here, deploymentmanagerroot is the directory that WAS-ND was installed to, servername is the name of the server you are installing the WSGW to, and nodename is the name of the WAS-ND node that the server is located on.

4 Channels carry requests and responses between Web services and the Web Services Gateway. When a request to the WSGW arrives through a channel, it is translated into a WSIF message, sent through any filters that are registered for the requested service, and finally passed on to the service implementation. Responses follow the same flow in reverse.

5 The install of the Web Services Gateway components is an option during the WAS-ND install. If you didn't select the WSGW components during your initial WAS-ND install, you will need to rerun the install, but you will only need to specify that the WSGW components be installed. You will need to reinstall any fixpacks as well.

> **NOTE**
> During the execution of the script, there may be some errors creating ObjectNames from empty strings; this is normal, and you may ignore these messages.

You will need to run this script once for each application server you are installing the Web Services Gateway on. After completion of the script, you will have installed three applications on each server:

- Web Services Gateway (wsgw.ear)
- Apache SOAP channel 1 (wsgwsoap1.ear)
- SOAP over HTTP channel 1 (wsgwsoaphttp1.ear)

Successful installation of the WSGW applications will result in the message shown in Code Snippet D-2 in the OS command shell (with an appropriate value for the servername parameter).

**Code Snippet D-2 Message indicating successful WSGW install**

```
GWIN0052I: WSGW successfully installed. Please restart server
➥servername to activate configuration changes. Value is:
➥servername=server1a
```

The results of executing the script twice, once for server1 and once for server1a, both located on the node sonoma, is depicted in Figure D-3. You'll notice that the installed application name is of the form applicationname.servername.nodename; this is the default behavior for the supplied script. This default overcomes the restriction in WAS-ND that precludes the installation of a given application name more than once in a non-clustered environment.

Before closing the admin console application, there is one key additional task that you'll need to perform for each application server that the WSGW is running on—adding a classloader on each application server, which points to WebSphere Shared Library that contains the Web service-specific Web services client classes[6] (e.g., the generated client stubs). If you don't perform this step, you'll encounter java.lang.ClassNotFoundException errors during configuration of the WSGW. An example error is depicted in Code Snippet D-3.

6 If you're not familiar with WebSphere Shared Libraries and classloaders, you might want to refer to Chapter 5 before proceeding. An alternative would be to add the JAR file containing the web service client classes to the wasinstall-root/lib/ext directory, which would make the client classes available to all server processes running on a node. This is not recommended since you can avoid class implementation conflicts by configuring a classloader specific to each application server.

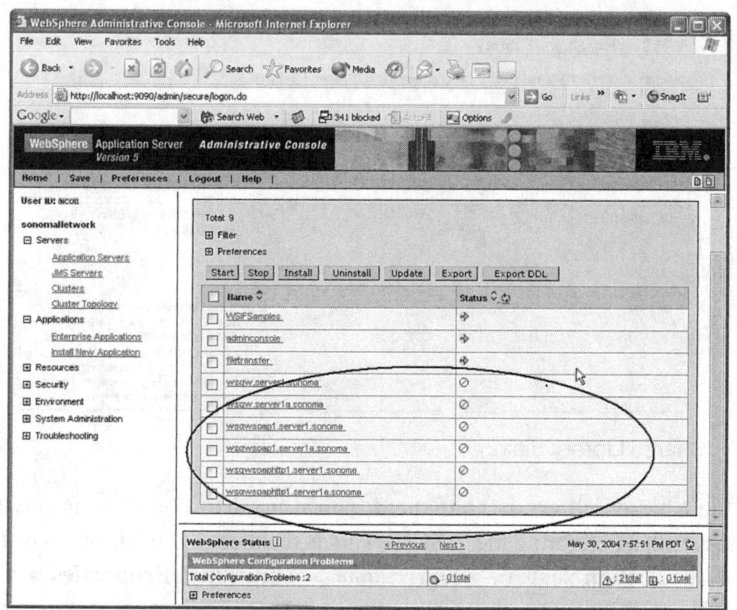

**Figure D-3** Installed Web Services Gateway applications in admin console.

**Code Snippet D-3** Example ClassNotFoundException

```
5/30/04 21:01:52:075 PDT] 7c785289 WSDDPort        E com.ibm.ws.
➥webservices.engine.deployment.wsdd.WSDDPort  TRAS0014I: The
➥following exception was logged java.lang.ClassNotFoundException:
➥wsifsales.addressbook.types.WSIFPhone
  at java.net.URLClassLoader.findClass(URLClassLoader.java(Compiled
  ➥Code))
  at  com.ibm.ws.bootstrap.ExtClassLoader.findClass
  ➥(ExtClassLoader.java(Compiled Code))
  at java.lang.ClassLoader.loadClass(ClassLoader.java(Compiled Code))
  at java.lang.ClassLoader.loadClass(ClassLoader.java(Compiled Code))
  at java.lang.Class.forName0(Native Method)
  at java.lang.Class.forName(Class.java:256)
  at com.ibm.ws.webservices.engine.utils.ClassUtils$2.run
  ➥(ClassUtils.java:239)
```

To add a Shared Library, navigate to the Shared Library dialog in the admin console **Environment > Shared Libraries** and select **New**. The resulting dialog is shown in Figure D-4, which shows a Shared Library named WebServicesSharedLibrary with a classpath value that corresponds to the directory where the Web services client JARs for your Web services are located.

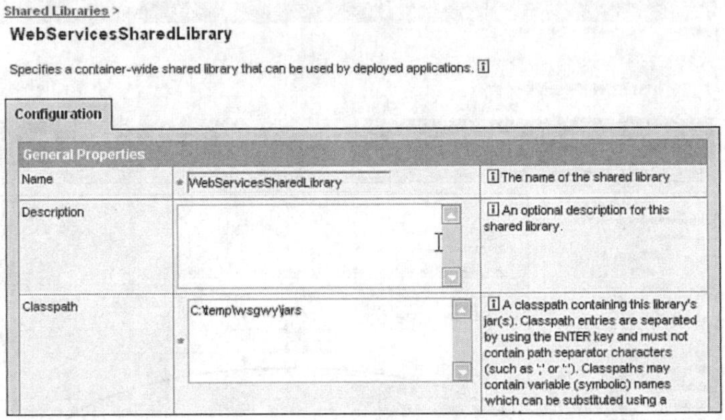

Figure D-4 Shared Library dialog.

Once the Shared Library is configured, you'll need to configure a classloader for each application server that is running the WSGW. This is reached in the admin console by navigating to **Servers > Application servers >** ***servername*** **> Additional Properties > Classloader** and then selecting **New**. This will create a unique classloader. Once that occurs, select the classloader in the classloader selection dialog (see Figure D-5), which will bring up the classloader configuration dialog. From that dialog, select **Libraries** on the **Additional Properties** to bring up the dialog for adding and removing Shared Libraries to the classloader. Select **Add** to bring up the Library selection dialog depicted in Figure D-6. Using the pull-down menu, select the Shared Library you just created and then click **OK** or **Apply**. Repeat the steps for each application server that you're running the WSGW on, and be sure to save the configuration changes when you're finished.

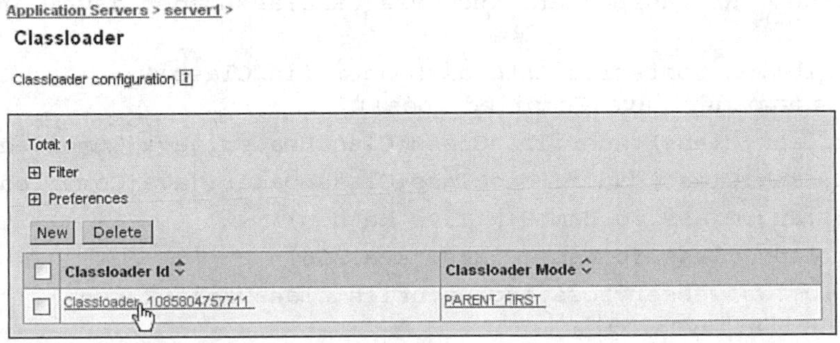

Figure D-5 Classloader selection dialog.

Application Servers > server1 > Classloader >

New

Library References specify one or more shared libraries used by this application.

Configuration

General Properties

Library Name | WebServicesSharedLibrary | The name of a shared library that has been defined in the one of the shared library configuration documents.

Apply | OK | Reset | Cancel

**Figure D-6** Library Name selection dialog.

Now that you have completed these steps, the WSGW has access at runtime to the client stubs it needs to contact your existing Web services. Obviously, if you update the Web services in the future, you'll need to update these JAR files with the latest versions of the client stubs.

## Web Services Gateway and Channel Configuration

Configuration of the WSGW and the associated channels is accomplished in the administrative portion of the wsgw.ear application. This requires that the application server that the WSGW is installed in be started. Once the application server (and application) is started, the administrative portion of the WSGW is accessed from a web browser with the URL http://hostname:portnumber/wsgw/, where hostname is the host that the application server is running on and portnumber is the HTTP transport for the web container in the application server. This is depicted in Figure D-7.

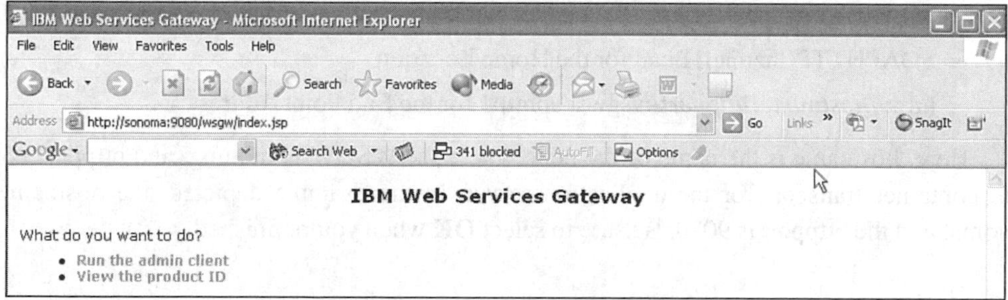


**Figure D-7** Web Services Gateway browser application client.

Selecting **Run the admin client** brings up the WSGW administration client, as shown in Figure D-8.

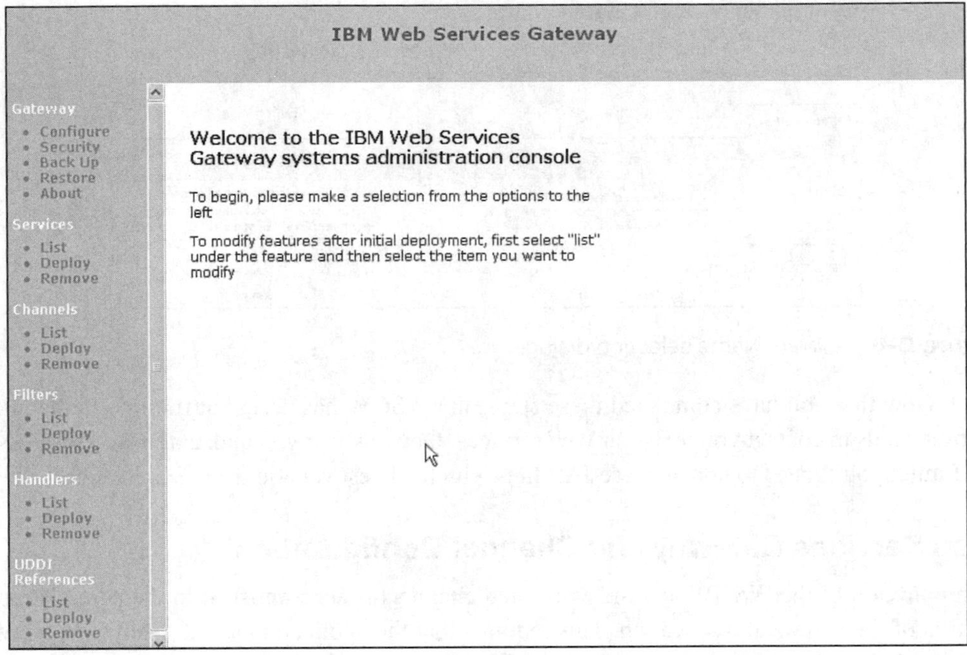


**Figure D-8** Web Services Gateway administration console.

First, you'll need to deploy a channel for the gateway to use. Select **Channels > Deploy**, which will bring up the dialog shown in Figure D-9. Enter the following values:[7]

- SOAPHTTPChannel1 for the Channel Name
- SOAPHTTPChannel1Bean for the Home Location
- http://***hostname:httpport***/wsgwsoaphttp1 for the End Point Address

Here, hostname is the name of the node where the WSGW is running, and httpport is the web container transport for the application server. In the example depicted, the hostname is sonoma, and the httpport is 9080. Be sure to select **OK** when you're finished.

7 The specific values required when deploying a channel depend on which of the four WebSphere supplied channels are installed. Refer to the article "Installing the Gateway Supplied Channels" in the WAS Info Center [WAS] for more information.

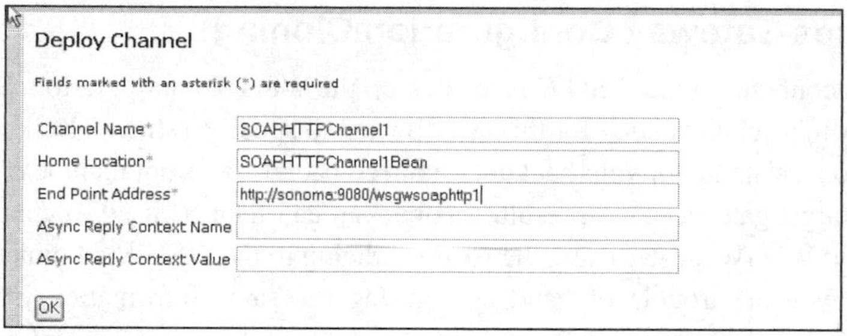

Deploy Channel

Fields marked with an asterisk (*) are required

| | |
|---|---|
| Channel Name* | SOAPHTTPChannel1 |
| Home Location* | SOAPHTTPChannel1Bean |
| End Point Address* | http://sonoma:9080/wsgwsoaphttp1 |
| Async Reply Context Name | |
| Async Reply Context Value | |

OK

**Figure D-9** Channel deployment dialog.

Once you've deployed a channel, you are ready to deploy the Web service in the gateway. This is accomplished by selecting **Deploy** under **Services**. The resulting dialog is shown in Figure D-10. At a minimum, you'll need to enter a **Gateway Service Name** for your Web service, **Message Part Representation**, and **WSDL Location** and **Location Type**. The first two properties will depend on the application and its associated WSDL. The second two properties will depend on where and how the target Web service is deployed to and corresponds to the "Internal WSDL" shown in Figure D-1. In this case, the Web service is deployed to an application server running on the node sonoma on port 9083.[8]

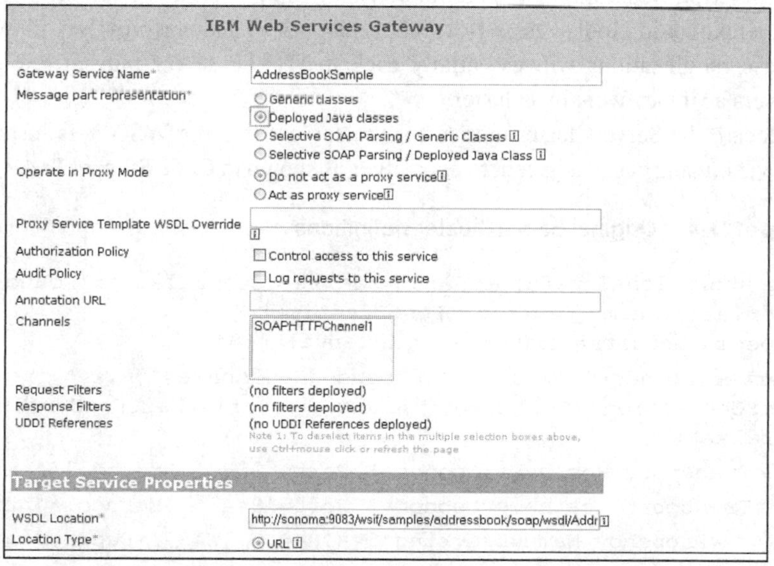

IBM Web Services Gateway

| | |
|---|---|
| Gateway Service Name* | AddressBookSample |
| Message part representation* | ○ Generic classes<br>◉ Deployed Java classes<br>○ Selective SOAP Parsing / Generic Classes<br>○ Selective SOAP Parsing / Deployed Java Class |
| Operate in Proxy Mode | ◉ Do not act as a proxy service<br>○ Act as proxy service |
| Proxy Service Template WSDL Override | |
| Authorization Policy | ☐ Control access to this service |
| Audit Policy | ☐ Log requests to this service |
| Annotation URL | |
| Channels | SOAPHTTPChannel1 |
| Request Filters | (no filters deployed) |
| Response Filters | (no filters deployed) |
| UDDI References | (no UDDI References deployed) |

Note 1: To deselect items in the multiple selection boxes above, use Ctrl+mouse click or refresh the page

Target Service Properties

| | |
|---|---|
| WSDL Location* | http://sonoma:9083/wsif/samples/addressbook/soap/wsdl/Addr |
| Location Type* | ◉ URL |

**Figure D-10** Web services deployment dialog.

8 In the case of a Location Type URL, the target application server and web service application must be running when configuring the WSGW. If Location Type were UDDI, then the UDDI registry would need to be configured for the web service and running.

## Web Services Gateway Configuration Cloning

The last step in configuring the WSGW is to back up the WSGW configuration. Select **Back Up** under **Gateway** to reach the dialog for this. You'll want to specify a **shared** backup and specify a valid file location and name for your backup. A **shared** backup does not include machine-specific values for the target gateways; as a result, this backup can then be used to configure the other gateways in your WSGW cluster using the **Restore** dialog in the WSGW administration console. This will save you the trouble of hand configuring the same information in every WSGW instance.

Once you've created a backup, navigate to the administration console on the other server(s) in your Web Services Gateway cluster and **restore** the configuration from the backup. Validate the configuration in each of the gateways and restart the application servers.

## HTTP Server Plug-In Configuration

The last step in creating a WSGW cluster involves modifying the plugin-cfg.xml file used by the HTTP server plug-in to reflect the implicit server cluster you've just created[9] by consolidating the multiple ServerCluster entries that exist for each application server running the WSGW into a single ServerCluster entry. Start by generating a new HTTP server plug-in, using either the genPluginCfg script, wsadmin, or the admin console. Once you have a new configuration file, open it with a text-editing tool such as Notepad, Emacs, or vi and perform the following modifications. These modifications will essentially trick the HTTP server plug-in into treating the WSGW servers as if they were in a cluster.

First locate the ServerCluster entries for the servers that the WSGW is installed on and place them, via cut and paste, adjacent to each other as shown in Code Snippet D-4.

**Code Snippet D-4** Original ServerCluster definitions

```
<ServerCluster CloneSeparatorChange="false" LoadBalance="Round Robin"
➥Name="server1_sonoma_Cluster" PostSizeLimit="-1"
➥RemoveSpecialHeaders="true" RetryInterval="60">
      <Server ConnectTimeout="0" ExtendedHandshake="false"
      ➥MaxConnections="-1" Name="sonoma_server1" WaitForContinue=
      ➥"false">
         <Transport Hostname="sonoma" Port="9080" Protocol="http"/>
         <Transport Hostname="sonoma" Port="9443" Protocol="https">
            <Property Name="keyring" Value="C:\WAS51\DeploymentManager\
            ➥etc\plugin-key.kdb"/>
            <Property Name="stashfile" Value="C:\WAS51\
            ➥DeploymentManager\etc\plugin-key.sth"/>
         </Transport>
```

9 You have not truly created a WAS cluster. Nothing in WAS realizes that the WSGW is part of a cluster. But, we want the HTTP server plug-in to treat the identical WSGWs as if they were a cluster. We do this here by modifying the plug-in configuration file.

```
      </Server>
      <PrimaryServers>
         <Server Name="sonoma_server1"/>
      </PrimaryServers>
   </ServerCluster>
   <ServerCluster CloneSeparatorChange="false" LoadBalance="Round
   ➥Robin" Name="server1a_sonoma_Cluster" PostSizeLimit="-1"
   ➥RemoveSpecialHeaders="true" RetryInterval="60">
      <Server ConnectTimeout="0" ExtendedHandshake="false"
      ➥MaxConnections="-1" Name="sonoma_server1a" WaitForContinue=
      ➥"false">
         <Transport Hostname="sonoma" Port="9084" Protocol="http"/>
         <Transport Hostname="sonoma" Port="9447" Protocol="https">
            <Property Name="keyring" Value="C:\WAS51\DeploymentManager\
            ➥etc\plugin-key.kdb"/>
            <Property Name="stashfile" Value="C:\WAS51\
            ➥DeploymentManager\etc\plugin-key.sth"/>
         </Transport>
      </Server>
      <PrimaryServers>
         <Server Name="sonoma_server1a"/>
      </PrimaryServers>
   </ServerCluster>
```

Second, delete the </ServerCluster> and <ServerCluster> entries that are lined through, as shown in Code Snippet D-5.

**Code Snippet D-5 ServerCluster entry deletion in plugin-cfg.xml**

```
<ServerCluster CloneSeparatorChange="false" LoadBalance="Round Robin"
➥Name="server1_sonoma_Cluster" PostSizeLimit="-1"
➥RemoveSpecialHeaders="true" RetryInterval="60">
      <Server ConnectTimeout="0" ExtendedHandshake="false"
      ➥MaxConnections="-1" Name="sonoma_server1"
      ➥WaitForContinue="false">
         <Transport Hostname="sonoma" Port="9080" Protocol="http"/>
         <Transport Hostname="sonoma" Port="9443" Protocol="https">
            <Property Name="keyring" Value="C:\WAS51\DeploymentManager\
            ➥etc\plugin-key.kdb"/>
            <Property Name="stashfile" Value="C:\WAS51\
            ➥DeploymentManager\etc\plugin-key.sth"/>
         </Transport>
      </Server>
      <PrimaryServers>
```

```
        <Server Name="sonoma_server1"/>
     </PrimaryServers>
  </ServerCluster>
  <ServerCluster CloneSeparatorChange="false" LoadBalance="Round
  ➥Robin" Name="server1a_sonoma_Cluster" PostSizeLimit="-1"
  ➥RemoveSpecialHeaders="true" RetryInterval="60">
     <Server ConnectTimeout="0" ExtendedHandshake="false"
     ➥MaxConnections="-1" Name="sonoma_server1a"
     ➥WaitForContinue="false">
        <Transport Hostname="sonoma" Port="9084" Protocol="http"/>
        <Transport Hostname="sonoma" Port="9447" Protocol="https">
           <Property Name="keyring" Value="C:\WAS51\DeploymentManager
           ➥\etc\plugin-key.kdb"/>
           <Property Name="stashfile" Value="C:\WAS51\
             ➥DeploymentManager\etc\plugin-key.sth"/>
        </Transport>
     </Server>
     <PrimaryServers>
        <Server Name="sonoma_server1a"/>
     </PrimaryServers>
  </ServerCluster>
```

Third, delete the first <PrimaryServers> and </PrimaryServers> entry, as shown in Code Snippet D-6, and add the Server Name entry from the deleted PrimaryServers entry to the remaining PrimaryServers entry for the ServerCluster.

**Code Snippet D-6** PrimaryServer entry deletion and movement

```
<ServerCluster CloneSeparatorChange="false" LoadBalance="Round Robin"
➥Name="server1_sonoma_Cluster" PostSizeLimit="-1"
➥RemoveSpecialHeaders="true" RetryInterval="60">
     <Server ConnectTimeout="0" ExtendedHandshake="false"
     ➥MaxConnections="-1" Name="sonoma_server1"
     ➥WaitForContinue="false">
        <Transport Hostname="sonoma" Port="9080" Protocol="http"/>
        <Transport Hostname="sonoma" Port="9443" Protocol="https">
           <Property Name="keyring" Value="C:\WAS51\DeploymentManager\
           ➥etc\plugin-key.kdb"/>
           <Property Name="stashfile" Value="C:\WAS51\
           ➥DeploymentManager\etc\plugin-key.sth"/>
        </Transport>
     </Server>
     <PrimaryServers>
```

```
        <Server Name="sonoma_server1"/>
    </PrimaryServers>
    <Server ConnectTimeout="0" ExtendedHandshake="false"
    ➥MaxConnections="-1" Name="sonoma_server1a"
    ➥WaitForContinue="false">
        <Transport Hostname="sonoma" Port="9084" Protocol="http"/>
        <Transport Hostname="sonoma" Port="9447" Protocol="https">
            <Property Name="keyring" Value="C:\WAS51\DeploymentManager\
            ➥etc\plugin-key.kdb"/>
            <Property Name="stashfile" Value="C:\WAS51\
            ➥DeploymentManager\etc\plugin-key.sth"/>
        </Transport>
    </Server>
    <PrimaryServers>
        <Server Name="sonoma_server1"/>
        <Server Name="sonoma_server1a"/>
    </PrimaryServers>
</ServerCluster>
```

Fourth, add a CloneID parameter and a LoadBalanceWeight parameter to each Server entry in the ServerCluster, as shown in Code Snippet D-7. The value for CloneID should be a unique value for each server. Since WAS normally generates a random 7 character value for this purpose, we also use 7 character values. The value for LoadBalanceWeight should typically be the same for each server, with the default of 2 used here. Refer to Chapter 21 for a discussion of possible values and the implications of different values.

**Code Snippet D-7** Plugin-cfg.xml with CloneID and LoadBalanceWeight added

```
<ServerCluster CloneSeparatorChange="false" LoadBalance="Round Robin"
➥Name="server1_sonoma_Cluster" PostSizeLimit="-1"
➥RemoveSpecialHeaders="true" RetryInterval="60">
    <Server CloneID="random1" ConnectTimeout="0"
    ➥ExtendedHandshake="false" LoadBalanceWeight="2"
    ➥MaxConnections="-1" Name="sonoma_server1"
    ➥WaitForContinue="false">
        <Transport Hostname="sonoma" Port="9080" Protocol="http"/>
        <Transport Hostname="sonoma" Port="9443" Protocol="https">
            <Property Name="keyring" Value="C:\WAS51\DeploymentManager\
            ➥etc\plugin-key.kdb"/>
            <Property Name="stashfile" Value="C:\WAS51\
            ➥DeploymentManager\etc\plugin-key.sth"/>
        </Transport>
    </Server>
```

```
    <Server CloneID="random2" ConnectTimeout="0" ExtendedHandshake=
    ➥"false" LoadBalanceWeight="2" MaxConnections="-1" Name=
    ➥"sonoma_server1a" WaitForContinue="false">
       <Transport Hostname="sonoma" Port="9084" Protocol="http"/>
       <Transport Hostname="sonoma" Port="9447" Protocol="https">
          <Property Name="keyring" Value="C:\WAS51\DeploymentManager\
          ➥etc\plugin-key.kdb"/>
          <Property Name="stashfile" Value="C:\WAS51\
          ➥DeploymentManager\etc\plugin-key.sth"/>
       </Transport>
    </Server>
    <PrimaryServers>
       <Server Name="sonoma_server1"/>
       <Server Name="sonoma_server1a"/>
    </PrimaryServers>
 </ServerCluster>
```

The last step is to delete the duplicate Route ServerCluster and URIGroup entries, as shown in Code Snippet D-8. These are the entries that correspond to the ServerCluster entry that was deleted in the second step. In this case the entries for server1a were deleted since we created a combined ServerCluster for server1 and server1a with the name of server1_sonoma_Cluster.

**Code Snippet D-8** Duplicate Route ServerCluster and UriGroup entries

```
<Route ServerCluster="server1a_sonoma_Cluster"
➥UriGroup="default_host_server1a_sonoma_Cluster_URIs"
➥VirtualHostGroup="default_host"/>
   <UriGroup Name="default_host_server2_sonoma_Cluster_URIs">
      <Uri AffinityCookie="JSESSIONID" AffinityURLIdentifier=
      ➥"jsessionid" Name="/wsif/samples/addressbook/soap/*"/>
      <Uri AffinityCookie="JSESSIONID" AffinityURLIdentifier=
      ➥"jsessionid" Name="/wsif/samples/addressbook/soap/servlet/*"/>
      <Uri AffinityCookie="JSESSIONID" AffinityURLIdentifier=
      ➥"jsessionid" Name="/wsif/samples/stockquote/soap/*"/>
      <Uri AffinityCookie="JSESSIONID" AffinityURLIdentifier=
      ➥"jsessionid" Name="/wsif/samples/stockquote/soap/servlet/*"/>
      <Uri AffinityCookie="JSESSIONID" AffinityURLIdentifier=
      ➥"jsessionid" Name="/wsif/samples/info/*"/>
      <Uri AffinityCookie="JSESSIONID" AffinityURLIdentifier=
      ➥"jsessionid" Name="/wsif/samples/infoservlet/*"/>
   </UriGroup>
```

Save the plugin-cfg.xml file and distribute it to each of the HTTP servers. For reference, complete copies of the "before" and "after" (modification) plugin-cfg.xml files are in provided in Code Snippets D-10 and D-11.

At this point, you're ready to invoke your Web service, pointing it to the HTTP server address. The plug-in will distribute the requests to the WSGW, and the WSGW will in turn send the request to the application server(s) running the Web service. An example Web service invocation is show in Code Snippet D-9. In this case, the Web service is a Java client.

**Code Snippet D-9** Example Web services invocation

```
C:\temp\wsgwy>launchclient WSIFSamples.ear -CCjar=AddressBookClient.jar
➥-W=http://sonoma:80/wsgw/ServiceDefinition?name=AddressBookSample
```

**Code Snippet D-10** Unmodified plugin-cfg.xml file

```
<?xml version="1.0" encoding="ISO-8859-1"?>

<Config ASDisableNagle="false" AcceptAllContent="false"
➥AppServerPortPreference="HostHeader" ChunkedResponse="false"
➥IISDisableNagle="false" IISPluginPriority="High"
➥IgnoreDNSFailures="false" RefreshInterval="60" ResponseChunkSize="64"
➥VHostMatchingCompat="false">
   <Log LogLevel="Error" Name="C:\WAS51\DeploymentManager\
   ➥logs\http_plugin.log"/>
   <Property Name="ESIEnable" Value="true"/>
   <Property Name="ESIMaxCacheSize" Value="1024"/>
   <Property Name="ESIInvalidationMonitor" Value="false"/>
   <VirtualHostGroup Name="default_host">
      <VirtualHost Name="*:9080"/>
      <VirtualHost Name="*:80"/>
      <VirtualHost Name="*:9443"/>
      <VirtualHost Name="*:9081"/>
      <VirtualHost Name="*:9446"/>
      <VirtualHost Name="*:9082"/>
      <VirtualHost Name="*:9083"/>
      <VirtualHost Name="*:9444"/>
      <VirtualHost Name="*:9445"/>
      <VirtualHost Name="*:9084"/>
      <VirtualHost Name="*:9447"/>
   </VirtualHostGroup>
```

```
<ServerCluster CloneSeparatorChange="false" LoadBalance="Round
➥Robin" Name="testcluster" PostSizeLimit="-1" RemoveSpecialHeaders=
➥"true" RetryInterval="60">
   <Server CloneID="vivjbv6d" ConnectTimeout="0" ExtendedHandshake=
   ➥"false" LoadBalanceWeight="2" MaxConnections="-1" Name="
   ➥sonoma_clusterserver1" WaitForContinue="false">
      <Transport Hostname="sonoma" Port="9081" Protocol="http"/>
      <Transport Hostname="sonoma" Port="9444" Protocol="https">
         <Property Name="keyring" Value="C:\WAS51\DeploymentManager\
         ➥etc\plugin-key.kdb"/>
         <Property Name="stashfile" Value="C:\WAS51\
         ➥DeploymentManager\etc\plugin-key.sth"/>
      </Transport>
   </Server>
   <Server CloneID="vivjbvs0" ConnectTimeout="0" ExtendedHandshake=
   ➥"false" LoadBalanceWeight="2" MaxConnections="-1" Name=
   ➥"sonoma_clusterserver2" WaitForContinue="false">
      <Transport Hostname="sonoma" Port="9082" Protocol="http"/>
      <Transport Hostname="sonoma" Port="9445" Protocol="https">
         <Property Name="keyring" Value="C:\WAS51\
         ➥DeploymentManager\etc\plugin-key.kdb"/>
         <Property Name="stashfile" Value="C:\WAS51\
         ➥DeploymentManager\etc\plugin-key.sth"/>
      </Transport>
   </Server>
   <PrimaryServers>
      <Server Name="sonoma_clusterserver1"/>
      <Server Name="sonoma_clusterserver2"/>
   </PrimaryServers>
</ServerCluster>
<ServerCluster CloneSeparatorChange="false" LoadBalance="Round
➥Robin" Name="server1_sonoma_Cluster" PostSizeLimit="-1"
RemoveSpecialHeaders="true" RetryInterval="60">
   <Server ConnectTimeout="0" ExtendedHandshake="false"
   ➥MaxConnections="-1" Name="sonoma_server1"
   ➥WaitForContinue="false">
      <Transport Hostname="sonoma" Port="9080" Protocol="http"/>
      <Transport Hostname="sonoma" Port="9443" Protocol="https">
         <Property Name="keyring" Value="C:\WAS51\DeploymentManager\
         ➥etc\plugin-key.kdb"/>
         <Property Name="stashfile" Value="C:\WAS51\
         ➥DeploymentManager\etc\plugin-key.sth"/>
```

```
        </Transport>
    </Server>
    <PrimaryServers>
        <Server Name="sonoma_server1"/>
    </PrimaryServers>
</ServerCluster>
<ServerCluster CloneSeparatorChange="false" LoadBalance="Round
➥Robin" Name="server2_sonoma_Cluster" PostSizeLimit="-1"
➥RemoveSpecialHeaders="true" RetryInterval="60">
    <Server ConnectTimeout="0" ExtendedHandshake="false"
    ➥MaxConnections="-1" Name="sonoma_server2"
    ➥WaitForContinue="false">
        <Transport Hostname="sonoma" Port="9083" Protocol="http"/>
        <Transport Hostname="sonoma" Port="9446" Protocol="https">
            <Property Name="keyring" Value="C:\WAS51\
            ➥DeploymentManager\etc\plugin-key.kdb"/>
            <Property Name="stashfile" Value="C:\WAS51\
            ➥DeploymentManager\etc\plugin-key.sth"/>
        </Transport>
    </Server>
    <PrimaryServers>
        <Server Name="sonoma_server2"/>
    </PrimaryServers>
</ServerCluster>
<ServerCluster CloneSeparatorChange="false" LoadBalance="Round
➥Robin" Name="server1a_sonoma_Cluster" PostSizeLimit="-1"
➥RemoveSpecialHeaders="true" RetryInterval="60">
    <Server ConnectTimeout="0" ExtendedHandshake="false"
    ➥MaxConnections="-1" Name="sonoma_server1a"
    ➥WaitForContinue="false">
        <Transport Hostname="sonoma" Port="9084" Protocol="http"/>
        <Transport Hostname="sonoma" Port="9447" Protocol="https">
            <Property Name="keyring" Value="C:\WAS51\
            ➥DeploymentManager\etc\plugin-key.kdb"/>
            <Property Name="stashfile" Value="C:\WAS51\
            ➥DeploymentManager\etc\plugin-key.sth"/>
        </Transport>
    </Server>
    <PrimaryServers>
        <Server Name="sonoma_server1a"/>
    </PrimaryServers>
</ServerCluster>
```

```
<ServerCluster CloneSeparatorChange="false" LoadBalance="Round
➥Robin" Name="dmgr_sonomaManager_Cluster" PostSizeLimit="-1"
➥RemoveSpecialHeaders="true" RetryInterval="60">
   <Server ConnectTimeout="0" ExtendedHandshake="false"
   ➥MaxConnections="-1" Name="sonomaManager_dmgr"
   ➥WaitForContinue="false"/>
   <PrimaryServers>
      <Server Name="sonomaManager_dmgr"/>
   </PrimaryServers>
</ServerCluster>
<UriGroup Name="default_host_server1a_sonoma_Cluster_URIs">
   <Uri AffinityCookie="JSESSIONID" AffinityURLIdentifier=
   ➥"jsessionid" Name="/wsgw/*"/>
   <Uri AffinityCookie="JSESSIONID" AffinityURLIdentifier=
   ➥"jsessionid" Name="/wsgwservlet/*"/>
   <Uri AffinityCookie="JSESSIONID" AffinityURLIdentifier=
   ➥"jsessionid" Name="/wsgwsoap1/*"/>
   <Uri AffinityCookie="JSESSIONID" AffinityURLIdentifier=
   ➥"jsessionid" Name="/wsgwsoap1servlet/*"/>
   <Uri AffinityCookie="JSESSIONID" AffinityURLIdentifier=
   ➥"jsessionid" Name="/wsgwsoaphttp1/*"/>
   <Uri AffinityCookie="JSESSIONID" AffinityURLIdentifier=
   ➥"jsessionid" Name="/wsgwsoaphttp1servlet/*"/>
</UriGroup>
<Route ServerCluster="server1a_sonoma_Cluster"
➥UriGroup="default_host_server1a_sonoma_Cluster_URIs"
➥VirtualHostGroup="default_host"/>
<UriGroup Name="default_host_server2_sonoma_Cluster_URIs">
   <Uri AffinityCookie="JSESSIONID" AffinityURLIdentifier=
   ➥"jsessionid" Name="/wsif/samples/addressbook/soap/*"/>
   <Uri AffinityCookie="JSESSIONID" AffinityURLIdentifier=
   ➥"jsessionid" Name="/wsif/samples/addressbook/soap/servlet/*"/>
   <Uri AffinityCookie="JSESSIONID" AffinityURLIdentifier=
   ➥"jsessionid" Name="/wsif/samples/stockquote/soap/*"/>
   <Uri AffinityCookie="JSESSIONID" AffinityURLIdentifier=
   ➥"jsessionid" Name="/wsif/samples/stockquote/soap/servlet/*"/>
   <Uri AffinityCookie="JSESSIONID" AffinityURLIdentifier=
   ➥"jsessionid" Name="/wsif/samples/info/*"/>
   <Uri AffinityCookie="JSESSIONID" AffinityURLIdentifier=
   ➥"jsessionid" Name="/wsif/samples/infoservlet/*"/>
</UriGroup>
<Route ServerCluster="server2_sonoma_Cluster" UriGroup=
➥"default_host_server2_sonoma_Cluster_URIs" VirtualHostGroup=
➥"default_host"/>
```

```
   <UriGroup Name="default_host_server1_sonoma_Cluster_URIs">
      <Uri AffinityCookie="JSESSIONID" AffinityURLIdentifier=
      ➥"jsessionid" Name="/wsgw/*"/>
      <Uri AffinityCookie="JSESSIONID" AffinityURLIdentifier=
      ➥"jsessionid" Name="/wsgwservlet/*"/>
      <Uri AffinityCookie="JSESSIONID" AffinityURLIdentifier=
      ➥"jsessionid" Name="/wsgwsoap1/*"/>
      <Uri AffinityCookie="JSESSIONID" AffinityURLIdentifier=
      ➥"jsessionid" Name="/wsgwsoap1servlet/*"/>
      <Uri AffinityCookie="JSESSIONID" AffinityURLIdentifier=
      ➥"jsessionid" Name="/wsgwsoaphttp1/*"/>
      <Uri AffinityCookie="JSESSIONID" AffinityURLIdentifier=
      ➥"jsessionid" Name="/wsgwsoaphttp1servlet/*"/>
   </UriGroup>
   <Route ServerCluster="server1_sonoma_Cluster" UriGroup=
   ➥"default_host_server1_sonoma_Cluster_URIs" VirtualHostGroup=
   ➥"default_host"/>
   <RequestMetrics armEnabled="false" newBehavior="false" rmEnabled=
   ➥"false" traceLevel="HOPS">
      <filters enable="false" type="URI">
         <filterValues enable="false" value="/servlet/snoop"/>
         <filterValues enable="false" value="/webapp/examples/
         ➥HitCount"/>
      </filters>
      <filters enable="false" type="SOURCE_IP">
         <filterValues enable="false" value="255.255.255.255"/>
         <filterValues enable="false" value="254.254.254.254"/>
      </filters>
   </RequestMetrics>
</Config>
```

**Code Snippet D-11** Modified plugin-cfg.xml file

```
<?xml version="1.0" encoding="ISO-8859-1"?>

<Config ASDisableNagle="false" AcceptAllContent="false"
➥AppServerPortPreference="HostHeader" ChunkedResponse="false"
➥IISDisableNagle="false" IISPluginPriority="High"
➥IgnoreDNSFailures="false" RefreshInterval="60" ResponseChunkSize="64"
➥VHostMatchingCompat="false">
   <Log LogLevel="Error"
Name="C:\WAS51\DeploymentManager\logs\http_plugin.log"/>
```

```
<Property Name="ESIEnable" Value="true"/>
<Property Name="ESIMaxCacheSize" Value="1024"/>
<Property Name="ESIInvalidationMonitor" Value="false"/>
<VirtualHostGroup Name="default_host">
   <VirtualHost Name="*:9080"/>
   <VirtualHost Name="*:80"/>
   <VirtualHost Name="*:9443"/>
   <VirtualHost Name="*:9081"/>
   <VirtualHost Name="*:9446"/>
   <VirtualHost Name="*:9082"/>
   <VirtualHost Name="*:9083"/>
   <VirtualHost Name="*:9444"/>
   <VirtualHost Name="*:9445"/>
   <VirtualHost Name="*:9084"/>
   <VirtualHost Name="*:9447"/>
</VirtualHostGroup>
<ServerCluster CloneSeparatorChange="false" LoadBalance="Round
➥Robin" Name="testcluster" PostSizeLimit="-1"
➥RemoveSpecialHeaders="true" RetryInterval="60">
   <Server CloneID="vivjbv6d" ConnectTimeout="0" ExtendedHandshake=
   ➥"false" LoadBalanceWeight="2" MaxConnections="-1" Name=
   ➥"sonoma_clusterserver1" WaitForContinue="false">
      <Transport Hostname="sonoma" Port="9081" Protocol="http"/>
      <Transport Hostname="sonoma" Port="9444" Protocol="https">
         <Property Name="keyring" Value="C:\WAS51\DeploymentManager
         ➥\etc\plugin-key.kdb"/>
         <Property Name="stashfile" Value="C:\WAS51\
         ➥DeploymentManager\etc\plugin-key.sth"/>
      </Transport>
   </Server>
   <Server CloneID="vivjbvs0" ConnectTimeout="0" ExtendedHandshake=
   ➥"false" LoadBalanceWeight="2" MaxConnections="-1" Name=
   ➥"sonoma_clusterserver2" WaitForContinue="false">
      <Transport Hostname="sonoma" Port="9082" Protocol="http"/>
      <Transport Hostname="sonoma" Port="9445" Protocol="https">
         <Property Name="keyring" Value="C:\WAS51\
         ➥DeploymentManager\etc\plugin-key.kdb"/>
         <Property Name="stashfile" Value="C:\WAS51\
         ➥DeploymentManager\etc\plugin-key.sth"/>
      </Transport>
   </Server>
   <PrimaryServers>
```

```
            <Server Name="sonoma_clusterserver1"/>
            <Server Name="sonoma_clusterserver2"/>
         </PrimaryServers>
   </ServerCluster>
   <ServerCluster CloneSeparatorChange="false" LoadBalance="Round
➥Robin" Name="server1_sonoma_Cluster" PostSizeLimit="-1"
➥RemoveSpecialHeaders="true" RetryInterval="60">
      <Server CloneID="random1" ConnectTimeout="0"
      ➥ExtendedHandshake="false" LoadBalanceWeight="2"
      ➥MaxConnections="-1" Name="sonoma_server1" WaitForContinue=
      ➥"false">
         <Transport Hostname="sonoma" Port="9080" Protocol="http"/>
         <Transport Hostname="sonoma" Port="9443" Protocol="https">
            <Property Name="keyring" Value="C:\WAS51\
            ➥DeploymentManager\etc\plugin-key.kdb"/>
            <Property Name="stashfile" Value="C:\WAS51\
            ➥DeploymentManager\etc\plugin-key.sth"/>
         </Transport>
      </Server>
      <Server CloneID="random2" ConnectTimeout="0" ExtendedHandshake=
      ➥"false" LoadBalanceWeight="2" MaxConnections="-1" Name=
      ➥"sonoma_server1a" WaitForContinue="false">
         <Transport Hostname="sonoma" Port="9084" Protocol="http"/>
         <Transport Hostname="sonoma" Port="9447" Protocol="https">
            <Property Name="keyring" Value="C:\WAS51\
            ➥DeploymentManager\etc\plugin-key.kdb"/>
            <Property Name="stashfile" Value="C:\WAS51\
            ➥DeploymentManager\etc\plugin-key.sth"/>
         </Transport>
      </Server>
      <PrimaryServers>
         <Server Name="sonoma_server1"/>
         <Server Name="sonoma_server1a"/>
      </PrimaryServers>
   </ServerCluster>
   <ServerCluster CloneSeparatorChange="false" LoadBalance="Round
➥Robin" Name="server2_sonoma_Cluster" PostSizeLimit="-1"
➥RemoveSpecialHeaders="true" RetryInterval="60">
      <Server ConnectTimeout="0" ExtendedHandshake="false"
      ➥MaxConnections="-1" Name="sonoma_server2"
      ➥WaitForContinue="false">
         <Transport Hostname="sonoma" Port="9083" Protocol="http"/>
```

```
        <Transport Hostname="sonoma" Port="9446" Protocol="https">
            <Property Name="keyring" Value="C:\WAS51\DeploymentManager\
            ➥etc\plugin-key.kdb"/>
            <Property Name="stashfile" Value="C:\WAS51\
            ➥DeploymentManager\etc\plugin-key.sth"/>
        </Transport>
    </Server>
    <PrimaryServers>
        <Server Name="sonoma_server2"/>
    </PrimaryServers>
</ServerCluster>

<ServerCluster CloneSeparatorChange="false" LoadBalance="Round
➥Robin" Name="dmgr_sonomaManager_Cluster" PostSizeLimit="-1"
➥RemoveSpecialHeaders="true" RetryInterval="60">
    <Server ConnectTimeout="0" ExtendedHandshake="false"
    ➥MaxConnections="-1" Name="sonomaManager_dmgr"
    ➥WaitForContinue="false"/>
    <PrimaryServers>
        <Server Name="sonomaManager_dmgr"/>
    </PrimaryServers>
</ServerCluster>
    <UriGroup Name="default_host_server2_sonoma_Cluster_URIs">
    <Uri AffinityCookie="JSESSIONID" AffinityURLIdentifier=
    ➥"jsessionid" Name="/wsif/samples/addressbook/soap/*"/>
    <Uri AffinityCookie="JSESSIONID" AffinityURLIdentifier=
    ➥"jsessionid" Name="/wsif/samples/addressbook/soap/servlet/*"/>
    <Uri AffinityCookie="JSESSIONID" AffinityURLIdentifier=
    ➥"jsessionid" Name="/wsif/samples/stockquote/soap/*"/>
    <Uri AffinityCookie="JSESSIONID" AffinityURLIdentifier=
    ➥"jsessionid" Name="/wsif/samples/stockquote/soap/servlet/*"/>
    <Uri AffinityCookie="JSESSIONID" AffinityURLIdentifier=
    ➥"jsessionid" Name="/wsif/samples/info/*"/>
    <Uri AffinityCookie="JSESSIONID" AffinityURLIdentifier=
    ➥"jsessionid" Name="/wsif/samples/infoservlet/*"/>
</UriGroup>
<Route ServerCluster="server2_sonoma_Cluster" UriGroup=
➥"default_host_server2_sonoma_Cluster_URIs" VirtualHostGroup=
➥"default_host"/>
<UriGroup Name="default_host_server1_sonoma_Cluster_URIs">
    <Uri AffinityCookie="JSESSIONID" AffinityURLIdentifier=
    ➥"jsessionid" Name="/wsgw/*"/>
```

```
        <Uri AffinityCookie="JSESSIONID" AffinityURLIdentifier=
        ➥"jsessionid" Name="/wsgwservlet/*"/>
        <Uri AffinityCookie="JSESSIONID" AffinityURLIdentifier=
        ➥"jsessionid" Name="/wsgwsoap1/*"/>
        <Uri AffinityCookie="JSESSIONID" AffinityURLIdentifier=
        ➥"jsessionid" Name="/wsgwsoap1servlet/*"/>
        <Uri AffinityCookie="JSESSIONID" AffinityURLIdentifier=
        ➥"jsessionid" Name="/wsgwsoaphttp1/*"/>
        <Uri AffinityCookie="JSESSIONID" AffinityURLIdentifier=
        ➥"jsessionid" Name="/wsgwsoaphttp1servlet/*"/>
    </UriGroup>
    <Route ServerCluster="server1_sonoma_Cluster" UriGroup=
    ➥"default_host_server1_sonoma_Cluster_URIs" VirtualHostGroup=
    ➥"default_host"/>
    <RequestMetrics armEnabled="false" newBehavior="false"
    ➥rmEnabled="false" traceLevel="HOPS">
        <filters enable="false" type="URI">
            <filterValues enable="false" value="/servlet/snoop"/>
            <filterValues enable="false" value="/webapp/examples/
            ➥HitCount"/>
        </filters>
        <filters enable="false" type="SOURCE_IP">
            <filterValues enable="false" value="255.255.255.255"/>
            <filterValues enable="false" value="254.254.254.254"/>
        </filters>
    </RequestMetrics>
</Config>
```

## Conclusion

This Appendix describes how to create a clustered Web Services Gateway implementation in WAS V5.x. For more information related to specific Web Services Gateway configuration options, refer to the WebSphere V5 Info Center [WAS].

# References


| Reference Key | Reference Data |
|---|---|
| [Alcott 2003] | Implementing a Highly Available Infrastructure for WebSphere Application Server Network Deployment, Version 5.0 Without Clustering. http://www-106.ibm.com/developerworks/websphere/library/techarticles/0304_alcott/alcott.html |
| [Barcia 2003] | JMS Topologies and Configurations with WebSphere Application Server and WebSphere Studio Version 5. http://www-106.ibm.com/developerworks/websphere/library/techarticles/0310_barcia/barcia.html. By Roland Barcia, Sree Ratnasinghe, and Benedict Fernandes. IBM DeveloperWorks. |
| [Barcia 2004: JSF Series] | Developing JSF Applications Using WebSphere Studio. http://www-106.ibm.com/developerworks/websphere/techjournal/0401_barcia/barcia.html. IBM DeveloperWorks. |
| [Botzum 2000] | *Enterprise Application Security* by Keys Botzum. |
| [Botzum 2002] | IBM J2EE Packaging and Common Code. http://www-106.ibm.com/developerworks/websphere/library/techarticles/0207_botzum botzum.html. IBM DeveloperWorks. |
| [Branson and Hao 2003] | Server Clusters for High Availability in WebSphere Application Server Network Deployment Edition 5.0. http://www-1.ibm.com/support/docview.wss?rs=180%26context=SSCVS22%26uid=swg27002473 |
| [Brown and Botzum 2003] | Deploying Multiple Applications in J2EE. http://www-106.ibm.com/developerworks/java/library/j-deploy/. IBM DeveloperWorks. |
| [Brown 2002] | Handling Static Content in WebSphere Application Server 4.0. http://www7b.boulder.ibm.com/wsdd/techjournal/0211_brown/brown.html |

| Reference Key | Reference Data |
|---|---|
| [Brown 2004] | *Enterprise Java Programming with IBM WebSphere, Second Edition*. Addison-Wesley Professional; (December 2003). ISBN 0-321-18579-X. |
| [buffer overflow] | Larry Rodgers. Buffer Overflows—What Are They and What Can I Do About Them?. CERT, 2001. http://www.cert.org/homeusers/buffer_overflow.html |
| [Cavaness 2002] | Cavaness, Chuck. *Programming Jakarta Struts*. O'Reilly & Associates; (November 13, 2002). ISBN 0596003285. |
| [Cundiff 2003] | *System Administration for WebSphere Application Server V5—Part 2: Writing Your Own Administration Programs*. WebSphere Technical Journal; (February 2003). http://www-106.ibm.com/developerworks/websphere/techjournal/0302_cundiff/cundiff.html |
| [Cuomo 2000] | "IBM WebSphere Application Server Standard and Advanced Editions: A Methodology for Production Performance Tuning." IBM Whitepaper. © Copyright IBM Corp. 2000. |
| [Fowler 1999] | Fowler, Martin. *Refactoring: Improving the Design of Existing Code*. Reading, Mass: Addison-Wesley, 1999. ISBN 0-201-48567-2. |
| [Fowler 2003] | *Patterns of Enterprise Application Architecture*. Addison-Wesley; 1st edition (2003). ISBN 0-321-12742-0. |
| [Gang 2003] | WebSphere Distributed Transaction Support for a Generic JMS Provider. http://www-106.ibm.com/developerworks/websphere/library/tutorials/0309_chen/chen_reg.html. IBM DeveloperWorks. |
| [Hatcher 2003] | *Java Development with ANT*. Manning Publications Company; (August 2002). ISBN 1930110588. |
| [IBM WAS 5 Handbook] | IBM WebSphere Application Server V5.1 System Management and Configuration WebSphere Handbook Series. SG24-6195-01, IBM Corp, 2004. http://www.redbooks.ibm.com |
| [IBM WAS AIX PD] | Problem Determination Across Multiple WebSphere Products AIX Platform. SG24-7043-00, IBM Corp, 2004. http://www.redbooks.ibm.com |
| [IBM WAS Security Redbook] | IBM WebSphere 5.0 Security Redbook. SG-246573, IBM Corp, 2004. http://www.redbooks.ibm.com |
| [java sec guidelines] | Java Security Coding Guidelines. Sun Microsystems, 2000. http://java.sun.com/security/seccodeguide.html |
| [Joines 2002] | Stacy Joines, Ruth Willenborg, and Ken Hygh. *Performance Analysis for Java Web Sites*. Addison-Wesley, 2002. ISBN 0-201-84454-0. |
| [Kovari 2003] | *Transactional Services in WebSphere Application Server Enterprise V5*. IBM RedPaper. http://publib-b.boulder.ibm.com/Redbooks.nsf/RedbookAbstracts/redp3759.html?Open |

| Reference Key | Reference Data |
|---|---|
| [Kreger 2003] | *Java and JMX, Building Manageable Systems*. Addison-Wesley; 1st edition (December 30, 2002). ISBN 0672324083. |
| [Mann 2004] | Mann, Kito D. *JSF in Action*. Manning Publications Company; (May 2004). ISBN 1932394125. |
| [Mitra 2004] | Using LDAP to Secure J2EE Applications in WebSphere Application Developer V5. http://www-106.ibm.com/Studiodeveloperworks/websphere/library/techarticles/0311_mitra/mitra.htm. By Tilak Mitra, IBM DeveloperWorks. |
| [Monson-Haefel 2002] | *Enterprise JavaBeans*. O'Reilly & Associates; 3rd edition (October 15, 2001). ISBN 0596002262. |
| [Oaks 2002] | Oaks, Scott. *Java Security*. O'Reilly & Associates; 2nd edition; (May 1, 2001). ISBN 0596001576. |
| [Perry 2002] | *Java Management Extensions*. O'Reilly & Associates; 1st edition (June 15, 2002). ISBN 0596002459. |
| [Smolenski] | *Transactions in J2EE*. IBM RedPaper. http://publib-b.boulder.ibm.com/Redbooks.nsf/RedbookAbstracts/redp3659.html?Open |
| [social engineering] | CIO Insight: What Is Social Engineering?. Computer Cops, 2003. http://computercops.biz/article2934.html |
| [Spille 2004] | XA Exposed Series. http://www.jroller.com/page/pyrasun/20040105#xa_exposed |
| [Vilaghy 2004] | WebSphere for z/OS V5 Connectivity Handbook. SG24-7064-00, IBM Corp, 2004. http://www.redbooks.ibm.com |
| [Wakelin 2002] | Java Connectors for CICS: Featuring the J2EE Connector Architecture Redbook. SG24-6401, IBM Corp, 2002. |
| [WAS] | WAS V5 Info Center. http://publib.boulder.ibm.com/infocenter/wasinfo/index.jsp |
| [Williamson 2003] | *How to Extend the WebSphere Management System (and Create Your Own MBeans)*. WebSphere Technical Journal; (April 2003). http://www-106.ibm.com/developerworks/websphere/techjournal/0304_williamson/williamson.html |
| [Williamson 2004] | *IBM WebSphere System Administration*. Prentice Hall PTR; (July 2004). ISBN 0-13-144604-5. |
| [XSS] | Malicious HTML Tags Embedded in Client Web Requests. CERT Advisory, 2002. http://www.cert.org/advisories/CA-2000-02.html |
| [Yusuf 2004] | *Enterprise Messaging Using JMS and IBM WebSphere*. IBM Press/Prentice Hall PTR; (February 25, 2004). ISBN 0131468634. |

# Index

## B

## S

## U

## X-Z